HISTORY OF ENGLAND

HISTORY OF ENGLAND

271/14

BY

GEORGE MACAULAY TREVELYAN

LATE FELLOW OF TRINITY COLLEGE, CAMBRIDGE

WITH MAPS

LONGMANS, GREEN AND CO. LTD.

39 PATERNOSTER ROW, LONDON, E.C. 4

NEW YORK, TORONTO

BOMBAY, CALCUTTA AND MADRAS

1926

Made in Great Britain

PREFACE

A BOOK that traverses so vast a field as the whole of English history in the course of seven hundred pages is apt to be either a text-book or an essay. It can in no case be a full narrative of events. This work is an essay in so far as it attempts to analyze the social development of the nation in relation to economic conditions, political institutions, and overseas activities. It is a text-book in so far as it preserves the narrative form in brief, deals in dates, and gives prominence to leading events and persons.

Scottish, Irish, Welsh, and overseas Imperial history are treated, I trust not in all cases from too English a point of view. But what unity the book has, especially in its earlier parts, is necessarily derived from England as the centre. Not to arouse expectations which I may not fulfil, I have called the book merely a History of England.

The original nucleus out of which the work has grown was the Lowell Lectures which I had the honour of delivering in Boston, Mass., in the spring of 1924. I therefore dedicate the book in its present form to President Lowell of Harvard and my other kind hosts on that occasion.

I am greatly indebted to two friends at the older Cambridge, Dr. Clapham of King's, and Mr. Claude Elliott of Jesus : to the former for allowing me to see the early part of his *Economic History of Modern Britain* before it went to press, a privilege of which I have made extensive use ; and to Mr. Elliott for reading the earlier half of my work and giving me valuable advice on numerous points.

G. M. TREVELYAN

BERKHAMSTED,
April 1926.

CONTENTS

BOOK I

THE MINGLING OF THE RACES. FROM THE EARLIEST TIMES TO THE NORMAN CONQUEST

ix

CONTENTS

CONTENTS xiii

BOOK V

FROM UTRECHT TO WATERLOO. SEA-POWER AND ARISTOCRACY. FIRST STAGE OF THE INDUSTRIAL REVOLUTION

CONTENTS

MAPS

GENEALOGICAL TREES

INTRODUCTION

THE history of civilized man in our country is very old ; it begins long before the reign of Alfred. But the history of Britain as a leader in the world's affairs is of much shorter date ; it begins with the reign of Elizabeth. The reason can be read upon the map. Map-makers, whether in ancient Alexandria or in mediæval monasteries, placed our island on the north-west edge of all things. But, after the discovery of America and the ocean routes to Africa and the East, Britain lay in the centre of the new maritime movement. This change in her geographic outlook was employed to good purpose by her inhabitants, who in the era of the Stuarts made her the chief seat of the new trans-oceanic commerce and of the finance and industry that sustained it. Next, with the aid of modern science, the land of Newton applied machinery to manufacture and began the world-wide Industrial Revolution. Meanwhile, Britain was peopling and giving laws to North America ; and after she had lost the Thirteen Colonies, she built up a second Empire, more widely scattered and more vast.

These latter centuries of material growth and leadership correspond with the period of greatest intellectual achievement. In spite of Bede, Roger Bacon, Chaucer and Wycliffe, Britain's contribution to mediæval science and literature is slight when compared to the world of her intellectual creation from the time of Shakespeare onward. The era when London awoke to find herself the maritime centre of the suddenly expanded globe, was also the era of the Renaissance and the Reformation—movements of intellectual growth and individual self-assertion which proved more congenial to the British than to many other races, and seemed to emancipate the island genius.

In the sphere of pure politics Britain is famous as the mother of Parliaments. In answer to the instincts and temperament of her people, she evolved in the course of centuries a system which reconciled three things that other nations have often found incompatible—executive efficiency, popular control, and personal freedom.

It is indeed in the Middle Ages that we must seek the origin of Parliament, and of the English Common Law which the ultimate victory of Parliament over the Royal power has made supreme in all English-speaking lands. The political merit of the Mediæval period lay in its dislike of absolutism in the Temporal sphere, its elaborate distribution of power, its sense of corporate life, and its consultation of the various corporate interests through their representatives. But, although Parliament was a characteristic product of the Middle Ages, the development of its powers in Tudor, Stuart and Hanoverian days, its resistance to the political theories of the Roman law received in contemporary Europe, and its transplantation to America and the Antipodes, are the great events which raised the political history of Britain into a sphere apart from the political life of the Continent. For, although France and Spain had a number of mediæval Estates and Parliaments, they failed to adapt them to modern conditions. On the passing of feudalism, the Latin peoples read despotic monarchy as the political message of the new era. Against Machiavelli's princely interpretation of the new nationalism, Britain alone of the great national States successfully held out, turned back the tide of despotism, and elaborated a system by which a debating club of elected persons could successfully govern an Empire in peace and in war. During the commercial and military struggles with foreign rivals which followed between 1689 and 1815, our goods, our ships, and our armies proved that Parliamentary freedom might be more efficient than despotism as a means of giving force to the national will. Nor, in the new era of man's life introduced by the Industrial Revolution, has this verdict yet been reversed.

In the Nineteenth Century the same Parliamentary institutions, while undergoing democratic transformation, were put to the severer test of coping with the new and bewildering conditions of social life created by the Industrial Revolution. At the same time the vast and ever-increasing Empire, of white, brown, and black communities, presented diverse and complicated problems, each one recurring in new guise every few years under the stimulus that modern economic conditions give to social and political change. Parliamentary government for the white races, and the desire to govern justly societies not yet prepared for self-government, have so far preserved this astonishing association of peoples.

Whatever, then, be our chief interest in the past—whether material progress and racial expansion, the growth of political and social institutions, or pure intellect and letters—it is the last four hundred years in British History which stand out. Yet I have not hesitated to devote a third of this work to a

survey of the pre-Tudor epochs. The mingling of the armed
races poured into Britain from the earliest times until 1066,
and the national temper and customs which they developed in the
shelter of the island guarded by the Norman and Plantagenet
Kings, alone rendered it possible for five millions of people,
ruled by Elizabeth, to lay hold on the splendid future offered
to themselves and their descendants by the maritime discoveries
and intellectual movements of that age.   If the hour then came,
the men, too, were ready.

Britain has always owed her fortunes to the sea, and to the
havens and rivers that from the earliest times opened her inland
regions to what the sea might bring.   Long before she aspired
to rule the waves she was herself their subject, for her destiny
was continually being decided by the boat-crews which they
floated to her shore.   From Iberian and Celtic to Saxon and
Danish settlers, from pre-historic and Phœnician traders to Roman
and Norman overlords, successive tides of warlike colonists, the
most energetic seamen, farmers and merchants of Europe came
by the wave-path to inhabit her, or to instil their knowledge
and spirit into the older inhabitants.   Her east coast lay obvious
and open to Teuton and Scandinavian immigrants ; her south
coast to cultural influences from the Mediterranean by way of
France.   From Teuton and Scandinavian she acquired the
more important part of her population and character and the
root of her language ; from the South she received the rest of
her language, the chief forms of her culture, and much of her
organizing power.

The Norman Conquest severed her ties with Scandinavia,
which Canute had drawn very close.   For several hundred years
the Nordic islanders were governed by a French-speaking aristocracy and a Latin-speaking clergy.   By a significant paradox
it was under this foreign leadership that the English began to
develop their intense national feeling and their peculiar institutions, so different in spirit from those of Italy and France.
Already among the fellow-countrymen of Chaucer and Wycliffe,
even when engaged in the disastrous adventure of the Hundred
Years' War, we see the beginnings of a distinct English nationality,
far richer than the old Saxon, composed of many different
elements of race, character and culture which the tides of ages
had brought to our coasts and the island climate had tempered
and mellowed into harmony.   At the Reformation the English,
grown to manhood, dismissed their Latin tutors, without reacting
into close contact with the Scandinavian and Teuton world.
Britain had become a world by itself.

It was at this crisis in England's cultural and political growth, when she was weakening her ties with Europe, that the union with Scotland came about, and at the same time the ocean offered the islanders a pathway to every corner of the newly discovered globe. The universality of the Englishman's experience and outlook—quite as marked a characteristic as his insularity—is due to his command of the ocean which has for more than three centuries past carried him as explorer, trader, and colonist to every shore in the two hemispheres.

Thus, in early times, the relation of Britain to the sea was passive and receptive ; in modern times, active and acquisitive. In both it is the key to her story.

HISTORY OF ENGLAND

BOOK I

THE MINGLING OF THE RACES. FROM THE EARLIEST TIMES TO THE NORMAN CONQUEST

INTRODUCTION

IT is a commonplace to say that the British are a people of mixed blood. I hope, in this First Book, to indicate a little how, when and why this mingling of races occurred.

It may be as well to say, at the outset, that the entrance into our island of the races who people it to-day was completed in main outline at the time of the Norman Conquest. With that event, which itself made less racial than social and cultural change, we come to an end of migratory invasions and of forced entry behind the point of the sword. Since Hastings there has been nothing more catastrophic than a slow, peaceful infiltration of alien craftsmen and labourers,—Flemings, Huguenots, Irish and others,—with the acquiescence of the existing inhabitants of the island.

To invade Britain was singularly easy before the Norman Conquest, singularly difficult afterwards. The reason is clear. A well-organized State, with a united people on land and a naval force at sea, could make itself safe behind the Channel even against such military odds as Philip of Spain, Louis XIV. or Napoleon could assemble on the opposite shore. In recent centuries these conditions have been fulfilled, and although an invading force has sometimes been welcomed, as when Henry Tudor or William of Orange came over, no invasion hostile to the community as a whole has met with even partial success owing to the barrier of the sea. But, before the Norman Conquest, there had been long ages when neither the island State nor the island navy was formidable; even in the days of Alfred and Harold they were inadequate to their task, and in earlier times they did not exist. Except when protected by the Roman galleys and legions, ancient Britain was peculiarly liable to invasion for geographic and other reasons.

The story of the Mingling of the Races in Britain, ending with the advent of the Normans, covers a thousand years of history very dimly descried, succeeding to many thousand more of archæological twilight. The era of Celt, Saxon and Dane is like Macbeth's battle on the blasted heath. Prophecy hovers around. Horns are heard blowing in the mist, and a confused uproar of savage tumult and outrage. We catch glimpses of giant figures—mostly warriors at strife. But there are ploughmen, too, it seems, breaking the primeval clod, and we hear the sound of forests crashing to the axe. Around all is the lap of waves and the cry of seamen beaching their ships.

CHAPTER I

Early Man.   Iberian and Celt

IT is not my purpose to describe pre-insular Britain and the great geologic changes, the volcanoes, the rise and fall of mountains, the tropical swamps in which the coal forests grew, or the industrious building of the chalk downs under the sea. Nor shall I attempt to distinguish the various races of primitive hunters, from ' Piltdown man ' onwards, who may have wandered over the land during the inter-glacial periods. It was probably at the great spring-time of Northern Europe, after the glacial epoch, that the soil of the future Britain was first trodden by ' Homo Sapiens,' unequivocal man. These early immigrants came over by the land-bridge from Europe as they followed northwards the last retreat of the ice; with them, or just before them, came the commonest of the wild animals, birds, flowers and trees. These hunters of the mammoth, the horse and the reindeer, have probably mixed their blood with some of the later races who are certainly among our ancestors. At the time of their coming overland, the chalk downs of Dover and Calais were still united in a continuous range ; the majestic Thames flowed into the lower Rhine ; and the Rhine itself meandered towards the Arctic Ocean through the marshy plain now submerged beneath the waves of the North Sea, where the bones of mammoth and reindeer are dredged off the Dogger Bank.

Since the flora and fauna which we call native to Britain came northward at this period to replenish a land swept bare by the snow cap of the last ice age, they are, therefore, closely identified with the flora and fauna of Northern Europe—except for the red grouse peculiar to the British Isles. Ireland was cut adrift from England before the piercing of the Dover Straits by the sea, and is, for that reason, poorer in mammals, plants and reptiles.

For many centuries after Britain became an island the untamed forest was king. Its moist and mossy floor was hidden from heaven's eye by a close-drawn curtain woven of innumerable tree-tops, which shivered in the breezes of summer dawn and broke into wild music of millions upon millions of wakening birds ; the concert was prolonged from bough to bough with scarcely a break for hundreds of miles over hill and plain and mountain, unheard by man save where, at rarest intervals, a troop of skin-clad hunters, stone-axe in hand, moved furtively over the ground beneath, ignorant that they lived upon an island, not dreaming that there could be other parts of the world besides this damp green woodland with its meres and marshes, wherein they hunted, a terror to its four-footed inhabitants and themselves afraid.

A glance at any physical map will show how Britain has always thrust out towards the continent of Europe a low coast with an undulating plain behind, easy of access through many havens and navigable rivers. It was only westward and northward, against the Atlantic, that the island presented a mountainous and iron-bound coast—though even there the mouths of Severn, Dee, Mersey, Clyde and other lesser inlets held the makings of future history. But, from the earliest ages the flat south and east coastlines with the plains and low ridges behind them presented, so long as they were unguarded by a fleet, a standing temptation to the migratory tribes, pirates, plunderers and traders roaming along the continental shores. See Frontis-piece and Map IV., p. 30, below.

The temptation to invade the island lay not only in the pearls, the gold and the tin for which it seems to have been noted among certain Mediterranean merchants long before the foundation of Rome ; temptation lay also in its fertile soil, the rich carpet of perennial green that covered the downs and every clearing in the forest, the absence of long interludes of frost that must have seemed miraculous in a land so far to the North before men knew the secret of the Gulf Stream.[1]

[1] Both Cæsar and Tacitus remark on the absence of severe cold in Britain, though Tacitus adds : ' the sky is overcast with continual rain and cloud.' The rapid changes of weather and temperature in Britain, a source of bitter merriment to its inhabitants in every age, stimulate the physical and mental energies, and ' make us Englishmen.' It is, in fact, one of the higher values of the land, but it can hardly have been one of the temptations to would-be invaders !

The forest of Britain swarmed with big and small game, and early man was a hunter. Whole districts, long since drained, were then shallow meres filled with fowl and fish ; the greatest of these fen lands stretched from future Cambridge to future Lincoln ; countless generations of early fowlers and fishermen dropped their tools and weapons of chipped flint in its waters, or on the sandy heaths round its margin, for the better instruction of archæologists. In the age of the shepherd the open chalk downs of the South were his wealth and his delight, while the more daring swineherd followed the hunter into the dark forest below.

See Map I., p. 8, below.

Flints lay about in profusion in many regions, but the best of them were buried in the chalk ; shafts thirty feet deep were sunk by the earliest island miners, who laboured down at the bottom with stag-horn picks and shoulder-blades for shovels, hewing galleries through the chalk and extracting the precious flints which then made man the master of the world. The ' palæolithic ' or ' old stone ' age, with its roughly chipped flints, fades by imperceptible degrees into the ' neolithic ' or ' new stone ' age, when men had learnt to polish their flint tools and weapons with an admirable perfection.

When, some 2000 years before Christ, the age of bronze gradually began in Britain, followed after more than a thousand years by the age of iron, the metals, too, were found in plenty, with timber at hand to smelt them. Timber grew everywhere for housing and fuel. Fresh water was widely distributed ; indeed before the age of draining and well-sinking, it was found more plentifully at high levels than in the South England of to-day. And village sites, from primæval hut circles to the Saxon townships of Domesday Book, were always chosen close to fresh water.

Last, but not least, when man took to ploughing and sowing, the soil was found to yield manyfold in the eastern and southern regions, those sunniest parts of the island where wheat-growing is still generally profitable under the very different world conditions of the modern grain market. Agriculture is the greatest change of all in the early life of man, for it enables him to multiply, fixes him to the home and to the soil, draws him into larger village communities, and thereby renders other inventions and changes more easy. The plough made but a slow conquest of Britain. It reached a definable stage in the latter part of the Saxon epoch, by which time the bulk of the present-day villages had come into existence, at least in embryo, as clearings in the forest. But agriculture had been first introduced in prehistoric times, when it could only be practised in certain carefully chosen localities that were neither marshy nor encumbered by trees, nor yet mere barren heath.[1]

Such were the attractions of this desirable land. And it stood, obvious to all, as centre to the grand semi-circle of the North European shore that stretches for two thousand miles from Norway to Ushant. From times long before the dawn of history until the Norman Conquest, all the various seafaring tribes who succeeded each other as nomads or settlers on any part of that great coastline regarded Britain as their natural prey. And Britain was the more subject to their attacks because the pressure of the folk wanderings was mainly from the East of Europe to the West. It followed, that for several thousands of years, wave after wave of seagoing adventurous races, or of races pushed behind by other adventurers, was flung upon Britain's southern and eastern shore.

See Map IV., p. 30, below.

Until each set of new-comers was half-way across the island, the worst natural obstacle they could meet was the widespread woodland and marsh. But where the forest was pathless or the valley too wet, the invader could either row up the river or trek round by the heaths and downs. The high-placed camps, roads and dew-ponds of the primitive peoples, often found where only the sheep and plovers now congregate, remind us of the greater part which the bare uplands played in the life of man, before the forests were felled and the valleys drained.

The first serious geographic obstacle appeared when the invader, perhaps in the second or third generation of his advance, at length approached the north or west of the island—the mountain ranges of Wales, of North-West England and of Scotland. Here the pursued might rally and the pursuers be forced to halt. If there had been no such mountain ranges, if England had been all one lowland, each successive invasion would have rapidly overrun the whole island. In that case no racial difference might to-day be discernible such as divides so-called Celtic Britain—Wales and the Scottish Highlands—on the one hand, from the Saxon districts on the other, for the primitive Saxons

---

[1] For instance, in Cambridgeshire, successive civilizations of flint-users had congregated on the sandy heath uplands on the border of the fens where Mildenhall now stands. See Map I., p. 8, below. But when the bronze and iron ages succeeded to the stone age, the centre of population shifted at last to the upper Cam valley, owing to the greater importance of agriculture. The shores of the upper Cam were not water-logged or forest-bound, and were better soil than the Mildenhall heaths ; so population gradually followed the plough upstream. But though the forest narrowly cramped the dimensions of this new domain, no attempt seems to have been made to encroach on the forest area till Roman and Saxon times. Yet this forest area occupied the greater part of the upland country which is now so bare of wood and so characteristic of agricultural Cambridgeshire. See the remarkable work of Mr. Cyril Fox—*The Archæology of the Cambridge Region.*

might have swept right over Wales and crossed into Ireland in the Sixth Century. But in fact the great plains of Ireland were only reached by the English of the Twelfth Century, marshalled under the feudal banner of Strongbow ; the mountains of Wales and the Pennines had impeded the first rush of the Saxon immigrants. Much the same thing must have happened long before in many unrecorded Celtic and Iberian invasions. History is governed by geography. If the mountain ranges had stood along the southern and eastern shores of England instead of standing far back to west and north, the tribal invasion of the island from the continent would have been so arduous a task that Britain would not have become the early receptacle for so many different races of vigorous barbarians. The physical formation of a country is the key to the history of its early settlement, especially in days before man had the mastery of nature which he now possesses.

And so, owing to these geographic features of Britain, the same phenomena of tribal invasion were repeated again and again on the same general scheme. Again and again, how often we know not, from the early stone age till the Danish invasions, some race of warriors crossing from some part of what we now call France, Holland, Germany or Scandinavia, has settled on the rich lowlands of southern and eastern Britain, killed or subjected many of the older inhabitants, and driven the rest into the mountains of the north and west or into the barren and remote peninsula of Cornwall.

It is thus that we must account for the variety and the present location of the races that were mingled in Britain so long ago. Cornwall, Wales and the Highlands of Scotland are inhabited by the oldest stocks ; we call them, to-day, ' the Celtic fringe ' of the island. But most of them are pre-Celtic —as also are the Irish. The Celts, late comers into western Europe, were tall men, fair or red-haired, who entered Britain and Ireland only a few hundred years before the coming of Julius Cæsar. The bulk of those whom we miscall ' Celts ' are for the most part dark-haired people whose ancestors had been in the island thousands of years before the red Celt was ever heard of. They were the folk whom Matthew Arnold in his poem describes as ' dark Iberians,' coming down, ' shy traffickers,' to chaffer with the Phœnician traders on the shore.

We may conveniently speak of these pre-Celtic peoples, collectively, as ' Iberians,' though in fact they consisted of many different races, not all of them dark-haired.[1] Some

---

[1] Some of the pre-Celts were of what archæologists call the ' Mediterranean,' others of the ' Alpine ' race.

'Iberian' blood probably flows in the veins of every modern Englishman, more in the average Scot, most in the Welsh and Irish. The Iberians were no mere savages. They raised themselves, during the long stone and bronze ages in Britain, from savagery onto the first steps of civilized life. At first hunters and users of flint, then shepherds also, they naturally learnt the uses to which man can turn the dog, the sheep, the goat, the ox, the pig; they adopted the use of metals; they became the men of the bronze age skilled in weaving and in crafts of many kinds, including agriculture. If in earlier times the largest political unit consisted of a tribe of a few hundred souls, living in dread of wolves and bears, and of their nearest human neighbours, the Iberians acquired in some parts of the country a much higher political organization, designed gigantic earthworks like the Maiden Castle near Dorchester on a scientific military plan, and reared Stonehenge, no mean engineering feat. Although the earliest of them had come over in coracles or canoes, they learnt to build the 'long-ship' or low war-galley.

Many of these improvements, especially agriculture, metal work and long-ship building, were probably taught to the islanders by merchants from the distant South, or by continental tribes who had learnt from those merchants. The Levant was the cradle of European civilization. The inhabitants of Mesopotamia, Egypt and Crete, in days before Tyre, Athens or Rome, evolved agriculture, metal-craft, shipbuilding and many other of the arts of life. Such Promethean secrets, starting on their journey from South and East, handed on from trader to trader and from tribe to tribe ever northward and westward across the forests of barbarous Europe, or travelling more quickly by merchant galleys round the Pillars of Hercules, reached at last those half fabulous 'tin islands' in the mists and tides of the northern seas.

The trade of Britain with the Levant, or rather of the Levant with Britain, is far older than the Celtic Conquest. English jet found in Spain is believed to date from 2500 B.C. and Egyptian beads found in England from about 1300 B.C. So early, perhaps much earlier, the Mediterranean traders had discovered the British islands with their wealth of pearls and gold, to-day long exhausted, and their metals, not yet at an end. But if these eastern merchants have the credit of bringing civilization to Britain, the Iberian tribesmen had the wit to adapt their teaching.

Either the traders, or else some conquering race, brought from overseas the first weapons of bronze that have been discovered in the island. But since copper and tin both lay near the surface in different parts of the island, particularly Cornwall, the natives were soon taught to smelt the two together and so

MAP I.—Iberian Britain

make bronze for themselves. After that, the end of the long stone age was in sight; it was only a matter of time before bronze, and iron after it, was lord of all. Some of the islanders attained high technical skill in metal working, and indeed some of the finest enamel work on bronze that the world contains was produced by these Iberian ancestors of ours. Many of the centres of this ancient civilization—Stonehenge perhaps—were placed on sites agriculturally barren, but once famous for the best flints or for surface gold, tin or copper, long since exhausted.

Trade routes and trade connections grew up within the island itself between very distant tribes; and there were ports trading with Ireland for gold, and others that shipped tin to the continent. Ancient trackways, running along bare downs and ridges, linked up the various centres of civilization which were otherwise separated by wide morasses and long leagues of forest. The fortifications were placed chiefly on the high bare land on the route of the trackways. They often ran along the edge of the chalk downs below the top of the tableland but above the marshy and tangled forest of the plain, like the track along the south edge of the North Downs, long afterwards known and used as the ' Pilgrims' Way ' to Canterbury, and still at places available to the pedestrian as it was four thousand and more years ago.

So too, ages before the arrival of the Celt, the Icknield Way ran along the chalk close under the ridge of the Chilterns, and was carried on westward by the line of the downs south of Thames; its object was to join up the fenland and agricultural civilization of East Anglia with the great downland civilization gathered round the circles of Avebury and Stonehenge, where man was most thickly congregated, because there he was most free from the impediment of forest and of marsh. The forest, still impenetrable save by a few daring hunters, lay deep on both sides of the Icknield Way. Ideas and arts of vast import to man have been carried along its springy turf by wayfarers listening anxiously to the noises of the forest, to distinguish the howl of wolves, the growl of bears or the yet more dreaded voice of hostile tribesmen.

From the seventh to the third centuries before Christ, the Celtic tribes, originally occupying North-western Germany and the Netherlands, were moving across Europe in many different directions. In the first centuries after Christ the Teuton tribes, starting from homes rather further to the East, were destined to move over much the same ground in much the same manner; but between the folk-wanderings of Celt and of Teuton was to be interposed the great event of the Roman penetration north of the Alps.

The Celts, in their earlier day, showed as much vigour in migration as any race that came after them. One great body settled in France and became an important element in the racial content of the Gaulish nation. A southern wing settled in the valley of the Po, put an end to the Etruscan hegemony in Italy, and about 387 B.C. sacked Rome, when the geese were said to have saved the Capitol. Others pushed into Spain, others into the Balkans. During the same centuries a northern wing of this great world movement overran our island and imposed Celtic rule and language on its inhabitants. The Celtic invaders of Britain came in successive tribal waves, kindred indeed but mutually hostile and each with a dialect of its own. Erse, Gaelic, and Welsh are still extant variations of the tongues which they and the Iberians evolved. Wave after wave of Celts, each entering Britain by the lowlands of south and east, slaughtered, subdued or chased across the island not only the Iberians but such of their own kinsfolk as had preceded them ; many of the pursued, as on all occasions in Britain, found refuge in the mountains to north and west.[1]

See Map II., p. 22, below.

At least two big waves of Celtic invasion can be distinguished : first the Gaels or Goidels, still found in Ireland and Scotland, some of whom may have come over as early as 600 B.C. ; secondly the Cymri and Brythons still found in Wales. Among the Brythonic peoples were the Belgæ and other tribes whom Cæsar found spread over Southern England ; they were closely related to the Gauls beyond the Channel. These Britons seem to have been already settled in the island that is still called by their name, at the time when Pytheas, the Greek traveller from Marseilles, recorded his visit to the ' Pretanic isle ' in the days of Alexander of Macedon.

circa 325 B.C.

The Celts who overran so much of Europe in the last six centuries before Christ were tall, light-haired warriors, skilful in ironwork, which was then replacing bronze, and in arts and crafts of their own, much admired by modern archæologists. Such was the outfit at any rate of the later among the Celtic invaders of Britain. The fair-haired Celts imposed themselves as an aristocracy on the conquered tribes throughout Britain and Ireland. In the end the races mixed, but what proportion the Celtic bore to the old Iberian blood it is impossible to say. In Wales, Cornwall, Ireland and the Highlands of Scotland, the

---

[1] Professor Chadwick appears to think that the Celts who came to Britain at various times, probably from Belgium, Holland and N.W. Germany, were (like the Anglo-Saxons after them) practically one race, but that they acquired different cultures and developed different dialects of Celtic, according to the varying dates of their crossing the sea, or the variations of their subsequent history and contact with the natives.

physique and colouring seem chiefly Iberian. The proportion of Celtic to Iberian blood is very small in the Welsh mountains. How far it was the same in the richer eastern portions of Britain at the time of Roman and Saxon invasions, there is no means of determining. It is equally impossible to know what form the Celtic conquerors gave to their economic and social relations with the conquered Iberians. In Wales there long remained traces, which some archæologists at least thought they detected, of a system by which certain hamlets were left to the conquered and others reserved for the conquerors, the former paying a heavier tribute. But it would be rash to conclude that such a system was universal in the island. Slavery or serfdom may have been commoner in the east.

The Celts, like the Iberians before them, remained tribesmen or clansmen, bound together by legal and sentimental ties of kinship as the moral basis of society. Unlike the Saxons after them, they developed no strictly territorial, still less any feudal organization. A thousand years after England had been subjected to Saxon conquest, Wales, Ireland and the Scottish Highlands were in different degrees still governed by the tribal rules of life. And we may be sure that in the palmy day of Celtic lordship in the British Isles, the Kings were tribal chiefs, rather than territorial or feudal monarchs. Justice was the justice of the clan, which punished and protected its members, exacting on their behalf from other clans either vengeance, or else payment in reparation for injuries done. The Celtic tribes, when the Romans came over, were perpetually at war with one another, but they formed large accretions, each tribe being spread over a considerable area, often equal to several modern counties.

Agriculture continued to progress slowly in the iron age under the Celts, as in the bronze age under the Iberians. Wheat was grown in the south, oats further north—as to-day. The Celt loved to cheer or fuddle his brain with mead—grain fermented with honey. But the acreage under plough was small, for the forests remained unfelled, and those river valleys, like Thames and Trent, where drainage was a necessary prelude to close habitation, remained marshy and sparsely peopled.

Herds of swine wandering by thousands through the virgin oak forests were a feature of Saxon and Norman times and must have been no less a feature of Celtic and pre-Celtic economy. Pig in various forms is still favourite feeding in England as contrasted to the continent of Europe, and in primitive times it was the staff of life not only in Ireland but in Britain. Sheep and oxen were perhaps the chief source of accumulated wealth and the chief means of barter. Horses were bred to drag the war chariots of the Celtic chiefs to battle, but the plough was drawn by oxen.

Taking the Celtic island as a whole, agriculture was not the pre-occupation it became in Saxon and mediæval times. Hunting, fishing, herding, weaving, bee-keeping, metal work, carpentry, and, above all, fighting occupied most of the time and thought of a small population scattered wide over a land not yet drained and deforested. The 'trevs' or hamlets of the Celtic families consisted of light structures of timber, wattles, or mud, easily and frequently destroyed in tribal wars. In the West, at least, the population readily moved the site of its 'trevs' to get fresh pasture and hunting ground, as the Welsh continued to do until late in the Middle Ages.

'Such agriculture as there was,' says Vinogradoff, 'did not make people strike deep roots into the soil.' This verdict, though certainly true of the West and of the Midlands, which the Celts left sparsely peopled and still under forest, is hardly applicable, perhaps, to certain wheat-growing districts in the South and East. Yet even in those regions it is by no means proved that the Celts ever adopted the open-field system of communal village agriculture and the large nucleated township which was established by the Anglo-Saxons when they, in their turn, occupied these corn-growing districts. In most parts of the island, at any rate, the tendency of the Celt was to scatter over the countryside in small family groups, continually subdividing, each group with its own 'trev' standing in the middle of its enclosed land, with the waste beyond.[1]

The most advanced regions of the Celtic civilization in Britain lay in the South and South-East. There were the best grainlands, the open pastures of the downs, the iron mines and forges of the Sussex Weald, the Channel ports and shipping (though London as yet counted for nothing), the easiest communications with the Mediterranean traders and with the Celtic kinsmen overseas. Though there was no town-life proper in the whole island, the largest assemblies of huts were probably to be found near St. Albans and Colchester. Already 150 years before Christ, south British tribes had a gold coinage of their own, imitated from the gold *stater* of the Kings of Macedon.[2] In the last century before Christ the British Belgæ and other southern tribes were in close political intercourse with their brethren of Northern Gaul ; some

[1] See note at end of chapter. Henceforth refer to Frontispiece Map of Celtic and Roman Britain.

[2] Examples can be seen exhibited in the coin room of the British Museum. The bronze shields, bronze and iron weapons, and gold ornaments in the neighbouring hall and in the iron-age room in the same Museum give some idea of the skill and wealth of the Iberian and Celtic civilizations in Britain.

of them had even for a few years acknowledged a King of the continental Belgæ as their suzerain. When, therefore, they learnt that the Romans were marching to subdue the north Gallic tribes, the Britons sent over ships and men who fought against Cæsar both by sea and land. It was one of the causes of his invasion of Britain.

Of Iberian and Celtic religion we know next to nothing save what little can be deduced from the fairy folk-lore of Celts in Christian times. Local gods and goddesses haunted particular springs, caves, mountains, forests and other natural objects, and easily became the local fairies and water-spirits of later times. The most detailed account of the old Celtic religion by a contemporary was written by Julius Cæsar. His imagination was stirred by the power of the organized caste of priests—the Druids —strong in Gaul and strongest in Britain ; they had all education in their hands, they administered justice in the courts, and placed recalcitrant laymen under interdict. ' Persons thus excommunicated,' writes Cæsar, ' are held impious and accursed; men will not meet or speak with them.' The power of the priesthood was distasteful to the Roman patrician, for Rome had not yet bowed her neck to the hierarchies from the East. ' All the Gauls,' he observes, ' are as a nation much given to superstition, and, therefore, persons afflicted by severe illness or involved in wars and danger either make human sacrifices or vow to do so, and use the Druids as their ministers in these ceremonies.' ' The Germans,' he adds, ' differ much from the Gauls in these customs. For they have no Druids to preside over their religion.' And if Cæsar had known the Anglo-Saxons and the Norsemen he might have said the same of them. The paganism of the Celts in France and Britain was a religion of fear and priestcraft as compared to the paganism of those other barbarian races destined to wrest from them the supremacy of the island.[1]

BOOKS FOR FURTHER READING

H. J. Mackinder, *Britain and the British Seas* ; Donald Mackenzie, *Ancient Man in Britain* ; Cyril Fox, *Archæology of the Cambridge Region,* Chapters I.–IV. ; Vinogradoff, *Growth of the Manor,* Bk. I., Chapter I., and Bk. II., Chapter II. ; Oman, *England before the Norman Conquest,* Chapters I.–II. ; Quennell, *Everyday Life in Prehistoric Times* ; Hippisley Cox, *The Green Roads of England.*

NOTE
(See p. 12, above.)

Celtic custom was probably one reason why the West of England has always been, from very early times, a land of enclosed fields and small hamlets. But much must also be allowed for the nature of the soil. For even the Nordic invaders did not establish the open-field system and the large nucleated township in districts not suited to agriculture on the large scale—not for instance on the

---

[1] *Cambridge Mediæval History,* Vol. II. Chap. XV.

moors of the North, or in the fruit gardens of Kent, or in districts that remained largely woodland. But the Saxons did establish the open-field and the large nucleated township in most of the East and Midlands. The question is—had the Celts the open-field system and the nucleated village in those eastern corn-lands, afterwards taken over by the Saxons? Seebohm thought that they had, and Vinogradoff that they had not. There is no certain evidence. ' Air photography' of areas in Wiltshire and Hampshire produces results said to be unfavourable to Seebohm's hypothesis, and to indicate Celtic methods of enclosure and agriculture which the Romans left unaltered but the Saxon conquerors superseded. See O. G. S. Crawford, *Air-Survey and Archæology.*

CHAPTER II

Roman Britain

See
Frontis-
piece
Map for
all this
chapter.

THE Roman occupation intervened between the coming of the Celt and the coming of the Saxon, and delayed the latter for perhaps two hundred years. Celt, Saxon and Dane came over to slaughter or expel the inhabitants and settle in their place, but the Romans came to exploit and govern by right of superior civilization. In this they resembled the Europeans in Africa rather than the Pilgrim Fathers in America. Yet the natives of Britain were white men, capable of adopting Latin ways more fully than most Africans are capable of adopting the ways of Europe. Nor, on the other hand, had the Gauls and Britons an elaborate civilization of their own, like the inhabitants of the Greek and Oriental lands subject to the Roman sway. And, therefore, once the Roman conquerors had glutted their first rage for plunder, their main effort was to induce their Western subjects to assimilate Latin life in all its aspects. Their success with the Gauls was permanent, and became the starting point of modern European history. But in Britain, after a great initial success, they had complete ultimate failure. ' From the Romans who once ruled Britain,' wrote Haverfield, the great student of the archæology of the occupation, ' we Britons have inherited practically nothing.'

In the end the Romans left behind them here just three things of value: the first of these would have amused or shocked Cæsar, Agricola and Hadrian, for it was Welsh Christianity; the second was the Roman roads; the third, a by-product of the second, was the traditional importance of certain new city sites, especially that of London. But the Latin life of the cities, the villas, the arts, the language and the political organization of Rome vanished like a dream. The greatest fact in the early history of the island is a negative fact—that the Romans did not succeed in permanently Latinizing Britain as they Latinized France.

Julius Cæsar won his place in the history of the world by a double achievement—the political renovation of the Roman Empire and its extension into northern Europe. He planted the power of the Mediterranean peoples broad and firm on the north side of the Alps, making Gaul a Latin country for ever. And he showed how the outworn machinery of the ancient world could be reconstructed on new principles, by converting the provincial-minded Roman Republic, tossed about between a selfish aristocracy and a debased city mob, into a disciplined and catholic-minded Empire of the Civilized World, at once popular and despotic. When his successors had rebuilt the Roman State on these lines, its life was renewed for another five hundred years in the West, and another fifteen hundred in the Near East. The Cæsarean Empire became the link between the ancient and modern world. It secured that enough of the influence of Greece and Rome should survive to give some degree of common culture to the races composing the future Europe. It became the arena for the propagation of Christianity, which travelled to the four corners of civilization by the roads built and guarded by the Roman soldiers.

In order of time, Cæsar's work in Gaul was the prelude to his work for the Empire as a whole. And the subjugation of Gaul was only half accomplished when he found himself one day gazing across the Dover Straits. He surveyed the white cliffs like Napoleon, but with other thoughts in his head: for there was nothing to impede a visit to the island and nothing to prevent his safe return; the only question was whether it was worth his while to make the voyage, with more important work on hand.

His decision to invade Britain was not taken in the hope of setting up a Roman administration on the spot. He had neither the time nor the men to spare for that; his military position in Gaul, his political prospects in Italy were too precarious, for the rulers of the Republic loved him as little as the Senators of Carthage had loved Hannibal. But as leader of the opposition party, playing to the gallery in Rome, he had need of showy exploits; and he had need of tribute and slaves to enrich his partisans, pay his soldiers and fill his war-chest. An invasion of Britain might answer all these requirements. Besides, the tribes of North Gaul and South Britain were so closely allied that Gaul would be more submissive if its neighbour were constrained to pay tribute and to fear the mighty name of Rome. At least some first-hand knowledge of the politics and geography of the island was necessary for the would-be governors of Gaul.

As a military undertaking his first expedition was a failure. He took too small a force, and scarcely moved ten miles inland from the Dover Straits. In the next year's invasion on a larger scale, he won several battles, forded the Thames in the face of the enemy, and penetrated into the Hertfordshire territories of Cassivelaunus, King of the Catuvellauni. That tribe was dominant in southern Britain, and the jealousies caused by its hegemony turned some of its rivals and subjects into allies of the Roman invader, both in the time of Julius and a hundred years later during the Claudian conquest. But many of the Britons, including the men of Kent, put up a stout fight against Cæsar, and though their undisciplined infantry were useless against the 'legion's ordered line,' the yellow-haired, athletic aristocracy of the Celts in their scythed chariots clattered down the war-ways of the battle like heroes of Homer, in a manner disconcerting even to the veterans of the Tenth. The chariot, however, had seen its day as a method of warfare; it had already been abandoned in Celtic Gaul as well as in the Hellenized East, and the British chiefs would have been more truly formidable if they had taught themselves to fight as cavalry. But the island never had the luck to be defended by an aristocracy trained to fight from the saddle, until the Norman conquest acclimatized the mediæval knight.

The expedition of 54 B.C., though not a failure like that of the year before, was no great success. As Cicero complained to his cronies, the famous British gold was secured in very in-adequate quantities; the slaves were too ignorant to fetch fancy prices in the market, and there had been neither the time nor the means to carry off rebellious clans wholesale to the auctioneer, as was Cæsar's practice in Gaul. The expedition had no permanent results, except as a memory on both sides of the Channel. The tribute soon ceased to be paid. The rising of Vercingetorix, which proved the real crisis of the war in Gaul, put an end to Cæsar's further plans for Britain, if he had any. Then the long Civil Wars, followed by the reorganization of the Empire under Augustus and Tiberius, gave the distant island a hundred years of respite.

The conquest of Gaul by Julius Cæsar, more decidedly than his invasions of Britain, had brought the South British tribes into the orbit of Latin civilization. They were of the same race and political group as the northern Gauls, and the Gauls were now Roman subjects, many of them Roman citizens. A peaceful penetration of the island resulted from the work of Cæsar, and prepared the way for the conquest under Claudius.

The hundred most important years in the history of the world were not wholly a blank even in Britain. While Julius was being murdered and avenged, while the loves of Antony and Cleopatra were raising the question of the relations of East and West inside the Roman world, while Augustus was cannily constructing the Empire, while Christ was preaching and while Paul was being converted, far in the north Roman traders and colonists, working from the base of the Latinized province of Gaul, were establishing settlements in the interior of Britain and gaining influence at the courts of its tribal Kings.

Shakespeare's Cymbeline, unlike his Lear, was no myth. From 5 to 40 A.D. he reigned over the Catuvellauni, and so far increased their hegemony in the south of the island as to style himself on his gold coinage ' Rex Brittonum.' The use of the Roman language in his title is all of a piece with the good relations he cultivated with the Emperors Augustus and Tiberius. Just as Edward the Confessor prepared the way for the Norman Conquest by introducing Norman knights and clergy into England and making French fashionable at Court, so Cymbeline encouraged Roman traders and craftsmen to colonize the towns of Britain, and familiarized the leading tribesmen with the Latin language and civilization. Cymbeline moved his capital from Verulamium [1] near St. Albans to Camulodunum (Colchester) in the territory of the subjugated Trinovantes, whence his mint poured out gold coinage of the Roman type in great profusion.

To his reign, perhaps, belongs the origin of London as a city. Finds have been made in the river bed which suggest that the first edition of London Bridge may have been erected in timber before the Roman Conquest but during the age of Roman influence. It was perhaps during this transitional period that London began to exist at the bridge-head on the northern shore. There was certainly a place of some kind known as London at the time of the invasion under Claudius.

In any case the city that was to play so great a part first in English and then in world history, attained its original importance under the Roman rule. The name of London is Celtic, but it was not a great centre of Iberian or of Celtic civilization : in Cæsar's time and long afterwards, Middlesex was a forest, and much of future London a marsh. [2] But a bluff of hard ground

[1] It is my general practice to use modern place-names as conveying more to the reader. But ' Verulamium' cannot be rendered ' St. Albans' without implying an identity of site which is remarkably not the case.
[2] The modern levels of London streets lie from five to twenty feet above the original London clay (or water). Town levels are always rising. Much of modern London was once a swamp or lake. On the difficult problems of London origins, see *London*, T. W. Page.

afforded a good bridge-head where roads from the Kentish ports could cross the river and spread out again thence on their journeys northward and westward over the island. It was also the best landing-place for continental commerce coming up the estuary of the Thames. The bridge and port coincided in situation, and their geographic coincidence made the greatness of London.

The Romans, after they had conquered the island, made the fortune of London Bridge by concentrating upon it one-half of their great roads, from both north and south. And they made the fortune of London port by creating an extensive commerce with the Continent, which found in the long-neglected Thames the best means of entry. London was the point at which goods from Europe could be unshipped well inside the land, and sent to its most distant parts by roads planned not for the local needs of tribes but for the imperial needs of the province. The principal exports of Roman Britain, with which she purchased the luxuries of the world, were tin, skins, slaves, pearls and sometimes grain.

London became larger and richer under the Romans than she ever was again after their departure, until near the Norman Conquest. The Roman walls enclosed an area corresponding very closely to the walls of the City in mediæval times, which were in fact only the Roman walls restored. In both periods London was a commercial, not a governmental centre. Officially she ranked lower in the Roman hierarchy than much smaller and less important towns.

It was under the Emperor Claudius, a century after Cæsar's exploring expeditions, that the actual conquest of the island took place. For many years it had been demanded and planned, as readers of Horace remember. As soon as there was an Emperor with a forward policy and leisure to carry it out, he was sure to annex those Celtic lands that lay beyond the Channel, and so round off his Gallic territories. Traders who had settled in Britain, courtiers and soldiers greedy for a fresh supply of slaves, lands and offices, were all agog for annexation. They were right in supposing it would not be very difficult. National resistance was out of the question among chiefs already half Romanized, and many of them bitterly resenting the domination of the Catuvellauni. A battle for the passage of the Thames estuary and a march on Colchester sufficed to reduce the old empire of Cymbeline in the south-east of the island. Another year or two of fighting reduced the Belgæ of Wilts and Somerset, and the Durotriges of Dorset with their great earthwork fortresses.

The Midlands, from Bucks to Warwickshire, were still forest land, too thinly peopled to resist. It was only when the legionaries found themselves on the edge of the Welsh mountains and the northern moors that the Romans, like every other successful invader of Britain, began to meet with serious difficulties. In 60 A.D. they were still struggling with the first stages of the Welsh problem ; after coasting round the edge of the Snowdon massif, the legionaries were engaged, on the low-lying island of Anglesey, in the slaughter of the Druids and their fanatical followers, when news reached them that a great rebellion had broken out in their rear.

The rising of Boadicea is the exception that proves the rule of the easy submission of East and South to Roman influence. It was due to the exceptionally gross misconduct of the first exploiters of the conquest, who treated the Iceni and Trinovantes, by no means altogether unfriendly to Rome, much as the worser type of Englishman treated Bengal after Plassey, before the proper organization of the British raj had been undertaken by Clive and Hastings. The anger of the Iceni against wholesale confiscation and plunder was given dramatic intensity by the personal outrages inflicted on their Queen Boadicea and her family. The Celtic [1] fury was roused against Rome and the Romanizing Britons congregated in Colchester, Verulamium and London, where the patriots put many thousands of men and women to death with savage tortures and mutilations. The great number of these victims, although the traditional 70,000 be an exaggerated estimate, confirms other evidence that the Latinization of these cities had been in process before the conquest of seventeen short years back.

Returning from Anglesey by forced marches, the legionaries, as so often before, broke in a great battle the undisciplined and short-lived ardour of the Celtic onset. The late massacre was avenged with frightful severity on the Iceni of Norfolk, whose land did not recover for generations from the destruction then wrought. Boadicea took poison. The Roman system was re-established in south and east Britain, and ere long was marked with more justice towards the natives. The towns which the Iceni had destroyed were soon more flourishing than ever, especially London, growing yearly as the centre of a new system of North European commerce. The leading Britons of the rising generation, abandoning the habits of free warriors, wore the toga with

[1] Henceforth I use the word ' Celtic' in its usual popular sense to denote the admixture of Celtic and older Iberian. Boadicea, with her golden hair, was of the Celtic aristocracy in the stricter sense. Her real name was ' Boudicca,' but Cowper and Tennyson have familiarised the world with the more euphonious ' Boadicea.'

pride and learned to take delight in Roman manners, language and art.

But there remained the problem of the North-West frontier. Until some effective system of military control had been established over the Welsh mountains and the northern moors, warlike tribes would be continually descending from those reservoirs of savagery to plunder the demilitarized inhabitants of city and villa in the plains below.

The Roman armies who for so many generations addressed themselves to this problem, were very different from the warrior swarms of Celt, Saxon and Dane, very different too from the feudal host of Norman times. A Roman army was a highly drilled, long-service force, held together under strict discipline all the year round and from year to year, accustomed, when not fighting, to fatigue duty in building roads, bridges and forts. Unlike the other invaders of Britain, the Romans did not achieve their conquests by indiscriminate slaughter and destruction, nor by ushering in a host of farmer immigrants, nor by the erection of private castles. Their method of conquest was to make military roads, planned on system for the whole island, and to plant along them forts garrisoned by the regular troops. It was thus that the legions were able, after a first check, to do what the Saxons failed to do, and the castle-building Norman Barons only did after long centuries, namely, to subjugate and hold down the Welsh mountaineers. They could not Romanize the mountains as they Romanized the eastern and southern plains, nor plant cities at the foot of Snowdon and Plynlymmon. But by means of roads and forts they had made an effective military occupation of Wales within five-and-thirty years of their landing.

Devon and Cornwall they neglected, as an area too small and isolated to be dangerous. Roman remains are scarce beyond Exeter. But Somerset played an important part in the new Britain. Within six years of the Claudian invasion, the new Government was working the Mendip lead-mines. And the waters of Aquæ Solis soon made Bath the centre of fashion, luxury and leisure for Romano-British society, desperately resolved to reproduce under leaden skies the gay, lounging life of Imperial Rome.

But the real difficulty of the frontier problem, never wholly solved, lay in the North. Between Tyne and Humber lay the moorlands of heather and white grass that we know, varied in those days by vast forests of brushwood, birch and dwarf oak destined to disappear before the nibbling of sheep when the wool trade developed in a later England. In those desolate regions the savage Brigantes refused to listen to the voice of the Roman charmer, or to lay aside their native habits and warlike aspirations. Beyond them, in modern Scotland, lay the Caledonians, of Pictish and other race, partly Celtic; they were no more submissive than the Brigantes, and were yet more formidable from the remoteness and the physical character of their territory.

It was not till a century and a half had passed after the Claudian conquest that the Emperor Severus marked the final limit of the northern frontier by renovating (210 A.D.) the wall that Hadrian had erected (123 A.D.) from Solway to the mouth of the Tyne. Several times the Romans had tried to conquer Scotland; once under Tacitus' father-in-law Agricola, the great Governor of Britain, with his victory at the 'Mons Graupius' somewhere on the edge of the Highlands (84 A.D.); once in the reign of Antoninus Pius (140 A.D.); and once again under Severus himself. But the Romans failed in Scotland as repeatedly and hopelessly as the English Plantagenet Kings. Their failure was due not only to the frontal resistance of the Picts in their water-logged straths and inaccessible mountains and forests, but to the frequent rebellions of the Brigantes in the rear. Until they abandoned Caledonia, the Romans' line of communication was too long, being exposed to the likelihood of attack all the way from the Humber northwards.

Some well-trenched camps and the ruins of Antoninus' turf wall from Forth to Clyde were all that the legions left behind them in Scotland—except indeed a greater sense of cohesion among the Pictish tribes, inspired by the common purpose of resisting and ruining the Roman Empire with all its walls and works. No attempt was made to add Ireland to the territory of the Cæsars.

The area of true Roman occupation was therefore confined almost exactly to modern England and Wales.[1] But this area was itself divided into two sharply contrasted regions, the Latinized South and East, the barbarian North and West.

North of Humber and Trent, west of Severn and Exe, Celto-Iberian tribalism survived in its more primitive form. This

---

[1] Except, of course, that the wall of Hadrian and Severus ran along the northern bank of the Tyne, instead of along the crests of the Cheviot Hills. Impressed by the wild moors stretching away from the northern foot of the wall, visitors speak of it as running through a wilderness. In a sense this is true, but the course of the wall is accompanied on the south by the Tyne valley, a natural line of civilization where the modern towns and railway are found. The Cheviot tops, and indeed almost any other line across North England, would have been more difficult for purposes of supply. The Romans, while occupying the wall as their line, normally held a few forts north of it, but south of Cheviot; 'indeed,' says Haverfield, 'we may call Cheviot then (as now) the dividing line between north and south.'

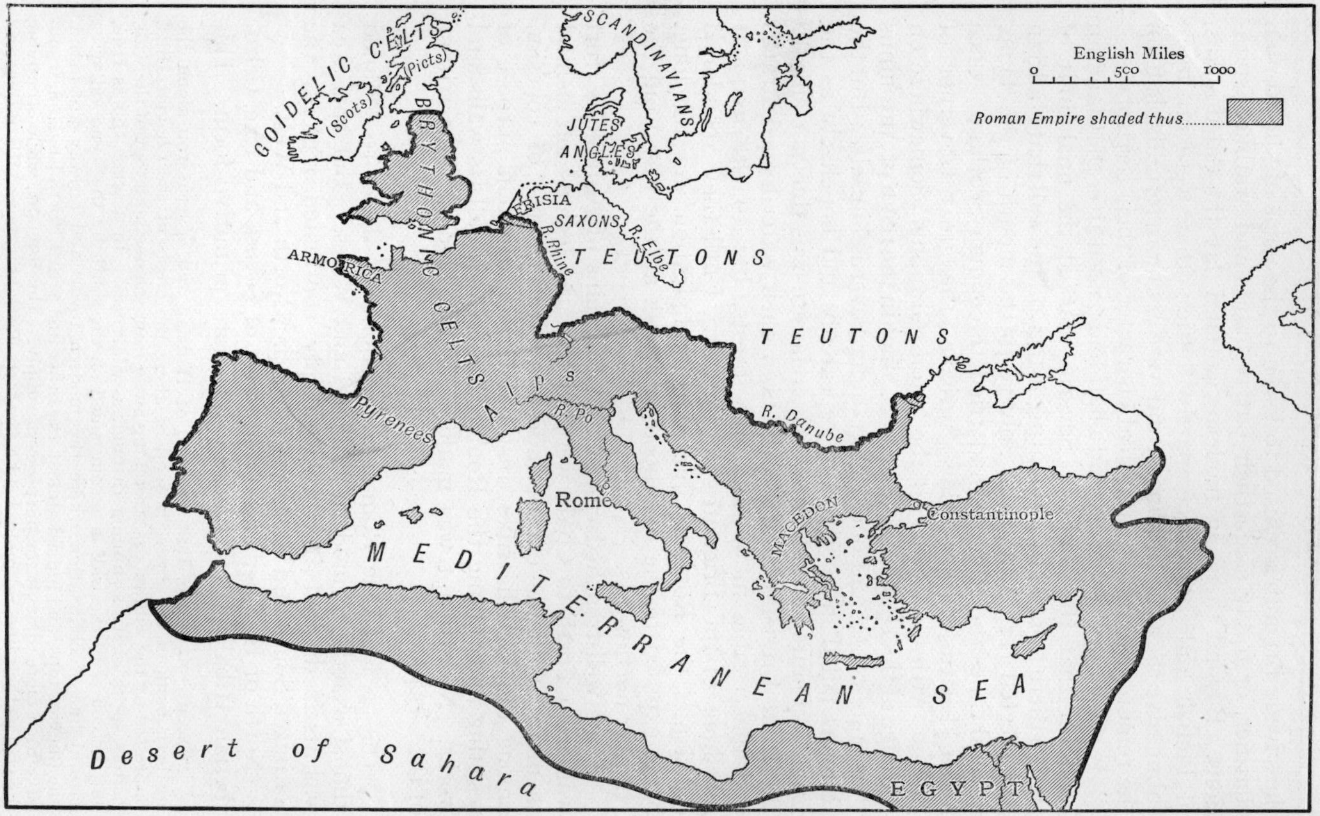

English Miles

0   500   1000

Roman Empire shaded thus.......

SCANDINAVIANS

GOIDELIC CELTS
(Picts)
(Scots)

BRYTHONIC CELTS

JUTES
ANGLES
FRISIA
SAXONS
R. Elbe
R. Rhine

ARMORICA

TEUTONS

TEUTONS

Alps
Pyrenees

R. Danube

R. Po
Rome

MACEDON

Constantinople

MEDITERRANEAN SEA

EGYPT

Desert of Sahara

Emery Walker Ltd. sc.

Map II.—The Roman Empire

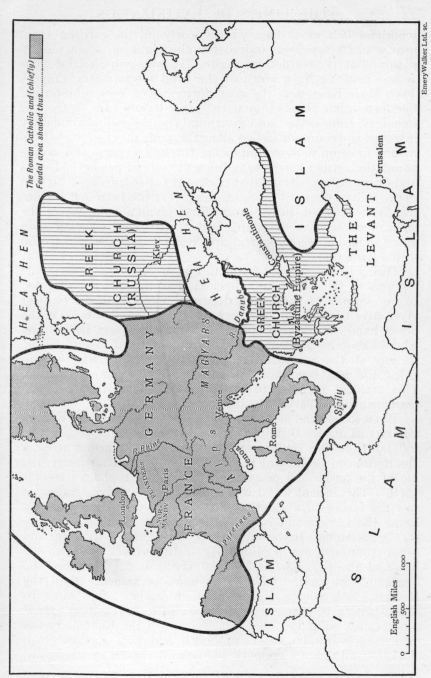

The Roman Catholic and (chiefly)
Feudal area shaded thus........

HEATHEN

GREEK
CHURCH
(RUSSIA)

Kiev

HEATHEN

R. Danube

GERMANY

MAGYARS

GREEK
CHURCH
(Byzantine Empire)

Constantinople

ISLAM

THE
LEVANT

Jerusalem

R. Rhine

Alps

Venice

Rome

Genoa

Sicily

FRANCE

London

FLANDERS

Paris

NOR-
MANDY

Pyrenees

ISLAM

ISLAM

ISLAM

English Miles

0   500   1000

Map III.—Mediæval Christendom (about 1100 A.D.)

moorland half of Britain, where nearly all the garrison spent nearly all its time, was indeed the chief area of military occupation, but it was nothing more. It was patrolled by some 40,000 men, nearly a tenth of the total forces of the Empire. Their three bases were the great fortresses of York, Chester and Caerleon, each the headquarters of a legion. In Wales, the Pennines, Cumberland and Northumbria, the mail-clad infantry marched and countermarched along the roads they had made from mountain camp to mountain camp, through a sparse and savage population, either hostile or indifferent to their passage. Devon and Cornwall were an isolated pocket of Celtic tribalism. It was in the fruitful plains of the South-East that the Latinized Britons were concentrated, in a peaceful and civilian land, where the sight of a cohort on the march was a rarity, but where Roman cities and villas were plentiful and Roman civilization powerful in its attraction.

Owing to this cultural distinction between the two geographic sections of the island, it happened that the districts destined to be overrun by the Saxon destroyer were the districts most given over to the Latin influences of city and villa life. On the other hand, Wales and Cornwall, Strathclyde and Lancashire, where alone independent Celtic life was destined to survive the coming of the Saxons, were precisely those districts wherein Celtic life had been least altered by the Roman occupation. This accident goes far to explain why Roman influence was permanent in no part of the island.

But a second and more general reason can be given for Rome's failure to Latinize Britain as she Latinized Gaul. Britain was too far from the Mediterranean. Southern France is itself a Mediterranean land. But the civilization of the Italian city, the life of the forum and piazza, shivers when transplanted too far north. The ancient world was a Mediterranean civilization. It was the mediæval world that first became truly European, by losing the Levant and North Africa and by winning Germany for Christendom. In the ancient world, Britain was a distant and isolated outpost; in the Middle Ages, it was much nearer to the heart of the Christian and feudal civilization. Therefore the Norman work in the island had more permanence than the Roman. Not enough Italian or Mediterranean folk came to Celtic Britain to change the character of its civilization except superficially. But the superficial success of the Romans in the richest agricultural districts of South and East was very remarkable, all the more remarkable since it proved so transient.[1]

See Maps, pp. 22, 23, above.

---

[1] By no means all the 'Roman' merchants, garrison and civil service came from Mediterranean lands. Especially after the first generation, many of the

The Mediterranean civilization, of which Rome had become the armed missionary, was based on city life. In that respect it differed from the Celtic civilization which it conquered and from the Saxon and feudal civilization that was destined to succeed it. The Roman Empire had grown out of a city state ; it had annexed a number of other city states in the Mediterranean, and had planted new cities among the tribes of Gaul. The true life of the Empire lay in the hundreds of walled towns, linked up by military roads, that held together its otherwise unwieldy bulk. From each of these cities it strove to govern and transform the surrounding countryside. And so in south Britain the first thing the Romans did was to build cities.

Besides London and the greater municipalities there were many lesser towns like Silchester, which the Romans planned out in their rectangular fashion, and in most cases protected with stone walls. In these towns even the common workmen talked Latin and were educated enough to read and write it, as we know from the words they scribbled for their amusement on tile and potsherd as they worked, which modern archæologists have dug up and interpreted. It was a high civilization, much more elaborate than anything seen again for many centuries in England. But it was not a native product, sprung from the soil; it was the life of the great cosmopolitan Empire oversea, of which the more progressive among the island tribes were content for a while to become a part.

Beyond the city walls Roman civilization petered away by degrees, through regions of Romano-British ' villadom,' into regions of mere Celtic tribalism. The countryside was sprinkled with smart Roman villas, built of stone in the Italian style, adorned with mosaics, frescoes and baths. Attached to each villa was an estate, worked by slaves, or by *coloni* who were bound to the soil and to its proprietor under rules as harsh as those which bound the mediæval villein. If there was not liberty there was peace. So real was the *Pax Romana* in the demilitarized districts of the South-East that these country-houses were not fortified or even protected by a moat, like the mediæval castle and manor house. The only people trained to fight were the soldiers of the regular army : this was one reason why Romanized Britain fell so easy a prey to the invader when men could no longer count on the protection of the legions.

soldiers were of Celtic, Teutonic or other northern origin ; in peace time perhaps 1000 to 1500 were paid off every year, but we do not know how many of them settled in the island after they had served their time. Nor is there evidence of any extensive immigration of civilians, though enough traders must have come to teach the language and civilization of the Empire to large sections of the natives. Persons of foreign origin were chiefly gathered in the towns.

In some of our southern counties, villas are constantly being unearthed ; in others they are seldom found. Celtic ' trevs ' of the Roman period are occasionally dug up ; the ground-plan of the hamlet and the form of the cottage are native, but the inhabitants used pottery and utensils of the Roman type. Celtic arts and crafts had been largely displaced by the prestige of the ' Samian ' and other Italian wares, just as European models drive out the native arts of Asia and Africa to-day, not always to the true enrichment of the world. But there is no evidence what language or languages the rural Celts talked, nor how far if at all their land system and habits of life and agriculture had been altered by contact with Rome. To resolve such questions we have little to go upon, and high authorities like Haverfield and Vinogradoff have held more or less divergent views.

The area of agriculture and the area of land reclaimed from forest and fen were both extended in Roman times, at least in some districts, as for instance in Cambridgeshire. But even there the work was only begun ; and the Midlands from Bucks to Warwickshire were still left in the main to the forest. The valleys of Thames and Trent, still water-logged, contained no connected line of important towns and villages as in later days. The Roman did something for deforesting and draining, but the yeoman's work in these matters was left for the stalwart industry of Saxon and Danish townships, extended over a thousand years.[1] Nevertheless in those districts which were already reclaimed for the plough, Roman Britain raised enough grain to export considerably to the continent.

The government of Britain was far from being a rigid and uniform bureaucracy. For the Roman Empire, though at bottom a military despotism standing on the social basis of slavery, was in some respects very liberal. In accordance with its custom, the privileged municipalities in the island not only enjoyed self-government but had jurisdiction each over a rural area about as large as a modern county. There were five such governing cities : Verulamium, Colchester, Lincoln, Gloucester and York ; mercantile London, though larger than any of these, had less official status.

The rest of civilized Britain was divided up into cantons, answering to Celtic tribal areas and bearing the tribal names. The cantonal administration was as far as possible centred on

---

[1] In discussing this matter, it is, however, dangerous to argue from the line of the known Roman roads, as though they indicate the line of cultivation and habitation. The Romans built their great roads from nodal point to nodal point, in order to link up the island regarded as a whole. Villages, villas and smaller cities were overlooked by the great road-builders and were served by smaller earth-roads not now specifically known as ' Roman.'

some Roman town not of municipal rank. It was characteristic
of the Romans that instead of trying to stamp out native tribalism
they used it as a means of government, while undermining its
spirit by contact with their own more attractive civilization.
Every inducement was offered to the Celtic chief to become
Roman in dress, language and heart ; on these conditions he
could remain a Celtic chief in relation to his tribesmen, exercising
his authority over them as a togaed Roman official. This policy,
which might appear to an iron bureaucrat to be a dangerous
concession to tribalism, became in fact the means of Romanizing
the Celt with his own good will. The same cantonal system was
established in Gaul ; but whereas the cantonal names and areas
survived the Frankish conquest of Gaul, they disappeared in the
more destructive Saxon invasion of Britain.

Just as the Roman Empire, in contrast to some modern
nationalist States, was easy-going in its dealings with racial
custom in the annexed provinces, and merciless only when its
political power was challenged—so in the sphere of religion,
in contrast to the Christianity of the Dark and Middle Ages,
the Empire put no shackles on philosophic speculation or on
variety in religion, and struck only at those organizations like
Druidism and the Christian Church which seemed to challenge
its authority as a government. When it persecuted it was not
from religious but from political motives. But the persecution
of the Christians was not for that reason any less odious or less
disastrous in its results, for the intermittent attacks made on
the early Church by the Empire must have greatly helped
to engender the persecuting spirit which the Church herself
showed the moment that she got the upper hand, and which
continued for fifteen hundred years to be the bane of Christendom. The persecution of Christians in Britain was probably
on a small scale, for the Church there was on a small scale, but
the story of St. Alban's martyrdom remains as the symbol of
the fact.
Where the Empire smelt no challenge to its authority, it
embraced with open arms all local variations of polytheism, and
attempted to identify the Celtic tribal deities and local nature-
spirits with gods of its own Græco-Roman pantheon—itself an
amalgamation made on similar principles. Zeus-Jupiter was
not ' a jealous God,' and polytheism in all its various forms
may almost be regarded as a single religion, whereas Judaism,
Christianity and Mohamedanism are mutually exclusive. Although the Druidical priesthood had been suppressed as politically
dangerous, the natives of Britain continued freely to worship

their old deities, together with those of the Romans, while the polyglot army on the wall honoured all the gods of the far-flung Empire, but most of all the Roman gods, and strange Oriental cults like Mithraism. These latter had become important in the life of the Western Mediterranean, and undoubtedly prepared the way for the general acceptance of another mystic religion from the East.

Constantine made Christianity the official creed of the Empire a hundred years before the withdrawal of the legions from Britain ; but even so the new cult does not seem to have spread rapidly in the most distant of the provinces, if we are to judge from the small quantity of Christian remains unearthed in Romano-British sites. There was, however, enough of it to survive among the Welsh when every other Roman institution disappeared, because after the departure of the Roman generals and officials, the Christian missionaries, alone among the emissaries of civilization, did not desert the Britons in their day of trouble.

BOOKS FOR FURTHER READING

Haverfield, *The Roman Occupation of Britain*, revised by G. Macdonald, 1924, and Haverfield in *Cambridge Mediæval History*, I., Chapter XIII. R. G. Collingwood, *Roman Britain* ; Hume Brown, *History of Scotland*, Chapter I. Roman chapters of works of Oman, Cyril Fox, Vinogradoff, as above, p. 13 ; R. E. M. Wheeler, *Prehistoric and Roman Water*, 1925.

CHAPTER III

Beginning of the Nordic invasions. The Anglo-Saxon Conquest

THE settlement of the Nordic peoples in our island is the governing event of British history. The various irruptions of Anglo-Saxons and Jutes, of Danes and Norsemen form a single chapter ; it has its prelude in the first plundering raids of Saxon pirates on the coast of Roman Britain well before 300 A.D., and it ends about 1020 when Canute completed the Scandinavian conquest of England by reconciling on equal terms the kindred races of Saxon and Dane. Between these dates the racial character of the inhabitants of the country was fundamentally altered. It has since undergone slight continuous modification by the arrival of Norman, Flemish, Huguenot, Hebrew, Irish and other immigrants. But the racial basis was fixed by the time of Canute.

The Nordic invasions are more important than the Roman interlude, more important even than the Norman Conquest. The attempt of the Romans to Latinize the Celtic civilization in Britain broke down because there were too few Romans. And the attempt of the Norman-French aristocracy and clergy to Gallicize England, though it had great and permanent consequences, was gradually abandoned in face of the facts of race, just as the attempt to Anglicize Ireland has recently been abandoned for the same cause. The Nordic conquest of England had larger permanent results than any of these conquests, because it was secured on a general displacement of Celtic by Nordic peoples in the richest agricultural districts of the island. The distinctive character of the modern English is Nordic tempered by Welsh, not Welsh tempered by Nordic. In Scotland the Celtic element is racially stronger, but in Scotland also the Nordic language and character have prevailed.

Objection may be taken to the word ' Nordic,' as to all terms invented in after times for historical purposes. But to give a just conception of British history, a single word must sometimes be employed to cover the German, the Anglo-Saxon and the Scandinavian races. And to use the word ' Teuton ' or ' German ' for this purpose is to give an undue prominence to one part of the whole. The Teutons or Germans whom the Romans knew and feared under those names on the Rhine border and in Southern Europe, were indeed of the same great stock and culture as the Anglo-Saxons and Scandinavians, and a common term must be employed for all three. But to employ for this purpose the word ' Teuton ' or ' German ' suggests to the mind a people with the characteristics of the landward tribes who were engaged in pushing down the barriers of the Roman Empire to south and west—the Franks who conquered and gave their name to Gaul ; the Goths, Vandals and Lombards who broke into Spain, the Balkans, Africa and Italy ; and the Germans who remained in the fatherland. But the Anglo-Saxons and Scandinavians, with whom our story is concerned, were the north-eastern and seafaring branches of this great family, with definite attributes of their own. Therefore to call the family as a whole by the name of Teutons or Germans is misleading in its suggestions when we are speaking of the conquest of Britain.

The ' Nordic ' race, then, had certain distinctive features which gave a family likeness to the innumerable and widely scattered tribes of Scandinavians, Anglo-Saxons, Franks and Teutons, who ranged, conquering and colonizing, from Ireland to Constantinople, from Greenland to the Desert of Sahara.

They had all originally come from the shores of the Baltic, though the ancestors of Franks, Goths and Vandals had wandered off west and south long before, in the course of the last millennium before Christ. All the kinsmen had much in common : allied languages ; the religion of Thor and Woden after which most of

the English and some of the German days of the week are called ;
a body of epic poetry celebrating common racial heroes, like
Sigurd or Siegfried known from Iceland to Bavaria, and Beowulf
who does in Denmark and Scandinavia deeds sung in an English
poem ; a common art for decorating weapons, jewellery and
objects in daily use, with patterns of great beauty and richness,
quite distinct from Græco-Roman art and rather less distinct
from Celtic ; and lastly, common customs of war and agriculture,
varying considerably according to local conditions. There
was much therefore to connect German, Anglo-Saxon and
Scandinavian. But there is danger in the practice, once prevalent
among historians, of applying to our Anglo-Saxon ancestors
living on the North Sea and the Baltic in the Fifth Century,
descriptions written by Cæsar and Tacitus of the German tribes
on the Rhine four or five hundred years before. Modern archæology, armed with the spade, enables us to check this somewhat
irrelevant literary evidence.

The Anglo-Saxons settled the greater part of Britain from
the Forth to the borders of Cornwall, and the Jutes settled
Kent and the Isle of Wight. Some modern scholars think of
the Anglo-Saxons as being substantially one people, while others
adhere to the distinction drawn by Bede between the Angles
and the Saxons. In any case, at the time of their migration to
Britain, Angles and Saxons were occupying parts of the coast of
modern Denmark and Germany on both sides of the mouth of
the Elbe, and the difference between them in language and
customs was slight. The Jutes were a smaller tribe, kindred but
distinct; they came to Britain either directly from their old
home in Jutland, in northern Denmark, or, as some think, from
their more recent settlements in Frisia and on the lower Rhine.[1]

Agriculture had been practised in the north-east of Europe
ever since the later stone age. Many of the Anglo-Saxon invaders of Britain were farmers seeking richer ploughlands than
the sandy dunes, heaths, marshes and forests of the north
European shore. But many of them were deep-sea fishermen,
seal-hunters and whalers, trained to hardihood in conflict with
the storms, the sea-monsters and the pirates then common in
the North Sea. Themselves pirates and plunderers when on
the war-path by sea or land, they had a high sense of honour
and much kindly good-nature in dealings with their own folk at
home, as the fragments of their epic poetry testify. Fierce,
courageous and loyal, they were accustomed to follow their
chosen chiefs with great fidelity on marauding expeditions along
all the coasts between Norway and Frisia.

[1] See Note (1) at end of chapter.

THE DESTRUCTION OF
ROMAN BRITAIN

MAP IV.

Land above 1000 Feet..............
  ,, between 500 & 1000 Feet.....
  ,, below 500 Feet..................

Note:—The arrows indicate the general direction
of the attacks on Roman Britain; not particular
expeditions, which are conjectural. Attacks from
E. to W. are Anglo-Saxon, the others Celtic.

English Miles
0   50   100   150   200

Longmans, Green & Co. Ltd. London, New York, Toronto, Bombay, Calcutta & Madras.

Emery Walker Ltd. sc.

Such were the migratory habits of these amphibious, restless folk in the first centuries after Christ; but we should not call them nomads, for wherever they settled they practised agriculture. The Anglo-Saxon form of government was autocratic Kingship, exercised by some member of a royal family supposed to be descended from the gods, although such autocracy was limited by the custom of the tribe, by the temper of the armed tribesmen, and by the personal qualities of the King himself. There was very little that was slavish in the Anglo-Saxon warrior. But the idea that our 'Teutonic' forefathers when they first came to England were in any formal sense a democracy appears to be erroneous. There were many grades of rank, wealth and freedom among them, and they were ruled by Kings.

Pre-eminent among many lesser Kings who bore rule among our ancestors before their migration to England, was Offa, King of 'Angel,' regarded by the best modern authorities as an historical character, though much poetry and legend accumulated round his name. He waged war on the shores of the river Eider, now in Schleswig, but then the southern boundary of the territories of the Angles, against Teutonic tribes to the South. The fanciful may, by a somewhat forced construction, regard Offa's campaigns as the last war waged by the English against the Germans

> Until a day more dark and drear,
> And a more memorable year.

The Anglo-Saxons at the time of their coming to England had both Kingship and aristocracy. They were not 'farmer republicans.' The only possible basis for a primitive democracy is the strict tie of kinship and the bond of mutual aid to be rendered between all members of a wide clan, for unless he is so protected and supported the peasant falls into debt and thence into dependence or servitude. But even before the migration to Britain, tribalism was yielding to individualism, and kinship was being replaced by the personal relation of the warrior to his chief, which is the basis of aristocracy and feudalism. And this tendency was greatly increased when parts of the tribe migrated from the old continental home, under leaders who had engaged the personal service of warriors of different clans and sometimes of alien race. The English of England have always been singular for caring little about their cousins and ignoring their distant relatives: the very different practice of the Scot is partly due to the fact that he carries more Celtic blood in his veins.[1]

[1] Chadwick, *Origin of English People*, Chap. XII.; Phillpotts, *Kindred and Clan*, pp. 205–276.

The naval and military organization of a group of migratory Anglo-Saxons, bound for the mouth of Ouse, Trent or Thames, was based not so much on kinship, as on the discipline of a ship's crew, and on the personal attachment of professional warriors to the chief who had organized the expedition.   The solid farmers of the tribe may follow afterwards, with the women and children, in case the raid leads to a successful land-settlement.   But the spear-head of the invasion is the chief and his followers.   He himself wears the boar-shaped helmet and shirt of ring-mail, and wields the jewel-hilted sword of his ancestors, the work of Wayland Smith ;   he has presented a sword to the captain of each galley, and has given to every man in his train a round wooden shield and a long spear with ashwood shaft and iron head. He has fed them bountifully all winter with flesh, bread and strong drink at the ' ale-board ' in his long timber hall, where they have praised him as their good lord, because like Beowulf he ' never slew his hearth-fellows in drunkenness.'   It is he who has undertaken to lead them this summer where good plunder and better lands are to be won by the shield-wall.[1]

Hengist, the Jute, the traditional conqueror of Kent, may or may not partake in his person of the mythical.   But at least he stands as the type of these great, forgotten makers of history, the men who in pursuit of their own hearty lusts for gain and for adventure—

> Sharked up a list of lawless resolutes,
> For food and diet, to some enterprise
> That hath a stomach in't,

and with such help unwittingly founded England and all that has since come of England in the tide of time.   The bones of these nameless chiefs are dug up to-day in ' early Anglo-Saxon graveyards,' lying between the rusted shield-boss and spear-head that expelled Rome from Britain and drove the Celt into the West.

---

[1] The poem of *Beowulf* describes the chief as constantly giving to his followers assembled round the ' ale-board,' not only spears, swords and shields but helmets and shirts or ' byrnies ' of ring-mail—the ' hard war-net.'   But *Beowulf* was written in an age well after the Conquest of Britain when armour was becoming more plentiful ;   also the poet would naturally tend to exaggerate the hero's wealth and munificence, like Homer describing the shield of Achilles or the hall of Alcinöus.   The early Anglo-Saxon graveyards in England, of the actual period of the invasion, contain iron spear-heads and the iron bosses and handles of the round wooden shields ;   swords less often ;   helmets and byrnies practically never.   Yet some of the invading chiefs must have worn helmets and byrnies, for these have been found in early treasure caches in the continental homes of the invaders.   Doubtless they were too rare and valuable to be buried—for the Anglo-Saxon is practical as well as pious !   Their axes were small and not very important weapons.   The big battle-axe of Harold and his guard at Hastings was of later Viking origin.

Some of these great unknown ones must have had what we should now call ' genius ' as ' men of action.' For the true life story of a single one of them, telling why he and his men decided to cross the sea, where they landed, and in what manner they fought and wrought and thought—for that how gladly would we give whole libraries of later record !

But the past is inexorable in its silence. There are no authentic chronicles of the Saxon Conquest. The Britons in their refuge among the Welsh mountains relapsed into Celtic barbarism, and if the priest Gildas wrote for them a Book of Lamentations in Latin, it answers few of the purposes of history. The heathen Saxon invaders had indeed a Runic alphabet ; it would serve for a charm on a sword or a name on a stone, but it was not used to take down annals, or to transcribe the long-lost epics sung by the gleemen in hall, of which more than one must have told the deeds of some hero who came seeking Britain over deep water.

The historian has two points of light, and even those are dim. He sees an orderly Romano-Celtic world late in the Fourth Century, beginning to fall into chaos. Two hundred years later he sees a Saxon-Celtic barbarism beginning to emerge confusedly into the renewed twilight of history, and he hears the marching chaunt of St. Augustine and his monks bringing back with them the Latin alphabet and the custom of written record. Between these points stretches a great darkness. The most important page in our national annals is a blank. The chief names of this missing period of history—Hengist, Vortigern, Cerdic, Arthur—may be those of real or of imaginary men. All that archæology and history together can do is to indicate—not the date, leaders, landings and campaigns—but only the general character of the warfare that destroyed Roman Britain and gave the land to the English.[1]

As early as the latter years of the Third Century, the Romans established a fleet specially charged to defend the Gallic and British shores against the plundering raids of Saxon pirates. The Empire was at the same time being disturbed from within

[1] The most fundamental points are in dispute. High authorities differ as to whether the Hengist and Vortigern story is true ; whether Wessex was settled from the southern coast or from north of the Thames ; whether there was ever a Roman army of occupation in Britain again after the ' withdrawal ' of 407 ; when and how London fell ; whether the invasion of the north of England was at all contemporaneous with that of the south. If anyone thinks that I am too cautious in refusing either to accept or deny so many well-known stories, let him read the last chapter of Haverfield's *Roman Occupation of Britain*, entitled ' Saxon England,' and the article by Ferdinand Lot at the beginning of *Mélanges d'histoire offerts à M. Charles Bémont*, 1913, besides the well-known passages of controversy by Sir Henry Howorth, W. H. Stevenson, Chadwick, A. F. Major, and Bury, *Later Roman Empire*, II. p. 201, etc.

by the wars of its own rival Emperors and armies. In this game the legions quartered in Britain often took a hand on behalf of their own chiefs. The most singular of these pretenders was Carausius, the warden against the Saxon raids, who from 286 to 293 A.D. ruled the island as a sovereign and independent section of the Empire, safe behind its own navy. Carausius has been called ' the first sea-King of Britain.' After the reform of the Empire by Diocletian and Constantine a few years later, the reincorporated province of Roman Britain enjoyed a last golden age. An official known as ' the Count of the Saxon shore' defended the coast from the Wash to Portsmouth, by the aid of ten large fortresses, of which Richborough in Kent was the chief, and a considerable garrison withdrawn for this new purpose from the military regions of the north-west. Each of the ten fortresses commanded a port, whence a fleet could issue to fight the invaders at sea. By this provision the civilized lowlands were rendered secure from Saxon attack for another half century. More villas appear to have been built and occupied in the island from 300 to 350 A.D. than at any other period ; while British grain was sold on the Rhine and British cloth in the Levant. Whether or not these symptoms of prosperity imply that British society was in a less miserable economic condition than that into which the ' decurions ' and ' coloni ' of other provinces of the Empire had by this time fallen, we have no evidence.

See Frontispiece Map.

In the last half of the Fourth Century the downfall began. As the spade of the archæologist gives proof, life and property then became insecure in the lowland area of Britain. Here and there villas were burnt or deserted, in the track of raiding bands of Picts and Brigantes from the North, or of the wild Irish tribesmen then known as ' Scots,' who swarmed in through the unromanized districts of the West. These local catastrophes were due to the great general cause : the heart of the Empire was weakening under attack nearer home ; fewer and worse soldiers and civilians were coming from the continent to serve in Britain. As a consequence, a Celtic revival began, slow at first, but visible even before the final Saxon onrush destroyed the centres of Latin influence in the island. The civil and military connections with the Mediterranean became every year more shadowy, and the unromanized Celts from Wales, Caledonia and Ireland poured down over the land. Before Roman Silchester was abandoned under Saxon pressure, an ' Ogam stone ' with a barbarous Celtic inscription had been set up in its streets, portentous to anyone who remembered what Silchester once had been.

In the course of the first thirty or forty years of the Fifth

Century, though by what exact stages it is impossible to say, the Romanized Britons found themselves left to their own devices by an Empire that confessed itself unable any longer to help. It was only then that the Saxons became the chief instrument in the destruction of Roman Britain, begun in the previous century by the Celtic barbarians of North and West. We do not know whether or with what success the Saxons had renewed their raids between 350 and 400, but it is clear that at the opening of the new century they came over with increasing numbers and boldness. The state of the island pulverized by Picts and Scots, the breakdown of the true Roman regime, the conduct of the defence by Christian missionaries of a practical turn like St. Germanus in the place of regular Roman generals,— such things must often have been the theme of excited debate in log-built halls of the Anglo-Saxon chiefs, after the return from each successful plundering expedition. Why, the pirate-farmers began to ask each other, as they quaffed the mead, why should we take only what we can carry away ? In these favourable new conditions the idea was mooted of wholesale immigration to these warm well-watered lands, rich in grain-fields and in pasture and in oak forests swarming with deer and swine.

As all evidence is wanting, we can only guess that the Saxon conquest was achieved by two distinct types of expedition. On the one hand, in view of the amount of fighting and destruction to be done, there must surely have been bands of warriors unencumbered by women and children, moving rapidly over the island by the rivers and roads, fighting the battles, storming the earth-work camps and stone-girt cities, burning the towns and villas, slaughtering and driving away the Romanized Britons, hurling back into the West the war-bands of rival barbarians from Caledonia and Ireland. But we must also picture to ourselves the shipping over of the families of the invaders, accompanied perhaps by the less war-like of the agricultural population, to take up new homes in the ground thus roughly cleared.

For the Anglo-Saxon conquest, like the Danish settlement in Alfred's day, had two aspects, and to omit either is to misunderstand the Nordic invasions of Britain. Like the Danes after them, the Anglo-Saxons were bloody-minded pirates, rejoicing to destroy a higher civilization than their own, and at the same time Pilgrim Fathers, come to settle on the land and till it themselves, not as mere exploiters and slave masters but as honest husbandmen. If they had not been barbarians they would not have destroyed Roman civilization ; if they had not been Pilgrim Fathers their race would not in the end have replaced it by something better.

The rivers, deeper and more navigable than they are to-day, were the main routes by which the English first penetrated into the interior of the country henceforth to be called by their name.[1] The undecked galleys of shallow draught, in which they had so daringly crossed the North Sea, could be rowed far upstream into the very heart of the country, and then left under a guard in some island among the marshes or behind a palisade of stakes hastily cut from the forest. The rest of the disembarked warband could then march across Britain with fire and sword. Such, as we know, was the method of the Danish invaders in the time of Alfred, and such probably was the method of the Anglo-Saxon invaders before them.

When once the Roman military system had collapsed, the Roman roads only served to hasten the pace of conquest and destruction. It was indeed by the side of rivers and not by the side of roads that the new race made its first settlements, as their earliest relics show, but the roads must greatly have assisted their wholesale conquest of the island.[2] One can see them, padding along the stone causeway, heavily laden with plunder but lightly burdened with the panoply of war. Laughing at their luck, they turn aside to sack a villa descried amid the trees. As the flames shoot up, the pampered cock pheasant, imported by the Roman to adorn his terraces, frightened now by the shouting of the barbarous seamen, scuttles off into the forest ; he will there become a wild bird of the chase, destined to play a great part in the social history of the island through many changing centuries.

We can say of these Saxon warriors, as they emerge for the first time on the great stage of history, that they, like their descendants, are ' a warlike but not a military people.' A spear and wooden shield apiece, with a few swords among them, here and there a helmet, and perhaps one mail shirt to every thousand men,[3] sufficed them to conquer the island. Yet the Latinized Britons should have been able to pit against them the disciplined infantry, the body-armour, the missile weapons and the cavalry of later Roman warfare. We do not in fact know whether the

[1] For this statement we have the direct archæological evidence of the early Anglo-Saxon graveyards, which are nearly all situated either on some navigable stream or on a tributary leading directly from it. See Thurlow Leeds, *Archæology of the Anglo-Saxon Settlements*, pp. 17–19.

[2] Mr. Thurlow Leeds (*History*, July 1925) argues that the primæval Icknield Way (see Map I., p. 8, above), which had been kept in use under the Romans, helped to draw the invaders along from the Wash to the upper Thames and so led to the foundation of Wessex from the North-East.

[3] See note, p. 32, above.

defenders fought principally in the Roman or in the revived Celtic fashion, when their half mythical King Arthur led them to battle against the ' heathen swarming o'er the Northern sea.' But in whatever manner the Britons fought they were conquered by foot soldiers without the discipline of the barracks, without body armour or missile weapons, but with prodigious energy and purpose. The defenders had the further advantage of formidable camps and steep earthworks crowned by stockades, very numerous all over Britain, besides the stone-walled Roman cities. But one by one all obstacles went down before the half-armed barbaric infantry landed from the long-ships.

We noticed in the last chapter, as a peculiarity of the Roman system in its best days, that no class in the peaceful South and East of the island had been trained to self-defence. The magnate of the villa, unlike the feudal lord of later times, was not a fighting man ; he had no fighting train and no fortified mansion. Many of the cities indeed were defended by magnificent stone walls, but their citizens were not accustomed to war like a burgher militia in the Middle Ages. If the Roman world was more civilized than the mediæval, it was proportionately more incapable of local self-help if anything happened to the central government and to the regular army. Indeed, the feudal system gradually arose out of the welter of barbarian invasions, precisely to remedy this vital defect in the social organism.

The most recent historical theory of the Saxon Conquest is that the great work of destruction was accomplished, not by each small tribal band as it settled down in its own particular district, but by a ' host ' of many bands acting together under a united military command. We know that the Danish marauders in Alfred's day were wont to sweep over the island in a composite ' host ' obeying for awhile a single leader. The Danish analogy, though suggestive, is not direct evidence as to the size of the Anglo-Saxon bands and their relation with each other. But Gildas, the vague and tearful British historian of these disasters, writing about 540 A.D., rather more than a hundred years after the serious beginning of the conquest, appears to believe that destruction advanced rapidly across the centre of the island till it touched the Western sea at some point, and that the invaders then withdrew to some extent from the West, leaving blank ruin behind. If this actually occurred in the middle and latter part of the Fifth Century, it would explain why the Roman cities and villas of the Midlands and the Middle West were destroyed long before the English invaders took up their permanent abode in those parts. Antiquarian research has proved that Bath, for instance, lay in ruins, its fashionable pools choked up with thickets and inhabited by waterfowl, long before the Saxons settled there, and long before the date 577, which the doubtful authority of the Anglo-Saxon Chronicle gives for the final capture of Bath. All this is easy to understand if there was a destructive rush of the invading ' host ' across the island at an early date, followed by partial withdrawal. The Midlands, sparsely peopled in Roman times, may have been left for awhile as no-man's land, a belt of destruction already lost to Latin civilization and not yet reclaimed by Saxondom. According to this theory the English ' host,' after its first great advance, retired from the West and dissolved into its component parts, of which each proceeded to found a Kingdom in the East of the island, and to busy itself with the work of land settlement, married life and farming.

Such then is the theory of the advance and retreat of the ' host,' based on the Danish analogy, on the hysterical expressions of Gildas, and on the established fact of very widely spread destruction at an early date. The theory cannot be regarded as either proved or disproved. It enjoys more favour at present than the older view enshrined in the classic pages of Green, which was based on the much later traditions or inventions of the Anglo-Saxon Chronicle.[1] This theory ascribed the work of destruction, as well as that of reconstruction, to isolated English bands, each working by itself in its own area. Possibly there may be some truth in both views. They are not mutually exclusive. During the conquest of the island from the Forth to the Channel, there was time and space for many different happenings. But it is wise to confess that we do not know.

Whether the bands of invaders were small or great, whether they acted separately or in concert, the destruction which they wrought was prodigious. The tradition of the Welsh Christian remnant is summarized in the words of Gildas the priest :—

Every colony is levelled to the ground by the stroke of the battering ram. The inhabitants are slaughtered along with the guardians of their churches, priests and people alike, while the sword gleamed on every side, and the flames crackled around. How horrible to behold in the midst of the streets the tops of towers torn from their lofty hinges, the stones of high walls, holy altars, mutilated corpses, all covered with lurid clots of coagulated blood, as if they had been crushed together in some ghastly winepress. . . . Of the miserable remnant some flee to the hills, only to be captured and slain in heaps : some,

---

[1] The Anglo-Saxon Chronicle, begun at King Alfred's order, is of course excellent authority for the Danish invasions and subsequent events with which its various authors were contemporary, but is not good for the conquest four hundred years before.

constrained by famine, come in and surrender themselves to be slaves for ever to the enemy. . . . Others wailing bitterly pass overseas.

The destruction of the Roman cities and villas was wholesale and almost universal. The early Anglo-Saxons were not city dwellers. They had no mercantile instincts except for selling slaves overseas, and they lost their old sea habits when they had won themselves good farm lands in the interior. The most civilized of their desires was to settle in large rural ' township ' and to till the soil on the open-field system of village agriculture. That was to be the sound basis of the new English civilization. Directed by this instinct, they began at once to build for themselves log houses grouped round the log hall of the lord. Split trunks of forest timber, set vertically side by side, composed the walls, for timber was there in plenty and they were no slovens at work.[1] Such were the homes in which they had lived beyond the sea, and they preferred the familiar touch and smell of the walls of split oak to the nice villas and town houses, fitted with every modern convenience, which they might have occupied at their will as soon as they had buried the corpses of the late owners.

We are told on the highest authority that ' no case is known where Saxons dwelt in a Roman villa.' [2] Time and spade may reveal some such cases, but they are scarcely likely to be numerous. And as with the villas so with the cities ; the newcomers showed the same unwillingness to live or to let anyone else live within the ramparts of stone. In some cases indeed the sites had been rendered so important by natural advantages or by the convergence of imperishable Roman roads, that they could not permanently be deserted. Chester, Bath and Canterbury were reoccupied in the course of time ; it is uncertain whether London, Lincoln and York were ever completely abandoned or not, though it appears that they ceased for some generations to be of any size or consequence. The junction of Roman roads and river passages ensured the ultimate greatness of London, Cambridge and various other places as soon as civilization began to make any recovery at all. There at least time and barbarism could not permanently obliterate the work of Rome.

But Silchester, Wroxeter, Verulamium and many other towns ceased for ever to be inhabited. St. Albans stands half a mile from the site of Verulamium, on the other side of the river ; it is as though the old site had been purposely avoided. Villas

[1] It was only as timber became rather more scarce, that houses began to be built of ' half-timber,'—a wooden ' framing ' to be filled in with cheaper material. Baldwin Brown, *Arts in Early England*, I., 26; II., 37–42.

[2] See note (2) at end of chapter, p. 48.

and cities are constantly being dug up out of the ground, in places given over to tillage, pasture or moor. But for some centuries the Roman ruins must have stood, as familiar a sight as the roofless abbeys under the Stuart Kings, a useful stone quarry sometimes by day, but at night haunted in the imagination of the Saxon peasant by the angry ghosts of the races that his forefathers had destroyed. Fear lest the dead should rise shrouded in their togas, may have been one reason why so many sites were never reoccupied at all.

In the course of the Sixth Century, after the first and most savage flood of destruction had ebbed, and while the western half of England still remained in Celtic hands, however barbarously most of it may have been ravaged,—a chain of separate but contiguous Anglo-Saxon kingdoms grew up, stretching from Northumbrian Bernicia to Wessex. For centuries they were shifting their frontiers like a kaleidoscope, but the names and positions of certain shires in south-east England, such as Essex, Sussex and Kent, recall some of these very ancient States.

These early English Kingdoms were periodically at war with one another, and with the wild Welsh.[1] The Welsh too were forever at one another's throats. The Romano-Britons of the ' Arthurian ' period had often been betrayed by the feuds and wickedness of their chiefs, if we are to believe Gildas. As Roman influence disappeared and Celtic tribalism revived, the intertribal warfare characteristic of the Celtic temperament revived with it, and according to Bede greatly assisted the Saxon Conquest.

The first result of that conquest was indeed to destroy the peace and unity of the old Roman province. Britain in the Fifth and Sixth Centuries must have been a fearsome chaos of warring tribes and kingdoms, while inside each of these loose political units, family carried on the bloodfeud against family, and was only sometimes persuaded to accept the ' weregild ' compensation in open folk-moot, in hope of bringing the series of murders to an end. Public and private war was the rule rather than the exception. But in the chaos the deep foundations were being laid.

As fast as their conquests were made good, the Anglo-Saxons brought over increasing numbers of their own women and children. The tradition in Bede's time was that the whole ' nation of the Angles ' had made the voyage, leaving empty the land whence

---

[1] Henceforward I begin to use freely the term ' Welsh,' the name given by the Saxons to the older races whom they drove into Strathclyde, Wales and the Devonian Peninsula. It is simply the Saxon word for ' foreigner.'

English Miles

0 10 20   40   60   80

R. Tweed

DALRIADA
(SCOTS)

Firth of Forth

R. Edinburgh
R. Clyde

STRATHCLYDE
(still Welsh)

GALLOWAY
(PICTS)

Melrose

Cheviot Hills

Lindisfarne
∴Farne Is.
Bamborough

BERNICIA

NORTHUMBRIA

Bewcastle Heavenfield
Roman Wall ✕ 635
(Broken) R. Tyne
Jarrow

CUMBRIA
(Lake District)

FURNESS

I. of
Man

R. Ribble

DEIRA

York

Streanaeshalch
(later Whitby)

R. Dee

R. Mersey

Heathfield ✕
633

R. Humber

✕ Chester
613

R. Ouse

LINDSEY

The Wash

WELSH MOUNTAIN REFUGE

✕ Maserfield, 642

WREO-
CEN-
SAETE

MERCIA

R. Trent

The
Wrekin

MAGE-
SAETE

○ Lichfield

R. Severn

HWICCE

R. Wye

R. Avon

MIDDLE
ANGLIA

R. Welland

EAST
ANGLIA

(NORTH FOLK)

(SOUTH FOLK)

R. Ouse

ESSEX
(EAST
SAXONS)

Deorham
✕ 577 ?

Ellandune
✕ 825

R. Thames

MID
SAXONS

R. Thames

London

I. of
Thanet

Canterbury

Bath

WESSEX
(WEST SAXONS)

Winchester

Forest of
Andredesweald

KENT
(JUTES)

SUMORSAETAN
R. Parret

WILSAETAN

SUSSEX
(SOUTH SAXONS)

WEST WALES

DORSAETAN

CORNWALL
(or Devonian Peninsula)

JUTES

MAP V.—England of the Heptarchy

Emery Walker Ltd. sc.

C 2

they came. Their royal family, of which the chief figure in story and legend had been the heroic Offa I, migrated from the old Kingdom of 'Angel' in Schleswig and became the Kings of Mercia in England ; the Danes poured in from what is now the Swedish mainland to occupy the parts of modern Denmark left unoccupied by the migration of the older inhabitants to the new 'Engle-land.' The shipping of many thousands of families from Southern Denmark to England was unique among the barbarian migrations of that period for the distance of sea traversed. When we remember that the emigrant ships in which they came over consisted of undecked galleys, we cannot withhold our admiration from these gallant women.

The colonizing energy of the English immigrants, combined with their savage destructiveness, altered the civilization and the racial stock far more than any other Nordic invasion of the period. Goth and Lombard in Italy, and Frank in Gaul had not destroyed the city life, the Christian religion or the Latinized speech of the conquered. But in Saxon England city life, Christian religion and Romano-Celtic language all disappeared, together with the native tribal areas and the Roman administrative boundaries ; the sites of towns and villages were generally, though not universally, changed, and their names are Saxon in perhaps nine cases out of ten. These things taken together imply a great alteration in racial stock, though the completeness of the racial change has sometimes been exaggerated.

It is, on the other hand, difficult to exaggerate the injury done to Romano-British civilization. It was crushed out between two barbarisms—invading Saxondom and the Celtic revival. For the lowland districts where it had flourished were exactly the districts swept by the besom of the Saxon destroyer. In the Welsh mountains and on the Cornish moors the civilized refugees, deprived of their cities and estates and surrounded by brother-Celts far less civilized than themselves, forgot in a generation or two the arts and traditions that had once enabled them to look down on the Saxon brute. The first result of the conquest was the loss of the crafts, science and learning of Rome ; in the island as a whole there was a sharp diminution in the numbers of the population and in the acreage of cultivated land. Surviving Celt and incoming Saxon alike were rude barbarians. Yet because the Saxon now lived in the lowlands, he began to evolve a civilization of his own, which was very soon superior to that of the Welsh mountaineers. Geography inverted the course of history, making the Celt barbarous and the Saxon civilized.

The removal of the Welsh from the richest districts in the island was in part due to their own temper. They had submitted to the civilized Romans as to superior beings, but these Saxon savages could not be accepted as lords. Better to die fighting or escape across the sea to the new Brittany in Armorica of Gaul, or retire among the wild hills of Wales. The Welsh hated the Saxons so much that they would not even attempt to convert them to Christianity. For this neglect the Saxons of Bede's time afterwards reproached them, when the gospel had come from Rome and from Scotland but not from beyond Severn. The semi-nomadic habits of the dwellers in some at least of the Welsh 'trevs' made it easy for them to shift their ground and to get away from the detested Saxon conqueror. The attachment of the Welshman was less to the soil than to the clan, and the clan can move where it likes.

I have said that after the first wild onrush was checked, the border war between Welshman and Saxon went on as the normal condition of life. The chief events of this age-long war were the debouchment of the English of Wessex at the mouth of the Severn (traditionally after the victory at Deorham in Gloucestershire, 577 A.D.), and the debouchment of the English of Northumbria at the mouths of Mersey and Dee, after a victory near the ruins of Chester, 'the city of the legions,' in 613. The arrival of Saxondom on the Irish Channel at these two points left the Welsh of Strathclyde, Wales and the Devonian Peninsula as three isolated pockets of Celtic tribalism, cut off from each other and from the life of the plains.

Thus in a succession of advances covering several hundred years, the Saxons, or later on the Scandinavians in their place, conquered and settled Cheshire, Lancashire, Cumberland and Westmoreland, the Severn valley, Somerset, and finally Devon, where the Saxon settlement was not completed till the Ninth or Tenth Century. But all the time the Saxons were getting more civilized and the Welsh more accustomed to them as neighbours. Long before the English advance had ended, both sides were Christian. Therefore, in these more westerly districts Celtic race and custom survived to a larger extent. But it was only in Cornwall and the unconquered Welsh mountains that language and civilization remained predominantly Celtic.

It is not possible to define accurately the proportion of Welsh to Nordic blood in any district. But it can be laid down as a general rule, good for both north and south of the island, that as we move from east to west we pass by successive stages from the Nordic to the Welsh. There are, however, exceptions to this rule : pockets of Welsh were left behind in the east, as in parts of the fen-country and of Hertfordshire ; and the Norsemen afterwards made settlements on the extreme west coast, as in

South Wales and North Lancashire, where the Vikings in their long-ships turned the rear of the Welsh from the sea.[1]

In Wessex and Mercia, though the language was changed, there were many more Welsh left alive than in the older Saxon settlements further to the east. In Wessex, which by that time included Dorset and Somerset, we find the laws of the Saxon King Ine in 693 acknowledging the rights of a separate class called Welshmen, sometimes as holders of land and military servants of the crown. But even in Kent and East Anglia some racial elements of the former population must have been transmitted through the women. It is not possible to suppose that the Jutish and Anglo-Saxon firstcomers would at once have brought over so many women of their own that they never mingled with the captive Welshwomen, the Andromaches of the conquered race.

The whole question of the number of Welsh spared by the conquerors is indeed very uncertain. The traces of Celtic in the language that was spoken in Saxon England are negligible, being confined to about half a dozen words. That proves much against Welsh survival. But it does not prove everything, for Celtic Ireland speaks English to-day ; and if that be attributed to schools and the printing-press we must remember that the population of South-West Scotland, who were to a large extent Celtic in blood, adopted the English language in the depth of the Middle Ages at a time when even the Scots were unlearned folk.

Another strong argument against extensive Welsh survival is the Nordic character of the place names in England. Some of the natural features, indeed, seem to have kept a Saxon variant of their old names,—as ' coombe ' for valley, and Bredon and Avon for certain hills and streams. Some even of the early Anglo-Saxon names for districts, like ' Deira,' ' Bernicia ' and ' Lindsey,' recall the Celtic past. But names of villages and homesteads are very seldom pre-Saxon, outside the regular Welsh areas ; and this fact is most significant of the completeness of the disturbance and resettlement effected by the Nordic conquerors. Yet even here we must be on our guard ; an Anglo-Saxon termination may conceal a Celtic root, as in

---

[1] Such a case is the Lake district. Its place-names are chiefly Norse, occasionally Celtic, but never early Anglo-Saxon. Chiefly between 900 and 1000, the Vikings came up the Solway and the estuaries of the Furness region, and thence settled the dales of Lakeland, being the first to clear and drain the valley bottoms and plant the still existing farms. The old Celtic tribes of the district had lived halfway up the fellside, on flat places of the moorland ; their traces are often found where no one would live to-day. They were not exterminated ; indeed, sheep on the fells used to be counted in Celtic numerals till quite modern times, so presumably the Norse farmers kept them as shepherd thralls. W. G. Collingwood's *Lake District History*, 1925.

*Trump*ington and *Mad*ingley; and purely Saxon names like Walton, Wallington and Walworth, and the Norse Birkby, are believed to mean the home of the Welsh or Britons.

Unlike the German and Scandinavian, the English is a mixed race though mainly Nordic—whatever the exact proportion may be. The Celtic and pre-Celtic blood, which probably flows to some extent in the veins of everyone who to-day claims English parentage, may have influenced the English temper. On the other hand, the difference discernible between modern English and modern German or Scandinavian might also be accounted for by the long centuries of residence in the very peculiar climate of Britain, and in the social and political security of an island that was well defended against invasion after 1066. But we still like to dream that English poetry owes something to wild Celtic fancy wedded to the deep feeling and good sense of the Nordic races. Shakespeare came from a shire that was close to the old Severn valley borderland of Welsh and Saxon conflict. All such speculations are fancy, in some indeterminate relation to fact.

The Celt remained with diminished lustre, but the Roman passed away out of the story of Britain. As has been said above, he left behind him three things as permanent legacies—the traditional site of London, the Roman roads and Welsh Christianity.

It is a moot point whether or not, during the fiercest time of the Saxon Conquest, London was ever completely abandoned. If, as is possible, it was at one time quite deserted, its re-establishment as a Saxon town on a more modest scale followed very soon, for by the time of Bede (700 A.D.) it was again spoken of as an important centre of commerce, as commerce was accounted in those barbarous times. We may fairly regard the Romans as the founders of London. The concentration of their road system at that point in the navigable Thames, made London's commercial revival certain, for the Romans, when they left England, did not take their roads away with them.

The importance of the Roman roads after their makers had gone, lay in this: no one made any more hard roads in the island until the turnpike movement of the Eighteenth Century. Throughout the Dark Ages and in early mediæval times, these stone highways still traversed an island otherwise relapsed to disunion and barbarism. The Roman roads greatly increased the speed of the Saxon, Danish and Norman Conquests, and aided, both in peace and in war, the slow work of Saxon and Norman Kings in uniting England as one State and making the English nation. Thanks to the Roman legacy, Britain had better national highways under the Saxon heptarchy than in Stuart times, though in the later period there were more by-roads. The imperial stone causeways, often elevated some feet above the ground, ran from sea to sea, generally keeping the higher land, but where needful marching majestically over bog and through forest. If the bridges soon fell in from neglect, the paved fords remained. For centuries wild tribes who only knew the name of Cæsar as a myth, trod his gigantic highways and gave them the fantastic names of Watling Street, Ermine Street and the Foss Way. Gradually the stones subsided and men were too careless and ignorant to replace them. Next, the road was used as a quarry, when the mediæval Englishman, having somewhat exhausted his timber, began to build for himself dwelling-houses of stone. From driving roads they declined into pack-horse tracks, finally disappearing for the most part in moor or plough-land. Stretches of them have been repaired and modernized, and the motor car now shoots along the path of the legions. But other stretches,—and those the best beloved,—are reserved for the Briton or Saxon who still fares on foot ; they are to be traced as green lanes, starting up out of nowhere and ending in nothing, going for miles straight as a die through the magical old English countryside.

The third legacy of the Romans was Welsh Christianity. Their latest importation into Britain survived all their older and more characteristic institutions. There are but few traces of Christianity in the Romano-British world revealed by the spade of the archæologist, and this makes all the more remarkable its survival as the only relic of that civilization among the Welsh. One reason was this : when the military and political system of the Cæsars departed from Britain, it never returned ; but missionaries of the Christian religion kept coming back from the Latinized continent to encourage the Welsh during the dark period after the Northumbrian wall was broken, when the Picts and Scots were attacking from north and west, and the Saxons from south and east. Deserted by the rest of the civilized world, the Welsh were not forgotten by the missionaries. Such a one was Saint Germanus, the traditional hero of the ' Hallelujah victory ' that he won over an army of combined Picts and Saxons in 430. The story tells how the Saint, formerly a distinguished soldier of Rome in Gaul, having come to Britain on a mission to put down Pelagian heretics, returned to his old trade, took command of the multitude of frightened Britons and led them to victory over the dreaded heathen invader. It may indeed be an exaggerated clerical account of a transaction that is otherwise totally lost to our knowledge, but it is highly characteristic of that period,— symbolic even. The Christian clergy, men of affairs and education when such qualities were becoming rare, stood in the gap whence the Roman soldier and governor were in retreat. In the day of trouble the Christian faith got a hold over the Welsh, which had not belonged to it as the official religion of later Roman rule in Britain. We shall see the same process repeated when the Saxons, newly Christianized, in their turn pass under the hammer of the heathen Danes and Norsemen. ' Give peace in our time, O Lord,' ' because there is none other that fighteth for us but only Thou, O God,' has a curious sound in the modern English liturgy ; it seems to speak of the Christian God as the only ally, but not a very formidable safeguard in a world all gone wrong. But to a Welshman dispossessed by the Saxons in the Fifth Century, or a Saxon dispossessed by the Danes in the Ninth, it would have appeared a very just statement of the case.[1]

In these circumstances, the Welsh of the Fifth and Sixth Centuries came to regard Christianity as their distinguishing mark which, together with their love of bardic music and poetry, enabled them still to feel superior to the Saxon savages who were exterminating them from the plains and confining them to the hills and moorlands of ' wild Wales.' The old Welsh bard's prophecy about the ancient races, once lords of Britain, thus describes their fate :—

> Their God they shall praise,
> Their language they shall keep,
> Their land they shall lose except wild Wales.

A similar development of Celtic Christianity took place in the remote peninsula of West Wales or Cornwall. On its tin-bearing moorlands and beside its woody streams running down to coves of the rocks, a race of local saints unknown to the rest of Christendom lived their lives and left their names to the villages of Cornwall, memorials of those stirring times when British civilization perished and British Christianity found creative vigour under the ribs of death. The lost history of the romantic age of Cornwall must have been largely maritime, for it was closely connected with the history and religion of Armorica on the Gallic shore opposite. Thither the Britons of the island fled from the Saxon invader, in such numbers that Armorica of the Romanized Gauls became ' Brittany ' of the Celtic revival, never to be fully absorbed in the life of Latin France, not even in the era of the French Revolution when the ' Bretons ' held out so fiercely against the great changes that the rest of France had ordained.

[1] How old the words actually are is uncertain,—possibly not older in fact than the Eleventh Century.

BOOKS FOR FURTHER READING

Professor Chadwick, *Origin of the English Nation* ; Haverfield, *Roman Occupation*, last chapter; Leeds, *Archæology of Anglo-Saxon Settlements*; Baldwin Brown, *Art in Early England* ; *Cam. Med. Hist.* I., pp. 380–391 ; Professor Chambers, *Widsith, a Study in Old English Heroic Legend* ; Oman and Cyril Fox, as before ; *Introduction to the Survey of English Place Names*, Place Name Society, Vol. I., 1925.

NOTES AT END OF CHAPTER III.

(1) For the origin of the Anglo-Saxons and Jutes see Chadwick, *Origin of the English Nation* ; *Cam. Med. Hist.* I., 384–5 ; Cyril Fox, *Cambridge Region*, pp. 238, 284–6, 296; Leeds, *Archæology of Anglo-Saxon Settlements*, and Chambers' *Widsith*, pp. 237–247.

(2) Haverfield, *Roman Occupation* (1924), p. 274. Haverfield's statement that 'no case is known where Saxons dwelt in a Roman villa,' is not contradicted, though it may be qualified by Cyril Fox, *Cambridge Region*, pp. 282–3. Mr. Fox there says : 'There is evidence of the superimposition of Anglo-Saxon settlements on Roman sites in the Cambridge Region. Apart from Cambridge itself, Roman houses at Litlington, Bartlow, Wymondley (H) and Stansted (E) are sited in or immediately adjacent to the Anglo-Saxon nucleus. But this is not necessarily to be regarded as evidence of continuity ; it may be merely a result of the operation of economic laws.'

CHAPTER IV

Mediterranean Influence again. The Return of Christianity

PRIMITIVE societies, if they are ever to move on towards knowledge, wealth and ordered freedom, are obliged to travel in the first instance not along the path of democratic equality, but along the path of aristocracy, kingship and priesthood. The heathen clan or tribe may be relatively equalitarian, and poverty may be more or less equally distributed among its members, but it can never move forward in mass order towards higher civilization and the freedom of the individual. When men collectively are very poor some few must be made rich if there is to be any accumulation of wealth for civilized purposes. When men collectively are very ignorant, progress is only possible through the endowment of an educated few. In such a world, organization can only begin through personal ascendancy and can only be rendered permanent through privilege. Education and spiritual religion are, in those primitive times, inextricably bound up with superstition and the ascendancy of the priest over the layman, as Bede's History so innocently and charmingly demonstrates on every page. In our own democratic and partially scientific age these conditions of progress in the past may seem strange to some, but they are a large part of the secret of early English history. The greatest student of those times has written :—

If we describe several centuries as feudal, then feudalism will appear to us as a natural and even a necessary stage in our history : that is to say, if we would have the England of the sixteenth century arise out of the England of the eighth without passing through a period of feudalism, we must suppose many immense and fundamental changes in the nature of man and his surroundings. If we use the term in this wide sense, then (the barbarian conquests being given us as an unalterable fact) feudalism means civilization, the separation of employment, the division of labour, the possibility of national defence, the possibility of art, science, literature and learned leisure ; the cathedral, the scriptorium, the library are as truly the work of feudalism as the baronial castle. When, therefore, we speak, as we shall have to speak, of forces which make for the subjection of the peasantry to seignorial justice and which substitute the manor with its villeins for the free village, we shall—so at least it seems to us—be speaking, not of abnormal forces, not of retrogression, not of disease, but in the main of normal and healthy growth. Far from us indeed is the cheerful optimism which refuses to see that the process of civilization is often a cruel process ; but the England of the eleventh century is nearer to the England of the nineteenth than is the England of the seventh—nearer by just four hundred years.

So Maitland wrote thirty years ago, and the chapters of this book which endeavour to sketch the Anglo-Saxon and Norman periods must be to a large extent a comment on this ' deep speech ' of his. Kingship, feudalism and ecclesiasticism grew together as harmonious parts of a general movement. King, thegn and Bishop, though often rivals, in the main fostered one another's power. All three were at once the exploiters and the saviours of an otherwise helpless society. The period during and after the Danish invasions will offer the best ground for describing the growth of feudalism and Kingship, the origins of which we have already noticed in the period of the Saxon Conquest. In the present chapter, covering the years between that conquest and the coming of the Vikings, we must attempt the difficult task of appreciating the change of religion as the first great step forward of the English people on the path of civilized life.

The Christian conquest of the island was the return of Mediterranean civilization in a new form, and with a new message. At the Kentish ports, through which the legions had come and gone, landed Augustine of Rome and Theodore of Tarsus ; they established here a hierarchy imitated from the officialdom of the defunct Roman Empire, and the English Kings in turn borrowed, from this new civil service of the Church, forms and policies fitted to the needs of the infant State. Christianity meant, also, the return of learning to the island, and the beginning among the barbarians of a political and legal civilization based on the arts of reading and writing in the practicable Latin alphabet.[1]

Christianity spoke also of strange matters, totally foreign to the Nordic mind, and in great part foreign to the mind of ancient Rome : it taught charity, humility, self-discipline, a concern about spiritual things, an active and uneasy conscience, an emphasis on the distinction between soul and body to the disparagement of the latter, a great fear and a great hope about the next life perpetually governing action in this one, the submission of the freeman to the priest,—partly as being the wiser man of the two, partly from superstitious awe,—great stress on dogma and consequently, as a strange corollary to the religion of brotherhood, the novel religious duty of persecuting every heathen and every heretic. Like Kingship and feudalism, mediæval religion was not an unmixed blessing. But the play of these forces upon the old easy-going Nordic character produced after a thousand years the Englishmen of Tudor times, and, without disrespect to our more distant ancestry, we may confess that they thought of more things in the Mermaid Tavern than in those Saxon mead-halls where Widsith, the minstrel, ' his word-hoard unlocked.'

The worship of Odin and Thor, the religion common to primitive Anglo-Saxon and Scandinavian, was pre-eminently a layman's religion, a warrior's religion, a religion of high-hearted gentlemen not overburdened with brains or troubled about their own souls. Its grand old mythology inculcated or reflected the virtues of the race—manliness, generosity, loyalty in service and in friendship, and a certain rough honesty. The social standards of the modern English schoolboy come nearest to it, as the most elementary expression of the racial character. The Danes had a word for acts of cowardice, desertion or dishonourableness of any kind—' nidings vœrk,'—as distinct from the ordinary breaches of the law, and more terribly punished by public opinion. It was worse to be a ' niding ' than a man-slayer. The liar, too, is rather despised than honoured. The Nordic race would not have found its hero in Jacob or even in Odysseus of the many wiles—in spite of many similarities between the society described in Homer and in *Beowulf* respectively. The favourite heroes of the northern warrior world, like Njal of Iceland on the

---

[1] It is with the arrival of the Christians in Saxondom that we begin to get *written* laws, chronicles and poems. One source, however, the historian loses,—the weapons and ornaments which the heathen Saxons buried with their dead, but which Christian custom omitted. ' Graveyards,' all-important for the heathen period, are of much less service in the Christian epoch. Fortunately, we have literary evidence instead.

eve of the coming thither of Christianity, are praised by their neighbours because they ' never lie.'

At the time of the first contact of the Odin worshippers with Christianity, the sacrifice of slaves and captives, common to all primitive religions, had not completely died out on the continent, though there is no evidence of it in Saxon England. The sacrifice of cattle or horses was very common, accompanied by sacred feasting and drinking, which, in accordance with Pope Gregory's advice, were converted into Church feasts and ' Church ales.'

The Nordic religion was not a religion of dread, or of magic formularies to propitiate hostile powers. Instead of covering its temples with frescoes of the tortures of the damned, it taught people not to be afraid of death. Its ideal was the fellowship of the hero with the gods, not merely in feasting and victory, but in danger and defeat. For the gods, too, are in the hands of fate, and the Scandinavian vision of the twilight of the gods that was to end the world showed the heroes dying valiantly in the last hopeless fight against the forces of chaos—loyal and fearless to the last. It is an incomplete but not an ignoble religion. It contains those elements of character which it was the special mission of the Nordic peoples to add to modern civilization and to Christianity itself.

But, when all is said, the old Saxon and Danish faith was a religion of barbarism with no elements in itself of further progress, and the spontaneous conversion of its adherents to Christianity seemed a confession of this fact. The old religion was merely a traditional expression of racial character, not an outside force at work upon that character. It did little for learning or art. It did not preach humility, charity, or anything else that was difficult. It did not foster religious ardour in any form. And it was not intolerant ; no missionary is recorded to have suffered martyrdom while converting the Anglo-Saxons. English heathenism had no defences, good or bad, against the Christian attack. Its scattered priesthood had no corporate consciousness, no privileged position. Coifi, the high priest of Odin in the Yorkshire region, when Paulinus first came preaching to Edwin of Northumbria, declared that he got nothing out of the service of his gods, not even the first place at the King's court, and forthwith rode at the head of the people to overthrow the shrine of which he was the keeper.

Bede also reports another and nobler speech in favour of adopting Christianity, delivered by one of King Edwin's thegns at the same Witan :

The present life of man upon earth, O king, seems to me, in comparison with that time which is unknown to us, like to the swift flight of a sparrow through the house wherein you sit at supper in winter, with your Ealdormen and thegns, while the fire blazes in the midst and the hall is warmed, but the wintry storms of rain or snow are raging abroad. The sparrow, flying in at one door and immediately out at another, whilst he is within, is safe from the wintry tempest ; but, after a short space of fair weather, he immediately vanishes out of your sight, passing from winter into winter again. So this life of man appears for a little while, but of what is to follow or what went before we know nothing at all. If, therefore, this new doctrine tells us something more certain, it seems justly to deserve to be followed.

The Christian missionaries had, indeed, an immense advantage in bringing a clear-cut cosmogony and definite doctrines about heaven and hell, how to attain the one and avoid the other. In contrast with these precise dogmas, the old religion only presented a vague and poetical version of popular superstitions about the next life. These are exemplified by the Icelandic story in *Burnt Njal*, where the newly slain warrior, Gunnar, is overheard by his son, Hogni, singing of his last fight from inside his burial cairn.

Now those two, Skarphedinn and Hogni, were out of doors one evening by Gunnar's cairn on the south side. The moon and stars were shining clear and bright, but every now and then the clouds drove over them. Then, all at once, they thought they saw the cairn standing open, and, lo ! Gunnar had turned himself in the cairn and looked at the moon. They thought they saw four lights burning in the cairn, and none of them threw a shadow. They saw that Gunnar was merry, and he wore a joyful face. He sang a song, and so loud, that it might have been heard though they had been further off :

> He that lavished rings in largesse,
> When the fight's red rain-drops fell,
> Bright of face, with heart-strings hardy,
> Hogni's father met his fate ;
> Then his brow with helmet shrouding,
> Bearing battle-shield, he spake,
> ' I will die the prop of battle,
> Sooner die than yield an inch,
> Yes, sooner die than yield an inch.'

After that the cairn was shut up again.

It may be taken as the swan-song of that fine old heathen society, for a few years later the Christian missionaries came to Iceland, one of the last strongholds of Nordic heathendom, and the best men of the island, including Njal the truth-teller, promised them backing.

Anglo-Saxon heathendom perished four hundred years before Scandinavian. From geographic causes England lay in the path of Christian influence long before it reached Denmark, Norway or Iceland. The English Woden was overthrown in the Seventh Century by a vigorous encircling movement from North and South at once, the religion of Columba and Aidan coming from Scotland, the religion of Gregory and Augustine coming from Rome. It might, indeed, have been expected that the attack would be launched from the West, but the Welsh Christians still hated the Saxon intruder too much to try to save his soul.

Nevertheless, the Welsh had indirectly assisted in the conversion of England, for St. Patrick was a Romanized Briton. Probably the lower Severn was the scene of his early home, whence raiding Scots of Ireland had carried him captive in the opening years of the Fifth Century. His subsequent conversion of Ireland (432–461) started Christianity on the long circuit by which it returned to Northern England. Columba carried it from Ireland to Western Scotland (563), and from Scotland it converted Northumbria through the mission of Aidan (635), a generation after the landing of Augustine in Kent (597).

Though the Irish Christianity of Columba and Aidan became a rival to the Roman Christianity of Gregory and Augustine, Patrick had not intended to found a Church hostile to Rome. Bearing a Roman name,—Patricius,—he was a citizen of the old Empire, as proud of his Roman rights as St. Paul himself. He studied in Gaul, and held his commission thence from a Church which already regarded the Bishop of Rome as an important adviser on doubtful religious questions, though not as lord paramount. Patrick, though not very learned himself, brought to Ireland the inestimable gift of the Latin language of which the Celtic genius soon made such good scholarly use in profane as well as sacred letters. He did not, like Cyril, the Apostle of the Slavs, set out to found a separate Christian civilization for the race he converted. He desired to make Ireland a part of Roman Christianity and civilization, at a moment when the Roman Empire in the West had scarcely yet breathed its last and was completely identified in the minds of men with the Christian religion. The acceptance of Christianity in Ireland, as later in England, was in part due to the admiration felt by the barbarians for the Empire even in its fall, and for all things appertaining to Rome, very much as Christianity is accepted by African tribes to-day as representing Europe.

Nevertheless, the Church which Patrick caused to triumph in Ireland developed after his death in a direction away from Rome. The fall of the Empire in the West, the extirpation of Latin institutions in the neighbouring island of Britain, and the barbarian conquests in France and Italy for awhile isolated

Ireland from Mediterranean influence, and gave opportunity for the rise of a native Celtic Church and civilization. The fact that the barbarian inroads did not reach Ireland till the coming of the Vikings in the Ninth Century, gave time for the efflorescence of the artistic, imaginative and literary life of early Irish Christianity.

But, though Irish Christianity flourished in the midst of Irish society, it did not transmute it as Anglo-Saxon Christianity transmuted Anglo-Saxon society. The social structure in Ireland offered no platform on which it was possible to erect a hierarchy of the Roman order, still less a parish system. Till the Vikings came there were no cities. Till Strongbow came there was no feudalism. The Irish were organized in a number of hostile and warring tribes, each tribe held together by the tie of kinship and each governed by its chief, over whom the ' High King ' at Tara was suzerain rather than sovereign. Irish Christianity was perforce tribal. It was not parochial, nor in the Roman sense episcopal, though there was a plethora of insignificant Bishops, mostly without sees. Its real life was monastic. The normal Irish monastery was connected with a single tribe, and acknowledged no ecclesiastical superior capable of controlling its Abbot.

Celtic monasticism did not represent the conventual ideal of St. Benedict. It was a congregation of hermits planted in some remote spot, often on a rocky mountain or island. Each lived in his own beehive hut of wattle, clay and turf ; but the huts had been collected together for mutual intercourse and security in a fortified village or *kraal*, under the command of an Abbot. The monks had many-sided activities, for they were hermits, scholars, artists, warriors and missionaries. The individual monk would sometimes go out into the world to preach, to compose tribal feuds or lead tribal wars ; sometimes he would copy and illuminate manuscripts in the monastery ; sometimes he would depart in search of a more complete seclusion, like St. Cuthbert when he left the company of his brother monks at remote Lindisfarne for the still deeper solitude of the Farne Islands.[1]

This Irish monasticism, both in its original home, and in its mission lands of Scotland and Northumbria, produced a rich crop of saints. The stories of their lives, many of them preserved by Bede, are singularly attractive. The freshness and the light of dawn glimmer in the legends of Aidan and of Cuthbert.

[1] St. Cuthbert submitted to Rome in 664, but the traditions of Scoto-Irish Christianity remained potent in his life ; nor were these traditions quite dead even in Bede—who was, therefore, eminently suited to write ' The Ecclesiastical History of the English People.'

To this form of monasticism we owe not only the Book of Kells but the manuscript art of Lindisfarne, wherein Celtic and Saxon native ornamentation were blended in perfect harmony with Christian traditions from southern lands. The Irish monks also revived a knowledge of classical secular literature, which had almost died out in Western Europe. While Pope Gregory the Great was reproving a Gallic Bishop for studying Latin grammar and poetry, the Irish Christians were busy saving it for the world in their remote corner where the Papal censure was unheard. Thence they carried it to the England of Benedict Biscop and Bede, where it greatly fructified ; finally, in the days of Charlemagne, it was taken back across the sea by Alcuin to begin its reconquest of the illiterate continent.

Scotland, England and Europe owe a great debt to the Irish churchmen. Yet they did little to civilize and nothing to organize the people of their own island, whose tribalism continued as before. The merits and limitations of the Celtic Church were closely connected ; the breath of freedom and individual choice implied a looseness of organization which left the Church little power when the first golden impulse had spent its force.

Such was the Christianity which invaded heathen Scotland from Ulster in 563, under the vigorous leadership of St. Columba, at once warrior, statesman, hermit and missionary—the greatest and most typical abbot of the Irish monastic ideal. On the small island of Iona off the West coast of Scotland he founded his cluster of beehive huts, whence the missionary monks swarmed over Northern Britain, and whither they returned periodically for repose, common counsel and solitary meditation.

In Columba's day the future Scotland [1] was already divided between Saxon and Celt. The Saxon had established himself in the south-eastern corner of the lowlands ; this rich district, afterwards known as Lothian, was then the northern part of the Kingdom of Northumbria, which at its greatest extent stretched from the Humber to the Firth of Forth. King Edwin of Northumbria was fortifying his ' Edwin's Burg ' on the famous rock, as the northernmost stronghold of Saxondom in the island. All the north and west, and most of the centre of the future Scotland was still Celtic ; yet it was destined in the long run to adopt the Saxon tongue and civilization, perhaps without great racial change. The history of Scotland is largely the history of that process of Anglicizing the Celt. Had it not been for the early

[1] The division between England and Scotland, though adumbrated in Roman times, see note, p. 21 above, was in abeyance during the Dark Ages. Saxon Northumbria overlapped the Cheviot border on the East, and Celtic Strathclyde overlapped it on the West. Scotland had even less pretension to internal unity than England.

English Miles

0 10 20 30 40 50   100

Hebrides

PICTS
(Goidelic Celts)

PICTLAND
PICTS (Goidelic Celts)

DALRIADA
Scots (Irish Goidelic Celts)

Iona   Mull

Dunkeld

Scone ○   R. Tay

R. Forth

R. Clyde

STRATHCLYDE
(Brythonic Celts)

○ Edwin's Burg (Edinburgh)

R. Tweed

Lindisfarne I.
·: Farne Is.

Melrose ○   ○ Bamborough Fortress

GALLOWAY
(Picts)

Cheviots

ROMAN WALL   R. Tyne
(Ruins)

SCOTS

NORTHUMBRIA
(SAXONS)

Streanaeshalch
(later Whitby)

(Saxons)

York ●

R. Ribble

R. Humber

MERCIA
(SAXONS)

Brythonic Celts

Emery Walker Ltd. sc.

MAP VI.—Scotland and Northumbria in the Dark Ages

settlement of the Anglo-Saxons in the south-eastern lowlands, Scotland would have remained a Celtic and tribal country, and its future history and relations to England might have borne more resemblance to the story of Ireland or of Wales.

In the days of King Edwin, the Saxons of Northumbria were still hostile intruders in Scotland, constantly at war with the Celtic world in the upper Tweed as well as farther north. And the Celtic world was constantly at war within itself. Apart from the innumerable tribal divisions and feuds, there were three main Celtic races—the Picts of North Scotland and of Galloway, probably most of them Goidelic Celts ; the Britannic Celts of Strathclyde ; and the latest comers, the Scots, from Ireland, settled in Dalriada, modern Argyllshire. The Scots from oversea were destined to give their name but not their civilization to the whole land. The history of these early times, no less than the settlement of Protestant Ulster in James 1's reign and the Irish immigration into Clydeside in recent times, reminds us that the connection between West Scotland and North-East Ireland is a constant factor in history.

Columba, himself an Irish Scot, gained great influence over his fellow Scots of Dalriada, and over the Picts of the North. The Britons of Strathclyde were more gradually brought under the influence of the new religion. At the opening of the Seventh Century the Christianity of Iona had a firm hold on many at least of the Chiefs and tribes of Celtic Scotland. But the Saxons of Northumbria still vacillated, according to the chances of battle or the personal beliefs of their Kings, between the worship of Woden and the Roman form of Christianity preached to them by Paulinus, one of Augustine's men. Before describing the conversion of Northumbria by Scoto-Irish Christianity, we must turn our attention to Augustine's mission in southern England, the other wing of the Christian invasion of the island.

Gregory the Great, the first of the great Popes, was the true founder of the mediæval Papacy. In 590 he received into his charge the defenceless and impoverished Bishopric of Rome, surrounded by triumphant barbarians amid the ruins of a fallen world. In a dozen years he had raised it up in the imagination of mankind as the heir to the defunct Empire of the West.

The change of European leadership from lay to clerical hands was reflected in the personal story of Gregory's life. Having begun his career as a wealthy Roman patrician, he employed his high administrative talents as Prefect of the City for awhile. Then he suddenly abandoned his social privileges and political duties to live as a humble monk on the Cælian Hill. Promoted thence to be Bishop of Rome, he exerted on behalf of the Church the genius of a Cæsar and the organizing care of an Augustus. His letters of advice to the Churches of Western Europe on every religious, political and social interest of the day, were accepted not indeed as having legal power but as having an unique moral authority. If the Papacy was, as Hobbes called it, ' no other than the ghost of the deceased Roman Empire, sitting crowned upon the grave thereof,' it was a living ghost and not a phantasm. Since the governing power of the Empire had perished in the West, a ghostly authority was welcomed by distant Kings, Bishops, monks and peoples, as giving some hope of progress, concord and righteous impartiality in a world of chaotic violence. This new conception of old Rome was about to take a strong hold of Anglo-Saxon England.

Augustine was no more than the worthy instrument of Gregory the Great. The impulse for the conversion of the ' Angles ' into ' angels ' came from Gregory in person. And, when Augustine and his fellow-missioners turned in despair back from their dangerous journey, he sent them on again with admonition and encouragement.

597. When Augustine landed in Thanet the Kingdom of Kent was evidently not unprepared to receive the gospel. It was the most civilized of the English States and had the closest connections with Christian France. The wife of King Ethelbert of Kent was herself a Christian Frank. Owing to the absence of deep attachment to the pagan religion which we have noticed above as characteristic of the Nordic world of that day, the Kings were often persuaded by their Christian wives to adopt the religion of the more civilized part of mankind, and their subjects seldom resisted the change.

Augustine did not convert England. He converted Kent, founded the see of Canterbury, and made it the solid base for the subsequent spread of Roman Christianity over the island. Outside Kent progress was at first slow. Augustine's claim to supremacy over all Christians in Britain by virtue of his Roman commission, was rejected by the Welsh clergy at a conference near the mouth of Severn where both parties lost their temper. Nearer home, the missionaries were, after some years, expelled from London, whose citizens now reappear in the page of history in a position partially independent of the small Saxon Kingdoms on either side of the lower Thames. The continued paganism of London was a chief reason why effect was never given to Gregory's plan to make London, and not Canterbury, the Metropolitan See.

The first striking success of Roman Christianity outside

Kent was Paulinus' conversion of the great King Edwin of 627.
Northumbria, again through the agency of a Christian wife.[1] As
Edwin was ruling from the Humber to the Forth, and had vassal
Kings in other parts of the island, it seemed for a moment that
England was already half won for Christ.

But the missionaries had as yet no deep hold on opinion
outside the Royal Court, and the fortunes of religion were for
a generation to come subject to the wager of battle, and to the
whims or deaths of rival Princes. For thirty critical years
Northumbria was fighting to preserve its supremacy in the island
from the rising power of Mercia, and these political wars affected
the issue between Christ and Woden. Woden was favoured by
King Penda of Mercia, while the champions of the Cross were
Kings Edwin and Oswald of Northumbria, who both lost their
lives fighting against him. Yet the ultimate triumph of Mercia
did not prevent the triumph of Christianity.[2] The struggle was
not a war of religion. Penda did not persecute Christianity and
passed no such laws against its practices as the Christians subsequently passed against the cult of Woden. ' King Penda,'
writes Bede, ' did not forbid the preaching of the Word even
among his people, the Mercians, if any were willing to hear it.
But, on the contrary, he hated and despised those whom he
perceived to be without works of faith, when they had once
received the faith of Christ, saying that they were contemptible
who scorned to obey their God, in whom they believed.'

Penda's allies against Northumbria were the Christian Welsh
under their King Cadwallon, savage mountaineers who revenged
the wrongs of their race on the Northumbrian Christians with a
cruelty far exceeding that of the heathens of Mercia against
their brother Saxons. Yet the fact that Penda sought Welsh
allies at all implies that the barrier between the two races was
becoming less impenetrable. It was during this period that
Mercia extended Saxon rule and Saxon colonization into the
Magasaetas, the lands beyond Severn, subsequently bounded to
the West by King Offa's Dyke.

See Map V., p. 41, above.

The political outcome of these wars was the decline of Northumbria and the rise of Mercia. In the course of the Seventh

---

[1] See p. 51, above.
[2] 633 Heathfield.   Penda defeats and kills Edwin.
634 Heavenfield.   Oswald defeats and kills Welsh Cadwallon, ally of Penda.
642 Maserfield.   Penda defeats and kills Oswald.
655 Oswald's brother, Oswy, defeats and kills Penda.
659 Wulfhere of Mercia throws off the Northumbrian yoke, but Christian-
izes Mercia.

It must be remembered that Mercia gets less than justice done to its importance and power in the history of Bede the Northumbrian, and in the Anglo-
Saxon Chronicle instituted by Alfred King of Wessex.

Century Mercia not only annexed the smaller Saxon States of Hwicce, Lindsey and Middle Anglia, but claimed lordship over East Anglia and Essex and began to thrust Wessex to the south of the Thames, struggling to wrest from her the Chiltern district. The smaller Saxon Kingdoms were being swallowed up, and the battle for their reversion lay between Wessex and Mercia. Although the independence of Northumbria as a separate Kingdom was maintained until the coming of the Vikings, she retired from the struggle for political supremacy, but retained the leadership in art, letters and religion throughout the period of Cuthbert and Bede. Not only the Lindisfarne gospels, but the Cross at Bewcastle and the ' Franks casket ' in the British Museum testify to the prolonged vigour of Northumbrian art, when the South European tradition of representing the human form had enriched the beautiful scroll and design work of Celtic and Saxon native art.

It is remarkable that until the middle of the Seventh Century, power in Saxon England had lain in the North, which never again claimed the leadership until the industrial revolution made coal and iron more valuable than cornfields. Archæological evidence suggests that the Anglo-Saxons were slow though sure in developing the agricultural wealth of the South ; and until they had done so it was always possible for the warriors of the northern moorlands to establish an ephemeral supremacy. London, too, though in a measure independent of the neighbouring kingdoms, was yet of small account. It was only after the coming of the Danes that the City of London stepped into her destined place as the leader of England, the principal seat of wealth and power though not of Royalty.

The religious consequences of the wars against Penda had been the disappearance of Paulinus' Roman Christianity from Northumbria, and its replacement by the mission of Aidan from Iona at the invitation of King Oswald in 635. Aidan founded the monastery of Melrose whence the Lothians were evangelized, and the monastery of Lindisfarne on Holy Island, a site chosen in obvious imitation of Iona. At Lindisfarne, Aidan was Abbot and Bishop in one. The ascetic yet cheerful life of these ardent, lovable, unworldly apostles of the moorland, who tramped the heather all day to preach by the burnside at evening, won the hearts of the men of the North. Indeed, Christianity had never, since its earliest years, appeared in a more attractive guise.

Until the Seventh Century was more than half spent, the monks of the Church of Iona did quite as much as the men of Canterbury to convert the English race. They re-converted relapsed Northumbria and Essex, and evangelized Mercia. Some

Irish hermits established their huts as far south as still heathen Sussex. But want of organization rendered the durability of their work doubtful, so soon as the zeal of their successors should decline. Already in Bede's time the historian noted how great was the falling-off in the spirit of Northumbrian religion, how lax the life of the monasteries had become, how much less the clergy were respected than in the days of Aidan and his first disciples. But by that time the organization of Rome had triumphed throughout England, and good organization can survive periodic lapses of zeal.

The success of the Iona mission on English soil revived the disputes between the Celtic and Roman Churches, which Augustine and the Welsh had defined without solving at their abortive conference on the banks of Severn. So long as the Celtic Church had remained in Celtic territory, Rome could afford to overlook its remote existence. But when rivalry began for the possession of Saxon England, the issue could no longer be evaded. The men of Iona, like the Welsh, had a date for Easter different from the Roman ; and their priest-monks shaved from ear to ear across the front of the head—possibly a reminiscence of Druidism—instead of making a round tonsure on the crown. These trivialities were the ostensible subjects of dispute and anathema. But behind lay far more important differences of spirit and organization, which in that epoch were involved in the question of submission to Rome.

Again the decisive event was brought about by a woman. The wife of Oswy King of Northumbria undermined her husband's faith in the orthodoxy of the Church of Iona, whose champion he had been ever since the death of his brother Oswald. Oswy summoned the Synod of Whitby [1] in 664, and gave his own judgment in favour of the claims of Rome as the inheritor of Peter's commission. The men of Iona, rejected in the house of their Northumbrian friends, could no longer maintain the struggle in England. Some, like St. Cuthbert, accepted the new order of things, others retired back into the Celtic wilderness. In the course of generations, Scotland, Wales and Ireland gradually came into line with the rest of Western Europe.

It cannot be denied that the decision of Whitby contained the seeds of all the trouble with Rome, down the ages to come. But men must live in and for their own epoch. The early

---

[1] The name Whitby, like other place-names ending in ' by,' is Danish, and therefore of later date. But the Synod which met at the monastery of Saxon ' Streanaeshalch ' is always called by the more familiar Danish name of the place.

adhesion of all the English Kingdoms to the Roman system of religion gave a great impetus to the movement towards racial unity, kingly and feudal power, systematic administration, legislation and taxation, and territorial as against tribal politics. The English, as we have seen, were already moving away from tribalism much more rapidly than the Celts ; the choice at Whitby may have been prompted in part by a desire to get away from Celtic and tribal things, and to imitate the superior organization of the Frankish Kingdom, where the Roman municipal system had not been extinguished by the barbarian invaders. The new Roman hierarchy would be a substitute for Roman bureaucracy and for municipal life which the Anglo-Saxons in their wilder days had destroyed, and were beginning dimly to regret.

A greater centralization and unity of system and purpose in ecclesiastical affairs throughout all the English Kingdoms led the way towards political unity under a single King. The administration of the Church became the model for the administration of the State. Methods and habits of mind based on discipline, system and the work of scribes were engendered in the life of the Church and spread thence to the secular world. And since the Churchmen, being the only learned men, were the chief advisers of the Crown and its first Secretariate, the new Roman ideas passed all the more easily from the sphere of the Church into the sphere of the State. Kingship gained new allies—men as skilled to serve with brain and pen, as the thegns with muscle and sword. Kingship gained also a new sanctity and a higher claim on the loyalty of the subject, through hallowing by the Church and by clerical theories of sovereignty drawn from recollections of the Roman law. It was only after the Norman Conquest and the days of Hildebrand, that Church and King became rivals as well as allies.

Christian leaders of the new type, by becoming statesmen and great prelates, did England yeoman's service. But the change put them in no small danger of becoming hard-faced officials, territorialists greedy above all things of lands and power for the Church. The old spirit of the Iona mission—humble, ascetic and full of brotherly love—had one last impersonation in Cuthbert of Lindisfarne, a convert to the Whitby decisions.

The man who organized the new hierarchy and brought all monastic and episcopal England under the dominion of Canterbury, was Theodore of Tarsus, Archbishop from 669–690. The first remarkable man among the successors of Augustine, he stands out as perhaps the greatest Prince of the Church in all English history. His career is the chief example of the value to England of her close relation to the Papacy of that day, which

supplied the northern island with the best that the Mediterranean civilization still had to give. At a time when France
and Germany were sunk in barbarous ignorance, the Pope sent
us Theodore, a Greek of Tarsus in Asia Minor, who brought with
him the African Hadrian as his lieutenant. Both men were
adepts in the best Greek and Latin scholarship of Italy and the
Levant. With the help of the Englishman, Benedict Biscop,
they brought over from the Mediterranean good store of books,
the indispensable but all too rare equipment of learning.
Canterbury became a school not only of Latin but of Greek.
The new influences from southern lands, combining with the
liberal traditions of Celtic scholarship in the north of England,
produced the school of Bede at Jarrow, and the library at York
where Alcuin studied. Thence religious and secular learning
migrated back to the continent and taught Latin literature to
the Empire of Charlemagne, when the Danish invasions for a
while extinguished the lamp of learning in the monasteries and
libraries of Northumbria.

The intellectual life of Bede (673–735) covered the whole
of the limited range of the learning of the Dark Ages. But
we moderns value him most as the ' father of English history.'
The first in the long roll of mediæval chroniclers of our island,
he told the tale of the Church of Iona in England and its rival
of Canterbury, writing at a place and time in which the memory
of both was still alive. He could not be unfair to the memory
of Aidan and his disciples, deeply as he deplored their unorthodoxy, for he was a Northumbrian well knowing how and by
whom his own people had been converted. His feelings towards
the schismatics of Wales were much less tender.

The spread of the Roman influence over the island from
Canterbury carried with it Church music, till then mainly confined to Kent. The Saxons took to it kindly and it greatly
strengthened the hold of Christianity on the people. The triumph
of Rome meant also the growth of ecclesiastical architecture.
Aidan's ' Scottish ' successors had been content with timber walls
and roofs of reed even for their cathedral on Lindisfarne. But
after Whitby the builders of the new regime aspired to give to
their churches something of the grandeur and permanence of
Rome. The roofless shells of Roman cities and villas with which
England was then so thickly sprinkled, afforded ready-hewn
quarries of squared stone, and were not without influence as
models to the church builders of the Seventh and Eighth Centuries,
who had also their memories of crypts and basilicas seen on
pilgrimage in Italy or in Merovingian Gaul. After the era of
Charlemagne, the influence of the romanesque Rhenish and

German architecture became strong in the England that recovered from the Danish invasions. Most of the Saxon churches, including all the largest, were eventually pulled down to make way for Norman or Plantagenet successors. But this should not blind us to the fact that stone churches were being multiplied in Saxon England at a time when the laity still built their halls and cottages of wood.[1]

The organization of the English Church was begun in 669 by Theodore of Tarsus as a man of sixty-eight, and was carried on by him for twenty years of vigorous old age. There was much opposition, and he beat it down. The essence of the reform was Theodore's creation of a sufficient number of Bishoprics, not of the roving missionary type of the Celtic Church, but with definite and mutually exclusive territorial sees, all subject to Canterbury. The monasteries were also subjected to the general ecclesiastical system ; they continued indeed to grow in wealth and numbers, but they were no longer independent and no longer the sole agencies of the Church, as they had almost become in Celtic Christianity.

After Theodore's day, as a result of his preparation of the ground on episcopal lines, the parish system began slowly to grow out of the soil, first in one township, then in another. Before the Norman Conquest most of the island was supplied with parish churches and parish priests, men who were not monks, and who in Saxon times were often married.

Just as in the mundane sphere the great work of Anglo-Saxon and Dane was to multiply townships in clearings made at the expense of the forest, so in the ecclesiastical sphere the work of the same pre-Norman period was to map out England in parishes, each with an endowed priest and a place of worship. The two movements together laid the foundations of the rural England we know. The parishes were often identical in area with the townships, in districts where the township was itself a large aggregate. But in North and West England we often find a number of townships in one parish, because the townships were mere hamlets or single farms.

The chief agents in the creation of the parish system were the Bishops and the thegns. The Bishops, no longer merely

---

[1] Most of the parish churches were still of timber at the time of the Norman Conquest, but some were already of stone. Wing church, in Bucks, remains as an example of a rural church built of stone on a large scale in Saxon times ; with its crypt it is an obvious imitation of Italian or Frankish models. So was the great Hexham Abbey, built by Wilfrid in the Seventh Century, in stone taken from the ruined Roman cities of the neighbouring wall of Hadrian ; the crypt still remains intact. At Brixworth, in Northamptonshire, the bricks from some neighbouring Roman ruin have been used by Anglo-Saxon builders.

monastic in their outlook, encouraged the growth of the secular, that is the non-monastic, clergy, who were more subject than the monks to episcopal authority, and were spread abroad in direct and continual contact with the laity. The thegn or local magnate gave the land or endowment. In the first instance the priest was often the private chaplain attached to the thegn's hall, but in the course of time his successor became the parson of the parish. The heirs of the original lay benefactor naturally claimed control over his nomination, but the Bishop was effectively his commanding officer.

A very large proportion of the sites of the parish churches of rural England are of Saxon origin, though not much of the Saxon building has survived the active piety of subsequent generations. The essential life of Saxon England was village life, and the parish church and the graveyard around it became the centre of the village for most purposes, mundane as well as spiritual. As the worship of Woden and Thor gradually died out, or was suppressed as devil-worship by the intolerant laws dictated by the victorious clergy, the whole population found its dearest associations in life and in death gathered round the parish church.

The growth of the power and influence of the Church, spiritual and progressive on one side, was feudal and aristocratic on the other. But it is only modern thought that speaks of the two aspects as distinct. It was one and the same movement, and contemporaries saw nothing incongruous. Ecclesiastical dues enforced by heavy penalties, the tithe or tenth of the gross produce of the soil, were necessary to build up the mediæval Church, with its art, architecture, leisure, learning and civilization. Yet these dues were a burden on the farmer, and helped to reduce many freemen to poverty and serfage.

Anglo-Saxon Kings, first of Mercia and Wessex, then of all England, at the instigation of their favourite prelates and to save their own souls, endowed Bishoprics and monasteries with a vast proportion of the soil. It was the clergy who first taught the Kings how to alienate lands and royal jurisdiction by written charters, for the benefit of feudal magnates both lay and clerical. It was the clergy who taught Anglo-Saxon proprietors how to make written wills, and wills often enriched the Church. The Church, in elaborating the legal and learned aspects of daily life, was thereby promoting the feudal system based on territorialism, the sharp distinction of classes, and the increasingly unequal distribution of wealth and freedom. ' Richly endowed churches mean a subjected peasantry,' writes Maitland. At the time of Domesday the ' four minsters, Worcester, Evesham,

Pershore and Westminster, were lords of seven-twelfths of Worcestershire.'

In Anglo-Saxon times, both before and after the Danish invasions, it is impossible always to distinguish clearly between Church and State. Not only did Bishops and clergy compose the principal part of the King's civil service, as remained the case throughout the Middle Ages, but before the Norman Conquest there were no separate Church Courts. The Bishop sat side by side with the Ealdorman or sheriff on the bench of the Shire Court, where spiritual and secular laws were indifferently administered. Those laws of the Anglo-Saxon Kings which the clergy first reduced to writing from popular oral tradition, are an example of this state of things. Written in the Anglo-Saxon language, but in the Latin alphabet of the clerical scribes, the laws have a dual character. They are, in part, a schedule of tribal custom, particularly as regards the price to be paid for injury to life and limb in the frequent barbarous quarrels of a primitive people : ' If one man slays another, 100 shillings wergeld,' ' if a bone is laid bare, three shillings,' ' if an ear is struck off, twelve shillings.' But the laws also register the high claims and privileges of the Church and her new jurisdiction over sin. All were enforced together in the Shire Court, at once a temporal and an ecclesiastical tribunal.[1]

---

[1] See Attenborough, *Laws of the Earliest English Kings*, 1922. A few quotations from the laws of Ine of Wessex (*circa* 690) will illustrate various points :—
' A child shall be baptised within 30 days. If this is not done the parent shall pay 30 shillings compensation. If, however, it dies without being baptised, he shall pay as compensation all he possesses.'
' If a slave works on Sunday by his lord's command, he shall become free. . . . If, however, a freeman works on that day, except by his lord's command, he shall be reduced to slavery.' This law and others show that the Church had not set its face against slavery as such. ' Church dues shall be rendered at Martinmas. If anyone fails to do so he shall forfeit 60 shillings and render 12 times the Church dues.'
' If anyone steals without the cognizance of his wife and children he shall pay a fine of 60 shillings. If, however, he steals with the cognizance of all his household they shall all go into slavery.' ' If a thief be taken [in the act] he shall die the death, or his life shall be redeemed by the payment of wergeld.'
' If anyone slays a foreigner [a man not of Wessex] the King shall have two-thirds of the wergeld and his son and relatives one-third.' ' The wergeld of a Welsh taxpayer is 120 shillings.' The ordinary punishments are death, slavery, scourging and fine—not imprisonment. Elaborate rules are laid down for sanctuary in a church.
In the contemporary laws of King Wihtred of Kent we read ' Men living in illicit unions shall turn to a righteous life repenting of their sins, or they shall be excluded from the communion of the Church.'
The written portions of Anglo-Saxon law which have come down to us are but fragments of the various ' customs ' that governed proceedings in the courts of that day.

The political influence of the Church was inextricably involved with the religious awe in which it was held by Kings
and people. When we read in the Anglo-Saxon Chronicle of
powerful rulers of Mercia and Wessex abandoning their thrones
to end their days as monks or as pilgrims to Rome, we cannot
wonder at the vast alienation of land to the monasteries, or at
the predominance in the courts of Offa of Mercia and Egbert of
Wessex of the only class who knew how to read and write, who
alone understood the administrative systems of the great Frankish
monarchy oversea, and who, moreover, were the only people
capable of instructing the King and his thegns in the formularies
necessary to avoid eternal torment and attain eternal bliss.

Yet the Anglo-Saxon world was by no means entirely given
over to the cultural and ethical ideas of Mediterranean Christianity. The new religion was to some extent affected by the
temper of its latest converts, the gallant thegns of the North,
nurtured on heroic poetry and legend. In the ' Dream of the
Rood ' the Christian poet, probably a Northumbrian of the
Eighth Century, has thus blended the two strains :—

> Stripped himself then the young hero,
> that was God Almighty,
> strong and brave :
> he mounted the high cross
> courageously in the sight of many,
> when he wanted to set mankind free.
> I trembled when the hero embraced me.
> I dared not bend to the earth.

The majority of the high-hearted Nordic warriors, though
generally respectful to the clergy, had not forgotten their ancestors,
and were moved by much the same ideals of conduct as before.
Anglo-Saxon poetry, like much mediæval and modern poetry,
is sincerely Christian in form when religion is specifically mentioned, but is pagan in tradition and pure human in feeling.
Only a few fragments of the wonderful Saxon epics have come
down to us, and there is no reason to suppose these fragments
were the best. The longest of them, the poem of *Beowulf*,
though the matter of the tale is as childish as the tales told by
Odysseus in the hall of Alcinöus, has something of Homer's
dignity of feeling and of style.

The principal virtues praised in the Saxon epics were the
loyalty of the warrior to his lord, the readiness of men to meet
death in battle, the courage, courtesy and magnanimity of the
lord himself. For it is the poetry of the hall, sung before Kings
and thegns. The typical hero of these poems is a man

unrestrained by tribal custom or religious observance, a man to whom the love of adventure is the breath of life, generous but passionate—Achilles or Hector but scarcely Odysseus. In many respects the life resembles that of Homer's day. Each was a free Heroic Age, wherein the warrior chief played his part unshackled. Even when Christianity and territorial feudalism were beginning to lay new restraints on the individual, Anglo-Saxon society had in it much that was disordered, fierce, noble and tragic. Here is a piece of it, taken from the Anglo-Saxon Chronicle, which gives a living picture of South England during the years when Offa was reigning over the Midlands.

This year Cynewulf and the West Saxon witan deprived his kinsman Sigebert of his kingdom, except Hampshire, for his unjust doings.

755. And Hampshire he held, until he slew the ealdorman who longest abode by him. And then Cynewulf drove him into Andred [the weald], and he abode there until a swineherd stabbed him at Privets flood, and avenged the ealdorman.

And King Cynewulf fought very many battles against the Welsh [on the Somerset border in Devon] ; and after he had held the kingdom about one and thirty years he purposed to expel an etheling, who was named Cyneard : and Cyneard was Sigebert's brother. And the

786. etheling learned that the King, with a small band, was gone to Merton [in Surrey] to visit a woman ; and he there beset him and surrounded the chamber on every side, before the men who were with the King discovered him. And, when the King perceived this he went to the door and there manfully defended himself, until he beheld the etheling, and then he rushed out upon him and sorely wounded him ; and they all continued fighting against the King until they had slain him. And, upon this, the King's thegns, having discovered the affray by the woman's cries, each, as he was ready, and with his utmost speed ran to the spot. And the etheling offered money and life to each of them, and not one of them would accept it ; but they continued fighting until they all fell, except one, a British hostage, and he was sorely wounded.

Then, upon the morrow, the King's thegns whom he had left behind him, heard that the King was slain. Then rode they thither. And, at the town wherein the King lay slain, they found the etheling and those within had closed the gates against them ; but they went then forward. And the etheling offered them their own choice of land and money if they would grant him the kingdom, and showed them that their kinsmen were with him, men who would not desert him. And they then said that no kinsman was dearer to them than their lord, and that they never would follow his murderer. And they, in turn, bade their kinsmen that they should go away from the etheling in safety. But the kinsmen said that the same had been bidden to those who before had been with the King, and that they themselves would now pay no more attention to such offers.

The etheling was killed in the fight that followed, and all

his men with him, because they chose death rather than show themselves less noble than the King's men the day before. In this incident we see how the ethics of Anglo-Saxon heroic poetry might be translated very accurately into terms of every-day life.

BOOKS FOR FURTHER READING

Baldwin Brown, *Arts in Early England*, Vols. I. and II.; Professor Bury, *Life of St. Patrick*; Mrs. Green, *The Irish State to* 1014; *Cam. Med. Hist.*, Vol. II., Chaps. VIII. B, XVI. B., XVII. and Vol. III., Chap. XIX.; Chadwick, *The Heroic Age*; W. P. Ker, *English Literature, Mediæval*, Chap. II.; Professor Chambers, *Widsith*, as before, especially Chap. VII.

CHAPTER V

The Second Nordic Invasion.   Viking Settlement and Influence

THUS far had the first Nordic settlers in Britain advanced on the path of civilization and national unity when the second wave of Nordic invasion broke upon them in their turn. The heathen Danes and Norsemen destroyed for awhile the higher civilization of the island collected in its monasteries, and for awhile increased its disunion by establishing the Danelaw over against the areas ruled by Saxon and Celt. Yet before a hundred years were out, the Scandinavian invasions were seen to have greatly strengthened the forces of progress. For the Vikings were of a stock kindred to the Saxon, but even more full of energy, hardihood and independence of character, and with no less aptitude for poetry and learning. They brought back to the island those seafaring habits which the Saxons had lost in their sojourn on up-country farms, and it was due to them that a vigorous town life revived in England for the first time since the departure of the Romans. Had it not been for the Scandinavian blood infused into our race by the catastrophes of the Ninth Century, less would have been heard in days to come of British maritime and commercial enterprise.

The deficiencies of the Anglo-Saxons, prior to this stern process of reinvigoration, were indeed many and great. They had so much forgotten their sea-craft that when Alfred sought to make a navy he sent for Frisian mercenaries. The Saxons had never developed town life, except to a slight extent in London. Their great economic service to Britain was their work as pioneer farmers and lumbermen, living in large townships or in isolated homesteads and ' dens ' in the clearings they made in the forest.

But the men of the township had little concern with what went on beyond the waste surrounding their lands, and regarded with suspicion every ' foreigner ' from beyond it. ' If a man from afar or a foreigner,' say the dooms of Kent and Wessex, ' fares through the wood off the highway and neither hollas nor blows a horn, he shall be counted a thief and may be slain or put to ransom.'

Kings and Bishops were striving to create a national or at least a provincial patriotism, but with very limited success. Northumbria was isolated, decadent, torn by feuds which were to leave her an easy prey to the Dane. Mercia had held the leadership in the glorious reign of Offa II (757–796), whose descent was traced through twelve generations to that Offa I, hero of many a tale and ballad, who had reigned over Angel, the old racial home in Schleswig four centuries back. But Egbert of Wessex had broken Mercia's power at Ellandune (825), and established instead the supremacy of his own Kingdom. But Egbert was no more King of all the English than Offa before him. These successive ' bretwaldas ' of the pre-Danish Hept-archy,—Edwin of Northumbria, Penda and Offa of Mercia, Egbert of Wessex,—had only the shadow of empire in Britain. Their supremacy depended on prestige which a single stricken field could make or mar. Machinery was lacking for the per-manent subjugation of distant provinces. The victors of the hour had no garrisoned forts and no standing army in the vassal States. The King's personal following of thegns, however devoted, was not large ; the ' fyrd ' could only be called out for a few weeks, and the Saxon farmers had no desire to colonize other Saxon Kingdoms as conquerors, though they were still busy invading and settling new lands in Welsh territory beyond Exe and Severn.[1]

In the hour of serious foreign invasion the English Kingdoms proved able to lay aside their feuds and help one another against the Vikings, more at any rate than the tribes of Ireland in like case. Nevertheless they fell one after the other without having evolved any coherent plan of national defence. The desire to be united in one State only came into being as a later consequence of the Danish wars, after Northumbria and Mercia had been destroyed by the heathen flood. Out of the stress of the same conflict arose new feudal and civic institutions which made

---

[1] The Magesaete and Wreocensaete (dwellers near the Wrekin) were early English settlements on the Wye and higher Severn valleys, in constant conflict with the Welsh. Their territory was delimited by Offa's Dyke, *circa* 784. See Map V., p. 41, above. The thegns of Wessex were in no less constant conflict with the Welsh of the Devonian border, which the Saxons were constantly thrusting back and back till it reached the present boundary of Cornwall.

Egbert's descendants more truly Kings of England than the founder of their line had ever aspired to be.

The course of history would have been very different had not the royal family of Wessex provided a long succession of able warriors and statesmen, including Alfred the Great. In the absence of elaborate institutions the affairs of a primitive society depend on the personal accident of the quality of its Kings. The richest and most populous part of old agricultural England —East Anglia—had failed in the race for leadership because it had no prince of the calibre of Edwin of Northumbria, Penda of Mercia or Alfred of Wessex. The Danes soon found how safe it was to land on the shores of helpless East Anglia and thence to overrun decadent Northumbria and declining Mercia. Wessex, the State that lay furthest removed from the landing bases of the invaders, happened at that time to have more resisting power than any other of the kingdoms, thanks to Alfred and his brothers, and it was apparently owing to this accident of historical geography that the Vikings just failed to complete their conquest of England.

Would things have been very different in the end, or very much worse, if the Scandinavians had extended their power up to the borders of Cornwall and Wales in the Ninth Century, as they did in the Eleventh under Canute? The question is not easy to answer, if we assume that once the Danes were established in England they would in any case, like the conquerors of Normandy, have soon abandoned Woden for Christ. But the might-have-beens of history are only the shadows attending on the triumphant event. The event decreed that the work of reconstructing civilization after the Danish raids, and reconciling the two branches of the Nordic race in England, should fall in the first instance to Alfred the Great and his progeny.

Although ' Viking ' means ' warrior ' and not ' creek-man,' the Vikings were men of the creeks. Denmark [1] was a land of sandy flats through which crept tortuous channels of the sea. Norway was a land of fiords—precipitous gorges in the mountain plateau, carrying the tide into the heart of the hills, in some places for a hundred miles. Here and there along the winding course of these fiords, a plot of fertile ground between the precipice and the estuary left room for cornfields and a group of wooden chalets. Hard by, a steep slope bore the dark forest down to the water's edge, inviting the lumberman and the shipbuilder. Above, on ledges of the fellside, among sounding streams and waterfalls,

[1] So called because Scandinavian Danes had settled in the districts left empty by the Angles who had gone to England. See p. 42, above.

the cattle lowed on the summer pastures. High over all, the barren mountain ranges, the breeding ground of Norse legend and poetry, rose up towards glacier and snow-field, dividing the settlements on the fiords one from another each as a puny kingdom, delaying for centuries the political union of Norway, and thrusting the hardy inhabitants out to sea to seek food and fortune there.

Fur-traders, whalers, fishermen, merchants, pirates, yet all the while assiduous tillers of the soil, the Scandinavians had always been an amphibious people. Ever since they had occupied their present homeland at some undefinable date in the stone age, the sea had been their road from settlement to settlement and their only communication with the outer world. But till the end of the Eighth Century the area of their piracy had been chiefly confined to the shores of the Baltic. They had been content to prey on one another and on their nearest neighbours. It was only in the age of Charlemagne that they began to cross the ocean and attack the Christian lands of the West.[1]

Why, it is often asked, were they suddenly inspired to go so far afield in such numbers ?

Several answers have been given, each containing perhaps some element of truth. Famine, following a bad harvest in those inhospitable climes, sometimes drove whole settlements to seek new lands. There were three classes among the Scandinavians— thrall, carl and earl. Polygamy, practised chiefly among the earls, produced a superfluity of landless young men, unwilling to be starvelings or dependents ; in love with war and adventure, though not above trade by the way ; proud of their swords and ring-shirts, of their red cloaks, gold ornaments and long yellow hair—for the Vikings were dandies rather than slovens, save when one of them felt the ' baresark ' fury upon him. Such were the raw materials of the Viking movement. It is also pointed out that in the last thirty years of the Eighth Century Charlemagne and his mailed Frankish horsemen approached the southern border of Denmark, on the cruel crusade which offered the Saxons

---

[1] Their amphibious habits they carried with them to their overseas settlements. See *Burnt Njal* for Iceland, and the Orkney Saga, where we read of Sweyn—'He had so great a drinking-hall that there was not another so great in all the Orkneys. Sweyn had in the spring hard work, and made them lay down very much seed, and looked much after it himself, but when that toil was ended he fared away every spring on a Viking voyage, and harried about the Southern Islands and Iceland and came home after midsummer. That he called Spring-Viking.' He then reaped his crops and ended the year with an Autumn-Viking. A strenuous and varied life !

The Viking has fared well in modern English fiction. Kipling's *Joyous Venture* in *Puck of Pook's Hill* has caught his historical character with rare felicity, and the first story in John Buchan's *Path of the King* is a fine piece of historical imagination.

of Germany the choice between baptism and death. The Danes gave asylum to the Saxon patriots and were naturally alarmed at Charlemagne's proceedings in their neighbourhood. Some have thought that the armed and threatening approach of the Christian warrior world aroused the Danish worshippers of Woden to raid the monasteries of the British Isles. But those early raiders came from Norway rather than Denmark, and the Scandinavians had no sense of political unity as a nation. Neither were they religious fanatics. They were savage robbers in an age of universal savagery, and they had what others had not—a noble joy in maritime adventure and exploration. It is probable that peaceful Scandinavian traders had visited England before the age of the Viking raids, but the evidence about them is so slight that nothing of importance can be deduced.

Many definable causes may have contributed to the Viking invasions, but the wind bloweth where it listeth and there is an element of chance in the rise and decline of great movements. The outburst of energy that carried the secluded inhabitants of the creeks to Constantinople and Greenland, that founded Normandy, the English Danelaw and the Irish towns, may have been due to the mere force of example and fashion, the cumulative power of a ball once set rolling by the casual success of a few adventurers.

At any rate, in the closing years of the Eighth Century, while Offa of Mercia was still alive, occurred the first recorded Viking raid in Western Europe. Three long-ships, with perhaps a couple of hundred rascals on board, landed somewhere on the peaceful coast of Wessex, killed the King's reeve who came to demand their business, and put to sea again before they could be caught. No more Vikings were seen in those parts for long years to come, but there followed in quick succession a series of similar raids on the coasts of Northumbria, Scotland, Ireland and Wales. The water-thieves plundered the monasteries temptingly situated, after the manner of the Celtic Church, on islands and capes peculiarly exposed to attack from the sea. Lindisfarne, Iona and many shrines of less name were robbed of their treasures, and the monks were either massacred or carried off to be bartered as slaves on the continent. The ill-guarded wealth of the shrines would fully account for these proceedings without our being forced to attribute to the pirates a fanatical hatred of Christianity provoked by Charlemagne's Saxon crusade. Nor was the gross cruelty of these raids anything exceptional. Even while they were in process the Anglo-Saxons were dealing out the same measure to one another. 'This year,' says the Chronicle for 796, ' Kenulf, King of the Mercians, laid waste

Kent as far as the marshes, and took Pren, their king, and led
him to Mercia and let his eyes be picked out and his hands
cut off.'

These attacks on the monasteries of the British coastline seem
to have been the beginning of the Viking movement. We can
imagine the next stage with likelihood enough, if we shift the
scene to Norway and Denmark. The successful raiders have
returned, loaded with gold and gems. Along every fiord and
estuary rumours run that the churches of the west are paved
with gold, that there are no warships in the western seas, and
that a new way has been found to get rich quick with a little
lively adventure. It is added that some of the ploughlands
out west seem richer even than those of Stavanger. The
needy Earls' sons talk over the tidings at the ale-board and look
round for leaders and followers.

Slowly, during the fifty years or more before the movement
reached its height, all Norway and Denmark awoke to the truth
that there was no sea-power to protect the British Islands or
the famous Carolingian Empire ; that the Anglo-Saxons and
Franks were land-lubbers, and that the Irish for all their missions
and colonizings used mere coracles and canoes. The world lay
exposed to the sea power of the Vikings, a prey for their greed
and a playground for their love of joyous adventure. Soon the
young man who had not been out a-Viking was chaffed at the
ale-board and scorned by the maidens, some of whom accompanied
their men folk oversea and fought fully armed in the shield ring.
As with the simple Swiss peasants after the easy victories of
Morat and Nanci, war and plunder abroad became the chief
national industry, absorbing the best energies of the rising
generation. The last and most important stage was reached
when permanent immigration and land settlement oversea took
the place of plundering raids.

The Scandinavians had always been traders as well as pirates
in their dealings with one another in home waters, and so they
remained in the larger field of foreign enterprise now open to
them. They combined the pride of the merchant with the very
different pride of the warrior, as few people have done. In a
tomb in the Hebrides a pair of scales has been found buried in
a Viking chief's tomb, alongside his sword and battle-axe. Their
first thought when they founded a colony in England or Ireland
was to build fortified towns and to open markets. By land or
sea they were prepared to trade with the newcomer or to cut
his throat according to circumstances or the humour of the hour.
Such indeed, for centuries to come, was the custom of sailors
from every port of mediæval Europe, not excluding Chaucer's

Shipman and some of the Elizabethan heroes. But the Vikings put an energy all their own into the practice both of piracy and trade, adding thereto great military qualities on land, unusual with Jack ashore.

As the Ninth Century wore on, a large part of the whole Scandinavian people had been a-Viking to the most various parts of the world. They carved their runes on the stone lion of the Piræus that now keeps guard before the Arsenal at Venice. They were known to avenge in the streets of Constantinople blood feuds begun among themselves in Dublin. Their far journeys brought them wealth, civilization and the knowledge of cities and men. The Saxon peasant, who regarded them as outer barbarians, was ignorant and provincial compared to them. Their Eddic poetry was succeeded by no less splendid prose Sagas, historical novels recording with extraordinary realism the romance of their heroic life.

There were three routes of Scandinavian activity in the Viking era. First there was the Eastern route, followed mainly by the Swedes, who penetrated the heart of the Slav territories, to Novgorod and Kiev; at Kiev they founded the original Russian State, and sailed thence down the Dnieper and crossed the Black Sea to annoy the walls of Constantinople itself.

The other two routes lay to the West. There was the route followed mainly by the Norsemen or men of Norway, which we may call the Outer Line. It led to the most adventurous sea-voyages, to the settlement of Iceland and Greenland and the discovery of North America. It led to the Orkneys, Caithness, Ross, Galloway and Dumfries, where large Scandinavian colonies brought the first Nordic element into the life of Highland and South-Western Scotland. The Isle of Man was occupied as the Malta of the new maritime power in the Irish Sea, which had become a Scandinavian lake. By this Outer Line important colonies of Norsemen were planted in Cumberland, Westmoreland, Lancashire, Cheshire, and on the coast of South Wales. Ireland was for a while overrun, and Dublin, Cork, Limerick, Wicklow and Waterford were founded as Danish towns, the beginning of Irish city life.

Thirdly, there was the Inner Line, mainly followed by the Danes from Denmark. By that way attacks were delivered on the north coast of Europe and the east and south coasts of England. That way went the largest hosts of Viking immigrants, in the days of Alfred of Wessex, seeking to win wide lands to plough and to rule. These great armies, composed of bands enlisted under many allied kinglets, learnt to obey a single war chief so long as the season's campaign lasted. The ' host ' passed freely from France to England and back again, according as the resistance was stronger or weaker first on one side of the Channel, then on the other. Their mighty and protracted operations ended in the creation of two Danelaws, each of the first importance in history. The smaller one, which they carved out of the Frankish Kingdom, was named after them Normandy ;

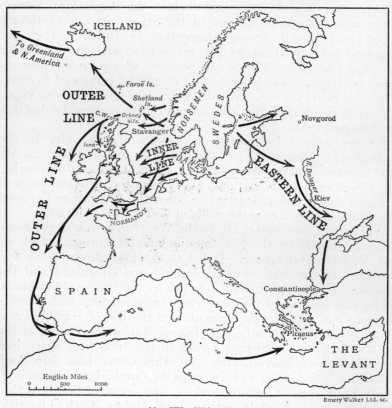

MAP VII.—Viking Routes

the larger Danelaw consisted of all eastern England between Thames and Tyne. Finally the Norse settlers in Lancashire and Cumberland joined hands across England with the Danish settlers from Yorkshire, so that at this point the Scandinavian race predominated from sea to sea.[1]

The Viking followers of the Outer and Inner Lines often crossed each other's path. Danes and Norsemen were found together in Normandy, in South Ireland and in North England,

[1] See p. 44, above, and note.

and both indifferently penetrated into Spain, the Mediterranean and the Levant. All this amazing exploration, which touched the coast of North America five hundred years before Columbus, this habitual and almost daily defiance of the storms of Cape Wrath and the Hebrides, was conducted in open long-ships, propelled by oars in the hands of the free warriors themselves, aided, when the wind served, by a single sail of striped colours and costly material. Over the low waist of the brightly-painted ship hung the line of round shields, yellow and black alternately, while the high dragon-prow broke the billows in front, a terror to Christian men who saw it coming. The courage and sea craft of sailors who could venture in such ships on such voyages has never been surpassed in maritime history. They often paid toll for their daring. Alfred's Wessex was saved once by the drowning 877. of a host, when a storm piled up 120 Danish galleys against the cliffs of Swanage.

The first bands of marauders who had come to plunder the seaward abbeys had little armour, and the better part of their tactics had been to sail off before any serious force could be assembled to catch them. But as the number of the Vikings increased, so did their military knowledge and equipment, after they had travelled and traded and fought in all the most civilized countries of Europe. Their fleets rose from three to forty, to a hundred or to three hundred and fifty ships, each ship carrying perhaps a hundred men. And in these great hosts body armour had become the rule rather than the exception. The Vikings in their mail shirts were irresistible for the strength with which they swung the long two-handed battle-axe, the skill with which they used the bow, and the regular wedge formation in which the disciplined ships' crews were taught to fight on land. Siege craft with mangonel and mine was an art they learned to perfection. Meanwhile the Saxon peasants, called from the plough in their woollen shirts, had no weapon but shield and spear.

In mobility the odds were no less great. Until Alfred built a fleet, the Danes could move where they pleased by river and sea. And on land, when they had left the galleys behind a garrisoned stockade, they soon learned to ' horse ' themselves from the breeding pastures of East Anglia. Thence, during the 866. five terrible years that followed, the ' host ' rode through the 866–871. length and breadth of England, destroyed first Northumbria, then Mercia, and finally invaded Wessex.

Until Alfred learnt to beat them at their own game, the strategy of the Danes lay in surprise attacks delivered on distant and unexpected points. It was impossible for the ' fyrd ' of English farmers on their slow feet to catch up these galloping warriors, or to fight armoured men if they ever got near them. It is even doubtful how often the ' fyrd ' or *levée-en-masse* of this primitive character was called out in Alfred's day. A dozen

877. years after the first ' horsing ' of the Danes, we read that Alfred with his forces ' rode ' in pursuit of them. To hunt down and fight the invaders, Alfred was driven more and more to rely on his mounted and armoured thegns and their vassals, the class that specialized in war. When war becomes serious, it necessarily becomes professional, and requires changes that re-act upon the whole social system. The Danish wars meant another advance on the road to feudalism in England.

Thus both sides became mounted infantry, but not yet cavalry. Although Dane and Saxon rode to the battle-field, and fled or pursued on horseback, they had not acquired the art of fighting from the saddle. But those Vikings who had become the ruling classes in Normandy learnt the value of shock-tactics on horseback from the Frankish knights who opposed them on the banks of the Seine. In the fullness of time the Franco-Viking cavalry returned under William to the conquest of the Anglo-Danish infantry at Hastings.

Alfred the Great is naturally to be compared to Charlemagne, after whom it is possible that he modelled many of his doings. Each was the champion of Christ against the heathen, of the new feudal kingship against chaos. Each had many-sided talents as warrior, administrator and scholar, suited to an epoch before professional men abound, when a king can himself teach, govern and lead his subjects in peace and in war. If Alfred's lot was cast in narrower geographic limits than the Napoleonic arena of Charlemagne's activities, his work has lasted longer. He and his sons made England one for ever. The memory of Charlemagne does not suffice to unite Germany and France.

871. By temperament a scholar, and of ailing health, Alfred was forced into the field in early youth to lead the grimmest warfare of that terrible epoch. But harsh experience schooled without souring his gentle qualities. At the age of twenty-two he was second-in-command in the campaign of Ashdown and the eight other ' folk-fights ' when Wessex was striving desperately to thrust the Danish host off the chalk ridges south of Thames ; England north of the river had already submitted to the Danes. The young man at once won the confidence of the army, and when in the middle of that year of battles his elder brother died, he was chosen king by the Witan. His nephews were passed over, for minors were excluded by custom and necessity in days when a king's first business was to lead the folk to war.

Seven years later came the crisis of his life. The Danes, 878.
secure in the possession of North, Midlands and East, at last
overran Wessex by an unexpected raid at mid-winter. Alfred's
subjects began to fly over sea. He himself with a small army of
Somerset warriors held out in the island fastnesses of the Parret
fenland. Fifty miles beyond lay the Cornwall of that day, where
the Welsh enemies of Wessex were often in league with the Dane.
On so narrow a thread hung the cause of English independence.
But the Saxon thegns who had recently colonized Devon stood
strongly for Alfred, and destroyed a Danish force that had been
landed in his rear. Such was the confidence inspired by his
leadership even in this desperate hour, that the thegns of conquered Wilts and Hampshire answered once more to his summons
and rode to rejoin his banner. The battle of Ethandune reversed
the whole situation, and the Danish leader, Guthrum, accepted
terms, known as the Treaty of Wedmore, whereby he and his
followers underwent baptism and agreed to retire into the
' Danelaw,' leaving Wessex free.

Having found the resistance of South England stiffer than
they had hoped, many of the ' host ' transferred their operations
to France. A few years later Alfred extracted from Guthrum
a still more advantageous treaty defining the southern frontier
of the Danelaw ; it was to run along Watling Street and the Lea
river from its source, leaving London to the English King.

Such was the political geography for the remainder of Alfred's 878-900.
reign. The Danes, on the way to become Christian, were settled
as acknowledged masters of North-Eastern England. All Saxon
territory to south of them was united under Alfred. If his
descendants should conquer the Danelaw, they would be the first
Kings of England, for Mercia, East Anglia and Northumbria had
disappeared from the list of sovereign states.

Only the wreck of old Northumbria—Bernicia beyond Tyne
—had not been conquered by the Vikings. This Saxon district
between Tyne and Cheviot assumed the name of Northumberland
and dragged on for many centuries a precarious existence between
England and Scotland. But Saxondom between the Cheviots
and the Forth, which now first began to be called Lothian,
became increasingly involved in Scottish history, because the
Danelaw cut it off from the main current of Saxon history to the
south. At the same time the Norse invaders of the western sea
cut the connections between the Scots of Ireland and the Scots
of Scotland. In these ways the Viking invasions drove Scotland
in upon herself, and hammered her warring tribes into something
a little more like union. It was in the Viking epoch that 844-860.
Kenneth MacAlpine became King of the united Picts and Scots.

He moved the relics of St. Columba and the centre of Scottish religion from Iona, with its backward glance over the sea at Ireland, to Dunkeld in the heart of his united kingdom.

After the Christening of Guthrum and the fixing of the limits of the Danelaw, Alfred's life entered a new and happier phase that lasted till his death. His position in southern England was relatively secure ; the tide of events flowed with him now ; he was regarded by all Saxons, both within and without the Danelaw, as their sole champion ; even the christened Danes, constantly increasing in number, felt reverence for this English Charlemagne. There were indeed more Viking invasions from over sea, but the Danes of the Danelaw backed the newcomers half-heartedly, for they themselves were now settled men with farms and wives, fearing reprisal since they now had lands of their own to be raided. And Alfred, copying Danish methods, had rebuilt London as a walled and garrisoned town, held by English burghers, whose duty it was to defend it against attack ; the chief gate of England was locked against the Danes.

878-900.

In the intervals of these later and less terrible wars, Alfred enjoyed whole years of respite in which he could indulge in tasks very near to his heart. He began English prose literature by translating Bede's Latin into Anglo-Saxon, and by translating and compiling handbooks of theology, history and geography for his subjects' use ; and he initiated the keeping of the Anglo-Saxon Chronicle, the first historical record ever composed in English. He fetched over foreign scholars, and welcomed learned refugees from Mercia and the North, in the hope of repairing, in Wessex at least, the desperate ravages of the Danish raids, which had swept away the libraries and learned men of the earlier England, and had left a clergy who no longer understood the Latin of the mass they sang. Alfred, moreover, founded the first ' public schools ' for teaching letters to the sons of noblemen and thegns, extending for the first time the gifts of learning to some of the higher laity, so as to fit them for the tasks of modern administration.

The revival of letters and religion was slow and artificial, the gift of an industrious king to an ignorant clergy and people. It was no longer the glad, confident morning of Cuthbert, Bede and Alcuin. Learning had indeed received a terrible blow in the sack of the Northumbrian and Mercian monasteries, but at least Alfred had set recovery afoot, and the new growth of city life due to the Danes would in the end do more for the higher civilization than monasticism at its best.

During the last twenty years of his reign, Alfred strengthened the institutions of Wessex both in peace and war. He created a fleet. He made an available army system, and put permanent garrisons into earthwork forts of the Danish type. He set up a sound administration worked through the shire and its officers. It was all very primitive, but better than anything there had been before in England. Thus armed, his son, Edward the Elder, and his daughter, the lady Ethelfleda of Mercia, proceeded after his death to the reconquest of the Danelaw, which Edward's son and successor, Athelstan, completed. The Danes of the Danelaw had shown themselves deficient in political unity as soon as they settled down upon the land. A number of rival settlements, each under a ruler styled King or Earl according to fancy, had less cohesion than the English of the remodelled Kingdom of Wessex. The Vikings had been apt to unite for offensive warfare under temporary war chiefs, but the oneness of the ' host ' that had trampled England under foot was not reflected in the political arrangements of the Danelaw, which therefore fell before the returning wave of Saxondom.

Edward Elder, 900–924.

Athelstan, 924–940.

Edward the Elder and Athelstan are the first whom we can justly describe as Kings of England. Edward's grandson Edgar, in a prosperous and peaceful reign, was clearly recognised as such. The Danelaw, after absorbing the other English kingdoms, had itself been absorbed by Wessex. Only Celtic Wales and Celtic Scotland were still independent, and even their kings and princes sometimes acknowledged a vague supremacy in Athelstan and Edgar, who for their part regarded themselves as ' Emperors of Britain.'

Edgar, 959–975.

A new unity had grown out of the cleaving and sundering of the Danish conquests. So long as the Viking battle-axe was crashing through the skulls of monks, and the English were nailing to their church-doors skins flayed off their Danish enemies, the hatred between Anglo-Saxon and Scandinavian was profound.[1] But it was not permanent. In days before the printing-press, the memory of inter-racial wrongs and atrocities was not artificially fostered. Green earth forgets—when the school-master and the historian are not on the scene. And these two Nordic races were of kindred stock, with many instincts and customs in common. After the Danes had accepted baptism, it was easy to merge them with the English under the rule of the House of Wessex, for they had not come over to found a Scandinavian Empire, but to seek good farm lands. So far were they from enslaving their neighbours, that their Danelaw contained

---

[1] There is no doubt about the Danes' skins. See H. St. George Gray's paper in the *Saga Book of the Viking Club*, Vol. V., anno 1906–7. It is only one of many reminders of the barbarism of heathen and Christian alike in that age.

many freemen and no slaves, in sharp contrast to Wessex. Settled down prosperously in their new quarters, under their own Danish laws and Danish earls and lawmen, they could tolerate the light rule of English Kings.

There was now only one King, but for generations to come there was a rich variety of customs and ' laws ' in the land. The Common Law—that is the law common to all England—was built up in Plantagenet times by the professional lawyers of the King's courts ; but in Anglo-Saxon times there was no such body of men and no body of case law for the whole nation. Certain written laws were sometimes issued by the King with the help of his Bishops, perhaps for the guidance of all courts. But every Shire or Hundred Court and every court of private jurisdiction might also have its own customary local laws. The Danes clung strongly to their own, and the region of the ' Dane law ' had its name thence.

Law, like many other good things, received a stimulus from the coming of the Danes. The very word ' law ' is Danish, and has survived its rivals, the Anglo-Saxon word ' doom ' and the Latin word ' lex.' The Scandinavians, when not on the Viking war-path, were a litigious people and loved to gather in the ' thing ' to hear legal argument. They had no professional lawyers, but many of their farmer-warriors, like Njal the truth-teller, were learned in folk custom and its intricate judicial procedure. A Danish town in England often had, as its principal officers, twelve hereditary ' law men.' The Danes introduced the habit of making committees among the freemen in court, which perhaps made England favourable ground for the future growth of the jury system out of a Frankish custom introduced later by the Normans. In the laws of Ethelred the Unready we read ' that a gemot be held in every wapontake, and the twelve senior thegns go out, and the reeve with them and swear on the halidoom that is given into their hand that they will accuse no innocent man nor conceal any guilty one.' This is Danish, and very near to a mediæval jury of presentment, though not its direct original.

The conception of justice in the Anglo-Danish period shows traces of three different origins. First the old idea, common to Saxon and Scandinavian, was the ' weregild ' or money compensation for a wrong, to be paid to the injured party or his kin to prevent feud, a conception once covering almost the whole field of justice, but on the wane as the power of the courts became stronger and the feeling of the clan weaker ; slowly, throughout the late Saxon period, ' slaying ' loses much of its character as a blood feud between families and becomes increasingly an affair between the community and the murderer.[1] Secondly, there was the new doctrine of the Church that wrong-doing had the further aspect of sin or moral wrong, to be expiated by penance. And thirdly there is the peculiarly Scandinavian view, found in Anglo-Danish laws, that certain acts such as cowardly flight or desertion of one's chief were dishonourable—'nidings vœrk'— to be punished as deeds unworthy of the free warrior. From the time of Alfred onwards, we find special penalties and special reprobation attached to the crime of treason to the King or to a man's lord ; the growth of the law of treason and petty treason is due, in part, to the increase in the power of the Crown and of the feudal lord, partly to the influence of Roman law coming in through the clergy, and partly to the strong ethical feeling of the whole Nordic race, expressed alike in Anglo-Saxon and Scandinavian literature, of horror of the man who betrays or deserts his chief.

The Danelaw, during its brief period of independence as a confederation of Scandinavian communities, had been organized round the life of its towns. The Roman walls of Chester were repaired first by a Viking chief, and the commercial life of Chester and York was revived by Scandinavian enterprise. Roads were scarce but rivers were deep, and commerce was borne in barges to the wharves of inland towns. The famous ' five boroughs ' of the Danes—Lincoln, Stamford, Leicester, Derby and Nottingham —served both as military garrisons and as trading centres. Each was protected by a palisaded mound and ditch ; each had its own ' law men,' its own army and its own sovereign ' Jarl ' or Earl. From the borough, the Earl and his army ruled a wide surrounding district. There is something analogous to Roman practice in the political importance of the Danish town, though it was purely Scandinavian in origin.

When Edward the Elder and his sister Ethelfleda of the Mercians set about conquering the Danelaw, they did it by imitating and taking over the Danish borough system. Alfred had set the example in London and elsewhere in Wessex, and his son and daughter spread the net of fortified English ' burhs ' up the Severn valley and across the Midlands. They repaired the

---

[1] How slowly the law got the strength to replace the blood-feud and to bring the accused into court otherwise than by the force of arms of the aggrieved party, we are reminded by Alfred's laws, *e.g.* ' If anyone chances to meet his enemy, not having known him to be at home, and if he will give up his weapons, he shall be detained 30 days and his kinsmen informed. If he will not give up his weapons, then he may be attacked.' ' A man may fight on behalf of his lord if his lord is attacked, without becoming liable to blood-feud.' The laws of Edmund and of Canute show that the blood-feud was still a custom even in their day.

stone walls of ruined Roman cities, or piled up new earth-works round tactical points unguarded before. In each fortress they planted a permanent English garrison holding lands on burgage tenure, with the duty of defending the place. As fast as they conquered the Danelaw, they divided it into shires like those of Saxon Wessex ; but each of the new shires was moulded round the administrative centre of some Danish borough, and its boundaries were probably those of the Danish military district attached thereto. Such is the origin of the shires of the east midlands—Lincoln, Derby, Nottingham, Leicester, Northampton, Huntingdon, Cambridge, Bedford. An ealdorman, with a shire-reeve beside him to represent King and people, answered to the King for one or more of the old shires of Wessex, or of the new shires of recovered Mercia. But a Danish Earl answered to the English King for each shire of the annexed Danelaw.

The new English Kingdom was thus equipped with a garrison system and with organs of administration which had been wanting to the shadowy empires ruled over by Offa and Egbert.[1] And so the familiar shape of modern England, with its famous shires and towns, comes out line by line under our eyes, as we watch the clouds drifting and lifting over the chaos of the Anglo-Danish wars. So much we can see even from far off, but if we could watch the Tenth Century map at closer quarters, we should see no less clearly one country village after another grow modestly into being along the newly drained river valleys and across the slowly diminishing area of forest.

Although the boroughs had been formed in the first instance to meet the military and administrative needs of both sides in the Danish wars, they soon took on a commercial character. The Danes were indefatigable traders, faring across the sea and claiming on their return to be ' thegn-right worthy ' in their honourable character of overseas merchants, all the more if some of the goods they brought back had been won by hard knocks rather than by hard bargaining. The Saxons caught up some at least of their commercial ideas and habits. The special peace of the King protected the borough and all within it. And, when Edward the Elder published a law that all buying and selling must take place in a market-town before the town reeve, he aided the concentration of business in the new boroughs. The citizens were at once warriors, traders, and farmers of the adjoining lands. In days to come, their milder descendants might find it enough to be traders and farmers only, when the mounted Norman knight took over the fighting part of their business and retired proudly into his stone donjon overlooking the town. And when, after

[1] See p. 70, above.

many centuries, specialization had been carried one step further, the citizens ceased to till the soil and confined themselves altogether to crafts and commerce.

Such, in one of its aspects, was the origin and development of the English town. But no English town has the same history as any other. And some of the larger stone-walled cities, particularly London, never completely submitted to the feudal world outside, but preserved down the ages an adequate military control of their own defence.

BOOKS FOR FURTHER READING

Gjerset, *History of the Norwegian People*, Vol. I. ; W. G. Collingwood, *Scandinavian Britain* (S.P.C.K., 1908) ; Beatrice Lees, *Alfred* (Heroes of Nations Series) ; Oman, *Art of War in Middle Ages* ; *Cam. Med. Hist.*, Vol. III., Chaps. XIII., XIV., XX.

CHAPTER VI

Life in Later Saxon England.   Feudalism encroaching.   Canute and the Nordic Maritime Empire.

WAR, invasion and bloodshed were normal conditions of life in Saxon England. Nor did the advantages of our island position begin to appear before the strong Norman Kings and their following had taken hold. So long as the sea was the highroad assistant to every invader, ' England bound in with the triumphant sea ' was bound a helpless victim, and her ill-defended charms were as well known to the warrior races of Northern Europe as were Italy's to those of the South.

Nevertheless the slayers and marauders could not be everywhere in the island at once. The habitations of man were more secluded then than now, surrounded by marshland and forest ; there were no maps to reveal their whereabouts and few roads to guide the spoiler to his prey. A story is told of times much more recent than the Danish raids, how Scottish moss-troopers failed for a whole day in their search for so important a place as Brinkburn Priory, amid the wooded dells of Coquet, until it was betrayed at the last moment by the sound of its own bells on the evening air. It is likely that, when the Danish ' host ' was riding through a countryside, people in quiet parishes were chary of ringing their bells.

An Anglo-Saxon lived in some respects an enviable life, so long as he could avoid being ' hewed amain with swords mill-sharp '—the ending of most folk in his favourite poems. We too seldom ask ourselves what his life was like, because, while the life of the later Middle Ages and even of Roman antiquity presents itself to the eye and the imagination through the work of masonry, the Saxon period has vanished from the landscape ; most preconquest churches have been rebuilt, and the wooden chalets and halls where life was spent have left neither trace nor tradition, unless it be in the architecture of some of our fine old English barns. But those halls were great places in their day. Lowland Switzerland can still show us how noble and spacious a wooden structure can be, when it is the natural product of a native art tradition, with no limit to the building material on the spot, save the labour of cutting it down. The log halls of Saxon thegn and Danish jarl were decorated with carving and paint both outside and in, and hung with burnished armour, though the smoke eddying under the rafters in search of the hole in the roof diminished the sense of luxury. The thegn and his family were resplendent in cloaks of many colours. Articles of daily use were fantastically carved by native craftsmen. The art of the English jeweller was very fine, as the ' Alfred jewel ' and others still remain to prove.

It was seldom that the thegn or his followers possessed any books, unless he were an assiduous courtier of King Alfred. But the bards every evening chanted their epics through the smoke drifts of the hall to an audience that loved noble and resonant language far more than their descendants of to-day. The form and colour of things seen and the sound of fine words were a greater part of the pleasures of life in that simple age than in our own more intellectual world.

Saxon and Dane each came of a thirsty race, and many an acre of barley went to fill the ale-horn. ' Yuletide ' feastings, common to the earliest traditions of both races, and rehallowed as ' Christ Mass ' by the Church, were as merry in the thegn's wooden hall as afterwards in the stone donjon of his Norman supplanter.

But in the main, life was an out-door affair for rich and poor, a constant hand-to-hand struggle of a hardy folk with untamed nature. In the intervals of peace, when neither public war nor private blood-feud were disturbing the district, the thegn and his personal retainers laboured at spearing and netting the wolves and foxes, and keeping down the deer, hares, rabbits and wild fowl, if the crops were to be saved and the larders well stocked with meat. Hunting was always a pleasure, but it was not then a sport. It was a duty, which, like the sterner duty of war, devolved more and more on the thegn and his attendants, as functions became more specialized. But every freeman could still hunt on his own land, and it is probable that many serfs and thralls suffered no rebuke in taking game off the limitless waste ; some were employed for no other purpose. It was still a hard struggle for man collectively to make head against the forest and its denizens. The King of England did not yet ' love the tall stags as if he were their father ' nor had the harsh code of the Royal Forest yet been imported from Normandy. Landlords were not yet tempted to strain their authority on behalf of game preservation, for the game could still preserve itself only too well. For ages still to come, a large proportion of the people's food consisted of wild game of all sorts, and the half-wild herds of swine in the forest. If Englishmen had been forced in the Tenth Century, as their more numerous descendants were for awhile in the Nineteenth, to live chiefly on such grain as they could grow in the island, those primitive agriculturists would have been hard put to it to live at all.

What a place it must have been, that virgin woodland wilderness of all England, ever encroached on by innumerable peasant clearings, but still harbouring God's plenty of all manner of beautiful birds and beasts, and still rioting in a vast wealth of trees and flowers,—treasures which modern man, careless of his best inheritance, has abolished and is still abolishing, as fast as new tools and methods of destruction can be invented, though even now the mere wrecks of old England still make a demi-paradise of the less inhabited parts of the island. We conjure up the memory of what we have lost in speaking of Robin Hood's Sherwood or Shakespeare's Arden, but it was older than Robin Hood and vaster than Arden. It was the land not merely of the outlaw and the poet but of the whole Anglo-Danish people. Had some of them at least the eyes to see the beauty in the midst of which they went about their daily tasks ? When Chaucer and the late mediæval ballad-makers at last found a tongue for the race, the first use to which they put it has recorded their joy in the birds and flowers, the woods and meadows. In Tudor times the popular songs of the day give the impression that the whole people has gone a-maying. Did not some such response to nature's loveliness move dimly in the hearts of the Saxon pioneers, when primrose, or bluebell, or willow-herb rushed out over the sward of the clearing they had made in the tall trees?

In certain respects the conditions of pioneer life in the shires of Saxon England and the Danelaw were not unlike those of North America and Australia in the Nineteenth Century,—the lumberman with his axe, the log shanty in the clearing, the draught oxen, the horses to ride to the nearest farm five miles across the wilderness, the weapon ever laid close to hand beside the axe and the plough, the rough word and ready blow, and the good comradeship of the frontiersmen. And in Saxon England, as in later America, there were also the larger, older and more settled townships, constantly catching up and assimilating the pioneers who had first started human life in some deep ' den ' of the woodlands. Every one of the sleepy, leisurely gardenlike villages of rural England was once a pioneer settlement, an outpost of man planted and battled for in the midst of nature's primæval realm.[1]

The work of colonization and deforestation in later Saxon England was carried on under feudal leadership. ' We wonder not,' wrote King Alfred, ' that men should work in timber-felling and in carrying and building, for a man hopes that if he has built a cottage on laenland of his lord, with his lord's help, he may be allowed to lie there awhile, and hunt and fowl and fish, and occupy the laenland as he likes, until through his lord's grace he may perhaps some day obtain book-land and permanent inheritance.' The feudal lord was to the Anglo-Saxon pioneer what the State was to his remote descendant in America and Australia. In those early times ' the State ' in the modern sense scarcely existed. A man looked to his lord for military protection, for justice or something more in court, and often for economic help as well; in return the lord restricted his freedom, became a large sharer in the profits of his labour, or claimed much of that labour for himself.

In the Anglo-Danish period the King's thegn, who is also the peasants' lord, is pre-eminently the armed warrior with helmet and chain shirt falling below the hips, the mounted infantryman in heavy armour on whom the King relies in case of invasion. The thegn devotes his life to hunting and war, and to the service of his own overlord,—the King it may be, or else some Bishop or Abbot, or some greater thegn than himself. Personal loyalty rather than abstract patriotism inspires his service, and it is not always the King to whom the personal loyalty is most felt or exclusively owed. In succession to the Saxon thegn, the Norman knight, still more completely armed and trained to fight from the saddle, will stand just one step higher above his neighbours as a specialist in war, and therefore feudalism as a social system will reach its climax after the Norman Conquest. It will decline with the advent of longbow and gunpowder. For feudalism, though a system of law and land tenure, really depends for its spirit on the military superiority of an aristocracy in arms.

---

[1] The termination ' den ' so common in our village names often denoted a swineherds' woodland colony of some mother village, which stood some considerable distance away in the better cleared country.

After the breakdown of the tribal and clan organization, and before the rise of the State, feudalism was the only method by which a helpless population could be protected, war efficiently conducted, colonization pushed forward, or agriculture carried on with increased profits. For it was a process of differentiating the functions of warrior and husbandman. The Anglo-Saxon ploughman was not only an unskilled but an unwilling soldier. He disliked being called out every few months. He wanted to be left alone in Cowstead or Nettleden to till the soil in which he had taken such strong root. He had forgotten the warlike desires of his ancestor who helped to sack the Roman villa hard by. His lord, the thegn in the high hall of the township, should protect him in local troubles ; and the King and the assembled thegns should protect him in the day of national danger. The thegn, for his part, ceased to handle the plough and spent his time in war and talking about war, in hunting and talking about hunting, and in doing rough justice among his neighbours accord-into to traditional law and custom. Already we have the embryo of the future squire and Justice of the Peace, except that the Anglo-Saxon prototype of the squire is pre-eminently a soldier.

So the ploughman ceased more and more to be a warrior, and the warrior ceased to be a ploughman. Differentiation of function led away from equality—away from liberty even. But it led to settled order, to civilization, to wealth, and finally in the course of centuries to a much fuller liberty for the individual than the freeman of a savage tribe can possibly enjoy.

Meanwhile the conditions of life were harsh enough on the lower classes of husbandman, the thralls and serfs whose labour was in different degrees required to support the thegns and the clergy in their specialized functions. There exists a dialogue of about the year 1000, which gives us, with a pathetic realism, a single glance behind the scenes of the national stage :—

*What sayest thou, ploughman ? How dost thou do thy work ?'
' O, my lord, hard do I work. I go out at daybreak driving the oxen to field, and I yoke them to the plough. Nor is it ever so hard winter, that I dare loiter at home, for fear of my lord ; but the oxen yoked, and ploughshare and coulter fastened to the plough, every day must I plough a full acre, or more.'
' Hast thou any comrade ? '
' I have a boy driving the oxen with an iron goad, who also is hoarse with cold and shouting.'
' What more dost thou in the day ? '
' Verily then I do more. I must fill the bin of the oxen with hay, and water them and carry out the dung. Ha ! Ha ! hard work it is, hard work it is, because I am not free.'

The shepherd in his turn answers :

' In the first of the morning I drive my sheep to their pasture and stand over them, in heat and in cold, with my dogs, lest the wolves swallow them up. And I lead them back to their folds and milk them twice a day ; and their folds I move ; and I make cheese and butter, and I am true to my lord.'

The oxherd says :

' When the ploughman unyokes the oxen, I lead them to pasture and all night I stand over them waking against thieves,'

for cattle-lifting was then a great part of life, not merely on the Scottish and Welsh borderlands as in later years, but in all the unquiet island.[1]

The peasants of this dialogue were evidently doing customary services upon their lord's home farm or domain land, under more or less servile conditions. In the Tenth and Eleventh Centuries there were many grades of servile and semi-servile tenure, varying according to the local circumstances, and according to Danish, Welsh or Saxon custom. There were ' geneats,' ' cottars,' ' geburs,' shepherds, bee-keepers (for honey was the only sugar), swineherds, and many others, each owing to the lord so many days' work a year for such and such purposes, or so much rent in kind. In the Danelaw the proportion of small freeholders was largest and the number of actual slaves a minimum, while in the Western and more Celtic shires the opposite was the case. In the districts where the incoming Danes settled, they tended to break up the encroachments of feudalism, lay and clerical, and to favour freedom; but the effect of their raids and ransomings on the other parts of England was to hasten the degradation of the peasant, who ' bowed his head ' for bread or protection to the thegn or the abbey, or was ruined and sold up owing to the burning of his farm by the Vikings, or the intolerable burden of the Danegeld. Thus when the Norman came he found the North and East freer than the South and West.

Taking the country as a whole, in spite of much local variation, there was a tendency in these later Saxon centuries towards the growth of a large class or classes of semi-free peasants, into which the slave or thrall rose, and the freeman sank. This important double process will come clearly to light after the Conquest, when the French feudal lawyers will give a definiteness and universality to this half-servile class under the title of ' villeinage.'

[1] The later English custom of leaving sheep and oxen to graze without a herd or watcher present, was remarked on in Tudor times by foreigner visitors as a custom peculiar to England. It argued a high degree of safety from robbers as well as wolves, that was only very gradually attained.

In the Anglo-Danish times it was laid down as a rule of law and police that 'every man must have a lord,' to be answerable in court for his misdoings. Only thus could the peace of the united English Kingdom be maintained, now that the old clans and kinships, long decadent, were ceasing altogether to function in the sphere of justice and police. Since a man's relations were no longer answerable for him, his lord must answer for him instead.

The lord, whether thegn or prelate, performed in each locality many of the functions, judicial, military and economic, performed by the clan in more primitive societies, and by the State in the modern world. The new Kings of all England could keep only a very rough and ready control over the general body of their thegns, for purposes of national defence and for little else. For local purposes they were fain to grant away rights of justice and administration which they had not the machinery to exercise from the centre, making them over to powerful local magnates, lay or clerical. It was only after the Norman Conquest and the growth of a more elaborate civilization, that the Plantagenet Kings gradually assumed administrative and judicial control over the localities, and formed the modern idea of the nation and the modern machinery of the State.

Saxon times witnessed the growth of feudal power, and witnessed also the growth of Kingship not as its enemy, but as its ally. The battle between the Crown and the centrifugal tendencies of feudalism was postponed till after the Norman Conquest. In the days when the Kings of Wessex became Kings of all England, greatly as the prestige of the Crown was thereby increased, the very extension of the boundaries of their realm compelled them to decentralize, leaving more power to local magnates. The shire machinery was the King's chief organ of administration. So long as the realm had been confined to the manageable area of old Wessex, a single magnate had answered to the King for each single shire. But with the formation of the new enlarged Kingdom, this machinery was compromised to meet the new facts. Edward the Elder and his sons, and even Canute himself, were fain to allow powerful subjects to be Ealdormen or Earls of two, three, finally half-a-dozen or more shires each.[1]

[1] A subordinate officer administered each single shire, under the Earl who ruled the group of shires. This shire officer became known as 'shire-reeve,' later 'sheriff.' He served in a dual capacity, primarily as the representative of the King's interests, but for some purposes as officer and agent of the Earl (W. A. Morris in *E.H.R.*, 1916). After the Norman Conquest the Earl (except in a few shires) disappeared, the Bishop retired with his spiritual cases to the new Church Courts; the Sheriff was, therefore, left as sole ruler of the shire for the King, and as agent of the King's orders only. The 'Hundred,' called in Danelaw the 'Wapentake,' was a territorial division of the shire.

United England, just because it was united, came to be administered in four, six or eight 'Earldoms,' as these large divisions were called.[1] To some extent they carried on the submerged life of the former political divisions of the island— Wessex, Northumbria, Mercia, East Anglia,—and thereby the more Danish districts were not in effect subjected to the direct rule of Wessex. Government by Earldoms, though feudal in form, had analogies to Home Rule in modern Empires too large and too little homogeneous for united administration. William the Conqueror, as we shall see, was destined to give the death blow in England to this centrifugal tendency, which continued for many centuries longer to divide mediæval Germany and France into great feudal provinces.

Such was the triumph of political feudalism in the newly formed Anglo-Danish Kingdom. And there was the same feudal tendency in the sphere of justice at the expense of the communal or public courts.

In the communal courts of Shire and Hundred, the law of the district—whether Danelaw, law of Mercia or of Wessex, or some obscurer provincial custom—was administered by the freemen suitors of the court as judges, presided over by the Ealdorman, Shire-reeve or Hundred-reeve on behalf of the King. There was as yet no 'common law' of all England, no Courts of King's Bench or Common Pleas, no Judges of Eyre or of Assize. These local communal courts were the Royal Courts, the courts of the land, so far as the King and the country as a whole can be said to have had courts at all.

But in the same period feudal justice was encroaching upon the communal courts. From the time of Edgar onwards, we find the King perpetually alienating the rights of the Crown, and particularly the power and jurisdiction of the Hundred Courts, to abbeys and feudal magnates. Whole districts are put under the judicial control of monks or Bishops, Earls or thegns, by grants of *sac and soc, infangthef* and *hamsocne*.[2] And with the judicial powers, the judicial revenues also—the valuable fees and fines of the courts—pass from the King to the private landowners whom he most fears or favours.

Private justice was encroaching on public justice. Was this reaction or progress? It was deplorable that the King should not be strong enough to enforce public justice through public courts. But if in fact he was not strong enough, it was better

---

[1] See Map IX., p. 110, below.

[2] *Sac and soc* = the right to hold a court ; *infangthef* = the right to try and to hang a thief taken on one's land ; *hamsocne* = house-breaking, or the right to try cases of it.

that justice should be administered somehow and by someone, than that thieving, manslaying and cattle-lifting should pass unpunished. Very possibly the change was often popular at the time it was made, if men got better and quicker justice from their strong neighbour lord or abbot than from their distant King or his weak ' reeve ' in the Hundred Court. But we cannot at this distance of time tell whether the lay and clerical beneficiaries of the grants of *sac and soc* were really the best people to hold the courts, or only the strongest and most cunning to seize the envied privilege. In any case it was to be the great merit of the Norman and Plantagenet Kings that they devised machinery by which the Crown was able gradually to reverse this Anglo-Danish alienation of royal rights, and to bring back public justice into public hands. That is one of the chief reasons why the name and office of King has been popular in England.

The latter half of the Tenth Century, between the first and second period of the Danish wars, witnessed an important crisis in religious history. The Danish invasions in the time of Alfred, so destructive to the monastic centres of Christian enthusiasm and learning, had completed the decadence of conventual and clerical life which Bede had noted in his own time. The burning of the great Northumbrian and fenland monasteries disorganized Christianity north of the Thames, and many districts were subjected to heathen jarls and ' hosts.' Even in Wessex it was long before Alfred's efforts to stimulate learning and religion led to any widespread movement among the clergy. The reconquest of the Danelaw and the partial conversion of the Danes were principally due to the Christian laity, the vigorous Kings of the House of Wessex and their thegnhood. There is no evidence that Alfred, Edward and Athelstan owed as much to clerical advisers as the Kings before and after their time.

Until the middle years of the Tenth Century the monasteries remained sunk in one of those ever recurring lapses by which human nature has always avenged itself upon the demands of asceticism. The monastic endowments were enjoyed by married clerks, many of whom lived in their own homes with large households and in considerable luxury. Monasticism had almost ceased to exist in any real sense ; it had certainly ceased to exert any great influence upon the island. Whether the growing movement for the foundation of parish churches and parish priests would have been able to make good in mediæval England if there had been no monastic revival, may be an interesting subject for speculation and controversy, but is not a question that history can attempt to answer.

The fact is that monasticism revived. A new spirit came over from the French Abbeys of Cluny and Fleury; this 'Cluniac' movement was one of the many offshoots of the great Benedictine rule. Under this inspiration certain reforming Abbots and Bishops, of whom Dunstan was one of the most effective, but by no means the most intolerant, re-enforced the conventual discipline and the ascetic ideal in many English convents, sometimes not without blows and turmoil. At the same time King Edgar (959–975) and his successors were persuaded to rebuild and re-endow the fenland monasteries such as Ely and Peterborough, and to enrich the monks of the new movement everywhere with vast territorial and judicial power over their neighbours.[1]

1073–1085. Under this new impulse English religion moved forward towards the more extended claims of the Church in the days of Hildebrand, Pope Gregory VII., whose ideals were to a large extent imposed upon England by her Norman Conquerors. In the end the movement enforced celibacy even on the parish priests, increased the international character of the Church under the Papal headship, and led to the full development of the doctrine of transubstantiation, the great importance attached to the worship of the Virgin Mary, and many other characteristic religious movements of the later Middle Age. The monastery in fact was destined to be the principal breeding ground whence religious idea and practice emanated for centuries to come, and to hold a great place in the economic and social life of feudal England.

924–988. Few would have prophesied such a future for monasticism when Dunstan was a boy. He himself took a leading part in the revival as the youthful Abbot of Glastonbury, and remained a sympathetic but less active friend to the movement when he became Primate. The stories of his clerical intolerance in this and other matters which once gave him his chief historical reputation are untrue. The son of a thegn of Somerset, Dunstan had a Celtic excitability of religious temperament remarkably blended with the cool and just judgment of a statesman. He was for many years the most influential of the advisers of the Crown. His power at Court was one of the many signs of the revival of the Church and was fully justified by the use he made of it. The disasters of the Kingdom began again when Ethelred the 'Redeless' ceased to enjoy the 'rede' or counsel of Dunstan.

The new feudalism made little distinction for its own pur-

[1] The fenland monasteries did much for the draining and colonization of the fen country. The grants of *sac and soc*, judicial in their most obvious aspect, were connected with another side of territorial feudalism, the aid given to reclaiming and colonizing waste land, by feudal lords, lay and clerical.

poses between cleric and lay. Thegns and prelates were alike lords holding lands of the King, and owing him service in war and peace. The revival of ascetic religion stimulated piety and fashion to reward the worthy monks who had thus forsworn the world afresh—with land, jurisdiction and treasure ! By the time of the Norman Conquest, shires like Worcester, Wilts and Dorset were as much owned and governed by churchmen as by barons and knights. The monks took to forging charters of the lands they claimed—the clerical method of 'estate jumping' to match the drawn sword of the baron.

The civil jurisdiction and temporal power of churchmen, not resented in those days, was sowing the seed of future evil on the grand scale. But the lavish monastic endowments prepared the way also for the architectural glories of the later Middle Age. And all the while the parish churches were rising, in village after village, and the impact of Christianity on the Nordic character was at work, unseen. Doubters may perhaps wonder whether the Church would have survived the rough feudal centuries if she had not herself acquired the feudal power that so sorely compromised her ideals.

During most of the Tenth Century the Viking movement was in abeyance. Emigration from the Baltic lands fell off, and the Scandinavian colonists spent their time in building up towns, farms and institutions in the lands which their fathers had won with the battle-axe. It was due to this ebb in the tide of invasion that Alfred's children had been able to effect a nominal reconquest of the Danelaw, on condition of leaving its Scandinavian character untouched. The era of Edgar and Dunstan followed as a brief period of peace and prosperity. And then, during the reign of the incompetent Ethelred the Redeless, the storm broke once more. 978–1016.

The Vikings were again on the war-path, and this time, under Sweyn Forkbeard, King of Denmark, they made South England the special object of their attack. Normandy and the English 988. Danelaw, being under Scandinavian rule, they naturally spared, while their cousins in Yorkshire and East Anglia equally naturally did nothing to thwart them or to help the decadent Saxon King to save his Wessex. The unity of Saxon and Dane in the island was still incomplete, and the weakness of the new Kingdom of England stood revealed. The Danelaw has been called ' the rock on which the old English Nationality foundered.' Ethelred was indeed a weak and foolish King and his reign was one long disaster, but there were other than personal and accidental causes for the collapse of England before the renewed Danish invasions.

In the long wars that ensued before Canute won the throne, there are two features of special interest,—the Danegeld and the part played by the city of London.

Danegeld had been levied and paid in Alfred's day, but in those primitive times the Danes had more often preferred to enrich themselves by direct plunder of place and person. Both sides were now rather more civilized, and the ransom in gold of the whole country became the more usual method of the latter-day Vikings. Nor does there seem to have been so much Danish demand for estates and land-settlement as in the time of Alfred. Many of the victors were content with enriching themselves out of the Danegeld, and spending the wealth so gained on houses and estates in Scandinavia. Historians are astonished at the sums paid to them in Danegeld, far exceeding what the same tax afterwards rendered to the Norman and Plantagenet exchequer, and out of all proportion to the rateable value of the land. No doubt the relative peace of the Tenth Century had enabled English thegns and churchmen to amass treasure and personal property of all kinds, especially the exquisite work of the English gold and silver smiths, which now went into the Danish melting-pot, as the plate and jewels of Renaissance England paid for the wars of Charles and Cromwell. Some of the vast ransom remained in England, being spent there by the freehanded and pleasure-loving Vikings, but much of it crossed the seas.

The sums extorted from the peasantry were ruinous, and hastened the decline of the freeholder into the serf. The Danegeld holds indeed a great place in our social, financial and administrative history. Direct taxation began in this ignominious form. Under the weak Ethelred it was the normal way of buying off the Danes. Under the strong Canute it became a war tax for the defence of the realm. Under William the Conqueror its levy was regarded as so important a source of revenue that the first great inquisition into landed property was made with this end in view. Domesday Book was originally drawn up for the purpose of teaching the State how to levy Danegeld. The collection of this great national burden, originally entrusted to the township, passed into the hands of the lord of the manor. First Canute, and then still more definitely the Norman Kings, preferred to deal with a single man rather than with the local community, thereby subjecting each village more than ever to its lord. For the lord became the tax-farmer. And the man who answered financially for the land tended to become in the eyes of the State the owner of the land and the lord of all who lived on it.

The other remarkable feature of the renewed Danish wars is the part played by London. The city magnificently fulfilled

the hopes entertained by Alfred a hundred years before, when he
fortified and colonized London as the guardian of England's
gate against the Danes. In Ethelred's reign her citizens were
the heart of English resistance, far more than the inept and
cowardly King. When at last he died, two years after his fierce April 1016.
Danish rival, Sweyn Forkbeard, there followed a brief struggle
for the throne of England between the two young heroes,
Edmund Ironside son of Ethelred and Canute son of Sweyn.
London was Edmund's rock of strength. But his death a few Nov. 1016.
months later ended the war; and the Saxon Witan, bowing to the
necessities of the case, chose Canute as King. The proximity of
the Danelaw on the flank of the contest in South England made
the choice of the Danish candidate natural, and after Edward's
death inevitable. Owing to the qualities latent in the young
Canute, it proved also fortunate beyond expectation.

The elective character of the English monarchy comes out
more clearly at this epoch than at any other before or after.
Canute, Harold and William the Conqueror had none of them a
valid legal title to the throne, save the choice of the Witan, or
acknowledgment by the individual magnates of the realm. But
such choice was enough to give legality to the results of conquest
or the wishes of the nation. The Witan was not the origin of the
later English Parliament, which grew up out of Anglo-Norman
institutions. Nor was the Witan a popular or representative
body. It was a haphazard assembly of Bishops, Earls, royal
officials and other magnates, who by no means always proved
themselves as 'wise' as their name suggests. When once a new
King was on the throne their power of controlling him depended
on character and circumstance, rather than on any 'law of the
constitution,' for none such existed. But they had by custom
the right to fill the throne vacated by death, and at the end of
the Saxon period that power was being exercised with an extraordinary freedom: not merely the order of succession but the
royal family itself was on more than one occasion changed. The
idea of a divine right of succession lodged in an individual and
not capable of alteration by any human authority was, so far as
English history is concerned, an invention of James I's over-busy
brain.

The part played in the later Danish wars by London as an
almost independent military and political power, is the more
remarkable because her municipal rights were, nominally, meagre
in the extreme. There was no Mayor or Alderman, and the port-
reeve was a royal official. Instead of the democratic 'wards' of
later London history, we find the City area divided into 'sokes'
or private jurisdictions granted by the King to lay and clerical

E

magnates. Municipal self-government was still in the future.
As yet even the freedom-loving Danish towns were ruled by hereditary ' lawmen,' and the other market towns and ' burhs ' of
England, scarcely yet distinguishable from rural villages or royal
forts, were subject each to its lord, whether King or thegn, or,
as often was the case, to a number of thegns.

But the real power, wealth and independence of the port of
London, alone of English cities, had far outrun her municipal
status in the eye of law. The fact that Winchester rather than
London was regarded as the official capital of the peripatetic
monarchy gave to the great port on the Thames a measure of real
political independence, and an attitude of external criticism
towards the royal power ; that spirit, kept in bounds by genuine
loyalty and patriotism, continued to inspire London down the
centuries until it culminated in the great doings of the Stuart
epoch. Very different is the history of Paris, the dwelling-place
of the Kings of France.[1]

The accession of Canute, though so stoutly contested by the
Londoners, was a blessing for them in disguise. Commerce
between his English and Baltic dominions grew very large, when
piracy was put down on the North Sea and the ports on both
sides were opened to mutual trade. The Danish merchants became the leading citizens in London, as they had long been in
York and the towns of the Danelaw. In the Eleventh Century
the Danish ' lithsmen ' and ' butsecarles ' of London took the lead
in transmarine trade, in the naval defence of the island, and in
disputes over the succession to the throne. Many of them at
first were heathen, but St. Clement Danes and dedications of City
churches to St. Olaf tell the tale of their conversion. ' Men of
the Emperor,' from Cologne and elsewhere, were also settled in
London with their own trading establishments. London regained
the place she had first acquired under the Romans as the chief
emporium of North European commerce.

1016–
1036.

Canute, the son of Sweyn Forkbeard the old Viking, became
an Emperor on the model of Charlemagne, and a King of England
following in the footsteps of Alfred along the path of reconciliation and renewal. Having won Kingship over the English
by force of arms, he put them on a real equality with the Danes,
and was loved by all his subjects alike. His father had been a
heathen more often and more genuinely than a Christian, and

---

[1] The Saxon Kings had palaces inside the London walls and sometimes
resided in them. The action of Edward the Confessor in building his palace
outside the walls, at Westminster, had immense unforeseen consequences in the
history of London and of England. See p. 112, below.

the boys had been brought up in the worship of Woden ; yet Canute died in the odour of sanctity, a high favourite with monastic chroniclers. For he became a great benefactor of abbeys, and his laws enjoined the more rigorous payment of tithe and Church dues, the observance of Sunday and the final suppression of the heathenism that lingered in parts of the Danelaw and still more among the new-comer Danes, whom he himself had led from oversea. The very ancient song that has given so pleasant a picture of Canute to many generations of Englishmen, shows how completely he obliterated in the imagination of men the record of his Viking youth :

> Merry sungen the monkës in Ely
> When Cnut King rowed thereby.
> Row, cnichts, near the land
> And hear we these monkës sing.

The monks of Ely would have sung a less merry tune if they had seen him coming as a boy in his father's war-boat along the channels of the fen. But the age of the Vikings was over at last ; Canute, King of Denmark, Norway, England and the Hebrides, had transmuted all that terrible energy into a beneficent Empire of the Nordic maritime peoples.

The more famous legend of his rebuke to preposterous courtiers by the seashore, though also very ancient, would more fitly have been attached to some wise King of lands nearer the sun, surrounded by his satraps and eunuchs. The hard-bitten housecarls and Vikings and Saxon thegns who guarded Canute had very different ideas of speech and service from those of Oriental hyperbole and servitude. Indeed it would be hard to find a local habitation for the story, because, in lands where courtiers flatter so grossly, the tide does not rise so fast or so far.

For the first few years after 1016 Canute was a foreign conqueror in England, holding his throne by the sword. But in 1020, after his return from a happy expedition oversea to secure his succession to the Danish throne, he adopted in England the policy of reconciling the two races on a basis of equality, and he began his famous alliance with the Church. In many vital respects his policy differed from that of the Norman who conquered England fifty years later. The Danish ' host ' who had won the throne for Canute was paid off in Danegeld instead of in confiscated estates. Anglo-Saxon and Danish were in equal favour as languages in the garth of the King's House at Winchester, and Canute issued a collection of Anglo-Saxon laws. The Church in Canute's reign was governed chiefly by Anglo-Saxon churchmen, whom Canute took into high favour as civil servants at his Court ;

thence he promoted them to Bishoprics. Under his patronage
churchmen from England went over to Norway and Denmark,
and played an important part there in the prolonged struggle
between Christian and pagan. There is no doubt that whereas
William the Conqueror found the French clergy abler and better
trained than the Saxon, Canute found the Saxon clergy less
badly trained than the Scandinavian. But the whole attitude
of the two Conquerors towards the leaders of the conquered
English was as different as possible. Not only in the Church,
but in the State and the army the Saxon thegns were trusted and
used by the Danish King. The great Earldom of Wessex was
governed by his favourite Saxon, Godwin, who now first rose
to fame.

After he had paid off the host and the fleet that conquered
England, Canute kept a navy of forty ships and a small standing
army of ' housecarls.' The ' housecarls ' were a bodyguard of
heavily-armoured, professional, mounted-infantry, drawing the
King's pay, and bound together in a military guild of which Canute
himself was a member. It was at once a ' cash nexus,' and a
brotherhood of honour and of personal service. The element of
feudal land-tenure was wanting, for although some housecarls
obtained estates in England they did not owe their service
as housecarls on account of their lands. At first entirely Scandinavian, the force soon included many Saxons. Essentially Viking
in origin and Anglo-Danish in development, the housecarls
perished with Harold at Hastings. The Norman conquerors did
not revive the force, for under their more purely feudal system
England was organized with land-tenure as the key to civil and
military institutions.

The supersession of Canute's work by the Norman Conquest
within a generation of his death makes it very difficult to estimate
either its importance or its excellence. If he had lived till sixty

1036. instead of dying at forty, he might have left a more permanent
mark on the world's affairs. He was a great ruler of men, and
he was on the way to found a Nordic Empire astride of the
North Sea, with Scandinavia for one pillar and England for the
other. Sea-power would have been its cement and its master-
spirit. If he had succeeded he would have changed the history
of the world. But the material difficulties of distance were too
great for the rude appliances of that age. In the Eleventh
Century it was as difficult to hold together an Empire astride of
the North Sea, as it was difficult in the Eighteenth Century to
hold together an Empire astride of the Atlantic. Indeed the
connection between Denmark, Norway, the Hebrides and England
was purely personal ; they were each of them ruled by the same

energetic man, but there was no Imperial machinery and no feeling of common patriotism. England herself had to be governed in four great Earldoms, and Norway was still very far from being a real political unit.

Canute's incapable Danish successors soon dissipated the loose confederation. Edward the Confessor, the restored Saxon monarch of independent England, looked no longer towards Scandinavia but towards French Normandy, and prepared the way for the Norman Conquest. Scandinavia and England, after being closely associated in hatred and in friendship for several centuries, drifted far apart, when England was drawn by the Normans into the orbit of France. Instead of remaining a maritime and Nordic State in touch with Scandinavia and only slightly connected with the main body of Europe, England became for many generations almost a part of French feudal civilization, engrossed either in her own island interests or in the continental ambitions of her French-speaking Kings. It is generally assumed that this change was quite inevitable and that on the whole more was gained than lost thereby. It may well be so. But the fact that Canute attempted a very different orientation for England is of profound interest, and though his Empire broke up, it was not without permanent effect, for it reinforced the Scandinavian and trading elements in the English nation.

1042–1066.

BOOKS FOR FURTHER READING

Gjerset and Collingwood, as for last chapter ; Larson, *Canute*, in *Heroes of the Nations* Series ; Vinogradoff, *English Society in the Eleventh Century* ; *Cam. Med. Hist.*, Vol. III., Chapter XV.

CHAPTER VII

The Norman Conquest up to Hastings. 1042–1066

FROM the time of Alfred to the time of Canute, the influences that refashioned Britain had come from Scandinavia ; for the next hundred years, dating from the accession of Edward the Confessor, they were to come from Normandy. The same is true in a less degree of European history as a whole.

1042.

The Norman aristocracy, Scandinavian by origin, retained all the Viking energy in colonization and in war, but had become converts to Latin culture. For that or other reasons the Normans were distinguished by a quality which the Scandinavians at home and in England lacked, the instinct for political unity and administrative consolidation. That instinct was the most valuable of the Conqueror's many gifts to England.

It was the Normans who turned back from Europe the tide See Map IX., p. 110, below. of Scandinavian influence. The province which their Viking ancestors had carved out of France as another ' Danelaw,' became the citadel whence the language, arms and manners of French feudalism sallied forth to the conquest of the world, more particularly of Naples, Sicily and the British Isles. Britain, not yet capable of becoming as in Shakespeare's day ' a world by itself,' had oscillated for two hundred years between Scandinavia and continental Europe. Her position was at length rudely determined for her by the French-speaking Norman Duke. The battle of Hastings was not only a great English but a great European event. For, with Britain closed to Scandinavia and opened to France, the Vikings were locked up in their fiords, and ceased to threaten or attract Christendom. The mounted spearmen who conquered at Hastings imposed their ' chivalric ' ideals and feudal relationships on the northern world, where the memory of Viking and thegn grew dim in the twilight of the past. Latin speech, literature and religion reigned unchallenged, until many centuries later the secession of Britain upon new lines of her own again redressed the balance of North and South.

Yet we must not too closely identify Norman with Latin civilization. The culture that the Normans imported into England was indeed Franco-Italian,—the culture of Taillefer, the French minstrel, and of Lanfranc and Anselm, the Italian Churchmen. But the monarchy brought over by the Normans was the monarchy of their own strong Dukes, not of the weak French Kings at Paris.

The Norman State was unique, and requires to be specially studied by searchers after the origins of things English. First founded by Danes and Norsemen, it had come to differ very widely from the districts similarly planted by the Vikings in Britain. It differed also from the rest of France. In Normandy the majority of the inhabitants were French peasants in origin and character, their backs patiently bent to the tillage of the soil. But the Scandinavian minority included the fishermen and merchants of the estuaries along the coast, and the feudal aristocracy of the land ; these grandchildren of the fiord still had their faces turned seaward with unabated ancestral love of roving and adventure, although they had adopted the speech, religion and customs of the French.

The jarl, in becoming a feudal baron, had learnt the new continental methods of war from the French enemies and allies whom he had met upon the Seine : instead of fighting on foot with the battle-axe of his fathers, he fought from the saddle with the spear and sword, and made his position in the country safe by piling up a high circular mound with a wooden fortress on the top, whence he could the more safely rule his peasants and defy his foes. Now heavily armed cavalry and private castles are the final flower of fully developed feudal society, and neither of them existed in England before the Normans brought them across the Channel.[1]

Norman feudalism had become strictly territorial, after the French model. The barons of the province owed military service to the Duke on account of the lands they held from him, and not, as many thegns in England still owed service, on account of personal or national obligation. The barons were bound to ride under the Duke's banner in his constant wars against Anjou, Maine or Brittany; each led his quota of five, ten or thirty knights due from his barony, the quota being always, for purposes of military convenience, assessed in units of five knights. This system the Conqueror afterwards imposed upon England with a remarkable uniformity.

The knights in their turn held their lands from the barons by the same military tenure. The knight, if he held a ' knight's fee ' of land, had to follow the banner of the baron from whom he held it, whenever the baron followed the Duke to the field or made war on his own account,—such at least was the custom in Normandy.

This military service was due nominally for forty days in the year, but it was possible sometimes to exact it for rather longer in order to finish the campaign. A few weeks would serve for the private wars of baron against baron, or for the Duke's campaigns in Brittany and Anjou. But for a prolonged adventure like the conquest of England a voluntary long-service agreement had to be improvised, distinct from the feudal obligation. The period of military service due was wholly inadequate for distant enterprises ; that is one of the chief reasons why feudalism broke down as communications improved. Feudalism had been originally devised for the defence of a countryside against Danish and other raids, and for the purposes of private war : it was not suited to the growth of great states or for the conduct of prolonged and extensive military operations.

[1] The mound castles of England are Norman (see Baldwin Brown, I. 106–110). The Saxons and Danes made earthwork enclosures to protect towns and royal forts, but not high mounds like those of the Norman barons. The English thegn's house was usually unfortified. Hence the English outcry against the high mounds crowned by timber forts which the Normans erected in great numbers immediately after their arrival in England. It was only gradually that stone replaced timber work in the Norman castle—except in a few special cases like the Conqueror's Tower of London, which was of masonry from the first.

From the top to the bottom of society the feudal relation of lord to man in Normandy was fixed, territorial and heritable—passing from father to son. At the top was the Duke, under him the barons, under each of them the knights, and under all the peasants. The peasant was a serf bound to the soil and to his lord as owner of the soil. In Normandy neither peasant nor knight could transfer his vassalage at will to another lord, as many freeholders were still able to do in the less territorialized feudalism of Anglo-Danish England. Norman society was therefore less free than Scandinavian or even Anglo-Saxon, but it was more stable, and more efficiently organized for peace and war.

Although in Normandy the social and military system was more strictly feudal than in Saxon England, the political system was less feudal, for the Duke had begun to impose on his barons an authority which the Kings of strictly feudal countries could never hope to wield. The feudal King of France claimed a vague suzerainty over the Norman Duke, but enjoyed no power in his territories, nor in any other province of France except in the small royal domain round Paris. On the other hand the Norman Duke was much more than feudal lord in his own remarkable Duchy. The traits of real monarchy in the Norman State were neither Scandinavian nor French in their character. They were peculiarly Norman. The Conqueror and his sons carried these monarchical peculiarities of their Duchy to the island soil, where they re-enforced the English Kingship and developed it into that great mediæval monarchy which had no parallel in France, Germany or Spain.

In the first place there were no large baronies inside Norman territory, and no single baron was strong enough to defy the Duke with impunity. Government by great feudal Earldoms, which prevailed in the England of Edward the Confessor and in contemporary France, had no place in Normandy. The Norman Duke had real administrative officers of his own who exercised functions properly public, as distinct from the work of a bailiff of the ducal domains. These officers were called *vicomtes* ; they collected the Duke's revenues, commanded his troops, held his courts and maintained his peace. The King of France had no such officers. The subsequent identification of the Norman *vicomte* with the old English sheriff greatly strengthened the position of the latter, and made the sheriffdom the chief pillar of the mediæval English monarchy. Norman finance was the best in Europe and the Duke was proportionately powerful ; he collected a revenue in hard money, while his suzerain King of France lived as best he could on rents paid in kind, moving round for his bed and board from farm to farm upon his domain.

In Normandy no one besides the Duke dared to mint money. Private castles could be erected only by his license, and were to be handed over on demand. Private war, though not yet illegal, was limited by the Ducal power.

It will therefore be seen that when England was invaded in 1066, she was being attacked not merely by a band of cosmopolitan adventurers enlisted for the nonce under a single war-chief—though that was one element in the affair ; England was also being attacked by the most highly organized continental state of the day, which possessed peculiar institutions capable of rapid development in the free field of a vast and inchoate conquered territory. And even more important to England than the institutions of the Norman State were the habits of mind and action which the Norman Duke and his subjects brought over with them. William, before ever he invaded England, had fought and conquered his rebellious barons in Normandy. A bastard, called to his doubtful inheritance as a boy of eight, he had seen feudal anarchy at its worst, trampled it down and taught men to obey.

Last but not least, the Church in Normandy was in league with the Ducal power. The later Dukes, zealous converts from Danish Woden to the French Christ, had restored and re-endowed the Abbeys and Bishoprics overthrown by their heathen ancestors. In return they appointed all the Bishops and most of the Abbots. The leaders of the Church were therefore servants of the Ducal policy. Some of them, indeed, were merely fighting barons dressed up as churchmen. The Conqueror's most powerful subject was his brutal and turbulent brother Odo, whom he had thrust into the Bishopric of Bayeux while still a boy. Odo led his own hundred and twenty knights to war, and since the Church objected to priests shedding blood with the sword, swung his mace in the thick of the melee at Hastings.

Others of the Norman prelates were of a higher type. Since the beginning of the Eleventh Century there had been a strong movement of reform, and the Cluniac monastic revival had been favoured and guided by the rulers of the Duchy. In a land remote from the Italian centres of religion and learning, a land where barbarism might long have reigned undisturbed under heathen or Christian forms,[1] there had grown up monasteries like that of Bec capable of attracting the greatest intellects of the day from beyond the Alps. Lanfranc of Pavia and Anselm of Aosta were successively Priors of Bec and Archbishops of Canterbury. No fact illustrates more clearly the cosmopolitan character of learning and religion in the Middle Ages, in striking

[1] As late as 1001 a Burgundian monk declared that scarcely a priest in Normandy could read. Haskins, *Normans in European History*, p. 164.

contrast to the isolation in which most men had to pass their lives, bound never to leave their native village, either by their legal status as serfs or by want of means to travel. The physical and social barriers that impeded the communication of man with man were very great, but national barriers scarcely existed. Lanfranc and Anselm, from far Italy, brought the knowledge of Roman and Canon Law, and the latest theology and philosophy of the day, first to Normandy and thence to England. And few complained of them as 'foreigners.' Before the age of Universities, monasteries like Bec served as the chief centres of learning. Meanwhile architecture was already laying its massive and imperishable impress on the Norman landscape. Though the great age of stone castles was delayed till the Twelfth Century, the Norman Abbeys and Cathedrals that we know were already beginning to rise when the Conqueror sailed for England.

Yet although the Normans were ahead of barbarous Europe in certain respects which proved of the first importance in the future development of England, they were not what we should recognize as a civilized people. In spite of a few learned priests, the upper class were ignorant of the rudiments of letters ; there were no lawyers and practically no professional men except the clergy ; the luxury, art, commerce and chivalry of the later Middle Ages had not yet come into existence, and nothing of that kind was to be found in the timber fortresses and occasional stone ' donjons ' of this primitive baronage. The Normans were quite as inhumane as the Anglo-Saxons or Danes of contemporary England, and being more active and industrious they committed many more deeds of revolting cruelty. The lopping-off of hands and feet and the gouging out of eyes of prisoners and rebels, wholesale massacre of populations, and deliberate devastation of whole districts, were among the Norman methods of warfare, as England was soon to learn to her cost. The Norman, devoted servant of the Church as he had now become, had advanced little if at all beyond the heathen Viking in point of humane conduct. But in knowledge and organizing power he had advanced. The Church taught barbarians to organize society, and it was this better organization of society, even more than the precept and example of the Church herself, that eventually taught men to take the first halting steps in the direction of humanity and justice.

Although the Ducal power in Normandy, when transferred to England, would help to make the King's Peace supreme there, the Normandy of the Conqueror was an unquiet land, perpetually disturbed by private and public war, violence and outrage of all kinds, like the typical feudal province of the Middle Ages.

It is an error to suppose that the mediæval world was safe and peaceful because its inhabitants were theoretically conscious of the unity of Christendom. It was indeed free from our modern dangers of race hatred and war organized on the national scale, for the low level of organization and transport prevented France and Germany from conceiving the idea of racial patriotism and making war on one another as nations ; but they were both in a state of constant internal war between the petty feudal powers composing them, wars conducted with the utmost ferocity, although for purely personal motives. In the feudal world the hand of neighbour was perpetually raised against neighbour, and death, injustice and outrage were the daily lot. But in the Norman Dukes' conception of their office there was that which looked distantly towards better conditions of life ; if this conception could be realized in the ring fence of an island State, it might lead in the course of a few generations to a better society than the chaos of the ordinary mediæval kingdom.

Meanwhile the inhabitants of England, left to themselves, were making little or no progress towards a more united island or a stronger monarchy. The failure of Canute's sons to perpetuate his Nordic Maritime Empire or to govern England as a Danelaw, had resulted in the restoration of the House of Alfred in the person of Edward, whom after ages called the Confessor. He was the son of Ethelred the Redeless and of Emma, daughter of a former Duke of Normandy. 1042-1066.

See p. 113 below.

The return of the English line to the throne, though it put an end to the Scandinavian supremacy, failed to set the Anglo-Saxon nation again on the path of progress. If an Alfred or even a Harold had inherited the unchallenged throne at a juncture so favourable, something at least might have been done to unite and reform England without Norman interference. But the Confessor was, at heart, not an English King but a French monk. He was entirely without political vision and almost without political ambition. What stirred his enthusiasm was the religious life as he had seen it lived among the new school of Norman clergy. He had spent among Norman monks his long years of exile, from boyhood to middle age, during the Danish rule in England. Norman by birth on his mother's side, he was at the moment of his restoration even less of an Englishman than Charles II when he landed at Dover. Edward spoke, and probably thought, in French. His rôle in English history was to prepare the way for the Norman Conquest, both by the little that he did and by the much that he left undone.

His only active policy was to introduce Normans into the high places of Church and State. He was prompted to show them favour not only by his personal tastes and friendships based on the experience of the best years of his life, but by the desire to find loyal and able adherents of his own to counterbalance the overpowering influence of Earl Godwin. Godwin had placed him on the throne, and like other kingmakers expected to act as Mayor of the Palace. Without his Normans, the King would have had neither the wit nor the strength of will to resist his too powerful subject.

Edward raised several Normans to be Bishops, and made one of them, Robert of Jumièges, Primate of England. A group of Sussex ports, the gateway of the continent, was placed in Norman hands. Herefordshire was entrusted to the Norman Earl Ralph ; his wardship of the Welsh March, which this post implied, enabled him to introduce the Norman military system into that remote woodland shire, while some of his followers gave the inhabitants a foretaste of Norman violence and greed. Ralph and his knights built private castles, a novel portent on which the Saxon freemen looked askance, and he attempted in vain to teach the thegns to fight from the saddle in their contests with the Welsh tribesmen. The characteristic refusal of the English to learn the now indispensable art of cavalry fighting from Ralph or anyone else, sealed their doom in the Hastings campaign.

At court the Confessor's secretaries and chaplains were Normans. In the heart of London, the wine merchants of Rouen held a wharf of their own at the mouth of the Wall Brook. When therefore the Conqueror landed at Pevensey, he set foot on an island where for a quarter of a century there had been a Norman party in politics, and where Norman methods and customs were known, feared and admired.

But what Edward left undone was even more important than what he did, in preparing the way for the Norman Conquest. In the first place he deliberately left behind him a disputed succession by his personal adherence to the monkish ideal of chastity, in spite of the fact that he went through the idle ceremony of marriage with Earl Godwin's daughter. Secondly, he never tried to unite the island administratively or to improve its laws and institutions. It would have been a hard task, impossible perhaps for anyone but an armed conqueror to complete, but Edward never even attempted it.[1]

---

[1] ' In after days,' writes Maitland, ' the holy but imbecile Edward won not only the halo of the saint, to which he may have been entitled, but the fame, to which he certainly was not entitled, of having been a great legislator. In the minster that he reared, king after king made oath to observe the laws of the Confessor. So far as we know, he never made a law. Had he made laws, had he even made good use of those that were already made, there might have been

The most serious bar to all national progress was the government of England in half a dozen great Earldoms, each presided over by a feudal magnate, instead of in single shires, each ruled by a royal official. It is true that the evil was no new thing in Edward's day, that England had never really been united since the departure of the Romans, and that a similar system prevailed in yet worse forms in Germany and France. But since England under the Confessor enjoyed more than twenty years of external peace, unassailed by Normandy or Scandinavia, a strong King would have used a respite so unusual to try at least to promote greater national unity, before the inevitable next onset of the foreign foe. But Edward's policy, so far as he can be said to have had any consistent plan besides the introduction of Normans, only served to encourage provincial feeling and to divide North from South. For he was fain to play off the power and the jealousy of the Northern Earls of Mercia and Northumbria against Wessex and the other Earldoms of the South presided over by the House of Godwin.

By this means the Confessor on one occasion succeeded in 1051. having Godwin and his family driven from the realm. But next year a counter-revolution took place. Godwin and his son Harold came back from their places of exile in Flanders and Ireland. They sailed up and down the Channel, landing at various points to ravage after the cruel manner of warfare in those days ; none the less South England rose to fight on their side. The seafaring population swarmed out of the Channel ports to join their flotilla, while forces from Sussex and Surrey marched on London, all vowing to ' live or die ' with Earl Godwin. When finally he floated up the Thames, the men of London let 1052. his ships pass unopposed under their bridge. Then and there he dictated terms to the King, for whom no one seemed eager to fight. Godwin's chief Norman enemies fled the land, and his House was restored to all its private estates and public offices.

The underlying motives of the politics of this troubled reign are obscure. The evidence we have is fragmentary, and modern historians equally well informed of all that there is to know have differed widely from one another in their estimate of the character and policy of the chief actors. It is probably safe to say that dislike of the Normans was a strong motive in the popular

no Norman Conquest of England. But then had there been no Norman Conquest of England, Edward would never have gained his fictitious glories. As it was, men looked back to him as the last of the English Kings of the English,—for of Harold, who had become the perjured usurper, there could be no talk,—and galled by the yoke of their French masters, they sighed for Saint Edward's law, meaning thereby the law that had prevailed in a yet unvanquished England.' *Social England*, I., p. 169.

English Miles
0 10 20 30 40 50   100

1. DURHAM, *County Palatine after Conquest till Henry VIII.*
2. CHESTER, *Palatine Earldom after Conquest.*
3. SHREWSBURY, *Palatine Earldom after Conquest till 1102.*
4. HEREFORD, *Palatine Earldom after Conquest till 1076.*

Edinburgh
LOTHIAN
SCOTLAND
NORTHUMBERLAND
Durham
DURHAM 1
CUMBRIA
WESTMOR-
LAND
NORTHUMBRIA
(Morcar)
Stamford Bridge
York
R. Humber
Lincoln
The Wash
CHESTER 2
WILD WALES
Offa's Dyke
SHREWS-
BURY 3
MERCIA
(Edwin)
(Waltheof)
EAST
ANGLIA
Peterborough
Ely Isle
t   h)
HERE
FORD 4
(G   y   r   (Leofwine)
Wallingford
London
R. Thames
R. Severn
Winchester
Westminster
Canterbury
Dover
W   E   S   S   E   X
Exeter
(Harold)
Bosham
Andredesweald
Lewes
Battle
Hastings
Pevensey
CORNWALL
FLANDERS
PICARDY
Jumièges
Rouen
Bayeux
Bec
R. Seine
NORMANDY
KINGDOM OF FRANCE
Paris
BRITTANY
MAINE

Emery Walker Ltd. sc.

Map IX.—England in Earldoms: Eve of the Norman Conquest

reception of the ambitious Earl, a year after his outlawry had
been so easily decreed.   But to speak of him and of his son Harold
after him as ' national heroes' may be misleading, because
' national' feeling as we know it had not come into existence.
The men of Wessex, of the Severn valley and of Danelaw might
each and all dislike the Normans, but they knew not one another
and had no common loyalty.   The appeal to unite in defence
of England as a whole was never made to them in the Eleventh
Century, because it would not have been understood.   If it had
been understood, a few thousand armoured cavalry would not
have been able to conquer and share up England after Hastings.

Godwin died the year after his triumphant return, bequeathing   1053.
to his ablest son Harold the chief direction of the King's government, the Earldom of Wessex, the affection of England south of
Thames, and vast estates scattered over many shires.   These last
had been accumulated in a single generation by arts which would
perhaps not bear too close an inquisition.   For Godwin's fortunes
were of his own making.   A simple thegn of Sussex, he had
not inherited but acquired the vast wealth and the power unparalleled in a subject, which he left to his son.   He must have
been a remarkable man, but we know too little about him to
estimate his character and career.

For the dozen years after Godwin's death, the King was never
able openly to defy Harold.   It was a state of equilibrium which
prevented any real steps towards national consolidation.   Not all
the Normans had disappeared, and, when Edward died, the two
great Earldoms of Mercia and Northumbria belonged to Edwin
and Morcar, representing interests alien if not openly hostile to
Harold's power.   The Earldom of East Anglia, indeed, had been
consigned to his brother Gyrth.   But the fact that two of his
brothers, Sweyn and Tostig, were ne'er-do-wells who proved unfit
for public trust had helped to prevent the closer union of the
whole island under the ægis of the House of Godwin.

Such was the political situation when the mild King died
in his new Palace at Westminster, after a futile reign in which   Jan.
Saxon England had wasted its last opportunity of setting its   1066.
own house in order.   The continued decadence of Anglo-Saxon
prose and poetry in this period had been all of a piece with the
political failure.   The Norman Conquest did not cause the decline
of Anglo-Saxon literature, though it may have prevented its
revival.   The decline might with more plausibility be ascribed
to the Danish conquest of half a century before.

Like the Third and Sixth Henries and other ' sore saints for
the Crown,' the Confessor left behind something that pleads with
posterity against his political failures.   Though Westminster

Abbey was destined to be rebuilt once more in a greater age of architecture, it was Edward's endowments and buildings that prepared for Westminster the high place that it holds in ecclesiastical history and its supreme place in the political development of England. He moved the King's dwelling from inside the walls of the City to a new Palace on the rural 'island of thorns' two miles up the river, in order to be near the great church that he was building there to St. Peter, an operation on which his whole heart was set. Mighty consequences flowed from the royal flitting to Westminster. As time went on, the centre of government was inevitably drawn more and more from the old Wessex capital at Winchester to the area of London. And if the strong Norman Kings, like their Saxon predecessors, had lived actually inside London walls whenever they were in the neighbourhood, the political independence of the City would have been nipped in the bud. Yet the political independence enjoyed by the Londoners was to be the bulwark of the liberties of England in times to come, from the days of King John to the Stuart era. It was well, therefore, for British freedom that the great Plantagenet bureaucracy which grew up round the King's Palace, struck root not in the City itself, but in Westminster; it was no far-seeing political philosophy that had fixed it there, but chance and Edward the Confessor's pious whim.

At the end of the Saxon period London was beginning again, for the first time since Roman days, to be a great centre of North European commerce. London was a whale among the fishes beside the other English boroughs. Within the circuit of its Roman walls, which five hundred years before had stood unrepaired and almost empty, the chief arteries of traffic and many of the narrow lanes were already laid out on the sites they occupy in 'the City' of to-day. The houses, indeed, were of wood, many of them mere market booths, and there was much open ground behind and around the buildings. But the busy, cosmopolitan character of the great port had already something about it prophetic of the future 'London.' Scandinavian, Fleming, German and Norman all had their share in the place, but the East Anglian type prevailed among the common people. Close outside the walls spread the ploughlands and pastures of Moorfields, Smithfield and other 'fields,' growing food for the citizens, and loud with the noise of water-mills turned by streams flowing to the Thames. On the northern horizon lay wooded hills, where the lords of the London sokes and the merchant warriors of the City hawked after herons and hunted the stag, the boar and the wild bull, in St. John's Wood, in Hampstead, in Enfield Chase, and in the Hertfordshire forests beyond.

The death of the immaculate Edward left the succession to the throne in a fine confusion. The nearest heir was Edgar the Atheling, but he was a boy. If, indeed, the English State had been more highly organized, and if Englishmen had been more conscious of their nationality, they would have proclaimed the boy King and rallied round him against all comers. But as the world went then, there was great fear of anarchy if a minor should ascend the throne, especially one who had no strong connections and no party of his own. It is small wonder that men turned rather to the tried ability and long established power of Harold. He was, indeed, more distant from the royal line, but the blood of Scandinavian Kings was in his veins through his mother's side; and with all his experience, and his wide family estates in Southern England, he bade fair to defend and rule the land in troubled times better than the Atheling.[1]

It may be that Harold would have done better if he had resisted the suggestions of vaulting ambition, and set himself as the guardian lion on the steps of the Atheling's throne. But his acceptance of the crown, even if ill-advised, cannot be stigmatized as a usurpation. England had never observed a strict law of hereditary succession ; the passing over of minors was quite usual though not obligatory ; the dying Confessor had named Harold his heir ; and, above all, the Witan chose him King. But his weak title invited Scandinavia and Normandy to compete for the conquest of England—as probably they would have done even if the Atheling had been chosen in his stead, though scarcely if the Confessor had left a son. The autumn of 1066 saw England attacked by Harald Hardrada, King of Norway, and by William, Duke of Normandy, in two almost simultaneous invasions. It was the dramatic climax of the long competition between Scandinavia and Latin Europe for the prize of England. Harold might have repelled either enemy alone ; he sank beneath the double attack, and the Norman, through luck and conduct, rose the only winner.

William's claims to the throne—if indeed we are willing to

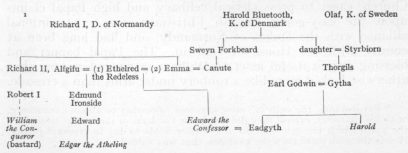

set aside the not altogether unimportant fact that he was a bastard—were genealogically better than Harold's, though worse than the Atheling's. But Harold had been chosen King by the Witan and William had not. William, however, won the sympathy of continental Christendom by certain arguments which appeal very little to modern minds, though they served conveniently to brand Harold for many centuries as a perjured usurper.

In the first place William declared that Edward had at one time named him as his successor. It may have been so, but it is more certain that Edward's last act was to recommend Harold, and in any case the Witan and not the late King had the disposal of the Crown. Secondly, William had, a couple of years before the death of Edward, compelled Harold, who had fallen by chance into his hands, to swear on certain relics to be his man and to support his claims to the reversion of the English throne. The solemn oath and its flagrant breach weighed heavily in the minds of contemporaries, in whose every-day lives and legal proceedings oaths sanctioned by religion played a very much larger part than in our own.[1] The less formal modern mind is more impressed by the fundamental injustice of William's proceedings ; he took advantage of an accident to compel his guest, as a condition of safe return home, to swear away his own chances of succession and those of Edgar Atheling, and his country's freedom to decide its own destiny. It is one of the points on which mediæval and modern ethics stand honestly at variance.

Last of all, William raised prejudice against Harold as the patron of Stigand, whom the Godwin faction had irregularly thrust into the Primacy of England, but who was regarded by the Papal party on the continent as little better than a schismatic on account of his dealings with an anti-Pope. The age of Hildebrand was approaching upon the continent ; that great man was not yet Pope, but he already enjoyed considerable influence at Rome, and he used it with effect on William's side at this crisis. The reforming and Hildebrandine party in the Church, eager to press clerical celibacy and high Papal claims upon the easy-going English Christians, was in traditional alliance with the Dukes of Normandy, and had long been at enmity with the House of Godwin. The Papal banner and blessing were a useful asset to William in an undertaking that otherwise looked more like a robbery under arms than a crusade.

---

[1] For instance, the oath of ' compurgators ' swearing to a man's innocence, or to his character, even if they did not know the facts of the case at issue, held the place which the examination of evidence holds to-day in criminal justice. It was the oath more than the evidence that was valued.

In that day of small feudal States, Normandy counted as a great European power, and its ruler was a statesman well versed in the intricacies of foreign politics. Like his namesake six centuries later, William prepared the way for his invasion of England by propaganda and diplomacy ably conducted in many distant countries, and by skilful settlements with his neighbours which rendered his homeland safe during his absence. Harold's case was unheard abroad and went by default. The French-speaking feudal world felt a glow of righteous enthusiasm for the bandits' league into which it entered under the great chief.

The armament that landed at Pevensey was not a feudal levy, though its members were strongly imbued with the feudal spirit and were to be rewarded by strictly feudal holdings in the con-quered land. William had no power under feudal law to call out his vassals to a campaign which must last a great deal longer than forty days. But many of the barons and knights, not only of Normandy, but of Brittany and of Flanders which owed him no allegiance, had voluntarily engaged themselves to serve under his flag. It was a joint-stock enterprise for the sharing out of the English lands. On much the same principle the conquest of Ireland in Cromwell's day—also regarded at the time as a great religious work—was carried through by military service to be paid in estates won from the conquered and by loans raised on the same speculative security. William and his confederates were at the expense of building a fleet of transports during the spring and summer of 1066, for it was essential to carry across not only the armoured men but the trained war-horses which gave them their chief hope of breaking the shield wall of Harold's famous housecarls.[1]

It was a great armament, but its strength lay in its training and equipment rather than its size. In those days even officials were unable to count large numbers accurately, but modern historians reckon that at the highest figure the expedition did not exceed 12,000 men, of whom probably less than half were cavalry. It is certain that when England had been divided up among the conquerors, many of whom came over after Hastings, the total number of knights enfeoffed did not exceed 5000.[2] That a country of a million and a half people should have been subdued, robbed and permanently held down by so small a band, gives the measure of the political and military backwardness of the English system as compared to the Norman.

[1] The invading Danes in Alfred's time could ' horse ' themselves in England, because they wished to march as mounted infantry, but not, like the Normans, to fight as cavalry.

[2] Round, *Feudal England*, pp. 265, 289–292. Haskins, *Norman Institutions*, p. 78. Oman, *England before the Conquest*, p. 641. Stenton's *William*, p. 196.

There was also an element of luck, decisive of the narrow margin by which William conquered at Hastings. For six weeks contrary winds had held him weatherbound in port. During that interim Harald Hardrada, King of Norway, landed with another great host to conquer England, and defeated Earls Edwin and Morcar and their local levies two miles from York. The English Harold had perforce to break up the armed watch he was keeping on the southern coast against the expected Norman armada, and hurry off to save the North. His house-carls,[1] the finest mounted infantry in Europe, began their last admirable and tragic campaign by riding hot-spur to the gates of York, and fighting foot to foot against the great Viking host

Sept. 28, 1066.

at Stamford Bridge until it was utterly destroyed. Three days later William landed at Pevensey.

Harold had removed from the Normans' path a most formidable opponent, and in doing so had reduced his own strength by many gallant warriors hewed down at Stamford Bridge. He and his housecarls rode back to London in four days, reaching it on October 6th. The battered forces of the North were following more slowly on foot ; the fyrd of the South-West had not yet arrived. Rightly or wrongly Harold determined to give William battle at once in Sussex, with the thegns and fyrd of the South-Eastern counties alone, gathered round the strong nucleus of his remaining housecarls. Since infantry contending against cavalry must needs stand on the defensive, he defied William from a well-chosen position on an isolated spur of hill six miles north-west of Hastings ; it stood on the southern edge of the great forest of Andredsweald from which the Saxon army had emerged. The hill, afterwards crowned by the village and Abbey of Battle, then bore no dwelling and no name, and was distinguished only by a forlorn feature on its skyline, ' the hoar apple tree.' [2]

Oct. 14, 1066.

The storming of that hill proved a day's task almost beyond the power of the invaders, in spite of their great superiority in arms and tactics. The two hosts represented different developments of the old Nordic method of war, the outcome, respectively, of two different social and political systems. Norman knights and English housecarls wore indeed much the same defensive armour ; the primitive shirt of ring-mail of their common ancestry had been lengthened into a garment of the same material ending in a divided skirt convenient for riders. Both sides wore

---

[1] For the Anglo-Danish institution of the housecarls see p. 100, above.
[2] In the Middle Ages the action was called either *Battle* or *bellum*, or the battle or *bellum* of Hastings. It was hardly ever called Senlac until the end of the Nineteenth Century by Freeman and his school. See Round, *Feudal England*, pp. 333–340. See the same authority on the course of the battle ; he has shown that the English had no artificial defences to their position.

the conical helmet and nose-piece then in fashion, and bore shields no longer round but in most cases of the new kite shape, long and tapering so as to protect the warrior's thigh when on horseback. Both armies contained also a number of unarmoured or half-armoured men with inferior weapons—the ' fyrd ' of the neighbouring shires swelling the ranks of the Saxons in this particular. But here the similarity between the opponents ceased. The Anglo-Danes, leaving their horses in the rear, still fought on foot in the shield-ring, and still used the long Danish battle-axe, which Harold plied so manfully in his last fight. The Normans fought from the saddle, casting and thrusting with the spear [1] and striking down with the sword. But even the shock tactics of their splendid cavalry proved unable to destroy the shield-wall on the top of the hill, without the aid of another arm. The Normans as warriors had not only learnt the new but remembered the old ; they had learnt cavalry tactics from the French, but they had preserved the old Scandinavian practice of archery which the Anglo-Danes had neglected. Between the charges of horse Harold's infantry were exposed to the shafts of archers, inferior indeed to the future long-bowmen of Crecy, but superior to any who drew bow for England that day. Infantry with only striking weapons fight at desperate odds against cavalry supported by missiles. At Waterloo the English squares had missile weapons on their side against the French cuirassiers ; it was otherwise at Hastings.

When night fell, Harold and all his housecarls around him were lying dead in their ranks on the hill-top, like the Scots round their King at Flodden ; and the surviving warriors of the ' fyrd,' battle-scarred and sick at heart, were trailing to their distant homes in every direction along the darkening tracks of the Andredsweald.

CHAPTER VIII

The Norman Conquest completed, and Norman institutions
established. 1066–1135

Kings : William I, 1066–1087 ; William II, 1087–1100 ; Henry I, 1100–1135

THE shock of the battle of Hastings would have rallied the forces of a well-organized feudal kingdom, and stirred the patriotic resistance of a nation. It had no such effect in the Anglo-

[1] The long heavy spear of the ' tourney ' type was a later development in mediæval war.

Danish realm.   Earls, thegns, Bishops, sheriffs, boroughs thought only of making their private peace with the Conqueror.   Even Stigand, the foremost man in Harold's party, and the special object of aversion to the Pope's Norman allies, vainly sought to retain the throne of Canterbury by an immediate submission, made while William was in the act of crossing the Thames at Wallingford.   Edwin and Morcar had come south too slowly to help Harold at Hastings—whether from treachery, slackness or unavoidable delay no one will ever know.   They now slunk back to the North, leaving Southern England to make the best of the situation.   Probably they reckoned that, whoever wore the crown in Wessex and on the banks of Thames, they themselves would continue to enjoy virtual independence as Earls of Mercia and Northumbria.   But it was not so that William conceived of the Kingship he had won.

South England meanwhile offered little resistance.   Winchester, the old Wessex capital, led the way in submission.   As to London, William had not force enough to be sure of taking it by storm, and he desired to enter it in peaceful guise as Edward's acknowledged heir.   He began therefore to make a wide circuit round the city to west and north, destroying as he went the villages of Buckinghamshire and Hertfordshire to hasten the surrender of the English.   The policy was successful.   London, after a few weeks' hesitation and a futile proclamation of Edgar Atheling as King, sent to acknowledge William and invite him to his coronation at Westminster.

There, on Christmas Day, 1066, he was crowned as lawful heir of the Confessor, while his followers, on a false alarm of treachery, were setting fire to the houses of the English outside. The noise of strife and outrage interrupted the service, and all save William and the officiating priests rushed out of the Minster to take part.   Here were grim realities, in dramatic contrast to William's theory of a lawful and natural passage of the Crown. The claim to be heir to the Confessor and guardian of his ' good laws ' thinly covered over the brute facts of conquest, and seemed of little avail to protect the country against French robbery and violence.   Nevertheless, in the days of the Conqueror and his sons after him, the occasional alliance of the Norman King with his Saxon subjects against rebellious members of the Franco-Norman baronage, and the revival and strengthening of the fyrd and the shire-court, gave importance to the constitutional formula on which William had based his claim to the throne of England.

In the first critical months after Hastings, when the English let slip the opportunity of united resistance, many of them hoped by submission to suffer no more loss of lands and liberties than they had suffered under the foreign rule of Canute and his men from Denmark. They were soon undeceived. On the ground that everyone who had acknowledged the usurper Harold had forfeited all his possessions, the confiscation of Saxon estates for the benefit of the foreign conquerors began directly after the battle, and went on year after year as rebellions or other less good reasons gave excuse.

Nor was the yoke of Norman King or Norman baron like the easy yoke of Canute and his Earls. The new monarchy and the new feudalism were riveted on the land by the new military system. Everywhere huge circular mounds, like those still visible at Lewes and in a hundred other places throughout the land, were piled up by the forced labour of Saxon peasants, and crowned by royal or private fortresses first of timber and ultimately of stone.[1] In front of the mound there was an outer court, called a 'bailey,' protected by an earthwork enclosure. From these impregnable citadels the armoured horsemen issued forth to dominate the countryside, sometimes in the interest of order, sometimes on errands of plunder and misrule. The Londoners saw with alarm the royal masonry of the Tower donjon gradually overtopping the eastern walls of their city, and curbing though not destroying their cherished independence.

After a successful campaign in the South-West, where the power and estates of the House of Godwin had chiefly been concentrated, William by the end of 1068 was true lord of Southern England, and in the North was at least acknowledged as King. But only a portion of the landed estates of the country had as yet changed hands ; in particular, Mercia and Northumbria were very much as they had been before Hastings. The *status quo* in the North would have lasted longer, had the two Earls, Edwin and Morcar, remained passively loyal. But they rebelled, were suppressed and pardoned, and then rebelled again. Their second rising was rendered formidable by the help it received from another Viking invasion, led by the sons of the King of Denmark. In Mercia the wild Welsh poured across Offa's dyke to aid the war against Norman rule. 1069.

Such was the occasion of William's great campaign in the North and of his cruel vengeance. Between York and Durham

---

[1] See note, p. 103, above. The mound was known as the 'motte' and the timber or stone tower on it as the 'turris,' 'donjon' or 'keep.' The Bayeux tapestry represents the throwing up of such a mound at Hastings to support a timber fortress. The character of the timber fortresses of the Normans is more exactly delineated in the siege of Dinant castle in the same tapestry. We see there the attackers applying fire to it ; that danger no doubt hastened the 'stone age' of Norman castle building in the time of Stephen.

he left no house standing and no human beings alive that his horsemen could search out. As Doomsday testifies, many scores of villages were still without inhabitant seventeen years later. Most of the North Riding and much of the East Riding of Yorkshire were depopulated by massacre. In Durham County the houses and cattle were destroyed, but the inhabitants had warning and escaped across the Tyne. Many sold themselves as slaves, not a few in the Lothian district of Scotland which thus obtained a strong infusion of Scandinavian blood. Devastation and massacre were let loose in more spasmodic fashion in Cheshire and the midland shires. The wooden hovels of that day could be rebuilt from the neighbouring forests more easily than houses in civilized times, but the loss in men, cattle and farm utensils could be less easily repaired. The ' harrying of the North ' was a vengeance Turkish in its atrocity, but fully in accord with the ideas and practice of the most zealously Christian warriors in mediæval Europe.

This foul deed served its purpose. There could be no more rebellions after such wholesale destruction. It decided the question whether William and a few thousand armoured knights could conquer all England and coerce her inhabitants into a new manner of life. It put an end to the age-old separatism of Northern England and of the Danelaw in opposition to the kingship seated in Wessex and London. And it broke the resistance of Scandinavian society to Norman feudalism. The Durham Castle and Cathedral that we know, rose as the symbol of a new Latin civilization, superimposed on these wild Nordic lands by a foreign soldiery and clergy : the splendid architecture that crowns the rock, much of it raised within one generation of the ' harrying of the North,' in a region that had been poor and barbarous to a degree even before that terrible catastrophe, bears witness to the energy of the French-speaking rulers, builders and churchmen, the handful of men whom William's Conquest sent to govern and transform those distant regions.

Not only the lands north of Humber, but Lincolnshire and East Anglia, the richest agricultural districts in England, received the new civilization, but at a heavy price in human freedom. The freemen of the Danelaw had hitherto kept at arm's length even the Anglo-Saxon forms of feudalism. Many of them could ' go with their land ' to what lord they would, and some villages had no lord at all. The proportion of freemen was much greater in the Danish and Norse districts than elsewhere in England. But the Normans put an end to these old-fashioned liberties, and imposed the French system of strictly territorial feudalism on the Scandinavian North and East as well as on the Saxon

South and West. The Danish freeman in most cases sank into the villein of the manor. Yet in prosperous Lincolnshire some of the villeins remained well-to-do and in certain legal aspects free men.

' The harrying of the North ' diminished the number of Danes in England and especially in Yorkshire. But it appears that, as time went on, the Norsemen who had settled so thickly on the Western coast in Cumberland and Lancashire moved eastward into the depopulated regions, so that the actual acreage of Scandinavian occupation in England was perhaps not greatly reduced in the end.[1] But Scandinavian ideals and civilization gave way to Norman. The North England of the Middle Ages, with its great families of Umfraville and Percy, its great York-shire Abbeys and its Palatinate of Durham, was a land very completely feudalized and Normanized in its governing class.

The same influences, by peaceful penetration across the Border in the reign of King David of Scotland, laid the impress of Norman ruling families on Scottish society and religion. The Bruces and Balliols, Melrose and Holyrood, were but a further extension of the Norman Conquest. South England, indeed, owing to more rapid economic progress, moved out of the feudal age in Tudor times more quickly than the northern part of the island. Yet the North, completely feudalized as it became and long remained in its social forms, retained the old Nordic temper of independent manhood all the while, underneath the feudal form of its society. The peasant of Scotland and North England, however much bound by law and attached by affection to his lord, seems to have suffered less degradation of spirit than the peasant of the Saxon South from the long centuries of feudal subjection. 1124–1153.

The military drama of the conquest closed with the vast 1070–1. siege operations conducted by William against the Isle of Ely defended by Hereward. Hereward was a man of the Fenland district, with a genius for amphibious guerilla warfare in that difficult country. But his resistance only began after the rest of England had been conquered, and the event was therefore never in doubt. It was but the last and noblest of a series of regional revolts undertaken too late. There had been no general movement of patriotism, no Wallace or Joan of Arc. England was still a geographical expression, an aggregation of races, regions and private jurisdictions. She still needed to be hammered into a nation, and she had now found masters who would do it.

[1] Lancashire as a county was only created after the Conquest : it is one of the newest of the Shires of England. The status of Rutland as a county is also post-conquest. For the movement of Norsemen from the West into the de-populated districts of Yorkshire, see W. G. Collingwood, *Scandinavian Britain*, pp. 176–181.

The fact that England had been conquered piecemeal, as a result of a series of spasmodic local rebellions, gave William an excuse for depriving English landlords of their lands, and glutting his followers, lay and clerical, with feudal baronies, till every shire was divided up into knights' fees held by French-speaking knights from French-speaking Barons and Prelates, who in their turn held of the King.

The gradual character of the conquest and of the confiscation, which had moved step by step across England during a number of years, was one cause of a peculiarity in English feudalism : each individual Baron held lands in many parts of the country ; his estates were not gathered in a single province as was frequently the case on the continent.   Because the possessions of the typical Norman magnate in England were scattered far and wide, the royal power remained stronger than that of any single subject within the boundaries of the shire.   It was therefore possible to govern it through the sheriff, a man usually of baronial rank, but removable by the King, and acting solely as his officer.   The old English ' shire-reeve ' was henceforth identified with the Norman *vicomtè*, and the old English ' shire ' was also known by the foreign title of ' County.'   The sheriffdom reached its moment of greatest political power as the instrument of the Norman Kings, alike against Saxon and French-speaking malcontents.[1]

See
Map IX.,
p. 110.

1069.

1075.

To make way for direct royal government in each shire, William deliberately broke up the half-dozen great Earldoms into which later Saxon England had been divided for purposes of administration.   First Wessex disappeared with the House of Godwin, and has never again been a unit except in Mr. Hardy's novels.   Mercia and Northumbria vanished no less completely on the fall of Edwin and Morcar after their second rebellion. East Anglia was preserved for a while under a Norman Earl, but was resolved back into its component shires after the Norman Earl had himself risen in revolt against the Crown.   When William Rufus died, there remained only three counties governed otherwise than by the King's officers,—the hereditary Earldoms Palatine of Chester and Shrewsbury, and the County Palatine of Durham, governed by its Prince Bishop, the secular and spiritual lord of the Border.   Such as they were, these exceptions were tolerated by the Norman Kings only to keep the military guard strong against Welsh and Scots.

Outside the Counties Palatine, William the Conqueror governed England by a dual system : indirectly through the feudal

---

[1] For the early history of the ' shire-reeve ' and *vicomte*, see pp. 91, note, and 104, above.

contract with his vassals, and directly through sheriffs and through special commissioners like those who made the Domesday survey. Those perambulating inquisitors recalled the *missi* of Charlemagne's Empire, and foreshadowed the Justices in Eyre and the Justices of Assize. There had been nothing like them in Saxon England. He would have been a bold servant of the Saxon Crown who had set out to enquire through the sheriffs and the good men of the townships into the affairs of Godwin's Wessex or Edwin's Mercia.

The French-speaking Barons had hoped to obtain in England the privileges usually enjoyed by their caste upon the Continent. Some of these men turned with fury upon William when they realized the restrictions he was laying upon their power. In the last dozen years of his reign he was frequently called upon to suppress their turbulence, with the help not only of the loyal members of their order, but of the conquered English themselves. Racial feeling was in those days little developed, and the Saxons had been schooled to suffer the tyranny of the strong even under their native rulers. The wrongs done by the French conquest were therefore soon forgotten, enough at least to permit of the combination of the disinherited English with William himself. Yet the great King had done them wrongs such as Irishmen never forgave to England in later and more sophisticated times.

The Barons' rising of 1075 and its suppression by the King shows that the Norman Conquest proper was already complete. The robbers could afford to fall out over the spoil, and to make appeal to their victim. The subsequent rivalry in arms of William's sons for the succession, compelled Henry I to appeal to the favour of his subjects irrespective of race and rank. Charters of liberties, general and particular, were the price by which the Kingship was purchased; and the special importance of London, as a makeweight in the balance of these disputes for the succession, removed any inclination that the Norman Kings might otherwise have felt to tamper with the privileges of the City.

The Conqueror, while establishing a rigorously feudal system of land tenure, had successfully prevented England from falling into the anarchy of political feudalism prevalent on the continent. And he had cleared the ground for the gradual development of a great monarchical bureaucracy. But he did not enjoy unlimited despotic power, nor by right did anyone who ever succeeded him on the throne of England. William was doubly bound by law, —by the old Saxon laws which he had ostentatiously sworn to observe, and by the feudal customs of continental Europe to which his followers from oversea were one and all devoted.

It was from the marriage of these two systems that in the course of long centuries the laws and liberties of modern England were evolved. The concentration of power in a single person ' carrying the laws in his own breast ' was opposed to the mediæval spirit, at least in secular affairs. The omnicompetence of the modern State, the omnipotence of the monarch who says ' *L'état c'est moi*,' would both have been alien to the mediæval mind, which conceived of public law as a mosaic of inalienable private and corporate rights. Between the King and the baronage stood the Church, who satisfied her interest and her moral sense alike by holding the balance between the two secular forces. Again and again, from the days of Lanfranc through Langton to Grossetête, we find the Church justly maintaining the balance of the constitution ; lay tyranny and lay anarchy were alike unwelcome to her, and therein she was able to speak for the dumb multitudes of the common people, in matters where her own privileges were not too directly involved to bias her judgment.

In the mediæval State anarchy was a greater danger than despotism, though the opposite was the case in the mediæval Church. The mediæval State was a ' mixed polity ' of King, Barons and Prelates. The relation between lord and man, which was the essence of feudal politics, was based on mutual obligation. A breach of contract on either side involved penalties, and as law was ill-defined and ill-administered, resort was continually had to war to decide points of feudal right. Non-resistance to the Lord's Anointed was opposed to the central current of thought and practice of the Middle Ages. In the mutual obligations of feudalism lay the historical reality of that 'original contract between King and people' long afterwards proclaimed by the Whig philosophers in reaction against the Renaissance despots.

It was at once the privilege and the duty of a feudal King to consult his tenants-in-chief,—that is the men who held land from him direct. It was at once the privilege and the duty of the tenant-in-chief to give advice to his lord the King. From this arose the royal *consilium* or *curia* common to all feudal states. Such was the ' Council ' or ' Court ' of William. The Witan, though not in the strict sense feudal, had been a somewhat similar body, but the strong and self-willed Norman monarchs were less governed by their vassals in Council than the Saxon Kings had been by the magnates of the Witan.

In Norman times the words *consilium* and *curia* were two words used indifferently for the general body of the advisers of the Crown, not yet divided up into administrative, judicial and legislative organs such as Privy Council, King's Bench and Parliament. Indeed no distinction was made in the minds of even the subtlest clerks between administrative, judicial and legislative acts. The King consulted whatever members of his ' Court ' or ' Council ' happened to be with him, on the question of the moment whatever its character. He appointed Committees and sent Commissioners down to the shires for this purpose or that, according to the apparent need of the hour, without being guided by rules. As yet there were no bodies, like the House of Lords or the Court of Common Pleas, consisting of definite persons, with a right and duty to meet periodically for special purposes with a fixed procedure. This very vagueness gave an able King immense power, but he needed it all to bring any semblance of order out of the chaos of the Anglo-Norman State.

The earliest step towards differentiation of function was taken in the reign of Henry I, when certain ' Barons of the Exchequer ' evolved a procedure and an office of their own, inside the larger Court or Council, for the purpose of dealing with the most important of all the royal interests, the proper receipt of his multiform dues and money payments from his sheriffs, feudatories, chartered boroughs and domain lands.

All other procedure in what we should now call legislation, administration and justice was left undefined. The form to be adopted in any given case was decided by the will of the King, subject to very strict practical limitations in a land full of armed barons accustomed to maintain their rights by the sword. But the theoretical obligation under which the King lay to consult his tenants-in-chief, however little defined by law, and however irregularly observed in practice, was never denied, and it was the seed out of which the liberties of England grew in the constitutional struggles of the Plantagenet epoch.

The greatest of the inquests carried through by the power of the King was the Domesday Survey of 1086. Its text is the surest proof we have of the obedience to which that ' stark ' man, the Conqueror, had reduced Norman, Saxon and Celt, from remote Cornish ' trevs ' hidden away in woodland creeks of the sea, to the charred townships and wasted dales of Yorkshire. No such uniform set of answers to an unpopular inquest could have been wrung from any equally large district on the continent, nor again from England herself until the days of Henry II's bureaucracy. ' So narrowly did he cause the survey to be made,' moans the Saxon chronicler, ' that there was not one single hide nor rood of land, nor—it is shameful to tell but he thought it no shame to do—was there an ox, cow or swine that was not set down in the writ.'

Domesday is primarily a ' geld book,' that is a collection of facts made for a fiscal purpose, the proper collection of the Danegeld. But although all the questions asked and answered may have helped the collection of the geld, it is going too far to say that William the Conqueror could have had no further end in view. The final form in which Domesday Book itself was laboriously recast out of the original returns, points to other objects and ideas besides the Danegeld. The Book presents to the King,—as lord paramount of the feudal system, from whom henceforth every acre in the realm is held,—an exact account of the power and resources of his feudatories and of their vassals in every shire. The government was engaged in supplementing the Saxon scheme of local adminstration by a network of new feudal bodies for military, fiscal, judicial and police purposes. Therefore,—although the original evidence for Domesday was taken by the Commissioners from sworn juries consisting of the priest, the reeve and six villeins of each township,—the form in which the returns were rearranged grouped every township or section of a township in its new position as a manor in the feudal system.

Domesday Book takes full cognizance of one organ of Saxon life,—the Shire. Everything is grouped under the Shire or ' County,' for it is through the Shire organization that the King intends to act. But inside each Shire the unit under which all the information is rearranged is the feudal holding of the tenant-in-chief, however widely scattered his lands may be over all the Hundreds of the County. And the lesser unit in Domesday Book is not the village regarded as a township, but the village regarded as a manor belonging to a lord, be he tenant-in-chief or vassal. Thus the final form in which the Report was drawn up established the feudal maxim—*nulle terre sans seigneur*,—' no land without its lord,'—with a uniformity unknown before.

In the collection of the Danegeld, the Norman King and Council laid on each Shire a round sum, which was reallotted locally among the Hundreds. But the officers of the Shire or Hundred made their demands not from the men of each township, still less from each peasant, but from the lord of each manor, who ' answers for the manor ' in the matter of taxation and must wring the geld from his tenantry as best he may. With that the Shire officers have nothing to do. In the eyes of the law the man who ' answers for the manor' becomes more and more the owner of the manor, and the old village organization slips ever more into the background. It was a process begun long before in Saxon times, but it now reached its theoretic perfection and was made uniform for the whole country, including the sullen Danelaw.[1]

The lowest unit of the new England was the lord's manor, into which the township had been transformed. Every manor had its manor court.[2]   Nor was that the only or the most important of the courts of private jurisdiction in Norman England. Other higher courts sprang up, as necessary adjuncts of complete feudal tenure : a tenant-in-chief could hold a court to decide questions of feudal law among his vassals.   Last, but not least, many valuable franchises, surviving from Saxon days, gave to Lords and Prelates criminal jurisdiction equivalent to that of the Hundred Court.   It was only very gradually, in the course of the three centuries following the Conquest, that the King's courts took the place of nearly all these private jurisdictions, because the King's justice was found to be a better and cheaper article than any which private courts could supply : but that was far in the future.   In Norman times the public courts were those of the Hundred and the Shire, and after the conquest the Hundred Court rapidly declined.   In the Shire Court the King's Sheriff presided, but the judges were the principal freemen of the County, administering the traditional law of the district, and such bits of law common to the whole realm as might be known and approved in that Shire.   But English Common Law and the great legal profession capable of administering it in the King's courts, were still in the womb of time.

One class of royal court was indeed brought into existence by the Conqueror,—the Forest Court—more odious to Norman and Saxon alike than any private jurisdiction.   For it represented the King only in his personal and selfish capacity.   The forest law and the forest courts of Normandy were transplanted to England, with lamentable results in human suffering and servitude. In the following century as many as sixty-nine forests belonged to the Crown, computed at almost a third of the whole acreage of the Kingdom.   Inside that vast but thinly inhabited area the King's peace indeed reigned, but in a form hateful to God and man.   The special courts of the forest deprived all who dwelt within their jurisdiction of the ordinary rights of the subject.   Poaching deer was punished under the Conqueror by mutilation, under his successors by death.

The alienation of so huge an acreage of land from national

[1] See p. 96, above. For a typical Domesday extract see note at end of chapter, p. 132, below.

[2] See pp. 147–151, below, where the agricultural methods and social structure of the manor are described.

uses and national liberties remained for hundreds of years a source of constant bickering between the King and his subjects. The gradual deforestation of district after district marked the economic and moral progress of the country. When in Stuart times the King's power passed to the squirearchy, the modern ' game laws ' grew up, like ' a bastard slip,' as old Blackstone called them, of the dying forest laws of the King, less ferocious indeed but equally opposed to the freer spirit of the English law of the day.

It was William the Conqueror who brought this plague into our island :

He made large forests for deer (wrote the Anglo-Saxon Chronicler), and enacted laws therewith, so that whoever killed a hart or a hind should be blinded. As he forbade killing the deer, so also the boars. And he loved the tall stags as if he were their father. He also appointed concerning the hares that they should go free. The rich complained and the poor murmured, but he was so sturdy that he recked nought of them.

In the Church the Conqueror effected a revolution hardly less important than in the State. Just as the French Barons and knights ousted the Saxon Earls and thegns, so foreign clergy replaced native Englishmen in Bishoprics and Abbacies and in the Chapters of Cathedrals. Obedience was enforced to the doctrines and standards of the reforming party on the continent in the age of Hildebrand. Some of these changes, particularly the change in the persons of the hierarchy, meant greater efficiency and a higher standard of learning and zeal. There followed four centuries of splendid ecclesiastical architecture, starting with the Norman builders, who hastened to replace the largest Saxon churches with structures yet more magnificent. But the changes effected by the foreign churchmen meant also the further Latinization of religion in ways not permanently endurable to the Nordic temper and genius.

' On the day King Edward was alive and dead ' a large proportion of the English parish clergy were living with their lawful wives. The compulsory celibacy of all priests was introduced at the bidding of the Pope, not without a prolonged struggle in the reigns of the Conqueror and his sons. It meant that not only the parish priests, but almost all professional or educated men could have no legitimate children. The monastic ideal of chastity, however suited to the more zealous churchmen of that age, was at total variance with the outlook on life of many types of useful citizens and public servants who were then as a matter of course numbered among the clergy. To prevent almost all educated men from having wives and lawful children scarcely tended to improve the breed of the race, and had lamentable results upon its moral standard.

The Conqueror's great ecclesiastical reform was his division of the spiritual from the secular courts. Hitherto Bishop and Sheriff had presided together over the Shire Court, where both spiritual and secular causes came up for decision. By William's order the Bishop now retired to hold a court of his own, concerned only with spiritual affairs. The separate jurisdiction of the Church covered great tracts of human life which in modern times have been made over to the King's courts and the law of the land,— such as felonies committed by persons in holy orders, and the great fields of marriage, testament, and eventually of slander. It included also many matters which are not now dealt with by any court at all, such as penance for sins and jurisdiction over heresy.

The differentiation of the functions of lay and spiritual courts was a long step towards a higher legal civilization. Without it neither Church nor State could have freely developed the law and logic of their position. The English Common Law could never have grown to its full native vigour, if its nursery had been a court shared by ecclesiastical lawyers and judges trying to measure English law by Roman rules. And the separate existence of her own courts rendered it easy for the Church to adopt the Canon Law, as fast as it was formulated on the continent in the great legal age now coming on. The Papal Canon Law was enforced in the Church Courts of England throughout the later Middle Ages. The Church as a spiritual body was subject to the Pope, but the King, representing the secular arm, dealt with the Papacy as with an honoured but a rival power. The limits to Papal power were therefore set, not by churchmen as such, but by the King acting in defence of his own authority, often with the good-will of many English priests.

It was essential to William's conception of Kingship that he should be able in practice to control the nomination of Bishops and Abbots. Without that privilege he might have reigned but could scarcely have ruled in England. He used this great power for the benefit of the reforming party in the Church, but he also used it in the secular interests of the Crown. His secretaries, his judges and most of his civil servants were churchmen, for there were no learned laymen. Men who were learned, took orders as a matter of course. The King and his successors, right down to the Reformation, used a large part of the wealth and patronage of the Church to pay for services rendered to the State. Judges and civil servants were rewarded with benefices and even with bishoprics. Viewed ecclesiastically by modern

F

standards, this was an abuse. But the system served the country well and rendered the enormous wealth of the mediæval Church useful and tolerable to a society that might otherwise have revolted against it before the age of the Tudors. The mediæval Church served not only the purposes of piety and religion strictly defined, but all the purposes of learning and knowledge. Only when learning and knowledge spread into the lay world, a new system had to be adopted involving a limitation of the sphere of the clergy and a consequent reduction of the wealth of the Church.

William the Conqueror, a generous patron of the Church, yet a strong protector of the rights of the Crown, had ruled the country with Lanfranc as his right-hand man, in spite of occasional quarrels. But William Rufus, though not without kingly qualities, was a ruffian only pious when on his sick bed. In pursuit of revenue he abused the position he had inherited from his father in relation to the Church, just as he strained his feudal rights over his lay vassals. After Lanfranc's death he refused to appoint a new Primate, and enjoyed for five years together the revenues of the See of Canterbury. At length he was taken ill, thought he was dying, and appointed the most unwilling Anselm. Then, to the surprise and grief of his subjects, he recovered, and for years led the saintly Archbishop such a life as fully explains the comic and almost cowardly reluctance that Anselm had shown to accept the post, to which the voice of the whole country had called him. The events of the reign show how the secular power, in the hands of a passionate and unscrupulous prince, could hamper the religious life of the country. Such facts must be borne in mind in judging of the undoubtedly extravagant claims put forward to secure the 'liberties' of the Church, the championship of which Hildebrand, the great Pope Gregory VII, had bequeathed to his successors.

In the reign of Henry I the inevitable clash came. Henry 'the clerk' was a very different person from his barbarian brother Rufus.[1] But though he did not abuse he steadily maintained the rights of the Crown, while Anselm stood for the new claims of the Church. The question was that of 'investitures,' then convulsing all Europe :—should prelates be appointed by the Crown or by the Pope? After a fierce struggle a compromise was arranged. The King of England ceded to the Pope the right of investing the new Bishops with the spiritual staff and ring.

1087–
1100.

1089–
1093.

1100–
1135.

1106.

---

[1] In the Middle Ages, almost every King of England who was a political failure left us something particularly good in stone. Rufus left us Westminster Hall, destined to be the spacious nursery of the English Common Law. Richard II gave it its present character by removing the pillars that once supported the roof. Henry III rebuilt the Confessor's Abbey. Henry VI began King's College Chapel.

But he retained the right of claiming their feudal homage as Barons. And the choice of the man who was to be Bishop tacitly remained with the King. The King's power of naming the Bishops whom the Cathedral Chapters were to elect, though not absolute and often subject to the approval or interference of the Pope, was the basis of the friendly relations of Church and State. During the centuries when laymen were ignorant and the States of Europe were small and weak, the mediæval Church was so truly ' universal,' so powerful in opinion, knowledge and wealth, so strongly organized under the Pope and dominant over so many sides of life that have since been left to the State or to the individual, that if she had then enjoyed all the ' liberty ' of a voluntary religious denomination of modern times it would have meant the complete enslavement of society to the priest-hood. That at least the mediæval Kings were able to prevent.

We have unfortunately no picture of the parish clergy, as they were in the days of the Normans, like the charming portrait of the village priest drawn three hundred years later by Chaucer. The poor parson was a Saxon and one of the conquered. The riches of the Church, distributed among the conquering race, concerned him not. His status in the manor was parallel to that of the villein.[1] The social class from which the parish priests in England were chosen, rose steadily from the Conquest until the Nineteenth Century. In the later Middle Ages, when the number of freemen was again on the increase, the Church attempted to lay down the rule that no villein was to be a priest, though with only partial success. In Tudor and Stuart times the parish priest was usually drawn from yeoman stock or from one of the numerous middle classes of that day, though not infrequently from the gentry. In the age of Jane Austen the wheel has come full circle, and the parson appears normally as one of the upper class, very often the son or the friend of the squire.

One outcome of the Norman Conquest was the making of the English language. As a result of Hastings, the Anglo-Saxon tongue, the speech of Alfred and Bede, was exiled from hall and bower, from court and cloister, and was despised as a peasants' jargon, the talk of ignorant serfs. It ceased almost, though not quite, to be a written language. The learned and the pedantic lost all interest in its forms, for the clergy talked Latin and the gentry talked French. Now when a language is seldom written and is not an object of interest to scholars, it quickly

[1] ' The parish priest with his virgate, half-hide or hide, appears as one of the villein shareholders of the township, though his tenement is held free of the common service on account of his special obligations.' Vinogradoff, *Eleventh Century*, p. 455.

adapts itself in the mouths of plain people to the needs and uses of life. This may be either good or evil, according to circumstances. If the grammar is clumsy and ungraceful, it can be altered much more easily when there are no grammarians to protest. And so it fell out in England. During the three centuries when our native language was a peasants' dialect, it lost its clumsy inflections and elaborate genders, and acquired the grace, suppleness and adaptability which are among its chief merits. At the same time it was enriched by many French words and ideas. The English vocabulary is mainly French in words relating to war, politics, justice, religion, hunting, cooking and art. Thus improved, our native tongue re-entered polite and learned society as the English of Chaucer's Tales and Wycliffe's Bible, to be still further enriched into the English of Shakespeare and of Milton. There is no more romantic episode in the history of man than this underground growth and unconscious self-preparation of the despised island *patois*, destined ere long to 'burst forth into sudden blaze,' to be spoken in every quarter of the globe, and to produce a literature with which only that of ancient Hellas is comparable. It is symbolic of the fate of the English race itself after Hastings, fallen to rise nobler, trodden under foot only to be trodden into shape.

BOOKS FOR FURTHER READING (FOR THE LAST TWO CHAPTERS)

C. H. Haskins, *The Normans in European History* (Houghton Mifflin, 1915) ; F. M. Stenton, *William the Conqueror* (Heroes of the Nations Series) ; Oman, *England before the Conquest*, and *The Art of War* ; H. W. C. Davis, *England under the Normans* ; J. H. Round, *Feudal England* ; Dean Church, *Anselm* ; J. F. Baldwin, *The King's Council*, Chap. I. ; Maitland, *Domesday Book and Beyond* ; Vinogradoff, *The Manor*, Book III., especially pp. 291–306 on Domesday, and his Chap. XVIII. of *Cam. Med. Hist.*, III., on Feudalism ; Pearsall Smith, *The English Language* (in the Home University Library).

NOTE ON DOMESDAY

Here is a typical Domesday extract, translated from the Latin ; it differs from the more usual purely agricultural Manor in that it also records the existence of a small market town of 52 burgesses.

' Earl Morton's land. In Tring hundred. Earl Morton holds Berkhamsted. It is rated for 13 hides. The arable is 26 *carucates*. In the lord's domain 6 hides, and there are 3 teams of oxen for ploughing : there is land for 3 more. Here is a priest with 14 villeins and 15 bordars, having 12 teams of oxen for ploughing and there is land for 8 more. There are 6 slaves. A certain ditcher has half a hide, and Ralph, a servant of the earl, one virgate.

' In the borough of this vill are 52 burgesses who pay 4 pounds a year for toll, and they have half a hide, and 2 mills of 20 shillings rent by the year. And there are 2 arpends of vineyard, meadow 8 carucates, common of pasture for cattle of the vill, wood to feed 1000 hogs, and 5 shillings rent by year.

' In the whole value it is worth 16 pounds. When he received it 20 pounds. In the time of King Edward 24 pounds. Edmar, a thane of Earl Harold, [= King Harold,] formerly held this manor ' [before it was confiscated for Earl Morton's benefit].

The ' certain ditcher ' mentioned is probably the local Vauban, who kept the earth-works of Berkhamsted Castle and its fine new Norman mound in a state of military preparedness.

BOOK II

THE MAKING OF THE NATION
FROM THE CONQUEST TO THE REFORMATION

INTRODUCTION

THE mediæval period, as distinct from the Dark Ages, may be said to begin about the time of the First Crusade, that start- 1095 ling outward thrust of the new Europe reorganized by the 1099 feudal system. Feudalism is the characteristic institution of the Middle Ages ; it implies a fixed and legal subordination of certain classes of society to certain others, to obtain civilized order at the expense of barbaric anarchy. Feudal society divided up the surplus product of the labour of the rural serf among Barons and knights, Bishops and Abbots. By stereotyping and regularizing the inequality of incomes derived from the land, it enabled wealth to accumulate in the hands of Lords and Prelates, and so stimulated the rich man's demand for luxuries, whence grew the trade and the higher arts and crafts of the merchant cities. In this way the Dark Ages progressed into the Middle Ages, and barbarism grew into civilization,—but decidedly not along the path of liberty and equality.

Another aspect of feudalism was that it organized military, political and judicial power on a local basis. Not the Empire as in Roman times, or the nation as in modern times, but the barony, or the manor was the unit of power. Feudalism was a confession of the disintegration of the Empire and the extreme weakness of the State. Over against this disintegrated secular society of feudal Barons and knights, each with an outlook limited to his province or his manor, stood the pan-European Church organized from Rome, as centralized as secular society was decentralized, and, therefore, if for no other reason, its master. Furthermore, since the clergy enjoyed an almost complete monopoly of learning and clerkship, the control of Church over State in the early Middle Ages was very great.

Mediæval society began as a rude arrangement, between knight, churchman and peasant serf, for the protection of a poverty-stricken rustic village against marauders and devils, in return for its due exploitation for the benefit of knight and churchman. It was an arrangement in the making of which

133

there were elements of force and fraud, as also of religious idealism and soldierly heroism in defence of the community. But gradually, out of these primitive arrangements of feudalism, the Middle Ages built up the Europe of Dante and Chaucer ; of the Cathedrals and Universities ; of the English monarchy and Parliament ; of the Canon, Civil and English Law ; of the merchant communities in Italy and Flanders, and of London ' the flower of cities all.' Which of these two pictures is the true Middle Ages ? The feudal village, with its ragged, frightened, superstitious, half-starved serf, leaving his chimneyless cabin to drive afield his meagre team of oxen, and fleeing to the woods at the approach of armed horsemen—or the Florence of Dante, the Flanders of Van Artevelde, the Oxford of Grossetête and of Wycliffe ? Which is the true Middle Ages, the barbarism or the civilization ? We may answer—' both.' The one was developed out of the other and the two continued side by side. The Dark Ages were in four hundred eventful years transformed into the full splendour of the Renaissance, although the darkness of poverty and ignorance still lay thick in many districts of the new Europe.

The aim of the greatest minds of the Middle Ages was to provide man upon earth with a permanent resting place in unchangeable institutions and unchallengeable beliefs ; but their real achievement was very different ; the true merit of mediæval Christendom was that as compared to Islam and Brahminism it was progressive, and that society moved constantly forward from 1100 to 1500 towards new things,—out of uniformity into variety ; out of feudal cosmopolitanism into national monarchy ; out of a hegemony of the priesthood into lay emancipation ; out of the rule of the knight into the world of the craftsman, the capitalist and the yeoman. The spirit of mediæval Europe was not static but dynamic. The best and the worst of the Middle Ages was that they were full of wolfish life and energy. Their sins were the vices not of decrepitude but of violent and wanton youth. It is useless to seek in the Middle Ages for a golden age of piety, peace and brotherly love. It is an equal mistake to fall back into the error of the Eighteenth Century, of despising the great epoch that led man back out of barbarism into the renewed light of civilization. We should think of the mediæval era not as a fixed state but as a living process ; we should not conceive it as a motionless picture in a Morris tapestry, but as a series of shifting scenes, some brilliant, some terrible, all full of life and passion.

Throughout the mediæval period the British islands were still in the extreme North-West angle of all things. No one dreamt there were lands yet to be discovered beyond the Atlantic rollers,

—unless indeed, in remote fiords of Iceland and Norway, tales about ' Vineland' lingered among the descendants of those bold Viking crews who, a thousand years after Christ, had beached their long-ships on some point of the North American shore.

But although, when William landed at Pevensey, Britain still seemed to be poised on the world's edge no less than when Cæsar first beheld the cliffs of Dover, the world itself had shifted its centre northward and drawn nearer to the British angle. Western civilization was no longer, as in Græco-Roman times, Mediterranean, but properly European. North Africa, the Levant and part of Spain had been lost ; they had become portions of Asia and of Islam. Germany had been gained instead, and was thenceforth the trunk of the body politic of Europe, with Britain and Scandinavia its northern limbs. The cultural leadership was divided between Italy and France, but political and military power lay decisively to the north of the Alps, among the feudal knighthood of the French and German states. Flanders, Normandy and Paris, closely connected with South England in commerce, politics and literature, did as much for the development of mediæval civilization as Italy herself. Because the centre had been shifted northwards from the Mediterranean, the Norman Conquest left more permanent traces than the Roman had done upon the life of our island.

See Maps II. and III., pp.22–23, above.

Until the middle of the Eleventh Century, both Scandinavia and Britain had been somewhat loosely attached to the civilization of Europe. They had their own Nordic traditions and literature, perhaps the noblest product of the Dark Ages,—the spirit of the Eddas and Sagas. But the Norman Conquest severed Britain from Scandinavia of the Vikings and connected her with France of the feudal knights.

The mediæval Europe to which England was closely attached for four hundred years after Hastings found its unity only in its social, religious and cultural institutions. Unlike the ancient Roman world, it was not held together as a single State. Its political structure was the legalized and regulated anarchy of the feudal system. The only name by which Europe knew itself was Christendom, and its only capital was Papal Rome. There was no political capital ; the so-called ' Empire ' existed in theory, but lacked administrative force. Real unity was given by the customs of feudalism, chivalry and Roman Christianity, which were then common to all lands from the Forth to the Tagus, from the Carpathians to the Bay of Biscay. The agrarian feudal economy with its lords and villeins, the orders of clergy with their judicial powers and social privileges, feudal custom and the Canon Law, were universally accepted, as no equally important institutions could be accepted after the rise of the middle classes and of nationality had given greater variety to European life. The English knight, speaking French, and the English churchman, speaking Latin, could travel through Europe from castle to castle and from abbey to abbey, and find less that was strange to them than Englishmen touring in the same parts in Stuart or Hanoverian times.[1]

Britain, reorganized after the Norman Conquest, became strong enough to defend herself behind the narrow seas ; henceforth they served ' as a moat defensive to a house,' and no longer as an open pathway to her enemies. As she gathered strength, she became the hammer instead of the anvil, the invader of France instead of the invaded. And as the French influences of the Norman Conquest became absorbed in the island atmosphere, the Norman overlords became identified with the life of their English neighbours, particularly after the loss of Normandy in the reign of John. Britain began, before any other European State, to develop a nationhood based on peculiar characteristics, laws and institutions. Because she was an island, her life drew apart once more. Already in the reign of Henry III, the Barons of the land, the descendants, or at least the successors, of those victors of Hastings fight who had scorned everything English, had learnt to say ' Nolumus leges Angliae mutari' (' We don't want the customs of old England changed ').

Foreign chivalry and foreign clericalism had been the two chief methods of progress for Englishmen under the Norman and early Plantagenet Kings. High above the wooden huts and thatched roofs of the Saxon villeins towered the great stone castle and the great stone cathedral : mighty works they were, and strong the arms and subtle the minds of the men who reared them and dwelt in them. Nevertheless it was the despised English people and not their alien tutors who would prevail in the end, emerging once more, strengthened, instructed, elevated, prepared for tasks that would have astonished William and Lanfranc.

The leaders in this great work of evolution were the Anglo-French Kings. The Norman Conquest and the Angevin succession gave us, by one of those chances that guide history, a long line of Kings more vigorous than any in Europe. They used the new feudalism to enforce national unity, though elsewhere feudalism meant disruption ; they built up a strong but supple administration, centralized, yet in touch with the life of the

---

[1] These remarks are of course quite untrue of that semi-detached portion of Christendom, the Byzantine or Eastern Roman Empire seated at Constantinople that ultimately fell before the advance of Islam. Its form of government was a bureaucratic, erastian despotism, inspired by Orthodox religion, Hellenistic culture, and Roman political tradition.

localities ; their courts evolved a single system of native law for the whole realm ; they stretched out their royal hands to the subjugated English, protected them against feudal oppressors, helped them to find new organs of self-expression in cities, law courts and Parliament, and even in foreign wars won by the long-bow of the English yeoman.

Under such kingly leadership England acquired, during these centuries of foreign rule and influence, great institutions undreamt of before in the life of man ; representative assemblies, Universities, juries and much else on which our modern civilization still rests. In the Middle Ages institutional and corporate life flourished and grew, while the individual was held of little account. Some of these institutions, like the Universities, the legal profession, the city guilds and companies, and Parliament itself, had their origin or analogy elsewhere ; they were characteristic products of mediæval Christendom as a whole. But our Common Law was a development peculiar to England ; and Parliament, in alliance with the Common Law, gave us in the end a political life of our own in strong contrast to the later developments of Latin civilization.

Yet even as late as the Fourteenth and Fifteenth Centuries, England was not yet fully conscious of her life apart, nor of the full value of her island position. Under the later Plantagenets, she abandoned her task of completing the British Empire by the assimilation of Ireland and Scotland, and tried instead to revive the Norman and Angevin Empire on the continent. The preoccupation of England with the Hundred Years' War secured Scottish freedom ; left half-conquered Ireland to permanent anarchy ; hastened the ruin of mediæval society in France and England, and stimulated the national self-consciousness of both —leaving to the victors of Agincourt memories on which two hundred years later Shakespeare could still look back with pride as the central patriotic tradition of his native land, only in part replaced by the Armada story.

At the same time in Chaucer and Wycliffe we see a new English culture struggling to be born, not the old Saxondom of *Beowulf*, Bede and Alfred, but something far richer and stronger, —thanks to the French and Italian schoolmasters, soon to be peremptorily dismissed by full-grown Tudor England. In the Fifteenth Century we see all the conditions of mediæval society silently dissolving, sure prelude to the coming revolution. The villein is achieving his emancipation under a new economic order. New middle classes in town and country are thrusting themselves in between lord and serf, the two isolated pillars of the old feudal structure. Commerce and manufacture are growing with the cloth trade, and are bursting the boundaries of mediæval borough and guild. Laymen are becoming learned and are thinking for themselves. Caxton's press is replacing the monastic scribe. The long-bow of the English yeoman can stop the charge of the feudal knight, and the King's cannon can breach his donjon wall. As climax to all these profound changes, slowly at work through many passing generations, the mist is suddenly rolled back one day off the Atlantic waves, revealing new worlds beyond the ocean. England, it seems, is no longer at the extreme verge of all things, but is their maritime heart and centre. She has long been half European; she shall now become oceanic—and American as well, and yet remain English all the while.

CHAPTER I

The Anarchy and the Restoration of Royal Power. Henry II. Knights and Villeins at the Manor. The Village Economy

Kings : Stephen, 1135–1154 ; Henry II, 1154–1189

THE Norman Kings had kept their Barons in order, revived the shire organization as the instrument of royal government, and established in the Exchequer an effective system of collecting the multifarious revenues of the Crown. But the peace of the land still depended on the personal activities of the King. As yet there was no automatic machinery of State that would continue to function even when the crown had been set upon a foolish head. Between the First and Second Henries, between the Norman and Anvegin Kings, intervened the anarchy known as the reign of Stephen.   It was, in fact, not a reign but a war of succession, waged by Stephen of Blois against Matilda, widow of the Emperor and wife of the great Plantagenet Count, Geoffrey of Anjou.[1]

1135-
1154.

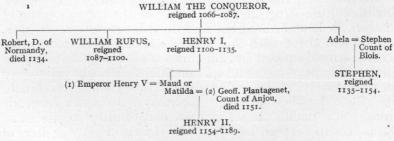

It is remarkable that the citizens of London, in support of Stephen, asserted

The miseries of this period prepared all men to accept the bureaucratic and judicial reforms by which Henry II afterwards extended the authority of the King's courts, and laid the basis of the Common Law, in a spirit alien to true feudalism. Of true feudalism England had enough under Stephen.

The feudal anarchy rose out of a disputed succession between a man and a woman equally unfit to fill the throne. Stephen and Matilda raised rival armies by giving a free hand to their baronial supporters, and by granting away to private persons those rights of the Crown which the Norman Kings had laboriously acquired. For two generations past, the sheriff had been a real King's officer, removable at will and subject to the inquisition of the central *Curia*. But the typical figure of the new age was Geoffrey de Mandeville, whom Matilda and Stephen in turn made hereditary sheriff and justiciary of Essex, granting to him and his heirs for ever the right of holding all the King's judicial and administrative power in the county. He was perpetually changing sides and perpetually raising the price of his allegiance. Finally he secured from Stephen these royal rights not only in Essex but in Hertfordshire, Middlesex and London, the very heart of the Kingdom. He was a ruffian of the worst order, and the most powerful man in the East of England, not excepting the King. But, in spite of the royal charters, ' his heirs for ever ' were not destined to rule those regions.

By men such as these, in local possession of sovereign power, whole districts were depopulated. The Thames valley, the South-West and part of the Midlands suffered severely, but the worst scenes of all were enacted in the fenland, where Geoffrey de Mandeville kept an army afoot on the plunder of the countryside. In the heart of this unhappy region, in the cloisters of Peterborough, an English monk sat tracing the last sad entries of the Anglo-Saxon Chronicle, first compiled under the patronage of the great King Alfred, now shrunk to be the annals of the neglected and oppressed. In it we hear the bitter cry of the English common folk against the foreign chivalry to whom the foreign Kings had for a while abandoned them.

They greatly oppressed the wretched people by making them work at these castles, and when the castles were finished they filled them with devils and evil men. They then took those whom they suspected to have any goods, by night and by day, seizing both men and women, and they put them in prison for their gold and silver, and tortured

with some success their right to choose who should fill the throne. This shows how little the crown was then held to devolve by divine right of hereditary succession. It shows also how the country as yet lacked an institution like Parliament to settle such disputes.

them with pains unspeakable, for never were any martyrs tormented as these were.'

Then follows the passage so often quoted in our history books, the inventory of the tortures used, of which the mildest were starvation and imprisonment in oubliettes filled with adders, snakes and toads. If we remember that two generations later King John starved to death a highborn lady and her son, we may well believe the worst of these tales of horror wrought under the anarchy upon the friendless and the poor.

While such atrocities were things of every day in the stone castles that now covered the land, the feudal nobility who had reared them were also engaged with a peculiar zeal in founding and endowing monasteries. In Stephen's reign a hundred new foundations were made. Those who caused and exploited the anarchy were foremost in making liberal grants to the Cistercian monks, who first came over from France at this period. We need not suppose that religious motives of a very high order were always at work, any more than that they were always absent. A Baron, whose imagination was perturbed by some rude fresco in the church of a long-clawed devil flying off with an armoured knight, would reflect that a grant to a monastery was an excellent way of forestalling any such unpleasant consequences that might follow from his own habits of torturing peasants and depopulating villages.

1153.   At length, by the help of Archbishop Theobald, an accommodation was brought about between the claimants. Stephen was to wear the crown till his death, but Matilda's son should succeed as Henry II. Meanwhile unlicensed castles, reckoned at over a thousand, were to be destroyed. It was a coalition deliberately made by both parties against the too apparent evils of unchecked feudalism. But Stephen was not the man to cure the ills of the State, and it was one of England's great good fortunes that he died next year. He was a gallant warrior, a knight-errant of the new chivalric ideal, capable of giving the Lady Matilda a pass through his lines to his own great disadvantage, but careless of the public welfare and wholly unfit to be King.

Of all the monarchs who have worn the island crown, few have done such great and lasting work as Henry Plantagenet, Count of Anjou. He found England exhausted by nearly twenty years of anarchy, with every cog in the Norman machine of State either broken or rusty with disuse, the people sick indeed of feudal misrule, but liable at any moment to slip back into it for want of means to preserve order. He left England with a judicial and administrative system and a habit of obedience to

1154–
1189.

government which prevented the recurrence of anarchy, in spite of the long absences of King Richard and the malignant follies of King John. After the death of the First Henry, the outcome of bad government was anarchy; after the death of the Second Henry, the outcome of bad government was constitutional reform. And the difference is a measure of the work of the great Angevin.

Henry II was as little of an Englishman as the Norman or the Dutch William. There are advantages as well as disadvantages in having a King who is a foreigner: he may see the wood more clearly for not having been born among the trees. The Angevin brought to bear on English problems not only his fierce and tireless energy and imperious will, but a clerkly mind trained in the best European learning of his day, particularly in the lore of the legal renaissance then spreading northward from the Italian Universities; he was able therefore to be the pioneer of the new jurisprudence in a land that only since his day has been famous for its native law. He was wise too in all the administrative arts of the various provinces of the empire that he ruled. For he was not merely Duke of Normandy but ruler of all western France. By marriage, diplomacy and war, the House of Anjou had accumulated such vast possessions that the Monarchy at Paris and the Holy Roman Empire itself were for awhile of less account in Europe.

Since Henry reigned from the Cheviots to the Pyrenees, he was the better able to control the English baronage, who dared not defy the lord of so many lands. The last baronial revolt of the old feudal type was in 1173, and Henry crushed it. In this way the continental power of the early English Kings was indirectly of service to the internal development of England, when the chief thing needed was a strong monarchy.

Henry's ever-moving court [1] was filled with men of business, pleasure and scholarship from every land in Western Europe. To the great King, who was to leave so deep an impress on English institutions, England was merely the largest of his

[1] It was no sinecure to be a courtier of Henry II. Here is an account of the life by Peter of Blois, who shared it : ' If the King has decided to spend the day anywhere, especially if his royal will to do so has been publicly proclaimed by herald, you may be certain that he will get off early in the morning, and this sudden change will throw everyone's plans into confusion. . . . You may see men running about as though they were mad, urging on the pack-horses, driving chariots one into another, and everything in a state of confusion. . . . His pleasure, if I may dare to say so, is increased by the straits to which his courtiers are put. After wandering about three or four miles in an unknown forest, frequently in the dark, we would consider our prayers answered if we found by chance some mean filthy hut. Often were there fierce quarrels over these hovels, and courtiers fought with drawn swords for a lodging that it would have disgraced pigs to fight for.'

The possessions of Henry II.

Boundary of nominal dominions of King of France

Lands directly ruled by King of France

MAP X.—The Angevin Empire

Emery Walker Ltd. sc.

provinces. The dominions which he administered were not divided by conscious national cleavage, but were all part of the same cultural civilization. In England the upper class still talked French, and continued to talk it till well on in the reign of Edward III. In the English village the distance between the lord and his villeins was accentuated, no longer indeed by racial feeling and the memory of Hastings, but by the ever-present barrier of a different language. The deep social gulf, characteristic of feudalism, was not in the Twelfth Century filled up by a numerous middle class of yeomen or traders. Such as they were, the bailiff, men-at-arms, and other go-betweens who linked the lord to the peasant serf, must have spoken both French and English. The priest dealt in yet a third tongue—Latin, which was therefore the language of official documents. Mediæval England was a polyglot community—even without taking account of the numerous provincial variations of ' old ' and ' middle ' English, or of the Celtic tongues spoken in Wales and Cornwall.

English snobbery was already at its beneficent task, unending down the ages, of spreading the culture of the upper class outwards and downwards among the people. As late as the reign of Edward III, a chronicler tells us that ' uplandish men will liken themselves to gentlemen and strive with great business for to speak French, for to be i-told of,' and we may be sure it was so even more in the time of the Angevin Kings. It is then no wonder that the great wave of French poetry and French narrative that was sweeping over Europe in the Twelfth Century, invaded and conquered England. The alliterative poetry of the school of *Beowulf* must have lingered on obscurely, since there was a modest revival of it two centuries later in the time of Langland's *Piers Plowman*. But the England of Henry II and his sons, inhabited by a good-humoured folk devoted, as foreigners remarked, to outdoor sports and games and jokes, was carried away by the lilt and swing of French songs for music and the dance, by the *verve* of French epics and tales, and by English songs made in imitation. Here we must seek the origin of the forms taken by the great English poetry of later times.

In remote Iceland a literature not inferior to the French romances and carols was flourishing and decaying, neglected by the world. If the prose Sagas had been known and appreciated in England, they might have changed much in the history of letters. But they were left to a little clan, hemmed in by the stormy seas, while England and Germany were conquered by the literature of Italy and France, which made all Europe one in culture no less than in religion. The Nordic humour and poetry, when it reawakened in Chaucer and Shakespeare, poured its impetuous forces into Latin forms, transmuting them into something rich and strange.

The progress of mediæval England in the arts and crafts, in wealth, civilization and good humour, was due to the relative peace that she enjoyed as compared to the rest of mediæval Europe. Her French-speaking Kings not only prevented the constant invasions which had characterized the Anglo-Saxon period, but after the reign of Stephen stopped the private wars which continued to be a feature of continental feudalism. In England, a Baron did not enjoy the right to wage war on another Baron; and the knights whom he had enfeoffed to render the services he owed to the Crown, were not permitted to fight in his private quarrels, least of all against the King.

The knights, in fact, were ceasing to be called out on any feudal service at all, even in the King's wars. A great foreign ruler like Henry II wanted troops whom he could take to Aquitaine or beyond, and keep on foot for more than the feudal forty days. He therefore extended a system begun by Henry I, by which payments called 'scutage' or 'shield-money' were, if the King wished it, received by the Exchequer from Prelates and Barons, in lieu of the military service of their knights enfeoffed upon their lands. The cash could be used by the King to hire mercenaries either foreign or English.

And so in the reigns of Henry II and his sons, an English knight, though trained to joust and fight from the saddle, might never have seen a siege or a stricken field. His interests were growing every day more peaceful and more agricultural. He was always plotting to improve the yield of his domain lands. watching the villeins at work upon them, and going the rounds with his friend and servant the bailiff, whom he could instruct to 'sow the headland with red wheat.' He was in process of becoming that pre-eminently English figure—the country gentleman.

For these reasons the stone castle typical of Stephen's reign was gradually replaced by the stone manor-house, typical of the Plantagenet epoch. The movement was hastened by Henry II's demolition of unlicensed castles and his unwillingness to grant new licences. The stark donjon-keep was replaced by a high-roofed stone hall of the type of a college dining-hall at Oxford or Cambridge, the lineal descendant of the high timber hall of the Anglo-Danish thegn. In front of it was a walled courtyard partly surrounded by buildings. The manor-house was only to be entered through the gateway of the courtyard, and was often protected by a moat. It was built to be defensible against a mob or a troop of horse, but could not, like the castle, stand a regular siege. The men who built the Plantagenet manor-houses lived among armed neighbours easily moved to violence, but they were not preoccupied with the thought of serious war, their chief desire being to enjoy in safety the fruits of the soil and to cultivate the arts and crafts of peace.

There were indeed infinite varieties and grades of manor-house and hall, and I have here described only those of the better-to-do gentry. But some must have been very humble abodes in the Middle Ages, for even in Tudor times there were some ' halls ' of the gentry that are now only used as barns, and very many that are now farmhouses.

English knights, down to the age of Chaucer and beyond, often hired themselves out to their own or other Kings to fight in Scotland, in France, or even as far afield as ' Alisandre when it was wonne.' But they were soldiers only when on campaign, and could return to their peaceful country homes. Others never left the manor except to ride to the Shire Court on county business. The more fashionable and adventurous were devoted to the sport of the tournament and to the trappings and romance of the new school of chivalry coming over from France, rather than to actual war.

Such at least was the state of the southern and midland counties, but the social landscape grew more grim as one approached the Welsh or Scottish borders. There dwelt the Marcher Lords in their high stone castles, soldiers ever on watch for the beacon fire and the raid of the racial enemy. It was these warrior nobles of the Welsh and Scottish Marches who supplied the chief fighting element in the constitutional troubles of Plantagenet times and in the pseudo-feudalism of the Wars of the Roses.

There followed, indeed, one remarkable consequence of the feudal and warlike origin of the English country gentleman. After the Norman Conquest the rule of primogeniture had gradually been adopted for land, to secure that a feoff should not be broken up among the sons of a vassal and so become unable to supply the military service due to the lord. In Saxon times an estate had normally been divided among the sons. In Plantagenet times it normally went to the eldest son alone. And therefore the younger sons, after being brought up as children of the manor-house, were sent out into the world to seek their fortunes. This had the effect of increasing the adventurous and roving spirit of the new English nation, and of mingling classes as they were not mingled in Germany or France. The English upper class never became a closed caste, like the continental nobles who married only inside their own order, and despised merchants and commerce. If English history followed a very different course, it was partly because the custom of primogeniture, though originated to meet a feudal requirement, had become part of the land-law of an England that was rapidly escaping from feudalism.

We are watching an important step towards the higher stages of civilization—the growth of a leisured class. At a time when the island held about as many people as New Zealand to-day, and when these few inhabitants were still so poor that we should not have expected any of them to be people of leisure, the feudal system had established a class of warriors living at the expense of the cultivators of the soil. And now that the Monarchy had caused war to cease in the island, this warrior class found its occupation gone. The time and endowments which it was to have spent on war and the preparation for war had become an endowment of leisure. In the Plantagenet manor-houses, time lay heavy on the peace-bound knights, and to kill time they took to a number of different devices, each according to his tastes,—to drink, sport, tournament, agricultural improvement, local administration and politics, music, letters and art. In the primæval Saxon forest, hunting had been the duty of the thegn ; it was now the pass-time of the disoccupied knight. As game and wasteland became more scarce, he struggled with the King above and with the peasantry below to preserve enough for his own diversion. Increasing wealth was supplied him by the manorial system of agriculture, by the rising population, by the increasing acreage under plough, and by the disinheritance of his younger brothers under the law of primogeniture ; he spent the surplus on comforts and amenities for his manor-house, on art and minstrelsy in the hall, in a thousand ways discovering for the behoof of a barbarous age what a spacious and beautiful thing man can make of life. The rich Abbot and Bishop did the like. The accumulated wealth of the feudal classes and their call for new luxuries caused the rise of the English towns, and the new middle classes engaged in manufacture, trade and overseas commerce. The arts of civilized life were forced into being in mediæval England by the unequal distribution of wealth under the feudal and manorial system, by the stability of these harsh social arrangements, and by the good peace which the King imposed on all.[1]

[1] Mediæval commerce chiefly supplied luxuries for the rich. The food, furniture and clothing of the poor were produced and manufactured locally in the villages. It was the Industrial Revolution of modern times that devised methods of mass-production and distribution of common articles for the common man.

It remains for us to examine the feudal system of the manor from the point of view of the peasant ; to him it was a less unmixed benefit than to the privileged classes, lay and clerical, whom it was specially designed to support.

In the Twelfth Century the proportion of freeholders in an English manor was very small. The day of the yeoman freeholder only came with the breakdown of the old manorial system and the feudal economy proper, which were still in full vigour under the Angevin Kings. The slave, who had composed nine per cent. of the population recorded in Domesday, had risen into the villein class, but the free man was not markedly on the increase. The lord and his villeins shared the manor and its produce between them.

The serf or villein was by birth and inheritance bound to the soil ; he and his family were sold with an estate when it changed hands. He could not marry his daughter save with the lord's consent and the payment of a heavy fine ; when he died, his best beast, sometimes his only cow, was seized as ' heriot ' by the lord of the manor. He could not migrate or withdraw his services at will. He could not strike. He must work on his lord's domain so many days in the year without pay, bringing his own team or half-team of oxen for the plough. It was by these services of the villein, and not by hired labour, that the lord's home farm was worked. The bailiff had to keep his eye on the unwilling workmen lest they should sit down for half-an-hour at a time at the end of every furrow.

But the villein, half slave as he was in these respects, held lands of his own which he tilled on those days of the year when his lord had no claim upon him or his oxen. And he had his share in the use and profit of the village meadow, the village pasture and the village woodland and waste, where the swine and geese were turned loose.

How was his position secured ? There was for him no ' equality before the law.' As late as John's reign the safe-guards given by Magna Carta to the ' free man ' touched him not at all. He could not sue his lord in the King's courts. But he had a double protection against ill-usage. First, the lord and bailiff found it to their interest to receive from him willing rather than unwilling work and to give him no motive to run away. For he could not be easily replaced, like an overworked slave in old Rome, or in the West Indies before Wilberforce ; nor might he be driven to work with the whip. And secondly, he had the security of village tradition, legally expressed in ' the custom of the manor,' and enforced in the Manor Court, which was held sometimes in the lord's hall, sometimes under the time-honoured oak tree in the middle of the village.

How much protection was the Manor Court to the villein? It was indeed his lord's court, not the King's. But at least it was an open court, in which there is reason to think that the villeins shared with the freemen the duty of acting as judges or assessors. It was at least better than the mere arbitrary word of the lord or his bailiff. Against a rapacious and wicked lord the protection seems but slender, and doubtless there was often terrible oppression, especially in Stephen's reign. But in Plantagenet times the English peasant never fell to the level of the French peasant of the *Jacquerie*.

No ancient system must be judged in the abstract, or by purely modern standards. The great merit of the manorial system in its day was this, that among men of primitive passions and violent habits it promoted stability, certainty and law. A court that focussed public opinion and tradition, and that actually kept written records from the Thirteenth Century onwards, was established as part of the normal life of the English village. When the system worked properly, a peasant knew what services he owed his lord, and he knew that the bailiff would exact those and no more. It is true that the peasant could not strike and could not legally emigrate without his lord's consent; but neither could his lord evict—in fact, whatever may have been the case in theory. Nor could the lord raise the rent or services due, once they were fairly established by custom of the Manor Court.

During the centuries when this system flourished in England, wealth slowly accumulated; more land came under plough; flocks and herds multiplied in spite of frequent murrain; and in spite of no less frequent famine and pestilence the population went up from perhaps one-and-a-quarter or one-and-a-half million when Domesday was compiled in 1086, to perhaps three-and-a-half or four millions when the Black Death of 1349 temporarily checked the increase.

But at the best of times life on the manor was hard, and the villeins were very slow in rising above the level of Anglo-Saxon rural barbarism towards the type of jolly English yeoman of later days. The serf was what poverty and submission made him, —shifty, fearful, ignorant, full of superstitions Christian and pagan, trusting to charms and strange traditions of a folk-lore of immemorial antiquity; cheating and sometimes murdering the lord or his officers; incompetent and fatalistic in presence of scarcity and plague in the village and murrain among the ill-kept beasts. The soil was undrained and sodden to a degree we can now hardly conceive. The jungle kept rushing in, weeds overspreading the ploughland, as bailiffs complained.

Under the open-field system with its unscientific farming, the soil after centuries of use became less fertile, and the yield per acre was reduced.

The English weather was at least as bad as it is in our day, and when the crop failed, as it often did after a wet summer, there was nothing to avert famine in the village. Animal food was less available than in Saxon times, for the vast forests of the Norman Kings and the private warrens of their vassals were guarded by cruel laws. The wild birds, the preserved pigeons and rabbits, and the other animals with which the island swarmed, often came marauding into the peasants' crops with the direst effects, and were taken and cooked on the sly in spite of laws and penalties. Cattle and sheep were not for the peasant to eat, though ' beef ' and ' mutton ' figured in the bill of fare of the French-speaking lords at the manor-house. Pig's flesh was commoner in the cottage. In fen regions fishers and fowlers supplied eels and water-fowl good and cheap.

The mediæval English village, at the end of its muddy riding tracks, with its villeins bound for life not to stray from the precincts of the manor, was subject to physical and intellectual isolation that governed its life in every respect. One result of isolation was that the village had to manufacture for itself. Among the villeins were craftsmen, who might or might not be husbandmen as well. The ' wright ' or carpenter could knock together the cottages, their furniture and the wooden part of the farm machinery; the thatcher and the blacksmith could finish his work. The women and children were all ' spinsters,' and village weaving of the coarser kind of cloth preceded fine weaving in England by many centuries—and indeed stretches back to prehistoric times. Much of the peasant's clothing was of hides roughly tanned. The neighbouring market town, itself an agricultural village, supplied what else had occasionally to be bought. Only the inhabitants of the manor-house were likely to go further afield in their purchases and to patronize the commerce of the towns and the traders oversea.

In Henry II's reign, the lord's dwelling, whether Abbey, castle or manor-house, was often built of stone. But the villeins' cottages were still hovels, without chimneys or glass, and some-times without any aperture but the door. They were built either of split logs, erected side by side in the old Saxon fashion, or, where timber became scarce, of ' half-timber ' walls, with mud filling in the oaken frame-work. The art of baking bricks had died with the Romans and had not yet been revived. The roof was of turf or thatch. A small orchard, garden or yard surrounded the villein's cottage, even when it faced the village street.

In the West and North and in districts still chiefly woodland, the cottages often stood in small hamlets of one, two, three, or half a dozen farms, and each little farm often had its own consolidated lands, sometimes surrounded by permanent enclosures.[1] But in the best agricultural districts in East and Middle England, the prevailing system was the large village of two to five hundred souls, grouped round the parish church and manor-house, in the middle of the open field. This 'open' or 'common field,' was not cut up by hedges into the chess-board appearance presented by rural England to-day. It was divided into hundreds of little strips each of an acre or half an acre, divided by 'balks' of grass or footpath. It must have looked somewhat like a group of allotments of our time, but on a gigantic scale, and all under corn.

Each of these strips was a separate holding, a unit of proprietorship as well as of agriculture. Each peasant had his property scattered about in the field in a number of separate strips, and a single freeman or villein might hold any number from one upwards ; thirty formed a usual holding. The lord's domain, though part of it might be in a continuous tract separate from the village field, was in part scattered about among the peasant holdings.

Lord, freeman and villein were perforce subject to the general village policy as to the cultivation of the 'common field,' of which the private strips were the component parts. There were in fact three separate fields, in each of which every man had his share, small or great. Each year one of these three huge fields lay fallow with the cattle grazing over it ; one was planted with wheat or rye, and the third with oats or barley. While under cultivation, the area was generally enclosed by hurdles. Agricultural improvements and private enterprise were severely handicapped by such a system, yet it lasted in some of the best agricultural districts of England from times long before the Conquest to the great age of agricultural change in the Eighteenth Century. The chief improvements took place in that part of the lord's domain which formed a self-contained whole, and could be enclosed, or let as a separate block to leasehold farmers.

Apart from the 'fields' lay the meadow, if possible down beside the brook. The meadow was common hayfield and common pasture, subject to elaborate rules and 'stints' discussed and enforced in the Manor Court. Astride of the brook or mill-stream stood the water-mill, usually belonging to the lord, who could make the villeins bring their own corn to be ground there at his price, which was sometimes so exorbitant that the right to use hand mills at home was striven for as a rare privilege.

[1] See above, p. 12, and note, p. 13.

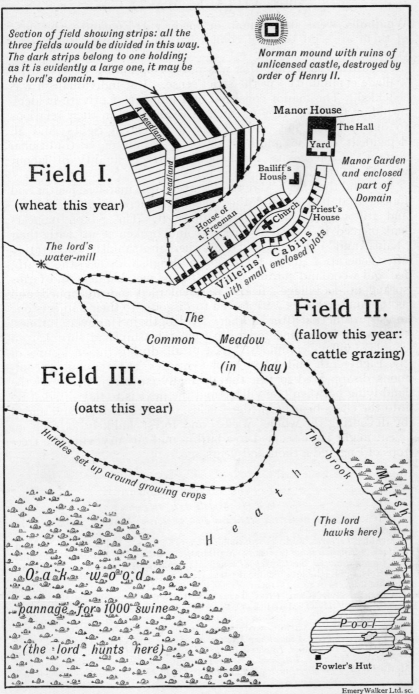

Section of field showing strips: all the three fields would be divided in this way. The dark strips belong to one holding; as it is evidently a large one, it may be the lord's domain.

Norman mound with ruins of unlicensed castle, destroyed by order of Henry II.

Manor House

The Hall

Yard

Manor Garden and enclosed part of Domain

A headland

A headland

Field I.

(wheat this year)

Bailiff's House

House of a Freeman

Church

Priest's House

The lord's water-mill

Villeins' Cabins with small enclosed plots

Field II.

(fallow this year: cattle grazing)

The Common Meadow (in hay)

Field III.

(oats this year)

Hurdles set up around growing crops

The brook

Marsh

H e a t h

(The lord hawks here)

O a k w o o d

pannage for 1000 swine

(the lord hunts here)

P o o l

Fowler's Hut

Emery Walker Ltd. sc.

MAP XI.—Cowstead: an Imaginary English Village under the Manorial System

Windmills were uncommon in mediæval England : the first of them are said to have come from the East after Richard I's crusade.

It will be seen that this was not a communist society, or a ' village community ' in the strict sense. But individualism was shackled. The manor consisted of a number of private holders, including the lord, very unequal in wealth and in their relations to one another, but with closely inter-related rights, and all dependent on one another for co-operation on a traditional system. Cash nexus, freedom of contract, fluidity of labour were the exception and not the rule.

Beyond the ' fields ' lay the ' waste '—the marshes, heaths and forests that had once clothed the whole acreage of the island, and still covered more than half of it. The Saxon pioneers had pierced its heart of darkness and broken it up with their ' hams ' and ' dens ' planted everywhere in its midst. Generation after generation, down the length of English history, the heath, fen and woodland shrank and shrank, as new hamlets and farms sprang up, as village ' fields ' were enlarged and multiplied, and as the hunter-Kings were forced to disgorge to their subjects one forest jurisdiction after another. At length, in Hanoverian times, the ' waste ' dividing township from township had shrunk to a couple of village commons. Last of all, during the enclosures of the Eighteenth and Nineteenth Centuries, the remaining commons disappeared so fast that in many cases every acre of the land lying between one village and the next is to-day divided up into the chess-board of hedged fields. The townships have ended by devouring the whole ' waste ' and forest, unlikely as such an event might have seemed to a bird in mid-air surveying the tree-tops of England a thousand years ago.

BOOKS FOR FURTHER READING

For Book II. (Middle Ages) in general

Davis, *England under the Normans and Angevins* ; Vickers, *England in the Later Middle Ages*.

Stubbs, *Lectures*, and *Constitutional History* (3 vols.) ; Pollock and Maitland, *History of English Law* (2 vols.) ; Maitland, *Constitutional History of England*, and *Canon Law in the Church of England* ; Holdsworth, *A History of English Law*, Vols. I., II. (the less technical parts are of great value to historical students, whether lawyers or not) ; Oman, *Art of War in the Middle Ages* ; W. C. Bolland, *The General Eyre* (Cam. Press, 1922) ; A. L. Smith, *Church and State in the Middle Ages* ; H. O. Meredith, *Outlines of the Economic History of England* ; Coulton, *Social Life in Britain from the Conquest to the Reformation*, and *The Mediæval Village* ; Various writers, *Social England* (ed. Traill), Vols. I.–II. ; W. P. Ker, *English Literature, Mediæval* (Home University Library) ; Tout, *Relations of France and England in the Middle Ages* ; Quennell, *A History of Everyday Things in England* ; J. F. Baldwin, *The King's Council* ; C. H. McIlwain, *The High Court of Parliament* (Yale Univ. Press) ; Stawell and

Marvin, *The Making of the Western Mind*; A. F. Pollard, *Evolution of Parliament*; Barnard's *Mediaeval England* (ed. 1924. H. W. C. Davis); M. Deanesly, *A History of the Mediaeval Church* (1926).

For Chapter I. only

Relative parts of general works above, especially Davis; J. H. Round, *Geoffrey de Mandeville, a Study of the Anarchy*; Hubert Hall, *Court Life under the Plantagenets* (reign of Henry the Second).

CHAPTER II

Henry II continued. The Cistercians in the North. Becket. The King's Courts. The Common Law and the Jury

King: Henry II, 1154–1189

SOME features in the manorial system described in the last chapter were only developed after the period of Henry of Anjou. It was in the reign of his grandson, Henry III, that the keeping of written records by the Manor Court became usual. And in the same reign scientific treatises on agriculture and estate management began to be circulated. The home-staying feudal knights began to imitate on their own estates the methods of account-keeping and record with which the King's Justices, Sheriffs and Barons of the Exchequer had made them unpleasantly familiar. They also took lessons from the managers of Church estates, particularly those of the Cistercian monasteries.

In spite of the enthusiasm with which abbeys were being founded and endowed in the reigns of Stephen and Henry II, and the puritan severity of the original English Cistercians, the monks of that order were not for long a great moral and intellectual force among the people of the land, such as the friars became in the following century. But they led the way in estate management, and especially in growing fine wool for the Flemish looms. If, as has been said in relation to the export of raw wool, Plantagenet England was the ' mediæval Australia,' the monks were among the first great ' squatters.' The famous monasteries under the steep, wooded banks of Yorkshire dales began the movement that in the course of four or five hundred years converted most of North England and Scotland from unused wilderness into sheep-run. By a process too slow to be observed or recorded, the nibbling flocks destroyed the dwarf oak-rods, birch and scrub which had cumbered the water-logged wastes of the North since time immemorial, leaving us instead the prairies of white grass and heather under the drying western wind.

The Cistercians in England perhaps did as much good by their methods of estate management as in any other way. Good and evil are hard to disentangle, for the order was most heartily abused by contemporaries for its proverbial greed, which led the monks into chicane, forgery and oppression, but led them also to keep estate accounts and to develop sheep farming sooner than most landlords. If it is once admitted that monks who have renounced the world and its vanities have nevertheless as good a right to acquire riches as people with fewer pretensions to virtue, then the same measure of mingled praise and blame must be allotted to the early Cistercians as to the improving lay landlords of Tudor times and of the Eighteenth Century.

Many of the new foundations were not subject to the control of the English Bishops, but only of their own Abbots and of the Pope—a liberty, of doubtful benefit to the Church at any time, that ultimately hastened the destruction of the monasteries in England. But some abbeys were within the jurisdiction of the Bishops, and the reports of the episcopal visitations supply the best evidence we have from which to form a judgment on the vexed problems of English monasticism.

In this connection, there is a story told by Giraldus Cambrensis in his malicious *Speculum Ecclesiæ*. One day when Henry II was riding back from the chase, the prior and monks of St. Swithin at Winchester fell on their knees before him and besought him with tears to save them from the Bishop, who proposed to cut down three out of their thirteen dishes at dinner. ' By God's eyes ! ' said the King. ' Look at these monks ! I thought from their howling, their abbey had been burned down. And this is all the story. May the Bishop perish if he does not cut down their dishes to three, with which I am content at my royal table.' Whether this tale be true or not, many similar stories, jests and sayings show that the popular reputation of the monastic body for sanctity was not very much higher in the reigns of Henry II and his sons than in the time of Chaucer. But in the early days some monasteries were of great service as centres of scholarship before the rise of the English Universities, and as the homes for chroniclers and copyists before the rise of lay historians, scriveners and printers. Carlyle's hero, the noble Abbot Samson of St. Edmondsbury, kept his monks on stricter fare than their contemporaries at St. Swithin's. But the scandals of the Evesham case in the reigns of Richard and John show how easy it was for the heads of monastic houses to abuse their autocratic powers, and how utterly unfitted some of them were for such trust. There was as much variety between one abbey and another as between one manor and the next. Idealization and sweeping censure are equally dangerous with regard to any period—whether Past or Present.

In deciding about the dishes proper to a refectory table, and in more weighty matters of the law, Henry II would have worked well enough with his Bishops, whom he had himself appointed, if he had not made the memorable mistake of naming his Chancellor and friend, Thomas Becket, to be Archbishop of Canterbury. The new Primate, freed from the King's service, held himself to be representative only of the Church and of the Pope. It rejoiced his combative nature and litigious intellect to 1162. stand up almost single-handed against a combination of King and Barons and a varying proportion of the Bishops themselves.

The sympathies of the English Church and nation were divided, but on the whole they inclined to the King—for Becket was both violent and inconsistent in his conduct of the case. Unfortunately Henry's ungovernable temper broke out in a cry of rage that inspired four of his knights to steal away from his court and 1170. murder his enemy in Canterbury Cathedral. The wave of re-action caused by this appalling deed deprived the State of many important rights only recovered at the Reformation. The cult of St. Thomas the Martyr remained for three centuries the most popular in England. So many myriads besides Chaucer rode to Canterbury ' the holy blissful martyr for to seek,' that the word *canter* passed into the language for the pace at which pilgrims bound thither should ride—presumably between one tale and the next. It was left for another masterful King Henry, in an age when much had changed, to grind the shrine to powder as being not only the chief centre of a relic worship which the pupil 1538. of the Renaissance reformers wished to destroy, but as the monu-ment of the famous triumph of clerical privilege over the King and the King's law.

The matter of the criminous clerks on which Henry II was worsted by the dead man was this. In the Constitutions of 1164. Clarendon, when a grand council of Barons and Prelates had defined the boundaries of Church and State, the King had success-fully claimed that clerks who committed felony should be accused first in the lay court, then handed over to the Church court for trial, and, if condemned and degraded from holy orders by their spiritual superiors, should finally be brought back by the King's officers to the lay court for sentence and punishment. This, he argued, was agreeable to ancient usage and not inconsistent with the Canon Law. He did not claim that lay courts could try persons in holy orders.

To many even of the clergy this had seemed a reasonable compromise. But Becket, after a temporary acquiescence, threw it over. His intransigence was approved by his martyrdom, and the result of his posthumous victory was that not only monks and parish priests, but professional men, and an enormous crowd of menials and minor officers of clerical establishments, and in later times anyone who could make some show of being able to read, were safe from the dread of any serious penalty for such crimes as burglary, rape and homicide, at any rate for the first offence. It was only too easy to obtain minor orders, and the attraction to baser spirits of such privileges and protection was great. ' One of the worst evils of the later Middle Ages,' wrote Maitland, ' was the benefit of clergy.'

Although Henry's rash outcry and the knights' wicked deed saved the skins of felonious clerks for more than ten generations to come, in many matters Henry successfully set up the barrier of the lay courts against the encroachments of the clerical power. During the atrophy of the State under Stephen, the Church had naturally and deservedly improved her position and prestige. Supported by the high Papal claims from oversea, the Church courts now threatened to invade many provinces not their own. Henry stayed this tide. The ' benefit of clergy,' that he was forced to concede, only affected cases of felony. For minor offences and in civil actions arising from contract and delict, clerks must appear as defendants in the lay courts of England, to the scandal of high churchmen.

Above all, advowsons were declared lay property and cases about Church benefices were to be tried in the lay courts. This victory of the Common over the Canon Law set some limit to the power of the Pope over the English Church. Cases decided in the spiritual courts could be carried by appeal to Rome, and the Pope was in the habit of stopping cases while they were still pending and calling them up to Rome or before tribunals appointed by himself in England. The Church was in no position to resist this procedure, for she admitted its legality. In matters spiritual she was subject to the Pope, and therefore the only way to protect her against him was to restrict the frontiers of the spiritual field, and compel her to take refuge behind the lay power in the King's courts.

Henry II's firm stand in the matter of advowsons, which he insisted were temporal property, prevented appointments to benefices in England from passing wholesale, by the route of the Church courts, into the hands of the Roman Court.

Even as it was, the Pope soon learnt how to make appointments by ' provisors,' largely for the benefit of Italian priests. The struggle between the Pope and the patrons of English livings, whom the King sometimes championed and sometimes betrayed, went on for centuries, and led to the Statutes of Præmunire and other anti-Papal enactments of Parliament under the later Plantagenets, all tending towards the far-off event of the full Tudor solution.[1]

The greatest of many benefits that Henry II conferred upon England was legal reform. The new judicial procedure that he introduced was destined to shape the future of English society and politics, and to give distinctive habits of thought to all the English-speaking nations ' in states unborn and accents yet unknown.' For the increase of power and jurisdiction that he gave to the King's central courts and to their offshoots travelling in the shires, rendered possible the rapid growth of English ' Common Law,' that is to say a native system ' common ' to the whole land, in place of the various provincial customs still administered in the Shire and Hundred Courts and in the countless private jurisdictions.

The organs of old Anglo-Danish life, the communal courts of Shire and Hundred, could never have become instruments for creating the supremacy of the Common Law. They were the courts of the middling class of gentry, and could not have been clothed with enough power and prestige to wrest jurisdiction from the feudal and ecclesiastical courts held by the great nobles and prelates. Moreover, the knights and freeholders who were judges in the Shire Court were themselves too much wedded to various local customs, and their intelligence was too untrained and too provincial to evolve by the light of their own wisdom a new jurisprudence for all England. Even the sheriffs who presided there were not lawyers bred in one great central school like the King's Justices. If a common law was to be created for the nation it must emanate from a single source. That source was the royal *curia*, the King's Court.[2]

Henry II, with his foreign legal learning and his gift for choosing men, made a famous bench of royal judges. Some were in holy orders, but others, like Glanvil himself, were of the feudal warrior class. These men and their intellectual progeny in succeeding reigns evolved the Common Law from the procedure of the King's central courts. And the same men went forth to every corner of the land as Justices of Eyre or of Assize, carrying with them the Common Law as fast as it was made, teaching its new doctrines and enforcing its new procedure among ' uplandish men ' in every shire.

The Common Law, the great inheritance of the English-speaking nations, has in modern times sharply divided them in their habits of thought from the world of Latin and Roman

[1] Maitland, *Canon Law in the Church of England*, especially pp. 57–75.
[2] See pp. 124–125, above.

tradition. Nevertheless it was an outcome of the Norman Conquest. The men who made it between the reigns of Henry II and Edward III were lawyers who thought and pleaded in French, while making their official records in Latin. ' How shall one write a single sentence about law,' said Maitland, ' without using some such word as *debt, contract, heir, trespass, pay, money, court, judge, jury*? But all these words have come to us from the French. In all the world-wide lands where English law prevails, homage is done daily to William of Normandy and Henry of Anjou.'

The Common Law owes only a little to the Anglo-Danish codes and customs with their barbarous procedure, their compurgation and their weregild, representing a bygone stage of society. It owes something to the feudal custom of all Europe, particularly as regards land tenure. But the favourite subject of study in the Twelfth Century was the ' Civil Law ' of the old Roman Emperors, and the Canon Law of the Church, then in process of elaborate definition. These two Roman ' laws ' served as the exemplar in legal method and science for the men who were making the very different Common Law of England. From about 1150 to 1250 the Universities of Bologna and Paris, where the ' two laws ' could best be studied, drew across the sea and the Alps young English clerks, lawyers and archdeacons by the hundred, who returned, as their countrymen complained, Italianate Englishmen full of foreign vices, but full also of strange legal learning. Oxford, almost as soon as she became a University, had flourishing schools of Civil and of Canon Law.

The question then arises—why did the law of England grow upon lines so native and so free in spite of the intellectual attraction exercised during the most critical century of its growth by these potent alien forces ? No doubt the Barons of the land, already an English and a conservative body, eyed the Civil Law askance as something foreign and as favouring autocratic kingship, and they had shown in the Becket controversy that they had no love for the Church courts. These feelings on the part of the grandees of the land had to be respected by the King's lawyers, who, moreover, shared them at least in part. And so, while they used the Civil and Canon Law as lesson books in method and spirit, they rejected their positive contents, all except a few great maxims. The English ' Common Law ' was not a code imitated from the Code of Justinian but was a labyrinth of precedents, cases and decisions of the various royal courts, a labyrinth to be unravelled by the help of clues held by the legal profession.

Throughout early Plantagenet times the King's *curia* or Court began to specialize its work among various subordinate committees, each gradually acquiring a special function and a procedure of its own, as the financial Exchequer had begun to do as early as the reign of Henry I. A bench of judges, known in after times as the Court of Common Pleas, was by John's reign fixed for the convenience of the subject at Westminster, where the Exchequer also sat, thereby ' giving England a capital.' Otherwise, parties to a suit in the *curia regis* had to chase the King about on his bewildering journeys. The King's courts were as yet judicial committees of the *curia*, rather than law courts in the modern sense. But they, and the itinerant justices in the shires, had enough regularity of procedure to manufacture ' case law,' the precedents which composed the Common Law of England.

By the procedure laid down in his writs, Henry II enabled the subject to bring many kinds of action in the King's courts rather than in the local and private tribunals. The Crown at this period had plenary power to issue what writs it would, and they form a great original source of English law. Only in the more constitutional times of Henry III and de Montfort, when the King's power was being limited, were the permissible forms of writ defined, and the power of issuing novel writs circumscribed. But by that time the King's courts were well on the road to become the ordinary courts of the land.

Partly by writs, partly by ' Assizes,' which were royal decrees issued in an ' assize ' or session of notables, the Kings from Henry II to Henry III enjoyed the power of creating new legal remedies, new modes of litigation, new forms of action, to the detriment of the feudal and ecclesiastical courts. Other ' legislation ' in our sense of the word there was none. But Henry II, by offering the subject alternative and preferable methods of procedure in the royal courts by his ' Assizes,' in effect stole from the feudal courts most of their jurisdiction as to the title and possession of land. He thereby threw the shield of the royal justice over small landowners whose estates were coveted by some great feudal neighbour.[1]

By this Assize legislation Henry II at the same time introduced the new procedure of trial by jury.

The barbarous Anglo-Saxon method of trial by ' compurgation,' when a man proved his case by bringing his friends and relations in a sufficient number to swear that they believed his oath ; the superstitious ' ordeal ' by hot iron, originally heathen, but latterly

---

[1] The Assize of Novel Disseisin (1166) and of Mort D'Ancestor protected the possessor and his heir against unwarranted eviction. The Grand Assize (1179) regulated proprietary actions, and the Assize of Darrein Presentment disputes as to advowsons. All these added greatly to the jurisdiction of the King's courts.

Christian ; the Norman warriors' favourite ' trial by battle,'
always unpopular with the English, when the parties knocked
each other about with archaic weapons of wood and horn, till
one of the two was fain to cry the fatal word ' craven'—all these
were methods which resulted perhaps as often as not in a wrong
verdict, frequently in an unjust sentence of mutilation or death.
In looking back over the martyrdom of man, we are appalled
by the thought that any rational search after the truth in courts
of law is a luxury of modern civilization. It was scarcely
attempted by primitive peoples. In mediæval England the
first step in that direction was taken by Henry II, when he
laid the foundation of the jury system in place of these antiquated
procedures.

The jury which he established was not the jury we know
to-day—persons empanelled to hear the evidence of others and
decide on the facts laid before them. Henry's jurymen were themselves witnesses to the fact. Yet even this was a great advance,
because hitherto courts had too seldom asked for witnesses to
fact at all. Henry's Grand Assize enabled a man whose right
Circa to property in land was challenged, instead of defending himself
1179. through trial by battle, to claim trial by jury. If such were his
choice, twelve neighbours who knew the facts were to testify
before the King's Justices as to which party had the better right
to the land.

Another kind of jury, the jury of presentment or accusation,
1166. was instituted by the Assizes of Clarendon and Northampton.
1176. Twelve sworn men representing each ' Hundred ' were to ' present '
to the court those of their neighbours who had committed crimes.
Like the jurors of the Grand Assize, these jurors of presentment
were not judges of fact but witnesses to fact—at least to the facts
of the local reputation of the accused. Their ' presentment '
sent the culprit to the ordeal, but even if the so-called judgment
of God was given for him, though he escaped the gallows, he was
to abjure the realm ! When in 1215 the Lateran Council abolished
the long-discredited ordeal, by forbidding priests any longer to
conduct the mummery of the hot iron, the way was opened in
England for further developments of the jury system. In the
course of the later Middle Ages the jury were gradually transformed from givers of sworn evidence to judges of the evidence
of others. In the Fifteenth Century the jury system, more or
less as we now have it, was already the boast of Englishmen,
proudly contrasted by Chief Justice Fortescue with French procedure where torture was freely used.[1]

---

[1] The jury system as created by the Plantagenet Kings and judges was
suggested by the methods used by Norman Kings to take the evidence of town-

Henry's new justice was popular and was eagerly sought. Cruelty, violence and oppression were things of every day in a society slowly emerging from barbarism, and the royal writ at least afforded to the defenceless occasional help and remedy. Yet there was a less attractive side to the justice of the King. His courts were a means of extortion, to fill his ever-gaping Exchequer. It was not only the disinterested desire to give his people true justice that caused Henry II to extend the profitable domain of the royal courts. Richard, John, and Henry III cared even less than he about abstract justice, and even more about money, and they all continued to foster the royal jurisdiction. The Justices were quite as busy collecting the King's revenues as enforcing the King's peace. They were two aspects of the same operation.

Specially extortionate, unpopular and monstrous, from the time of Henry III onwards, were the proceedings of the 'General Eyre,' when a King's Commissioner was sent down to some unhappy shire to overhaul every judicial and financial action of the sheriff and freemen since the last Eyre perhaps seven or more years before, and extort heavy fines for every trifling oversight. In 1323 the men of Cornwall fled with their families to the moors and woods to escape the dreaded visitation. In Edward III's reign, partly on account of their unpopularity, the General Eyres came to an end—the itinerant Justices thenceforth holding smaller commissions. Although royal justice was the chief method of progress under the early Plantagenets, it no more deserves unqualified praise than other human institutions.

Henry II was an autocrat, but like his Tudor namesakes he lived in times when people wished for strong government more than anything else. And like them he was an autocrat who ruled by law, who trusted his people, and who had no standing army, but encouraged his subjects to be armed, as unpopular tyrants dare not do. The Assize of Arms of 1181 decreed in detail what weapons and armour the men of every rank to the lowest freeholders and artisans must keep ready for the King's service in time of need. It was a measure anti-feudal in tendency, looking back to the Saxon fyrd, and forward to the new England in the making.

It was owing to Henry of Anjou that anarchy was quelled in the early morning of our history, instead of the late noon, as happened in the feudal lands of the continent. And it was

ships on the Domesday and other inquests. But Anglo-Danish customs had already in Ethelred's time a system curiously like Henry II's jury of presentment. See p. 82, above.

G

due to him that the King's Peace was maintained through a native Common Law, which, unlike the systems more directly drawn from the civil law of the Roman Emperors, made law itself the criterion, and not the will of the Prince.

CHAPTER III

Richard I and the Crusades.   Hubert Walter and the Middle Classes. Constitutionalism grows out of Feudalism.   John and Magna Carta. Henry III and Simon de Montfort.

Kings : Richard I, 1189–1199 ; John, 1199–1216 ; Henry III, 1216–1272

CHRISTENDOM in the Ninth and Tenth Centuries had been ringed round by foes encroaching upon her from east, from south and from north.   Europe had been, not the attacker, but the attacked ; not the explorer, but the explored.   If her enemies no longer, after the days of Charlemagne, threatened her very life, they bade fair to deny her the use of the sea, the possession of her own coasts, and therewith the prospect of the commerce and the world expansion which we associate with the destiny of the European peoples.   In the North, the heathen Vikings held both sea and shore.   Most of Spain and Sicily were under Saracen rule. The Mediterranean was swept by Moslem and Viking craft. From the lower Danube the heathen Magyars pushed into the heart of Germany and across the Lombard plain.   Both by sea and by land Western Europe was being cut off from everything outside herself, even from Constantinople, the hearth of Eastern Christianity and learning.

In the course of the Eleventh and Twelfth Centuries the situation was reversed.   The slow conquest of Spain from north to south began.   Norman instead of Saracen reigned in Sicily. The Vikings were repelled or converted, and their splendid energies, renewed in Norman warriors and statesmen, became the spearhead of Christian chivalry.   The Magyars too were baptized, and their kingdom of Hungary gave the crusading armies free access by land to the Balkan territories, the Byzantine Empire, and thence into Asia Minor and on to the Holy Land. Sea power passed into the hands of the Italian maritime Republics of Genoa and Venice, who were therefore able to convoy the soldiers of the Cross to the Levant.

See Map III., p. 23, above.

This brilliant change in the prospects of Europe had been achieved in the main by feudalism.   Feudal Christianity, for all its faults, had imposed its ideals on Viking and Magyar as something superior to their own social order. And it had turned back the Moslem advance. When the feudal knight charged, as he had now learnt to do, with heavy lance in rest, no one could resist his onset. Infantry were no longer of great account till the rise of the English bowmen. And during the Twelfth and Thirteenth Centuries the military power of feudalism was crowned by improvements in the science of castle building. Richard I's famed Château Gaillard in Normandy and the fortresses of the Crusaders in the East were vastly superior to the mound-and-stockade castles with which the Normans of the Conquest had held down England. They were superior even to the square donjon-keeps whence the anarchy of Stephen's reign had emanated, for the scheme of the new military architecture was a long curtain wall, defended by towers placed at intervals along its circuit, and enclosing a single great courtyard. The type is to be seen in Conway, Carnarvon and Harlech, with which Plantagenet England held down the Welsh, and in Bodiam Castle in Sussex.

In these altered circumstances and with these improved methods of warfare, the recovered self-confidence of feudal Christendom was bound to seek outward expansion. The Crusades satisfied at once the dictates of piety and the craving for battle, exploration and plunder. They were the policy not of the national statesman but of the knight errant, a characteristic figure in real life during the Twelfth and Thirteenth Centuries. The Crusades were the first phase in that outward thrust of the restless and energetic races of the new Europe which was never to cease till it had overrun the globe. It was the same spirit which had inspired the Vikings, but it was directed no longer inwards against the vitals of Europe, but outwards against her Asiatic neighbours.

As yet these adventurous energies, which were one day to cross the Atlantic and Pacific Oceans, were turned to the South-East, by the reopened routes of Danube and Mediterranean. England, in the North-West corner of the world, was left in a backwater. Individual English knights long continued to go on crusade, but the movement never became a national undertaking and tradition, as it did in France. The reason is obvious. France had a Mediterranean seaboard and England had not.

England, then, had practically no share in the First and most successful of the Crusades, when Godfrey of Bouillon liberated Jerusalem and set up the Frankish states of Syria. In the Third Crusade, for the recovery of these territories most of which had been lost to Saladin, King Richard Cœur de Lion won personal glory as the greatest of knight errants. He took with 1095-1099.

1190-1193.

him other Englishmen of an adventurous disposition, but not the solid part of the baronage, who stayed at home to govern the island in his absence. As for the English common folk, the emotions of the Third Crusade touched them just enough to produce some shocking pogroms of Jews.

But indirectly the effects of the Crusades upon England were very great, because they enriched and enlarged the mentality of mediæval Christendom, of which England formed part. They brought many of the ablest men of the half-developed society of the West into fruitful contact with the trade, arts, science and knowledge of the East. Both Saracen enemy and Byzantine ally were the heirs of civilizations older and better equipped than that of contemporary Europe. Even the art of fortification was largely imitated from the castles the Crusaders found in Asia. The settlements and ports founded by the Franks in Syria gave a great impetus to commerce between the two continents. The Crusades raised Venice, as the principal carrier of that commerce, to the pinnacle of her wealth and glory, enabled her citizen Marco Polo and many Italian traders and missionaries to traverse the heart of Asia sometimes as far as the Chinese littoral, and flooded Europe and England with luxuries and crafts imported or imitated from the East ; while the nascent intellectual curiosity of the West, taking shape in Universities and in heresies, was deeply affected by Eastern philosophy and science. The rich, many-coloured fabric of later mediæval life, the world of Dante and of Chaucer, would never have come into existence if barbarous Europe had remained as much shut in upon herself as she had been before the Crusades.

Such were the prizes that Europe carried back from the East. Her ardour was not rewarded by the permanent liberation of the Holy Sepulchre ; nor by the fraternal unity of Christendom, of which the tale of the Crusades is one long negation ; nor did she permanently strengthen the Byzantine Empire, the true bulwark of our civilization against Islam, which the Crusaders of 1203 basely betrayed for their own ends. What the blood and the zeal of the Crusaders really purchased for their descendants was the increase of commerce, craftsmanship and luxury, the lust of the eye and of the ear, the pride of intellect, the origin of science, everything that was most despised by Peter the Hermit and the zealots who first preached the movement in the simpleness of their hearts.

1189–
1199.
Richard as King of England was a negligent, popular absentee, as befitted the character of knight errant. He left the island on his long Crusade, after making provisions for the government that

ensured its disturbance by his brother John. In the hands of that man, already a proved traitor and ne'er-do-weel, he placed half a dozen counties, which were to pay nothing into the Exchequer, and which no royal justices were to visit. It was a dangerous blow at the system of direct royal government built up by Henry II, but that system had taken such firm root that even a rebellion plotted by John against his absent brother failed to shake the State. Richard had just appointed Hubert Walter to be Archbishop of Canterbury and Justiciar or Chief Officer of the Crown. Hubert, backed by the official baronage and by the Mayor and Citizens of London, suppressed the treason of John, and purchased Richard's deliverance from the Austrian prison into which his fellow crusaders had thrown him on his way home. He rewarded England's loyalty by draining her of money once more, and going off again at once to defend his Angevin inheritance. He never returned to England. Five years later he received his death wound in some obscure dispute with a vassal, beneath the walls of a petty fortress.

1193–
1194.

1199.

Hubert Walter, indeed, governed England better than Richard would have done in person. He not only enforced the King's Peace, but began a new policy of trusting the middle classes of town and country, an important preparation for the great constitutional changes of the next two reigns.

With the doubtful exception of London and one or two more, the English towns were not, even those few of them that stood on Roman sites, survivals of Roman *municipia*, as were the French and Italian cities. They were for the most part villages or forts that had grown into market-towns in Saxon times.[1] In the Twelfth Century, therefore, the towns still lay under seignorial, prelatic or royal government, according to the owners of the land on which they were built. The era of their emancipation now began, but most quickly on royal land.

It had not, indeed, been any part of Henry II's policy to favour municipal any more than feudal autonomy. Both had been equally suspect to him as encroachments on the direct authority of the Crown. But, if we may guess at Hubert Walter's mind by his actions, that wise prelate and statesman perceived that, while the power of the State would be weakened by feudal privilege, it would be increased by municipal growth.

He granted charters to various towns, conveying the privilege of self-government through elected officials. The old English word ' Alderman ' and the word ' Mayor,' imported from France, reflect the dual origin of the liberties of the mediæval English towns. Hubert, indeed, like Henry II before him, seems to

[1] See p. 84, above.

have feared the peculiar power which the citizens of London derived from their wealth, numbers and geographic position. Nevertheless, during the period of disturbance caused by John's intrigues, the Londoners had secured once for all the right of electing their own Mayor—the first officer so called in England. When John came to the throne he continued and expanded the policy of selling municipal independence to the towns.

But Hubert Walter's policy of trusting and using the middle class as instruments of government was no less observable in the affairs of the shire. The class of rural gentry, the knights who were settling down on their manors to agricultural and peaceful pursuits, were increasingly employed for county business by the wise Justiciar. It is here that we see the first sure signs of that peculiarly English system of government whereby the Crown depends largely on the amateur services of the local gentry for the enforcement of the King's Peace, instead of depending wholly on the sheriff and Judges, or on a centralized bureaucracy of the later continental type. The new policy reached its full development in the Justices of the Peace of later times. In Richard I's reign the gentry were not yet performing their tasks under that name, but already, if not earlier, they were being compelled by the government to act as Coroners to ' keep the pleas of the Crown,' that is to defend the King's judicial and financial rights in the shire. Their services were not always voluntary ; it was indeed a function of the mediæval Kingship to force the English to acquire the habits of self-government. The Crown found in the knights of the shire a useful check upon the sheriff, who was suspected by both King and people of frequently abusing his great powers.

Nor did Hubert Walter keep the appointment of Coroners in his own or in the sheriff's hands. He ordained that the suitors of the Shire Court, in other words the local gentry, should choose four of their own number to serve as Coroners. On the same principle, he ordered that the juries, instead of being chosen as heretofore by the sheriff, should be chosen by a committee of four knights who also were to be chosen in the Shire Court.

Here we have the self-government of the shire not through its great Barons but through its gentry, and here also we have the principle of representation. Thus by the end of the Twelfth Century, two hundred years before the Franklin of Chaucer's *Prologue*, a rural middle class was arising in England, accustomed to the transaction of public business and to the idea of electing representatives. When these local activities of the smaller gentry and the idea of representation were carried up to the larger

1194–
1198.

sphere of a national Parliament, mighty consequences followed to England and to the world.

In the reign of John the feudal resistance of the Barons to the exorbitant demands of the Crown began gradually to turn into constitutional resistance, embracing all other classes of freemen. The King by his plenary power had familiarized the country with the idea of a Common Law of the land. In the reigns of John and Henry III after him, men began to formulate more precisely the conception of law as something with a life of its own, distinct from the regal power—something above the King, by which he must rule. {1199–1216.}

What we should now call ' constitutional ideas ' were growing, slowly but steadily, all through the Thirteenth Century. Our constitution was the child of Feudalism married to the Common Law. For feudalism is the opposite of despotism. It may often be tyranny and it may sometimes be anarchy, but it is never despotism ; for it is an elaborate balance of defined rights and duties as shared by the King and the various holders of land. The Barons and knights were protected from the King by feudal law and custom. When he claimed service, aids or reliefs on a scale larger than the custom allowed, they resisted him on point of feudal law. That was the beginning of the Constitutional and Parliamentary movement. The King, instead of arguing each disputed case with each separate lord, found it quicker to come to an agreement with them collectively in Council or in Parliament.

Moreover there is another sense in which English constitutionalism was feudal in origin. The resistance to royal despotism in the Thirteenth Century was successful because the feudal class, unlike the squires of later times, was still to some extent a warrior class. Although, as we have seen, many of them were unused to war, they all had chain-armour and war-horses, some had gone on the Crusades, and many lived in a state of chronic skirmishing with their Welsh and Scottish neighbours. That is why the Barons of Magna Carta and the followers of Simon de Montfort were able to put up a fight against the King. That is why Barons Bohun and Bigod so confidently replied to the threats of Edward I ' By God, Sir King, we will neither go nor hang.' Sir John Eliot would never have dared to answer Charles I in such terms ; Pym and Cromwell had to tread the paths of revolution in order to procure the armed force which the Parliamentarians of the Middle Ages normally and legally possessed.

John was the very man to arouse a movement of constitutional resistance. A false, selfish and cruel nature, made to be hated, he showed pertinacity and tactical ingenuity in pursuit of his designs, but he had no broad political strategy or foresight. He strained the feudal law and misused the splendid machinery of State, to extort money from all classes of his subjects, lay and clerical, rich and poor, burgher and Baron—and then spent it in clumsy and unsuccessful attempts to defend his Angevin inheritance against the rising power of the Capet Kings of France. The loss of Normandy to Philip Augustus took place in 1204, and ten years later John's scheme to recover it through a grand European coalition against France was shipwrecked by the defeat

1214.

of his German allies at Bouvines. These events, together with the long-drawn-out quarrel of John with the Pope involving the interdict on England, were the prelude to Magna Carta. John's prestige was shattered, and the strength which previous Kings of England had drawn from their foreign possessions was turned into weakness.

Bouvines, besides helping England to become a constitutional country, ensured the reunion of France under the monarchy of Philip Augustus. The poetry-loving French Court, and the University and architectural schools of Paris, were the cultural centre of chivalric and crusading Europe. It was but natural that the Court should also become, after Bouvines, the political centre of the French feudal provinces. But it failed to develop administrative institutions like those with which Henry II had strengthened the English throne, and the French monarchy was therefore destined, in the days of Crecy and Agincourt, to go down once more before renewed English attack from without and feudal treason from within.

But meanwhile, between the reigns of John and Edward III,

See Map X., p. 142, above.

the possessions of the English Kings abroad were reduced to reasonable dimensions. Their Angevin Empire was no more ; but they still retained Gascony and the port of Bordeaux, a stimulus to overseas trade, supplying cheap and excellent wine to replace mead and ale on the tables of the English middle class, and so putting an end to the pathetic efforts of our ancestors to grow grapes under our sunless sky. But the connection with Gascony had not the intimate character of the old connection with Normandy, when so many Barons had lands or relations on both sides of the Channel. During the century and a quarter that intervened between the loss of Normandy and the beginning of the Hundred Years War, the English Kings, nobles and knights, though still talking a caricature of the French tongue, interested themselves in questions proper to England—her relations with Wales and Scotland, and the development of her law and of her Parliament. This return to a more insular outlook

saved us from too close an identification with France. If
the England of the Thirteenth Century had been occupied in
defending the Angevin Empire against the French Kings, the
energies and thoughts of our leaders would have been drawn
away from national interests and internal problems. When at
length, in 1337, Edward III resumed the conquest of France,
the English law had already acquired, and Parliament was fast
acquiring, well-defined native forms, and the English people had
become conscious of its own identity.

The first great step on the constitutional road was Magna **1215.**
Carta. The Barons in arms who extorted it from King John at
Runnymede were none of them, so far as we know, remarkable
men, but their ally, the Archbishop Stephen Langton, had both
moral and intellectual greatness. He was all the greater man
because his support of the constitutional cause was contrary to
the wishes of the great Pope Innocent III, who, in return for
John's politic submission in 1213, backed him at every turn in
his quarrel with his subjects and declared Magna Carta null and
void. Considering that Stephen Langton owed his election to
Canterbury to the Pope's support, his stoutness on political
questions in England was doubly remarkable.

The Barons were acting selfishly and class-consciously to just
the same degree—no more and no less—as other English
classes and parties who in successive centuries have taken part in
developing ' our happy constitution ' by self-assertion ending in
a practical compromise. Doubtless they would have sworn
mouth-filling oaths if they could ever have been made to comprehend the idealised misinterpretations of the Charter which held
the field in Stuart and Hanoverian times—such for instance as
the belief that Clause 39 demanded trial by jury for the meanest
villein, and that Clauses 12 and 14 required all taxes to be voted
by a national Parliament. Their demands were more limited
and more practical, and for that reason they successfully initiated
a movement that led in the end to these yet undreamt-of liberties
for all.

The Barons had come together to prevent the King from
abusing feudal incidents and from raising aids and reliefs on their
lands beyond what feudal custom allowed. It has been called
a ' tenant-right ' movement on the part of an oppressed upper
class against their landlord the King, though it must be remembered that what the King unjustly extorted from the Barons had
most of it to be extracted by them from the classes below. The
Barons also wished to put some limit to the King's plenary power
of withdrawing case after case from their courts to his own,

through the procedure of writs. We may sympathize less with the latter object than with the former. But, taking the situation as a whole, it was time that the King's plenary powers were curbed or nationalized, and no one but the Barons could have made such a movement effectual.

Stephen Langton was an enlightened guide to his baronial allies, but even without him the circumstances of the age in England were forcing them into the path of true progress. For the strength of the Plantagenet State machinery precluded a return to pure feudalism, nor had the Barons any such thought in their hearts. They had no desire to destroy the work of Henry II which had become a part of their own and of the nation's life. Knowing it to be indestructible, they desired to subject it to some form of common control, to prevent it from being any longer the instrument of one man's will.

In England a hundred years before, and still in Scotland and on the continent, the policy of the Barons was each to maintain his individual independence and private 'liberties' upon his own estates to the exclusion of the King's officers. But in England after Henry II, that was no longer to be dreamt of. The new English baronial policy, enshrined in Magna Carta, is designed to obtain public 'liberties' and to control the King through the Common Law, baronial assemblies, and alliance with other classes. When the Barons extracted the famous concession that no extraordinary 'scutage or aid shall be imposed on our kingdom, unless by common council of our kingdom,' 'and in like manner it shall be done concerning aids from the City of London,'—although they proceeded to define the 'common council' as a strictly feudal assembly of tenants-in-chief—they were none the less taking a step towards the principle of Parliaments and of 'no taxation without representation.' It was a very short step, but it was the first, and it is the first step that counts.

Moreover the Barons of Runnymede were not strong enough to rebel against the son of Henry II without the aid of the other classes whom John had oppressed and alienated. The Londoners opened their gates to the baronial army and took the field in warlike array. The clergy gave their moral and political support. The *liberi homines* or freemen—roughly including all classes above the unregarded villeins—aided with their passive sympathy; it was useless for John to call out the fyrd of all freemen under the Assize of Arms, as Henry II would have done against baronial rebellion. The English people for the first time sided with the Barons against the Crown, because they could do so without fear of reviving feudal anarchy.

Each of the classes that aided or abetted the movement had its share of benefits in the clauses of the Great Charter. In that sense we may call it a national document, though no claim was made on behalf of ' the people ' or ' the nation ' as a whole, since those abstractions had not yet begun to affect the minds of men. Protection against the King's officers and the right to a fair and legal trial were assigned to all ' freemen,' The term was of limited scope in 1215, but owing to the economic and legal evolution of the next three hundred years it came to embrace the descendant of every villein in the land, when all Englishmen became in the eye of the law ' freemen.'

Several clauses in Magna Carta give expression to the spirit of individual liberty, as it has ever since been understood in England. And the constant repetition of these brave words in centuries to come, by persons who were ignorant of the technical meaning they bore to the men who first wrote them down, helped powerfully to form the national character :—

No freeman shall be taken or imprisoned or disseised or exiled or in any way destroyed, nor will we go upon him nor will we send upon him except by the lawful judgment of his peers or (and) the law of the land.

Numerous other clauses apply sharp checks to various lawless and tyrannical habits of the King's officers, both in his forests and elsewhere, which, if patiently suffered, would have created a tradition of the worst type of continental *droit administratif*.

The Charter was regarded as important because it assigned definite and practical remedies to temporary evils. There was very little that was abstract in its terms, less even than later generations supposed. Yet it was the abstract and general character of the event at Runnymede that made it a great influence in history. A King had been brought to order, not by a posse of reactionary feudalists, but by the community of the land under baronial leadership; a tyrant had been subjected to the laws which hitherto it had been his private privilege to administer and to modify at will. A process had begun which was to end in putting the power of the Crown into the hands of the community at large.

It is for this reason that a document so technical as the Charter, so deficient in the generalizations with which the Declaration of Independence abounds, so totally ignorant of the ' rights of man,' has had so profound and lasting an influence on the imagination—in every sense of the word—of succeeding ages. Throughout the Thirteenth Century the ' struggle for the Charter,' with its constant reissues, revisions, infringements

and reassertions, was the battleground of parties—although
both sides were drifting away from the feudal 'consilia' of
Clauses 12 and 14, towards the larger ideal of a national Parliament. But until the Edwardian Parliaments were fully established, the Charter remained in the foreground of men's thoughts.

In the Fourteenth and Fifteenth Centuries it fell into the
background, its task apparently accomplished. Parliament held
the place in men's minds which the Charter had once occupied.
The later copyists and the early printers were never called upon
to issue popular English versions of the great document. In
Tudor times the Charter was even more utterly out of fashion,
because it emphasized the distinction between the interests of
Prince and people, which throughout the Sixteenth Century
Prince and people were equally anxious to deny. Shakespeare's
King John shows that the author knew little and cared less
about the Charter; though he treated fully and freely the human
tragedy of Richard II's deposition and death.

But when, under James I, Prince and people again began to
take up opposing ground, Magna Carta came quickly back into
more than its old splendour. The antiquarians and lawyers who
asserted our Parliamentary liberties in the age of Coke and
Selden, saw looming through the mists of time the gigantic
figure of Magna Carta as the goddess of English freedom. Their
misinterpretations of the clauses were as useful to liberty then
as they are amazing to mediævalists now. Under the banner of
Runnymede the battle of Parliament and the Common Law was
fought and won against the Stuarts.

In the Eighteenth Century, the era of unchallengeable
chartered liberty and vested interest, the greatest charter of
all was worshipped by Blackstone, Burke, and all England. It
had become the symbol for the spirit of our whole constitution.
When, therefore, with the dawn of a more strenuous era, the
democracy took the field against the established order, each
side put the Great Charter in the ark which it carried into battle.
Pittites boasted of the free and glorious constitution which had
issued from the tents on Runnymede, now attacked by base
Jacobins and levellers ; Radicals appealed to the letter and the
spirit of 'Magna Charta' against gagging acts, packed juries and
restrictions of the franchise. America revolted in its name and
seeks spiritual fellowship with us in its memory. It has been
left to our own disillusioned age to study it as an historical
document, always remembering that its historical importance
lay not only in what the men of 1215 intended by its clauses,
but in the effect which it has had on the imagination of their
descendants.

The Barons, having no idea of Parliamentary institutions, could only devise the most clumsy means to enforce the treaty they had wrung from the momentary need of their shifty and able adversary. By one of the final clauses of the Charter, John was forced to concede to a revolutionary committee of twenty-five Barons the right, if he broke any of the terms, ' to distrain and distress us in all possible ways, namely by seizing our castles, lands and possessions and in any other way they can.' The situation immediately after Runnymede was as black as it could well be : John was incited by the Pope and his legate to repudiate the Charter, while the Barons called in the armed intervention of the French Prince. We were saved from having to choose between a cruel despotism and a foreign dynasty, by that fortunate surfeit of ' peaches and new cider.' John's death afforded a last **1216.** chance to reunite the nation on the principles of Magna Carta.

In the hands of patriotic statesmen like William Marshall and Hubert de Burgh, with Langton as mediator between parties, the cause of the infant King Henry III made successful appeal to the nation. In a few years the land was pacified. The Charter was reissued with modifications ; the Frenchmen were expelled on the one hand, and on the other the growing Papal influence on our politics was kept in check. Castles which the feudal classes had built for themselves or seized from the Crown during the civil war, were pulled down or resumed into royal hands, in many cases after serious siege operations. The minority **1216-** of Henry III, which began in the midst of war and bade fair **1227.** to see a revival of anarchy, was turned to good account, thanks to the honesty and ability of the statesmen exercising power in the name of a King who never afterwards used it well for himself. This period saw an increase in the authority of the King's Council, through whom Marshall and de Burgh had to act during their regencies. Yet even so the Council was still a wholly indefinite body of men.

Henry III had so great a veneration for the memory of Edward the Confessor, whom he resembled in more ways than one, that he pulled down the church which it had been the chief life's work of the Confessor to erect, and built in his honour and round his high raised shrine, the Westminster Abbey that we know.

Henry's personal piety controlled his political action. It made him the instrument of the Pope's ambitions in England and in Europe. Since the clergy had no means of protection against the Pope except only the royal power,[1] the King's defection

1 See p. 156, above.

exposed them to the full blast of Roman covetousness. Italians and other foreigners, often of bad character, generally absentees, and nearly always unfitted for the cure of souls in England, were foisted into innumerable benefices by Papal 'provisions.' On one occasion the Pope rewarded the loyalty of the Romans with the promise of the next 300 benefices that should fall vacant in our country. Meanwhile the English clergy were pitilessly taxed to support the political schemes of the Papacy against the Emperor Frederic II and others. These experiences set going an anti-Papal current in English popular feeling, that went on increasing in force until it had accomplished the Reformation. In earlier times the English people, at least since the Norman Conquest, had been regarded as peculiarly loyal subjects of the Pope. Their new-born hostility to the Roman Curia, though shared by many of the clergy, had no logical basis in ecclesiastical theory until the time of Wycliffe, but could find occasional expression through the acts of the State.

1255.

1257.

In further pursuance of the Pope's ambitions in Europe and Italy, Henry III allowed his second son Edmund of Lancaster to assume the disputed Crown of Sicily, and his brother Richard of Cornwall to be a candidate for the Imperial throne, England being expected to pay for the war of succession of the one and the election bribery of the other. These demands, unconnected with any conceivable English interest, roused the baronage and the nation to fury.

1258–
1265.

Thus, for a whole generation after the King had come of age, misgovernment continued, keeping up discontent, till it burst out in another period of civil war and constitution-making. It was still 'the struggle for the Charter,' a continuance of the issues raised in John's reign, but with a significant difference. In the reign of John it had been a duel between the King on one side and the baronage supported by the people on the other. Under Henry III it was a triangular conflict. The 'bachelors,' that is the rising class of knights and gentry, accustomed to local work as Coroners and jurymen, now took a line of their own in national politics. Discontented with the selfishness of the Barons as displayed in the Provisions of Oxford, they demanded and in the end obtained, that the baronage should concede to them as vassals and tenants the privileges that it extorted on its own behalf from the supreme landlord the King. And in the matter of royal against seignorial justice, the 'bachelors' favoured the King's courts.

1258.

The real strength of Henry's party lay in this division of its adversaries, which his able son Edward was eager to exploit. In opposition to the more popular movement, many of the

Barons eventually went over to the King's side, while the constitutional or reforming party, that continued to follow the flag of Simon de Montfort, was almost as much democratic as baronial. The contest became, like the Civil War of Stuart times, less a class war than a war of ideas.

In the final crisis, centring round de Montfort's victory at Lewes, and his overthrow in the following year at Evesham, his party consisted of the reforming section of the Barons ; the more politically minded of the knights and gentry ; the best of the clergy in revolt against the unnatural combination of Pope and King ; the students of Oxford University ; and the other popular elements to whom the preaching friars made appeal in the heyday of their democratic zeal for work among the poor. Though the Pope excommunicated him, Simon had the more potent religious forces upon his side. And among his partisans must be numbered the citizens of London, whose flying ranks Prince Edward at Lewes pursued in the fashion of Rupert, while Simon like Oliver was destroying the main of the King's army. *1264, 1265.*

The political rhymes and treatises of the hour show that this reforming party of Simon's last years clearly conceived law as a thing above the King.[1] And many of them were filled, like their leader, with a religious spirit which they devoted to the cause of reform as being the will of God.

Simon de Montfort, Earl of Leicester, was of French extraction and education, but in an age when the English upper class talked French in its familiar intercourse, that did not prevent him from becoming an Englishman at heart. He was one of those commanding natures, like Cromwell or Chatham, who cannot play the second part, whom to accuse of ambition seems almost irrelevant. Like many such men he was not overscrupulous. But he too learnt to identify his cause with his country's, and the country felt it and knew it. He derived his broader conception of patriotism not a little from his long friendship with Grossetête, Bishop of Lincoln, one of the noblest, wisest and most learned men of that remarkable century, who for many years stood out as the critic of royal and papal misrule in England. Simon was Grossetête's friend and successor, as Cromwell was Hampden's, and who shall say whether the forerunner would have approved all had he lived ? *Died 1253.*

The party that Simon led in his last two years was indeed remarkably like the Cromwellian both in its strength and its weakness. Democrats before an age of democracy, they were in

---

[1] *E.g.*, from a political song of the time of Lewes :—
'Nam Rex omnis regitur legibus quas legit.
Rex Saül repellitur, quia leges fregit.'

an impossible position, and could not themselves have effected any settlement. But their action dictated the future, at least negatively. Lewes, won like Naseby with prayer, psalm-singing and cold steel, was, like Naseby, a fact that could never be obliterated. The restoration of Henry III was no more a return to the old despotism than was the restoration of Charles II. In each case restoration was adopted as the only possible way to obtain government by consent.

But there were also differences. More of what Cromwell valued perished with him than in the case of de Montfort. It is no paradox to say that this was partly because Oliver had greater success than Simon as a ruler of the land. The Cromwellian rule was protracted by force for a dozen years, so that in the end the popular reaction against everything associated with it was much stronger. Simon's rule lasted hardly more than a year, and in fact he was never able to impose order on the North and West. And so it was Simon, dying for freedom on the field of Evesham, who became the beloved martyr in popular imagination—a part which Cromwell made over to Charles I.

There was a further reason why Simon's work profited by his death ; he had made an intellectual conquest of his greatest enemy, the victor of Evesham. Henry III's son and heir Edward ' was one of those people whom revolutions teach.' He had learnt that the King must reign under and through the law, and that the Crown opposed to the nation was less strong than the Crown in Parliament.

What then was Parliament ? The name ' Parliamentum '— ' talking shop ' as Carlyle translated it, ' parley ' or ' discussion ' as it might more fairly be rendered—was first applied in Henry III's reign to the purely feudal assemblies of tenants-in-chief sitting with the other members of the King's Curia. The name ' Parliament ' as yet carried no idea of election or representation, nor did it necessarily imply a legislative or tax-voting assembly. It was simply the King's Curia or Council, that elusive Proteus, in the largest and most majestic of its forms, when Barons and King's servants met together to ' talk,' to debate high politics foreign and domestic, to discuss petitions, grievances, ways and means, and new forms of writ, and to conduct State Trials. It was not more legislative than administrative, not more financial than judicial. Having ' talked,' it acted, for it was an epitome of all the powers in the State. But the method of selecting its members had not yet been defined.

In the course of Henry III's reign it became an occasional but not an invariable practice to summon to this great assembly two or more knights elected in each Shire Court to represent the county. This was not to create a new assembly, or to 'originate Parliament'; it was merely to call up some new people to the plenary session of the old *curia regis*. Neither was it a party move either of the King or of his opponents; both sides felt that it was best to know what the 'bachelors' were thinking. It was a natural evolution, so natural as scarcely to attract notice. For two generations past, knights elected in the Shire Court had transacted local business with the King's judges and officers.[1] It seemed but a small step to summon them collectively to meet the King among his judges and officers at some central point. Moreover representatives from individual shires and boroughs had long been in the habit of attending the King's Curia to transact the business of their community. To us, with our knowledge of all that was to come, the step of summoning them collectively and officially may seem immense. But in the mediæval world the representation of communities was a normal way of getting business done, and its application to the central assembly of the realm was too natural to cause remark. When the wind sows the acorn the forester takes little heed.

Then and for long afterwards the summons to Parliament was often regarded as a burden, grudgingly borne for the public good, much as the companion duty of serving on a jury is still regarded to-day. Communities, particularly boroughs, often neglected to send their representatives; and even the elected knights of the shire sometimes absconded to avoid service. Doubtless it was galling, when you looked round the Shire Court to congratulate the new member ironically on his expensive and dangerous honour, to find that he had slipped quietly on his horse and ridden for sanctuary, leaving the court to choose you in his stead! 'The elective franchise' was not yet a privilege or a 'right of man.' In Edward III's reign, the borough of distant Torrington in Devon obtained by petition the 'franchise' of not being required to send members to Parliament; for the payment of members' expenses then fell on the communities that sent them up.

Nevertheless the presence of the knights of the shire strengthened the authority and aided the counsels of the Parliament of magnates. The Government found it convenient and advantageous to enforce the presence of the 'communities' or 'commons' of the realm through their representatives. And so in the year of revolution after Lewes, Simon de Montfort summoned not only 1265. the knights of the shire, but for the first time two representatives from each of the chartered boroughs. He probably knew that

---

[1] See p. 166, above.

the burghers would be of his faction, and he was the first of our rulers to perceive that the general position of a party government could be strengthened by calling representatives of all the communities together and talking to them.   It was a form of ' propaganda,' over and above any financial or judicial use that was made of the Assembly.   We learn from the writs that the burghers were summoned, but we do not know how many came, or what, if anything, they did.   That particular Parliament was a revolutionary assembly to which only those Barons were summoned who were of Simon's party, but it set a precedent for the summoning of burghers which was imitated in the more regular Parliaments of Edward the First.

The English Parliament had no one man for its maker, neither Simon nor even Edward.   No man made it, for it grew.   It was the natural outcome, through long centuries, of the common sense and the good nature of the English people, who have usually preferred committees to dictators, elections to street fighting, and ' talking-shops ' to revolutionary tribunals.

BOOKS FOR FURTHER READING

Kate Norgate, *John Lackland* ; F. M. Powicke, *The Loss of Normandy* ; McKechnie, *Magna Carta* ; Lives of *Simon de Montfort* by Creighton, Charles Bémont and G. W. Prothero.   Also see p. 152, above.

CHAPTER IV

The Corporate Sense of the Middle Ages.   The Universities.   The Friars. The Jews.   The Common Law and Lawyers.   Parliament under the Edwards.   The House of Commons.   The Justices of the Peace

Kings : Edward I, 1272–1307 ; Edward II, 1307–1327

IN the Middle Ages men thought and acted corporately.   The status of every man was fixed by his place in some community —manor, borough, guild, learned University or convent.   The villein and the monk scarcely existed in the eye of the law except through the lord of the manor and the Abbot of the monastery. As a human being, or as an English subject, no man had ' rights ' either to employment or to the vote, or indeed to anything very much beyond a little Christian charity.   The unit of mediæval society was neither the nation nor the individual but something between the two,—the corporation.

By thus strictly formulating on the group principle the

relation of every man to his fellows, civilization emerged out of the Dark Ages into the mediæval twilight. Only in the later age of the Renaissance and Reformation, after the emancipation of the villeins had shattered the economic system on which the feudal world rested, was it possible to take another step forward towards personal freedom. Then indeed many of the mediæval corporations went down before the omnipotent State on the one hand and the self-assertive individual on the other. The monasteries and orders of friars disappeared from England, and the town corporations and guilds saw their more important functions divided between the individual and the State. But some mediæval institutions survived unimpaired. The secular clergy, the lawyers and the Universities adapted themselves to the service of the new nation, and the ' House of Commons,' where the ' commons' or ' communities' of the Realm were represented, became the chief organ of the national life.[1] Such has been the priceless legacy to England of the mediæval genius for corporate action.

In this chapter we are concerned with the rise of four great institutions, of which three have survived and one perished in England—the Universities, the orders of friars, the lawyers incorporated in the Inns of Court, and Parliament, more especially the House of Commons. The monastic and the feudal systems had arisen in the struggle against barbarism during the Dark Ages; but these newer institutions were the ripe fruit of mediæval society at its culminating point.

Universities, like Parliaments, were an invention of the Middle Ages, unknown to the wisdom of the ancients. Socrates gave no diplomas or degrees, and would have subjected any disciple who demanded one to a disconcerting catechism on the nature of true knowledge. Philosophy and science rose in the Hellenic world to a point far above any regained in the Middle Ages. But ancient learning and wisdom were never organized in Universities. Partly for this reason they decayed, and fell before the attack of the regimented Christian priesthood.

After that, during the long centuries when the Church supposed that all necessary knowledge was a simple matter, and the world agreed with her, no need was felt for any organization of learning outside the occasional efforts of monastic cloisters and Cathedral chapters. But the Twelfth Century saw a Renaissance

---

[1] Originally the House of ' Commons ' represented, not as to-day statistical aggregations of individual voters, but certain definite communities—the City of London, the Shire of York—somewhat as the United States Senate represents the separate States.

of learning and thought, partly owing to the contacts set up by the Crusades, partly to the automatic increase of mental activity in a richer and safer Europe. The study of Civil and Canon Law, of classical Latin, of philosophy based on Aristotle, of mathematics and medicine based on Arabic numerals and treatises, seemed to require a new corporate life of their own.

The zeal for learning, like the contemporary zeal for the Crusades, was compounded of many diverse elements—pure fire of the spirit, professional ambition, greed for benefices, curiosity high and low, love of adventure and of travel. Like the Crusades, the impulse was international, leading men to desert their own country and wander over Alps and seas. Out of this intellectual ferment over the face of Europe, the Universities suddenly arose, first in Italy, then in almost all the lands of Christendom. Such was the genius of the Middle Ages for giving corporate life to an idea. Even when each land had set up its own Universities, the more famous centres of learning still had ' nations ' of foreign students in their midst, for, so long as all educated persons talked and wrote in Latin, learning remained cosmopolitan in spirit.

The mediæval as distinct from the modern University was ' built of men ' alone, not of stone and mortar, of colleges, laboratories and libraries, of endowments from capitalists and grants from the State. Nor was it burdened with overmuch examining or too many regulations. It would have been the freest of all human societies had it not been for the control of the Church over heresy, which drove the keenest speculative abilities into narrow and arbitrary channels.

Just because the original Universities were not dependent on endowments or buildings, they were able to propagate their species all over Europe in the Twelfth and Thirteenth Centuries with amazing rapidity, without waiting for the patronage of wealth. Thus it was that, owing to trouble between Henry II and the King of France, the English students at the University of Paris lightly migrated to their native island and founded a University at Oxford. It was a convenient spot, easy of access to all Southern and Western England, with houses where the scholars could lodge half a dozen in a room; taverns where they could sit drinking, arguing, singing and quarrelling; churches which could be borrowed for University functions ; rooms where the Masters could lecture, each with some precious volume open before him, while the students on the floor took notes and applauded or hissed him like a rowdy audience at the theatre.

1209.   So too, it was probably an enforced migration from Oxford, the result of town and gown feuds of the murderous kind then usual, that gave birth to the rival University. Cambridge was a meeting-place of waterways and Roman roads convenient for the North and East of England. Both Oxford and Cambridge were each just over fifty miles from London, which had no University of its own until the Nineteenth Century. Wales went to Oxford, and Scotland to Paris and Padua, until at the beginning of the Fifteenth Century the Scots set up a University of their own at St. Andrews.

The early Universities were neither assisted nor corrupted by great endowments, nor by the presence, as in later times, of ' the noblest youth of the land.' Mediæval Oxford and Cambridge belonged to the poor, in the sense that the upper classes had as yet no use for them. The knights and Barons thought themselves above University education. But the villeins, bound to the soil of the manor, were below it. The actual students were for the most part the cleverest sons of yeomen, retainers, and citizens. When, abandoning their fathers' farms and crafts, they took minor orders as the first step in the pursuit of knowledge, they became indeed ' poor clerks ' and ' poor scholars,' the chartered beggars of learning.

For such men the University was the way to professional honour. It was almost the only path to high promotion in the Church for those who were not of noble family. And all who aspired to rise by their wits to be civil servants, secretaries of great men, physicians, architects or ecclesiastical lawyers, must needs take holy orders and pass through the University. The first profession to be laicized was the Common Law bar and bench, in the course of the Thirteenth Century. Yet even they were largely recruited from men who had once been at Oxford and Cambridge, in such minor orders as gave no indelible character of ' clergy.'

When, therefore, we imagine what the first English under-graduates were like, we must think of them as nearly all ' clerks ' of a sort, under lightly taken vows of celibacy, protected by the shadow of Becket from the King's courts and hangman, but by no means of a type in which we should recognize the characteristics of a modern ' clergyman.' Any time before the Fifteenth Century, the typical student was a poor, clever lad of lower middle-class origin, coming up to Oxford or Cambridge at fourteen and staying probably till he was twenty-one or more, sub-jected all the while to slight discipline either of school or ' college ' character. His morals have been depicted by the author of the *Miller's Tale* and the *Reeve's Tale* and by many others of less note, though Chaucer has also given us a nobler type in the Scholar of the *Prologue*. The songs of the student, Latin rhymes common to all the Universities of Europe and known as ' goliardic ' verses, boast his resolution to ' die in a tavern,' and meanwhile to enjoy all the sweets of a vagabond life, now on the road, now in the city. They have small savour of any religion save that of Bacchus, Venus, and the heathen hierarchy as pictured by Ovid. Yet many of the students were pious, and all were devoted, at least in theory, to learning.

The atmosphere was that of the *Quartier Latin* rather than that of the later Oxford and Cambridge of the collegiate life, half aristocratic and half respectable. The mediæval student was neither. When Simon de Montfort raised his banner, the Oxford undergraduates flocked off in ragged regiments to fight for the cause of freedom, in the same mood as the undisciplined students of France, Italy and Germany fought on the barricades of 1848. In Simon's day it was still possible for youth to be the sectary at once of learning, licence, liberty and religion, and to feel no contradiction.

A sound and generous instinct has led people in modern times to compare themselves unfavourably with the ' poor clerks ' of mediæval Universities who faced the direst poverty in pursuit of knowledge. But there was another side to the picture. Boys of fourteen sent, with little or no money and no advice or protection, to fend for themselves in a scene of riot, of debauchery, and frequently of murder, among practised extortioners who lived by cheating the ' silly scholars,' might often get as much harm as good from academic life.

When, therefore, the first Colleges were started, towards the end of the Thirteenth Century,[1] originally to provide food and maintenance for scholars to be placed ' on the foundation ' of the College, it was soon perceived that the protection and control of the boys were hardly less valuable than the financial assistance afforded them. Careful English parents became more and more anxious to put their sons into one or other of these arks of safety ; an increasing number of undergraduates who were not scholars ' on the foundation ' sought and obtained a place in the envied life of the Colleges. The number, wealth and importance of these institutions increased generation after generation to meet a natural demand, characteristic of the English craving for the comfort and security of a settled ' home.' From the Fifteenth Century onwards an additional motive in the endowment of Colleges was to preserve the youth from the

---

[1] Balliol, Oxford, 1261-6, and Merton, Oxford, 1263. Peterhouse, Cambridge, 1284. The numbers of mediæval Oxford students were probably always below 3000, and at Cambridge they were still smaller. There has often been gross exaggeration of this as of other mediæval figures.

influences of Lollardry, Popery, Puritanism, Arminianism and similar evils of each passing age. Where a fold and shepherds were provided, the wolf could less easily prowl.

It is a mistake to suppose that Colleges were always peculiar to Oxford and Cambridge. Italian Universities had many Colleges or endowed residences for students, which have since disappeared with a very few exceptions. At Paris University upwards of fifty Colleges were founded between 1180 and 1500. But they never attained to the size, wealth and importance eventually reached by the corresponding institutions in England. They withered away and failed to preserve their property, and what was left of them finally disappeared in the French Revolution. The English Colleges grew in wealth and numbers until in Stuart times they had devoured their mother the University.

The chief study of mediæval Universities was a peculiar school of logic, much needed to reconcile Aristotle with the unchallengeable doctrines of the Church, a feat which St. Thomas Aquinas accomplished to the general satisfaction. A promising revival during the Twelfth Century of classical Latin on its literary side, took feeble root in the new Universities and withered away. The time for the poets, orators and historians of Greece and Rome was not yet. True vision of the ancient world, especially that of Hellas, only came with the second Renaissance in the Fifteenth Century. When it came, it gave the spiritual death-blow to the whole mediæval system, for men saw, or thought they saw, far back in time, something more wise, more noble and more free than the world of their own experience. The early doctors and students had no such disturbing vision.

Physical science did not get far in theological swaddling-clothes; the genius of friar Roger Bacon of Oxford shone like a star in the night, but with only scientific weapons he was, as Newton would have been in the Thirteenth Century, a powerless and unpopular victim of the prejudices of his age. Wycliffe, being a master of scholastic reasoning, was far more formidable a century later in his influence upon the minds of men.

The great work of mediæval logic and scholasticism was to train and subtilize the crude intellect of Europe. The intellectual progress of the Middle Ages is to be measured not by results in original thought, which was under an interdict, or at least in strict confinement, but by the skill with which men learned to handle their philosophic material. Though much of the subject-matter of their disputes seems to us as vain and nugatory as the much-debated problem ' how many angels can stand on the point of a needle,' the debt we owe to these ancient choppers of logic is none the less great for being strictly inestimable.[1]

Another great social change in Thirteenth Century England, besides the growth of the Universities, was the coming of the friars. We cannot indeed say of England, as was said with more plausibility of the continent, that the orders of St. Dominic and St. Francis saved the tottering Church. In the England of Henry III the Church as an institution was safe enough. There was much ignorance, neglect and practical heathenism, but there was no heresy and little anti-clerical feeling. There was nothing comparable to the Albigensian, Waldensian and other continental movements which were persecuted with ruthless and wholesale cruelty by the Inquisition, largely under the inspiration of the friars of St. Dominic. The Dominicans flourished in England, but as yet there were no heretics for the ' hounds of God ' to hunt. It was the gentle Franciscans and their Umbrian evangel that most completely and rapidly won the hearts of the English after their landing in 1224.

Nor can the friars be said to have saved the Papal power in England. It is indeed remarkable that the anti-Papal feeling first grew strong over here in those very years of Henry III's reign when the friars were obtaining their greatest hold over the people. The two movements were not antagonistic. Grosse-tête took a leading part in both, and the commission which the friars held from the Pope did not prevent them from giving rein to their democratic sympathies and joining with the party of Simon de Montfort, which though religious and orthodox was openly at feud with the Roman court.

But if in England the friars cannot be said to have saved either the Papacy or the Church, they gave to religion a new spirit and new methods. The earliest Franciscans, themselves converts from the class of gentry, made a great religious revival among the poor, comparable in more ways than one to the Puritan, Wesleyan and Salvation Army movements. In the spirit of their founder, they sought out the poorest, the most

[1] Mr. Pearsall Smith, in his excellent work on the *English Language*, p. 187, says : ' If we were to study the history of almost any of the great terms of ancient or mediæval philosophy, . . . we should be able to observe the effect of the drifting down, into the popular consciousness, of the definitions of high and abstract thought. We should find that many of our commonest notions and most obvious distinctions were by no means as simple and self-evident as we think them now, but were the result of severe intellectual struggles carried on through hundreds of years ; and that some of the words we put to the most trivial uses are tools fashioned long ago by old philosophers, theologians and lawyers, and sharpened on the whetstone of each other's brains.'

neglected, the diseased, especially in the slums of the larger towns, insufficiently provided for by the parish system.

The secret of the friars' propaganda was preaching, in words which the common people could feel and understand. Parish priests were then seldom competent to preach, while the higher clergy had their heads full of matters of Church and State, and the monks abode in their convents or rode about on mundane business and pleasure. Before the coming of the friars, religion relied too exclusively on the sacraments she dispensed, nor were they always at hand for those who needed them. The friars not only made the sacraments more available, but erected preaching and religious instruction into a popular system. It was the destined method of the Lollards and Protestants in later times. By enhancing the importance of the pulpit the friars prepared the way for those who were to replace and destroy them, for they brought religion to the common people, endeavouring to make it intelligible to their minds and influential over their lives.

The monastic movement from the Fourth to the Twelfth Century had been the desperate resource of pious men in ages of decadence or of barbarism, to save their own souls and to make a garden of God in the midst of the world's wilderness. The garden had often served as a useful model for the cultivation of the wilderness, but the wall between the two had always been maintained. But now the friars, in a somewhat more hopeful and better ordered world than that which had generated many successive orders of monks, regarded the world itself as God's garden. They went down into the market-place and the slum to wrestle for the souls of men and women. The monk remained, theoretically at least, shut up in his cloister ; when he wandered abroad, as he frequently did, he was more often than not breaking rules to escape the monotony of a life to which he had no real vocation. But it was the duty of the friar to walk from town to town, nursing the sick, preaching, and hearing confessions. The monk was supported by the income of broad acres and sheep-runs ; but the friar was to live on the alms he received from door to door.

In theory, indeed, the friar might hold no property. But, contrary to the original intentions of St. Francis, his disciples acquired not only priories but libraries and great churches of their own. As their popularity increased, the ideals of their founder were forgotten or explained away with mediæval subtlety, until those who still stood by his tenets of evangelical poverty were persecuted inside his own order. Learning, which he had deprecated as a snare to the purity of the evangelical mission, was taken up with splendid results by the Grey Friars of Oxford

University, under the patronage and guidance of Bishop
Grossetête. His friend Adam de Marsh and Roger Bacon himself were among the earlier Oxford Franciscans ; and in a later
generation came Duns Scotus and William of Ockham. Philosophy, physical science and medicine owed much to the English
followers of St. Francis.

As with all such movements, the true apostolic spirit gradually
sank into its embers, while the institution survived. In the
Fourteenth Century the English friars, Franciscan and Dominican,
were two powerful corporations with a host of enemies. The
secular clergy in whose parishes the friars poached, carrying off
their flocks and their fees under their very faces, hated the friars
scarcely less bitterly than did the Wycliffite reformers, who saw
in Franciscan and Dominican their chief popular rivals ; men
of the world like Chaucer laughed at the hypocritical devices
of ' brothers ' who made gain out of popular superstition while
pretending to observe rules of evangelical poverty ; and the pious
and orthodox Gower could write of the friars : ' Incest, flattery
and hypocrisy and pandering to vices, these are the qualities
have raised their minsters, their steeples and their cloisters.'

But even at the end of the Fourteenth Century the friars
still had a strong popular following ; to die in a friar's dress was
still held by many to be a passport to heaven. During the
Fifteenth Century, though they saw their Lollard enemies
crushed, their own influence was declining. When the storm
of the Reformation broke they were almost without friends.
The secular clergy had always regarded them as interlopers and
rivals. And when Henry VIII set out to destroy the Papal
power, the disbandment of the friars was an essential part of
the policy, for they were the Pope's special protégés and
servants.

The coming of the friars was the last great wave of the flood
of foreign influence that had been washing over England ever
since the Norman Conquest. After that the waters recede,
leaving a rich sediment, while the wind shifts and blows from
inland woods. In the Edwardian and later Plantagenet period,
England, instead of perpetually receiving, gives out of her own
plenty. She becomes profuse in the creation of native forms.
Her own law and Parliament develop under the First Edward,
her own language and literature arise under the Third ; and with
Chaucer comes also Wycliffe and the beginning of the distinctive
English contribution to religion. Meanwhile the English yeomen
conquer France with the island weapon ; and the archer en-
shrines himself in the general imagination of a woodland people

of sporting instincts, fun and good-nature, as that exclusively English figure of the jolly outlaw and radical—Robin Hood.[1]

All this was accompanied and aided by the growth of English liberty in the emancipation of the villeins, and the increase of English wealth in the substitution of the manufactured cloth trade for the export of raw wool. At the same time, English finance and money-lending passed into English hands in the course of the Fourteenth and Fifteenth Centuries; the way for that development was prepared by Edward I's expulsion of the Jews.

The Jews, like so many other foreigners, had come into England in the wake of the Conqueror. Saxon England had been so primitive as to require few money-lenders. But the Norman and Angevin kings, like other continental princes, employed the Jews to supply them with ready cash in anticipation of revenue. The Jews throve on money-lending for interest, a practice forbidden by the Church, which Christian traders, having no gold to lend, were fain to abandon with a curse to the infidels who had it. The Jews were the King's sponges. They sucked up his subjects' money by putting their own out on usury, and were protected from the rage of their debtors solely by the strong arm of the King, who in his turn drew what he wanted from their ever-accumulating wealth. They stood to the King as the villein to his lord; all they had was, theoretically, his. His 'exchequer of the Jews' aided them to collect their debts. They were utterly at his mercy, for he was their only friend in a hostile land. Their unpopularity was twofold, for were they not the arch-creditors when no one else had money to lend on usury, and the arch-infidels when everyone else, of course, believed?

Their operations in England, besides their dealings with the King, consisted very largely in lending money to the baronage and the warrior class. They supplied the sinews of war and government, but not yet of commerce and industry, for the day of commercial capitalism was still in the future.

Some of the English Jews became very rich, like Aaron of

[1] Robin Hood, originally a woodland elf of infinite antiquity, was a 'good yeoman' in his greatest days towards the close of the Middle Ages. He only became vulgarized as a disguised Earl of Huntingdon late in the Sixteenth Century. His story, as it is known to us to-day, dates from late Plantagenet to early Tudor times. The King with whom the early ballads connected him was not Richard I, but an Edward, probably the First. Robin's feats with the long-bow (see pp. 210–211, below) and his animosity against rich Churchmen bespeak a period subsequent to the Thirteenth Century, and his 'friar' Tuck has had time to acclimatize himself to the island atmosphere. Maid Marian, who seems to have had an earlier existence on her own account, did not join Robin's troupe before 1500; yet the fully developed idea of her is as distinctively English as any part of the legend. Perhaps she owes most to Peacock in the Nineteenth Century!

Lincoln in the reign of Henry II, who had the honour of a special department of the Exchequer, ' *Scaccarium Aaronis*,' to wind up his affairs. In the towns of wealthy East Anglia, the stone houses of the Jews, not easily broken open, stood as rivals to the stone castle and the stone church among the mud and timber hovels of the poorer Christians. But whenever the King drew in his protecting arm, horrible pogroms put an end at once to the Jews and their tell-tale parchments.

1290.   In Edward I's reign this unhappy system came to its cruel end. Edward, perhaps, was only acting up to the best lights of his time, in driving the Jews out of the island. The expulsion was praised as an act of self-sacrifice on his part, and was of course intensely popular. It was a feasible policy because the time had come when it was just possible for a King and his nobles to get money elsewhere, from ' usurious ' Christians. At first the money-lending business in England passed largely into the hands of the Flemings and Italians, like the great Florentine firms of Bardi and Peruzzi, from whom Edward III borrowed. Then English capitalists gradually became more important. Merchants like William de la Pole of Hull, the first commercial founder of an English noble family, and Richard Whittington, Mayor of London and hero of the cat-myth, became money-lenders to the King and baronage, financing the Hundred Years' War and the Wars of the Roses. Edward IV lived on intimate terms with the great London citizens, not only because he liked their wives but because he borrowed their money. When, therefore, under the Tudors the age of commercial capitalism slowly dawned, high finance was in native hands.

When the Jews returned to England in the Stuart and Hanoverian era, they found the English in control of their own money-market and of the other intellectual professions. And by that time the new Bible-reading culture of the English had diminished the religious hatred against the Chosen People. For these reasons the relation of the Jews to the English was renewed under happier auspices than even now prevail in lands where the natives have not had the wit or the opportunity to contract the habit of managing their own affairs.

1272–
1307.
527–565.   Edward I has been called ' the English Justinian,' in refer-ence to the Emperor who carried through the codification of old Roman law on the eve of its decline. It has indeed been said that to compare the English law of Edward's time with the Roman law of Justinian is to compare childhood to second childhood. But Edward at least resembled his prototype in being a royal definer of things legal. He did not, it is true,

perpetrate anything so definite as a code, which is unsuited alike to the childhood of a nation and to the plastic genius of English law. But he gave closer definition to our land law, our public law and our Parliament. Under him the institutions of the mediæval State, hitherto fluid, began to take form. Henceforth the distinction between Parliament and Council is, for practical purposes, clear.

The first eighteen years of Edward I saw the beginning of our Statute Law. Surrounded by great lawyers, native and foreign, the legal-minded King, in the prime of his magnificent manhood, passed Statute after Statute through his Parliaments, with a legislative vigour comparable, according to Maitland, only to that of the Whigs in the first few years after the Reform Bill.

These Statutes are a new phenomenon, for they alter the very substance of the law. Hitherto there has always been ' law,' Anglo-Danish in origin, traditional, customary, unwritten, much of it local, most of it obsolete ; and there has been feudal law, also customary ; more recently there has been ' case law,' made by pronouncements of famous royal judges, and commented on in professional treatises like those of Glanvill and Bracton ; there have been public treaties, like the Constitutions of Clarendon and Magna Carta, purporting only to restate and re-enforce the law, though perhaps in fact enlarging it ; there have been royal Assizes or ordinances altering legal procedure, substituting for instance trial by jury for trial by battle. But now under Edward I we get for the first time ' laws ' undoubtedly competent to alter ' law ' itself—with the exception of an undefined residuum of ' fundamental law,' for neither King nor Parliament are as yet ' omnicompetent.' [1]

In these first Statutes of the Realm, especially *De Donis Conditionalibus* and *Quia Emptores*, feudal law was restated with alterations, in such fashion as to become the starting point of our modern land law. Indeed the two great Statutes of Edward I remained so long the basis of our law of real property that a knowledge of them has remained necessary for English lawyers up till our own day. *De Donis* originated the practice of entailing estates, **1275.** which for so many centuries wrought widespread mischief in

---

[1] ' The vigorous legislation ' of Edward I ' has an important consequence in checking the growth of unenacted law.' Maitland, *Const. Hist.*, p. 21. While there was still no Statute Law the law courts had been more free to mould the law than they ever were again ; *e.g.*, from the Eleventh to the Thirteenth Centuries it had lain with the King and his Judges to decide whether murderers and felons should be blinded or otherwise mutilated, or hanged. William I had decided for mutilation, the Judges of the Thirteenth Century for death. But in later times the list of capital offences is settled by Parliamentary Statute, in obedience to which the Judge must put on the black cap.

1290.   rural England. *Quia Emptores* was passed by Edward I and his tenants-in-chief to preserve to themselves the full value of their feudal dues by preventing subinfeudation. But in fact this only hastened the decay of feudalism. For when the tenants-in-chief wished to dispose of land, they had in future to make the purchaser become a tenant-in-chief like themselves. This caused a great multiplication of persons holding land direct from the King, and a consequent levelling of classes and a further disintegration of the feudal spirit.[1] Before long a man was more proud of being summoned to Parliament than of being one of the innumerable tenants-in-chief. And the King had more prestige as head of the executive and as the holder of Parliament than as the supposed universal landlord. From a feudal society we were becoming a Parliamentary nation.

Edward defined the land law, and the process of defining the law courts was always going forward, not least in his reign. In the course of the Thirteenth and Fourteenth Centuries, the Exchequer, Common Pleas, and King's Bench, one after the other, became distinct courts, each with its own records, procedure, permanent officers and judges. The rise of the Court of Chancery was later and more peculiar.[2]

From the time of Edward I onwards the courts of Common Law, as distinguished from the Court of Chancery and the Church courts, were manned by persons not in holy orders. The Pope had for some time past taken objection to the service and teaching of the secular law by the priesthood. The King's judges were ceasing as a rule to be ecclesiastics like Bracton, or warrior-statesmen like Glanvill. The normal movement of legal promotion in England was no longer from outside, but from bar to bench, whereas in many countries of Europe to this day judge and pleader belong to two distinct and mutually exclusive professions. In the professional atmosphere of the King's courts in Westminster Hall, where English law was perpetually on the anvil red-hot, the corporate sense of the Middle Ages was forming pleaders and judges into a single self-conscious society. Jealous of outsiders, rivals to the ecclesiastical lawyers, ' learned brothers ' to one another, makers and guardians of a great intellectual and moral tradition, acquiring too all the faults and all the unpopularity of a powerful and highly organized profession, they were not a close ' noblesse of the robe,' but offered to any Englishman

---

[1] *Quia Emptores* allowed land to be freely sold, but the purchaser must hold it as the vassal of the King or of the lord from whom the vendor held it, and not as the vassal of the vendor himself. Scottish law continued to permit subinfeudation—one reason why Scotland remained more feudal than England.

[2] See note, pp. 199–200, at end of this chapter.

of brains and industry a ladder to wealth and greatness as attractive as the Church herself.

The common lawyers were, as a class, the first learned laymen, and as such were of great importance to the growth of the nation. Their place in English history is only a little lower than that of the Parliament men. Without the lawyers neither the Reformation nor the victory of Parliament over the Stuarts would ever have been accomplished. Yet their tradition and their society are a highly characteristic product of the Middle Ages, closely comparable to the Universities.

And as the English Universities developed Colleges, so the English lawyers built their Inns of Court. During the reigns of the first three Edwards they grouped their halls, libraries and dwelling places in and around the deserted groves of the Templars. Their place of public performance lay two miles further westward, in the shadow of the royal residence, where they were royally accommodated in Westminster Hall, the magnificent excrescence which William Rufus had added to the Confessor's Palace, as it were in rivalry to the Abbey. But the lawyers slept, dined and studied in their own Inns of Court, half-way between the commercial capital at London and the political capital at Westminster, a geographic position that helped the English lawyer to discover his true political function as mediator between Crown and people.[1]

In the reign of Edward I the famous Year Books begin. They were unofficial verbatim reports of legal proceedings, taken down in court in the French tongue, which was then spoken by the upper classes and therefore by the lawyers in their pleadings. There was no such full reporting in any other country or in any other sphere of English life, political or ecclesiastical, for centuries to come. All that is of professional and much that is of purely human interest is recorded word for word as it was uttered, ' the shifting argument, the retort, the quip, the expletive.' These reports, carried on for generation after generation, stood in the place of the Code of Justinian or the Decretals as the authority and inspiration of the great students who, in apostolic succession through the ages, built up English law.

Proud of his courts of law, and jealous of any baronial franchises more extensive than the usual manor court, Edward I instituted a formal enquiry, known as the *Quo Warranto* inquest, 1278- into the origin of the higher private jurisdictions, demanding to 1279. see a charter where in many cases there was only the prescriptive

---

[1] In the latter part of Queen Victoria's reign the Law Courts themselves were moved from Westminster to the neighbourhood of the Inns of Court at Temple Bar.

right of immemorial custom. The attempt was premature, seeking to achieve by a bold stroke of political authority what could more safely be left to the invisible action of time. The story goes, with somewhat doubtful authenticity, that in answer to the questions of the Justices, the Earl Warenne drew his old, rusty sword and told them that he held his land and franchises by that charter. King Edward did not press the issue, for he had seen enough of Barons' wars in his youth. But the *Quo Warranto* inquest at least put a stop to recent or future encroachments on the sphere of the King's tribunals, and the preference felt by suitors for royal justice gradually brought private courts to an end. When, during the Wars of the Roses, anarchy raised its head for the last time, the great lords no longer claimed extensive jurisdictions of their own, but were content to employ their retainers to overawe judge and jury in the King's courts.

1455-
1485.

England's characteristic institution, Parliament, was not devised on the sudden to perpetuate a revolution in which one power rose and another fell. It grew up gradually as a convenient means of smoothing out differences and adjusting common action between powers who respected one another—King, Church, Barons, and certain classes of the common people such as burgesses and knights. No one respected the villeins and they had no part in Parliament. Knowing that Parliament was hostile, ' labour,' as soon as it began to be self-conscious, preferred ' direct action ' like the rising of 1381. But, setting the villeins aside, Parliament represented a friendly balance of power. The English people have always been distinguished for the ' Committee sense,' their desire to sit round and talk till an agreement or compromise is reached. This national peculiarity was the true origin of the English Parliament.

It was during the reigns of the first three Edwards that Parliament gradually acquired something like its present form. After his experiences in the time of de Montfort, Edward I saw in frequent national assemblies the best oil for the machinery of government. His object was not to limit the royal power or to subject it to the will of the commonalty. His object was to make the royal power more efficient by keeping it in constant touch with the life of the governed. And like Henry VIII, the only other monarch in our annals who did as much to increase the prestige of Parliament, he knew the value of the support of the middle classes in shire and town.

Edward I, therefore, decided to continue and popularize the experiment that had occasionally been made during his father's turbulent reign, of summoning representatives of the counties and boroughs to attend the great conferences of the magnates of the realm. He wanted, for one thing, to collect certain taxes more easily. The difficult assessments could not be well made without the willing help and special knowledge of the local knights and burgesses. Their representatives would return from the presence of King and assembled magnates, each to his own community, awestruck yet self-important, filled with a new sense of national unity and national needs. In that mood they would help to arrange the assessments locally, and facilitate payment. And they would explain the King's policy to their neighbours, who had no other means of information.

When there were no newspapers and few letters, and when travel was difficult and dangerous, the King's rigid insistence on the perpetual coming and going of ever fresh troops of knights and burghers between Westminster and their own communities began the continuous political education of Englishmen, and perhaps did more to create the unity of the nation than Chaucer or the Hundred Years' War. Nor, without such a machinery for the easy levy of taxes, could the great Scottish and French wars of the Edwardian period have been fought. It has been said that it was not England who made her Parliament, but Parliament that made England, and there is an element of truth in the epigram.

Financial need was not the only reason why the King summoned the representatives of town and shire. Indeed Edward I sometimes called them together on occasions when he asked for no money at all. For he had another end in view, to gather together the petitions and grievances of his subjects, so as to be able to govern in accordance with real local needs, and to keep a check on the misdeeds of local officials. Thus a large part of the business of these early Parliaments consisted in receiving piles of petitions for redress, mostly from private persons or single communities, but increasingly as the Fourteenth Century went on, from the House of Commons as a whole. In the reign of Edward I these petitions were directed, not to Parliament, but to the King or Council. They were dealt with in Parliament either by the King, by his ministers, or by committees of councillors, judges and Barons, known as ' Triers.' The redress afforded to the petitioners in these early times may now be regarded as either judicial, legislative or administrative ; the distinction was not then made. But, as time went on, while many of the private petitions were referred to judicial processes in the Chancery Court or elsewhere, the more important class emanating from the Commons' House as a whole began in the reign of Henry VI to take the form of ' bills ' to be passed

H

into law by Parliament. Such was the origin of the right of the House of Commons to initiate legislation.

But we must not speak of 'Houses' of Parliament as early as the reign of Edward I. There was then but one assembly, presided over by the King from his throne, or by his Chancellor from the woolsack; the rest of the chief officers of State were present *ex officio*, together with the Barons, lay and spiritual, summoned each by special writ; there were also present, humbly in the background, the representative knights and burghers summoned through the sheriff of each shire, not likely to speak unless they were first spoken to in such a presence. This was the 'High Court of Parliament,' which is still visible to the eye in the modern House of Lords with its throne and woolsack, although the Chancellor alone of the King's Ministers can now attend *ex officio* even if he is not a peer, and although the throne is now occupied only when Parliament is opened or prorogued. Then, when the Commons flock to the bar to hear the King's words, we have the original Plantagenet Parliament reassembled.

In the reign of Edward I the representatives of the Commons were not yet a separate House. And though they often attended the sessions of the Parliament one and indivisible, their presence there was not essential for much of the important business transacted by the magnates. Their consent to legislation was not always asked. The great Statutes for which the reign was famous were some of them, like *Quia Emptores*, passed when no representatives of the Commons were in attendance. And it is probable that if knights and burgesses were present at all when high matters of foreign and domestic policy were debated by the Ministers, Barons and Prelates, it was but as 'mutes and audience.'

The House of Commons as a separate Chamber originated in unofficial meetings of the knights and burgesses, discussing anxiously behind closed doors what collective reply they should give to some difficult question or demand with which they had been confronted by the higher powers. They were so careful to leave no reports of these proceedings that we know nothing of the internal development of the early House of Commons. We do not even know how and when the Speaker became its chairman. For the Speaker was originally the person appointed to 'speak' for the Commons in full Parliament, the other knights and burgesses being silent in presence of their betters. But until Stuart times the Speaker was a servant of the Crown much more than a servant of the House. As early as the reign of Edward III we find some of the King's household officers sitting as knights of the shire, very possibly to direct the debates and decisions of the House of Commons in the interest of the Crown, as Privy Councillors continued to do with very great effect in Tudor times. It was also in the reign of Edward III that the Chapter House of the monks of Westminster came to be regarded as the customary meeting place of the Commons.

The most important fact in the early history of our institutions is that the English Parliament, unlike analogous assemblies of the same period in Europe, divided itself, during the later Plantagenet reigns, not into three Estates of clergy, nobles and bourgeois, but into two Houses of Lords and Commons. The greater part of our constitutional and social history is in some sense either cause or effect of that unique arrangement.

In the continental system of ' Estates,' all the ' gentlemen,' as we should call them, were represented in the estate of the ' *noblesse.*' But the ' *noblesse,*' in the large sense which the word bears on the continent, was in the English Parliament divided in two. The *barones majores*, each summoned by special writ, sat in the upper house. The *barones minores*, even though tenants-in-chief, shared with knights, gentry and ' franklins ' the liability to be elected as knights of the shire. Thus the forms of English Parliamentary life abolished the distinctions of feudalism. Even a tenant-in-chief might be found sitting and working with the burghers of the towns.

This strange and significant arrangement of the Fourteenth Century English Parliaments was rendered possible by earlier developments which we have already noticed. The active part taken by the smaller gentry in shire business had often brought them in contact with the burghers as well as with the humbler rural freeholders.[1] The English rule of primogeniture, which sent the cadets of a noble family out into the world, had given the inhabitants of castle and manor-house a friendly interest in trade and commerce. The inter-marriage of classes and the constant intercommunication of the upper and middling ranks of society were already much more marked in England than elsewhere. Ages long ago, before the battles of Bannockburn or Crecy, the House of Commons already reflected these English peculiarities. Already the knights of the shire, a semi-feudal class, were acting as elected representatives of the rural yeomen, and were sitting

---

[1] See p. 166, above. The members of the Lower House, including the burghers, were all summoned through the sheriff, not by special writs directed to individual towns. This made a connection between burgher and knight—they were both in a sense representatives of the shire, in its rural and urban aspect respectively. The sheriff and the shire had played so great a part in royal government that the arrangement seemed natural to all.

cheek by jowl with the citizens of the boroughs. That is why the House of Commons was able to assert its importance at a very early date, when burghers and yeomen had small political prestige unless they were acting in association with knights. That also is why the English Civil War of Stuart times was not a class war ; and why the English of Burke's time could not understand what in the world the French Revolution was about.

Neither was any Estate or House of the Clergy formed as part of the English Parliament. Not only did the spiritualty refrain from drawing together as a separate clerical ' Estate ' in Parliament, but they voluntarily abandoned all their seats among the Commons and many of their seats among the Lords.

In the Upper House, indeed, the Bishops and certain of the greater Abbots continued to sit in their secular capacity as holders of baronies in a feudal assembly. Moreover some of the Bishops were royal ministers and civil servants. But the Prelates who were churchmen first and foremost took little stock in Parliament. The majority of the Abbots and Priors, wrapped up in local monastic interests, disliking the trouble and expense of long journeys, and feeling more bound in duty to the Pope than to the King, would not be at the pains to attend. They fell out of the national life and abandoned their places in Parliament, with results that became apparent in the Parliamentary Statute Book of Henry VIII.[1]

So, too, the representatives of lower clergy did not become a permanent part of the House of Commons, and gradually ceased to attend Parliament at all. The business of voting the ' fifteenths ' and ' tenths ' of clerical property to the King was conducted instead in the Convocations of Canterbury and York. Those assemblies were and are ecclesiastical, not political. They were in no sense an Estate of Parliament like the French Clerical Estate which figures in the original session of the *États Généraux* of 1789. The English clergy, on the principle that the things of Cæsar and the things of God were best kept apart, deliberately stepped aside from the political life and growth of the nation in the later Middle Ages. But since they also preserved their great and envied wealth and many ancient privileges, which came to be regarded as abuses in a changed world, their position was one of isolation, peculiarly exposed to attack when the Reformation began.

From humble beginnings in the reign of Edward I the House of Commons attained in the next hundred and fifty years

---

[1] The number of Abbots and Priors attending Parliament declined from about 70 in the reign of Edward I to about 27 under Edward III and his successors.

to a great place in the constitution.   The consent of its members
became necessary for all making of Statutes and for all extraordinary taxation ;   their own petitions very frequently received
the assent of the King in Parliament ;   and even the highest
acts of State like the deposition and election of Kings took place
with the Commons as parties to the deed.   Their constitutional
power when the Wars of the Roses broke out was indeed more
apparent than real, for the strongest forces in politics were
Crown, Barons and Church, not Commons.   But their recorded
position in the public law of the country supplied invaluable
precedents for the assumption of real power by the Lower House
after the Tudor monarchs had clipped the wings of Church and
baronage.

If in later Plantagenet times the Commons increased in real
power much, and in nominal power more, the reason is not far
to seek.   They were a third party, holding the balance, and
courted by the principals in the warfare of State.   The constant
struggle between King and Barons under the three Edwards,
the equally constant struggle between the great families around
the throne in the days of the House of Lancaster, put the Commons almost into the place of umpire.   They were well fitted
to take advantage of the position, because their interests were
not wholly bound up with either Barons or King.

Edward I had probably looked to the Commons to support
him against the baronage.   But the townsfolk, too, had their
own griefs against the King.   It was his habit, when in need of
instant supply for Gascony or Scotland, to seize a larger share
of the exports of wool than was warranted by the ' customs.'
These ' maltoltes ' or ' ill takings ' of wool were declared illegal, 1297.
after the burghers, on a famous occasion, had joined the opposition of the Barons and clergy, who were suffering from grievances
of their own with regard to the King's hasty demands.

Nevertheless, when Edward I died he was on the way to 1307.
make himself absolute master of England and of Scotland both.
He had in the last years of his life gone far to break the baronial
opposition at home, and to tread out the embers of the fire that
Wallace had kindled and that Bruce was trying to fan.   An able
successor might have destroyed constitutional liberty in England
and national liberty in Scotland.   Parliament might have
become, not an opposition or a critic to be conciliated, but a
useful cog in the machine of royal government—as no doubt
Edward himself regarded it.   The reign of his innocent-minded 1307–
but lazy and incapable son, Edward II, saved the situation. 1327.
It is not good to have an unbroken succession of great rulers
like Henry II, Edward I, or the Tudors.   John, Edward II,

and the Stuarts had their appointed place in the destiny of Britain.

The lax rule of two people of such unbusinesslike and artistic temperaments as young Edward II and his friend Piers Gaveston, presented the Barons with another chance. Gaveston was by no means the first nor the worst ' upstart,' nor the most alien ' foreigner ' who had risen to the head of affairs in England, but he had no prudence, for he gave nicknames to the leading Barons. In return, some of them took his life by treachery. Edward II and Gaveston were perhaps as unfit to govern England as Charles I and Buckingham. But the leaders of the baronial opposition, especially Earl Thomas of Lancaster, were stupid, selfish and brutal men, swollen with the pride of birth. The King's next favourite, Despenser, was not an ' upstart ' like Gaveston, but he developed into a tyrant. And yet the struggle between such unpromising opponents worked out to the advantage of the nation. The machinery of administration was improved, not by subjecting it to the clumsy control of the Barons, but by certain bureaucratic reforms. And the powers of Parliament were much increased, for on several great occasions it was called upon, now by Edward II, and now by the baronial opposition, to regularize their alternate victories by vote and Statute. In this new prestige of Parliament the Commons had their share.

The net result of the baronial tumults—they can scarcely be called baronial wars—during the reign of this unhappy King was not to increase the power either of Crown or of baronage. Throughout the Middle Ages the Barons were never able, in spite of repeated efforts, to dominate the King's counsels on any regular plan, though they held that on feudal principles he ought always to be guided by their noble advice, instead of by the advice of trained clerks and civil servants whose only qualification was that of understanding the King's business. The Barons failed to establish their claim to govern, because government means steady application, which a Baron could seldom give. His castles, his hunting, his estates, his retainers, his habits of life, his manors scattered over half the counties of England, very properly took up his time. He could not be the King's responsible Minister or attend at the regular sessions of the Council, because he had other duties and other pleasures.

A second reason why the Barons failed to control the government except in moments of revolution, was that the King's Court and household were too large and complicated to be easily subjected to control. If one office—say the Chancery with its Great Seal—was secured by the baronial opposition, the King could dive underground and still govern the country through the

1312.

Wardrobe with its Privy Seal. The King's Court was plastic and adaptable in its organization, yet highly specialized as a civil service, full of trained and able men who went on quietly governing, while far over their heads fools or scoundrels like Gaveston and Thomas of Lancaster, Despenser and Mortimer, ranted and killed each other for the benefit of posterity and the Elizabethan dramatists. Meanwhile peaceful stone manor-houses could rise in quiet corners of the land, the export of wool could increase, the population could go up, all classes could grow less poor and less ill-fed, because all the while the King's Peace was indifferently well enforced.

In the reign of Edward III an addition was made to the State machinery, significant of much. Keepers or Justices of the Peace were set up in every county to help the central power to govern. Like the Coroners before them, they were not bureaucrats but independent country gentlemen. As typical of the rising class of knights and smaller gentry, the Justices of the Peace took over more and more of the work previously done by that great man the Sheriff, or by the Judges on circuit. The ' J.P.'s ' seemed to strike root in the shire and grow as a native plant, equally popular with their neighbours and with the King's Council, between whom it was their task to interpret. For four hundred years their powers continued to increase, both in variety of function and in personal authority, till in the Eighteenth Century they were in a sense more powerful than the central government itself. This would not have happened if they had not responded to the needs and character of the English over a long period of time. According to Maitland, the respect in which the English hold the law was generated not a little by this system of ' amateur justice.' For the magistrate who expounded and enforced the law for ordinary people in ordinary cases may not have known much law, but he knew his neighbours and was known of them.

BOOKS FOR FURTHER READING

See p. 152, above. Also Rashdall, *The Universities of Europe* ; Haskins, *The Rise of the Universities* (Holt, New York) ; Reginald Poole, *Illustrations of the History of Mediæval Thought* ; Jessopp, *The Coming of the Friars* ; Sabatier, *Life of St. Francis* ; A. L. Smith, *Church and State in the Middle Ages* ; Tout, *Edward I*, and *Place of Ed. II. in Eng. History* ; Maitland, *Year Books of Edward II*, Introd. (Selden Soc.), and *Memoranda de Parl.*, 1305 (Rolls Series), Introd. ; Pasquet, *Essay on the Origins of the House of Commons* (translated, 1925, Cam. Press).

NOTE ON THE COURT OF CHANCERY

From the time of Edward I's friend Robert Burnell, if not before, the Lord Chancellor was the chief officer of the Realm, for his office, in charge of the King's Great Seal, was necessarily as much in touch with all departments of

State as the Treasury in our own day. Until the Reformation, the Chancellor was frequently an ecclesiastic as well as a lawyer. In the course of the Fourteenth and Fifteenth Centuries, his Chancery Court became a definite tribunal where equitable remedies were provided for unforeseen abuses in the working of the courts of Common Law. His court, on behalf of the King's Council, answered petitions of the aggrieved subject in a judicial manner. Since Parliament now prevented the King from altering procedure or calling up cases by the issue of unauthorized writs, and since the Common Law was rapidly becoming a law unto itself, a rigid system independent of the King's volition—this equitable and correctional jurisdiction of the Chancellor was invaluable to the King as a method by which he could turn the flank of the common lawyers and of the Parliament men. But no strong objection was taken, because the relief it often afforded to individual subjects was so great. Before the accession of the Tudors the Chancery Court had become a recognized part of the Constitution, and was destined to survive later royal expedients for supplementing the Common Law, such as the Court of Star Chamber.

In the Fifteenth Century, Chancery had been a method of appeal to commonsense from the technicalities of the other law courts. Four centuries later, in the days of Eldon and Charles Dickens, it had become the slave of its own technicalities, and the subject's remedy lay rather in the modern habit of frequent remedial legislation by Parliament.

CHAPTER V

Celt and Saxon. Attempts to complete the Island Empire. Causes of Failure in the Middle Ages. Ireland, Wales, Scotland

THE England of the later Middle Ages, the most highly organized of the larger States of Europe, lay alongside of Wales and Ireland, each a congeries of Celtic tribes, and abutted on Scotland, a poor and thinly inhabited Kingdom, racially divided between Celt and Saxon, but already becoming Anglo-Norman in language and institutions. In such circumstances it was inevitable that attempts should be made to round off the island empire on the basis of conquest by England.[1]

The Romans in Britain had been faced by precisely the same geographic problem. Their good genius prompted them to leave Ireland alone ; they tried repeatedly and vainly to conquer Scotland ; but they quickly subdued Wales by their system of military roads and forts, without, however, inducing the mountaineers to adopt the Latinized civilization of the plains. Mediæval England had much the same measure of success as Roman Britain. More slowly indeed than the legions, English feudal chivalry with its network of castles made a military conquest of Wales, but the full adjustment of Welsh to Saxon civilization was left over till Tudor and Hanoverian times ;

---

[1] I use the word Celtic in this chapter, as elsewhere, to designate the mixture of Celtic and earlier ' Iberian ' races.

the attempt to subdue Scotland was a complete failure ; while beyond St. George's Channel, England effected not a conquest, but a lodgment in mediæval Ireland, and hung on like a hound that has its fangs in the side of the stag.

A main reason why the mediæval English failed in Scotland and Ireland, and never reduced even Wales to good order, is to be sought in their continental entanglements. Till the loss of Normandy in John's reign, the energies of the Norman and Angevin Kings of England had been occupied in the recovery or defence of provinces in France. The only time that the Plantagenet Kings were able to devote the best part of their thoughts and resources to purely British problems was during the century that followed the final loss of Normandy and preceded the outbreak of the Hundred Years' War. During that period there was only one great King, Edward I, and in his reign, as we should expect, the power of mediæval England in Wales, Ireland and Scotland reached its high-water mark. After his death, the incapacity of Edward II, and the preoccupation of all later Kings before the Tudors with the extravagant attempt to conquer France or with resultant civil troubles at home, destroyed English rule in all Scotland and in nearly all Ireland, and weakened it even in Wales. *1214–1337.*

When we last looked towards Ireland it was in the heaviest midnight of the Dark Ages, when the light of learning sparkled in that distant corner of the world, casting back gleams on the opaque ignorance of Scotland and England, Germany and France.[1] The saints, artists and learned men of Irish monasticism shone by their individual merits and were free from the bondage of organization. Institutionalism was as abhorrent to the early Irish Church as to the tribal system from which it sprang. It followed that the Irish clergy never helped, as the Saxon clergy had done, to organize their race in a united Church and a single State. When the zeal and inspiration of the early saints died away, they left nothing behind but memories, and Ireland was little less dark and distracted than she had been before.

Even the suzerainty formerly exercised over the other chiefs by the ' High Kings ' at Tara had become in the Eleventh Century a mere title. The career of Brian Boru, King of Cashel in Munster, the racial hero against the Viking invaders, did not permanently strengthen the ' High Kingship ' or unite the Celts. But the victory of Clontarf on his death's day saved Ireland from the Norsemen and confined the Danes to the towns they had founded such as Dublin, Waterford and Limerick. Town life and trade *1014.*

[1] See p. 55, above.

H 2

had no attraction for the native. Cattle-feeding and cattle-lifting, tribal war and family feud, minstrelsy and a little agriculture still occupied the time and thoughts of the Celtic tribes, as of many other tribes all the world over for many thousand years in times gone by. It is a matter of opinion whether or not these simple folk were better employed than the new restless Europe with its Crusades and Hildebrandine movements, its stone castles and cathedrals, its feudalism, its charters, its trade-routes and all the stir of modernity. But for good or for evil the time had gone by when a European race could, with impunity, remain primitive. To eschew defensive armour, castles and feudalism in the days of Strongbow was as dangerous as to eschew machine guns and the industrial revolution in our own.

The Irish, therefore, were regarded as savages, almost outside the pale of Papal Christendom. It is true that in the first half of the Twelfth Century Saint Malachy and other Irishmen began a movement for Church reform. The excessive number of Irish Bishops was reduced, in order to enhance the episcopal authority ; a gallant attempt was made to rekindle the religious zeal of the laity, to enforce the payment of tithe, and approximate the Church a little to the Roman model. But it was the armed invaders from England who gave full power to the influences which in the end attached Ireland irrevocably to Rome. The reforming Church party in Ireland was willing, in the absence of any strong national feeling, to welcome and abet Strongbow and the English. Adrian IV, the only English Pope in history, had commissioned Henry II to conquer the island if he liked, as the best means of bringing it into the Roman fold.

Henry II was too busy on the continent to take up the Irish question himself. The conquest was, however, begun in his reign by private adventurers from Wales, led by Richard de Clare, Earl of Pembroke, nicknamed Strongbow. His partners in this last of the Norman conquests were not pure Normans, nor pure Anglo-Normans. Many of them, like the famous Fitzgeralds, were sons of Welsh mothers. They were a special border breed, these ' Marcher lords ' ; and their soldiers were many of them Welsh or Flemings. Perhaps the Celtic element in the blood and experience of these first ' English ' conquerors of Ireland helped their descendants to mingle only too easily with the native Irish and adapt their own feudal institutions to the tribalism of the Celtic world beyond the Dublin ' pale.' Possibly pure Normans or Anglo-Normans might have stamped more of their own character and institutions on this land, as they did on so many others.

But no Norman intruders in England, Sicily or Scotland ever

1169–
1171.

showed themselves superior in warlike efficiency to the followers
of Strongbow. His chain-clad knights were supported by archers,
whose skill was then the speciality not of England but of Wales.
The unarmoured infantry of the Irish tribes, fighting with the
Danish battle-axe and hurling stones and javelins, were helpless
against the best archers and some of the best cavalry in Europe.
The only refuge of the natives was the marshes, woods and
mountains of their roadless and unreclaimed island. They knew
all the arts of guerrilla war, using felled trees and earthworks to
block the narrow passages through forest and bog. But the
opposition to the invaders was not truly national. They found
many allies both among tribesmen and churchmen. Dermot,
who had invited over Strongbow, was not in his own lifetime
universally execrated as the traitor that he appeared in the
distant retrospect.

Castle-building was the cement of Anglo-Norman rule in
Ireland, as in the sister island. Here, too, the Celt was at a
great disadvantage, for the only resistance behind permanent
fortifications which the invaders had to encounter was in the
port-towns of the Danes. But since the battle of Clontarf, the
Danes in Ireland had become peaceful traders instead of warrior
Vikings, and moreover they were few in number. Their towns
were easily captured, and were transformed at a stroke from
Scandinavian to English. The citizens of Bristol were given
the right to inhabit Dublin. Dublin Castle, first erected by the
Vikings, became the centre of Saxon rule in Ireland from the
Twelfth to the Twentieth Century.

The Danes were massacred or returned to Scandinavia, making
way for the conquerors, who henceforward held in these port-
towns the keys of entry into the island. Celtic town life did not
yet exist. Even towns like Galway in the far west were of Anglo-
Norman origin. Only towards the end of the Middle Ages, the
English inhabitants of the towns outside the Dublin pale gradually
adopted the speech of the surrounding population with whom they
bartered, and became by intermarriage and otherwise scarcely
less Irish than English.

At the time of Strongbow's conquest and for long afterwards,
national feeling did not exist, and foreign rule would have been
accepted on its merits. All that was then necessary to put the
races on a friendly understanding was strong and just government. But throughout the Middle Ages the government was
neither strong nor just. Henry II, the father of rebellious sons,
and the embarrassed ruler over half of western Christendom, had
perforce to limit the liabilities which Strongbow had created
for him, for he had neither time, money, nor men to establish

his own rule in the island, in anything more than name. Yet, while he could not afford to keep up an effective royal government, he dared not let Strongbow or any of the feudal leaders obtain Viceregal authority. The adventurers therefore continued to prey on the natives, and to carve out baronies for themselves, fighting for their own hands without either proper support or proper control from the English King. For more than a century the Conquest went forward, slowly enlarging its boundaries westward, meeting no determined resistance from the natives, but divided and uncertain in its own purpose, and bringing in its train neither justice nor even a strong tyranny.

In these circumstances there grew up that three-fold division of the island which, with continual variation of boundary, held good throughout the rest of the Middle Ages. There was the ' Pale ' round Dublin, where English law was administered as in an English shire. Far in the west lay the purely Celtic chiefs and tribes, threatened but still untouched by the invasion. And between these two Irelands, and intermingled with them both, lay the areas of mixed rule, the baronies where the descendants of the great adventurers bore sway from their castles over the native population. But their Norman-Welsh feudalism was gradually transformed into something very like the Celtic tribalism which it was intended to replace. If, long afterwards, with all the differences of religion, the descendants of so many of Cromwell's soldiers were quickly absorbed into the Celtic atmosphere around them, it is no wonder that the same evolution took place in the case of the Anglo-Irish Barons. Throughout the greater part of the island English rule had been built upon the foundation of an Irish bog.

In the reign of Edward I, the greater attention paid at that period to insular affairs enabled Ireland to enjoy a brief spell of prosperity, especially in Leinster and Meath where the English interest was strongest. Villages sprang up and agriculture spread under the protecting shadow of the castles. Trading towns like Dublin, Waterford and Cork pushed their commerce oversea.

Then came one of those rapid wrong turnings, so habitual in Irish history. Edward I's attempt to conquer Scotland led to reprisals under his feeble son. Immediately after Bannockburn the Scots under the Bruce brothers broke into Ireland through Ulster, where in all ages they have had strong connections. The delicate prosperity of the new Ireland was destroyed with fire and sword, and the English influence never recovered for two centuries. The invasion of the Bruces was rather the occasion than the cause of the collapse. At bottom it was due to the

1315–
1318.

character and power of the Anglo-Irish baronage, ever less distinguishable from the Celtic chiefs, and ever enlarging the boundaries of their rule at the expense of the genuinely English colony.

The Pale grew narrower both in space and in spirit. The English settlers and officials, increasingly conscious that they were a garrison in an alien land, cooped up and hard beset, drew in upon their own company and their own ideals of life.

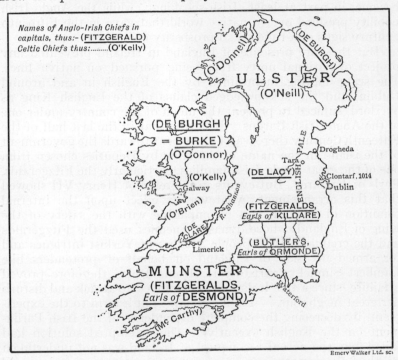

Names of Anglo-Irish Chiefs in capitals, thus:- (FITZGERALD)
Celtic Chiefs thus:.........(O'Kelly)

ULSTER
(O'Neill)

(DE BURGH
= BURKE)
(O'Connor)

(O'Kelly)
Galway

(O'Brien)

(FITZGERALDS,
Earls of KILDARE)

(BUTLER'S,
Earls of ORMONDE)

Limerick

Drogheda
Tara
(DE LACY)
Clontarf, 1014
Dublin

MUNSTER
(FITZGERALDS,
Earls of DESMOND)

(McCarthy)

Emery Walker Ltd. sc.

MAP XII.—Ireland towards the close of the Middle Ages

They came to regard almost everyone and everything outside the Pale ditch as belonging not to the 'English' but the 'Irish' interest. The distinction set the tone to a policy that for centuries was fruitful of mischief. The colonists drew ever more rigidly the line between the two races, and proscribed native law, language and custom, so far as their little power extended in pre-Tudor times.

The Hundred Years' War with France distracted England's attention yet further from the overseas possession where her real duty lay. In the interval between the two parts of that long struggle, Richard II came with an army to Ireland. Then he

fell, and no English King set foot in Ireland again until William
of Orange. The utter neglect of Ireland by the rival Houses
of Lancaster and York completed the relapse to Celtic tribalism
outside the Pale, and, in spite of the efforts of one section of the
colonists, Irish language and custom spread among the English
of the Pale itself. The native civilization had indeed profited
by the conquerors whom it had absorbed. Town life had been
started ; most of the towns founded by Danes and English had
become, in part at least, Irish-speaking ; while the Anglo-Irish
nobility presided over a native world that gave in the Fifteenth
Century signs of a rude social prosperity of its own.

But the bare presence of England in Ireland prevented any
project of national unity from being pursued on native lines.
The scant footing maintained by the English in and around
Dublin, and the acknowledged claims of the English King as
overlord, sufficed to prevent the union of the country under one
of the Anglo-Irish Barons. It is true that in the last half of the
Fifteenth Century there was a movement towards the government
of the island in the name of the King by Deputies chosen from
one of the great Anglo-Irish families, particularly the Fitzgeralds,
Earls of Kildare. But events in the reign of Henry VII showed
that this arrangement, whatever its effect upon the internal
condition of Ireland, was incompatible with the safety of the
King of England, whose dynastic enemies used the Fitzgeralds
and the credulous Irish people as allies of Yorkist intrigues and
1487.   for armed invasion of England on behalf of pretenders like
Lambert Simnel. ' Aristocratic Home Rule' therefore proved
a failure, since a free Ireland was employed to attack and disturb
1494.   her great neighbour. ' Poynings' law ' put a term to the experiment, by decreeing the complete dependence of the Irish Parliament on the English executive. The attempted solution had
failed, but the actual reconquest of Ireland was not undertaken
till the following century.

England had proved too weak to conquer and govern Ireland, but strong enough to prevent her from learning to govern
herself. It is significant that the island which had once been
the lamp to Europe's ignorance was almost alone of European
countries in having no University when the Middle Ages came to
an end. It was a sorry heritage overseas which the mediæval
English handed on to the English of the Reformation. They had
neglected Ireland for centuries when a forward and active policy
might have saved the situation ; when the policy of real conquest was adopted under the Tudors it was in an age too late,
an age of religious cleavage, commercial competition and national
self-consciousness all in their crudest form.

The relation of the Celt to his neighbour has proved more happy in Britain than in Ireland. And again we must look to mediæval history to see why.

In the latter stages of the Anglo-Saxon conquest, the remaining territories of the Cymri or Welsh had been cut by the English advance into three separated parts—Strathclyde in the north, Wales in the centre, and the Devonian-Cornish peninsula in the south. See Map V., p. 41, above. Their collective power of racial resistance was greatly reduced by their geographic isolation from one another, which was rendered complete by their enemies' command of the sea from the Isle of Man, the Vikings' centre of operations, and from the great port-towns of Chester and Bristol. Before the Norman Conquest, Scandinavian settlers had already given a thoroughly Nordic character to the Lake District and North Lancashire,[1] while Devon had been so far colonized by the Saxons of Wessex that it has ever since been regarded as an integral and characteristic part of the life of England. Cornwall remained as a pocket of Celtic race and language, but too small and isolated to give trouble on that score. Conquered in Anglo-Saxon times and closely annexed to the English Crown, it was subjected to Norman feudalism as Domesday Book records, and subsequently to mediæval English law. But it spoke a Celtic tongue of its own until Stuart times, and it preserves a regional and Celtic character in its population to this day.

The larger problem of Wales remained. The wide extent of its mountain area had brought the Saxon Conquest to a halt behind Offa's Dyke. But the mountains which kept back the English prevented the union of the Welsh. In Edward the Confessor's reign, Harold made headway westward, and secured the alliance of some of the Celtic tribes ever at feud with one another, thus opening a road to further advance under the Normans.

From William the Conqueror till the accession of Edward I the most successful efforts to subdue Wales were made, not by the Kings of England, but by the ' Marcher Lords ' and their private armies, men of the type of Strongbow and the Fitzgeralds. In blood a mixture of Norman, English and Welsh, they represented feudal government and English economic penetration rather than the English monarchy. At one time there were reckoned to be 143 Lords Marcher, and wherever a Marcher Lord carved out for himself an estate with the sword, he built a castle and proceeded to exact feudal dues from the inhabitants, and to enforce in his own court feudal law, English law or fragments of Welsh tribal custom. Under his protection English-speaking

[1] See note, p. 44, above.

colonists,—military, farming and trading,—settled on the land he ruled. He was in reality a petty sovereign, representing the intrusion of a new race and a more elaborate civilization.

The Anglo-Norman invasion conquered the lowlands and penetrated up the valley bottoms, because the valleys were the only gates of entry into the roadless mountains, and because they contained the arable land. But as the valleys themselves were frequently choked up with forest and marsh, the process was slow. The English had to play the part of pioneer farmers, as well as of warriors ever on the alert.

Before the coming of the Anglo-Normans, the Welsh had been a pastoral rather than an agricultural people. They did not inhabit towns, villages or even houses, but lived in huts of boughs which they twisted together for a few months' occupation, as they followed their flocks and herds from winter to summer ground upon the mountain side. But whenever these simple tribesmen saw their valley dominated by a Norman castle of timber or stone, with a feudal court and an English-speaking agricultural village attached, one part of them fled higher into the neighbouring hills in pursuit of freedom. Others remained below as vassals of the new lord, but were often at heart faithful to the tribal chief exiled onto the neighbouring mountains, whence he was perpetually returning in destructive raids upon the vale.

To imagine such a situation in fifty different valleys is to get some idea of the chaos that Wales must have presented in the Twelfth Century. Tribalism and feudalism were struggling for the land. And mountain barriers separated district from district, increasing the tendency inherent in both tribalism and feudalism to divide political authority into fragments. In the hills tribe fought against tribe, and in the valleys Baron fought against Baron, while every baronial valley was at war with its tribal hills.

Yet civilization was advancing, however slow and however bloody the process. Time was on the side of the invaders, who were near to their own bases and were perpetually recruited by sea and land, unlike the forlorn hope of Anglo-Norman civilization, derelict among the bogs of Ireland. Ships from the great ports of Bristol and Chester commanded all the valley mouths of Wales that ran into the sea; while, inland, the upper valley of the Severn gave the invaders an easy route from Shrewsbury into the heart of the country, enabling them to overrun Powys and cut off Gwynedd in the North from Dinefawr in the South. Pembroke was planted from the sea by so many industrious English and Flemings that it lost the use of the Celtic tongue and became known as 'little England beyond Wales.' But even at the height of their power the Lords Marcher were never able to subdue the Gwynedd district centred round the impenetrable fastnesses of Snowdon.

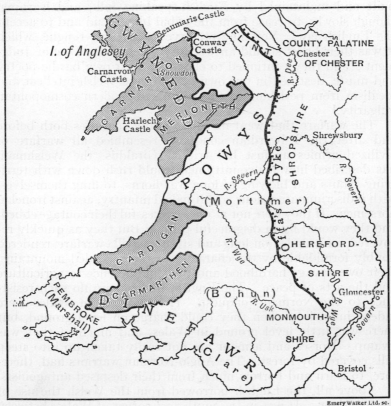

The Principality (shaded) as delimited by Edward I. is in two parts, Gwynedd, and Cardigan-Carmarthen

All except the Principality and the English border counties may be regarded as normally Marcher Lordships.

Names of some of the chief Marcher Lords in brackets thus:- (Bohun)

MAP XIII.—Mediæval Wales

The Lords Marcher represented a type of government more backward than that of England but more advanced than that of tribal Wales. Bohun, Mortimer and the other Marcher families were an element of disturbance in the English polity, because they were accustomed to fighting and feudalism while the nobles and gentry of England proper were becoming accustomed to peace and centralized government. But to the tribal Celts the

civilization forcibly imported by the Marcher Lords meant progress. All through the Middle Ages the native Welsh, in imitation
of their English lords and neighbours, were slowly taking to
agriculture, erecting permanent houses, trading in market-towns
built and maintained by English-speaking folk, and learning,
though slowly, to cease from the tribal blood feud and to accept
the English law. Yet they preserved their own tongue, which
it was their boast should answer for Wales at the Day of Judgment ; and they continued to elaborate their own bardic poetry
and music, destined in our own day to save Welsh intellect and
idealism from perishing in the swamp of modern cosmopolitan
vulgarity.[1]

The warfare that went on for so many centuries both before
and after the Edwardian conquest, resembled all warfare of
civilized armies against hill tribes. Giraldus, the Welshman,
has described how his countrymen would rush down with terri-
fying shouts and blowing of long war horns, to fling themselves,
with indiscriminate valour, a half-naked infantry, against ironclad
horsemen. If they were not at once successful their courage ebbed,
and they would fly in disgraceful panic. But they as quickly recovered, and carried on long and stern guerrilla warfare, rendered
doubly formidable by the character of their wooded mountains,
their own savage hardihood and their indifference to agriculture
and the arts of peace. The English had put up no such resistance to the Norman Conquest. The invaders of Wales were
indeed invincible when they could charge on level ground, but
there was little level ground in Wales, and much of that was
swamp. Horses and armour are not easily taken up into steep
hills covered by forest. The Anglo-Norman warriors had, therefore, to learn and borrow much from their despised antagonists.

Above all, the English borrowed from the Welsh the use of
the long-bow. It was in the south-east corner of Wales, between
the upper waters of the Wye and the Bristol Channel, that this
famous weapon first emerged into local fame. As early as the
reign of Henry II it had been known, in Welsh hands, to pin a
knight's armoured thigh through his saddle to the horse's side.
Eighty years later there were Welsh archers with de Montfort
at Lewes, but they still attracted less notice in England than the
crossbowmen. It was Edward I's experience in Welsh campaign-
ing that determined him to adopt the long-bow as the special
weapon of his infantry in his Scottish wars. It is true that in an

[1] About 1200 A.D. Giraldus the Welshman wrote of his countrymen words
which are equally true of them to-day : ' In their musical concerts they do
not sing in unison like the inhabitants of other countries, but in many different
parts ; so that in a company of singers, which one very frequently meets with in
Wales, you will hear as many different parts and voices as there are performers.'

Assize of Arms of Henry III's reign certain classes of English freemen had, for the first time, been required to possess bows of some sort. But it was the Welsh who taught Edward I and his subjects what a ' long-bow ' really meant. Not till the Fourteenth Century can it fairly be called the English national weapon, when it crossed the seas to affright the feudal chivalry of Europe at Crecy and Poitiers.

In the early years of the Thirteenth Century a Welsh national revival took place. It was displayed not only in a fresh effervescence of bardic poetry, but in a movement to unite all the tribes under the hegemony of the Llewelyn princes, who ruled over Gwynedd, among the fastnesses of Snowdon and in the rich grain-bearing island of Anglesey, sheltered behind that lofty barrier. North Wales summoned all Wales to unite and be free. Llewelyn the Great reconquered much of Powys from 1194–the Marcher Lords. He was a prudent diplomatist as well as 1240. a great warrior, for while he called on his countrymen to rally round him as the native Prince acclaimed by the Bards, he never forgot that he was also a great feudal magnate, owing allegiance to the Crown, and could as such play a part in English faction most helpful to his other rôle as Welsh patriot. By the judicious policy of joining the Barons' party in England, he secured for Welsh rights three clauses of John's Magna Carta.

His grandson Llewelyn ap Griffith carried on the same double policy and allied himself with Simon de Montfort. He still 1246–further enlarged the area of his Welsh Principality at the expense 1283. of the ever divided and quarrelsome Lords Marcher, many of whom were forced to do him homage. At length he began to dream of complete separation from England. He went out of his way to defy Edward I, who was more than ready to take up the challenge. That was the beginning of the end of Welsh independence.

In the greatest of Edward's numerous Welsh campaigns he 1277. surrounded the unapproachable Snowdon fastnesses by sea and land and starved Llewelyn and his mountaineers into surrender. After another rebellion, provoked by harsh government regardless of Celtic laws and susceptibilities, another war resulted in 1282–another conquest and a better settlement. Royal castles such 1284. as Conway, Carnarvon, Beaumaris and Harlech rose to make the King's authority in North Wales as secure as feudal authority in the centre and south. Edward divided up Llewelyn's ' Principality ' into shires on the English model,—Carnarvon, Anglesey, Merioneth, Flint, Cardigan and Carmarthen,—and soon afterwards gave to his infant son, Edward, born at Carnarvon, the title of ' Prince of Wales.' But the ' Principality ' was not yet a part of England, and all the rest of Wales remained to the Lords Marcher.[1]

Edward I would fain have abolished the feudal independence of the Marcher Lords, by subjecting their jurisdictions to a strict *quo warranto* inquiry. But he had not the power to do it, and he had need of their co-operation to keep down the spirit of the Welsh, perpetually incited by Bards recounting the glories of the House of Llewelyn. Until the Tudor reforms, Wales remained divided between the feudal territories of the Lords Marcher on the one hand, and on the other the Celtic Principality, ostensibly governed by English law, but with a large allowance for tribal custom. In both districts English and Welsh were slowly learning to mix and to co-operate. Civilization was creeping forward with the growth of towns, trade and agriculture.

Nevertheless, by any standard of English comparison, Wales in the Fourteenth and Fifteenth Centuries was a scene of tribal feud, baronial violence and official tyranny and extortion. In the troubled times of Henry IV, Owen Glendower, reviving the policy of Llewelyn the Great, made play with the rivalries of English factions while appealing to the hopes and grievances of his race. This wonderful man, an attractive and unique figure in a period of debased and selfish politics, actually revived for a few years the virtual independence of a great part of his country, at the cost of wars that proved utterly disastrous to the economic life of Wales, both in the Principality and in the Marches. The Welsh and English districts, which were then found side by side in the same county and even in the same feudal manor, were again set by the ears, and the necessary amalgamation of the two races into the modern Welsh people was further delayed. Even after the death of Glendower and the re-establishment of English rule, the King's Peace was but poorly enforced. Between Celtic and feudal anarchy, Wales remained a paradise for the robber and the homicide, so long as the Crown was preoccupied with adventures in France and dynastic strife in England.

The disorders alike of the Principality and of the March lands preserved the military habits of the Welsh so long, that even after the Tudor pacification poets still regarded them as

> An old and haughty nation, proud in arms.

They followed the military life not only at home but in the King's armies in Scotland and France, while in every English Civil War from Henry III to Charles I it was always found

---

[1] The whole of Wales is now often called the ' Principality,' but in Edward's time the ' Principality ' contained only these half-dozen counties.

easier to recruit infantry among the poor of Wales than among the settled and peaceable English. The Wars of the Roses were to a large extent a quarrel among Marcher Lords. For the great Lords Marcher were closely related to the English throne, and had estates and political interests both in England and in the Welsh March. Harry Bolingbroke of Hereford and Lancaster was a great possessor of Welsh lands, as also were his rivals, the Mortimers. The House of York, Warwick the Kingmaker, and Richard III's Buckingham were all in one way or another connected with Wales and the Marches. Such men brought a fighting element into English constitutional and dynastic faction. Because mediæval England had left half done its task of conquering Wales for civilization, Welsh tribalism and feudalism revenged themselves by poisoning the Parliamentary life and disturbing the centralized government of its neglectful overlords. But when at length a Welsh army put a Welsh Tudor Prince upon the throne at Bosworth Field, Wales supplied a remedy to those ills in the English body politic which she had helped to create.

The history of Scotland presents yet another version of the contact of Saxon with Celt. Wales and Ireland were both eventually forced to submit to England's rule more completely and for a longer time than Scotland, yet they both remain to this day far more Celtic in character. The apparent paradox is explained if we remember that the wealthiest and most important districts inhabited by the Celt in Scotland had already adopted Anglo-Norman language and institutions before the struggle for national independence began in the time of Edward I. Resistance to England was not therefore identified with Celtic speech and tribal traditions, as in mediæval Ireland and Wales. The wars of the Edwards against Wallace and Bruce were a struggle between two kindred nations, each organized as a feudal monarchy. The analogy to Irish or Welsh mediæval history is to be found rather in England's conquest of the Highland tribes after Culloden.

It had indeed seemed likely, in the Dark Ages, that Scotland would emerge as a Celtic Kingdom with a Saxon fringe along the lowlands of her eastern coast. For the union of the Picts and Scots under the Scot, Kenneth Macalpine, had enabled them to impose a name and a dynasty on the land from the Celtic capital at Scone. But history began to revolve in the other direction when Lothian, the part of Saxon Northumbria that lay to the north of Tweed and Cheviot, was detached from its southern connections and converted into an integral part of Scotland.[1]

844.

See Map VI., p. 56, above.

[1] See p. 79, above.

English Miles
0 5 10 20 30 40 50 60

Orkneys

Hebrides

NORSE SETTLEMENTS

THE GAELIC SPEAKING

TRIBAL

HIGHLANDS

beyond the "Highland Line"

as it was defined in later times.

Inverness

The "Highland Line"

Aberdeen

Iona

Scone Dundee
Perth   *R. Tay*
        St. Andrews

×Stirling, 1297   *R. Forth*

Bannock-
burn, 1314   ×Falkirk   Leith
             1298   ×Pinkie
R. Clyde   1547
Glasgow   Edinburgh   LOTHIAN

Holyrood
Lanark   Melrose   Berwick
         Peebles   *R. Tweed*   ×Flodden, 1513
         Selkirk   EAST
                               MARCH
Ayr   Jedburgh   *Cheviots*   Alnwick
                                      Castle

         Liddisdale Otterburn
         WEST MIDDLE MARCH 1388
Annan MARCH

GALLOWAY Dumfries   Newcastle *R. Tyne*

              Hexham
      Carlisle   COUNTY PALATINE
      Nevilles Cross 1346 × Durham
Naworth Castle   OF DURHAM
         R. Eden   *R. Tees*

                    Northallerton
              Battle of the Standard
                          1138 ×

Emery Walker Ltd. sc.

MAP XIV.—Mediæval Scotland and North England

The change was a natural result of the dissolution of the Kingdom of Northumbria under the blows of the Viking invasions. After many generations of warfare between Celt and Saxon in the heart of Scotland, Lothian was acknowledged, in the time of Canute, to be a possession of the Scottish Crown.

1018.

It was in the newly acquired territory of English-speaking Lothian, with its rich agricultural soil and its rock-fortress of Edinburgh, that the Scottish Kingship, which had been Celtic, tribal and North-Western in origin, became Anglo-Norman, feudal and South-Eastern by choice. Led or driven by the monarchy, Strathclyde and Galloway, though very largely Celtic in race, eventually adopted English speech and feudal organization. We can only notice one or two of the more obvious stages in that long, complicated and obscure process of evolution.

First, before the period of Anglo-Norman influence, came the period of purely English influence in the last half of the Eleventh Century. Malcolm III, before he dethroned Macbeth, had spent his boyhood in exile in the England of Edward the Confessor. The English proclivities of his education were enhanced in later life by his second marriage with the saintly and strong-minded Margaret, sister of Edgar Atheling. As Queen of Scotland she did much to strengthen the English language and the Roman ecclesiastical system against Celtic tradition. Her pertinacious efforts, far from popular with the tribes and priests of Celtic Scotland, were helped by the catastrophe that had befallen her own race and lineage in England after the battle of Hastings. The first result of Norman conquest down south was to drive over the Border troops of Saxon and Scandinavian exiles of all classes, from Margaret herself to the hinds of Yorkshire and Durham fleeing from the red wrath of William and his 'harrying of the North.' The Nordic element in Scotland, based on the Saxons of Lothian, was greatly strengthened by these refugees.

Reigned 1057–1093.

English influence prepared the way for Anglo-Norman penetration that followed hard on its heels. David I, a worthy son of Malcolm and Margaret, took advantage of the paralysis of England under Stephen to build Scotland anew in the form of a Norman feudal monarchy, and to appropriate as much as possible of the disputed territories in Cumberland, Northumberland and Durham. His successes beyond Tweed and Cheviot were not permanent, and the Border between the two Kingdoms gradually took its present shape when England recovered her strength under the Plantagenets. But David's invasions of North England during the anarchy of Stephen had served to reveal how vain was the courage of the disorderly and savage clansmen of Scotland charging with their claymores, as compared to mail-clad feudal

1124–1153.

knights, whether of England or of Scotland. This had been
1138. demonstrated at the Battle of the Standard, near Northallerton.
There is no wonder that the Scottish Kings embarked on a
policy of change deliberately aimed at the extinction of tribalism
and Celtic institutions.

Warriors of Norman or English race, like the Bruces and
Balliols, were invited over the Border by King David, and given
by him baronies in Scotland, to be held on terms of feudal
service. There was no large displacement of existing proprietors,
as in conquered England after Hastings ; for this was Norman
penetration, not Norman conquest. Estates of the Crown
and unused lands, both very extensive, enabled David to create
baronies for the new-comers without resorting to wholesale confiscation. But the Celtic tribal inhabitants, or the colonists of
newly occupied waste land, found themselves placed in a strictly
feudal relation to their Anglo-Norman overlords, who knew how
to make their new-fangled claims respected. Everywhere, as in
contemporary England, rose the circular mound with the timber
or stone tower on the top, whence the armoured cavalry ruled
and judged the countryside.

And beside the castle rose the parish church, for the
country was divided under Anglo-Norman auspices into parishes
on the English system. The parish was often coterminous with
the fief of the new lord. Religion as well as government was
territorialized, and St. Columba's Church became a ghost and a
memory, like the tribes to which it had ministered. King David
and his nobility vied with each other in pious bequests and endowments of the feudal type. The Twelfth and Thirteenth Centuries
were the great age of ecclesiastical architecture in Scotland.
Stately Cathedrals and Abbeys rose, destined to perish at the
hands of English moss-troopers or Scottish reformers. From the
first the people resented the tithes and other novel burdens laid
on them in David's reign for the benefit of an alien clergy. And
ere long the attitude of the Barons to the Church became little
more than a desire to secure the ecclesiastical endowments for
their own families,—a desire gratified by many curious devices,
such as warrior nobles masquerading as churchmen, until the
Reformation introduced more direct methods.

David and his immediate successor, William the Lion, re-
produced many of the features of the English State with remarkable success. The Shire system and the King's justice were
brought in gradually, though much limited by the franchises of
the Barons. Scottish ' burghs ' received royal charters to elect
their own magistrates, even more freely than the wealthier and
more populous ' boroughs ' of England.

The new Scotland was able to take shape and solidify, because she remained so long on tolerable terms with England. During the century and a half before the era of the wars of independence, the nobles of Scotland served King and country better than they ever did again. They and their vassals spread the use of the English language, nomenclature and institutions so successfully that these were the institutions for which Scots under Wallace and Bruce were prepared to die. The world of Celtic tribalism passed away out of the Western Lowlands, making less armed resistance than we should expect, save in fierce Galloway, where things Celtic lived longest and died hardest. With his formidable following of mail-clad feudal cavalry, the King could disregard those Celtic tribal chiefs who refused to become feudal lords. The old order gradually shrank into the mountain area of the Northern Highlands, where tribal Scotland survived intact until 1746. South and east of the Highland Line men gradually adopted the names, manners and language of the new regime. *[1124–1286.]*

While these great changes were in process, Crown and baronage were still necessary to each other, and both were still necessary to the best interests of the youthful nation. It was only when the war of independence against Edward I put that new-made nation to the test, that the Barons proved less responsive than the commons to the novel creed of patriotism, because feudalism is international, and their estates in England involved them in a dual allegiance. And it was only after the Scottish monarchy had established itself in the hearts and habits of the people, that the baronage became its constant and most dangerous foe.

The golden age of mediæval Scotland came to an end when Alexander III's horse carried him over a sea-cliff. His surviving heir was his grand-daughter Margaret, ' the maid of Norway,' a girl who resided in Scandinavia during her brief reign. By the Treaty of Brigham it was arranged that she should marry the first English ' Prince of Wales,' afterwards Edward II of England. The peaceable union of the whole island was close in sight. The crowns of Scotland and of England would meet on one head, but the two countries would be administered as separate realms, much as afterwards took place when James VI of Scotland became James I of England. But the course of history was not to be thus foreshortened. The Scots have seldom had luck with young Queens brought from oversea. That very autumn the Maid of Norway died in the Orkneys on her voyage home. *[1286.] [1290.]*

The chance of a peaceful solution died with the Maid. Edward I, pressing the claims of ancient English Kings to be

overlords of Scotland, asserted his right to act as arbitrator between the various claimants to the vacant throne, of whom the chief were John Balliol and Robert Bruce. He decided in favour of Balliol, justly it would appear. But, not content with that, he treated Balliol as a puppet and Scotland as a subject land. Balliol, goaded to desperation, renounced his allegiance to his oppressive overlord. But he received little support from
1296. a divided and jealous baronage, and was easily deposed by Edward, who marched in triumph through the land, carried off the coronation stone from Scone to Westminster, and made himself direct King of Scotland. The Ragman Roll contains the long list of the Scots nobles who did him homage.

All seemed finished. All in fact was about to begin. Deserted by her nobles, Scotland discovered herself. The governors whom Edward I left behind him were incapable and cruel, and the foreign soldiery made the Scots feel their subjection
1297. In the following May a guerrilla chief of genius, a tall man of iron strength, who suddenly appears on the page of history as if from nowhere, defeated at Stirling Bridge end an English army under its blundering feudal chief the Earl of Warenne, of *quo Warranto* fame. Thence William Wallace broke ravaging into Northumberland and Cumberland.

This unknown knight, with little but his great name to identify him in history, had lit a fire which nothing since has ever put out. Here, in Scotland, a few years before the very similar doings in Switzerland, a new ideal and tradition of wonderful potency was brought into the world ; it had no name then, but now we should call it democratic patriotism. It was not the outcome of theory. The unconscious qualities of a people had given it reality in a sudden fit of rage. Theories of nationhood and theories of democracy would follow afterwards to justify or explain it. Meanwhile, it stood up, a fact.

Edward I had thought that he was going to yoke Scotland to England through the ordinary feudal apparatus of the time. His mistake was very natural, for by the accepted standards of the day, his proceedings were less abnormal than Wallace's amazing appeal to the Scottish democracy to save the Scottish nation. Nowadays, indeed, we expect as a matter of course to find both national feeling and democratic instincts in every part of Europe. But in mediæval times things were very different. Society was divided, not perpendicularly into nations, but horizontally into feudal strata. And Edward I had the feudal magnates of Scotland mainly on his side. Anglo-Normans, owning estates in England as well as Scotland, were excusably lukewarm in their Scottish patriotism and anxious not to quarrel

with England's King, from whom they held their English
lands.

But the Scottish people had national feeling and democratic
feeling, both hitherto unconscious and unexercised. Wallace
called them into activity. The burghers and peasants, led
by the lairds or small gentry of whom Wallace himself was
one, defied the power of England and when necessary defied the
power of their own Scottish nobles. The 'schiltrons,' thick
masses of plebeian spearmen, standing shoulder to shoulder,
withstood on many a field the onset of the armoured English
knights and their horses, who had made short work of the Celtic
clan charge in Wales and Ireland. Here was a steadier spirit,
and the discipline of a more settled civilization. But on other
occasions the Scottish schiltrons were broken by the irresistible
combination of feudal chivalry with Welsh or English long-
bowmen, whose arrows prepared a passage for the horsemen
through the ranks of death. Falkirk, which put an end to **1298.**
the effective part of Wallace's career, was but the first of
many English victories won by these tactics.

But to defeat the Scottish army now and again was not to
conquer Scotland. The common people were accustomed to the
state of war, and every peasant was a warrior. In that at least
Scotland resembled rough Wales rather than peaceful England.
The Scots were ready to fire their huts and lay waste their
country in front of the invader rather than give in, and again
and again they were called on to put this stern virtue into practice.
Two things decided the long-doubtful issue in favour of Scottish
independence : the personality of Robert Bruce, and after his
death the distraction of Edward III with the Hundred Years'
War in France.

Robert Bruce, grandson of the claimant of 1290, had been
brought up in no tradition of high-flown Scottish patriotism.
Both he and his father had adopted the trimming politics common
among the nobility ; he had changed sides more than once in the
days of Wallace. But he was betrayed into the path of duty and
heroism by his own fiery temper. When once he had cut the **1306.**
throat of the Red Comyn in the church, he was a hunted outlaw,
and had no choice but to throw himself on the patriotic section
of the Scottish people, and revive the Wallace tradition. In
that he found salvation for himself and his country. To the
democratic traditions of Wallace were now added a much needed
element of feudalism which Bruce and 'the good Sir James'
Douglas could supply, and an element of true Kingship to be
found in Bruce and in Bruce alone.

When the timely death of Edward I left the Scots matched **1307.**

with Edward II, the desperate conditions of their struggle for freedom became more equal. One by one the castles from which the English held down the land were captured and destroyed by those redoubtable men of war, Douglas and Bruce. The crowning victory of Bannockburn, in which the English failed properly to deploy their masses of cavalry or to use their archers to advantage, enabled the homely Scottish schiltrons to thrust the English baronage and knighthood at the spear's point into marsh and stream. Never before or after was there such a destruction of English chivalry. After that, the English carried off the main of their archers and men-at-arms oversea to southern lands where the peasantry had no such spirit.

1314.

The Border warfare of England and Scotland during the centuries that followed Bannockburn went best for the Scots when they fought it with guerrilla tactics. Some rude rhymes known as ' good King Robert's testament ' handed on the supposed advice of Bruce to his people to avoid the open field,—in spite of the great exception of Bannockburn,—and to sacrifice their homes and property again and again to foil the invader. The conditions were indeed unequal for the Scots, demanding in them a marvellous patience, for while they could only raid the comparatively barren lands of Northumberland, Cumberland and Durham, the English moss-troopers and armies again and again harried the richest parts of Scotland, lying as they did within two days' ride of the Cheviot Border.

Scottish independence was won at a heavy price, as most things worth having are won. For two centuries and a half after Bannockburn, Scotland remained a desperately poor, savage, bloodstained land of feudal anarchy, assassination, private war and public treason, with constant Border warfare against England, with a peculiarly corrupt Church, with no flourishing cities, no Parliament worth calling such, and no other institutions that seemed to give promise of a great future. Her democratic instincts had prevented her from being annexed to England, who would have given to her wealth and civilization. But her democratic instincts had done nothing else for her politically, had not kept her feudal nobility in order, still less found expression for the national feeling in any representative system. Her alliance with France, useful militarily against England, was unnatural culturally, and could be no true substitute for the broken connection with her nearer neighbour. What then had Scotland gained by resisting England? Nothing at all,—except her soul, and whatsoever things might come in the end from preserving that.

NOTE

Lines from Bruce's ' testament ':

> ' On fut suld be all Scottis weire,
> By hyll and mosse themselff to reare.
> Let woods for wallis be bow and speire,
> [Let woods instead of castle walls
> be their weapons of defence]
> That innymeis do them no deire.
> In strait places gar keip all store,
> And byrnen ye planeland thaim before.
> Thane sall thai pass away in haist
> When that thai find na thing but waist.
> With wyles and waykings of the nyght
> And mekill noyis maid on hytht
> Thaim sall ye turnen with great affrai,
> As thai were chassit with swerd away.
> This is the consall and intent
> Of gud King Robert's testament.'

But in spite of the first line, the Scottish picked troops, when they raided England, were a *mounted* infantry, riding to battle and dismounting to fight. Froissart has described them on these raids in the reign of Edward III, ' for they are all a horsbacke, without it be the traundals and laggers of the host who folow after, a foote. The knightis and squicrs arc well horsed, and the comon people and other on litell hakeneys and geldyngis ; and they carey with them no cartis, nor chariettis, for the diversities of the montaignes that they must pass through in the countrey of Northumbrelande.' He goes on to describe how each horseman carries a little sack of oatmeal and a metal plate on which to cook it ' in maner of a cracknell or bysket, and that they eate to comfort of all theyr stomakis.' Otherwise they lived on the half-sodden flesh of the cattle they captured *en route*. (Froissart. Lord Berners' translation.)

Froissart also tells us how on one occasion in the reign of Richard II, when the French knights found the Lowlands apparently ruined by an English invasion, ' the people generally made light of it, saying that with six or eight stakes they would soon have new houses, and that they should have cattle enough for provisions from the forests, whither they had been driven for security.' This illustrates the working of the policy of ' Good King Robert's testament.' There was much more woodland in North Britain at that time than in the era of the Stuarts.

BOOKS FOR FURTHER READING

Professor E. Curtis, *History of Mediaeval Ireland* ; Stephen Gwynne, *History of Ireland* ; Mrs. J. R. Green, *The Irish State to* 1014, and *The Making of Ireland* ; Giraldus Cambrensis, *Description of Wales* (trans. *Everyman* Library) ; W. Ll. Williams, *Making of Modern Wales* ; Rhys and Jones, *The Welsh People* ; W. Rees, *South Wales and the March* 1284–1415 ; Tout, *Edward I* ; Hume Brown, *History of Scotland*, Vol. I. ; Andrew Lang, *History of Scotland*, Vol. I. ; Oman, *Art of War in the Middle Ages* ; Scott's *Tales of a Grandfather*, Vol. I.

CHAPTER VI

The Hundred Years' War. Its causes and effects. The Birth of Nationalism. Archery and Yeomanry. English language and patriotic feeling

Kings : Edward III, 1327–1377 ; Richard II, 1377–1399 ; Henry IV,
1399–1413 ; Henry V, 1413–1422 ; Henry VI, 1422–1461

IT is sometimes held that the unity of mediæval Christendom
prevented such wars as those which have devastated Europe at
intervals from the Sixteenth to the Twentieth Century. But
there was, in fact, no unwillingness on men's part to wage war
on one another, and the cruelty with which war was waged
was even greater than in our own day. The desire to kill
was under less restraint of conscience or of custom, but the
means of killing were more restricted. It was not the unity
of Christendom but the limit of man's control over nature,
the inferior methods of locomotion, and the want of political,
administrative and financial machinery to keep and feed large
bodies of men in distant campaigns that prevented wars on the
colossal scale. Europe, still very poor and with no elaborate
system of credit, could not pay for the withdrawal from agriculture of a large proportion of her youth to engage in destruction
as a skilled trade. The small warrior class of feudal Barons and
knights were all-powerful, because they and their paid followers
held a monopoly in the profession of arms. From the Eleventh
to the Fifteenth Century, wars on the continent were numerous
and local, instead of few and large like those of modern times.
The arm of Mars was short, but it was kept in continual practice,
and the peasant suffered more constantly from the soldier than
he does to-day.

Perhaps the first European war that can be called national
was the Hundred Years' War as waged by England. The armies
she sent year after year to lay waste and plunder France were
indeed very small, but their efficiency was the outcome of a
national organization and a national spirit. England, on account
of her insular and remote position, and her strong kings, had
since the Norman Conquest outstripped the rest of Europe in
obtaining a certain measure of internal peace, and was passing
from feudalism to nationhood. As soon as King and Parliament
had endowed her with administrative machinery and national
self-consciousness, she exercised these new powers at the expense
of that clumsy giant, the French feudal Kingdom. She became
for a while the plunderer and bully of her continental neighbours,
not because she had less conscience than they, but because she

had more power. In Tudor times the position was to be reversed, when united France and united Spain became each more powerful than England; but her island position saved her from reprisals, and suggested a more profitable outlet to her national energies in commerce and discovery beyond the ocean.

The Hundred Years' War was therefore a question of political dynamics. It is useless to idealize it. The fact that the plundering expeditions of four generations of Englishmen were supposed to be justified by the genealogical claims of Edward III and Henry V to the throne of France, no more proves that the Middle Ages had respect for ' the idea of right,' than the similar dynastic claims of Frederic the Great on Silesia can help the Eighteenth Century in like case. Froissart, much as he admired the English performance which it was his life's work to record, was under no such delusion.

' The English,' he wrote, ' will never love or honour their king, unless he be victorious and a lover of arms and war against their neighbours and especially against such as are greater and richer than themselves. Their land is more fulfilled of riches and all manner of goods when they are at war than in times of peace. They take delight and solace in battles and slaughter : covetous and envious are they above measure of other men's wealth.' ' The King of England must needs obey his people and do all their will.'

Indeed no King could have constrained an unwilling people to wage war oversea for four generations. The Hundred Years' War was not, at bottom, the result of dynastic ambition, but of national, popular and Parliamentary institutions. The new England passed through a phase of expansionist militarism, profitable at first, in the end disastrous.

It was early in the reign of Edward III that English ambitions were diverted from Scotland to France. To pick the famous lily was an enterprise of more profit, ease and honour than to pluck the recalcitrant thistle. When English noblemen, younger sons and yeomen returned from oversea, each brought back his share of booty, perhaps the gold vessels of an abbey, the tapestry of a merchant's house, or a brace of wealthy French knights to ransom ; and each had his stock of tales for an admiring audience, in days when tales held the place in society that books and newspapers hold to-day,—rich tales of adventure, battle, free quarters and free love in the most famous cities and best vineyards of Europe. That way a man cut a finer figure in his own and his neighbour's eyes than when he returned from harrying a thrice-harried Scottish moorland, where he had burnt some empty huts and a few stooks of oats or barley, but found nothing to carry away save the skin of a cow too lame to hobble to the hiding place in the wood.[1]

The modern mind, nursed on the theory and practice of racial nationalism, is astonished that the English should ever have thought it possible to annex France. But for many years the French resisted us less heartily and hardily than the Scots who spoke our own tongue. For Scotland was already a nation in spirit, while France was a loose collection of feudal fiefs. Moreover, when the Hundred Years' War began in 1337, Edward III and his nobles spoke French and were more at home in Gascony than in Scotland.

There were deeper causes of the breach with France than Edward III's dynastic claims to her throne. His possession of Gascony, the last wreck of the old Angevin Empire, was coveted by the French King, who aided the Scots against us. France, moreover, had designs in Flanders against the burgher democracy of Van Artevelde, and we could not brook French predominance in those parts because of our trade interests: our chief export, English-grown wool, was sold to feed the looms at Ghent, Bruges and Ypres, for our cloth manufacture at home was still in its infancy. At sea the English and French traders were perpetually cutting one another's throats, in the Channel and on the route across the Bay to fetch the Gascon wines. The first great action of the war was the battle of Sluys, won by the English merchant navy. After that, Edward III claimed to be lord of the English sea, and the gold noble he struck represents him standing armed and crowned in a ship.

1340.

> Foure things our noble sheweth to me,
> King, ship and sword and power of the sea,

wrote the author of the ' Libel of English Policie,' who in the latter part of the Hundred Years' War put out the first reasoned case for the necessity of sea-power to England. Sea-power was one of the objects of the war, but unfortunately not the chief object.

[1] Froissart's accounts of English proceedings in France and in Scotland, respectively, make this very clear. In the invasion of 1346 he tells us in great detail how ' by the Englishmen was brent, exiled, robbed, wasted and pilled the good, plentiful country of Normandy.' ' The soldiers,' he tells us, ' made no account to the King nor to none of his officers of the gold and silver that they did get. They kept that to themselves.' There is abundant evidence that the English armies of the Fourteenth Century frequently behaved like the Turkish bands to-day, robbing, massacring and burning. Yet the English were not specially inhumane. In mediæval warfare humanity and courtesy were not shown to ' your even Christian,' but only to members of the knightly class male and female, and to clergy and nuns, who often, though by no means' always, obtained respect for their persons, but less often for their property.

Because the struggle was much more than feudal or dynastic, it lasted intermittently for over a hundred years. John had failed to compel the English to fight in defence of his Norman and Angevin possessions. But from Edward III to Henry VI Parliament after Parliament voted supplies for the war, and called to

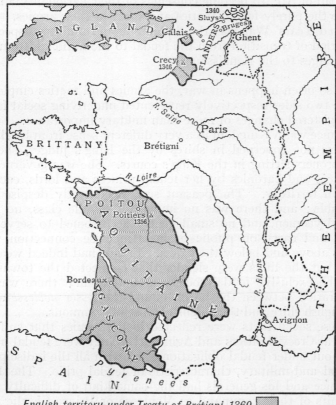

English territory under Treaty of Brétigni, 1360
Boundary of French Kingdom ...._._._.

MAP XV.—France: First Part of Hundred Years' War. Height of Edward III's Power

account Ministers who failed to conduct it with success. Pride in the triumphs of the English archer ' for all the French boast,' the joy of seeing—

> Our King go forth to Normandy
> With grace and might of chivalry,

and return with the proudest princes and nobles of Europe as captives in his procession through London streets, intensified the patriotic sentiment that united all classes of the nation. Hatred

I

of the French was even stronger among the common folk than in the bi-lingual upper class. Therefore we persisted so long in this disastrous enterprise, till our own well-ordered mediæval society was ruined, and till we had twice goaded the French themselves, once under Du Guesclin and again fifty years later under Dunois and Joan of Arc, to become conscious of their nationality and to change the purely feudal tactics and spirit of their armies. The Hundred Years' War was the diplomatic and military aspect of the period of transition from the feudal to the national, from the Middle Ages to the Renaissance.

As so often happens in war, the armies and tactics employed by the two sides respectively represented underlying social facts, and registered changes of more than military importance.

France was a Kingdom in a very different sense from England. She was not governed in shires by the King's judges, sheriffs and coroners sitting in the King's courts. She was governed in provinces and baronies by her feudal princes and lords, each in his own territory. The peasant serf was bitterly despised by the noble ; and there was no important middle class, no substantial yeomen, and no small gentry accustomed to serve the Crown and carry on public business in close connection with classes above and below their own. France had indeed wealthy cities, but the links were slender that connected the townsfolk with the exclusive feudal society around them ; there was no co-operation between the burghers and the lesser *noblesse* as in the English shire and the English House of Commons.

These social facts were reflected in the armies that suffered defeat at Crecy, Poitiers and Agincourt. They were feudal hosts, called out under feudal obligations, and with all the indiscipline, political and military, characteristic of feudal pride. The King of France and his generals had the same kind of difficulty with the units of their command as Montrose or Prince Charlie with the Highland chiefs. The feudal army had no idea of tactics except the unsupported cavalry charge. Its shock had decided the issue of battle for many centuries past, but the English archers put a term to its supremacy on the day of Crecy.

1346.

The best missile troops the French had were Italian mercenaries,—crossbowmen from Genoa. The French peasant, despised in peace, was little regarded in war. His part was to pay the ransom from the estate, when his lord had been carried off to an English manor-house, to hawk and flirt with his captor's family till the money arrived. This method of securing ' reparations ' during the war itself, especially the ransoms extorted

1356.

for the great haul of highborn prisoners at Poitiers, in addition

to the terrible plunderings of the soldiery, goaded the starving
peasants of France into the revolt of the *Jacquerie*, a gesture of 1358.
mere despair.

The English social system was no less faithfully reflected
in the organization and tactics of the invading armies. In the
England of the Edwards, Piers Plowman was in better plight
than Jacques Bonhomme across the Channel. Even the villeins
were relatively wealthy and well-fed, and the proportion of
free-men agriculturists above the status of villein was on the
increase. Indeed the Hundred Years' War covers the greater
part of the period of servile emancipation in England. Now the
Plantagenet Kings had compulsorily organized all the freemen
for training in military service, not on a feudal system but on the
principle of the Saxon fyrd brought up to date by the Assizes
of Arms. A large body of militia were kept familiar with the
use of those weapons which each man was compelled by the State
to possess. The fact that so many of the common folk had arms
in their cottages which they knew how to use, was a chief cause
why the island atmosphere breathed something of political and
social freedom.

In the Fourteenth Century the longbow became more and more
the prescribed weapon, and the practice at the butts behind the
churchyard became the chief sport and excitement of village life.
Edward III encouraged it by royal proclamations, prohibiting
under pain of imprisonment—

handball, football or hockey (*pilam manualem, pedivam, vel bacularem*) ;
coursing and cockfighting, or other such idle games,

which drew men away from the butts. In a later age Hugh
Latimer used to tell from the pulpit the tale of his father the
yeoman—

He taught me how to draw, how to lay my body in my bow, and
not to draw with strength of arms as divers other nations do, but with
strength of the body. I had my bows bought me according to my
age and strength ; as I increased in them, so my bows were made
bigger and bigger. For men shall never shoot well unless they be
brought up in it.

We may be sure that Crecy and Agincourt had been vicariously
won by just such careful fathers as old Latimer. For the art
of the longbow was so difficult that foreigners never learnt the
knack that would send an arrow through plate-mail, and though
the longbow was for more than a century the acknowledged
master-weapon in European war, it never ceased to be an English
monopoly. And even in England its gradual supersession by the
less efficient hand-gun of Tudor times appears to have been

due to the village neglect of archery for 'football and other lewd games,' or as Latimer thought, for 'bowling, drinking and whoring,'—Statutes and Proclamations notwithstanding.

In Edward III's time this formidable militia was at the height of its efficiency and could on occasion be called out. When in the year of Crecy the Scots thought to make an easy prey of a land whose King and nobles were in France, the democratic levy of the shires taught the invaders, at Neville's Cross near Durham, the lesson they had learned at Northallerton and were to learn once more at Flodden, that England,—though she had no national motto to remind her of it,—can no more be 'provoked with impunity' than Scotland herself.

1346.

From this large body of armed and half-armed freemen, Edward III selected, by Commissions of Array addressed to each shire, a picked host to wage war oversea. For this purpose he resorted at first to conscription, eked out with volunteers. But as the French war went on, the Commissions of Array and the principle of compulsion were abandoned in favour of the system of hiring private 'companies' of professional warriors.

These 'companies' were the backbone of the long English warfare in France. They were not feudal hosts or conscript levies, but long-service professional soldiers, enlisted for pay by some noble or knight who had determined to push his fortunes in politics and in war. The King could contract with their leaders for their services at easy rates, because they counted on enriching themselves further with plunder, ransom and free quarters. Sometimes, especially during the intervals of truce between France and England, they fought and ravaged on the continent for their own hands, like the famous Hawkwood and his English Company in Italy. When driven back to England in the reign of Henry VI, the 'companies' became a chief cause of the social and political disruption at home, which provided them with fresh occupation as 'retainers' in the Wars of the Roses.[1]

The tactics of the English implied trust in the yeoman as a fighting man and in the longbow as a weapon. Those lessons had been learnt in the Scottish campaigns of the first two Edwards. The feudal warriors of the continent had taken no interest in such obscure and barbarous wars, and were stricken with amazement when, on the field of Crecy, the despised islanders revealed themselves as the masters of all Europe in the art military.

---

[1] Conan Doyle's *White Company* gives a spirited and well-informed if somewhat idealized picture of one of these 'companies' abroad, while Stevenson's *Black Arrow* describes Sir Daniel Brackley and his retainers at home, with a great measure of historical truth.

The lesson learnt in the Scottish wars had been twofold. At Stirling Bridge and Bannockburn the schiltrons of Scottish spearmen had shown that under favourable circumstances a self-respecting infantry could defeat feudal knighthood hand to hand, while the English victories, such as Falkirk, had taught the value of the longbow. From these two lessons of the Scottish war put together, the army chiefs of Edward III deduced a new method of warfare, combining the archer and the feudal knight in a single unit of battle, formidable alike for its missiles and its sword play. The English chivalry, perceiving that they had not the numbers to meet the French chivalry in the shock of horse and lance, consented to dismount and to fight in their full armour as a ' stiffening ' to the line of half-armoured archer infantry, who were to win the battle by the rapidity of their penetrating volleys of cloth-yard shafts. Those of the French knights who struggled alive through the arrow-storm, came to hand grips with the English line, where the archer, drawing his sword, stood shoulder to shoulder with the armoured knights and nobles, sometimes behind a hedge or a line of portable stakes.[1]

The French were so hopelessly defeated by these tactics at Crecy that they determined so far to imitate the victors as to fight on foot. But that by itself was not the secret, as Poitiers proved. Their other remedy against the arrows was to increase the thickness of their armour and to substitute plate for chain mail over all parts of the body. But they lost as much in mobility as they gained in protection, and the absurd helplessness of the Fifteenth Century knight, in a case too heavy for him to carry, only hastened the decline of chivalry.

The French in fact never devised a means of successfully attacking the English infantry line, once it had taken up chosen ground with flanks protected. But the English system elaborated by the Black Prince had one great defect. It was not mobile on the field of battle, like the ' thin red line ' of Wellington. It could not advance to attack the mounted knights without exposing itself to be outflanked and ridden down. In short it could only win victories when the French were foolish enough to attack it in position.

The first deliverance of France was made by Du Guesclin, the man who grasped the full meaning of these facts. It was he who, in the last years of Edward III, overthrew the compromise treaty of Brétigni, which in 1360 had assigned south-western

1369–1377.

See Map XV., p. 225.

---

[1] The archer, when his value as a fighting man had come to be fully recognized, was often supplied with defensive armour and a horse, so that the whole army of mounted infantrymen would scour through France on their raids. But all from King to scullion, dismounted to fight if occasion demanded.

France to England. Du Guesclin hired the service of ' free companies ' instead of relying on the undisciplined feudal host, and he avoided battle, except when he could surprise the English or take them in some circumstance of special disadvantage. His principal work was to besiege the castles from which the English ruled the country, and in that the French were our match, for they excelled in the early use of cannon. Gunpowder, not yet used effectively in the open field, was already revolutionizing siege operations. It helped to liberate France, but it sapped the power of feudalism, for the King, who could best afford to pay for a train of artillery, would in the end put down the feudal Baron, if he could blow a hole in his castle wall.

Yet even so feudalism died very hard in France. After Du Guesclin had freed his countrymen by finding substitutes for the feudal tactics which had failed at Crecy and Poitiers, a growth of French national monarchy at the expense of feudalism might have been expected during the generation of uneasy truce and intermittent warfare that divided the two halves of the Hundred Years' War. But no such development took place. When
1413. Henry V, on his accession, revived Edward III's pretensions to the French Crown in order ' to busy giddy minds with foreign quarrels,' the English, going out to fight with the tactics of the Black Prince, found themselves opposed, not by the proved methods of Du Guesclin, but by the idiotic feudal array of Crecy
1415. and Poitiers. Agincourt was the natural result.

Indeed the similarity of the second to the first half of the Hundred Years' War is extraordinary, as regards the military methods of both sides. For a long time the French refused to learn or to remember anything. Henry V, being a great soldier, —he has been called ' the first modern general,'—secured the English hold on Normandy as an occupied province, and thence extended his power to the banks of the Loire. The quarrel between the great feudal Houses of Orleans and Burgundy tore France in two, and brought about the alliance of Burgundy and Flanders with England, to the delight of wool merchants on both sides of the Channel. In 1420 Henry V was acknowledged heir to the French Crown by the Treaty of Troyes. Two years later he died, leaving his ill-gotten inheritance to an infant, who was acknowledged by Northern France.

During the minority of Henry VI came the second French revival, following tactically on the lines of Du Guesclin. His successor was Dunois, who had a harder task to face and was not his equal. But Dunois obtained a most unexpected and extra-
1429– ordinary ally. In one year of glory and one year of martyrdom
1431. Joan of Arc evoked a national tradition and sentiment in France

which has never since looked back. Spiritually she was the
Wallace of France. But more than twenty years passed after
her death, before the English power had been completely worn
away by the Fabian tactics and siegecraft of the Dunois era.
When English Talbot and his son perished in the last battle 1453.
down in Gascony, the Hundred Years' War drew to a close ; its

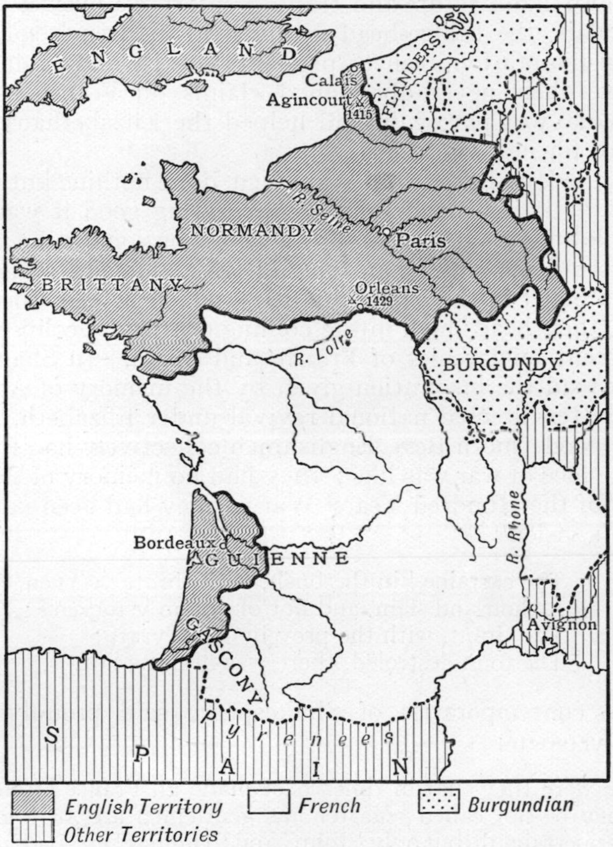

MAP XVI.—France: Second Part of Hundred Years' War. Height of Henry VI's Power

aftermath in England, the Wars of the Roses, began two years
later at St. Albans. So little rest had England in the ill-governed
Fifteenth Century.

What had we gained by the long, persistent endeavour to
erect an English Empire in Europe ? We had most justly earned
the break-up of our own mediæval society and a period of anarchy
and moral prostration. We had gained the port of Calais which

we kept for another hundred years, the solitary pledge of England's foretime rule in France, as Berwick-on-Tweed of her lost Scottish dominion. Calais was used as a port of vent for our raw wool abroad, where it was gathered and taxed before sale. The staple was fixed there by the King of England for that purpose. But the use of the staple gradually declined with the increase of our cloth manufacture and trading enterprise oversea. Meanwhile Calais, the bridge-head firmly held in French soil, was a standing temptation even to prudent Yorkist and Tudor Kings to revive their never abandoned claims on France. Its loss under Mary was pure gain and helped the Elizabethans to look westward for new lands.

Had the Hundred Years' War, then, done nothing but harm to England ? If it brought any compensating good it was of the intangible and intellectual order—a strong national self-consciousness, more democratic than feudal ; great memories and traditions ; a belief in the island qualities, which helped Englishmen to carry their heads high in the coming century of eclipse behind the crescent monarchies of France and Spain. In Shakespeare we may read the inspiration given by the memory of Agincourt to the better-directed national revival under Elizabeth. In the days of good Queen Bess, Englishmen collectively had forgotten what the face of war was like ; they had no memory of the bitter realities of the Hundred Years' War as they had been painted in Chaucer's vision :—

> The carraine [1] in the bush, with throte ycorven,
> A thousand slain, and not of qualm ystorven [2] ;
> The tirant, with the prey by force yraft ;
> The toun destroiëd, there was nothing laft.

But the contemporaries of Shakespeare said proudly of the English yeomen :—

These were they that in times past made all France afraid. And albeit they be not called ' Master ' as gentlemen are, or ' Sir ' as to knights appertaineth, but only ' John ' and ' Thomas ' etc., yet have they been found to have done very good service. The kings of England in foughten battles were wont to remain among them who were their footmen, as the French kings did amongst their horsemen, the prince thereby shewing where his chief strength did consist.

From the Hundred Years' War onwards, the ' yeoman *motif* ' runs through English thought, literature and politics with a potent and life-giving force, right down to the coming of the Industrial Revolution.

---

[1] Carrion, corpse.   [2] Not dead of sickness.

In earlier mediæval times hostility was normally felt against the natives of a neighbouring town, shire or village. This un-neighbourliness diminished as insular patriotism enlarged the mind and pointed out the Frenchman or the Spaniard as the true ' foreigner.' The habits of thought and feeling that were contracted during the Hundred Years' War with France—a period of ' hate' less intensive but twenty-five times longer than our recent war with Germany—sharply defined the new patriotic feeling in the form of racial hatred of the French. It was intensified in the era of Du Guesclin by destructive enemy raids on our South coast and not unsuccessful warfare against our shipping. The feeling against the French outlasted the war, and helped to put an end to that subordination of English to French culture which the Norman Conquest had established. From this time forward foreigners complained of the insular and surly exclusiveness of the English common people. In Henry VII's reign the Venetian envoy noted that :—

They think that there are no other men than themselves, and no other world but England; and whenever they see a handsome foreigner, they say ' he looks like an Englishman ' and that ' it is a great pity that he should not be an Englishman '; and when they partake of any delicacy with a foreigner they ask him ' whether such a thing is made in his country ? '

In the middle of the Tudor period a French visitor wrote :—

The people of this nation mortally hate the French as their old enemies, and always call us ' France cheneve,' ' France dogue.' (French knave, French dog.)

In the reign of Elizabeth these feelings were turned for awhile against the Spaniard. Yet there was often an element of good-nature in English nationalism. At the height of the Elizabethan struggle with Spain, Shakespeare's kindly caricature of Don Armado, ' a fantastical Spaniard,' in *Love's Labour's Lost*, does credit to the mentality of our people at war.

The upper classes followed more slowly in the wake of the common people in the repudiation of everything from beyond the Channel. Squire Western was in process of evolution, but not yet evolved. Ever since the loss of Normandy and the Angevin Empire, the French-speaking upper class had been cut off from estates and connections oversea, and their culture, severed from its roots in France, was clearly exotic. A hundred years before the days of Chaucer's Prioress, Frenchmen ' of Paris ' used to laugh at the strange hybrid that passed for their tongue in the mouths of English gentlefolk. Yet, such as it was, it was their everyday speech till the reign of Edward III, and was regarded as the hall-mark of a gentleman, till the increasingly racial character of the war compelled all men to regard French as an enemy language.

Six years after Poitiers a statute was passed through Parliament declaring that since the French tongue was ' much unknown in this Realm,' all pleading and judgments in the law courts should be spoken in the English tongue and enrolled in Latin. ' Men of lawe fro that tyme shold plede in her moder tunge,' it was said. ' Their mother tongue ' ! Here indeed is a new and significant order of ideas ! If the statute was imperfectly obeyed at first, it was obeyed before long, although lawyers, with professional conservatism, long continued to write documents in the ' law French' in which their predecessors had addressed the court.

A still more fundamental revolution was taking place in regard to the language used in the schools. English was becoming once more the tongue of the educated and of the upper class, as it had never been since Hastings :—

Children in scole (thus wrote John of Trevisa in 1385), agenst the usage and manere of alle othere naciouns, beeth compelled for to leve thire own langage, and for to construe thir lessouns and there thynges in Frensche, and so they haveth seth (*since*) the Normans come first in to Engelond. Also gentil men children beeth i-taught to speke Frensche from the tyme that they beeth i-rokked in their cradel. . . . This manere was moch i-used to fore the first moreyn (*before the Black Death*, 1349) and is siththe sumdel (*since somewhat*) i-chaunged. For John Cornwaile, a maister of grammar chaunged the lore in gramer scole and construccion of Frensche into Englische ; and Richard Pencriche lerned that manere teaching of hym, and other men of Pencriche. So that now, the yere of oure Lorde a thowsand thre hundred and foure score and fyve, and of the secounde Kyng Richard after the conquest nyne, in alle the gramere scoles of Engelond, children leveth Frensche and construeth and lerneth in Englische. . . . Here avauntage is that they lerneth ther gramer in lasse tyme than children were i-woned (*used*) to doo ; disavauntage is that now children of gramer scole conneth no more Frensche than can thir left heele ; and that is harme for them and (*if*) they schulle passe the see and travaille in straunge landes and in many other places. Also gentil men haveth now moche i-left for to teche ther children Frensche (*have much left off teaching their children French*).

Thus did these humble schoolmasters, John Cornwaile and Richard Pencriche, prepare the road for Chaucer and Wycliffe in their own century, for Shakespeare and Milton in time to come, for the English Reformation and Renaissance, and the whole development of English national life and letters as something other than a northern offshoot of French culture. Some may regard the transaction thus casually recorded by the chronicler as more important than Magna Carta or the Declaration of Independence.[1]

During the formative period of the English language, the centuries after the Conquest when it was out of fashion with the learned and the polite,[2] in the chrysalis stage between Saxon caterpillar and Chaucerian butterfly, it was divided into many regional dialects, of which the chief were Wessex, Northumbrian, East and West Midland. The Wessex had been the Court language in Alfred's time, but the Norman Conquest had relegated it for ever to the cottage and the plough-furrow. It was the speech of the East Midlands that became the ancestor of modern English, triumphing over the other dialects, partly because it was spoken in London, Oxford and Cambridge ; partly because it was employed by Chaucer, who enriched it with many French words, and by Wycliffe, who enriched it with many words from the Latin Vulgate. Both Chaucer and Wycliffe founded a school of imitators who used mainly the same dialect. Their writings and translations were for awhile widely circulated in manuscript. Then in the later Fifteenth Century came Caxton's printing press at Westminster, under the patronage of the Yorkist Kings ; it further popularized Chaucer, and spread through the land translations of various works done into English of the same type.

In this way a standard of English was being formed for all those who could read, and for all, even beyond Trent and Avon, who wished to be regarded as educated men and women. In Tudor times the Bible and the Prayer Book in the same dialect —already regarded as ' the King's English '—obtained a diffusion and authority quite unparalleled by any works in earlier times, and firmly fixed the standard. During these two centuries from Chaucer to Elizabeth, the language in question, living on the tongues of men no less than in their books, was moving forward from strength to strength and from beauty to beauty, enriching itself with Latin words expressive of all the joy and learning of the Renaissance, until it fell into the perfecting hands

---

[1] The linguistic situation about the year 1375 is thus summed up by William Nassington :—

> ' Some can French and no Latin,
> That have used courts and dwelled therein :
> And some can of Latin a party,
> That can French full febelly :
> And some understandeth English
> That neither can Latin nor French :
> But lerid and lewid, old and young
> All understanden English tongue.'

lerid and lewid = learned and ignorant.

[2] See pp. 131–132, above.

of the man of Stratford. Since his day its adaptability to exact scientific statement has increased, and its poetic and literary quality has decreased, answering to the changes in the mind and life of the people who use it.

CHAPTER VII

The Black Death. The Emancipation of the Villeins and the fluidity of labour. The Rising of 1381. The Church and the Laity. Wycliffe and Lollardry

IN a previous chapter we considered the life of the mediæval English village.[1] We saw it, self-sufficing in its labour and its poverty ; often suffering from famine but never from unemployment ; little connected with the world beyond its own forest bounds, except through the personal activities and requirements of its lord ; supplying nearly all its own simple needs ; containing its own miller, craftsmen and spinsters ; feeding itself by tilling, on traditional methods, the strips owned by the villeins in the open field, and by sharing the common rights over meadow and waste. We saw too that the village was a ' manor ' held by some lord, resident or non-resident, lay or spiritual. We noted the relations between the lord and his villeins, who composed the great majority of the village, and by whose compulsory labour his domain was tilled under the supervision of his bailiff.

This system, found with variations all over feudal Europe, served no less than the sameness of religious observance to give unity to Christendom. In every land there was the same scheme of society resting on two pillars—the lord and his serf, and in every land the lord and the serf respectively had much the same outlook on life. Change and variation began with the rise of the yeoman, the free labourer, and a number of active and intelligent middle classes, towards the end of the mediæval period. The citizens of Paris differed widely from the citizens of London, the yeomen of Tudor England from the peasantry of Valois France. And so the feudal unanimity of old Europe was at length broken up into nations, each with a character of its own.

The manorial system had led England out of the Dark Ages and had enabled man to conquer the forest, subdue the soil, and colonize the land. In ages of brute force it had protected the weak behind the shield of custom, even while making them half

[1] See pp. 147–152, above.

slaves. It gave stability and peace, but checked progress and denied freedom. Its part in English history had been great, but its use was at length exhausted.

Already before the close of the Thirteenth Century the beginnings of change were perceptible. Lords and their bailiffs occasionally found it more convenient to take money rents of a penny or a half-penny instead of the day's work due. But the villeins who thus commuted did not necessarily become freemen in the eye of the law, and were in most cases still bound to the soil; indeed the commutation was often made in a form revocable by the lord. The change from servile to hired labour went quietly forward on some estates during the first half of the Fourteenth Century, but the old system was still prevalent though not universal when in 1348–9 occurred the most appalling of national catastrophes.

The Black Death, on its first visitation of Europe from some mysterious fountain-head of disease in the undiscovered East, swept off perhaps a third, possibly a half, of the compatriots of Boccaccio, Froissart and Chaucer. The most terrible feature of its first advent was its ubiquity. In the most secluded English hamlets we often read, in the list of vicars in the parish church, the names of *two* incumbents under that fatal year. Some villages and hamlets ceased to exist, the whole population having died. In the winter of 1349 the plague was stayed, but it remained in the island, and was perpetually breaking out in one insanitary township after another. Its last appearance, as Charles II's ' Plague of London,' seems to have been little, if at all, worse than several plagues that had devastated the capital in Lancastrian, Tudor and Stuart times, with no Defoe to celebrate them. Plague was a black cloud, ever hovering over the filthy streets and brief lives of our ancestors. It was a frequent sequel to the famine of a bad harvest year.

The reduction of the English subjects of Edward III. in sixteen months, from perhaps four million to perhaps two and a half million souls, precipitated the class struggle, and embittered the process of emancipating the villein. In a society accustomed to very slow changes in conditions of life, the market value of labour had been doubled at a stroke. The consequence was twofold. The labourer who was already free struck for higher wages, while the villein whose labour was not free struggled against the legal demands of the bailiff for customary services which were now worth more to both parties; gradually he was led on to demand his full freedom, the right to take his labour where he would, to plead in the King's Court even against his own lord, and to be free of irksome feudal dues.

Lords and bailiffs were in a terrible dilemma. Half the domain land, half the rent-paying farms were lying untilled, turf and bushes overgrowing the strips, the ploughmen dead, the thatch falling from their deserted hovels. And the survivors were rising in open mutiny against law and custom, and sometimes also against what was economically possible. The world seemed coming to an end, yet it never occurred to the governing class to stop the French war, which was still regarded as a source of profit and plunder. Poitiers followed Crecy, as though half the world had not died in the interval.

Part of their difficulties the landlords solved well and wisely, by substituting sheep-pasture for tillage. It was not till a hundred years later, when the population had nearly filled up the gaps left by the Black Death, that there was any need for landlords to evict ploughmen in order to make room for the shepherd. In 1350 death had evicted the ploughmen, and 'the deserted village' was ready to hand. In such circumstances, the multiplication of sheep-runs was pure gain to a community in distress. The export of raw wool to the Flanders looms, and the concurrent growth of cloth manufacture in England, aided by Edward III's importation of Flemish weavers to teach our people the higher skill of the craft, made demand for all the wool that English flocks could supply. In this way a national policy and distant markets were beginning to disturb and to improve the parochial economy of the old manor, and to offer alternative occupations for the emancipated or the runaway villein.

Other steps taken by the landlords in distress, though very natural, were less in harmony with the destined course of affairs. An endeavour was made to keep down wages and prices by law, to limit the mobility of the free labourer in search of highly paid employment, and to prevent the further emancipation of the villeins. But even in making these efforts to stop social and economic change, the landlords recognized the new and national character of the situation, for they legislated through Parliament. The conflict was moving away from the old manor court, which the peasant was learning to defy, to the arena of Parliament, which was already beginning to take over control of economic affairs from municipal and manorial authorities— a nation-making process completed under Queen Elizabeth. Unfortunately Parliament represented too exclusively the landed 1351. gentry and the employing classes of the towns. Their Statute of Labourers, following up the King's Ordinance of two years before, showed a desire to be fair, and endeavoured to fix not only wages but prices of provisions at the old standards. But no

Statute could make two loaves or two labourers where there was only one. No Act of Parliament could repeal the Black Death or abolish the spirit of the age. The statutory limitation of wages, and the refusal to complete the emancipation of the villeins aroused a fierce struggle which lasted for the remainder of the century, and culminated in the drama of the Peasants' Revolt.[1]

Nothing is more remarkable than the change in the temper and mental activity of the lower orders during the Fourteenth Century. Professor Davis has summed up the reign of Henry III with the words : ' Of all the contrasts which strike us in mediæval life, none is so acute as that between the intellectual ferment in the upper class and the oriental passivity of their inferiors.' But in the reign of Edward III the peasants could no longer be accused of ' oriental passivity,' and the ' intellectual ferment ' in their ranks reminds us of a modern labour movement. Village unions strike for higher wages, villeins demand freedom in return for 4d. an acre rent, and men ask each other in every field that deep-probing question—

> When Adam delved and Eve span,
> Who was then the gentleman ?

The agitation was Christian in its form and language, but hostile to the Church authorities, whether as monastic landlords [2] or as royal Ministers. It had lost sympathy with the mediæval order in Church and State, drawing its inspiration from the equalitarian element in earlier Christian teaching. Some of the poor parish priests, some of the friars, and some of the Wycliffite preachers helped to fan the flame—Wycliffe himself maintaining a middle attitude sympathetically critical of both sides, which contrasts favourably with Luther's heated partisanship in the very similar case of the Peasants' Revolt in Germany.

Exalted by this new order of ideas, the peasants carried on the struggle for their freedom. The free labourers attempted to ignore the Statutes fixing their wages, and conducted strikes that were frequently but not always successful. Those who had no land of their own often emigrated to towns or manors where their

---

[1] Bertha Putnam, *Enforcement of the Statutes of Labourers*, 1349–59 (*Columbia University, Studies in History, etc.*, Vol. XXXII., 1908).

[2] There was no tendency on the part of the monasteries or other ecclesiastical lords to manumit serfs more rapidly than the lay landlords. Manumission of serfs was stigmatized as embezzlement of ecclesiastical property except when freedom was purchased as part of a business transaction. Corporate bodies, like monasteries, tended to a more conservative, though not necessarily a more oppressive policy than individual lords.

illegal demands were accepted. Their prosperity in good times
is thus described in *Piers Plowman* :—

> Labourers that had no land to live on but their hands,
> Deigned not to dine to-day on night-old worts.
> May no penny-ale please them, nor a piece of bacon,
> But it be fresh flesh or fish, fried or y-baked,
> And that *chaud* and *plus chaud* for the chill of their maw.
> But he be highly hired, else will he chide, . . .
> Then curses he the King, and all his Council after
> For making such laws, labourers to grieve.

But the Justices entrusted with the enforcement of the Statute
of Labourers often succeeded in keeping wages from rising as
high as they would have gone in an open market.

Meanwhile the villeins, still bound to the soil, slacked or
refused the unpaid labour which they owed on the lord's domain.
Some of them fled to the woods and became Robin Hood bandits,
helping to build up the legend of that friend of the poor peasant
and enemy of rich churchmen. Other villeins fled to distant
estates, where in the general dearth of hands they were received
as free labourers, no questions asked. Their former masters
strove to drag them back to servitude and to exact the ancient
dues from those who had remained behind, by employing the
' rusty curb of old father antic the law.' The activity of the
lawyers and well-to-do juries on the side of the landlords exposed
the learned profession and its satellites to the popular hatred,
as not a few judges and jurymen learnt to their cost in the days
of June 1381.

The dramatic events of that summer had their roots in social
rather than political causes, though the revolt was precipitated
by the Poll Tax, a method of taxing the poor for the French war
at a moment when it was singularly unsuccessful and therefore for a while unpopular. The incompetent government of
Richard II's minority was hated and despised. But what chiefly
brought the men of East Anglia and the Home Counties trooping
up to London was their own grievances and ambitions as peasants.
It was a rising, more or less concerted and prepared by John Ball
and his agents, against the gentry, the lawyers and the wealthy
churchmen. The rebels' chief demand was for the commutation
of all servile dues throughout the land for a rent of fourpence an
acre ; many of them also demanded the disendowment of the
Church, free use of forests, abolition of game laws and outlawry
—a ' Robin Hood ' programme suggestive of the life recently
led by some of those who were taking a leading part in the
revolt.

The rising took the upper class by surprise, and for some

days there was little resistance, either central or local. Admitted into London by the 'prentice mob and by certain democratically minded aldermen, the rebels held the capital and the government at their mercy. The King was in the Tower, which his subjects proceeded to blockade. The situation was saved—but by very base means. Richard II was sent to a conference at Mile End with the rebels, where he made them promises of pardon and emancipation from villeinage, which his counsellors had no intention of carrying out. It was easy thus to beguile the moderate section of the rebels, who had a simple-minded belief in the King as distinct from his Council, Parliament, lawyers, Church and knighthood. Yet in fact the Crown of England was identified with those interests. *June 13, 1381.* *June 14.*

Having received grants of emancipation and pardon hastily drawn up by the King's clerks, many of the insurgents set off home to their villages, deceived and happy. But meanwhile others had broken into the Tower and executed Sudbury, the Archbishop of Canterbury, on Tower Hill before a vast concourse of people who greeted the ferocious act with yells of triumph. They were incensed against him as Chancellor and chief Minister of the King, but the fact that he was Archbishop gave him no sanctity in their eyes. The relation of Church and people had undergone a profound change, since the ancestors of these same men had knelt beside their ploughs to pray for the Holy Martyr, Thomas Becket.

Other murders stained the rising, both in London and in the country, but there was no general massacre of the upper class such as characterized the French Jacquerie twenty years before. For the Jacquerie had been a gesture of savage despair, but the English revolt was the offspring of hope and progress, and was designed to hasten the advent of a freedom already on the way. It was one of the growing pains of the new England.

The forces of order were now beginning to rally. Another conference in the presence of the King, held in Smithfield, resulted not in further concessions, but in the slaying of a rebel leader, Wat Tyler, by the Mayor of London. After that, the insurgents soon dispersed before a mixture of force and cajolery. The revolt went on spreading over the country till it reached from South Yorkshire to the South-Western counties But when it had lost its hold on London it was doomed. *June 15.*

Whether the rising of 1381 actually hastened or retarded complete emancipation it is difficult to say. The immediate result was a strong and cruel reaction, when every promise made to the peasants in the hour of need was broken, and a bloody assize made mock of the pardons granted by the King. But a class that could give its rulers such a fright could not ultimately be held down. As compared to Peterloo, or to the rick-burning and the ' peasants' rising ' in 1830, the revolt of 1381 was extremely formidable. Thistlewood talked about taking the Tower, but John Ball took it. For the peasant of the Fourteenth Century was not unused to arms and archery; he had the leasehold farmer in his ranks instead of against him, and he was in close touch with the turbulent democracy of the towns. In the battle for the preservation of order at home, the feudal class of the Hundred Years' War had no such allies and no such organization as the gentry in the time of Castlereagh and Wellington.

The failure of 1381 by no means ended the strikes, labour troubles and riots against serfdom. It must have been difficult to get a good day's work on the domain out of such surly fellows. Partly for this reason, partly in obedience to the general economic tendencies of the age, landlords gradually ceased to work the domain by the forced service of villeins, and let it instead to farmers who produced for the market, and so obtained money to hire free labour. In most cases the villeins bought their emancipation from serfdom, a process facilitated by the growing wealth of the country and of the peasants, and by the increasing quantities of coin of the realm. The emancipation took place mainly in the Fifteenth Century, and was completed under the Tudors. It was hastened by the changed attitude of the King's law courts, which became surprisingly liberal, and ' strained the law in the interests of the humbler classes.' [1]

The emancipated villein filled many rôles in the new society. He became a small yeoman farmer, whether freehold, leasehold or copyhold ; or else he became a labourer for hire, or else he drifted into the towns or village workshops, or took to the wars or to the life of the high seas. He retained valuable rights of his own in the open field and the waste, to induce him to stay in the village : but he was now free to go if he wished. ' The world was all before him where to choose,' and the modern English proved themselves great adventurers, both in the material and the spiritual world.

The fluidity of labour had come, altering the whole outlook of economic society. The change from the fixed and limited

[1] Holdsworth, III. 505. On the whole question of emancipation see ' Oxford Studies in Social and Legal History,' Vol. V., Black Death, etc., by Miss Levett and A. Ballard, with introduction by Vinogradoff. Also T. W. Page, End of Villeinage in England, and Maitland, History of a Cambridgeshire Manor (Collected Papers, Vol. II.). ; Ashley, Economic Organization of England, Chap. III. ; G. G. Coulton, The Mediaeval Village, especially Chaps. XII., XIII., on monks and serfs.

rights and duties of the serf to the competition and uncertainty of the open labour market was by no means wholly to the labourer's advantage, though for a hundred years after the Black Death the dearth of labour enabled him to command a high price. But in the later part of the Fifteenth Century, when the population had recovered, wages fell. Under the modern regime, though famine was more rare and the average standard of life was raised, the horrors of unemployment became known, and the ' sturdy beggars ' of Tudor times had little joy of their freedom. But the change was necessary if the English race was to be anything better than a race of serfs, if it was to make vast increase in numbers, wealth and knowledge, if it was to take to industrial and maritime adventure and people the lands beyond the ocean. The power, liberty and progress that we associate with modern England, America and Australasia, required as a precondition the emancipation of the serfs. Emancipation and the consequent fluidity of labour formed the necessary prelude to the growth of trade, manufacture and colonization, as well as to the intellectual and political developments of Tudor and Stuart England.

One feature of the old village economy lasted on in whole districts until the reign of George III. In the best wheat-growing belt of the midland and eastern shires, the open village field, with its queer strips, involving enforced adherence to early Anglo-Saxon methods of cultivation, survived in many places to shock the sensibilities of Arthur Young and his ' improving landlords.'

If the Fourteenth and Fifteenth Centuries saw the emancipation of the serf and the birth of English language, literature and national feeling, they witnessed also, in consonance with those great movements, the failure of the cosmopolitan Church of the Middle Ages to meet any longer the conscious requirements of the new nation.

It may be questioned how far the loss of moral and intellectual leadership by the Church was due to greater corruption or inefficiency than of old. It was not so much that the clergy had sunk as that the laity had risen. In Norman and early Plantagenet times, when the Church reigned supreme in the minds of men, the mass of the clergy had—as compared to the modern English clergy whether Protestant or Catholic—been very ignorant and often very irregular in their lives. The ecclesiastical machinery was not strong enough to enforce the full programme of Hildebrandine celibacy upon the unwilling English priests. But in those days the laity were even more ignorant and brutal than the clergy, and probably even more immoral. A more or less barbarous Church had easily maintained its leadership over a laity still more barbarous. But times had changed. In the days of Chaucer, though neither laity nor clergy led very reputable lives, there was a more widely diffused standard of civilized conduct, much more learning and a more intellectual outlook. It was a sign less of clerical decadence than of general progress that a new generation of laymen were alienated by abuses in the Church that were not new : orthodox Gower and Langland and humanist Chaucer were no less severe on the churchmen than Wycliffe the heretic.

In earlier days, whatever the average priest may have been like, the Church had supplied the intellectual and moral leaders of the country, from Lanfranc and Anselm to Langton and Grossetête. But in the course of upward evolution this had ceased to be the case. It reflects no discredit on the Church that she had so well played her part as schoolmistress of the nation that her scholar was beginning to think for himself. Except Langland, the most influential literary men of the new era, such as Froissart, Chaucer and Gower, were not clergy at all, while Wycliffe and his Oxford following, though clergy, were heretics in the eye of the Church. The lawyers, the gentry and the rising middle classes of town and country had not the unquestioning minds of their forefathers. They were beginning to think for themselves. The pious Langland tells us :—

> I have heard high men eating at table
> Carpen (talk) as they clerkes were, of Christ and his might,
> And laid faults upon the Father that formed us all
> And carpen against clerkes crabbed words—

to the effect that we ought not to be damned for the fault of Adam.

> At meat in their mirth when minstrels be still
> Then tell they of the Trinity a tale or twain,
> And bringen forth a bald reason and take Bernard to witness,
> And put forth a presumption to prove the sooth.

Times were ripe for ecclesiastical reform and religious growth, no less than for social and political change. But whereas Parliamentary institutions and servile emancipation were developing apace, religious reform was impossible. The Church in England had no power to reform herself, because she had no autonomy. She was part of a cosmopolitan organization centred abroad, of enormous prestige and power, knowing nothing of English needs and of set purpose to resist change. If in England the Church had retired step by step before the rising tide of lay emancipation, there would have been no violent overturn in Tudor times. But pent waters gather force. In the Fourteenth and Fifteenth Centuries the Church refused every concession, effected no reform, and called in brute force to repress heresy. If an opposite course had been followed ; if the rights of sanctuary and benefit of clergy had been modified ; if ecclesiastical property had been redistributed more fairly to the poor parson ; if priests had been permitted to marry their wives as in Saxon times ; if the Pope had ceased to job rich places of the Church for foreign favourites ; if the ecclesiastical authorities had withdrawn their countenance from the sale of pardons and relics and other superstitious practices that revolted the better sort of laity, orthodox as well as heretic ; if the Church courts had ceased to make a trade of spying on the lives of the laity in order to extract fines for sin ; and finally if Lollardry had been tolerated as Dissent, there would have been religious evolution spread over several centuries, instead of the religious revolution which we know as the Reformation.

But the doctrine of persecution was an integral part of mediæval Christianity. To the men of the Middle Ages, life outside the Church in disobedience to her doctrines was no more conceivable than life outside the State in disobedience to its laws. Religious persecution was therefore as much a matter of course as civil police. It was a tradition some thousand years old, and only a long course of very bitter experience has in modern times gone far to eradicate the doctrine of persecution from the Christian mentality. It is necessary to understand this before we can be fair to the conduct of any of our ancestors in the terrible religious struggles that began for England with the rise and suppression of Lollardry. There was never any serious question of tolerating Wycliffe's doctrines, if he could not get them accepted by the Church. There is no need to ascribe evil characters to the energetic Kings and Bishops who persecuted the Lollards, any more than to the members of the court that sentenced Joan of Arc. But neither is there any need to approve of the doctrine of persecution, because it was at that time very ancient, very respectable and universally held. It was none the less erroneous, and was destined to cause incalculable evil for centuries to come. That we should ever have cast out so deeply ingrained and so specious an error, is perhaps the most solid piece of human progress to which Europe can point.

We may, on similar principles drawn from the history of the case, understand why the Church refused to make concessions to the laity on points of clerical privilege, and why the monasteries

and the highly endowed clergy refused to redistribute tithe
and endowment for the benefit of the parish priest, before the
Tudor squirearchy laid hands on the spoil. Men cannot so
easily shake off the past. In the Dark Ages that followed the
fall of the Roman Empire, the Church, struggling for existence
in a world of barbarous and lawless force, had learnt how to bring
the enginery of excommunication and the whole power of the
united Church of Christendom to defend every right claimed by
the clergy and every piece of property acquired by any specific
clerical corporation, as if the foundations of Christianity were
involved in their conservation. In an age too late the Church
still held to these customs, which had become a part of her nature.
She would not treat with the State on the basis of concession.
She would not reform herself from within. The complete triumph
of the State over the Church was needed to effect any appreciable
measure of change.

The Church of England, indeed, was in no position to reform
herself, had she wished, because she had no independence, and
indeed no corporate existence. All the friars and most of the
monks in England were subject not to the English Bishops, but
only to the Pope ; to him, not to the Church of England, they
owed loyalty and obedience. Ecclesiastical law was the Roman
Canon Law which the English Church was not competent to
change. Appeal in ecclesiastical causes lay to the Papal courts.
The Bishops were therefore without power to set the English
house in order.

Nor in any case did the episcopal bench contain men fitted
for such a task. Appointed by collusive arrangement between
the King and the Pope, many of the Bishops were royal civil
servants—like William of Wykeham, the great builder of colleges,
and the Chancellor Archbishop Sudbury, the victim of the rebels
of 1381. They were excellent and useful men, but they served
the State rather than the Church,—Cæsar rather than Christ as
contemporaries said,—and their ecclesiastical duties were often
committed to subordinates. No one could look to them to reform
the religious life of the country.

The Papal nominees were even less adapted to such a task.
The Pope no longer sent men of the stamp of Theodore of Tarsus
or Stephen Langton to govern the English Church. His modern
favourites were most numerous in the ranks of the higher clergy
just below the episcopate ; many of them were foreigners who
resided abroad and regarded England as a source of income.

While plurality and simony were rife among the upper clergy,
native or foreign, the best element in the Church in the last two
centuries before the Reformation were the poor parish priests.

Miserably starved as many of them were for the benefit of the monks and higher clergy to whom the tithe was ' appropriated,' and often very ignorant, they were in close touch with their flocks, and not a few of them, no doubt, resembled Chaucer's poor parson. Would that we had their annals !

The collusion between the Pope and the later Plantagenet Kings was injurious to the Church, which had no defence at all if the King deserted her. And the collusion was highly unpopular with Parliament. Yet it continued more or less until Henry VIII's change of front. The Pope, who alone had the power to reform the Church, was deeply interested in the ecclesiastical venality and corruption of which Englishmen, orthodox and heretic alike, complained. The chief centre of the traffic of simony was the Papal Court, held during the Fourteenth Century at Avignon on the borders of France, where the association of the Pope with the national enemy during the first part of the Hundred Years' War helped to turn English national feeling against the Papacy and all its works. Nor did the schism that followed between rival Popes increase respect for the institution.

But so long as mediæval theories of the relation of Church and State held good, England was without a remedy. She might grumble, but no one at Rome or Avignon cared. The ' English asses ' might bray, but they must still bear the load. Parliament might pass Acts of Provisors and Præmunire to limit the Papal power as against the rights of the Crown. But these laws were largely inoperative, and at the most served the King as an asset in his perpetual bargaining with the Pope. They were, however, a remarkable sign of the movement of opinion among the laity, and formed a precedent for much stronger action to be taken some day by the King in Parliament.[1]

John Wycliffe, a Yorkshireman by birth and an Oxford don by profession, pointed out to England a remedy for her griefs, and found what had hitherto been lacking, a theoretic basis for denying the Papal authority. His ' theory of dominion ' taught that the authority of the wicked could not come from God. The Pope's power was derived from the Cæsars of Rome, not from Christ or Peter. It is remarkable that an academician whose methods of thought and expression were involved in the technical labyrinths of later mediæval philosophy, should have foreseen so accurately many of the general lines of development which

---

[1] The Statute of Provisors (1351) protected the rights of English patrons against Papal ' provisions ' to English benefices. The Statutes of Præmunire (1353, 1365, 1393) were of much more limited scope than was supposed in later times. So far as they went they provided a machinery to check Papal interference with royal rights in England.

England was destined to follow between one and two hundred years after his death. The Anglican, the lay [1] and the Protestant positions are all prominent in Wycliffe's teaching, and it was by a mixture of these three different points of view that the affairs of Church and State were ultimately rearranged in England.

The first important stage of Wycliffe's career as a reformer, in the last years of Edward III, brought him in touch with politicians. He was employed to state the case of the nation against Papal encroachments, and his attack on the ' possession-ate ' and ' Cæsarean ' clergy not only won him much popular support, especially in London, but found for him powerful but unpopular allies in John of Gaunt, Percy of Northumberland and the party of lords and knights who were already nosing after the spoils of the Church. And at this stage he also found defenders where he was afterwards to find his bitterest enemies ; the friars [2] were always on bad terms with the rest of the Church in England and were still theoretically advocates of poverty and therefore of disendowment. Some of them found in Wycliffe an ally against the landed classes of monks and Bishops, until his denial of transubstantiation and his attacks on their patron the Pope became more than the mendicant orders could endure.

1377.

The peasants' rising in 1381, in which he was not involved on either side, did not directly affect Wycliffe's position, except by removing from the world the mild Archbishop Sudbury who had shown no desire to persecute him. The new Primate, Courtenay, was his bitter and energetic enemy, and the period of active repression was at hand. At the same time the Reformer broke with John of Gaunt, the politicians and the friars, by arguing against transubstantiation. His propositions as to the nature of the sacrament were indeed very moderate, but for those days bold in the extreme ; his followers in the next generation went farther.

In the last years of his life Wycliffe became less political and less strictly academic. He retired from Oxford to his last home, the Rectory at Lutterworth, in Leicestershire, and there developed further his popular methods of appeal, through English tracts written either by himself or his companions. He attacked,

1382–
1384.

---

[1] ' Erastian ' in the strict sense of the word Wycliffe perhaps was not. ' He was no Erastian,' Dean Rashdall writes, ' since while he held strongly a distinction between the clergy and the laity, he asserts very emphatically the priesthood of the laity, and insists that he is only calling on one part of the church to remove the evils due to the misconduct of the other.' But he did so call on the laity to reform the Church, as occurred in Tudor times, and many people would call that Erastianism. The tendency of his argument was to make the King the head of the Church, though he does not say so definitely. But the stress he lays on the individual conscience or priesthood of every lay person would have left him dissatisfied with the ' Tudor ' solution.

[2] On the friars see pp. 184–186, above.

and taught his disciples to attack, the Pope, the monks, the friars
and the 'Cæsarean clergy,' and many of the religious practices of
the day such as the worship of images and relics, sale of pardons
and masses for the soul.   He appealed for the direct relation
of the individual to God without mediators, declaring that
'each man that shall be damned shall be damned by his own
guilt, and each man that is saved shall be saved by his own
merit.'

He demanded a service in English, and he produced,
chiefly through the agency of his Oxford follower and secretary,
Purvey, the first full English translation of the Bible, an admirable
and scholarly piece of work, a great event in the history of
English language as well as religion.   The Bible was not to
Wycliffe, as it was to some later Protestants, the sole basis of
his doctrine and his sole canon of appeal.   But his doctrines led
him to perceive the practical need of a diffusion of the Scriptures
in modern English, and the reading of the English Bible became
the distinctive practice of his sect.   The Church, which permitted
under special licence the use of vernacular versions to wealthy
persons and to nuns, continued during the Fifteenth Century to
deny its possession to the laity in general and to make possession
of the Scriptures in English a charge against Lollards.[1]

Meanwhile a great disaster had befallen Wycliffism, which
was in origin an Oxford movement.   The University, and even
its officers, were to a large extent Wycliffe's partisans, at least
in regard to many of his theses.   The monks and friars of
Oxford were now solidly against him, but the secular clergy and
undergraduates were largely on his side.   Archbishop Courtenay
intervened in the quarrel, and with the help of the King overrode   1382.
the liberties of the University and silenced or expelled the
Wycliffites.   This purge, which had to be repeated in the reign
of Henry IV, cut off Lollardry from its roots in the best culture
of the day, and helped to turn it into a popular evangelicalism,
hiding from authority and propagating itself among the poor.
Courtenay's suppression of the liberty of academic thought doomed
the University to a hundred years of intellectual stagnation, in
curious contrast to its great productivity in the relative freedom
that it had enjoyed during the first two centuries of its existence.
No single act had more to do with the barrenness of English
mental and spiritual life in the Fifteenth Century.

Yet the dragooning of Oxford and Cambridge by the orthodox
had one good side.   It afforded an additional motive for the
foundation and endowment of Colleges, because they were useful

[1] On this question see Deanesly, *The Lollard Bible* (Cam. Univ. Press, 1920),
in answer to Cardinal Gasquet's *The Old English Bible*.

for secluding the students from heretical contagion.[1] The peculiarly English growth of the College system within the University made great strides in the period between William of Wykeham and Wolsey. The foundation by Henry VI of King's College, with its magnificent chapel, was one of the events that tended to bring Cambridge into prominence as a rival to the senior University. At the Reformation this famous rivalry became every day more marked.

Even after the intellectual roots of the Wycliffite movement had been cut by the hand of authority at Oxford, the influence of Wycliffe increased in the land till it was said, though with gross exaggeration, that every second man you met was a Lollard. Parts of Wycliffe's doctrines no doubt found favour with many who would have repudiated other parts. Thus in the reign of Henry IV the knights of shire in the Commons proposed that the King should seize the Temporalities of the Church to relieve taxation and the poor, and endow new lords and knights—the policy of Henry VIII. But they do not appear to have opposed the Statute *De Heretico Comburendo*. The Lollard movement was suppressed by persecution in the days of Henry IV and Henry V, who sought security for their questionable dynastic claims in the powerful support of the Church. Some heretics were burnt, more recanted under threat of burning. During the rest of the Fifteenth Century Lollardry survived underground in the towns and villages of England. In the reigns of Henry VII and Henry VIII the recrudescence of this native heresy began to alarm the orthodox and to provoke a very active persecution, marked by many martyrdoms, before it became merged in the return wave of Protestantism from Luther's Germany. But every important aspect of the English Reformation was of native origin. All can be traced back as far as Wycliffe, and some much farther.

1401.

BOOKS FOR FURTHER READING

See notes pp. 239, 242, above, on rural problems.

Vickers, *England in the Later Middle Ages* ; Kingsford, *Henry V* ; Coulton, *Chaucer and his England* ; Trevelyan, *England in the Age of Wycliffe* ; Dean Rashdall's article in *Dict. of Nat. Biog.* on Wycliffe ; *The Lollard Bible*, Margaret Deanesly (Cambridge, 1920), especially Chap. IX. ; R. Lane Poole, *Wycliffe and Movements for Reform*.

---

[1] See p. 182, above.

CHAPTER VIII

Parliamentary development from Edward III to Henry VI.   Aristocratic
Anarchy.   Some aspects of English Life in the later Middle Ages.
Wars of the Roses.   The Yorkist Kings

Kings : Edward III, 1327–1377 ; Richard II, 1377–1399 ; Henry IV
(Lancaster), 1399–1413 ; Henry V, 1413–1422 ; Henry VI, 1422–
1461 ; Edward IV (York), 1461–1483 ; Edward V, 1483 ; Richard III,
1483–1485

BETWEEN the accession of Edward III and the deposition of 1327–
Henry VI,[1] the English Parliament became fixed in its bicameral 1461.
form, and acquired the outline of its modern procedure, while the
House of Commons developed its financial and legislative powers
and even asserted an occasional control over the executive by
impeachment of Ministers before the Lords, and by insisting that
redress of grievances should precede supply.   In all these ways
precedents were furnished for the future use of Stuart Parliaments,
no less valid than the precedents of an opposite tenor quotable
by royalist lawyers.

But at the close of the Middle Ages the Lower House was not
yet an independent power representing the chief political forces
in the country, as it was under Charles I.   The mediæval nobility
and the mediæval clergy stood between Commons and King,
and dwarfed the stature of both.   The Lower House enjoyed,
indeed, great influence in the State, but only on condition of
becoming to a large extent the tool of rival factions among the
nobility who were fighting each other for the control or possession
of the Crown.   At the close of Edward III's reign, the ' good
Parliament ' of 1376 aided the triumph of the popular cause of
the Black Prince and the Earl of March, and impeached their
enemies, but the next year's Parliament was packed by the
opposing faction of John of Gaunt.   Similarly in Richard II's 1377–
reign the Commons had no consistent policy of their own, but 1399.
were made the instrument of a series of State convulsions, con-
trived by the higher powers in deadly strife with one another.
In the following century the premature experiment in Parliamentary control of the executive ended in the aristocratic anarchy
which we know as the Wars of the Roses.

Before the Commons could aspire to take authority out of the
hands of the King, an interlude was necessary of increased royal
power under the Tudors, to strengthen the framework of the
State and reduce the nobles and clergy to the level of other

[1] See pp. 192–199, above, for Parliament under the first two Edwards.

subjects. But there was never any complete break in the forms or in the spirit of the ' mixed ' English Constitution. The most masterful of the Tudor monarchs used Parliament as the instrument of a revolution in Church and State which would, under the so-called ' Parliamentary' regime of the House of Lancaster, have been regarded as utterly beyond its competence. The complex forms and the free spirit of English government persist from century to century with continuity in change.

The Hundred Years' War, following on the Welsh and Scottish campaigns, rendered it more than ever impossible for the King to ' live of his own,' for in time of war the State expenses could not be met from the proceeds of the royal estates, law courts, feudal dues and other customary levies. It was found increasingly convenient for all parties that the King should raise extraordinary taxation, not by bargaining with individual merchants, cities and counties, but by meeting their spokesmen in the national Parliament. The voting of taxes on the wool trade, then the easiest way of collecting large sums in a hurry, gave to the burgher representatives a certain importance, in an age when they had no desire to meddle in affairs of State, or even, if they could help it, to attend Parliament at all. The financial importance of the modest burghers increased the financial and political importance of the knights of the shire, at whose side they sat in the Westminster Chapter House.

The success of the warfare waged against France and the power of the Commons who voted the taxes depended upon one another, no less in the days of Sluys, Crecy and Agincourt than in the days of La Hogue, Blenheim and Waterloo. Only when the King bade fair to become ruler of France in good earnest did the Commons take momentary alarm at the prospect : what indeed would become of the liberties of England if her monarch ruled Western Europe from Paris ? But the sudden death of Henry V and the career of Joan of Arc saved the British Constitution.[1]

1420.

1422–1429.

The mediæval English Parliament was not only a tax-voting and law-making assembly ; it was also ' the High Court of Parliament,' charged with judicial functions, not all of them distinguishable in those days from its legislative powers. The lawyers practising in Westminster Hall regarded the national assembly, so often held in their neighbourhood, as the greatest

---

[1] In 1420, when the French had acknowledged Henry V as heir to their throne, the English Commons withheld a money grant till the King returned from France, and called for a republication of the Statute of 1340, guarding against any subjection of the people of England to their King quâ King of France. The danger was much greater in 1420 than in 1340.

of all law courts, and were, for that reason, the more ready to assist its development. The alliance of the common lawyers with the Parliament men can be traced back to Plantagenet times.

The lawyer-like respect for precedent and procedure that has always characterized the House of Commons was a great strength to it from the first. It began its life, not as a mere ' debating assembly,' but as part of the King's ' High Court ' of Parliament, with the formality and the privilege of a law court. By the help of the lawyers among them and around them, the knights of the shire learnt many indispensable arts, foremost among these the drawing up of well-drafted ' bills ' ready to become Statutes, instead of mere petitions for redress. This change seems to have begun towards the end of Henry VI's reign, and gave the Commons greater control over the Acts to which their assent was asked, and even some power of initiation. Without the active help, continuous down the ages, of some of the best legal brains in the country, the House of Commons could never have become the principal source of legislation, nor have argued the constitutional case against the Crown lawyers and the royalist judges in the century of Coke, Selden and Somers.

The early connection of the Inns of Court with the House of Commons increased a tendency, apparent in students of the English Common Law, to regard the King himself as subject to law, and not as the absolute monarch envisaged by the Roman Code and its students. And so, at Richard II's deposition, it was formally imputed against him as a crime that he had declared the laws to be ' in his own breast,' and himself alone competent to frame and change them at will. This issue was not finally decided until the revolution that drove James II from the throne, but a preliminary judgment was passed upon it when a similar fate befell Richard Plantagenet.

These two revolutions, separated by almost three centuries 1399, of time, have an extraordinary likeness in their constitutional, 1688. and to some extent in their personal and accidental circumstances, although the great religious and international issues which make 1688 an era in European as well as English history were lacking in the quarrel between Richard and his subjects. Three years before the event, neither revolution could have been prophesied by the keenest observer, without an exceptional inner knowledge of the King's character. In 1396 Richard, as in 1685 James, still had a tolerable public record, strong partisans and adequate popularity, and though each had bitter enemies, those enemies had been subdued. Richard, indeed, had already governed well for half-a-dozen years, so long as his violent passions had been restrained by his affection for his first wife, Anne of Bohemia.[1] But after her death some obscure psychological change destroyed his nerve and judgment, just as advancing years, sudden power, and religious fanaticism seemed to make another and a worse man of James.

Three years sufficed to unite against either monarch his old friends and his old foes. For each suddenly entered on a course of open tyranny; each, after packing Parliament in vain, tried to govern without it; each broke law on law, and finally frightened every freeholder in the country by depriving people of their estates, without pretence of right. 'Richard the Redeless' was not more bloodthirsty than the clique of domineering nobles whose power he had quelled in former years. But for ill-advisedness, not even the ejection of the Fellows of Magdalen by James surpassed Richard's seizure of the estates of the House of Lancaster, a family, till then, by no means inveterately hostile to his person. The light-hearted folly of the act is heard in the jingle of Shakespeare's rhyming couplet :—

> Think what you will : we seize into our hands
> His plate, his goods, his money and his lands.

The return of Henry of Lancaster from abroad, claiming his paternal estates, rallied the whole country round him, like the coming of William of Orange. Richard, like James, made every possible mistake at the crisis, could get no one to fight for him, and was deposed by Parliament on the express ground that he had broken the fundamental laws of the Kingdom. And Henry, like William, was called to the empty throne partly indeed by hereditary right, but yet more by Parliamentary title, for neither Henry IV nor William of Orange was the nearest heir.

The result of the Revolution of 1399 was to set the power of the two Houses of Parliament on ground at once higher and firmer than ever before. They had not only deposed a King— as had happened when Edward II was forced to yield the throne to his son—but this time they had chosen the successor. The Lancastrian, like the Hanoverian Kings, ruled by Parliamentary title, and under them the power and privilege of both Houses must needs be respected.

It is not, therefore, surprising to find that the political theories of the Fifteenth and of the Eighteenth Centuries both lay great stress on the legal limitations of the Crown's power, and proudly contrast the freedom of the English subject to the slavery of

---

[1] It is supposed that some of her Bohemian (Czech) countrymen who came over with her, must have taken back copies of Wycliffe's works to Bohemia— with the result of the great Hussite movement there in the Fifteenth Century.

the French. Such was the constant theme of the contemporaries of Hogarth, Blackstone and Burke, and such, three hundred years earlier, was the boast of the typical common lawyer of the Fifteenth Century, Chief Justice Fortescue, a patriot who loved his country as being the land of liberty. Though he was driven into exile with the Lancastrian party after Towton, he 1461 sat down abroad to write the praises of the English constitution: ' For the King of England,' he writes, ' cannot alter nor change the lawes of the Realme at his pleasure. For why, hee governeth his people by power, not only royall, but politique '—' constitutional,' as we should say. The spirit of the English Common Law, writes Fortescue, is repugnant to the theory of the Civil or Roman law, dominant in other countries, that ' The Prince his pleasure hath the force of a law.' He goes on to contrast, from personal observation, the misery of the French common people, continually robbed and insulted by the King's soldiers and servants, to the ' Realme of England, where no man sojourneth in an other man's house without the love and the leave of the good man of the same house '—in other words, the Englishman's house is his castle.

It is very remarkable that Fortescue should have used such language at the height of the Wars of the Roses, and the more so since he was bitterly conscious of what was wrong in contemporary England. He diagnosed the ' lack of government,' tracing the evils of the day to their true source in ' the perils that come to the King from overmighty subjects,' and he demanded a richer and stronger monarchy and poorer and less powerful nobles. He foreshadowed, in some detail, the policy actually carried out by Henry VII.

The great nobles and their satellite gentry, who disturbed the England of the Fifteenth Century with their lawless brawls, had at least accepted the fact of the unity of the national State. They did not aspire to govern whole provinces with feudal or princely sway, like the French nobles whom it was the task of Louis XI to subdue after the final departure of the English invaders. In England the rival King-makers did not seek to destroy or divide the royal authority, but to control and exploit it. They did not even attempt to restore the now obsolete ' franchises ' or private courts which de Warenne had so noisily maintained against Edward I's *Quo Warranto* enquiry.[1] The latter-day noble knew how to get what he wanted in the King's courts, by bribing and intimidating county jurors and royal Judges and Justices of the Peace. Indeed, the law-breakers often held the King's commission in the shires. The records of

[1] See pp. 191–192, above.

the period sometimes give a curious picture of a set of country gentlemen now enforcing the King's Peace and the Statutes of Labourers, now charged with robbery, piracy and murder, now sitting on the Bench, now sent to prison.

While too many of the smaller gentry acted in this fashion in the country-side, their patrons and paymasters, the great nobles, were quarrelling with each other for the control of the central government, as the fount of power, honours and wealth. The battlefield was the King's Council, where the executive power was lodged. The nobles regarded the Council as a body representative of the forces in the State, or at least of the higher aristocracy, a sort of Parliament in permanent session, where each of the great lords had a personal right to sit whenever he felt so disposed. The King, on the other hand, regarded the Council as personal to himself, to be filled by whom he would, not necessarily by great nobles ; under a foolish King this meant the rule of favourites, under a wise King the rule of trained, professional experts.

Conflict between the King's view and the nobles' view of what the Council should be, had often led to strife, particularly in the reign of Richard II. And in a sense Henry IV's wars with the Percies, Mortimer and Scrope had been fought on the same issue, complicated by Welsh and northern border problems, and by the dynastic question never wholly at rest. But neither the royal nor the aristocratic theory as to the proper constitution of the Council had completely extinguished the other, for each had a solid basis in the actual needs and forces of that age. Only during the long minority of Henry VI the Council inevitably fell into the hands of the great nobles, and when Henry grew to manhood he lacked ability and character to resume authority as Richard II had in like circumstances done. The personal feuds of the great nobles with each other for supremacy at the Council board and in the bedchamber continued as before, until at length they plunged the country into the Wars of the Roses.

The weakness of the saintly Henry among the rival factions in the Council was translated into lawless violence in the country-side by the privileged clients of the great families. Parliament should have supplied a remedy, and strengthened the power of the King against the nobles. But it did not even attempt the task. In Henry VI's reign the mediæval House of Commons reached its highest point of constitutional privilege, but failed to use it for the benefit of the nation. There was no friction between Parliament and Council, because both were controlled by the same aristocratic cliques, whose only contests were against one another.

In 1430 an Act of Parliament took away the county franchise

1402–
1405.

1422–
1437.

1455.

from the general body of freemen suitors in the Shire Court, and limited the right of voting for knights of the shire to the class of forty shilling freeholders. So the letter of the law remained until the Reform Bill of 1832. But in Lancastrian times a freehold worth forty shillings a year was a much higher qualification than it became after the value of money had fallen. For some generations, therefore, the disfranchising law of 1430 excluded, as it was confessedly designed to exclude, almost everyone below the small gentry, and the result of a diminished county electorate was to increase the power of the great nobles over Parliament. The House of Commons, in aristocratic leading strings, was getting ever more out of touch with the people, while driving the theory of Parliamentary government to extremes in an age too soon. Because the nobles could use the House of Commons for their purposes, they were not jealous of its growth. Here again, we find a parallel, in certain respects, to the Eighteenth Century, when the power and prestige of the House of Commons were on the increase, at the very time that it was becoming an aristocratic assembly on the basis of a franchise tending to become rather less than more popular.

It is significant that the last of the English were driven out of France in 1453 and that the Wars of the Roses began only two years later in the streets of St. Albans. The return of the garrisons and armies from oversea filled England with knights and archers, accustomed to war, licence and plunder, and fit for any mischief. The unemployed and starving veteran was dangerous enough, but yet more dangerous was the ' company ' of warriors in private employment, kept together by its paymaster when the French war was over, to further his political ambitions or his designs upon his neighbours' estates.[1]

Nor was the Hundred Years' War injurious to English society only when it came to an end. Throughout its whole course it had bred habits of lawlessness and violence at home. The Parliaments of Edward III had complained of estate-jumping, carrying off of heiresses and breach of the peace by gentlemen and their retainers as a new and growing evil. And to the influence of the foreign campaigns must be added the older and more permanent influence of the Welsh and Scottish Borders, where the Marcher Lords in their castles, like Mortimer in Wigmore and Percy in Alnwick, lived constantly under arms, preserving the feudal customs and spirit that had disappeared from the more civilized South and East. Wales and the North between

---

[1] See p. 228, above, for the ' companies ' in the Hundred Years' War, who now became the ' retainers ' at home.

K

English Miles
0 10 20   40   60   80

*Names of great families with influence
in a district are in brackets thus:-* (PERCY)

SCOTLAND

I. of Man
(STANLEY)

(CLIFFORD)

Hedgeley Moor
(PERCY) ✗ 1464
○ Alnwick Castle

Hexham
1464 ✗
Newcastle

(NEVILLE)

(NEVILLE)

(DUCHY OF
LANCASTER)

York
✗ Towton, 1461

Wakefield
1460

R. Humber

Ravenspur
*Henry IV landed 1399
Edward IV ,, 1471*

(STANLEY)

(LANCASTER)

(OWEN
GLENDOWER)

WALES

AND ITS MARCH

Mortimer's Cross

Shrewsbury
○ ✗ 1403

(MORTIMER)

Wigmore
Castle

(STAFFORD)

Stoke
1487 ○

(YORK)

Bosworth
✗ 1485

○ Lutterworth

Caister
Cas. ○

Norwich

(LANCASTER)

○ Cambridge

Tewkesbury
✗ 1471

Milford
Haven
Henry VII landed 1485

Bristol

R. Severn

St.Albans, 1455, 1461
○ ✗
○ Oxford

Westminster

Barnet, 1471
✗

Eton ✗ London
Windsor
Northampton
1460

R. Thames

Blackheath
1497

(BEAUFORT)

○ Winchester

Plymouth
Warwick landed 1470

Emery Walker Ltd. sc.

MAP XVII.—England in the Fifteenth Century

them caused the troubles under Henry IV; and the Wars of the Roses were to a large extent a quarrel between Welsh Marcher Lords, who were also great English nobles, closely related to the English throne.[1]

A characteristic feature of this revival of anarchy in a civilized society was the combination of legal chicanery with military violence. It was an age of litigation tempered by house-breaking. In Stephen's reign the barbarous Barons had had no need to be lawyers; but under Henry VI every ambitious noble, and every country gentleman who aspired to found the fortunes of his family, was well versed in the processes of law as well as in the siegecraft of forcible entry into a moated manor-house. Such a man kept in his pay not only archers but lawyers and jurymen. The correspondence of the Paston family has made us familiar with the type in reality, and Stevenson's Sir Daniel Brackley in fiction. The law-breakers were often Justices of the Peace, and some of the worst ' ambushes ' were committed by royal judges and by nobles high in office. The operations of purely private war were sometimes on a scale that matched the more regular dynastic struggle. In 1469 a dispute over Sir John Fastolf's will led to a five weeks' siege of Caister Castle by the Duke of Norfolk with 3000 men, finally ended by cannon to breach the walls—and this in East Anglia, the richest and most settled part of the island.

Juries were as regularly intimidated in Fifteenth Century England as in Nineteenth Century Ireland. ' Maintenance ' was the recognized duty of the great man to protect his client in the King's courts from the consequences of illegal action, and since the English courts already insisted on the unanimity of the twelve jurymen, it was seldom possible to get verdicts against the friend of a great man. Maitland has expressed the opinion that more injustice was done at this period by wrongful acquittals than by wrongful condemnations. The subsequent Tudor practice of making jurors answer for their verdicts before the King's Council, though incompatible with the full freedom of the subject, was at one time regarded as a much needed reform. At the outbreak of the Wars of the Roses the grievances of quiet people were summed up in these rude verses :—

> In every shire with jacks and salads [2] clean
> Misrule doth rise and maketh neighbours war.
> The weaker goeth beneath, as oft is seen,
> The mightiest his quarrell will prefer.

---

[1] See p. 213, above.   [2] Cuirasses and helmets.

They kill your men alway one by one,
And who say aught he shall be beat doubtless.
For in your realm Justice of Peace be none
That dare aught now the contesters oppress.

The law is like unto a Welshman's hose,
To each man's legs that shapen is and meet ;
So maintainers subvert it and transpose.
Through might it is full low laid under feet.

What are we to think of this outbreak of savage wrong-doing
in the highest ranks of a society so far emerged from feudal
barbarism, and artistically so much the superior of our own in
the arts and crafts of daily life ? But contrast is the essence
of social history, and particularly of mediæval history. We
think of the Fifteenth Century as the era of chivalry : for did
not its knights wear the plate armour in which modern artists
depict Sir Galahad with his pure, schoolboy face, and was it
not the century when Sir Thomas Malory produced his ' Morte
Arthur ' ? But the actual contemporaries of Malory would,
at close quarters, have seemed to us singularly deficient in
' chivalry ' according to modern notions. It was not that in
England ' chivalry ' any longer looked with unmitigated scorn
on burgher and villein, as it still did in the yet more ' chivalrous '
society of France and Flanders recorded by Chastellain. Peasant
emancipation, burgher wealth and the prudent mixing and inter-
marriage of all the well-to-do classes were in England tending to
fill up the chasm that elsewhere divided the gentles from common
folk. But ' chivalry ' was, in England as elsewhere, compatible
with brutal violence and calculating materialism, not least in
the treatment of women.

1470.

Wife-beating was a recognized right of man, and was practised
without shame by high as well as low. The woman's defence was
her tongue, sometimes giving her the mastery in the household,
but often leading to muscular retort. One of the Fifteenth
Century English translations of the fashionable manual of the
Knight of La Tour Landry thus describes the proper treatment
of a scolding wife :—

He smote her with his fist down to the earth. And then with his
foot he struck her in the visage and brake her nose, and all her life
after she had her nose crooked that she might not for shame show her
visage it was so foul blemished. . . . Therefore the wife ought to suffer
and let the husband have the word, and to be master.

Similarly, the daughter who refused to marry the gentleman
of her parents' choice was liable to be locked up, beaten and

flung about the room, without any shock being inflicted on public opinion.[1] Marriage was not an affair of personal affection but of family avarice, particularly in the ' chivalrous ' upper classes. ' For very need,' complains a member of the noble family of Scrope, ' I was fain to sell a little daughter I have, for much less than I should have done by possibility.' Betrothal often took place while one or both of the parties was in the cradle, and marriage when they were scarcely out of the nurse's charge. It was sometimes difficult to get a little fellow to say the necessary words of the ceremony, before running back to his toys.

The elaborate literature of love, French in origin, of which Chaucer's *Troilus and Cresseyde* was the finest flower, was concerned with marriage principally as a disturber thereof, though the old ruling of the Court of Love ' that no married pair can really be in love with each other ' admitted in the world of reality of countless exceptions. And, indeed, Chaucer, who saw human nature not merely through the stained glass of literature, has drawn in his *Franklin's Tale* a beautiful picture of wedded faith and love alongside of the professional ' lover's ' torments. And though child-marriage and forced marriage were accursed customs, there were cases of young people successfully defying the heartless plans of their elders, even in the prosaic society of the Pastons. Side by side with the violence and materialism of mediæval life, there was much also of the 'good nature and integrity of the English people ' which was not a thing of yesterday.

Civilization and knowledge were all the while encroaching on the realm of ignorance. For although Oxford in the Fifteenth Century decayed in intellectual vigour prior to the blossoming of the New Learning, the end of the Middle Ages was a great period for the foundation of schools, besides William of Wykeham's Winchester and Henry VI's Eton. Guilds and private persons were constantly endowing chantries with priests to say masses for souls, and schools were often attached to them. Other schools were being founded on an independent basis, sometimes with lay headmasters. All this was over and above the Collegiate, Cathedral and parish church schools of earlier foundation.

Reading and writing, therefore, had quite ceased, in the days of York and Lancaster, to be the monopoly of the clergy. Not only the merchants but the bailiffs of manors kept good accounts and often wrote tolerable Latin in their business documents. Members of landed families like the Pastons corresponded with

---

[1] Locking up a daughter to force her to a loathed match was not impossible in squires' families as late as the middle of the Eighteenth Century, as we know from Squire Western's proceedings in the case of a daughter to whom he was much attached. A Fifteenth Century Squire Western would have beaten Sophia into the bargain.

one another by letters written in their own hands, usually on legal or other business or to convey political news.

For several generations after Chaucer's death in 1400, English literature remained under Chaucer's domination. The chief poets were of his school, and in the latter part of the century Caxton made haste to print him for a public that could not get enough copies of him in manuscript.

The works of Chaucer and his numerous imitators expressed to the satisfaction of the society of that age its delicate sense of the beauty of natural sights and sounds in the orchards and artificial gardens where it passed so many hours of dalliance, or in the wild wood beyond. To-day we like our gardens and parks to appear wild, because we have so terribly tamed the land outside, but from the Fifteenth to the early Eighteenth Centuries they liked artificial gardens because they had so much of wild nature elsewhere, in which their souls rejoiced no less than in the gardens. The song of birds, the run of water, the flowers in bloom and the woods in leaf gave those country-dwellers a joy of which they were fully conscious. It is in nature that the lover seeks ease from his ' love-longing ' :—

> And the river that I sate upon
> It made such a noise as it ron,
> Accordaunt with the birdës' armony
> Me thought it was the best melody
> That might ben heard of any mon.

The medicine recommended for the wounds of despised love is—

> Go looke on the fresh daisie!

Or again—

> A wind, so small it scarcely might be less,
> Made in the leavës green a noisë soft,
> Accordant to the fowlës song aloft.

The beauty of the domestic architecture of the manor-houses, then coming to perfection in stone or the new-fangled brick, the artistic merit and originality in dress, furniture and articles of common use for farm, barn and household, enriched life with joys that have disappeared from it, both for the craftsman who created and the owner who used his creation. Altogether a marvellous place was England at the end of the Middle Ages, so full of what we have lost, so empty of what we now have, and yet, as Chaucer and the Pastons have written and shown us, so English and so like us all the while.

1455. When the Wars of the Roses at length broke out in form, no question of principle or even of class interest was involved in the quarrel between Lancaster and York. It was a faction fight between the families allied to the royal house, contending for power and wealth and ultimately for the possession of the Crown. On each side was ranged a group of great nobles. And each noble had his *clientèle* of knights, gentry, led captains, lawyers and clergy, some attached to his person, some living in distant manors, but all conscious that their fortunes were involved in the rise or fall of their ' good lord.' Changing of sides was more frequent in this civil war than in others, because there was no principle to desert. The mass of the people looked on with indifference, the towns and villages only bargaining that they should, as far as possible, be spared the horrors of war. Even London, for once, remained neuter in the civil strife convulsing England. In return, the armies were much less destructive than in France, because their chiefs knew well that if the neutrals were roused by ill treatment they could soon dispose of the few thousand partisan soldiers, who scoured the country in hot pursuit of one another from Plymouth to the foot of the Cheviots, making and unmaking the short-lived fortunes of Lancaster and York. So in spite of the wars, which were at the worst inter-mittent, the neutral majority suffered little, and trade followed its usual course along the rivers and riding tracks with not much more than the usual amount of disturbance from high-waymen and water-thieves.[1]

But the actual combatants suffered severely. The fighting nobles were savage in their treatment of one another. There were many sudden turns of fortune's wheel, and each meant a fresh confiscation of great estates, and a new batch of noble heads for the block, over and above the heavy proportion of leaders killed upon the field of battle. The Crown was enriched by these confiscations and the nobles were impoverished, while their numbers, never great, were much reduced. The way was thus prepared for the Tudor policy of bridling ' overmighty subjects.' The Wars of the Roses were a bleeding operation performed by the nobility upon their own body. To the nation it was a blessing in disguise.

The hosts engaged in battles like Towton, Barnet and Tewkes-

[1] In the Middle Ages roads were little more than riding-ways, but rivers were deeper and more navigable than now. York, Lincoln, Doncaster and other inland towns depended on the water for their trade. As early as the Fourteenth Century, London consumed coal as its normal fuel, because it could come by sea from Tyneside. The traders of the English towns had a great interest in keeping the rivers on which they stood open to barges, by removing weirs and bridges that impeded traffic. Partly for this reason fords or ferries were preferred to bridges even when, as seldom happened, money was available to build a bridge. In the Middle Ages to travel by land meant to walk or ride, and to cross a stream or river meant to splash through a ford or to hail the ferryman.

bury were partly professional mercenaries, partly friends and tenants hastily called out ; they were serving under private paymasters, at whose behest they marched under the banner of York or Lancaster. The tactics were those employed by the same leaders in the recent French war. Cavalry fighting was the exception rather than the rule, the normal soldier being a mounted infantryman. Cannon and the new hand-guns were sometimes used in the field, but the longbow was still the lord of weapons. The archer still fought on foot, in line beside the knight. But the battles had not the same character as Crecy or Agincourt, because in England there was little to choose between the archery on the two sides, and rather than stand long under the arrow-storm, men came as soon as possible to close quarters and hacked out a decision with sword and bill.

1461–1483.

The figure that rose victorious from the murderous mêlée of the Wars of the Roses was Edward IV, heir of the House of York, the best soldier produced by those rough-and-tumble campaigns. The battle of Towton, fought in a blinding Yorkshire snowstorm, placed him on the throne. He was the first English Prince of the Renaissance type, so familiar to us in Louis XI of France and the Tudor Henries, though Edward was too lazy and self-indulgent to have served Machiavelli for a perfect model.

These faults once cost him dear. Warwick the King-maker, of the great House of Neville, type of the noblemen who were England's bane, had done much to set Edward on the throne of the incompetent saint of Lancaster. Ten years later, in a fit of jealousy for unrewarded service, analogous to the jealousy of the Percies against Henry IV, Warwick dragged Henry VI out of the Tower and made him King once more. But in the campaign of Barnet and Tewkesbury the luxurious Edward showed that when aroused he was still the better soldier. The deaths of Warwick and of Henry VI and his son were the results of the affair, leaving the House of York firmer than ever on the throne, whence nothing could have dislodged it but its own intestine broils and treacheries.

1461.

1471.

Edward IV's policy was a faulty and incomplete rehearsal of the policy afterwards pursued by Henry VII. Edward had no desire for 'overmighty subjects' in his kingdom, least of all on the steps of the throne. His own brother, ' false, fleeting, perjured Clarence,' soon followed Warwick to the further shore of the Styx, where the shades of England's noble and royal families were collecting in troops. And since Edward had made good his claim rather by conquest than by Parliamentary title, he had not the Lancastrian respect for Parliament, nor is there any evidence that people thought the worse of his rule for that. It was, indeed, a dangerous moment for Parliamentary institutions. Edward seldom summoned the Houses, and he began to rely less on taxes voted by the Commons and more on carefully modulated 'benevolences' or forced gifts from individual subjects.

A chief instrument of aristocratic power under Henry VI had been the King's Council.[1] It was, therefore, in little favour with Edward IV until in the latter part of his reign he saw reason to revive it as the instrument of the King's personal rule, a policy carried much further by the Tudors after him.

Edward had less inclination to the society of the great nobles than to that of the merchant princes of the rising plutocracy. London, ' the flower of cities all ' as it was now becoming in the whole world's esteem, was growing in wealth and outward beauty and inward intelligence, while the nobles were cutting each other's throats and the Church was losing its moral and intellectual leadership. The monastic scribes could no longer meet the nation's needs, and indeed the abbey chronicles were growing more meagre than of old. A new class of ' scriveners ' or 'stationers' copied books in an attempt to keep level with the growing public demand for poetry of the school of Chaucer, and for chronicles, histories and other works in prose. In these circumstances the setting up under Edward IV's patronage of Caxton's printing-press at Westminster was perhaps the greatest English event of the century. Edward, who wanted the money and liked the company of intellectual men and sprightly women, both from policy and choice lived much with the great citizens of London and their wives.

But with all this Princecraft of the modern order, Edward IV failed to establish the King's Peace in the counties, and to ' bridle stout noblemen and gentlemen.' That great work was left to the Star Chamber of Henry VII. No effective plan for strengthening the executive in the enforcement of order was conceived by the House of York. Private war, maintenance, and estate-jumping flourished only a little less after Towton and Tewkesbury than while Henry VI still sat on the throne. Moreover, Edward IV, instead of being content to govern through a professional civil service of clergy, lawyers, bourgeois and gentry, made the mistake of raising up his wife's relations, the Woodvilles and Greys, as parvenu nobles.

On Edward's death, the jealousy felt by the remnant of the **1483.** old nobility against the upstart Woodvilles and Greys, enabled Edward's brother, Richard Duke of Gloucester, to usurp the

[1] See p. 256, above.

L

throne. Edward V was a child, and his mother and her relations were odious to the nobles and not popular with the nation. This intestine feud was the ruin of the House of York. Richard was no monster born ; there is no clear evidence that he was more responsible for the deaths of Henry VI and Clarence than the rest of the Yorkist party, nor, prior to his usurpation of the throne, was his record as treacherous as that of his brother Clarence or as bloody as that of his brother Edward. But the glittering bait of the crown ensnared his soul : he murdered his two nephews under trust, and the disappearance of the Princes in the Tower, following on the violence of the usurpation, lost him the loyalty of the common people. The English had not been wholly debased by the wars and murderings of their ruling class, and the revulsion of feeling against Richard was the beginning of better things.

The claimants to the reversion of the throne, Yorkist and Lancastrian alike, had disappeared so fast in the battles and executions of twenty-five years that, on the death of Edward V, a Welsh gentleman named Henry Tudor, Earl of Richmond, was able to put up a very respectable case for himself on the Lancastrian side. After the custom of opposition leaders in those brisk times, he had sought refuge abroad, first in the Court of Brittany, then in France. Taking advantage of the unpopularity of the child-murderer, he landed with a slender and untrustworthy force, at Milford Haven, on the coast of his native Wales. The racial enthusiasm of the Welsh for a descendant of their ancient British Princes,—marching, as Henry was careful to march, under the red-dragon standard of Cadwallader,—broke out into prophecy and song, and enabled him to raise in little more than a week a small army of zealous supporters as he traversed that ever warlike land. They, with the help of a few French and English adventurers, won Bosworth Field against a King for whom the mass of his English subjects were ashamed to fight. Here, indeed, was one of fortune's freaks : on a bare Leicestershire upland, a few thousand men in close conflict foot to foot, while a few thousand more stood aside to watch the issue, sufficed to set upon the throne of England the greatest of all her royal lines, that should guide her through a century of change down new and larger streams of destiny, undreamt of by any man who plied bow and bill that day in the old-world quarrel of York and Lancaster.

Margin notes: 1483.   Aug. 22, 1485.

BOOKS FOR FURTHER READING

C. L. Kingsford, *Prejudice and Promise in* 15*th Century England* (Ford lectures, 1925) ; James Gairdner, *Richard III* ; Sir James H. Ramsay, *Lancaster and York*, 2 vols. ; Vickers and other works already mentioned, pp. 152 and 250, above.

Begin here.

BOOK III

THE TUDORS

RENAISSANCE, REFORMATION AND SEA POWER

INTRODUCTION

THE Europe of to-day is divided perpendicularly into a number
of separate States, each absolute sovereign in its own territories,
and each purporting to represent a racial or national idea. But
in the Middle Ages, Europe was divided horizontally into Estates
and corporations of clergy, nobles, villeins and burghers,—governed
locally by their own domestic laws, in convents, castles, manors
and walled cities. In the shelter of that framework the arts of
civilization, torn up by the barbarian inroads, took root again
and flourished in new forms. But the individual had little freedom in the feudal village and less in the monastery ; while, even
in the chartered town and guild, initiative was checked and the
unprivileged stranger excluded. Expansion, progress and individuality were hampered, until these rigid corporations had lost
some of their power, and until the close control of the mediæval
Church over the lives and thoughts of all men had been loosened.

Middle Age
hampered
life

The only power strong enough to effect a social revolution
of such extent and gravity was the power of the national State.
The despotism of the State laid indeed restraints of its own upon
liberty, but it cleared more elbow room for the individual than
he had enjoyed in the mediæval world. The era of private enterprise and expanding genius associated with Drake and Raleigh,
Shakespeare and Bacon, was the outcome of two hundred years
of social disruption and rebirth, of the appeal of Renaissance and
Reformation to the individual mind and conscience, and the
subjection of corporate power to the national will embodied in
Crown and Parliament.

Corporate
power of
State
favoured
individual

The mediæval system passed away, not by chance or by the
whim of a King impatient to be divorced, but on account of
profound changes in the habits of the English people, most of
which we have seen already at work in the Fourteenth and Fifteenth Centuries. The emancipation of the villeins ; the growth
of London ; the rise of educated and active-minded middle
classes ; the spread of cloth manufacture and other trading

activities outside the chartered towns; the unifying effect of the Common Law, the royal administration and the national Parliament; the national pride engendered by the Hundred Years' War and the democratic triumphs of the English archer over the mounted aristocrat; the adoption of the English language by the educated classes; the invention of cannon to shatter the noble's stronghold, and of the printing-press to undermine the churchman's monopoly of learning; the studies of the Renaissance, which on the one hand set religion in the light of a scholarly examination of the Scriptures, and on the other revealed in ancient Greece and Rome ideals unknown to mediæval Christendom; the discovery of the ocean trade routes and of the New World, which had held no place in the intellectual outlook or commercial habits of any former age—all these changes, spiritual and material, combined to dissolve the fabric of mediæval society in England.

At the same time all Western Europe was tending to group itself into national States—France, Spain, Portugal. Inside each modern State, power was increasingly concentrated in the King's hands. But whereas in France and Spain the new monarchy was allied with the old Church, in England it was allied with the old Parliament. In France and Spain mediæval religion was preserved, while mediæval Parliaments decayed and the Roman Imperial law was received as the basis of the Prince's absolute power. In England mediæval religion was changed, while we preserved mediæval Parliaments, native Common Law, and the constitutional character of the Kingship. The distinction between England and continental Europe, particularly Latin Europe, which the Norman Conquest had obscured, was emphasized once more by these opposite developments on the two sides of the Channel. English and French civilization, at one time not very easily distinguishable, became not only separate but mutually repellent.

Tudor England, while effecting a great revolution in the social system, characteristically preserved the form and even the spirit of much that was old. Most of the orders, corporations and institutions which had been the principal channels of mediæval life, remained intact on condition of submitting to the sovereign authority of the State. Universities, nobles, lawyers, Bishops, secular clergy and town corporations survived ostensibly in the old forms. Some institutions, like the cosmopolitan orders of monks and friars, could not be fitted into the new national scheme of things, and were ruthlessly destroyed by the State. Rights like those of Sanctuary and Benefit of Clergy were reduced or abolished, because they set limits to the execution of the national law. Noble and commoner, clergy and laity were made equal before the law of the land. The class of villeins excluded from these benefits disappeared, and the nobleman's coercion of the royal courts through his retainers became a thing of the past. The ecclesiastical courts exercised diminished powers over the laity, by the authority no longer of the Pope but of the Crown. Cosmopolitan feudalism and the cosmopolitan Church went down before the new idea of a national State with a national Church attached. The 'liberties' of the mediæval clergy and aristocracy, slices of sovereignty held in private or corporate hands, were resumed in favour of the liberty of the ordinary English subject, sheltered behind the power of the State.

So, too, the regulation of trade, instead of being as formerly an affair of each chartered town or guild, became the business of the national authorities. We have already seen Plantagenet Parliaments trying to regulate wages and prices by their Statutes of Labourers, to be enforced by the King's Justices of the Peace. In Tudor times this national control of economy was carried still further. The law of apprenticeship was regulated no longer by each local guild, but by the Statute of Artificers passed by Queen Elizabeth's Parliament. The provision for the poor, formerly left to the monasteries and guilds and to private charity, was provided for as a duty incumbent on society at large, and enforced by the State. The chief agents of this statutory control of the nation's economic life,—as also of its political and judicial life,—were the unpaid Justices of the Peace appointed by the Crown, who formed the link between the views of the central authority and the facts of local administration. They performed as servants of the State many functions which the feudal baron had performed in his own personal right.

When the Crown in Parliament effected a series of revolutions in ecclesiastical and religious affairs, it was demonstrated beyond all question that the State had acquired unlimited sovereign authority. In the Middle Ages such radical legislation would have been regarded as altogether beyond the legal and moral competence of any power in England. But in the Tudor epoch the nation asserted its new strength, and, expelling all foreign authorities and suppressing all local immunities, claimed the right to do whatever it liked within its own frontiers. These novel claims of complete independence for the nation and omnicompetence for the State, were embodied in the person of the Prince. This is the general cause of the Kingworship of the Sixteenth Century.

The plenary powers of the new State could, in that age, have been exercised only by the King. Parliament, half debating society and half court of law, had neither the strength nor the ambition for such a part. Indeed it was a main function of the Tudor Kings and their Privy Council to teach to the Parliament men at Westminster and to the Justices of the Peace in the countryside the work of real government, which had been so sadly neglected in the previous century. Parliament was ready to be the scholar and servant of royalty, like a prentice serving his time and fitting himself to become partner and heir.

So, too, the peculiar religious circumstances of that age of transition favoured the power of the Crown in England. By putting himself at the head of the Anti-clerical revolution that destroyed the mediæval power and privilege of the Church, Henry VIII not only became the heir of much of that power, but set the new Monarchy in alliance with the strongest forces of the coming age,—London, the middle classes, the seagoing population, the Protestant preachers, the squirearchy bribed and reinforced by the abbey lands ; together they proved more than a match for the forces of the old world,—the monks and friars, the remnant of the feudal nobility and gentry in the North, and popular Catholic piety which was strongest in districts farthest removed from London. The secular clergy acquiesced, at first as neuters; but in the course of the long reign of Elizabeth, the parish clergy and the schoolmasters became the chief instruments of Protestant propaganda and instruction.

Roman Catholic zeal in England was at its lowest ebb when Henry struck at the mediæval Church, and it failed to revive when his daughter Mary gave the old religion another chance. It only recovered vigour with the Jesuit reaction well on in the reign of Elizabeth. That revival came a generation too late for success, and it came from continental sources that infuriated the rising nationalism of the English. Catholic was identified in the vulgar mind with Jesuit, and Jesuit with Spaniard. The issue became involved in the struggle of our seamen for the free use of the ocean and the world beyond, which the Pope had divided with a stroke of the pen between Portugal and Spain. The new commercial and naval aspirations of England, embodied in the Tudor Royal Navy, in Drake and his captains, and in the trading companies of London,—and Raleigh's prophetic visions of colonial Empire, were all arrayed against the old religion and sailed under the banner of the new monarchy.

In the Tudor epoch as a whole, Catholic zeal had the feebleness of age and Protestant zeal the feebleness of immaturity. Neither dared to defy the Crown, as Catholics and Protestants then defied it in France and in Scotland, and as the Puritans afterwards defied it in England. Hence the bewildering changes

of religion with every fresh Tudor monarch were accepted by
laity and clergy alike much as a change of Cabinet is accepted
to-day. The only successful defiance of the Tudors' claim to
settle the faith of their subjects was the passive resistance of
the three hundred Protestant martyrs burned in Mary's reign,
and that was successful only on condition of being passive.
Wyatt's Protestant rebellion failed as hopelessly as the Catholic
Pilgrimage of Grace and the rising of the Earls. It was not
an age of religious zeal in England, like the age of Becket or
the age of Cromwell, yet the greatest of all religious questions
then came up for decision. It was, therefore, the supreme
moment for the Erastian Prince, who stepped into the place
whence the Pope had been deposed, fully prepared, with the help
of Parliament, to define the faith of all his subjects, as the great
mass of them heartily desired that he should do. So long as
men persisted in the mediæval error that there should be only
one religion tolerated, so long the only alternative to priestly
rule of society was the Erastian State. Liberty of conscience
slowly grew up out of the struggles between the Erastian State
and the various phases and sects of religious enthusiasm.

Only towards the end of Elizabeth's reign are there indications
that the House of Commons might some day acquire enough
political strength and enough religious conviction to dispute the
control of ecclesiastical affairs with the Crown. In that case
the ensuing confusion might enable the individual conscience to
come by its own. The assumption by the State of the persecuting
powers of the old Church was, as we can now see, provisional in
its nature ; however little questioned for the moment, it was
bound to break down in the end if persistently challenged by the
private conscience.

The Tudors gave a new direction to the external and expansive
energies of the English people. The attempt to conquer France
was not seriously resumed ; little England, with its four to five
million inhabitants, was thrown upon the defensive in Europe
by the strength of the new French and Spanish monarchies.
Her rising school of diplomacy, from Wolsey to Cecil, pursued the ' Balance of Power ' as England's only chance of
security in face of the great continental States now being formed.
Partly owing to these apprehensions, Henry VIII made, for the
first time in our history, a really fine Royal Navy. Celtic Wales
and the anarchic Welsh March were reduced to order and annexed
on terms of equality to England,—the first successful act of English
Imperialism of the modern type, due to Henry VIII and his
inherited understanding of things Welsh. Scotland he misunderstood, but under Elizabeth the future union of the two

Kingdoms was prepared, when Scotland was detached from her old French connections and bound in friendship to England on the basis of common Protestant interests. The future Great Britain, the heretical sea-power on the flank of the great continental despotisms, was already clearly visible in outline. At the same time the conquest of Ireland, after being neglected by England for four hundred years, was at length undertaken in earnest, in an age too late for the happiness of either party.

Last, but not least, just when social and economic change at home was setting free individuals of all classes to wander and seek fortune afar, the new paths of the ocean were opened to the adventurous, the avaricious and the valiant, where the restless spirit of the race could find better work to do than vexing France with fresh Agincourts and England with fresh Towtons and Barnets. The descendants of the archers and retainers thronged the decks of the privateers bound for the Spanish Main, and manned the merchantmen trading to Muscovy, the Levant and the further East. England had ceased to be at the world's extremity and was found, as the new *mappa mundi* yearly unfolded itself, to be each year nearer to the strategic centre. While the Armada was going to pieces on the rocks, England was at last entering on the wider spaces of her destiny ; and the sense of adventure in untrodden regions of mind and matter inspired the rising generation, who went out in the spirit of free individual initiative to explore new worlds of land and water, knowledge and imagination. At that propitious moment the English language reached its perfection of force and beauty in the mouths of men, and at that moment Shakespeare lived to use it.

CHAPTER I

Henry VII. The machinery of Tudor government. Economic and
social change. Cloth trade, Poor Law, and farming

Kings : Henry VII, 1485–1509 ; Henry VIII, 1509–1547

SHAKESPEARE was well advised to leave the reign of Henry VII as a blank in the sequence of his historical plays. For, having once drawn Richmond, the open-hearted young champion of Bosworth Field, gambling gaily with his life and addressing his little band of brothers with the ingenuous fervour of the Prince in the fairy tale, how would he have reconciled that portrait with the character in which Henry as King impressed himself upon posterity, as the English counterpart of Louis XI, cautious and thrifty to a fault, moving silently about with keen, inscrutable glance, opening his heart to no man and to no woman? There may have been a certain truth in both pictures, each in its turn, for life is long and ' one man, in his time, plays many parts,' especially if he is an able man with an eye for the change of circumstances. After Bosworth, England wanted, not more adventures in shining armour, but peace, retrenchment and, above all, the enforcement of order. It was by putting these prosaic ideals on to a new institutional basis that Henry VII left England in a position to seize her great opportunities in the coming era.

The Tudor monarchy had a pedestrian beginning, and became a very far-shining affair under Queen Elizabeth, but she would have been the last to deny that her glory was founded on the spade-work of her shrewd, patient grandfather, to whose character her own bore a family likeness for double-dealing, caution and thrift as to means, and clear, tenacious purpose as to ends. Had they not both been cruelly schooled to self-suppression by long experience of the world's treachery and danger before ever they came to the throne ? And if Elizabeth's other name and nature was that of ' Gloriana ' or ' the good Queen Bess,' Richmond too had known how to win the people's love in showing the high courage of his race on that gallant Bosworth campaign.

Henry VII, like his grand-daughter, ascended a throne surrounded by snares and challenges, domestic and foreign; but whereas Elizabeth's dangers could largely be traced to the religious differences of her subjects, Henry's arose from the social state of the country. Habits of disorder were general among high and low. ' There is no country in the world,' wrote the Venetian envoy to his masters, ' where there are so many thieves and robbers as in England ; insomuch that few venture to go alone in the country excepting in the middle of the day, and fewer still in the towns at night, and least of all in London,'— although the English appeared, to this representative of the Venice of Carpaccio, to be richer than any other people in Europe, especially the merchants and the clergy, and to wear the finest clothes in the world.[1] Robin Hood bands, with masked or blackened faces, were destroying the deer in royal forests and private parks, with none to say them nay. In most houses and castles, the retainers down the long hall tables pricked up

---

[1] Another Italian visitor, Polydore Vergil, had a similar impression of the wealth of early Tudor England, and the thriving condition of a meat-fed peasantry, as compared to those of the continent.

their ears as they heard their lord discussing with guests on
the dais the likelihood of fresh dynastic disturbance, and meanwhile contented themselves with occasionally beating the men
and robbing the granges of a neighbouring squire, or carrying
off the cattle and burning the gate of an abbey with whose
servants they had some quarrel.   Benefit of Clergy and the Right
of Sanctuary greatly impeded the execution of justice in every
shire, and juries were still intimidated or bought.

Closely involved in these habits of disorder was the dynastic
question, not yet at rest.   Sone fifteen years passed before it
was certain that Bosworth Field had ended the Wars of the
Roses.   By marrying the heiress of the House of York, Henry
somewhat strengthened his own title to the throne, more by
offering to the nation a prospect of reconcilement and peace,
through the blending of the Roses, than by securing an indis-
putable hereditary claim.   For in fact several persons still alive
could show a better title by lineal descent.   It was on the popular
will and *de facto* occupation that the Tudor claim to the throne
rested, not on the hereditary right divine, invented later by the
Stuarts and their partisans.

The lords and gentlemen who were gambling on a Yorkist
restoration were not to be appeased by Henry's marriage.   They
remained bold and confident in the North, much like the Jacobite
party in days to come.   In Ireland they were for awhile supreme.[1]
It was perhaps fortunate for Henry that they twice over chose
to pin their fortunes to impersonators like Lambert Simnel
and Perkin Warbeck, but the trouble which these sorry knaves
caused for years on end, reminds us how weak was the habit
of loyalty and how feeble the arm of the State when the Tudor
rule began.

There was no standing army, beyond a bodyguard of ' beefeaters.'   Only the rallying of gentlemen, yeomen and burghers
to the King, enabled him to defeat at Stoke the army of Irish
adventurers and German mercenaries who were parading Lambert
Simnel about in the North as Edward VI, and to round up at
Blackheath the Cornishmen who had marched unimpeded to
within sight of London by way of protest against taxation.[2]
Small bodies of foreign mercenaries were occasionally hired by
the Crown for a campaign in Scotland or elsewhere, but there was
no money to keep them in pay as a regular force.

---

[1] See p. 206, above.
[2] Latimer long afterwards told the real Edward VI from the pulpit, ' My
father was a yeoman. . . . He had a walk for an hundred sheep, and my mother
milked 30 kine.   He was able and did find the King a harness, with himself and
his horse, while he came to the place that he should receive the King's wages.
I can remember that I buckled his harness when he went unto Blackheath field.'

Neither Henry VII nor any Tudor after him made a standing army, or paid a centralized bureaucracy to govern the countryside. Tudor policy differed from that of contemporary despots on the continent. Henry and his descendants preserved the old mediæval institutions—King's Council, Parliament, Common Law, Justices of the Peace and jurymen—but breathed into them all a new vigour and compelled them all to become no longer checks on governmental efficiency, but instruments of royal power. In this way the English were trained in the habits of obedience to law necessary to modern civilization, without forfeiting their ancient liberties or breaking the continuity of their national life. The Venetian envoy had observed—' If the King should propose to change any old established rule, it would seem to every Englishman as if his life were taken from him,' and wondered how then Henry VII would be able to enforce order, which to the Latin mind could only be done through the setting up of despotism. Nevertheless another way was found, for the Tudors understood the people they ruled.

The pivot of this new constitution working through the old forms was the King's Council. Under the House of Lancaster, the Council had become, even more markedly than Parliament, a battle-ground of aristocratic factions.[1] The presence of great nobles at the Council-board had in itself secured that the arm of the State should not be exercised against them. But Henry VII and VIII, following up the beginning made by Yorkist Kings, excluded from the Privy Council all nobles save those of the King's own choice and obedience.

This exclusion of the aristocracy remained a first principle of Tudor statecraft: the list of sixteen regents named in Henry VIII's will to govern on his son's behalf, contained not a single peer of twelve years' standing. Very different had been the complexion of the Council during the minority of Henry VI. The change was partly the fault of the nobility themselves, for in the first Parliament of Elizabeth it was stated that ' the wanton bringing up and ignorance of the nobility forces the Prince to advance new men that can serve,' and Latimer declared in the reign of Edward VI that ' the only reason why noblemen be not made Lord Presidents is that they have not been brought up in learning.'

Under the first Tudor the chief Privy Councillors were middle-class clergy of the civil-servant type, such as Morton and Fox, or lawyers like Empson and Dudley; these men owed all to Henry VII, and were valued by him for their skill in filling his

---

[1] In the reign of Henry VII the term ' Privy Council' becomes usual for the more confidential and political body inside the larger Council.

exchequer by means however extortionate.[1] After the Reformation the lawyer element remained, but the clergy became less prominent in the Council and the civil service. There arose a new type of Privy Councillor, men like the Cecils, Walsinghams and Bacons, aspiring to be numbered among the country gentlemen, but connected with the trading community; these men pushed their fortunes at Court, after training themselves at the Universities and by foreign travel and legal study for all diplomatic and political business. The great successes of government under Elizabeth were largely due to such men, who were more enlightened and independent in spirit than the councillors of Henry VII, but not less loyal servants of the Crown.

In working out the policy dictated by the Tudor monarchs the Council displayed great legislative activity, partly by ordinances and proclamations which had an authority and a scope not yet seriously challenged by Parliament, and partly by Bills which the Councillors promoted in Parliament itself. For Parliament was an essential part of the Tudor system, especially after Henry VIII broke with Wolsey and embarked on his Reformation policy. The reign of Henry VII and the early years of his son were not a great Parliamentary period; the Houses were occasionally summoned, but there was little popular interest in Parliament, no resentment at its abeyance for half-a-dozen years on end, no competition for seats even when it met, and no constitutional resistance to Henry VII's exaction of unauthorized ' benevolences ' from the wealthy. This indifference disappeared as Parliament became more important under the later Tudors, and was made the instrument in constant changes of religion. Privy Councillors took seats in the Lower House and guided its proceedings, somewhat as the Ministerial Bench does to-day, save that their power depended not on the Commons, but on the Crown, whose wishes they interpreted to their fellow-members. This leadership was the chief process of education by which the House of Commons was trained to face the real problems of government and to deal with high affairs of State. It is partly for lack of such an intervening period of tutelage that some Parliaments in other countries than our own, when

---

[1] Bacon's *Henry VII* tells us : ' There is a tradition of a dilemma that Bishop Morton used to raise up the Benevolence to higher rates, and some called it his " fork " and some his " crotch." ' For he had couched an article in the instructions to the Commissioners who were to levy the Benevolence, that if they met with any that were sparing, they should tell them that they must needs have because they laid up ; and if they were spenders, they must needs have because it was seen in their port and manner of living.' Empson and Dudley ' being lawyers in science and privy councillors in authority turned law and justice into worm-wood rapine.'

suddenly entrusted with power, have failed in the practical qualities necessary for the conduct of affairs.

Besides greatly increased legislative activity in its own right by Ordinances, and indirectly through Parliamentary Statutes, the Council under the Tudors organized its ancient judicial authority anew so as to bring it to bear with more weight and frequency. It delegated a sub-committee of its own members to exercise its judicial power, which was as old as the Curia Regis of the Norman Kings. This new 'Star Chamber,' as it was called, in which some of the greatest men in the Privy Council had seats, was a court which no subject in the land could hope to overawe. It was popular because it protected the weak against the strong. It was the chief instrument by which Henry VII at length put down the illegal habits of riot, retainers and maintenance. Nor, as readers of the *Merry Wives* will remember, was this use of the Star Chamber yet exhausted in Shakespeare's day :

Shallow : ' I will make a Star-Chamber matter of it : if he were twenty Sir John Falstaffs he shall not abuse Robert Shallow, esquire. . . . The Council shall hear it : it is a riot. . . . Knight, you have beaten my men, killed my deer, and broke open my lodge.'
Falstaff : ' But not kissed your keeper's daughter ? '
Shallow : ' Tut, a pin ! This shall be answered. . . . The Council shall know it.'

Largely through the wholesome fear that the Star Chamber instilled into the minds of men, the ordinary law-courts recovered their real independence, and were no longer intimidated by sinister local influences. Juries became less afraid of giving verdicts against powerful neighbours, and more afraid of being called to answer before the Star Chamber for verdicts not in accordance with the facts of the case or with the wishes of the Crown. Another expression of the judicial power of the Council, analogous to that of the Star Chamber, was found in the prerogative courts of the Councils of Wales and of the North, districts where the feudal and military traditions of borderland would have made a mock of the unsupported courts of Common Law.[1]

Under Henry VII the jurisdiction of the prerogative courts and of the King's ordinary courts grew together in harmony under the shadow of the throne. But by the end of Tudor times, a sharp antagonism was felt between the courts where the Common Law was administered and the prerogative courts emanating from the Council, because the latter strove to introduce the Roman Civil Law as studied by the jurists of the Renaissance. By the end of Tudor times the prerogative courts were many and active : Star

---

[1] For the settlement of Wales by the Tudors, see pp. 358–60, below.

Chamber, Requests, Admiralty, Councils of Wales and the North, and the ecclesiastical Court of High Commission, an outgrowth of the royal Reformation.   All these courts were giving a favoured position to the King's servants as against the common subject of the land, according to the principles of continental law, known in France as the ' *droit administratif* ' ; some of the prerogative courts used the procedure of the *ex officio* oath by which the prisoner was constrained to bear sworn witness against himself ; and the Privy Council on occasion used the Tower rack, though torture was illegal in the English Common Law.   The battle of the Common Law against its rivals, first clearly ranged by Coke in the reign of James I, was one of the chief issues of the struggle between the Stuart Kings and their Parliaments. The victory of Common Law was decided in 1641 and confirmed in 1688.   It was well for the liberties of the subject that the future of English law did not lie with the prerogative courts, but the great part they played in Tudor times was neither unpopular nor unnecessary.

In the Sixteenth Century the English resented high taxation as quickly as in the next century they resented taxation not voted by Parliament, and the result was scarcely less effectual in limiting the power of the Crown.   Since the people were armed and the government was not, the Tudor monarchs had to be thrifty.   When Cornwall alone rose against the taxes in 1497, the State was seriously shaken.   Partly, then, to keep down expenses, Henry VII and his successors, instead of setting up a paid bureaucracy in the countryside, laid more and more duties upon the unpaid and therefore independent country gentlemen, who held the royal commission as Justices of the Peace.   Tudor England was governed by the Privy Council through the Justices of the Peace, and this involved a measure of agreement between the King and the gentry which the Crown had to consider in framing its plans for Church and State.

Every new reign added to the duties of the Justices of the Peace, until, when Elizabeth died, hardly anything in the countryside was alien to their province.   They tried small offences in petty sessions.   They kept up roads, bridges and prisons so far as they were kept up at all, they licensed ale-houses, they arrested criminals.   They became the agents of the vast and intricate economic control taken over by the State from the old corporations—regulation of wages and prices, relations of master and apprentice.   They enforced the new Poor Law.   Even Elizabeth's religious policy, involving hunts after Jesuits, recusants and nonconformists, depended largely on their activity and good will.

The Privy Council saw that all these multifarious duties were well and truly performed by the local magistrates. In Elizabeth's reign they were probably performed with more efficiency than at any time before, or for many generations after. The function of the Tudor Privy Council was to teach not only Parliament to legislate but Justices of the Peace to govern, and judges and juries to execute justice. The habits of self-government in England gained far more than they lost by the Tudor rule. This great process was set going by Henry VII, and was carried on with ever-increasing momentum by his son and grandchildren.

We may well ask why did the nobles submit to be thus supplanted alike in the Privy Council and in the countryside. It is not enough to point out that the Wars of the Roses had temporarily reduced the numbers of the aristocracy.[1] It was of more permanent importance that the expense of those campaigns and the confiscations that followed each of them had impoverished the noble houses, while the same confiscations had so enriched the Crown that Henry VII, by careful 'husbanding,' found the means to carry out his system of good but cheap government through unpaid Justices of the Peace. Furthermore the middle classes of town and country were heartily with the King against the nobles ; the squires, merchants and yeomen, who often intermarried with one another, were acquiring greater wealth and more trained intelligence, and could no longer be relegated to a subordinate part in the national life. It is time to examine the industrial and agricultural changes which were giving these classes a new importance.

The history of the change from mediæval to modern England might well be written in the form of a social history of the English cloth trade.

From prehistoric times coarse cloth had been manufactured in our island, and under the manorial system the mediæval villagers not only span but wove much of their own poor clothing. But in those days little was woven fit for export, or even for the home market, so that our well-to-do classes must needs bring English wool home again in the form of Flemish cloth. The export of raw wool to the looms of Flanders and Italy gave a modest trading wealth to Plantagenet England, besides helping her to pay the Pope's agents the sums which their master

---

[1] The number of Earls and Barons summoned to the Parliament of 1454, the last before the outbreak of the Wars of the Roses, was 53 ; in the last Parliament of Edward IV, 45 ; in the first of Henry VII, 29, partly because there were so many attainted or under age. As the minors grew up and a few new peerages were created, the average number of lay peers in the Tudor epoch rose again to about 50.

extorted.   But when at last the English themselves learnt to weave
fine cloth for the foreign market, unexpected consequences
followed in every department of life and thought.

The great change began when, under the patronage of Edward III, a large number of Flemish weavers brought their skill to
this island.   Many of them were refugees and allies of the English
cause in the Hundred Years' War, for the French feudal nobility
was constantly at war with the liberties of the burgher democracy
of Ghent and the neighbouring cities led by the Van Arteveldes.
The Flemish immigrants were, indeed, so little popular over here
that some hundreds were massacred by the London mob in the
rising of 1381, but the survivors were protected by the wise
policy of the King, until their descendants became by inter-
marriage indistinguishable from the other English.   The gift of
their skill became a national treasure, destined to multiply a
thousand-fold.   The French and Flemish Huguenots who flocked
over in Elizabethan and Stuart times found more popular
favour, as being sufferers in the Protestant cause, and they
were no less helpful than their mediæval forerunners in developing ever new branches of the English weaving industry.

In the Fifteenth and Sixteenth Centuries, East Anglia, with
Norwich for its capital, was greatly enriched by the cloth
trade, as its many fine churches bear witness.   Its example was
followed by Taunton and the western Cotswolds, Kendal and the
Yorkshire dales, and favoured spots in Hants, Berkshire and
Sussex.   East and West, North and South saw weaving colonies
spring up, not only inside old walled towns, but even more in
rural villages like Painswick and Chipping Campden.   Thence
new wealth and new ideas spread among the yeomen and squires,
drawing the whole countryside into a conspiracy to produce
cloth.   In such districts ' speed-the-shuttle ' became as popular
as ' speed-the-plough,' and sheep had a new value in the farmer's
eyes.   Stone villages of the noblest Tudor architecture, encircled
for miles round by Tudor farms built in the same lavish style,
tell the tourist on Cotswold the tale of the ancient prosperity
of the loom.   And the history of the Kendal cloth trade can
still be read in the stout stone walls and oak furniture of Westmoreland and Cumbrian sheep-farms.

The weaving industry was conducted on ' domestic ' lines,
that is, the weavers and their families worked their looms in
their own cottages and were supplied with material by middlemen who disposed also of the finished goods.   The long trains
of pack-horses, each animal with a wool-sack or a bale of cloth
slung across its back, were shuttles for ever moving across the
warp and woof of English life, drawing distant regions and

English Miles

0 10 20 30 40 50   100

SCOTLAND

Highland Line

Leith
Edinburgh ✗ Pinkie
Holyrood 1547

✗ Flodden
1513

Newcastle

NORTHUMBERLAND

CUMBERLAND   DURHAM

WESTMORE-
LAND
Kendal

Y O R K
York   Hull

CLOTHING
DALES

R. Humber

LANCASTER

ANGLESEY

FLINT   CHESTER   DERBY
Chester

LINCOLN

CARNARVON   DENBIGH
MERIONETH

SALOP   STAFFORD
NOTTINGHAM

✗ Stoke
1487

MONT-
GOMERY

WARWICK   LEICESTER
RUT-
LAND

Lynn

N O R F O L K
Norwich
Yarmouth

RADNOR

WORCESTER
NORTHAMPTON

HUNTING-
DON

CAMBRIDGE

SUFFOLK
Ipswich

CARDIGAN

BRECKNOCK

HEREFORD

Chipping
Camden
Cotswolds

BEDFORD

HERTFORD

E S S E X

PEMBROKE

CARMARTHEN

Gloucester
GLOUCESTER

Painswick

OXFORD   BUCKS

MIDDLESEX

London

GLAMORGAN

MON-
MOUTH

Bristol

BERKS

SURREY   K E N T

Dover

WILTS

SOMERSET
Bridgwater

HANTS

S U S S E X

Bideford

D E V O N   DORSET

Portsmouth

Exeter

CORNWALL

Fowey
Plymouth

Falmouth

Hampstead

London

R. Lea

R. Thames

Whitehall   Tower
Westminster   Southwark   R. Thames
Chelsea   Lambeth

Deptford   Greenwich

Woolwich

R. Thames

✗ Blackheath
1497

TUDOR LONDON

Emery Walker Ltd. sc.

Map XVIII.—England and Wales in Counties, Tudor Period.   (Inset—Tudor London)

classes together in a solid national texture. The farmer in Lincolnshire was growing fine wool for looms in Yorkshire, while the merchants and seamen of Hull and London were busy finding new markets for it in the Levant and Baltic, in the East and West Indies, and finally in Virginia and Massachusetts. The Cotswold shepherds and weavers had Gloucester and Bristol at hand in the plain below to push their wares across the sea.

All this widespread energy was taken into account by the statesmen of the Privy Council, who framed the nation's policy, foreign and economic. For all these various individual interests looked one way, when wisely guided by Cecil and Elizabeth. The town corporation and local guild could not command so wide a field of national vision as the State. Indeed the municipalities did little to control the new movement, for even when the cloth manufacture was not conducted, as it usually was, in rural surroundings, it was often set up in the 'liberties' just outside the borough jurisdiction, in order to avoid the pettifogging rules that hampered commerce within the walls. The great days of mediæval corporate life in guild and borough were on the downgrade throughout Tudor times, so far as economic regulation was concerned. On the other hand, there was a great increase in the wealth and political power of London and other towns, particularly the sea ports, for the cloth trade and the discovery of the ocean routes combined to make a new era in English maritime commerce.

The influence of the cloth trade was national and individualist, not cosmopolitan or corporate. All through the Wars of the Roses, through the changes and violences of Henry's Reformation and Mary's Counter-Reformation, in the golden days of Elizabeth, on through the civil wars of King and Parliament, enterprising cloth merchants, weavers and sheep-farmers were making and spreading wealth among many classes high and low, by their own individual initiative, subject only to State protection and control. They were at once more individualist and more nationalist than the mediæval churchmen and nobles whose place they were slowly taking as leaders of the English, for they had no corporate sense of belonging to a cosmopolitan order, like the mediæval Bishop, monk, noble and burgher. They had therefore no jealousy of the Tudor national monarchy, until the House of Commons engendered in them a new sentiment of democratic co-operation on a purely national basis.

The Protestant religion, setting up the domestic and individual forum for conscience and Bible-study, suited these men and their character well. In the Fifteenth Century great founders of chantries to save their own souls and perpetuate their own fame, with a strong tendency to anti-clericalism in early Tudor times, they became Bible-readers and Reformation men for the most part as the Sixteenth Century drew on. The richer of them, buying land and intermarrying with needy squires, founded new ' county families.' Not a few shared in the Abbey lands, having ready cash with which to join in the fierce land speculation that followed the dissolution of the monasteries. At the Universities and Inns of Courts their sons trained themselves to public service. The men of the new wealth were an indispensable mainstay first of Elizabeth and then of the Parliamentary cause in the era that followed. Through them the Tudor and Stuart navy came to rule the seas. For one chief advantage that England had over Spain in the exploitation of the New World, was that we had cloth to sell there in exchange for its goods, while the Spaniards had nothing to send out except soldiers, priests and colonists.

The effect of the cloth trade on rural development was not wholly for the good. The employment and wealth that it created for high and low greatly surpassed what it destroyed. But, like every other process of economic change, it had its army of victims and its tale of agony. Since it overthrew status and custom in favour of cash nexus and the fluidity of labour, it brought to the newly emancipated villein great opportunities and great risks, and to the capitalist farmer and landlord temptations to grow rich quickly at the expense of others. In certain districts there was ' enclosure ' of the open fields of the village for pasture, implying the eviction of many ploughmen to make room for a few shepherds. The Tudor Privy Council frequently interfered to prevent enclosure leading to depopulation, though its efforts were neither continuous nor always successful. The centre of the evil was Leicestershire and Northamptonshire, and to a less degree the counties bordering on them to the south and east.[1] Thence many of the evicted ploughmen wandered off to swell the ranks of the ' sturdy beggars,' ' staff-strikers,' and ' rogues forlorn,' who figure so largely in the literature and the Statute Book of Tudor times.

The ' beggars ' were the characteristic evil of the Sixteenth Century as the ' retainers ' had been of the century before ; and enclosing landlords who set them adrift on society were denounced by moralists like More and Latimer, just as the

---

[1] On the other hand, Somerset, Devon, Cornwall, Suffolk, Essex and Kent were counties largely enclosed in pre-Tudor times by the peasants themselves, because of woodlands, physical conditions, fruit-farming, or local circumstances now forgotten, and in the West partly because of old Celtic custom.

noblemen who kept the retainers had been denounced by Fortescue and his contemporaries. Many of the sturdy ' beggars ' were *quondam* retainers, robbers and outlaws, who had not thrown off the lawless habits of Fifteenth Century society. Under a stronger government they began to figure less often as bullies and more often as victims ; the stocks, the whip and the bed of ' short and musty straw ' became their lot, instead of the fellowship of the merry green wood or the licence to rob in their lord's livery. With them were joined the innocent sufferers from seasonal unemployment in the cloth trade and other industries of a modern character, and, last but not least, the evicted ploughmen of the Midlands. But unless tramps were very different in the Sixteenth Century from those of later date, many ne'er-do-wells must have claimed commiseration by posing as evicted ploughmen, in an era when everyone was talking of the wrongs of that much injured class.

The promiscuous charity distributed at the monastery door bred beggars as well as relieved them. And the sudden suppression of the monasteries, before the Poor Law had been fully developed to take their place as an agency of relief, naturally increased distress, as much perhaps by turning adrift the large companies of monastic servants, as by stopping the monastic alms; these had latterly been a much smaller proportion of the conventual income than is often assumed.[1] The ' beggars ' became the objects both of fear and of pity. Their entry into a village (usually called a ' town ' by our Tudor ancestors) has been immortalized in nursery rhyme :—

Hark ! hark ! the dogs do bark ; the beggars are coming to town.

and then we know how —

Some gave them white bread, and some gave them brown,
And some gave them a good horsewhip, and sent them out of the
    town.

Both bread and whip, at first the expression of individual charity and self-protection, were organized as compulsory social duties by the series of Tudor poor laws culminating in the Poor Law and parish Poor Rate of Elizabeth. Gradually the distinction between the able-bodied who would not work, the aged and feeble who could not work, and the unfortunate who could not find work, became clear to Tudor society and took its place in the Poor Law. The abolition of the monastic dole had helped to make England consider the problem in a national light and

---

[1] See pp. 112–118 of R. H. Snape's *English Monastic Finances in the Later Middle Ages* (Cam. Press, 1926).

to make scientific provision for the poor a civic duty enforceable by law. With all its imperfections the Elizabethan Poor Law marked a step forward in social organization, and by the end of her reign foreigners marked with surprise an absence of beggars to which they were unaccustomed in other lands.[1]

To regard ' enclosure ' of open land by permanent walls and hedges as a thing invariably or even usually bad in itself, would be to misinterpret the whole history of British agriculture. In the first place, by no means all enclosure, even in the Sixteenth Century, converted arable into pasture. Much of it was directed to convert unused land into pasture, or to improve the method of arable farming, processes essential to increase the wealth, trade and population of the island. In the second place, many of the Tudor enclosures were made, not by ' engrossing landlords ' or ' capitalist farmers,' but by small yeomen. By enclosing modest portions of the domain or of the open village field into compact farms and hedged fields, they increased the employment and wealth of the humble. The good farmer was freed from the drag of his slovenly, dishonest or less skilled neighbours in the common field. The constant quarrels and litigation due to the removal of balks and boundaries of the scattered strips came to an end. The free individual initiative given by enclosure to the yeoman farmer was an advantage to himself and to everyone else. The pity is that so much of the best land in the Midlands was still left ' open field,' till in the Eighteenth and Nineteenth Centuries it was enclosed under economic and social conditions more generally unfavourable to the small farmer than those of the Tudor age.[2]

Hugh Latimer's pulpit eloquence was fearlessly directed against enclosure accompanied by eviction on behalf of engrossing capitalist landlords ; but it is probable that his own father, whom he held up as the type of yeoman of the true breed,

---

[1] See p. 358 and note, below. Actually several Poor Laws had been put on the Statute Book before the dissolution of the Monasteries. ' The Dissolution no doubt made a Poor Law more necessary, but they do not stand to each other in the simple relation of cause and effect.' Tanner, *Documents*, 470.

[2] The Elizabethan agricultural poet, Tusser, thus describes the advantages of enclosure ' in severall,' as against the open field (' champion ') :—

> ' More profit is quieter found
>   (Where pastures in severall bee)
> Of one seelie aker of ground,
>   Than champion maketh of three,
> Againe, what a joie is it knowne
> When men may be bold of their owne !'

The extent of the Tudor enclosures is often exaggerated. The shires where there was most of it, Leicester and Northampton, were still very largely open and ' champion ' at the time of the enclosing movement of the Eighteenth Century.

had an ' enclosed ' farm of the right sort. We know at least that his leasehold farm, containing 200 acres arable, fed also 100 sheep and 30 milch cows besides the oxen for the plough, enabled him to employ six men besides women servants, to give his daughters portions of £50 apiece and to send Hugh to school, college and ultimately to bishop's bench and martyr's stake. It was such yeomen who bred the new England, a better England on the whole than that of mediæval lord and villein. These yeomen with small copyholds or moderate-sized leasehold or freehold farms, were as important a feature in the new rural economy as were the engrossing landlords with their large estates. The great importance of the yeomen, particularly the freeholders, in the wars and politics of Stuart times, was an outcome of the economic changes of the Fifteenth and Sixteenth Centuries.[1]

Nor must we judge the enclosure movement entirely by its immediate social consequences. There is also its agricultural and economic justification. The historian of British farming has pointed out that the exhaustion of the corn-land, especially in open-field farms, by centuries of use, in many cases necessitated the restoration of its fertility by a long period of rest under grass ; and moreover that the enclosures as a whole so benefited corn-production, that whereas in Tudor times men feared that bread would grow scarce if the open-field farms were broken up, the Hanoverians had learnt from experience that only by further enclosure could their over-populous island be saved from starvation.[2]

Tudor times saw not only the segregation of compact yeoman farms for the occupier, but the formation by proprietors of great landed estates, to which the superb country houses of Elizabeth's richest subjects bore monumental evidence. This movement, that made a few men ' spacious in the possession of dirt,' was destined to culminate in the Eighteenth and Nineteenth Centuries at the expense of the smaller freeholds; but in Tudor and Stuart England large and small properties flourished side by side. The concentration of landownership was furthered by the English custom of primogeniture, which remained a social habit long after it had ceased to be a legal obligation. The country gentlemen in their wills provided only the eldest son with land, having previously sent his brothers out from the manor-house door to seek their fortunes as apprentices in trade or manufacture, in the liberal professions or in overseas adventure. This custom, so

---

[1] The word ' yeoman,' prior to the late Eighteenth Century, was normally used for a free peasant farmer, irrespective of whether his land were freehold or held on lease. A villein was not a yeoman, nor was a landless labourer.
[2] Lord Ernle, *The Land and the People*, Chaps. I. and II.

different from that of the continental nobility, destroyed class barriers and greatly helped to build up English commerce and Empire. It built up also the great landed estates.

Sheep-farming and enclosure were not the only signs of a new spirit in the English countryside. Formerly, the object of 'subsistence agriculture' was to enable each village to grow its own food ; but many men, small and great, were now investing capital in land with their eyes on the national market and its ever-growing demand for corn, wool, cattle, horses, poultry, dairy produce, and a hundred other requirements. Throughout Tudor and Stuart times the old subsistence agriculture and the new capitalist agriculture were flourishing side by side, but the latter was always gaining ground. One of its earlier triumphs was the introduction of hops from Flanders, which in Tudor times went far to change the drink of the Englishman and the appearance of Kent. The feeding of cattle and sheep during the winter began to be seriously studied ; turnips were known over here in time for Shakespeare to mention them, and under the Stuarts artificial grasses and other methods were slowly introduced in imitation of the scientific farmers of Holland. Horses were slowly taking the place of oxen at the plough.[1]

Books for Further Reading

Tudor Period generally

I. Political and General :

H. A. L. Fisher, *Political History of England,* 1485–1547; A. F. Pollard, *ditto*, 1547–1603 ; Innes, *England under the Tudors* ; Tanner, *Tudor Const. Documents* ; Holdsworth, *History of English Law,* Vol. IV. (admirable on this period) ; Pollard, *Factors in Modern History* ; McIlwain, *The High Court of Parliament* ; *Tudor Studies,* by twelve colleagues of Professor Pollard, 1924.

It does not seem necessary to refer readers to the well-known controversial histories of the period by Froude and his opponents, who between them have elicited so much information. The present generation of historians seems to be in a calmer and more judicial mind.

II. Economic and Agricultural Changes :

Ashley, *Economic Organization in England,* and *Economic History,* Pt. II. ; Ernle, *British Farming,* and *The Land and the People,* Chap. II. ; Tawney, *Agrarian Problem in 16th Century* ; A. H. Johnson, *Disappearance of the Small*

---

[1]   ' Hops, Reformation, bays and beer
       Came into England all in one year '

is as truthful as such traditional rhymes can be expected to be. Put ' era ' for ' year,' and it is correct. ' Bays ' were a new kind of cloth introduced by Flemings into Norwich. There are various versions of the rhyme, some of them mentioning ' turkeys,' which came from America.

It is Anne Page in the *Merry Wives,* who declares that sooner than marry Dr. Caius, she

       ' had rather be set quick i' the earth,
    And bowl'd to death with turnips.'

Freeholder ; Gonner, *Common Land and Enclosure* ; Leonard, *English Poor Relief* ; Tawney and Power, *Tudor Economic Documents*.

III. EDUCATION, ETC. :

Leach, *English Schools at the Reformation* ; Foster Watson, *English Grammar Schools to* 1660 ; Einstein, *Tudor Ideals* ; Seebohm, *The Oxford Reformers*.

CHAPTER II

The revival of Lollardry. The Renaissance scholars. Wolsey and the Balance of Power. The era of discovery. The Cabots. Henry VIII founds the Royal Navy

Kings : Henry VII, 1485–1509 ; Henry VIII, 1509–1547

THE Fifteenth Century, if we exclude its last twenty years, was intellectually barren beyond any other epoch in our history since the Norman Conquest. The violent suppression of freedom of thought at Oxford and subsequently throughout the country by the persecution of Wycliffism, was not made good by any moral or intellectual revival of a more orthodox character. There was nothing analogous to the ' coming of the friars ' of two hundred years before. The triumph of mere obscurantism reached its height in the trial and imprisonment of poor Bishop Pecock, because in arguing against the Lollards he had appealed partly to human reason instead of wholly to the authority of the Church. Among the laity, the same period was unproductive of great literature, if we except some of the popular ballads. Chaucer had readers, reproducers and imitators, but not successors. There was, however, the new printing-press, and an adequate supply of new schools for the middle classes ; though the education given was of poor quality, the number of educated people in the island offered a wonderful field for the sower of wheat or tares. And Henry VII's reign was a season of seed.

The restoration of peace and order was a condition favourable to intellectual revival. We observe two portents in the early Tudor world, before the Lutheran controversy arose,—first a revival of Lollardry and Bible-reading among the poor, and secondly the coming of the Renaissance learning from oversea. To these two movements we should perhaps add another tendency, that favoured them both, the sheer anti-clericalism of large sections of the population : it was said that, if Abel had been a priest, Cain would have been acquitted by a jury of London citizens. The squires and nobles, though none of them were any longer Lollards, cared so little for the Church that they were prepared to support a policy of spoliation provided the spoils

1382.

1457.

came their way. Ecclesiastical privilege, left intact for centuries while all else had been changing in England, had aroused an anti-clerical temper in the ordinary Englishman which rendered him ready to listen to the new doctrines. The Church had lost her moral and intellectual leadership, while retaining to the full her privileges, her wealth and her persecuting power. Her decision to defend herself against Wycliffism by repression unaccompanied by reform, though successful for a while, was fraught with danger.

A generation before Luther sprang to sudden fame, Lollardry, long suppressed, had come into the open once more. It was native to the soil of England, and had been faithfully preserved in cottage and workshop as a poor man's tradition, by the spiritual ancestors of John Bunyan. Peasants in the Chilterns and other parts of the Home Counties, humble persons in London, Bristol and other towns, with here and there a priest and here and there a man of means, met secretly to read ' the epistles and gospels in English and Wycliffe's damnable works,' and to strengthen one another's faith in what we should now call ' Protestant' doctrine. Between 1490 and 1521 many of the Lollards actually went to the stake, while more recanted to save their lives. The persecution was hotter than ever before, but this time failed of its purpose.

In the same years a different movement was stirring the Universities to fresh life. Italy was the land of the Renaissance, and thence the new studies came to Oxford in the last two decades of the Fifteenth Century.[1] From Italy, Grocyn, Lily and Linacre brought home a new interest in Greek literature, Latin grammar and scientific medicine. Slowly the long-lost world of Hellas began to take shape, as in a glass darkly, revealing to a few ardent minds a world of thought not bounded by the mediæval heaven and hell, just as the material world was expanding beyond all the limits of mediæval cosmography, with every new voyage of Columbus and Cabot. At the same time, studies conducted in Ciceronian Latin, replacing the useful but inelegant Latin of the Middle Ages, suggested ideals of conduct on the ' antique Roman ' pattern. If these influences should once spread from Court and college into common grammar schools at Stratford and elsewhere, life even here, upon this bank and shoal of time, would become a gracious and noble adventure.

[1] Early in the reign of Henry VI, Humphrey Duke of Gloucester, an English statesman allied to the Royal House, had patronized Italian scholars of the new classical renaissance. His gift of ' Duke Humphrey's Library' to Oxford proved the beginning of the Bodleian collection, but some time passed before the classical writers were studied there in the unmediæval spirit of Duke Humphrey and his Italians.

M

Another element formative of modern England was introduced by young Colet, a London merchant's son. On his return from Italian groves of Academe, he astonished Oxford by the announcement that he would lecture on St. Paul's epistles. By sheer force of genius he compelled not only the enthusiastic undergraduates but the disapproving Abbots and doctors of divinity to listen to a young man scarcely yet ordained priest, while he set aside every landmark erected by the scholiasts, and gave straight from the Greek text a realistic and humanist exposition of the life and teaching of St. Paul. He was seeking to discover what the Epistles had meant to him who wrote and to those who received them, not at all what they had meant to the dialecticians of the last three hundred years. The studies and learning of the Middle Ages crumbled like a corpse exposed to the air. Duns Scotus had once been in the van of intellectual advance, but those who were still faithful to the Subtle Doctor were now held in derision as ' dunces ' by the rising generation at Oxford and Cambridge, and presently on every school bench in the land.

Dutch Erasmus was rapidly rising by the help of the printing-press to a European reputation without previous parallel. He was much in England, and both he and Sir Thomas More were Colet's friends and allies. Between them they gave a new character to the Renaissance studies, making them moral and religious in Northern Europe, instead of artistic and pagan as in Italy. To the Italian scholars and their patron Princes and Cardinals, the Renaissance meant the ancient poets and philosophers, marble nymphs and ' brown Greek manuscripts.' To Colet and Erasmus, and through them to the English generally, the Renaissance meant these things indeed, but it meant also the New Testament in Greek and ultimately the Old Testament in Hebrew. The difference was profound, and produced yet another rift between England and the Franco-Italian civilization which had nurtured her childhood. For the men of the Italian Renaissance lived, and their spiritual successors in France and Italy have lived ever since, in a world of art, letters and science seldom touched by religion, in effect abandoning ecclesiastical affairs to the unaided efforts of the monks and clergy. But in England the men of the Renaissance, following the lead of Colet, used the study of Greek and Latin to reform not only the schools but the Church herself, and called on clergy and laity to act together in the task.

This movement, at once moral and intellectual, classical and Christian, did not, as is sometimes said, perish in the storms of the English Reformation. On the contrary, its spirit found expression in the educational and religious policy of the reformed

schools and of the reformed Church of England that emerged
under the later Tudors from the confused violence of the earlier
struggle. If Colet had seen a typical Elizabethan grammar
school, he would have been well pleased. If the old endowments
that were confiscated under Henry and Edward are set against
the new endowments that were made under Elizabeth, the
quantity of educational provision was little if at all increased
under the Tudors ; but the quality was immensely improved.

These Oxford Reformers, as Colet and Erasmus were called,
began, in the names of scholarship, religion and morality, a
series of bitter attacks on the monks as obscurantists, on the
worship of images and relics, on the extortion of the ecclesiastical
courts and the worldliness of the clergy. On these matters no
Lollard could use stronger language, although they were no
Lollards. Their influence was spreading from Oxford to London,
to the Court, and ere long to Cambridge. Colet became Dean of 1505.
St. Paul's, and delighted the citizens and perturbed the clergy
of the capital by sermons denouncing Church abuses and practices
in a manner not heard from the official pulpit since the silencing
of Wycliffe's priests a hundred years before. Colet also founded,
in the shadow of the Cathedral, St. Paul's School with Lily as its
first headmaster, to teach Greek and Ciceronian Latin, and to
become the prototype of the reformed grammar school.

What would be the attitude of the new monarchy towards
the New Learning ? Much indeed turned upon that, for in the
situation then reached by England, the nation could do nothing
against the will of the Crown, and the Crown nothing against
the will of the nation, but the two together could do anything
they chose, even to the altering or preserving of religious doctrine
and ecclesiastical privilege.

Henry VII was too busy in his great task as England's
policeman to concern himself with the New Learning. The clergy
to him were useful civil servants, the Pope a figure on the
diplomatic chessboard. For the rest he was orthodox ; he once
took part in converting a Lollard at the stake, and leaving him
to be burned in spite of his recantation, such being the standard
of Christian charity of those times.

But what of the younger Henry ? In 1509 he succeeded to
the throne and to the marriage with Catherine of Aragon, since
his elder brother Arthur who was to have enjoyed the lady and
the realm had prematurely died. The young King of eighteen
exceeded the ordinary run of his subjects in body and in brain.
He was a paragon of Princes, the patron alike of all true English
sportsmen and of the men of the New Learning. Succeeding with

a clear title to the peace, wealth and power that his father had painfully accumulated, and cutting off the heads of Empson and Dudley as an earnest of the great love he bare his people, he won their hearts from the first. He was as true an Englishman as 'Farmer George,' but on a more brilliant pattern. He could bend a bow with the best forester in the realm, and when ·complimented on his archery by the French Ambassador could reply 'it was good for a Frenchman.' His colossal suit of tilting armour in the Tower reminds us that once he flashed through the lists like Launcelot, laying low his adversaries and calling for more. He was a champion at tennis and a mighty hunter. Orthodox like his father, he continued to encourage the burning of Lollards, wrote his book against Luther, and was dubbed by the Pope *Fidei Defensor*. But he was also a friend to Colet and More, forcing the latter to take up the dangerous profession of courtier, and defending Dean Colet against the obscurantist clergy, with the declaration 'Let every man have his doctor, this is mine,' even when the fearless Dean denounced his war against France as unchristian. For 'Henry loved a man.' And 'pastime with good company he loved,' as we read in the song which he is said to have composed and set. Among other accomplishments this Admirable Crichton was no mean musician, and played well on all known instruments. Poetry and music flourished in his Court, when the English lyrical and the English musical genius were moving forward again towards the moment of their fine flowering under Elizabeth.

It was said that Henry's Court had better store of learned men than any University. These early friends of his implanted in his mind a dislike of monks, of image worship, of relic worship, and a respect for the study of the Bible—all perfectly compatible with doctrinal orthodoxy on the Eucharist, as his subjects were to find out in days to come when this handsome young athlete and lover of all things noble had been turned by thirty years of power and worship into a monstrous egoism moving remorselessly over the bodies of old friends and new foes towards a clearly conceived middle policy in religion, with the Royal substituted for the Papal power. All the various aspects of that later policy can be traced to opinions imbibed during his early life, and to the movement of the age in a nation which, even in his days of bloated and ferocious tyranny, Henry understood with an instinct that even Elizabeth never surpassed.

For the present those days were far ahead. As yet the Cardinal ruled—the last Cardinal and almost the last churchman ever to rule over England. While 'Harry our King was gone hunting' morning after morning, or was holding high festival at

1521.

1513.

night 'with masque and antique pageantry,' Wolsey was
labouring over the details of home and foreign policy which in
later years Henry took into his own industrious hands. But
youth must be served, at least such a youth as Henry's, and that
was the Cardinal's day.

Wolsey, like all the greatest servants of the Tudor monarchy,
was of comparatively humble birth—his father was probably
an East Anglian grazier or wool merchant—but he was haughty
and ostentatious to a degree that would hardly have been tolerated
in a Prince of the Blood. He ' is the proudest prelate that ever
breathed ' reported a foreign observer, and such was the general
opinion. The one blot on his splendid equipment as a diplomatist was the fury of his temper ; one day he laid violent hands on
the Papal Nuncio and threatened him with the Tower rack over
some dealings with France. The state which Wolsey kept, in
the high hall at Hampton Court or when he travelled, for a while
pleased his master and dazzled his countrymen, but in the end
helped to turn them all against him, and pointed for poets the
moral of his fall.

In his hands the Balance of Power in Europe first became
clearly defined as the object of England's foreign policy. It was
dictated by the rise of the great monarchies of France and Spain,
for if either of these overcame the other, it would be lord paramount of Europe, and little England's position would be ignominious and unsafe. For several years Wolsey kept the balance with
consummate skill and with a minimum of expense to English
blood and treasure. In 1513 the double victory over the
invading Scots at Flodden and over the French at the Battle of
Spurs near Guinegatte on the Netherland border, raised England
to a strong position as holder of the balance. But after 1521
Wolsey's skill and foresight failed him. He backed Charles V,
monarch of Spain and the Netherlands and Emperor in Germany,
at a time when he should rather have supported the weakening
cause of France. At the battle of Pavia the capture of Francis I 1525.
and the destruction of his army laid Italy at the feet of Spain for
the next 180 years, reduced France and England temporarily to
impotence, and began that Hapsburg supremacy in Europe which
in the days of Philip II and Elizabeth almost proved the destruction of England, and would have destroyed her but for the
growth of popular, maritime and religious forces in the island
which Wolsey overlooked or opposed.

The power of Spain was not confined to the Old World. The
era of ocean discovery and commerce had begun, replacing the
ancient trade routes across Asia and Egypt, of which the European

end had been in the hands of Genoa and Venice. From the Italian cities and the land-locked Mediterranean with its oared galleys, power and wealth were passing to the lands of Western Europe, which could send out a new type of seaman and new type of ship to sail the far ocean, to reach the markets of Asia by sea, and to discover Africa and America on the way.

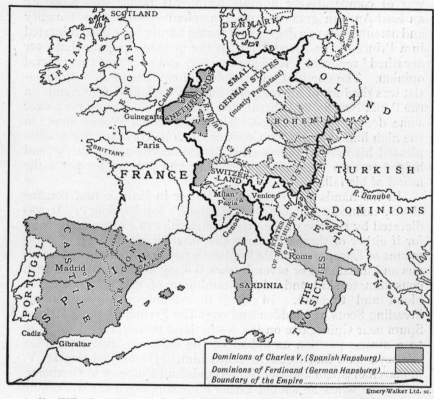

MAP XIX.—Europe in the Time of Henry VIII. Rise of the Great Continental Monarchies

It did not seem at first that England would be the chief gainer by this change. In the Fifteenth Century, Portuguese seamen, under Prince Henry the Navigator, had been beforehand along the coast of Africa and round the Cape route to India, founding a Portuguese Empire on the African littoral, destined to survive till the present day. Spain was long disunited and struggling with the Moors, but when joined into one State by the marriage of Ferdinand of Aragon with Isabella of Castile, she soon made an end of the Moors on her own side of the Straits of Gibraltar, employed Columbus and sent out the Conquista-

See
Map XX.,
p. 338,
below.

1492.

dores, who made her a present of the mines of Mexico and Peru 1519–
and the wealth of the Spanish Main.   1535.

The Pope had risen to the occasion. He had drawn a line
down the globe from pole to pole, a hundred leagues west of the
Azores, giving all lands discoverable to the west of it to Spain, 1493.
and on the east to Portugal. The competition thus set on foot
had incited the great voyagers in the pay of the two Iberian
monarchies, had sent Magellan round by the Horn and across the
Pacific, and set Amerigo Vespucci to trace the southern coastline
of the continent that bears his name. As yet no one openly
impeached the validity of the Pope's division. As yet Portugal
and Spain had no rivals on the ocean and in the lands beyond.
The Italian maritime States supplied the master mariners—
Columbus, Vespucci and Cabot—but neither Venice nor Genoa
ventured upon their own account on the new ocean traffic. It
was as if the heart of Italy had been broken by the decline of the
old Asiatic trade-routes of which she had been mistress ; neither
Venice nor Genoa, as communities, had the requisite vitality
to build the new type of ocean-going ship and train the new
type of ocean-going sailor : it was enough for their declining
powers to carry on the wrecks of the old Levant trade, and
engage galley to galley with the Turkish war fleets.

Neither as yet was France or England ready to challenge the
commercial and colonial monopoly of Spain and Portugal in
Africa, Asia or America. In Henry VII's reign John Cabot and
his boy Sebastian, sailing in a cockle-boat with 18 gallant men 1497.
of Bristol, visited certain regions in Labrador, Newfoundland or
Nova Scotia. They had sailed west to find the fabled Cathay
and the Seven Cities of the East, with their spices and their gold,
and found the way blocked by the foggy cod banks and drip-
ping pine forests of North America—a better heritage for the
English had they known it. But England dared not yet arouse
the wrath of Spain by laying hands on this heritage ; her time
was not yet. Henry VII had encouraged maritime adventure,
but Wolsey discouraged it. The voyages of the Cabots and the
men of Bristol to North America merely staked out a claim that
lay dormant for several generations as regards inland discovery
or plantation, though before the middle of the new century the
Newfoundland fisheries had become an important nursery of our
seamen.

Such was the situation with which Henry VIII had to deal.
His policy was both wise and strong. While not encouraging
transoceanic adventure in the face of predominant Spanish
power, he made possible the future liberation of his country's
energies by the only means—the foundation of a Royal Navy.

The ' narrow seas ' had been held during the Hundred Years' War—so far as they had been held at all—by the pugnacious seamen of the merchant navy, fighting sometimes as individual pirates, sometimes, as at Sluys, united under the royal command. Henry V had begun to build a royal fleet, but his work had not gone far and had subsequently been neglected.   Henry VII had encouraged the mercantile marine, but had not built a fleet for fighting purposes only.   It was Henry VIII who built an effective fleet of royal fighting ships, with royal dockyards at Woolwich and Deptford ; he also founded the corporation of Trinity House.

Henry's maritime policy had a double importance.   Not only did he create ships specially manned and commissioned to fight, and to fight in the public service alone, but his architects designed many of these royal ships on an improved model. They were sailing vessels better adapted to the ocean than the rowed galleys of the Mediterranean powers, and better adapted to manœuvring in battle than the more clumsy ' round ' ships of the mediæval type in which the English merchants sailed the sea, and in which the Spaniards crossed the Atlantic.   The new type of English warship was three times the length of its beam or more, while the normal ' round ' ship was only twice the length of its beam.   Hitherto sea-battles had consisted of ramming, archery and boarding, very much like the battles of the old Greek and Roman navies.   But a new age was at hand.   From the port-holes of Henry VIII's fleet protruded the iron mouths of great cannon in a row, ready to give the shattering ' broadside,' the operation of war to which, more than to any other, British maritime and colonial power owe their existence.   It was Henry VIII himself who had insisted that his naval architects should mount heavy cannon in the body of the ship ; they had devised the expedient of piercing apertures in the very hold itself through which the great shot could be discharged.[1]

In 1545, at the end of Henry's reign, a French armada attempted to invade England, but was foiled by the Royal Navy. England was saved from invasion, and the same year a baby called Francis Drake was born on a farm near Tavistock.

The Royal Navy was Henry's creation, and it saved both

[1] On the technical question of the build of the ships in Henry VIII's navy see Callender, *Naval Side of British History*, Chap. IV, and the Introduction to Corbett's *Drake and the Tudor Navy*.   The word, as well as the deed, ' broadside ' often occurs in Hakluyt's accounts of our ships fighting in Queen Elizabeth's reign.   ' I commanded to give the broadside, as we terme it,' says Captain Downton, describing his destruction of ' the Portugalls' mightie carack of the East Indies ' in 1593.

himself and his daughter after him when they adopted an island policy and defied the Catholic powers of Europe. Wolsey had no notion of the importance of sea power to England. He was a great mediæval churchman, a civil servant of the old school, and a diplomatist of the Renaissance type. But of the future development of England at home and on the sea Wolsey had no vision at all. His master, with that curious instinct of oneness with the English people which was the secret of Tudor greatness, saw deeper. He could use Wolsey's consummate administrative powers during the years of his own apprenticeship in statecraft, and then pass over him along a path of his own which no Cardinal could be expected to tread.

Wolsey was a great man, but it was not he who made modern England. He had no interest in the navy and no trust in Parliament. He had indeed an active distrust of it, because the growing anti-clericalism of the country had been demonstrated in the Parliament of 1515 by an attack on Benefit of Clergy, mortuary fees, and the currency of Papal decrees in England. There had been strange talk on the judicial bench of the penalties of *præmunire* incurred by Convocation. Judges and Parliament had stood up for the royal power, as representing popular rights against clerical privilege. Neither Wolsey nor his master had been unobservant of these things. For the present indeed the Cardinal ruled and Henry watched. So Parliament was not summoned again for eight years. But if ever Henry should tire of the Cardinal and desire to rob or to reform the Church and to defy the Pope, he would know to what institution he could look for support.

CHAPTER III

The Royal and Parliamentary Reformation under Henry VIII

THOSE who conceive of opinion in Tudor England as sharply divided between two mutually exclusive and clearly defined parties of Catholic and Protestant, can never understand the actual course taken by the Reformation before the latter years of Elizabeth. Opinion was in the making, not yet made. Honest men, as well as time-servers, were perpetually altering their views. Few held a consistent body of doctrine which would have satisfied the Catholic or Protestant partisans of a later day. Sir Thomas More, a scathing critic of the religious orders and the popular superstitions they fostered, became the martyr of Papal

Supremacy, whereas Bishops Gardiner and Bonner, though famous as Papalists under Mary, had defended Henry's original breach with Rome. Queen Elizabeth herself would have preferred a celibate priesthood. Opinion among the mass of men was more interested in preserving the King's Peace than in raising difficulties over his religious policy.

In the North and extreme South-West, considerable zeal was shown for the defence, not indeed of the Papal jurisdiction, but of the monasteries and the old forms of religion. In London and the neighbourhood the party of change prevailed. The contrast between the citizens of Tudor London and those of Valois Paris, in their attitude towards the clergy and the doctrines of the mediæval Church, goes a long way to explain the different fortunes of the Reformation in England and in France.[1]

But the party of change, in London and elsewhere, was not wholly inspired by Protestantism or by the New Learning of Dean Colet and his friends. It was also under the influence of a passion which can best be described as anti-clerical. Anti-clericalism was in some persons a greedy desire to plunder the Church for the benefit of their own families. In others it was a rational and honourable dislike of the powers and privileges enjoyed by the priesthood. For the clergy still had the legal right to extort money in innumerable ways, and to adjudicate in their spiritual courts on points of doctrine and morals for all men, in an age when the laity had become well able to think and act for themselves. The change from mediæval to modern society in the sphere of religion, consisted mainly in a reduction of the power of the priesthood, and the raising up of the laymen, first collectively through the action of the State, then individually through the freedom of private conscience. It was the first of these movements that took place under the Tudors, in the subjection of the Church to the State, and it was a movement quite as much anti-clerical as it was Protestant.

Henry VIII burnt Protestants, while hanging and beheading the Catholic opponents of an anti-clerical revolution. And this policy, which appears so strange to-day, then met with much

---

[1] Professor Pollard has written :—' Tudor despotism consisted largely in London's dominance over the rest of England,' and Miss Davis has added, ' The history of the English Reformation might well be rewritten from that point of view. Almost all its changes were anticipated there (in London), and Henry VIII, Elizabeth and Burghley succeeded, where Wolsey, Cromwell, Somerset and Mary failed, because they seldom flouted the City and never lost its allegiance.' For a monarch without a standing army, the presence of such a storehouse of wealth, arms, and men, two miles from his Palace gate, was a chief consideration in policy. *Tudor Studies*, pp. 287–8. Moreover, in the Sixteenth and early Seventeenth Centuries, London had a practical monopoly of the printing-press, except for Oxford and Cambridge ; Elizabeth actually forbade printing outside London and the two Universities.

popular approval in England. In the babel of voices heard during his reign, the strongest note is a Catholic, Nationalist anti-clericalism. It was only after Henry's death that the logic of the new situation at home and abroad drove the English Anti-clericals and Nationalists to defend themselves against Catholic reaction by alliance with the Protestants, to whose doctrines they became, in Elizabeth's reign, very fair converts.

Anti-clericalism, in fact, was not destined to become the shibboleth of a permanent party in England, as it became in France and Italy from the time of Voltaire onwards. Dislike of clerical domination and respect for religion are both more general in England than in most parts of Europe, and both found satisfaction in our post-Reformation churches and sects. The spirit of opposition to clerical predominance sometimes supported Anglicanism against Roman or Puritan claims to govern men's lives, and sometimes joined Nonconformity against the pretensions of the State clergy. But while the power of the Pope and the mediæval Church was being broken by Henry VIII, anti-clericalism appears as an independent force on the flank of both Catholicism and Protestantism, and for a few decisive years it was the strongest of the three.

The prelude to Henry's breach with the Pope was the German Reformation under Luther, which for some years almost annihilated the prestige of Rome as a centre of religious authority. In 1527 the Holy City was sacked by the armies of Charles V, Emperor in Germany and King of Spain. German heretics and Spanish Catholics rivalled each other in looting churches, raping nuns and besieging Pope and Cardinals in the Castle of St. Angelo, while a Roman Catholic wrote thus to Charles V :— 1519.

Everyone considers that this has taken place by the just judgment of God, because the Court of Rome was so ill-ruled. Some are of opinion that the Holy See should not continue in Rome, lest the French King should make a patriarch in his Kingdom, and deny obedience to the said See, and the King of England and all other Princes do the same.

If ever there was a moment when European opinion made it easy for England to break with the Papacy, it was the generation that followed the revolt of Luther and the sack of Rome.

The Lutheran doctrines had no sooner been proclaimed at Wittenberg than they became a power in England, though still under the ban of Church and State. They at once absorbed the Lollard into the Protestant movement. Their effect on the men of the New Learning was twofold : some, particularly the younger men, eagerly joined the more thorough-going movement; others, particularly the older men who had brought the Renaissance to England, shrank back and reacted towards orthodoxy. Erasmus feared Protestantism, and More persecuted it, dreading toleration anywhere nearer to Europe than Utopia. Oxford, where so much had been done for progress in the past, held back in doubt, but Cambridge stepped for the first time into the van of the national movement. From 1521 onwards, students met at the White Horse tavern in that town, to discuss Luther's propositions.[1] The tavern was nicknamed 'Germany' and the scholars who haunted it 'Germans,' but they were the makers of the new England—Tyndale and Coverdale who first gave her the Bible in Tudor English, Cranmer who gave her the Prayer Book, Latimer the soul of the popular movement, and many other future apostles and martyrs.

Latimer and Cranmer represented, each very nobly, the two aspects of the reformed English Church of the future—the moral and the reflective. Latimer was as fearless as Luther on points of religion, and was far less timorous than the German Reformer on social questions and in face of secular power. Cranmer, mild and cautious, a student scrupulously slow to choose between two sides in intellectual controversy, was a man of perpetual moral hesitations and mental revisions, but with occasional bursts of courage on behalf of his hard-won opinions, like the courage of a timid woman turning to bay in defence of her children. Both men won Henry's regard, and though Latimer's views were too uncompromising to suit the King's purposes for long, Cranmer's favour lasted through all the violent changes of royal affection and policy, to which Wolsey, More, Cromwell and so many others of both sexes fell victims. Cranmer, indeed, remained the last personal friend that Henry cared to keep : the brutal and self-willed King was to die murmuring of his faith in God, his hand lying trustfully in that of the gentle and perplexed founder of Anglicanism. If one could rightly interpret the inner meaning of that scene one would know much of the curiosities of human nature.

But Henry had a good deal to do before he came to die. At the time of the sack of Rome he was thirty-six years old, and had reached in his slow development the prime of his intellectual power. Hunting and tournaments could no longer be a substitute for politics and government as an outlet to his immoderate

1527

---

[1] There was, of course, nothing disreputable about a ' tavern ' in those days ; it had not the associations of a modern ' public house.' Gentlemen often took their wives to spend the evening at the ale house, as a natural place to meet friends. ' Mine host ' held an important social position, for instance in *The Merry Wives of Windsor*.

energies. He was, at last, prepared to take over from Wolsey the heavy burden of administration. Moreover, like all his subjects, he was getting tired of the Cardinal, who had failed abroad and given personal offence at home, and whose fall could scarcely have been delayed much longer, even without the question of the Royal Divorce.

That question, the immediate cause of the breach with Rome that had been preparing for centuries in England, was not, strictly speaking, a question of 'divorce' at all. Technically, it was a question whether or not Henry had ever been properly married to Catherine of Aragon, since his brother Arthur had been her first husband. A former Pope had granted a dispensation for her marriage to Henry, but Clement VII was now asked to declare that the marriage had never been valid, and that Henry was yet a lusty bachelor. For he desired to marry Anne Boleyn. Like the generality of monarchs of that era and of many eras before and after, he would have been perfectly content with her as his mistress, which she soon was, had he not desired a legitimate male heir to secure for England an undisputed succession and strong rule after his death. He could expect no more children from Catherine, and the Princess Mary was their only child. There had never been a Queen Regnant in England, and the unfamiliar idea of a female succession seemed to threaten the country with civil war or the rule of a foreign Prince as Consort.

The refusal of the Pope to liberate Henry was not due to scruples : he had only recently divorced Henry's sister Margaret, Queen of Scotland, on a far less reasonable excuse, and his predecessors had released monarchs like Louis XII of France, when they desired divorce on no grounds save reasons of state. But he could not oblige Henry, because after the sack of Rome he was in the power of Charles V, who was Catherine's uncle and zealous protector. The Temporal Power of a Pope, so far from giving him freedom, made him a slave to mundane considerations, then as in other ages. Because he was an Italian Prince, Clement could not afford to displease the *de facto* lord of Italy.

To Henry it seemed intolerable that the interests of England should be subjected, through the Pope, to the will of the Emperor. In his anger at this personal grievance, he came to see what many Englishmen had seen long before, that England, if she would be a nation indeed, must repudiate a spiritual jurisdiction manipulated by her foreign rivals and enemies. The full-grown spirit of English nationalism, maturing ever since Plantagenet times, asked why we should look abroad for any part of our laws, either matrimonial or religious. Why not consult our own churchmen ? Why not act through our own Parliament ?

1530. Wolsey's failure to obtain the 'divorce' from Rome sealed his doom. His death in disgrace saved him from preceding to the scaffold many high-placed victims of the Terror that now began to walk by noonday. Cranmer, learnedly arguing in favour of the 'divorce' and of England's competence to decide the question for herself, rose thereby to royal favour and became 1532. Archbishop of Canterbury, the first who never acknowledged allegiance to the Pope. But Henry needed also a rougher and less scrupulous servant and found one in Thomas Cromwell. The revolution—anti-Papal, anti-clerical, Anglican and Erastian all in one—was launched on the flood-tide, and was carried through with the accompaniment of violence and injustice that usually attends all great social revolutions, whether the driving force be a man or a mob.

What was the attitude of the English people towards the question? The average Englishman retained the feeling of his ancestors against the Pope's interference in England, but held it more strongly than ever in the light of the new times, and supported Henry in his decision to settle the question once for all. The nationalism of England was fully grown; she would no longer submit to be governed by a religious authority that was seated a thousand miles beyond seas and mountains, and that judged English questions by Italian, Spanish, Imperial and occasionally by French standards and interests, but never by English. On the other hand, even in London, the sympathies of the common people went out to the blameless and injured Catherine and her daughter Mary. Anne Boleyn was unpopular. A mistress raised to be a wife at another's expense can scarcely win respect, and Anne was a light woman with no claims of her own for a reversal of so natural a verdict.

But the political and ecclesiastical sides of the question soon swallowed up the personal, and as this change took place, Henry's position with his subjects grew stronger. In the great revolution, by which he freed the English Church and State from the bonds of Rome, suppressed the monks and friars who represented the old cosmopolitan order, and reduced the power and privilege of the clergy, he had the support of London and the South. The unpopular divorce policy involved the popular breach with Rome, and the breach with Rome involved the anti-clerical revolution at home, which enlisted in its defence the most powerful forces in the country. But neither Henry nor his subjects yet understood that these changes must lead in turn to the toleration of the 1533–1547. Protestant religion. It was the hour of a persecuting Catholic anti-clericalism as peculiar, some would say as monstrous, as Henry himself. But for the moment it won more support than any other more logical or more merciful policy. Henry, sending the noble Sir Thomas More to the scaffold for his refusal to repudiate the Papal authority, and poor Protestants to the stake for their denial of transubstantiation, moves the angry disgust of readers accustomed to religious toleration as the basis of modern society. But these tragic scenes affected the minds of contemporaries in a different manner,—with pity indeed for the victims, but with respect for a Government that was keeping order in Church and State according to the persecuting standards inherited from the past of Christian practice and never yet called in question.

King-worship under the Tudors reached its culmination in these years, in the acceptance of one man's will as the *salus publici*. It was disastrous to the character of Henry, whose egoism became a disease. But the disease affected the heart and not the brain. One result of King-worship under a strong King was that England secured the great change in her institutions without civil war, though Henry had no army with which to keep order. Brave blood was shed, but it was not shed in rivers, as in France, Holland and Germany during the wars of religion.

The instrument chosen by Henry to effect his Royal Reformation was Parliament. It could scarcely be Convocation : the ecclesiastical assemblies of Canterbury and York wherein there was no representation of the laity, could not be made active instruments in an anti-clerical revolution. The mediæval Church was organized as a purely clerical body and therefore the laity could only assert themselves from outside, through Parliament and not through Convocation.

In both Provinces Convocation acquiesced only under threat of the penalties of Præmunire. Yet we must not suppose that the whole body of secular clergy were adverse to all the changes which they were compelled to accept. They had little love for the monks and friars. They bitterly grudged the Annates and other heavy tolls levied from them by the Pope. Many in Convocation recognized that Benefit of Clergy, sanctuary and the abuses of the spiritual courts must be reformed. There was also a small but growing party of more advanced reformers like Cranmer and Latimer, whence Henry chose several of his bishops.

The attitude of the English clergy, though not heroic, was more patriotic, more useful and more morally sound than fanatical intransigence and the preaching of civil war in defence of outworn privileges. Because the clergy accepted much which they could not be expected to like, they saved England from a war of religion, and they soon recovered what they had long lost, a great place in the affection of the country, under a new regime suited to modern times.

To be freed from the Pope was well perhaps ; to be subjected to the King was perhaps less well. But the clergy had no third choice. Convocation acknowledged with a sigh that Henry was Supreme Head of the Church of England, with the scrupulous addition ' so far as the law of Christ allows,'—an elastic phrase that was stretched far in the next few years.[1] The clergy had thus forsworn the authority of the Pope and accepted that of the English State in its place. But Henry must seek elsewhere than in Convocation the active instrument of the layman's revolution that followed. He found it in Parliament.

The Reformation had the effect of doubling the importance of Parliament. Hitherto it had been almost as much a court of law as a legislative assembly, and under Henry VII and Wolsey its importance was on the decline. If English history had remained a branch of European history instead of going off on a course of its own, that decline would have continued until the English Parliament had followed into oblivion the mediæval Estates of France and Spain. But Henry VIII chose otherwise.

The Reformation Parliament was not packed. It was not necessary to pack it. The legislation that completed the breach with Rome, destroyed the monasteries and established the supremacy of the State over the Church in England, was prepared by Privy Councillors and passed after discussion by both Houses. The Reformation Parliament, unlike its predecessors, sat for seven years, and in the course of its eight sessions acquired a continuity of personal experience among its members which helped to build up the traditions of the modern House of Commons as a great instrument of government. In Henry's Parliaments debate was fairly free, at least on subjects with which the King wished the Houses to deal ; he knew the value of genuine advice and criticism,—provided always that he had his way in the main, and that was ensured by the nature of the times and by the character of the royal programme. Yet, in Henry's reign, several measures desired by government were rejected, and others amended by the Commons.

Louis XIV is commonly believed to have said ' L'état, c'est moi,' and he certainly acted as if he thought so. Henry's authority was of a different kind, as he was the first to acknow-

1531.

1529–
1536.

---

[1] In the Act of Supremacy, passed by Parliament in 1534, this qualification was omitted, and Henry was styled ' only Supreme Head in earth of the Church of England called *Anglicana Ecclesia*.'

ledge. In 1543 he told the Commons, while confirming them in the valuable privilege of freedom from arrest :—

We be informed by our Judges that we at no time stand so high in our estate royal as in the time of Parliament, when we as head and you as members are conjoined and knit together in one body politic.

And indeed, when a series of Royal Parliamentary Statutes had revolutionized the fundamental law of Church and State, which had from time immemorial been set high above the competence of Crown or Parliament to alter, then indeed the ' Crown in Parliament ' had more than doubled its power. It had become, what it had never been before, ' omnicompetent' to make any law it would within the Realm of England.

But while Parliament, and particularly the House of Commons, was gaining a new position in the State, it remained in royal leading strings. The Reformation Parliament and the ' Tractable Parliament ' that followed it, seem to have been unduly dazzled by the right divine of the new Pope-King of England. The Statute of Treasons of 1534 spread the net far too wide for the safety of the loyal subject, and in the hands of Henry VIII and Thomas Cromwell such a weapon was not left in the sheath. Fortunately it was repealed under the liberal Protector, Somerset, at the beginning of Edward VI's reign, and the relation of Crown to Parliament found its normal Tudor level once more.

The suppression of the orders of monks and friars, and the secularization of their property did much to secure the Royal Parliamentary Reformation on a basis of vested interest. 1536–1539.
Henry VIII sold great part of the confiscated Abbey lands to Peers, courtiers, public servants and merchants, who at once resold much of it to smaller men.[1] Syndicates of middlemen of the commercial class bought the lands to speculate in real estate. It was largely owing to these transactions that, when the Papal reaction began under Mary, it was suspect to this new element in the squirearchy. Many an Abbey had become a manor-house, or the quarry out of which a manor-house was being built, and the squire had no wish to see it an Abbey again. Such persons, though they themselves were never found at the martyr's stake, learnt the wisdom of encouraging the Protestant preachers who were more willing to serve God for nought.

In those days land meant power of a direct kind over those who lived upon it. The Reformation would never have been permitted to flourish among the tenants on monastic estates.

[1] See H. A. L. Fisher's volume of the *Political History of England*, pp. 496–9, for an interesting table of the disposal of the monastic lands.

But when land in every shire changed from the hands of corporations devoted to the Papal authority and the old religion, into the hands of laymen bound to the new order of things by the very fact of their possessing land confiscated by sacrilege, the influence exerted over a very great body of tenantry was reversed.[1] In London, as in every other town, valuable and conspicuous sites of religious houses and much house property belonging to them passed into lay hands, removing the last check on the ever-increasing Protestantism, anti-clericalism and commercialism of the capital. At Oxford and Cambridge the monks and friars had been very numerous and had formed the backbone of resistance to the New Learning. The first result of their disappearance was a fall in the numbers of those attending the Universities, which alarmed Latimer ; but ere long the ranks of the students were swelled by an increased proportion of gentlemen's sons. This new class of lay undergraduate made the Universities a path to court favour and public service. The Cecils and Bacons fitted themselves by their academic studies to govern the country under Elizabeth, and to foster a new order of intellectual ideas which would never have taken root if Oxford and Cambridge had been left to the guidance of the monks and friars, checked only by the secular clergy.

Nevertheless, the way in which the monastic lands were distributed was a crime against education. The wealth of the monasteries, and after them of the chantries which suffered like spoliation in the last years of Henry and the first of Edward VI, should have gone to multiply and enlarge the schools formerly attached to a few of the monasteries and many of the chantries. The example had already been set, for Wolsey had used the wealth of religious houses which he suppressed for the benefit of his Cardinal College, afterwards Christ Church. At Cambridge, a nunnery put down on account of scandals had been converted into Jesus College as early as 1496. Henry VIII made, indeed, the splendid foundation of Trinity College, Cambridge, largely out of monastic lands, a deed that should never be forgotten if only to remind us what might have been done with the rest of the monastic spoil. England might have become an educated democracy before the Industrial Revolution, and she might in that case have been able to direct that great change into nobler and more humane channels. But in the corrupted currents of the world such a scheme for the bestowal of these Abbey and chantry

1545–
1549.

---

[1] The strongly Protestant family of which Francis Drake was born in 1545 held a farm on the Russell estates in Devonshire confiscated from Tavistock Abbey. Francis Russell stood godfather to the baby, and gave him the Christian name which he was to make famous in two hemispheres.

lands ,wholesale on the public seemed a 'devout imagination,' in England and in Scotland both. The Exchequer was empty and the courtiers greedy, and a hasty sale of the lands to private persons was the course adopted.

The monks had not been good managers of their property, for they were terribly in debt. In relation to their tenants they were on the average neither much better nor much worse than laymen. As is the way with corporate bodies, they were often conservative in their policy as landlords—that is less efficient, but less severe. But even this rule had many exceptions. Enclosure with depopulation had taken place on many monastic estates, and Bishop Langland in 1526 said of some monasteries that ' more than the seculars or the laity, they flay their tenants ' (' excoriant firmarios suos '). It is true that when the monasteries were dissolved, many of the tenants suffered by a rise in rents, due to land speculation and frequent sales of the confiscated estates among the class of laity who were scrambling for them. But this, too, was far from being always the case ; very often the monks had wholly dissociated themselves from the management of their lands, letting them on long leases which necessarily remained untouched when the estates changed hands.[1]

Both the monks and the nuns, and those of the laity who lived upon pensions and ' corrodies ' charged on the monastic endowments, were to a large extent aristocratic and well-to-do in their origin and connections.[2] The monasteries were no longer either a democratic or an intellectual force. The proportion of their income that actually went in alms to the poor had become scanty. The chronicle-writing which had distinguished the English cloister in the past had practically ceased, and no other form of intellectual activity had taken its place. To Colet, More and Erasmus the monk was an obscurantist, and the friar an exploiter of the worst popular superstition. The revived classical and biblical scholarship of the Renaissance found scarcely an echo in the monastery. Manual labour had died out among the monks, and the ascetic life which had formerly given them so much influence over an admiring world was now neither admired nor practised. Occasionally there were bad scandals, both in monasteries and in nunneries, but for the most part the ' religious' on the eve of the Dissolution lived a life of easy sauntering comfort, without grave offence but without marked benefit to the world around them. For several generations pious endowments

---

[1] See note at end of chapter, p. 311.

[2] On this point see Professor Savine's *English Monasteries at the Dissolution* (Clar. Press, 1909), pp. 240–5 and 263–7. On English Nunneries see Miss Power's *Mediæval English Nunneries* (1922). There were never more than about 2000 nuns in mediæval England. On poor relief see pp. 284–5, above.

had been going no longer to monasteries, but to chantries and elsewhere. The numbers of the monks had fallen by some twenty-five per cent. in three hundred years, and stood at about 7000 at the time of the Dissolution. Years before the breach with Rome the movement for suppressing monasteries was being carried on by orthodox Bishops and Cardinals.

There was, in fact, a strong case for applying their endowments to other public purposes more suited to the new age, and if the breach with the Pope was to be permanent his militia must be disbanded. But there was nothing to be said for collecting vile charges on insufficient evidence,[1] judicially murdering the Abbot of Glastonbury and several other 'religious' in order to hasten the surrender of their property, and letting it nearly all pass into private hands in return for a merely temporary relief to the exchequer.

The monks and the old religion were still beloved in Lincolnshire, Yorkshire and the counties of the Northern border where feudal and mediæval society still throve. The rising known as the Pilgrimage of Grace was the result. Henry had no troops save a few Yeomen of the Guard. If the rest of the country had risen, or had refused to support him, he must either have fallen or reversed his policy. But London, the South and the Midlands stood by him and the storm was weathered. Nor is this popular attitude surprising : long before the King and the gentry rose against the monasteries, the peasants and townsfolk had so risen in 1381, at St. Albans, Bury St. Edmunds and elsewhere.

Neither did the rest of the Church feel called on to espouse the quarrel of the 'religious.' The secular clergy had for centuries regarded the monks and friars as their rivals, who took from them tithes and fees, competed against their ministrations, and rejected the jurisdiction of their Bishops. These feelings of rivalry between the two parts of the Catholic Church in England were just as strong on the eve of the Reformation as at any former time, and this fact largely accounts for what followed. The cosmopolitan orders which stood isolated alike from the clergy and the more progressive of the laity, and looked to Rome for protection, could not possibly survive when the spirit of nationalism undertook in earnest the formation of an English Church.

In that Church the Bishops retained their place, little altered in form or in law. It was easy for them to take King instead

---

[1] No historian goes to the reports of Henry VIII's Commissioners for evidence about the state of the monasteries. But there is plenty of good evidence in the Episcopal Visitations of those monasteries which were subject to them. See Tanner, *Constitutional Documents*, pp. 50–7, for an excellent summary.

of Pope for master, for they had long been accustomed to act as Royal rather than as Papal servants. The typical English Bishop of the Middle Ages was not Becket but William of Wykeham. Their experience as civil servants, their active part in Parliament and Privy Council, the habit of compromise between the rival claims of Church and Crown, helped the Bishops to accommodate themselves and their office to the great change. But the Abbots had, most of them, stood outside the national life, few of them attending Parliament, and hardly any of them mixing with business outside their own conventual affairs. It was natural then, that in modern England there was a great place found for the Bishop but none for the Abbot. The disappearance of those Abbots who had sat beside the Bishops in the House of Lords left the spirituality in that Chamber in a minority instead of a majority, a change of great significance.

Henry, as Supreme Head of the Church, proceeded to reform the religion of his subjects and so complete the breach with Rome. The study of the Canon Law, that intellectual link with Papal Europe, was suppressed.[1] There were also changes of a more purely devotional character. In his morose and terrible old age, Henry put into effect the ideals which he had imbibed from the Oxford reformers in his fresh and generous youth, the more readily as he could thereby counteract the influence of monks, friars and Papalists over the multitude. Relic-worship, image-worship and pardon-mongering, the grosser forms of popular superstition and pious fraud which Colet and Erasmus had attacked, were put down by the heavy hand of the royal authority. All over the country relics were being destroyed, miracle-working images taken down, and their crude machinery exhibited to the people on whose credulity it had imposed. ' Dagon is everywhere falling,' said the reformers ; ' Bel of Babylon is broken in pieces.' The shrine and cult of Thomas Becket, so long the chief centre of English pilgrimage, was utterly and easily suppressed, in a new age which spoke of ' the holy blissful martyr ' as ' a rebel who fled the realm to France and to the Bishop of Rome to procure the abrogation of wholesome laws.'

Meanwhile, under the influence of Cranmer, an approach was being made towards a new type of appeal to the religious instincts of the masses. The Archbishop himself was drawing up

[1] An indirect effect of the Reformation was to reduce not only the independence of the Church Courts, but the scope of their jurisdiction over the ordinary affairs of life. For instance, actions for defamation or libel gradually passed to the lay courts during the Tudor and Stuart epochs. See *Holdsworth*, III. 410–11, V. 205–6.

forms of prayer in English which found their places in the Prayer Book of the next reign. But, meanwhile, Henry ordered priests to recite to their congregations, and fathers to teach their children the Lord's Prayer, the Commandments and the Articles of Faith in English. Above all, at Cranmer's instigation, the Bible in English was not only permitted to circulate freely, but was ordered to be set up in every parish church. A version based on that of Tyndale, the noble scholar and martyr, and on another by his less learned successor, Miles Coverdale, became known, as Tyndale had desired, to craftsmen and to 'the boy that driveth the plough.' The English Reformation, which had begun as a Parliamentary attack on Church fees, and proceeded as a royal raid on Abbey lands, was at last to find its religious basis in the popular knowledge of the Scriptures which had been the dream of Wycliffe. In this way it acquired the strength that resisted the Marian persecution, when cobblers, clothiers and poor women willingly offered themselves for a cause they at last understood.

Henry, having thus let in the sea, proceeded to ordain the limits of the flood. The disagreeable appearance of one of his later brides, Anne of Cleves, whom Cromwell brought over from anti-Papal Germany, helped, together with graver considerations of European policy, to remind the King that things were going too far, or at least too fast. Cromwell was beheaded. The Act of Six Articles had already been passed decreeing death against any one who denied Transubstantiation, or the necessity of auricular confession and clerical celibacy. A man was hanged in London for eating flesh on Friday. The burning of Protestants proceeded quietly, but with no indecent haste. Latimer was permitted to retire to private life, but Cranmer remained Archbishop. It was an oscillation, not a reversal of policy. Catherine Howard, the fifth wife, was a Catholic Anne Boleyn, who had much the same faults and suffered the same fate as her Protestant prototype. Catherine Parr, the famous survivor, was a moderating influence on religious policy, inclining cautiously to the Reformers.

Henry in fact was trying to prevent further change and to frighten people who were too prone to discuss religion, a subject on which the King's Grace had finally pronounced—at least for the present. Meanwhile men could read the Bible and think what they liked in silence. The Act of Six Articles was not unpopular, for at the moment the great majority were neither Papalists nor Protestants, and no one believed in toleration. The Act was not rigorously or regularly enforced. Henry was still in touch with the desires of the generality of his subjects, and he had their loyal support against hostile foreign powers in the last

1540.
1539.

1542.

years of his reign.   But times were bound to alter, and there are
signs that he was meditating yet another move forward, when he
was called before the only spiritual authority that was any longer **1547.**
competent to summon a King of England.

BOOKS FOR FURTHER READING

Pollard, *Henry VIII* and *Cranmer*, and books in list, pp. 287-8, above.

NOTE (to p. 307 above), MONKS AS LANDLORDS

Mr. Leadam, in his close analysis of Wolsey's *Domesday of Enclosures* of 1517
(I. pp. 48–9, 263), comes to the conclusion, based on statistics, that ' leaving
out of account the question whether the evictions were the work of landlord or
tenant, there was no superior security, as fancied by later generations, for the
cultivators of ecclesiastical soil.'   It is not surprising therefore that, while the
monasteries still existed, they had no such reputation for good landlords as
they acquired in the sentimental retrospect.   In Sir T. More's *Utopia* we read :
' noble men and gentlemen, yea, and certain Abbots, holy men God wot, not
contenting themselves with the yearly revenues and profits that were wont to
grow to their forefathers and predecessors of their lands, . . . leave no ground
for tillage ; they enclose all in pastures ; they throw down houses ; they pluck
down towns (= villages), and leave nothing standing but only the church to make
of it a sheepcote.'

On the whole subject of monastic landlord policy and finance see the *Eynsham
Cartulary*, edited by H. G. Salter (Clarendon Press), especially his summing-up
on p. xx.   See also Tawney, *Agrarian Problems in* 16*th Century*, pp. 382–3 ;
A. Savine, *English Monasteries on the Eve of the Dissolution* (Clarendon Press);
R. H. Snape, *English Monastic Finances* (Cambridge Press) ; Leadam, *Domesday
of Enclosures* (Royal Hist. Soc.) ; Tanner, *Const. Documents*, pp. 50–7, and
H. A. L. Fisher, *Political History, passim*.   All these must be compared to
Cardinal Gasquet's *Henry VIII and the English Monasteries*.   A more general
review of monastic and ecclesiastical estate policy in relation to the peasants
in Europe throughout the Middle Ages will be found in G. G. Coulton's *Mediæval
Village* (Cambridge Press, 1925).

CHAPTER IV

Interludes, Protestant and Catholic.   Edward VI (1547–1553) and Mary I
(1553–1558)

THE patient craft of Henry VII and the imperious vigour of
Henry VIII had laid the foundations of modern England.   Order
had been restored, the nobles and their retainers had been suppressed, royal government through Council and Parliament had
become a reality in every corner of England and even of Wales,[1]
the Royal Navy had been founded, the independence of the
country had been established in the face of Europe, secular and
spiritual, and the lay revolution in the relations of Church and

---

[1] For Henry VIII's settlement of the Welsh problem see pp. 358–9, below.

State had been carried through. But all this, though accomplished, had not been secured. When Henry VIII died, the State was heavily in debt, the coinage had been debased, and the religious feuds which he seemed to have suppressed by violence were bound to break out afresh with increasing fury. The work of the Tudors might yet be ruined, unless the country could be governed on a method at once effective and cheap, and unless a form of religion was found for the new State Church sufficiently acceptable to prevent civil war leading to anarchy or counter-revolution. These problems were eventually solved by Elizabeth, a wise woman and something of a sceptic. But in the dozen years between her father's death and her own accession, government remained in the hands of fools and adventurers, foreigners and fanatics, who between them went near to wrecking the work of the Tudor monarchy, and who actually reduced England to a third-class power, torn by religious feud, a mere appanage of Spain on land and sea.

And yet this inglorious period was by no means barren of results. Religious parties and issues became more clearly defined. It was demonstrated that Henry's half-way tabernacle was not permanently habitable where he had pitched it, but that the country must choose between reunion with Rome and further advance in a Protestant direction. At the same time the national resistance to the Pope became identified in the popular mind with another issue—independence of Spain. The Prayer Book under Edward and the Protestant martyrology under Mary raised the English Reformation onto a new intellectual and moral plane, and rendered it possible for Elizabeth in 1559 to make a permanent settlement of religion, a feat that no human wisdom could have achieved in the drifting chaos of opinion that still obscured the land a dozen years before.

1547–
1553.

Edward VI, son of Henry VIII and Jane Seymour, was nine years old at his accession. He was an invalid child, intellectually precocious, earnest and severe, with more conscience than his father but scarcely more softness of heart. So far as we can judge of one who died before he was sixteen, he might, if he had lived longer, have ruined the Reformation by overdriving, much as his half-sister Mary ruined the Catholic cause. So long as he lived, two men in turn guided the State in his name. First his uncle Seymour, the Protector Somerset, a rash idealist ; and after him John Dudley, Earl of Warwick and Duke of Northumberland, a man of no principle at all except selfish ambition.

But Edward's reign was saved from futility by the two dominating figures of its religious life. The first of these was

Archbishop Cranmer, whose Prayer Book, based largely on his translations from late Latin into the purer English of the Tudor age, harmonized the old and the new, and appealed successfully to the temperament and higher emotion of large sections of the population who without this rallying point might have flown off into mutually hostile factions. Henceforth the Church of England was something more than a remnant spared by the royal and anti-clerical revolution : it had found what it so sorely needed—a positive religious atmosphere of its own. The final triumph of the Prayer Book was postponed till Elizabeth's reign, but it made its first voyages on the stormy seas of opinion under Edward. Cranmer, timid and time-serving at the Council Board, as soon as he took his pen in his hand in the freedom of his own study was like a man inspired.

Very different was his friend, Hugh Latimer. He did not resume the episcopal office which he had been obliged to relinquish on account of his Protestantism in Henry's reign, but remained as the free lance of the Reformation under Edward, free even to ' cry out against covetousness ' in the Lords of the Council. Preaching at St. Paul's Cross to the citizens and in the King's garden to the courtiers, Latimer, by his rough, homely sermons, set the standard of that English pulpit oratory which, together with the Bible and the Prayer Book, effected the conversion of the people to Protestantism in the course of the next hundred years.

Meanwhile he did his best to redeem the crimes of the Royal Reformation by the honesty with which he denounced them. Edward's reign opened with the completion of Henry's plan for the robbery of the guilds and chantries, ostensibly for the sake of putting down ' superstition ' and paid prayers for the dead, but trespassing far outside these limits in order to load the courtiers with fresh spoil ; the schools attached to the suppressed corporations were in the first instance abolished and were not in all cases re-established as ' King Edward Grammar Schools.' To Latimer and his contemporaries education was a part of religion, and he saw that without education Protestantism could never take root. The learning for which the English Church became afterwards so distinguished, the long array of divines and scholars from Jewel and Hooker to Westcott and Hort, were yet in the future, while in the present the sharers of chantry lands ' crammed their rich thievery up,' they cared not how.

Schools are not maintained (cried Latimer). Scholars have not exhibition, the preaching office decayeth. Men provide lands and riches for their children, but this most necessary office they for the most part neglect. It will come to pass that we shall have nothing but a little English divinity that will bring the realm into a very barbarousness and utter decay of learning. It is not that, I wis, that will keep out the supremacy of the Bishop of Rome. Here I will make a supplication that ye would bestow so much to the finding of scholars of good wits, of poor men's sons, to exercise the office of salvation, in relieving of scholars, as ye were wont to bestow in pilgrimage matters, in trentals, in masses, in pardons, in purgatory matters.

It was because many of the middle classes learnt this new conception of piety and good works that the rapacity of the courtiers was made good in the course of years, and the land saved alike from ' barbarousness ' and from ' the Bishop of Rome.' Yet the great chance for endowing education from the confiscated lands had been let slip, because England was then neither democratic nor in love with learning.

The Protector Somerset, in spite of the protests of Cranmer, had pushed on the spoliation of the guilds and chantries largely for private interests ; he had secured his own share of the spoil, out of which the original ' Somerset House,' too princely for a subject, rose on the banks of the Thames. He aimed at monopolizing power to an unwise degree for a statesman who had at his back no monarch of age and authority to support him against a revolt of his fellow-Councillors. Nevertheless he was a strange mixture of pride and humility, selfishness and pure public spirit. He was more honest, humane and democratic in sympathy than the other politicians of that time.[1] He believed in toleration in both Church and State. He encouraged Parliament to repeal the oppressive laws of Henry's later regime, the Statutes of Treason and Act of Six Articles. Under his influence Parliament legitimized the marriage of clergy in response to their petition, and issued the first edition of Cranmer's Prayer Book, which was enforced by the mildest Act of Uniformity ever issued by a Tudor Parliament.

Somerset persecuted neither Catholics nor Protestants on account of their opinions, and permitted free discussion of religious differences. The result was not altogether encouraging. The moment the heavy hand of government was raised, the religious parties everywhere flew at one another's throats. ' Hot gospellers ' matched against ' suppressed ' monks and friars led

1547.

1549.

---

[1] The extraordinarily low level of the past in humanity and decency is often forgotten by controversialists who judge it as if it were a struggle under modern conditions between the well-behaved sects and parties of to-day. In the last year of Henry VIII's reign Wriothesley, the Lord Chancellor, and Rich, the Solicitor-General, with their own hands turned the screws of the Tower rack while torturing the Protestant lady, Anne Askewe, in hope of extorting confessions. Her shattered body was afterwards tied to the stake at Smithfield and burnt.

on the rival crowds. Brawling in church and street over the removal or the non-removal of images, the reading of Mass or Prayer Book, Protestant preaching or Catholic processions, seemed the prelude to civil war.

There were serious disturbances in Oxfordshire, put down by the hanging of priests. The North was fairly quiet, perhaps because the Catholics there had not recovered from the severity of the repressions that followed the Pilgrimage of Grace a dozen years before. But only in the extreme South-West did anything that could be called a religious rebellion come to a head. The men of Cornwall still spoke their old Celtic language, and of two services in unknown tongues preferred the sound of the familiar Latin to the ' Christmas play,' as they termed it, in English. In Devon also the peasantry rose under their priests, but the mariners rescued Sir Walter Raleigh's father out of their hands, and the citizens of Exeter stood a six weeks' siege on behalf of Protestantism. In Elizabeth's reign the squires and the new clergy succeeded in bringing round the peasants to the point of view of the seamen and townsfolk, in that shire which more than any other was to challenge Catholicism upon the high seas.

Elsewhere the numerous local risings that disturbed Somerset's Protectorate were not religious but agrarian. Times were bad, Henry VIII had debased the coinage and the consequent rise and uncertainty of prices caused great distress. The most formidable outbreak was in Norfolk, where the Reformation was generally popular, but where enclosures for sheep-farming had exasperated the peasantry. The armed commonalty, under their leader Kett, captured Norwich and camped outside its gates 1549. upon Mousehold Heath, afterwards so famous a spot in English landscape. There they slaughtered and devoured 20,000 of the offending sheep ! Their spirit was democratic, not unlike that of John Ball's men in 1381, or of the German peasants who rose in Luther's time. One of their demands was the emancipation of all who were still villeins—an aspiration that was fulfilled in the reign of Elizabeth, who characteristically compelled all the villeins she could find on her royal estates to purchase their freedom at a swingeing rate.

Like all unassisted risings of peasantry, that of 1549 was soon put down by the better organized classes. Its chief result was a reaction in favour of ' strong government ' and the fall of the too liberal Somerset, who had sympathized with the popular complaints. Under the influence of Latimer and the party of social reform known as the ' Commonwealth's men,' the Protector had endeavoured to induce Parliament to pass effective statutes to control enclosures, but members elected on the strictly limited franchise of that day [1] were too deep in the business themselves, as also were many of Somerset's colleagues on the Council. It was easy for them now to lay at the Protector's door the blame for Kett's rising and the similar troubles elsewhere. He had, moreover, alienated the magnates of the City, though he was popular with the mob of the London streets. The affection of the peasantry stood him in little stead in a struggle for power.

1549. A combination of the Catholic and Protestant parties in the Council effected his overthrow, after he had made a wild appeal to the people to rise on his behalf against ' the great.'

The Catholic party looked to benefit by the change which they had helped to bring about, but they found themselves deceived. Somerset's supplanter, Dudley, Earl of Warwick and afterwards Duke of Northumberland, had no sincere religious opinions of his own, but he elected to work with the Protestants, and the Reformation was pushed on with greater vigour and less discretion than before. Toleration in Church and State, and popular sympathy in social questions had been tried by Somerset and found a failure by the upper classes. Encouraged by the set of opinion in Parliament, Dudley revived some of the harsher methods of Henry VIII, but this time in connection with a more advanced Protestant doctrine. No one indeed was put to death for religion, except Joan Bocher who denied the humanity of Christ and a Dutchman who denied His divinity. But some leading Catholics were deprived and imprisoned.

The Prayer Book was reissued with Protestant emendations —substantially in its present form (1925). Since Lutheranism had gone to sleep in the arms of the German Princes, Strasburg and Switzerland were the hearth of the Protestant flame, and the gathering places for English religious exiles, whence many now returned to speed the work at home. A breath from the lands on which the Alps look down began to make itself felt in England. As yet that influence came from the milder Zwingli of Zurich rather than from Calvin of Geneva, but both of these reformers were democrats, as anyone appealing to the Swiss must needs be. German Protestantism had become official and princely, but Swiss Protestantism always strove to arouse a lively sense of religion in the common people, whether in Holland, Scotland or England. It thereby contributed a useful element to the English Reformation, which went on its course gathering fruit off many trees old and new, but never entirely pleasing anyone outside its native island.

1549–1553. The ascendancy of Dudley, who became Duke of Northumberland in 1551, was as unpopular as it deserved to be. It was the

---

[1] See pp. 256–7 for the disfranchising Act of 1430.

high-water mark of corruption and greed among courtiers with
the country in their power and no King to keep them in order.
Northumberland, a purely self-seeking man, built his schemes of
ambition on the narrow basis of personal influence over a dying
boy, who took him for an earnest Protestant. But outside the
King's sick chamber, people of all religions soon recognized that
Dudley rang as false on the counter as one of the bad coins issued
by his government. The Protestants of London and East Anglia
liked him as little as the Catholics of the North and West. In
warfare and in political intrigue he had both skill and courage,
but these availed little to save a man without statesmanship,
whom all detested. For he had not even the art, by which
many political adventurers have prospered, to arouse the devotion
of a small personal following, and in the day of crisis Northumberland found himself deserted by all.

On the death of Edward VI he sprang his audacious plot
to exclude both of Henry VIII's daughters, Mary and Elizabeth,
and to place on the throne a distant heir, Lady Jane Grey, his
own daughter-in-law. He had induced the dying Edward, by
fears of a Catholic reaction under Mary, to sign a will to that
effect, and the Council was terrified into lending it a certain
measure of support. The plot had been well staged, but London
and all England rejected it with scorn, and Northumberland himself was fain to throw up his cap with a hoarse cheer for Queen July
Mary. . 1553.

That did not save him from the axe on Tower Hill, after a
public recantation of Protestantism as insincere as his original
adherence, and as vain to achieve its purpose as all the clever
schemes he had spun. The vision of Northumberland kneeling
on the scaffold, looking round vainly for the reprieve he had
purchased by apostasy, and at the last flinging himself down with
a gesture of irritated despair, remains in dramatic contrast to the
dignified resignation of Lady Jane Grey, the modest and studious
girl of sixteen, whom he had inveigled into a false position.
Her execution six months later aroused in the people of England
exactly opposite feelings to those aroused by the death of her
father-in-law. As learned as any of the Tudor sovereigns, this
gentle Grecian had a more perfect character than the best of them;
but whether she could have borne the weight of sovereignty as
well as Elizabeth may well be doubted.

Mary, through the mistakes and violence of her enemies, 1553–
began her reign in an atmosphere of popular enthusiasm, which 1558.
she dissipated almost as quickly as James II, when he sacrificed
a like initial advantage on the same altar of fanaticism. But

in character Mary was the superior of James. She showed the high Tudor courage in time of danger, and she had no personal vindictiveness ; if she had been a sceptic or even a moderate in religion she might in after years have been remembered as Mary the Humane. But the narrow understanding of the daughter of Catherine of Aragon had been educated by brooding in secret, a neglected girl, over her mother's wrongs and her mother's religion, while her mother's Spanish origin drew her affections with fatal magnetism towards Southern Europe. She had no national pride on behalf of the country she ruled. She cared only for the souls of the English, and believed they would be safer in Italian and Spanish hands. From her chapel she had as little vision of the real England as her brother from his sick bed. Wrapt in doctrinal studies or religious ecstasies, neither brother nor sister had an eye for the great outlines of Tudor policy, for the broad prospect of England's ploughlands and pastures, thronged marts and manor-houses, and England's ships tossing on distant seas ; no instinct told them what all those busy far-scattered subjects of theirs were thinking and needing day by day. But that vision and that instinct were the secret of all successful Tudor rule, and never deserted Elizabeth in her closest councils of State, in her devotions or her studies of theology, in her interviews with flattering foreign envoys, or even in the more dazzling presence of favourite suitors.

Identification with the Pope and Spain soon clouded the fortune that had seemed to shine upon the Catholic cause while Mary was being welcomed as Queen by the shouting 'prentices of London. On that day the Protestant cause had been associated in men's minds with violence and unrest. The robbery of the guilds and chantries, the continuous troubles of Edward's reign, above all Northumberland's headlong career ending in treason and crowned by apostasy, made the new religion for a while odious and despicable to the great body of floating opinion. It would have been safe and popular for Mary to return to the religious compromise of her father, to restore the Latin Mass, and discreetly to burn a dozen Protestants a year. If she had been content that England should rest there, at least for a while, there would have been no such revulsion to heresy as actually took place in the decisive first year of Elizabeth. But when **1554.** Mary insisted on marrying Philip of Spain in flat disregard of her subjects' wishes, making England the cockboat tied to the stern **1555.** of the great Spanish galleon, when she insisted further on reviving that Papal jurisdiction over the realm which even Gardiner and Bonner had helped Henry to abolish, she twice challenged the national pride in a way her father and sister would never have dared. And when, to crown the work, she burnt 300 Protestants 1555–1558. in four years, she made the old religion appear to the English as a foreign creed, unpatriotic, restless and cruel, an impression more easily made than eradicated.

It is common to speak of the 'Tudor despotism,' but the English were never 'mutes and audience' to the acts of their sovereigns, as the French were to the doings of Louis XIV. Henry VIII's policy had been in touch with general opinion and particularly with those parts of it which were represented in Parliament. In Edward's reign Parliament had played an independent if not a popular part, for Somerset's government had been foiled in its endeavour to carry democratic agrarian legislation through the Houses. And now popular acclamation had vetoed the will and testament of Edward VI and the action of the Council, and had prevented the substitution of the Dudley line for the Tudors. What would happen next? For Mary's policy of submission to Spain and Rome was contrary to the wishes both of Parliament and of people.

Parliament had no constitutional power to prevent the Queen from marrying whom she would, and the Commons' address against the Spanish match was therefore unavailing. The Kentish rising under Wyatt gave expression to the national 1554. feeling against a Spanish King, but though Wyatt obtained popular sympathy he missed popular approval, for men regarded rebellion as the sin of witchcraft. The horror of armed rising against the Crown was stronger in London and the South than in the wild North and West. Nor had Mary yet dissipated the personal popularity with which Northumberland's crime had endowed her. Protestant London refused to join Wyatt's forces when they cut their way along Fleet Street to Ludgate; he was overpowered, captured and executed.

Wyatt had intended to place Elizabeth on her sister's throne. But the young princess had already learnt the lesson of caution from some harsh personal experiences in girlhood, which had taught her that there were tricks in the world. With regard to Wyatt's rebellion, nothing could be proved against her, for she was innocent. Her sister was not wicked. The nation was on her side. After long weeks of anxiety in the Tower, during which Renard the Spanish ambassador clamoured for her blood, she was at length released, to the lasting regret of some in after years.[1] The Catholic prelate and statesman Gardiner, though he

---

[1] In the first Parliament of Elizabeth's reign John Story, an active persecutor under Mary, ' being at the Parliament House, did with great vehemency speak against the Bill that was there exhibited for the Restitution of the Book of Common Prayer, and said these words, " I did often-times, in Queen Mary's time, say to the Bishops that they were too busy with chopping at twigs, but

had opposed the Spanish match, would have had Elizabeth excluded from the succession, for he suspected the quality of her devotion as she knelt at the Mass. But Parliament protected her reversionary claims, and in the matter of the succession its constitutional rights were undeniable and its will prevailed. People and Parliament stood by Elizabeth against Spanish ambassador and Catholic Bishop. She silently took note where her strength lay.

1555–1558.

With Philip of Spain husband to a doting queen, England was for three years vassal of the great Spanish monarchy.[1] So long as Mary lived and loved, all thought of a foreign policy anywhere opposed to Spain must be set aside, together with all hope of trade with America—which Philip strictly denied to his island subjects—and all dreams of colonization or sea power. The terms of the royal marriage were most injurious to England, and the Venetian envoy declared that Mary was bent on nothing but making the Spaniards masters of her kingdom. Only revolution or the Queen's death could open England's path to the freedom and greatness that awaited her upon the sea.

1555.

The next step was reunion with Rome. The experience of Edward's reign had convinced Bishops Gardiner and Bonner that Catholic doctrine could not be safe under the Royal Supremacy, and Mary, as her mother's daughter, had always been a Papalist. A new Parliament yielded to the pressure of Crown and Privy Council, while imposing restrictions and conditions that bitterly galled the devout Queen. It was indeed an ignoble compromise. Matters of faith and spiritual jurisdiction were restored to Rome, but the material interests of the lay revolution were saved entire. Title-deeds of monastic lands, tithes and all Church properties that had found their way into the coffers of warm gentlemen were to lie there untouched, while the Queen had her way about Papal jurisdiction, and while the revived heresy laws allowed the spiritual courts and the Privy Council to burn alive believing Protestants at their pleasure. While cobblers and clergymen died in agonies for their faith, no gentleman who was not also a priest suffered in Mary's reign. The lay beneficiaries of the ' great plunder ' conformed to the service of the Mass, to save their skins and their lands. But they began to perceive that both would be more safe under a thorough change of system.

I wished to have chopped at the root ; which if they had done, this gear had not now come in question," and herein most traitorously he meaned the destruction of our dear and sovereign lady Queen Elizabeth. For which words spoken, in such an audience and in such a vehement manner, there was no honest nor true heart that heard him but did utterly abhor him.'—*State Trials* and *Strype*, I. i. 115.

[1] In 1556 Philip succeeded his father, Charles V, as King of Spain.

'God save the Princess Elizabeth' became the prayer of many a squire, dreaming on things to come. The Venetian envoy wrote home that, 'with the exception of a few most pious Catholics, none of whom are under thirty-five years of age, all the rest make this show of recantation yet do not effectually resume the Catholic faith.' The opportunity that Mary's State action gave to the old religion was lost for want of a corresponding religious revival to support it among the rising generation.

When Mary's Parliament consented to the revival of the heresy laws, it put the lives of the English out of its own keeping 1555. into the hands of the spiritual courts and a Privy Council chosen by Mary. There can be little doubt that in so doing the members expected such a moderate amount of persecution as the country had approved under Henry. Edward's reign, for all its faults, had seen almost nothing of fire and faggot, and the shock was the greater when some three hundred men and women were 1555– burnt in less than four years. The persecutors grossly mis- 1558. calculated the trend of public opinion, as honest fanatics are liable to do. Mary herself and her ecclesiastical advisers, Pole and Bonner, were responsible for the fatal policy, and to a less degree Gardiner, who died during its inception. The shrewd and scheming Spaniards, anxious mainly to keep their hold on England, warned Mary in vain that the burnings were making her unpopular. The Spaniards themselves were burning and burying heretics ten times as fast in the Netherlands, but in England there were as yet no Spanish troops ; let her beware. But on this she would not listen even to her husband, for did she not hear the voice of God ?

The prelates who encouraged her on this fatal course were Englishmen of an older generation, who failed to realize that there was no longer Catholic zeal enough to support anything but a temporizing policy on the part of government. Nor were they aware of the Protestant zeal latent in the common people, which this persecution brought to the surface and converted into a great political force in deciding the future of Church and State. The reforming party, as Mary and her advisers had known it all their lives at court, had been self-interested, time-serving, at best honestly Erastian and willing to conform to the Prince's religion. The very different popular resistance that the Catholics now encountered was a hidden reef on which their cause was shipwrecked beyond all recovery.[1]

---

[1] The growing importance and temper of Protestantism was shown by the fact that as many as 2000 out of some 8000 beneficed clergy had to be deprived. When Elizabeth changed the Church back to Protestantism, the number of clergy deprived as obstinate Romanists was much smaller.

They had miscalculated also the more humane feelings slowly growing in the English people. The repeated sight of prolonged agonies voluntarily endured and purposely inflicted, would have shocked people less in the Middle Ages. In Mary's reign it aroused some at least of the pity and anger that such exhibitions would arouse to-day. This nascent humanitarianism set people upon the first stage of the road towards toleration. It created for the first time in England a sentiment against putting people to death for their religious opinions as distinct from their political acts—a sentiment which greatly affected the practice of all subsequent governments.

In the hands of able propagandists like John Foxe, the memory of the martyrs bred a hatred of the Church of Rome, which proved the one constant element in English opinion during the coming centuries of civil and religious faction. For the next two hundred years and more Foxe's *Book of Martyrs* was often placed beside the Bible in the parish churches, and was read in manor-house and cottage, by Anglican and Puritan, in an epoch when there was relatively little else to read and when interest in religion was profound and widespread.

Most of the victims were inhabitants of London or the Home Counties, and most of them were humble folk. But Latimer died as he might have desired, lighting the candle of his own clear certainty to illuminate the more complex and hesitating opinion of others. In an age of mixed measures, confused counsels and compromise, he had held a straight course which the English of the new era could understand and imitate. Cranmer's example was of equal but different potency, for he was one of the doubters taking a line at last. He had honestly held that the Crown ought to decide on religion in England. Was he then to obey Mary or was he to stand up for his own convictions? It was a real dilemma for a convinced Erastian who had also become a convinced Protestant. Roman Catholics could only be in a like difficulty if the Pope were to turn heretic. There is no wonder that his timid nature hesitated and recanted in the presence of a terrible death. It is more wonderful that he saw his way so clearly in the end, and held the hand, which had signed the recantation, in the fire until it was consumed. Had the men of those days a less highly strung nervous system than ours, or can the power of a scholar's mind be so triumphant over physical pain? In that magnificent gesture the Church of England revived.

The capture of Calais by the French in a war fought by England to please Spain, and fought very ill, added to the heavy weight of Mary's unpopularity. Yet the loss of this cherished

1555.

1556.

Jan.
1558.

bridgehead on French soil, bitterly humiliating to national pride, was a blessing in disguise to an island whose future did not lie on the continent of Europe.

Childless after all, hated by her people, slighted by her husband whose favour was already turning towards the sister who must survive and succeed her, fearful that Elizabeth would quickly ruin her work for God, the most honest and ill-advised of the Tudors turned away to die. Never for centuries had Nov. 17, England been at a lower ebb; the country was not only ill- 1558. governed and disgraced in peace and in war, without arms or leaders, unity or spirit, but it was, to all intents and purposes, an appanage of the Spanish Empire. With a hope too like despair men turned passionately to a young woman to save them, the third and last of Henry's progeny, of whom two had failed their need; by the strangest chance in history, no elder states-man or famous captain in all broad Europe would have served so well to lead Englishmen back to harmony and prosperity and on to fresh fields of fame.

CHAPTER V

The policy and character of Elizabeth. The Elizabethan Church Settlement. Spain and France. The Scottish Reformation and the future
Great Britain. The ' Rising of the Earls ' and the end of feudalism
in England

FOR centuries past many different forces had been slowly drawing the English towards a national or patriotic conception of man's duty to society, in place of that obedience to cosmopolitan orders and corporations which had been inculcated by the Catholic Church and the feudal obligation. Among the forces creative of the sense of nationhood were the English Common Law; the King's Peace and the King's Courts; the frequent intercourse of the representatives of distant shires and boroughs in the national council of Parliament; the new clothing industry based on national rather than municipal organization; the new literature and the new language common to all England. Finally, the action of the Tudor monarchy had abolished or depreciated all loyalties that intervened between the individual and the State, much as Protestantism purported to eliminate all that stood between the individual and God. The Elizabethan age is at once intensely national and intensely individualistic.

Mary, indeed, had attempted to re-establish the rule of the

cosmopolitan Church, which employed a foreign tongue in its services, looked across the Alps for its laws, and was itself organized on Latin and Cæsarean principles of government very different from the national and Parliamentary polity which the English laity were evolving in the conduct of their secular affairs. The Marian restoration was welcomed by a large section of the clergy, and by the semi-feudal society of Northern England, but it was unpopular with the Londoners, with the sea-faring population and with the more enterprising of the squires who were most in touch with the rising middle class; these men had no wish to have their beliefs dictated and their lives supervised by the clergy, least of all on orders from oversea.

With the help of these elements as represented in the House of Commons, Elizabeth in the first year of her reign re-established the supremacy of the national, laic State, with a national Church engaged as its servant upon honourable terms. The rest of her long life was spent in cautiously adapting the habits of the whole people to this new settlement, and defending it against internal malcontents and foreign aggressors. For many years the dangers seemed greater than the chances of success, until a new generation had grown up under the influence of the Bible, the Prayer Book and loyalty to the Queen. The contest finally resolved itself into a maritime war against Spain as the head of the Catholic reaction in Europe and the monopolist of the ocean routes to the New World. In the heat of that struggle English civilization was fused into its modern form, at once insular and oceanic, distinct from the continental civilization of which the Norman Conquest had once made it part.

Not only was modern England created, but the future of Great Britain was mapped out. The exigencies of the struggle for island independence against the Catholic powers of the continent put an end to the long hostility between the peoples of Scotland and England, while the same causes dictated the ruthless and ill-fated conquest of Catholic Ireland.

Amongst the Elizabethan English, by land and by sea, individualism became the ally of nationalism on free and equal terms, for the national State could not afford to pay for an army and a bureaucracy to bend the individual to its will, like the France and Prussia of later days. The poverty of the Elizabethan State explains many of its worst failures and meanest shifts, and not a few also of its greatest merits and noblest attitudes. A Queen whose revenue in war time did not reach half a million pounds a year must needs be 'niggardly'; but since her subjects would not be taxed to give her adequate supply, she was fain to appeal to their free loyalty to fight her battles and to wear themselves out in her service for love. They gave her their lives and affections more readily than their cash. For the rest, her great object, as defined in a political poem she herself wrote,[1] was ' to teach still peace to grow,' till men treasured the life of their Queen because it meant for them peace and prosperity at home while the neighbour nations were ablaze with religious war. Many who disliked her ecclesiastical compromise as being too Protestant, or not Protestant enough, accepted it as the condition of tranquil government, which in an age of rival fanaticisms seemed, and perhaps was, a miracle of statecraft.

When Elizabeth became Queen at the age of twenty-five the country was in no condition to resist a foreign invader. Not only was it divided by fierce religious feuds such as opened contemporary France to the foreigner, but it had for several years been treated as an appanage of Spain ; its financial credit, its warlike stores and its militia, were at the lowest ebb, and if there were any men capable of leading it in peace or in war, it was left to this young woman to find them out. It was rumoured in the Spanish Embassy that the coming man was Sir William Cecil, a politician of the rising middle class of smaller gentry, a pestilent heretic at heart, the more dangerous because he was no zealot but had, like Elizabeth herself, deemed life to be well worth a Mass. Nov. 1558.

Yet Philip of Spain protected the new Queen's accession and extended his protection for years after she had fulfilled his worst fears on the score of religion. For the next heir to the English throne was Mary Queen of Scots, a devout Catholic indeed, but married to the Dauphin of France. Throughout Elizabeth's reign it was the rivalry of the two great Catholic powers, France and Spain, that saved the heretic island from conquest, till it was too strong to be conquered. Neither rival could allow Britain to be subdued by the other. The rebellion of the Netherlands against Spain and the religious wars in France were further safeguards, and Elizabeth frequently sent men and money to keep both movements alive. But in the early years of her reign the Netherlands were not yet in open revolt and her part was still to cajole Philip. This she did by holding out hope that she would marry either him or a man of his choice, though she had no real intention of slipping any such noose over her head.

Yet anxious as she was to stand well with the Spaniards, she would not allow their ambassador to say that she in any

---

[1] ' The Daughter of Debate, who discord eke doth sow,
    Shall reap no gain where former rule hath taught still peace to grow.'
The ' Daughter of Debate ' is Mary Queen of Scots.

degree owed her life, liberty or throne to the goodwill shown
her by his master in Mary's latter days. She owed all, she
said, to the English people. If this was not the whole truth,
it was the part of the truth that mattered most. It was one
of those lightning flashes of sincerity that so often burst from
the cloud of vain and deceitful words in which Elizabeth loved
to hide her real thought and purpose. Sometimes, indeed, she
lied for amusement rather than in hope of deceiving, as when
she told the envoy of Spain ' she would like to be a nun and
live in a cell and tell her beads from morning to night,' on which
his only comment was ' this woman is possessed by a hundred
thousand devils.'

To her own people she boasted on her accession that she was
' mere English.' Her mother had been no foreign princess but an
English flirt, and her father, the founder of England's Navy and
of England's religious independence, had possessed a sixth sense
whereby he understood the English people, even in the highest
rages of his tyranny. She inherited from both, but most from
her father in whose steps it was her ambition to walk. If she
was heir to her mother's vanity and coquetry, she heeded the
warning of her fate ; and her own bitter experiences as a girl,—
disgrace, imprisonment and danger of death,—had taught her,
as Frederic the Great was taught by similar experiences in
boyhood, that private affections and passions are not for Princes.
She had learnt every lesson that adversity had to teach, and she
would leave it to her rival to lose the world for love.[1]

There was in her a certain hardness and coarseness of fibre,
necessary perhaps for her terrible task in life. As a private
person she would scarcely have been lovable, perhaps not even
very admirable. But lonely on the throne she knew all the arts
to make herself adored by her Court and her people. Without
ceasing to be a woman, and while loving life in all its fullness,
she made everything subservient to purposes of State. Her
learning endeared her to the Universities, her courage to the
soldiers and sailors. Her coquetry became a means of keeping
her nobles and courtiers each in his place, and exacting from
each one the last ounce of personal devotion in the public service.
Leicester's neck might be tickled by the royal hand, but his
rival Cecil would be trusted in matters of high policy. And
Cecil too might serve her the better for a shrewd spasm of fear
that she would marry the worthless and intriguing Leicester,

---

[1] It is possible, though not certain, that Elizabeth knew she was incapable
of child-bearing, and never had any real intention of marriage, or desire for
anything beyond flirtation. It would have been characteristic of her to guard
this invaluable political secret like death—even from Cecil.

who, though sometimes posing as patron of the Puritan party, had offered Philip to restore the Roman Church in England if Spain would secure his marriage with Elizabeth. Her love of hunting and dancing, masque, pageantry and display, was used to strengthen the wider popularity which was her ultimate strength; her public appearances and progresses through the country, which she thoroughly enjoyed, were no dull and formal functions, but works of art by a great player whose heart was in the piece, interchanges of soul between a Princess and her loving people.

Her speeches to Parliament were very different from the official ' King's Speech ' of our modern constitution. ' Though I be a woman,' she told a deputation of both Houses who had come to urge measures about the Succession, 'I have as good a courage answerable to my place as ever my father had. I am your anointed Queen. I will never be by violence constrained to do anything. I thank God I am endued with such qualities that if I were turned out of the realm in my petticoat, I were able to live in any place in Christendom.'

Men, they say, have been worn out by high office in a few years or even months ; this heroic woman was her own Prime Minister in war and peace for forty-five years, most of them fraught with danger both to the State and to her own much threatened life. And all the time she was an invalid—suffering, and subject to moods, caprices and nerve-storms that shook her but never shook her from her course. It may be true that her heart was cold, but it was a heart of oak.

' Mere English ' as she was, her education had been the broadest that modern and ancient Europe could afford. She discoursed in Greek and Latin to the Universities of Oxford and Cambridge, and in fluent Italian to the natives of the land of Machiavelli. Her enemies might have called her, in the phrase of that day, ' *Inglese Italianata*,' though she never in her long life quitted the English shore. She had been influenced by the Italian heretics, such as Vermigli and Ochino, who were more philosophers than zealots. She was a child of the Renaissance rather than of the Reformation, so far as the two movements could any longer be distinguished. She approached religion in the modernist spirit of Colet and Erasmus ; but two generations after their time, to a mind of their disposition, Rome of the Jesuits was abhorrent and transubstantiation incredible. The Church of Geneva attracted her as little, with its usurpation of the province of the State and its democratic republicanism. If it was left to her successor to say ' No Bishop, no King,' she had thought it and acted on it long before.

Sceptical and tolerant in an age of growing fanaticism, all English in feeling but pan-European in education, she was born and bred to re-establish the Anglican Church, and to evade religious war by a learned compromise between Catholic and Protestant that would leave Crown and laity masters in their own island. She regarded her action as a revival of her father's policy, but changed times demanded a larger infusion of Protestantism, for the Jesuit propaganda and the spearmen and sailors of Spain were not to be conquered save with the help of men who regarded the Pope as anti-Christ and the Mass as an abomination. Cranmer's revived Prayer Book was the golden mean. It served well on board Drake's ships before and after battle with the idolaters, and in parish churches where Bernard Gilpin and other earnest Protestant clergy laboured to instil the new religion into rustic ignorance. Yet the concealed Catholic, doubtfully attending church to avoid the twelve-penny fine, was often less shocked than he feared, and could remind himself that they were still the old prayers, though in English. The book was a chameleon which could mean different things to different people—an advantage in the eyes of this wise young woman, who herself had as many different explanations of her policy as she had dresses in her wardrobe, and loved to display them all in turn.

The Parliament of 1559 restored the Reformation in its Anglican form by passing the Act of Supremacy which abolished the Papal power, and the Act of Uniformity which made the Prayer Book the only legal form of worship. These Statutes represented the will of Crown and House of Commons. The Queen was a restraining force on the zeal of her faithful Commons, as for instance in declining to adopt for herself in full the title of Supreme Head of the Church, although she assumed the name and function of its Supreme Governor. The House of Lords was with difficulty brought to accept extensive changes in ritual and doctrine. The lay peers, lukewarm and divided on the religious issue, attempted in vain to induce the Commons to accept large amendments in a Catholic sense. But the victory lay with the Lower House and the classes it represented, who were already more important in the State than the nobility, and were in this matter acting in concert with the Queen and her Council.[1]

---

[1] This House of Commons was not packed. There is evidence that the elections were at least as free as those for the parliaments of Elizabeth's father, brother, and sister Mary. See *English Hist. Review*, July and October 1908, Mr. Baynes' articles.

The Bishops in the Upper House were against all change, but were voted down, partly because an unusual number of sees happened to be empty. Outside Parliament, the Convocation of the Clergy of the Province of Canterbury reaffirmed the supremacy of the Pope and the doctrine of transubstantiation. Their will was overridden and their protest ignored by Parliament.

The Reformation was in short a lay revolution carried by Crown and Parliament—more specifically by Crown and Commons—against the will of the Church authorities. But it was not therefore contrary to the will of the religious-minded laity who had no representation in Church assemblies; and out of 8000 beneficed clergy at least 7000 acquiesced in the accomplished fact, some gladly, some with indifference, some in hopes of another reaction that never came; whereas there had been as many as 2000 deprivations of obstinately Protestant clergy under Mary. But with one exception the whole bench of Bishops refused to conform to the Elizabethan settlement and were deprived. In the reigns of Henry VIII and Edward VI the Bishops and the Convocations of Clergy had acquiesced in the changes made. The increased stubbornness of official clerical opposition in the first year of Elizabeth may be ascribed to two causes: in the age of the Jesuits and Council of Trent the parties of Reformers and Romanists were becoming more distinct and mutually exclusive, even in the remote island of compromise. Furthermore Queen Mary had weeded out the Protestants from the official body of the Church. The Convocation of 1559 gave no fair representation to the large and active Protestant body among the priests. It followed that the Parliamentary proceedings of that year, even more than those under Henry VIII, wore the appearance of a coercion of the clergy by the uprising of lay opinion.

But in England the laity did not proceed, after the manner of the contemporary Scottish reformers, to secure lay representation in the ecclesiastical assemblies and to associate the clergyman in every parish with a board of lay ' elders.' The internal organization of the English Church was left in its mediæval form, entirely clerical in composition. For this very reason it was felt to be the more necessary to subject the Church to the external control of Crown and Parliament. The bulk of the clergy loyally accepted that control from outside as the necessary condition of the large franchises still left to them, among others the national monopoly of all religious rites, which the Crown and Parliament secured for them at the expense of all would-be Dissenters, Romanist or Puritan. No one dreamed of permitting a variety of religions. No one therefore could reasonably deny to the nation the right of deciding in Parliament what its one and only religion was to be.

This external control by the laity was applied to the Church through laws passed in Parliament defining doctrine and ritual, and through Commissioners and Bishops appointed by the Queen who inspected and administered the Church according to her orders. Towards the end of her reign, and still more under her two successors, the Puritan party in the Church appealed to Parliament for help, and the Anglican party to the Crown. Neither school of thought attempted to take up the high religious ground of the Scottish Church, which claimed to be entirely autonomous, and even to dictate on matters of policy to the feeble Scottish Parliament and to ' God's silly vassal,' the King.

Rome and Geneva, Loyola and Knox, claimed for the Church freedom and even superiority in relation to the State, the claims of Rome resting on sacerdotal authority, those of Geneva on religious democracy. The English Church made no such claims, for in England the days of sacerdotal authority were numbered in a land where men had learned to think for themselves, and the spirit of democracy, so far as it yet existed, found its expression and organ in the House of Commons and not in any assembly of the Church. The arrangement suited the Tudor English well, for they were interested in many other things besides religion ; when in succeeding centuries the spirit of democracy required expression in religion, it found it in the safety-valve of the Non-conformist sects. The Elizabethan religious settlement, tempered by successive doses of Toleration, has held a permanent place in the institutions and still more in the spirit of modern England.

If the year 1559 is to count as the first of modern England, it is still more decidedly the birth year of modern Scotland. The precise coincidence in time of the final breach with Rome to north and to south of the Border, though largely accidental, was of great consequence. The double event secured the unbroken permanence of the Reformation in both countries, and drew English and Scottish patriotism, which had hitherto thriven on mutual hostility, into an alliance of mutual defence. In both countries the Reformation meant release from continental dominion, secular no less than spiritual. In the autumn of 1558 England was a Roman Catholic country virtually subject to Spain, and Scotland was a Roman Catholic country virtually subject to France. Two years later each was a Protestant country cleared of foreign soldiery and rulers, and closely identifying its newly chosen religion with its national independence. The double rebellion succeeded because Spain and France remained rivals, while England and Scotland became friends for the first time since the reign of Edward I. In the stress of that twofold crisis the foundations of Great Britain were laid by William Cecil and John Knox.

England approached the Reformation through the Renaissance ; Scotland approached the Renaissance through the Reformation. Catholicism as a religion had meant less to the Scots, for with them the Church was more corrupt and inefficient as a spiritual power than to the south of the Border. After the slaughter of so many leading nobles at Flodden in 1513, the secular power in Scotland was wielded more than ever by the prelates, cadets of noble families, living like laymen and fighting each other with sword and gun for the abbeys and benefices of the Church. The vernacular poetry of Sir David Lyndsay and other makers of ' godly ballads ' prepared the way for the Reformation by holding up to popular contempt the lives and pretensions of the Churchmen.

It is the less surprising that Protestantism obtained under the leadership of Knox the same hold on the intelligence and moral feeling of the common people in Scotland, as it obtained more gradually in England by the middle of the following century. In England the Reformation was promoted by the Crown and its satellites, while the old feudal nobility were lukewarm or hostile ; in Scotland the opposite was the case. But in both countries the genuine core of the movement lay in the burghers, yeomen and artisans and in the smaller landed gentry—the squires of England and lairds of Scotland.

It was only in the years immediately preceding 1559 that the Protestant party in Scotland had the advantage of figuring as patriots. In the 'forties it was the Catholic party that led the national resistance to English interference. For Henry VIII, though wisely aspiring to the union of the whole island through the marriage of his son Edward to the infant Mary Stuart, Queen of Scots, foolishly sought to force the policy on Scotland by the sword. Destructive raids in the valley of the Tweed and in the Lothians made the Scots curse the English tyrant and heretic, and frown upon his supporters in their own midst. When Henry died, the Protector Somerset carried on the same disastrous policy in the campaign of Pinkie, a dire defeat for Scotland, but a still worse blow to Somerset's prophetic daydreams of a united Great Britain, ' having the sea for wall and mutual love for its garrison.' To keep Mary Stuart out of

See Map XIV., p. 214, above.

1547.

the way of this rough and pertinacious wooing on behalf of
Edward VI, the Scots sent the impressionable little girl to
the court of Valois France, to learn in that most unsuitable
atmosphere the art of governing their dour and stubborn
selves.

But the insolence of the French army of occupation, which
was the price of the French alliance, did not long suit the proud
stomach of the Scots. Gallic domination became as unbearable
in Scotland as Spanish domination in contemporary England.

In her sixteenth year Mary Queen of Scots was married to the
Dauphin of France, and became party to a secret compact whereby
her native country was to go as a free gift to the French King
in case of her death without heirs. The able Regent who governed
Scotland in her absence, Mary of Guise, relied on French troops,
and thought of the land of Bruce as a Protectorate to be administered in the interests of France. In these circumstances
the Protestants in their turn became the champions of national
independence, while the Catholic party became unpopular
as the catspaw of French aggression. Under Mary of Guise
and Mary Tudor both North and South Britain lay beneath
the ' monstrous regiment (rule) of women,' which Knox be-
wailed all too loudly, improvident of his future relations with
Elizabeth.

In these circumstances a section of the Scottish nobles,
accustomed in that land of feudal anarchy to form ' bands ' for

the coercion of the Crown, formed a ' band ' to protect the new
religion. The confederates were bound together by the first
of Scotland's many ' covenants ' with God. This ' Congregation
of the Lord,' as it styled itself, was organized as an assembly
of estates, in which each Protestant notable took his place as
minister of religion or as noble, laird or burgess. It was more
representative of the political forces of the country than Scotland's Parliament, which was feudal in its form and served for
little more than a court of registration. The ' Congregation
of the Lord ' was army, Church and political assembly in one.
It formed the transition stage between Scotland's feudal warrior
past with its ' bands ' of rebel nobles, and her democratic religious
future with its Kirk Assembly. Nobles, styled ' Lords of the
Congregation,' were its leaders, but the popular and religious
elements were heard in its counsels, especially as they spoke
through the voice of John Knox.

The Moses of Scotland was a very rare combination of genuine
prophet and successful statesman. He who ' never feared the
face of man ' could calculate chances and consider ways and
means as the utterly fearless and the ' God-intoxicated ' are very

seldom able to do. He had been hardened by grim servitude and meditation at the oar of a French galley, and had since been founding Church congregations all over Southern Scotland. He knew the people well and saw that the hour had come to strike.

In 1559 a democratic religious revolution, preached by Knox and accompanied by image-breaking, swept through the Scottish burghs, beginning with Perth. It was thus that Calvinist revolutions began, whether in the Netherlands or in French-speaking countries, but they were as often as not suppressed with fire and sword. In Scotland, however, the ' Congregation of the Lord ' came with arms in their hands to defend the insurgent populace from the French troops and from Mary of Guise. There followed a spasmodic and ill-conducted war, in which little blood was shed ; it was going ill for the Scottish Protestants when it was decided in their favour by the intervention of England. Cecil had persuaded Elizabeth to take one of the few great initiatives of her reign. The English fleet appearing in the Firth of Forth, and an English army joining the Scottish Protestants before Leith, saved the cause of the Reformation. This *coup de théâtre* being followed by the death of Mary of Guise, led to the evacuation of Scotland by the French troops in accordance with the terms of the Treaty of Edinburgh. *1559.*

July 1560.

The Scottish Reformation was singularly bloodless, in spite of the violence of the language used on both sides. Very few Protestants had been burnt, and no Catholic was executed on account of his religion. Continental Europe, and even England in Mary Tudor's reign, presented a far bloodier spectacle of religious fanaticism.

Another Catholic force soon landed from France to take the place of the Regent and the soldiers. Mary Queen of Scots herself and a train of pleasure-loving ladies and favourites came over to try issues with that harsh land of old feudal power and new popular theology. An able, energetic and attractive widow, Mary Stuart was little likely to submit her royal will to Knox and the Lords of the Congregation. They had many enemies in the land—personal, political and religious—who would rally to the banner of the young Queen. Moreover, her eager eyes scanned horizons far beyond the borders of barren Scotland. The Catholics of Europe looked to her as their chosen champion to win back Britain to the faith. France and Rome were at her back. A great party in England hoped and intrigued to see Britain united by a counter-revolution, which should dethrone the illegitimate daughter of Henry VIII and place

1561.

the English crown on the head of the rightful heir, Mary Queen of Scots.[1]

The Protestant party in Scotland could not therefore afford to quarrel with Elizabeth, nor she with them. Little as she wished to abet feudal nobles and Calvinist peasants in resistance to their lawful sovereign, that sovereign was her open rival for the throne on which she sat. The situation was the more dangerous because the Catholic and feudal part of England lay precisely in the moorland counties nearest to the Scottish Border. Catholicism and feudalism were so strong to the north of the Humber that early in her reign Elizabeth was fain to employ the Catholic grandees of that region as her officials, in which capacity the Percies, Dacres and Nevilles continued to exert their old feudal influence and to thwart the policy of the government they served. 'Throughout Northumberland,' it was reported, 'they know no other Prince but Percy.' Bernard Gilpin, a mild and Anglican John Knox, was indeed busy helping the new Bishops to found the Protestantism of North England. But for many years there was the greatest danger of a feudal and Catholic reaction uniting all Britain north of the Humber in a single Kingdom governed by Mary Stuart. Northern England, like Scotland, was inhabited by a race of hardy and lawless fighters, bred to Border war, not easily kept in order by a distant government that had no army. But, fortunately for Elizabeth, Northern England, like Scotland, was very thinly inhabited and very poor. Until the Industrial Revolution, wealth and population were concentrated in the South, and most of all in and near London.

Grave as were her motives for dreading any increase in the power of Mary, Elizabeth was too cautious and too short of revenue

[1]

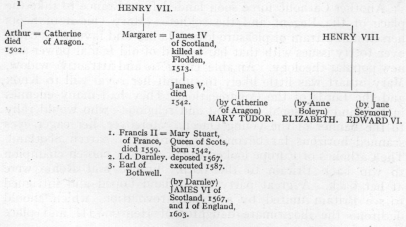

HENRY VII.

| Arthur = Catherine died 1502. of Aragon. | Margaret = James IV of Scotland, killed at Flodden, 1513. | HENRY VIII |

561-7.

to involve herself deeply in Scottish politics. For six years of
high romantic history, the struggle for power between Mary,
Knox and the nobles continued with little interference from
England. There was no organ of constitutional opposition to
the Catholic Queen, for the Scottish Parliament, after putting
the Reformation into legal shape in 1560, had sunk back into
a negligible quantity, a mere court of record once more. Mary
might therefore have triumphed over the feudal aristocracy
divided as it was on the religious issue in spite of its firm ad
herence to the abbey lands, had not John Knox and his party
created other organs of national life, and put a new spirit in
the educated middle class which inspired it to compete with
the old feudal power. In parish after parish arose a democracy
of laymen, who elected their own minister and found a nucleus
for self-expression in the Kirk Session of the parish. Nor was
a national organization lacking for long : in the General Assembly
of the Church, ministers and lairds sat side by side, representing
clerical and lay forces of a very different social class from the
high-born prelates and noblemen who had ruled Scotland for
centuries past. The General Assembly of the Church became
the centre of Scottish life almost to the extent to which Parliament
was the centre of English life, and the Church became the focus
of resistance to the Crown.

The Church brought Scotland freedom and bondage in one.
A spirit not of sacerdotal but of democratic tyranny strove to
dictate the dogma and discipline of the new religion to the
government of the land, to the peasant in his cottage and the
laird in his hall. This zealous and uncompromising spirit was
intolerable to many ; it was a chief cause of the faction and
blood-feuds of Scotland for a hundred years to come. In the
end the power of the Church was subordinated to that of the
State, but not before it had wrought a remarkable change. It
transformed the lowland Scot from a fierce feudal vassal, ignorant
of all save sword and plough, into the best educated peasant
in Europe, often plunged in solitary meditation and often
roused to furious argument on points of logic and theology
which few Englishmen had the mental gifts or training to
understand. Times and the Church have changed, but the
intellectual and moral vantage-ground won by the Scot in that
hard school has not yet been lost.

But the making of modern Scotland had only begin when
Mary reigned at Holyrood, and she might perchance have stopped
it all at the outset by winning her battle against Knox, if she
had been as ready as Elizabeth to control her private passions in
deference to her public policy. But her marriage with Darnley,

his murder by Bothwell at the Kirk of Field, and her too hasty marriage with the murderer, led her subjects to suppose her precognizant of the deed. True, assassination was still a custom of the country. Knox had not disapproved the slaughter of Cardinal Beaton, and Darnley had conducted the tragedy of Rizzio. But people had a prejudice against the killing of husbands by their wives. Innocent or guilty, Mary had by her marriage with Bothwell delivered her reputation and her kingdom into her enemies' hands. After some confused fighting and some romantic and luckless adventures, she was obliged to fly from Scotland. She elected, with characteristic rashness, to take refuge with Elizabeth whose throne she challenged and endangered. What did she expect ? If she looked for romantic generosity she had come to the wrong door. Or did she trust her own sharp wits to fool her rival ?

1567.

From the moment that Mary made herself Elizabeth's captive, the politics of England, and indeed of all Europe, turned on the hinges of her prison door. Since she had thrown away her own liberty and her own power of initiative, Philip began to think that she might be used to serve the purposes of Spain instead of those of France. Urged by the Pope, Spain, and the Jesuits, the more extreme English Catholics laid plot after plot to place her on Elizabeth's throne, through assassination, rebellion and foreign conquest. The first great crisis was the ' Rising of the Earls ' of Northumberland and Westmorland, followed by Dacre's rebellion. The Catholic feudal chiefs of North England, the Percies, Nevilles and Dacres, took up arms on behalf of Mary and the Mass, calling on the Catholic nobles of Scotland to cross the Border and join them. The crusaders marched under the banner of the Five Wounds of Christ, and tore up the Bible and Prayer Book in Durham Cathedral. But the Scottish government prevented the Scottish Catholics from crossing the Border, and South England rose eagerly to defend Elizabeth. The feudal spirit was no longer sufficiently sure of itself to look the national spirit in the face on the field of battle. Even the borderers were no longer at ease in following the modern Percy against the Crown, as their forefathers had followed Hotspur. A single skirmish sufficed to disperse the feudal and Catholic armies.

1569, 1570.

Instead of being thankful for a victory which demonstrated to a surprised world the solidarity of her position in her subjects' hearts, Elizabeth took a cruel vengeance on the feudal tenantry, of whom 800 were executed. But she was wise in her further arrangements. The problem of North England was liquidated at last. The Council of the North[1] and the Wardenships of the Marches could now be manned entirely by loyal officials ; it was no longer necessary to defer to territorial magnates who were rebels at heart. The cessation of Border war with Scotland created new conditions of life that enabled government in the coming epoch to wean the North from its military and feudal traditions. The great-hearted but tragic society of Border ballad and blood-feud was gradually transformed into that of the law-abiding and Bible-reading shepherds who peopled the moorlands in the days of Thomas Bewick and Walter Scott.

The internal unity of the new England had been demonstrated by the failure of the Northern rebellion, and foreign dangers might now be faced with a good courage. They came thick and fast. In 1570 Pope Pius V excommunicated Elizabeth and the Jesuit mission was launched on England. In 1572 the Duke of Norfolk was executed for plotting with the agents of Philip, Alva and the Pope to set Mary on the throne, this time as the puppet not of France but of Spain. She was to have Norfolk for her husband, the Pope undertaking to divorce her from Bothwell. The assassination of Elizabeth was henceforth a customary part of these discussions among the secular and religious chiefs of continental Europe, to whom the murder of heretics seemed a holy work.

The execution of Norfolk, the greatest nobleman in the land, following close on the fall of the Northern Earls, marked the final victory in England of the new regime over the old feudalism. It was indeed a changing world. In the same year the Massacre of St. Bartholomew, which crippled but did not destroy the **1572.** Huguenot cause in France, was counterbalanced by the effective rebellion of the seamen and towns of Holland against the cruelties of Philip of Spain. The Commons of England, full of rage and fear, were petitioning for the execution of Mary Queen of Scots as though she had not been anointed with oil. For fifteen years longer Elizabeth, obeying her pacifist and royalist instincts, stood between her people and Mary's life. She liked not the killing of Queens, and the deed would mean formal war with Spain. So long as Mary was her next heir, she might hope that Philip would bear yet a little longer with her and her seamen. But if Mary disappeared, Philip might claim England for himself and launch the invasion. Only sixty miles lay between the shores of Kent and the yet unvanquished veterans of Alva in the Netherlands. Fortunately those miles were of salt water, and turbid salt water was an element of increasing importance in this new age so disrespectful to the feudal past and to all the chiefs of chivalry.

[1] For the Council of the North, see p. 277, above.

CHAPTER VI

The Origin of English Sea-Power

' Which of the Kings of this land before her Majesty had their banners ever seen in the Caspian Sea ?   Which of them hath ever dealt with the Emperor of Persia, as her Majesty hath done, and obtained for her merchants large and loving privileges ?   Who ever saw, before this regiment, an English Ligier (Ambassador) in the stately porch of the Grand Signor of Constantinople ? Who ever found English Consuls and Agents at Tripolis in Syria, at Aleppo, at Babylon, at Balsara, and, which is more, who ever heard of Englishmen at Goa before now ?   What English ships did, heretofore, ever anchor in the mighty river of Plate ?   Pass and repass the impassable strait of Magellan, range along the coast of Chili, Peru and all the backside of Nova Hispania further than any Christian ever passed ? '—*Hakluyt*.

THROUGHOUT ancient and mediæval times Britain was cramped onto the edge of the *Mappa Mundi*.   Since there was nothing beyond, every impulse of private adventure and national expansion on the part of the islanders had to expend itself upon Europe.   Yet old Europe was no longer malleable stuff and could take no impress of British language and customs, even from the most vigorous efforts of young England, as the barren close of the Hundred Years' War had very clearly shown. And now the gate of return that way was bolted and barred by the rise of the great continental monarchies, so that Englishmen seemed shut in upon themselves, doomed for ever to an insular and provincial existence, sighing in old manor-houses for the departed glory chronicled by Froissart, and the spacious days of Harry the Fifth.

But it was the most unexpected that occurred.   Gradually, during the Tudor reigns, the islanders became aware that their remote situation had changed into a central post of vantage dominating the modern routes of trade and colonization, and that power, wealth and adventure lay for Englishmen at the far end of ocean voyages fabulously long, leading to the gold-bearing rivers of the African anthropophagi, to the bazaars of jewelled Asia, and to the new half-empty continent which was piecing itself together year by year under the astonished eyes of men, upsetting all known ideas of cosmogony and all customs of commerce.

In mediæval, as formerly in ancient times, the great trade of the world and the centre of maritime power had lain in the Mediterranean Sea.   The external trade of Europe, which in modern times traverses the ocean in European vessels, was formerly carried overland by caravans across the heart of Asia, or was taken by Oriental shipping up and down the Persian Gulf and the Red Sea.   The precious goods from China and India

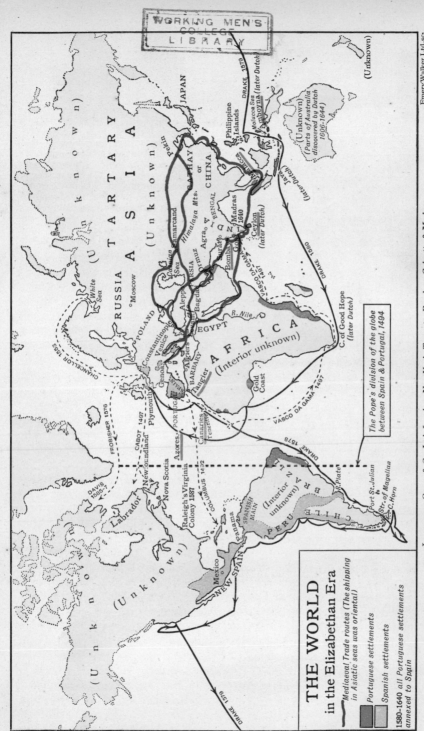

JAPAN

(Unknown)

DRAKE 1579

(Unknown)

Philippine
Islands

Molucca Sea
Amboyna (later Dutch)

(Unknown)
(Parts of Australia
discovered by Dutch
1606-1644)

R U S S I A   T A R T A R Y   A S I A   (Unknown)

(Unknown)

°Moscow

White
Sea

Pekin

Samarcand

CATHAY
or
CHINA

Himalaya Mts.

Agra°

BENGAL

Madras
1640

Caspian
Sea

PERSIA

Ormuz

Madras
Bombay
Delhi
Agra°

I N D I A

Ceylon
(later Dutch)

Javan
(later Dutch)

POLAND

°Bagdad
Aleppo

Constantinople

Venice
Genoa

Milan

BARBARY

Algiers

Tangier

EGYPT

R. Nile

GOA

VASCO DA GAMA 1497

AFRICA
(Interior unknown)

C. of Good Hope
(later Dutch)

DRAKE 1580

Gold
Coast

The Pope's division of the globe
between Spain & Portugal, 1494

PORTUGAL

Azores

Plymouth

FROBISHER 1576

CABOT 1497

Canaries
Teneriffe

VASCO DA GAMA 1497

DAVIS
1585-7

Labrador

Newfoundland

Nova Scotia

Raleigh's Virginia
Colony 1587

COLUMBUS 1492

CHANCELLOR 1553

(Unknown)

NEW SPAIN

Mexico

Panama

SPANISH MAIN

NEW SPAIN

B R A Z I L
(Interior unknown)

P E R U

C H I L E

R. Plate

DRAKE 1578

Port St. Julian

Str. of Magellan

C. Horn

DRAKE 1579

THE WORLD
in the Elizabethan Era

—— Mediaeval Trade routes (The shipping
in Asiatic seas was oriental)

▨ Portuguese settlements

▨ Spanish settlements

1580-1640 all Portuguese settlements
annexed to Spain

Emery Walker Ltd. sc.

Longmans, Green & Co. Ltd. London, New York, Toronto, Bombay, Calcutta & Madras.

MAP XX.

and the Spice Islands were dumped off the backs of camels onto the wharves of Levantine ports for shipment in Italian vessels to Venice and Genoa, whence they were distributed to the rest of Christendom.

Neither the Venetian traders, nor the Romans and Phœnicians before them, had been obliged to cross the ocean at any point. Ships were only required to traverse the shallow Mediterranean waters, and to coast along round Spain and France to the ports of England, Flanders and Northern Germany. The navies, whether commercial or military, consisted chiefly of oared galleys. This state of things lasted from prehistoric times till the latter part of the Fifteenth Century. Then the discovery of the Cape route to India and the revelation of the American continent destroyed the trade and the maritime supremacy of the Italian cities. Thenceforward Europe went round by sea to fetch its Asiatic, African and American goods, and on those ocean voyages the oared galley would be useless. The contest for commercial and naval leadership under the new conditions would clearly lie between Spain, France and England ; each of them faced the Western ocean which had suddenly become the main trade route of the world, and each of them was in process of being united into a modern State, with aggressive racial self-consciousness under a powerful monarchy.[1]

Spain and her small neighbour, Portugal, were the first to exploit the new situation on a great scale. They led the way in discovery along the African and American coasts. They planted South and Central America with their own people, enough at any rate to close them to Anglo-Saxon settlement, so that the English, when their turn came to colonize, would have to be contented with the colder and less envied climates to the north, where the white man must dig with his own arms, and not for gold.

France seemed half-inclined to follow the suit of Spain, and

---

[1] See pp. 294–6, above. It is not safe to assert, as has often been done, that the Portuguese and Spanish discoveries were due to ' the closing of the mediæval trade routes by the barbarous Turks.' On this subject see Mr. Lybyer's article in the *Eng. Hist. Rev.*, 1915. The Turk, though less liberal than the Tartar who had controlled the central Asiatic route in the time of Marco Polo, put fewer obstacles in the way of commerce with and through Europeans in the Fifteenth Century than the ' Young Turk ' of to-day (1925). The trade by way of Egypt was flourishing until the Cape route supplanted it. The Cape route in ocean-going ships could take bulky goods on a much greater scale than any of the mediæval routes. Mediæval Europe was being constantly denuded of precious metals because she had to pay for Asiatic spices etc. in gold and silver, for the camels could not carry back Europe's bulky goods. Relief came, none too soon, when the American mines produced abundance of gold and silver, and at the same time the ocean routes to the Eastern markets rendered it possible to send thither bulky articles in the holds of sailing ships.

compete for supremacy at sea and in America.   But already, by
the time of Columbus, her efforts were distracted by preoccupation
with European conquest towards the Rhine and beyond the Alps.
England, on the other hand, had learnt the lesson of the Hundred
Years' War, for the glories of which she had been punished by
a long period of anarchy and weakness.   She steadily refused
to be drawn again down the blind alley of continental ambition.
From Tudor times onwards, England treated European politics
simply as a means of ensuring her own security from invasion
and furthering her designs beyond the ocean.   Her insularity,
properly used, gave her an immense advantage over Spain and
France in the maritime and colonial contest.

The other distraction which impeded France in the race for
the New World was religious war, raging in her midst during the
precious years when Elizabeth kept England free from that
blight.   The French Huguenots, like the Protestants of Holland
and England, were the commercial and sea-going folk.   If they
had won, they might have made France mistress of the ocean.
But Admiral Coligny and his followers were massacred on St.
Bartholomew's Day, while Francis Drake and the Protestant
sailors whom he led became the servants of the English monarchy
and the heroes of the English people, turning England's main
thought and effort to the sea.

The square, unbroken mass of rural France, with its long land
frontiers, rendered it inevitable that the old feudal life should
be the prevailing social element, and set the fashion for the
territorial activities of the new national monarchy.   But in
England, with its narrow, irregular outline, almost surrounded
by a well-indented coastline, at peace at last with her only land
neighbour the Scot, well supplied with harbours great and small
thronged with mariners and fishermen, the State was subjected
to the influences and ideas of the commercial and naval men,
who formed one society with the best county families in seaboard shires like Devon.   The old song expressed a feeling very
general among our ancestors :

> We care not for your martial men
> That do the State disdain.
> But we care for your sailor lads
> That do the State maintain.

Indeed England's success against Spain after the defeat of the
Armada was limited not so much by want of naval power as by
want of military organization and tradition to seize the opportunities created by the Senior Service.

Since no point in England is more than seventy miles distant from the coast, a large proportion of her inhabitants had some contact with the sea, or at least with seafaring men. Above all, London herself was on the sea, while Paris lay inland and Madrid was as far from the coast as it was possible to be. London was Protestant, while Paris was enthusiastically Catholic. And London was so great in population and wealth as compared to the rest of the country that she gave the lead to all England. La Rochelle, the seaport of the Huguenots, was insignificant compared to a dozen great cities of the French interior. For these and other reasons France, in the Sixteenth Century, failed to compete in earnest for maritime supremacy. The best part of her sea-force acted in religious and political alliance with the English and Dutch in preying on the Spanish ships as they passed between Cadiz and the Netherlands.

If France was more feudal than England, Spain was yet more feudal than France. Spain, indeed, when she had annexed 1580. Portugal, was almost as much surrounded by the sea as England, and she had, moreover, a war fleet with a naval tradition. But it was a fleet of slave-rowed galleys and its traditions were those of the Mediterranean. The fleet that triumphed over the Turks at Lepanto, with the tactics of Salamis and Actium, would be of 1571. little avail against Drake's broadsides ; it could not cross the Atlantic and would be of limited use in the Bay of Biscay and the Channel. Spain had, indeed, her ocean-going vessels sailing up and down the Pacific coast of America, or crossing the Atlantic between Cadiz and the Spanish Main. They served to carry out emigrants and to bring back silver and gold, but they were not warships, and therefore fell an easy prey to the English pirates. Spain, in fact, began to build ships capable of fighting England only on the very eve of the outbreak of regular war. The Armada was not the last but the first of her oceanic fighting 1588. fleets. The English, on the other hand, though their total population was small compared with French or Spaniards, had a large sea-going community, accustomed for centuries to sail the stormy tidal ocean of the North. And ever since the reign of Henry VIII they possessed a royal fighting navy built and armed on modern principles, which gave a professional stiffening to the warlike efforts of private merchants and pirates. When Philip married Mary it had been his policy to rely on the English war navy because he could not hope to get its equal from Spain.[1]

---

[1] For Henry VIII's navy, see pp. 295–7, above.

Sir William Monson, the great Elizabethan naval authority, wrote : ' To speak the truth, till the King of Spain had war with us, he never knew what war by sea meant, unless it were in galleys against the Turks in the Straits or in the islands of Terceras (Azores) against the French, which fleet belonged to him by his new-gotten kingdom of Portugal. The first time the King showed himself

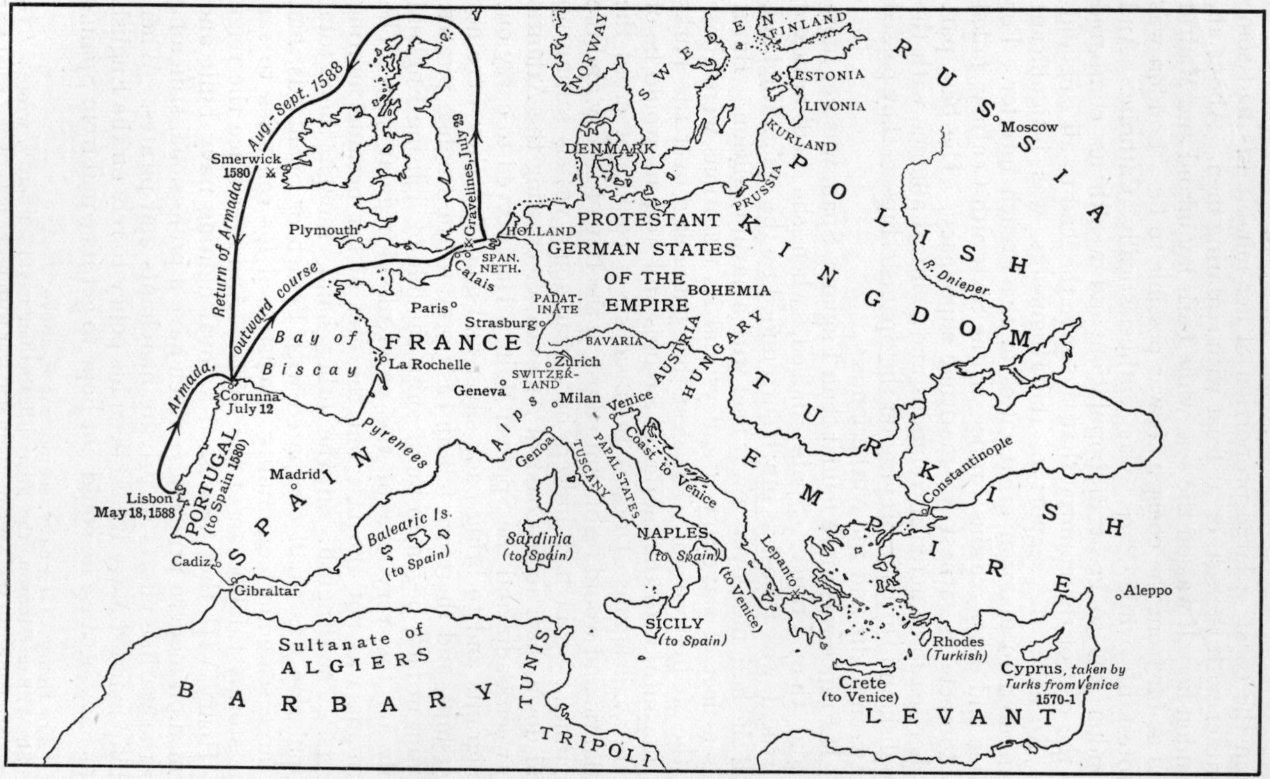

Map XXI.—Europe in the time of Elizabeth

Labels on the map:

RUSSIA

o Moscow

R. Dnieper

FINLAND

SWEDEN

ESTONIA

LIVONIA

KURLAND

PRUSSIA

POLISH KINGDOM

NORWAY

DENMARK

HOLLAND

PROTESTANT GERMAN STATES

BOHEMIA

OF THE EMPIRE

AUSTRIA

HUNGARY

TURKISH EMPIRE

Constantinople

o Aleppo

Cyprus, taken by Turks from Venice 1570-1

Rhodes (Turkish)

Crete (to Venice)

LEVANT

Lepanto

Coast to Venice

NAPLES (to Spain)

SICILY (to Spain)

PAPAL STATES

TUSCANY

Milan

Venice

Genoa

Alps

Sardinia (to Spain)

BAVARIA

PALAT-INATE

Zürich

SWITZER-LAND

Geneva

Strasburg

Paris o

FRANCE

La Rochelle

Bay of Biscay

Pyrenees

Balearic Is. (to Spain)

Sultanate of ALGIERS

TUNIS

BARBARY

TRIPOLI

SPAN. NETH.

Calais

Gravelines, July 29

Plymouth

Smerwick 1580

Armada, Aug.-Sept. 1588

outward course

Return of Armada

SPAIN

Madrid o

Coruña July 12

PORTUGAL (to Spain 1580)

Cadiz o

Gibraltar

Armada

Lisbon May 18, 1588

Naturally, the Spaniards, even when they came to build an ocean-going war-fleet in earnest, were hampered by the feudal and military ideals that permeated their social life, and by the Mediterranean traditions of their navy, adorned with the fresh laurels of Lepanto. Whether on oared galley or on wind-driven galleon, the instinct of the Spaniard at sea was to sail or row straight in, get to close quarters and either ram or board the enemy. The Spaniards, in short, like the Greeks, Romans and Venetians before them, wanted to make sea warfare as much like land warfare as the elements would permit. They stowed their ships with soldiers, who despised the sailors and ordered them about as if they too had been galley slaves. The ' mariners,' said one who knew, ' are but as slaves to the rest, to moil and toil day and night, and those but few and bad and not suffered to sleep or harbour themselves under the decks.'

It was the English who led the world in the evolution of a new kind of warfare at sea, decided by cannon fired through the portholes in the side of the ship. Drake's guns were not much smaller, though they were less numerous, than those on board Nelson's three-deckers. To serve them the seaman was more important than the soldier, because the success of the cannon-fire depended on manœuvring the ship into favourable positions to rake the enemy, and on aiming the guns with a sailor's instinct for calculating the roll of the two vessels. To Sir Francis Drake the warship was a mobile battery ; to the Duke of Medina Sidonia it was a platform to carry the swordsmen and musketeers into action. English naval history tells, indeed, of many a gallant boarding episode, from those of Drake and Hawkins themselves to Nelson at St. Vincent and ' brave Broke who waved his sword ' ; yet it was not the boarder but the broadside that made England mistress at sea.

While the Spaniards with their feudal prejudices and Mediterranean methods of sea-warfare subordinated the sailor to the soldier even when afloat, Drake worked out the proper relation to be observed between the military and maritime elements on board ship. When he quelled the party of insubordination among the gentlemen adventurers on his voyage round the world, he laid **1578.** down his golden rule to prevent ' stomaching between the gentlemen and the sailors ' :—' *I must have the gentlemen to hale and draw with the mariner.*' Starting from that point of new departure the ' gentlemen ' gradually learnt their place on board English

strong at sea was the year 1591, when the *Revenge* was taken.' Philip annexed Portugal, its navy and its overseas possessions in 1580. It remained attached to the Crown of Spain till 1640 ; after that it maintained its recovered independence, often through alliance with England.

men-of-war, and in the course of a long evolution became
' mariners ' themselves. By the time Nelson was born, each of
the King's naval officers united the character of ' mariner ' and
' gentleman,' and the sailing and fighting service was one and
indivisible.

Drake, who was first the greatest of privateers and afterwards
the greatest of Royal Admirals, established as no one else could
have done a complete understanding between the Royal Navy
and the merchant adventurers who carried on the unofficial war
against Spain. The Spaniards had slaves to row their galleys
and magnificent soldiers to fight from their ships, but for the
more indispensable supply of mariners they had no large and
energetic class of private merchants and seamen, such as those
who were the wealth and pride of England.

For indeed the technical differences between the personnel
and tactics of a Spanish and an English ship represented something more profound—the difference of social character between
Spain and the new England. Private enterprise, individual
initiative and a good-humoured equality of classes were on the
increase in the defeudalized England of the Renaissance and
Reformation, and were strongest among the commercial and
maritime population. The most energetic spirits of the gentry,
the middle and the lower classes were taking to the sea together
in a rough *camaraderie*, for purposes of war and of commerce.
In Spain the ideas and manners of society were still feudal,
though in politics the King had become absolute. Discipline, as
Drake well knew, is needed on board ship, but not feudalism and
class pride. The hierarchy of the sea is not the same as the
hierarchy of the land.

The Spaniards at the height of their power were great soldiers
and colonists, less great sailors, unenterprising merchants,
execrable politicians and rulers. Catholic enthusiasm drove them
to expel or kill out from their own peninsula just those classes
and races which might have enabled them to seize their new
commercial opportunities. No country could flourish for ever
on the importation of gold and silver from the American mines,
even if the English did not waylay the cargoes. Furthermore,
in their zeal for religion, the Spaniards murdered the prosperity
of the great cities of Flanders, which might otherwise have been
England's rivals in the new age. The mariners of Holland, who
inherited the commerce lost by the Flemish merchants, were
compelled by Spanish cruelty to become England's allies. If
ever there was a victory of the spirit of social and intellectual
freedom over its opposite, it was the maritime victory of England
and Holland over Spain.

The success alike of maritime warfare under Elizabeth and of colonization under the Stuart Kings rested on the growth of English commerce. For lack of a native commerce to feed it, the Spanish marine power, for all Philip's political and military strength and his empire over uncounted millions scattered round half the globe, went down before the attack of a small island State and a few rebel towns among the mudflats and sand dunes of Holland. For, unlike the Spaniards, the English and Dutch learnt how to trade with the newly discovered regions of the world.

To find vent for the new cloth manufacture [1] the Merchant Adventurers of England had from the beginning of the Fifteenth Century onwards been vigorously searching for new markets in Europe, not without constant bloodshed by sea and land in an age when piracy was so general as to be scarcely disreputable, and when commercial privileges were often refused and won at the point of the sword. Under Elizabeth they went further afield to find new markets in Africa, Asia and America.

Hakluyt laboured to inspire the English with a consciousness of their country's destiny at sea, by patiently recording the stories that the survivors of each notable voyage had to tell. His book serves to remind us that, side by side with the more warlike enterprises of Drake in robbing the Spaniards and opening trade with their colonies at the cannon's mouth, there was much traffic of a more peaceable character in Muscovy, Africa and the Levant. Besides Hawkins and those who dealt in the slave-trade, other English merchants preferred to develop the Guinea trade by giving the negroes fairer treatment than they got from the Portuguese and by trying to avoid unnecessary conflict with either black or white.

Yet it is impossible to draw a clear line between the peaceful and the warlike traders, because the Portuguese attacked all who came near the African and Indian coasts. They were no less determined than the Spaniards in America to exclude all foreigners, especially heretics, from the lands and seas which the Pope had assigned to them for ever.[2] Not seldom the African Gold Coast re-echoed to the noise of battle between English interlopers and Portuguese monopolists, and by the end of Elizabeth's reign the same sounds were already breaking the silence of the Indian seas and the Malay Archipelago. A sea fight with a pirate or a foreign rival was an unavoidable incident in the life of the most honest trader, whether in time of peace or in time of war. Companies were formed in the City to bear the expense and the risks of necessary hostilities, and were

---

[1] See pp. 280–2, above.   [2] See p. 295, above.

granted charters by the Queen giving them diplomatic and military authority on the other side of the world, where neither royal ships nor royal ambassadors ever came. Private English merchants, travelling on their lawful occasions, were the first men to represent their country at the Court of the Czar at Moscow and of the Mogul at Agra.[1]

Commerce was the motive of exploration as well as of warfare, and all three were combined in some of the greatest deeds of that generation. Romance and money-making, desperate daring and dividends, were closely associated in the minds and hearts of men. There was no line drawn between the bread-and-butter facts of life, and the life of poetry and imagination. The transactions of the money market and the war plans of sober statesmen turned on expeditions resembling those which in our own day explore Everest and the South Pole for naught save honour. Partly for that reason the Elizabethan age aroused the practical idealism of the English genius to its greatest height. Drake, Sidney, Spenser, Raleigh, and Shakespeare himself passed their lives among men to whom commerce was a soul-stirring adventure of life and death—

> As full of peril and adventurous spirit,
> As to o'erwalk a torrent, roaring loud,
> On the unsteadfast footing of a spear.

To the men of London and of Devon the unmapped world beyond the ocean seemed an archipelago of fairy islands, each hiding some strange wonder of its own, each waiting to be discovered by some adventurous knight vowed to leave his bones far away or to come back rich and tell his tale in the tavern.

To such a generation of men it seemed a light thing to find a passage through the Arctic seas by which the markets of India might be reached behind the backs of ' Portugalls ' and Turks. Sebastian Cabot in his old age revived the idea in English minds in the reign of Edward VI, and in 1553 Richard Chancellor sought the North-East Passage by the White Sea, and found instead the Czar keeping barbarous state over fur-clad tribes at Moscow; returning, he revealed to his countrymen the possibilities of a great Russian trade, and three years later perished on a second voyage. And so in Elizabeth's time the English Muscovy Company were the first Westerners to organize trade with the interior of Russia, though early in the following century they lost

---

[1] The ' Chartered Companies ' formed to develop the interior of Africa in the later Nineteenth Century were a revival under somewhat similar circumstances of the powers of the Elizabethan Muscovy Company, Levant Company, and East India Company.

it for a while to the Dutch. The corresponding attempts of 1576–8.
Frobisher and of Davis to reach India by the North-West Passage 1585–7.
led to the Hudson's Bay fur trade of Stuart times, one of the
main streams of British Canadian history.

Neither did Elizabethan merchants hesitate to traverse the
Mediterranean in spite of the war with Spain. The Levant
Company traded with Venice and her Grecian isles and with the
Mahomedan world beyond. Since the naval enemies of the Turk
were the Venetians and Spaniards, the Sultan welcomed the
heretic English at Constantinople. But on the way thither they
had to defend themselves against Spanish galleys near the Straits
of Gibraltar and ' Barbary pirates ' off the Algerian shore. Such
were the beginnings of English sea-power in the Mediterranean,
though it was not till Stuart times that the Navy followed where
the merchant service had already fought many a battle.

While the Armada was attacking England, one of these
Turkey merchants named Ralph Fitch was travelling in the Far
East, having started from Aleppo overland to India. After
eight years of wandering he brought home reports on the Persian
Gulf, Hindoostan and Malacca, which greatly encouraged the
promoters of the East India Company. They obtained a Charter
from Elizabeth in 1600, and proceeded to trade in the Indian
seas by rounding the Cape of Good Hope in tall ships laden
with goods and well armed to defend themselves against the
' Portugall.' Not lust of conquest but vent of merchandize
first drew our countrymen to the great peninsula which their
descendants were destined to rule. Hakluyt already had his
patriot's eye on lands still further afield :

Because (he wrote) our chiefe desire is to find out ample vent of
our wollen cloth, the naturall comoditie of this our Realme, the fittest
place which in all my readings and observations I find for that purpose
are the manifold islands of Japan and the Northern parts of China
and the regions of Tartars next adjoining.

All these trade routes and distant markets, sketched out
by the daring of the Elizabethan merchants, led in Stuart times
to an immense volume of commerce, particularly in the export of
cloth. The Queen and her ministers understood the mercantile
community and served it well. Unlike her brother and sister,
Elizabeth was in close touch with London opinion, a condition
of successful rule in Tudor England. She and Cecil were both
personal friends of Sir Thomas Gresham, the founder of the
Royal Exchange. She used him to raise State loans at home
and abroad, and took his advice on financial questions. The
chief of these was the difficult problem of the recoinage, which

she effected at the beginning of her reign, successfully relieving her subjects of the burden laid on every-day life by her father's wanton debasement of the currency.

Elizabeth's financial difficulties were increased by the continued fall in the value of money. Prices had been rising all through Tudor times, especially after Henry tampered with the coinage. And just when his daughter had applied a remedy to that, the flow of silver and gold into Europe from the Spanish-American mines began to act as a further cause of high prices. This may not have been bad for the merchant, but it was bad for hired labour, and for the Queen in whose revenue many of the items were fixed amounts. Even in war time barely a quarter of the royal income was derived from extra taxation put on by Parliament ; the Parliamentary ' subsidy ' was assessed in such a manner as to produce sums altogether incommensurate with the increasing wealth of the nation. The art of taxing the subject was not taken seriously in hand until Parliament had to find the sinews of its own warfare against Charles I.

Some historians, in their imperialist or Protestant zeal, have blamed the Queen for her parsimony, and have wondered why she did not send more men to the Netherlands, to France, to Ireland ; why she lied and prevaricated so long instead of challenging Philip to open war early in her reign ; and why, after the Armada, she did not seize the Spanish colonies and strike down the Spanish power. The royal accounts give a sufficient answer. The year after the Armada her total revenue was less than £400,000, of which the sum of £88,362 came by way of Parliamentary taxation. In the last five years of the war and of her reign, her average annual revenue was still well below half a million, the ' subsidies ' voted by Parliament still bearing the same small proportion to the whole. If anyone is to answer at the bar of history for Elizabeth's ' parsimony,' Parliament and the taxpayer must take their place there beside the Queen and her Ministers. What little money her subjects allowed her, she laid out with great wisdom for their safety and benefit. Because she refused to crusade hastily on behalf of Protestantism abroad, she was enabled to save the Reformation. Because she was a ' little Englander ' and an economist in the day of small things, she laid the sea-foundations of the Empire, on which those who came after her could build.[1]

Regular war between England and Spain was postponed until the eve of the sailing of the Armada, because Philip and Eliza-

[1] See note, pp. 356–7, below, for Elizabeth's revenue and war expenditure.

beth were both of them cautious and pacific by temperament.
Yet both were inflexibly set upon policies that could not fail to
end in war. Philip held to the right of excluding all foreigners
from approaching the newly discovered shores of Asia, Africa
and America, assigned by the Pope to Spain and Portugal. He
held to the right of handing over English merchants and sailors
in his dominions to the Inquisition. Nor would he tolerate
an England permanently severed from Rome, though he was
prepared to wait long in hopes of the death of Elizabeth, and
artificially to hasten that event. Within a dozen years of her
accession he was discussing plans of assassination and invasion
against her, and thenceforward more and more assumed the role
of executor of the Pope's decree of deposition. Yet his temperamental hesitation long restrained him from declaring open war,
and compelled him to swallow many affronts and injuries at the
hands of Hawkins, Drake, and the Queen herself. Probably he
hoped each year that the resistance of the Dutch under William
the Silent would collapse, and that then Elizabeth would become
submissive or England fall an easy conquest.

The Queen saw that this delay was to her advantage, because
each year made England stronger and more united. But she
traded somewhat boldly on Philip's unwillingness to fight. On
one occasion she laid hands on the pay for the Spanish troops 1569.
in the Netherlands when the ships that carried it sought shelter
in English ports ; three years later she secretly connived at the 1572.
capture of Brill by the Sea Beggars that founded the Dutch
Republic,[1] and she permitted English seamen to assist the rebels. See Map
In those early days the effective resistance of the Dutch was p. 350.
not in the open field, but on water and in the heroic defence of 1573-
their amphibious walled towns like Haarlem and Leyden. 1574.

Above all, Elizabeth abetted the piratical attacks of Hawkins
and Drake on the Spanish ships and colonies, by which the fighting
power of England was trained during the years of public peace
and private war. The chief scene of these irregular hostilities
was Spanish America. Its ports were officially closed to foreign
trade, but its inhabitants were not unwilling to purchase, under
a show of compulsion, goods with which Spanish merchants
were too unenterprising to provide them. Besides more innocent
traffic, Hawkins dealt with them largely in negroes whom he had
kidnapped in Africa. It would have been difficult to find anyone
in Europe to condemn the slave-trade from the point of view of
its victims, and for two hundred years England, being the most
energetic maritime community, took as much the leading part

---

[1] Motley, who is often very unfair to the English, mistook Elizabeth's part
in the Brill episode. See Pollard, *Pol. Hist.*, pp. 331–2.

in the development of this curse of two continents as she finally took in its suppression.

Drake was less interested in the slave-trade, but he attacked and robbed Spanish ships, towns and treasure caravans, along the American coasts. His proceedings were much in accordance

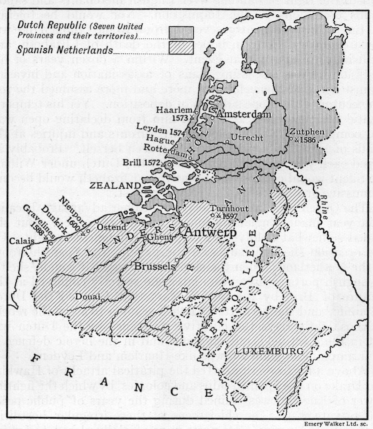

Dutch Republic (Seven United Provinces and their territories)............

Spanish Netherlands............

Haarlem 1573 X Amsterdam

Leyden 1574
Hague Utrecht Zutphen X 1586
Rotterdam

Brill 1572 X

ZEALAND

Nieuport
Gravelines 1588
Dunkirk 1600
Ostend Turnhout X 1597
Calais Ghent Antwerp
FLANDERS BRABANT LIÉGE

Brussels

Douai

B P OF

R. Rhine

LUXEMBURG

F R A N C E

Emery Walker Ltd. sc.

MAP XXII.—Spanish and Dutch Netherlands

with the practice of European sailors of all countries in days before the growth of international law. But they were dis-approved on moral and prudential grounds by some of Elizabeth's advisers, especially by Cecil,[1] though he himself had seized the Spanish treasure in the Channel.

In one sense England was the aggressor. But if England had not taken the aggressive she would have been forced to

[1] William Cecil became Lord Burleigh in 1571, but I continue to call him Cecil for the sake of clearness.

accept exclusion from the trade of every continent save Europe, to abandon her maritime and colonial ambitions, and to bow her neck to reconquest by Spain and Rome as soon as the resistance of Holland collapsed. A world of sheer violence, in which peaceful Englishmen were liable to be imprisoned or put to death in any Spanish possession, the world of the Inquisition and the Massacre of St. Bartholomew, of Alva's appalling devilries in the Netherlands, and the Pope's deposition of Elizabeth which Catholic Europe was preparing to enforce, left no place for twentieth-century standards of international conduct.

It was Sir Francis Walsingham who urged upon the Queen that her throne could be saved from the slow closing of the Spanish net only if she encouraged the lawless acts of Drake and his companions. A share in their plunder was a strong additional argument to a ruler with an insufficient revenue. The influence of Walsingham was rising at Court, not like Leicester's as a star hostile and co-rival to Cecil's, but as the complementary influence of a younger man who supports his elder but sees some things that the older man cannot see. Walsingham carried weight, for the system of spies he had organized repeatedly saved the Queen's life from the assassins set on by Philip and the Jesuits, who destroyed William the Silent for want of such a guard. Walsing- 1584. ham, inspired by a Puritan zeal against the Catholic reaction then raging on the continent, was impatient with the greater caution of the Protestant Nationalist Cecil and the 'mere English' Queen. He was ever for action, at all risks and at all expense of treasure. If Elizabeth had taken Walsingham's advice on every occasion she would have been ruined. If she had never taken it she would have been ruined no less. On the whole she took what was best in the advice of both her great Ministers.

The situation reached its crisis over Drake's voyage round the world. Cecil was an enemy to the expedition, but Walsingham had persuaded Elizabeth secretly to take shares in the 1577. greatest piratical expedition in history. 'Drake!' she exclaimed. 'So it is that I would gladly be revenged on the King of Spain for divers injuries that I have received!' She had applied to the right man.

Since Magellan had discovered a way round the southern 1520. end of America, the passage had been generally avoided as too stormy and dangerous for the tiny vessels of the day. The Spanish ships on the Pacific coast were built *in situ*, and communication with the Atlantic went overland by the isthmus of Panama. When therefore Drake appeared from the south 1578– upon the coast of Chile, he seemed 'like a visitation from heaven' 1579.

to the secure and lightly armed Spaniards, who had learnt to think of the Pacific as an inland lake closed to the shipping of the world. Although he had less than a hundred men in the *Golden Hind*, which alone of his tempest-tost squadron had held right on past the Horn and the Straits of Magellan, it was the easiest part of his task to rob the long coast-line of its fabulous wealth, and ballast his little bark with the precious metals. Then he turned homewards across the Pacific Ocean, bound for the Cape of Good Hope.

Such was the importance attached in Spain and England to these proceedings, of which word came to Europe by Panama, and so loud was the outcry raised by the Spanish ambassador, that if Drake had failed to return home safe and rich, the victory at court might have rested with Cecil's more timid policy, and the victory in the world-contest might have fallen to Spain and Rome. Drake had told his companions that if they failed in their venture ' the like would never be attempted again.' When the *Golden Hind* grounded on a shoal in the uncharted Molucca Sea and hung for twenty hours on the edge of apparently certain destruction, to glide off safe into deep water at the last moment, vast destinies depended on the relation of a capful of wind and a tropical sandbank to a few planks of English oak.

1580.

As Drake entered Plymouth Sound after nearly three years' absence from Europe, his first question to some passing fishermen was whether the Queen were alive and well. Yes, in spite of all her enemies, she was still alive, and well enough to come next year and knight him on board his ship at Deptford. It was the most important knighthood ever conferred by an English sovereign, for it was a direct challenge to Spain and an appeal to the people of England to look to the sea for their strength. In view of this deed, disapproved by her faithful Cecil, who shall say Elizabeth could never act boldly ? Her bold decisions are few and can be numbered, but each of them began an epoch.

1587.

After the accolade at Deptford, events drifted towards open war as fast as Philip's slow spirit could move. England's final act of defiance to all comers, the execution of Mary Queen of Scots, was the volition of the people rather than of their sovereign. Elizabeth long resisted the outcry, but her subjects forced her hand when the discovery by Walsingham of Babington's plot to murder her revealed Mary as acquainted with the design. Mary's prolonged existence raged like the fever in men's blood, for if she survived Elizabeth, either she would become Queen and the work of the Reformation be undone, or else there would be the worst of civil wars, with the national sentiment in arms against the legitimate heir backed by the whole power of Spain. The prospect was too near and too dreadful to leave men time to pity a most unhappy woman. Parliament, people and Ministers at length prevailed on Elizabeth to authorize the execution. Her attempt to avoid responsibility for the death warrant by ruining her Secretary Davison was in her worst manner, as the knighting of Drake was in her best.

Mary's execution made it certain that Spain would at once attack England, but it united England to resist. Moderate Catholics who might have drawn sword for Mary as being by their reckoning the legitimate sovereign, stood for Elizabeth against Philip of Spain when he claimed the throne for himself. Nor had Elizabeth driven moderate Catholics to despair. Beyond fines for non-attendance at church, irregularly levied, she had not persecuted the Catholic laity for their opinions.[1]   A more ultra-Protestant Prayer-Book or a harsher persecution of 'Popish recusants,' such as her Parliaments demanded, might well have led to civil war in face of the Spanish attack. As it was, a united people faced the storm of the Armada. For the Puritans, whatever they on their side suffered from Elizabeth in Church and State, would fight for her among the foremost.

The crews who manned the Invincible Armada, collected from half the sea-going populations of the Mediterranean, were many of them novices in the management of sailing ships in the open Atlantic, and acted as mere underlings of the soldiers, whom it was their privilege to carry from Spain to England. Very different was the opposing fleet. In those days the Lord High Admiral must needs be a great nobleman, but Lord Howard of Effingham, a Protestant though related to the Duke of Norfolk, was a fine sailor like his father before him, and well knew the value of the group of great seamen on whose services he could rely. Like Hawkins and Frobisher, he looked without jealousy on Drake as the master mariner of the world, who only the year before had ' singed the Spanish King's beard,' destroying with his broadsides the finest war galleys afloat, in the harbour of Cadiz itself.

The numbers of the rival fleets under Howard and Sidonia were not unequal. The English, combining their Royal Navy with their armed mercantile marine, had an overwhelming mastery in weight of gun-metal, as well as in seamanship and

---

[1] On the question of the treatment of Catholic 'Recusants' see Mr. Merriman's article in the *American Hist. Rev.*, April 1908, and W. P. M. Kennedy, *Elizabethan Episcopal Administration*, Alcuin Club, 1924. The 12d. fine of 1559 for non-attendance at church was often exacted, but the ruinous fine of £20 a month ordained by later statutes of 1581 remained *in terrorem*, a dead letter. For the persecution of the Jesuit missionaries, see pp. 363-4, below.

the art of gunnery. The Spaniards were superior only in the tonnage of their secondary craft and in their soldiers, who stood ranked on deck, musketeers in front of pikemen, waiting in vain for the English to draw near according to the ancient rules of warfare at sea. But as the English preferred that it should be a duel between artillery and infantry at range chosen by the artillery, small wonder that the Spaniards, as they passed up the Channel, underwent terrible punishment. Already demoralized when they reached Calais roads, they mishandled their vessels in face of Drake's fire-ships, and failed of any attempt to embark the waiting army of Parma in the Netherlands. After another defeat in the great battle off Gravelines, they were thankful to escape total destruction on the Dutch sand-dunes owing to a change in the wind, and ran before the tempest, without stores, water or repairs, round the iron-bound coasts of Scotland and Ireland. The winds, waves and rocks of the remote North-West completed many wrecks begun by the cannon in the Channel. The tall ships, in batches of two and half-a-dozen at a time, were piled up on the long lee-shore, where Celtic tribesmen who knew little and cared not at all what quarrel of civilized men had flung this wreckers' harvest on their coast, murdered and stripped by thousands the finest soldiers and proudest nobles in Europe. Out of 130 great ships scarce the half reached home.

See Map XXI., p. 342, above. July 29, 1588.

Profoundly moved by a deliverance that perhaps only the seamen had confidently expected, the English took for their motto ' *He blew and they were scattered,*' ascribing to the watchful providence of God and His viewless couriers a result that might without undue arrogance have been in part attributed to their own skill and courage at sea.

The first serious attempt of Spain to conquer England was also her last. The colossal effort put forth to build and equip the Armada, the child of such ardent prayers and expectations, could not, it was found, be effectively repeated, although henceforth Spain kept up a more formidable fighting fleet in the Atlantic than in the days when Drake first sailed to the Spanish Main. But the issue of the war had been decided at its outset by a single event which all Europe at once recognized as a turning point in history. The mighty power that seemed on the eve of universal lordship over the white man and all his new dominions had put out its full strength and failed. One able observer, Cardinal Allen, was quick to recognize in the Armada campaign the ruin of his life's work, to which he had sacrificed the ordinary feelings of patriotism by urging on the invasion of England.

When, some years later, the traveller Fynes Moryson entered Rome in disguise to view its antiquities, he found that the Cardinal had ceased to persecute his Protestant fellow country-men who visited the city, having changed his conduct in this respect 'since the English had overthrowne the Spanish Navy in the yeere 1588, and there was now small hope of reducing England to papistry.'

The defeat of the Armada ensured the survival of the Dutch Republic and the emancipation of France under Henri IV from Spanish arms and policies. Less directly it saved Protestant Germany, whose Lutheran Princes, at this crisis of the onslaught made by the organized and enthusiastic forces of the Counter-Reformation, had shown themselves more interested in perse-cuting their Calvinist subjects than in helping the common cause.

The fate of the Armada demonstrated to all the world that the rule of the seas had passed from the Mediterranean peoples to the Northern folk.   This meant not only the survival of the Reformation in Northern Europe to a degree not fully determined, but the world-leadership of the Northerners in the new oceanic era.

The regular war between England and Spain continued till the death of Elizabeth in 1603.   She regarded it as a first charge on her slender war-budget to see that French and Dutch in-dependence were maintained against Philip.   This was secured, partly by English help and by the holding of the seas, and partly by domestic alliance of the Calvinists with Catholic 'politiques' averse to Spanish domination ; it followed that an element of liberality and toleration very rare in the Europe of that day made itself felt in France and in Holland in a manner agreeable to Elizabeth's eclectic spirit.

The fine English regiments in Dutch pay, led by ' the fighting Veres,' helped to defeat, in the battles of Turnhout and Nieuport, the infantry of Spain, till then unconquerable in the open field. Under Prince Maurice of Nassau, the son of William the Silent, the Dutch army was becoming a school of scientific warfare for all Europe, and these Englishmen in that foreign service have some claim to be regarded as founders of the modern military traditions of their native land.[1]

1597.
1600.

What martial force Elizabeth herself could afford to pay, was for the most part sunk in the Serbonian bog of the Irish

---

[1] Three fine old ballads, printed together in Percy's *Reliques*—*Brave Lord Willoughby*, *The Winning of Cales* (Cadiz) and *The Spanish Lady's Love*, will give the reader an idea of the national spirit in this war and of the ideal of conduct in the English soldiery.   Vere's *Commentaries* give the spirit of the English regiments in the Dutch service; the ' Buffs ' trace their regimental traditions to Nieuport and Vere's campaigns.

tragedy. Partly for this reason it was impossible, in spite of our naval supremacy, to dismember the Spanish empire or even to release Portugal from Philip's grasp. There were fine episodes, like the last fight of the *Revenge* off the Azores, which poetry has not greatly exaggerated, and the plunder of Cadiz, the maritime base of Spain. But England made no permanent conquests, such as were won for her by the United Services in the wars of Marlborough, Chatham and Napoleon. The war party led by Drake had saved England and much else besides, but in the day of their apparent triumph they found themselves in eclipse. The regular war, for which they had waited and wrought so long, brought them, when it came, grave disillusionments.

England had yet to evolve a financial and a military system adequate to support her new-born naval power. Nor at the end of Elizabeth's reign, with scarce five million inhabitants, was she wealthy and populous enough to seize Spanish possessions or to found a colonial empire of her own. Even Raleigh's plantation at Virginia was premature in 1587. When in the Stuart epoch England's accumulated wealth and superfluous population enabled her to resume the work of colonization in time of peace with Spain, the path of the Puritan and other emigrants led necessarily to the Northern shores of America where no Spaniards were to be found. That way a greater future lay before Anglo-Saxon colonization than if the Elizabethans had risen to the opportunity offered by the war to annex the tropical settlements of Spain and Portugal, and had thereby directed the stream of English emigration into those deeply demoralizing climates. Here too Elizabeth's ' little Englandism ' served the future of the Empire well. The limitations imposed on the scope of the war, against which Drake and Raleigh fretted, may be counted among the blessings of a reign on which Englishmen have reason to look back as the most fortunate as well as the most wonderful in their history.

NOTE (see p. 348, above)
Elizabeth's Revenue and Expenditure

For the year Michaelmas 1588 to Michaelmas 1589 the Queen's total *ordinary* receipts were £294,819, including the fines and ancient customs and imposts, which increased somewhat with the trade of the country ; to this was added extra-ordinary Parliamentary taxation of £88,362 by ' subsidies,' besides £4410 by benevolences and £4878 for ' prizes.' The average annual revenue for the last five years of the reign and the war was :—

	£
Ordinary revenue	360,519
Subsidies and tenths	125,000
Total . £485,519

See pp. 516–17, W. R. Scott, *Joint Stock Cos. to* 1720 (Cam. Press, 1911).
The following is a table of extraordinary war expenditure throughout the
reign, drawn up by officials in 1603 :—

	£
Leith, in Scotland, 1559–60	178,820
Newhaven (Havre), 1562	246,380
Rebellion in the North, 1569	92,932
Shane O'Neill's rebellion, 1573	230,440
Desmond's rebellion, 1579	254,961
Tyrone's rebellion, etc.	1,924,000 [1]
Netherlands, 1585 to 1603	1,419,596
Aid of the French King, 1591 and later . .	297,480
Spanish Armada, Tilbury Camp.	161,185
Voyages to Cadiz and the Islands . . .	172,260

Besides these sums, ordinary recurrent expenses, including upkeep of the
fleet, were to be met out of the permanent sources of royal revenue not voted
by Parliament like the subsidies, but including the ancient customs and imposts.
The total sum obtained throughout the reign by extraordinary Parliamentary
taxation in subsidies and fifteenths was about 3½ millions (spread over more than
forty years) ; this went to meet the extraordinary war expenses tabled above.

CHAPTER VII

The great Elizabethan era. Wales. Ireland. Religion. The boundaries
of Elizabethan freedom. The Bible, poetry and music. Apprenticeship and some conditions of industry. The gentry and Parliament

FORWARD from the time of Elizabeth, warfare against some
great military empire is a recurrent *motif* of British history,
but because such warfare was conducted from behind the shield
of the sea and the Royal Navy, the island has never become
the scene of foreign invasion, nor until the novel circumstances
of 1914–18 was it ever found necessary to sacrifice a large part
of the manhood of the country abroad, or to interrupt the usual
course of business and pleasure at home. Such continuous
security, a privilege usually confined to countries either very
humble or very remote, but enjoyed in this case by a Great Power
on the very highway of the world's affairs, is the secret of much
in British character and institutions. It enabled us to evolve
Parliamentary government and the freedom of the subject before
any other great country, and even to pride ourselves on a
diversity of eccentric opinions and habits of life in our midst.
Its first good gift was the rich harvest of the Elizabethan
Renaissance.

The advantage of the ' moat defensive to the house ' was
fully understood by Shakespeare's contemporaries. During

[1] Such is the sum in the original MS., misprinted as 192,400 in the *Cal. St.
Papers, Dom.*, 1603.

1587–
1603.
fifteen years of open war with Philip, his veteran infantry were unable to cross from Antwerp to London, and England enjoyed greater security from ' foreign levy ' and ' malice domestic ' than during the three decades of troubled and dangerous peace with which Elizabeth's reign had begun. Nor did the state of war involve anything serious in the way of increased taxation or economic disturbance. A comparison may be made with the situation during the struggle with Napoleon : that later period was indeed a golden age in England for landscape-painting, poetry, novel-writing, boxing, hunting and shooting, but it was a dark time for the mass of people owing to the economic reactions of the war, and during it the seeds were sown of future social cleavage. But during the Elizabethan war the social and economic problems of the Tudor period continued to grow less acute. Since employment increased side by side with population, it was possible for Parliament, Privy Council and Justices of the Peace to cope with the problem of public provision for the poor. In the last year of the war a foreign traveller observed with surprise the absence of the plague of beggars which infested continental countries, and which had so gravely disturbed England in the earlier Tudor reigns.[1]

One cause of Elizabethan security and well-being was the fact that the outline of a united Great Britain had at length been drawn. There was lasting peace on the Scottish Border and a friendly State beyond it, as there had never been since the days of Edward I. And the Tudors had solved the problem of Wales, by which the mediæval English had been baffled only less completely than by the Irish question itself.[2]

1485–
1509.
In dealing with Wales, Henry VII had begun with two great advantages. First, he was a more powerful Marcher Lord than any of his predecessors, uniting in his own person the Marcher Lordships of the Houses of York and Lancaster to the number of some fifty. In the second place, he was a Welshman educated in Wales and retaining all his life a love of Welsh poetry and tradition. His fellow-countrymen considered that they had

---

[1] *Diary of the Duke of Stettin's Journey*, 1602 (R. Hist. Soc., 1892), pp. 11–12. ' It is a pleasure to go about [at the Royal Exchange] for one is not molested or accosted by beggars, who are elsewhere so frequently met with in places of this kind. For in all England they do not suffer any beggars except they be few in number and outside the gates. Every parish cares for its poor. Strangers are brought to the hospital, but those that belong to the Kingdom or have come from distant places are sent from one parish to another, their wants being cared for, till at last they reach their home.'
This would not be worth quoting if it did not bear out what we know from other sources as to the working of the Elizabethan Poor Law and compulsory Poor Rate, in which England was ahead of other countries. See pp. 284–5, above.
[2] See pp. 207–13, above, for mediæval Wales.

recovered their independence by placing one of their own Princes on the throne of England at Bosworth Field, and they flocked to his court as the Scots a century later to the court of James Sixt and First. With these advantages the prudent Tudor King was able to introduce a little order into the bloodstained anarchy of Wales, and his son completed the work.

Henry VIII, who mishandled Scotland and Ireland, understood Wales and solved its problems by a policy which combined 1509–1547. repression of disorder with justice to the Celtic population. Rowland Lee, Bishop of Lichfield, the energetic President of the Council of the Marches, hanged thieves and murderers without mercy, and made the King's authority feared by great and small, Saxon and Celt. His methods would shock us to-day, but he gave peace to a land that had never known it before. Like many great administrators he had little faith in the future of the rude people he kept in awe, and it was contrary to his advice that Henry VIII incorporated Wales in England on equal terms. 1535. This bold measure was the first and not the least successful Act of Union in British history. Henry abolished both Principality and Marcher Lordships, dividing the whole land into twelve See Map counties, to be governed like English counties through the Justices XVIII., p. 281, of the Peace, subject to the orders of the King's Council and above. the laws made in Parliament. The Welsh shires and boroughs were henceforth represented in the English House of Commons. The authority of the King's Council, very necessary in those disturbed districts, was brought to bear through its local offshoot the Council of Wales and the Marches, a body corresponding to the Council of the North.[1]

Thus supported by the strong arm of the central government, the Justices of the Peace were able to rule in the wild hill region where tribalism and feudalism had run riot for centuries. These magistrates, under the system inaugurated by Henry VIII, were not Englishmen imported to hold down the natives, but Welsh gentlemen who were the natural leaders of the people. In Wales the English government made friends with the native upper class, instead of destroying it as in Ireland.

The sight of the House of Tudor occupying the English throne enabled Celtic pride to accept union on these terms, and kept Wales loyal throughout the dangerous storms of the Tudor period. When Shakespeare represents Captain Fluellen boasting of the Welsh birth of the hero King Henry V, we suspect that the poet had overheard some honest Welshman boasting in similar terms of the racial origin of Queen Elizabeth. It was well that the Celtic population had this personal feeling for the House of

[1] See p. 277, above.

Tudor, for a great strain was put on their loyalty by the English Reformation. It is true that, after the Methodist revival, Wales became the most Protestant part of Britain, but in the Sixteenth Century this was far from being the case. Protestantism under the Tudors first came to Wales in an official Anglican dress, with a Prayer Book and Bible in a tongue as little known to many Welshmen as the Latin of the Mass. And the new religion was preached at first by an alien official clergy, many of whom were absentees and sinecurists. It was a great opportunity for Rome to capture the Celtic nationality and temperament in Wales, as she was doing so successfully in Ireland under very similar religious conditions. But the Jesuit missions in Elizabeth's reign neglected Wales, partly owing to a fierce domestic quarrel between the Welsh and English in the continental seminaries.

Thus left to themselves, the Welsh people regarded the Reformation changes with apathy. While their educated and landlord classes were becoming English in speech and habits of life, while their native language was discouraged in Church and State, intellectual torpor settled down for awhile on the quick-witted mountain peasantry. But though the Celtic language was neglected as an instrument of education, it survived among them more than among the Irish. At length in the Eighteenth and Nineteenth Centuries there was a great revival of national feeling and culture in connection with Puritan religion, education, music and Celtic poetry. In the history of the Welsh people the tribe has died, but the bard still reigns. Fortunately this later Celtic renaissance did not, like the contemporary movement in Ireland, take a form hostile to England. Henry VIII's Act of Union had been justified by leading to a union of hearts.

Very different was the outcome of Tudor policy in Ireland, inspired by an ignorance of local conditions comparable to that of Philip in his dealings with the Netherlands. In the Fifteenth Century, Ireland had been governed on the principle of ' aristocratic Home Rule ' through the great Anglo-Irish families, particularly the Fitzgeralds of Kildare. But the system had begun to break down in the reign of Henry VII,[1] and it came to a violent end when Henry VIII hanged the Earl of Kildare and his five uncles at Tyburn. No other system of government was immediately substituted. Although the Earl of Surrey reported to Henry that English conquest and colonization had become

1537.

---

[1] See p. 206, above.

indispensable, that dread alternative was not seriously applied before the later years of Queen Elizabeth.

Henry VIII, however, contributed something to the development of the Irish tragedy besides the hanging of the Fitzgeralds. He subjected Ireland, as a matter of course, to the religious revolution that he had devised to suit conditions in England. At first, indeed, the abolition of Papal Supremacy meant little to the Celts, to whom Rome had always remained a somewhat alien power, more closely allied to the Anglo-Irish nobles than to the people at large. The simultaneous abolition of the monasteries destroyed centres of culture more valuable to Tudor Ireland than to Tudor England. For though many of the Irish monks were as worldly and useless as the Bishops and parochial clergy, they were certainly no worse, and what little education there was in the island owed much to monastic centres. Popular religion was maintained chiefly by the itinerant friars, who also fell under Henry's ban. The English brought nothing that could effectively replace that which they destroyed. They founded no University and no schools to replace the monasteries.[1] Henry's English Bible and Edward's English Prayer Book were in a tongue then unknown to the Celt, who had moreover stood outside the current of the European Renaissance and the New Learning. But the old religion too was decadent, and there was little active resistance made to the official acts of the Reformation, until the Jesuits from abroad came to the aid of the wandering friars, whom government might proscribe but could not suppress.

Largely owing to the activity of the Jesuits, who turned to full account the English ' lack of governance ' secular and spiritual in Ireland, the situation became full of danger to Elizabeth. ' Ireland hath very good timber and convenient havens,' it was observed, ' and if the Spaniard might be master of them, he would in a short space be master of the seas, which is our chiefest force.' The Pope himself sent armed invaders to Ireland bearing his commission, six hundred of whom were captured and massacred by the English at Smerwick. Ireland was the danger 1580. point in Elizabeth's dominions, and when her enemies attacked her there she was compelled most reluctantly to undertake its conquest. Because her military and financial resources were inadequate to the task, her lieutenants used great cruelty in destroying the people by sword and famine, and in making a desert of districts which they had not the power to hold.

At the same time the policy of English colonization was favoured by government as the only means of permanently holding down the natives, who were growing more hostile every

---

[1] Trinity College, Dublin, was not founded till late in Elizabeth's reign.

year. This opened the door to a legion of ' gentlemen-adventurers ' and ' younger sons ' from the towns and manor-houses of England. It has been said that the Elizabethan eagles flew to the Spanish Main while the vultures swooped down on Ireland ; but they were in many cases one and the same bird. Among the conquerors and exploiters of Ireland were Humphrey Gilbert, Walter Raleigh, Grenville of the *Revenge,* and the high-souled author of the *Faery Queen.* They saw in America and Ireland two new fields, of equal importance and attraction, where private fortunes could be made, public service rendered to their royal mistress, and the cause of true religion upheld against Pope and Spaniard. When Raleigh and Spenser were stone-blind to the realities of the Irish racial and religious problem under their eyes, it was not likely that the ordinary Englishman at home would comprehend it for several centuries to come.

And so, in the last thirty years of Elizabeth's reign, Irish history, till then fluid, ran into the mould where it hardened for three hundred years. The native population conceived a novel enthusiasm for the Roman religion, which they identified with a passionate hatred of the English. On the other hand the new colonists, as distinguished from the old Anglo-Irish nobility, identified Protestantism with their own racial ascendancy, to maintain which they regarded as a solemn duty to England and to God. Ireland has ever since remained the most religious part of the British Islands.

In such circumstances the Irish tribes finally became welded into the submerged Irish nation. The union of hatred against England, and the union of religious observance and enthusiasm became strong enough to break down at last the clan divisions of dateless antiquity, which the English also were busy destroying from outside. The abolition of the native upper class to make room for English landlords, begun under the Tudors and completed by Cromwell, left this peasant nation with no leaders but the priests and no sympathizers but the enemies of England.

The conversion of England to Protestantism, which can be traced to origins in the time of Wycliffe, was substantially effected during the long reign of Elizabeth. When she came to the throne, the bulk of the people halted between a number of opinions, and the anti-Catholic party still consisted of anti-clericals as much as of Protestants. When she died, the majority of the English regarded themselves as ardent Protestants, and a great number of them were living religious lives based on Bible and Prayer Book.

There were two stages in the home policy of Elizabeth's

reign. During the first dozen years, although the Prayer Book was the only ritual sanctioned by law, Roman Catholics were not persecuted except by moderate fines irregularly exacted.[1] No one in that period was put to death on account of religion, and a great deal of private Roman Catholic worship was winked at by the authorities, even among persons in high State employ. But when in 1570 the Pope excommunicated the Queen, and absolved her subjects from their allegiance, the second period begins, and soon we breathe a harsher air. Jesuits from abroad travel through the island, passed on in disguise from hall to hall, hiding in ' priest-holes ' behind the wainscot, infusing into the quiescent body of old English Catholicism the new zeal of the European Counter-Reformation. They checked the peaceful process by which the Catholic squires were gradually becoming habituated to the English ritual. The Jesuits' mission was religious, but, if it should succeed, its political consequences must be the deposition of the Queen and the end of everything on which the new England had set its heart, at home or beyond the seas. The Jesuits preached spiritual obedience to the Pope-King who was at war with Elizabeth, and who invaded Ireland with his own armed forces. Crown and nation struck back savagely at his missionaries, who were hanged as traitors to the English State, but were regarded by their co-religionists as martyrs to the Catholic Church. Of the two most noted leaders of the Jesuit mission in England, Campion, who cared more for religion than 1581. politics, was unfortunately caught and hanged, while the indubitable traitor Parsons escaped abroad to work for a Spanish invasion.[2]

On the average, four Catholics suffered for every year of Elizabeth's reign, as against 56 Protestants for every year of Mary, and the charge was no longer heresy but treason. It was a tragic business, and no doubt many English Catholics who would fain have been patriotic and loyal, but who craved for the offices of their own religion, were ground small between the upper millstone of their spiritual lord, the Pope, and the lower millstone of their temporal lord, the Queen. Both sides had declared the two loyalties to be incompatible one with the other. There were many innocent victims of this tremendous conflict, wherein for the moment no compromise was possible. In the middle of Elizabeth's reign England was in a state of siege, and adopted

---

[1] See p. 353, above. and note.
[2] Parsons, debating the use to be made of the conquest of England, queries ' What form or manner of Inquisition to bring in, whether that of Spain (whose rigour is misliked by some) or that which is used in divers parts of Italy (where coldness is reprehended by more).' The Catholic Bishops were to have the power to negative or confirm elections to the House of Commons.

something of the discipline of a besieged town. Until the Roman Church throughout the world ceased to use the methods of the Inquisition, the Massacre of St. Bartholomew, the deposition and assassination of Princes, the States which she had placed under her formidable ban did not dare to grant toleration to her missionaries. To do so would have been to invite defeat by pitting a naked man against a fully armed and ruthless warrior.

Under these conditions the propaganda of the Protestant religion in England went forward apace. It was favoured by the alarmed authorities; and it was identified in the minds of Englishmen with patriotism, with defiance of Spain, with sea power and Drake's American adventures, with the protection of the life of the Queen from assassins. The remodelled Grammar Schools familiarized the young with the Classics taught in the spirit of Erasmus and Colet, and with the Bible and Catechism, and so produced the men of the new English Renaissance in literature, and the champions of Protestant Anglicanism in religion. During the death-struggle with Rome, Anglo-Catholicism could not flourish, and the new generation of clergy and scholars were ardent Protestants.[1]

The Puritans were most of them inside the Church, using it to convert the country to Protestantism and hoping ere long to change the Church's ritual and government more in their own direction. Elizabeth indeed had difficulty in getting Bishops who were not too rigidly anti-Catholic for her own instincts and policy, until she made the able Whitgift Archbishop of Canterbury, and with his help took a firm stand against the Puritanizing of the Church. Whitgift indeed was on many doctrinal points a Calvinist, but he opposed the democratization of Church government and stood stiffly for the Royal and Episcopal power as against Parliament, laity and Presbyterian clergy.

In her double resistance to returning Romanism and encroaching Puritanism, Elizabeth employed the power of the old Church courts and authorities, backed by the High Commission, a kind of ecclesiastical Star Chamber, by which the novel control of the Crown over the Church was very effectually maintained.

1583.

---

[1] The following account of the English parish churches early in Elizabeth's reign is by Harrison (*Holinshed*, II. 1): ' Whereas there was wont to be a great partition between the choir and the body of the church, now it is either very small or none at all : and to say the truth altogether needless, sith the minister saith his service commonly in the body of the church, with his face toward the people, in a little tabernacle of wainscot provided for this purpose ; by which means the ignorant do not only learn divers of the psalms and usual prayers by heart, but also such as can read do pray together with him : so that the whole congregation at one instant pour out their petitions on to the living God for the whole estate of his church in most earnest and fervent manner.' Such at any rate was the ideal aimed at in many churches, increasingly as the reign went on.

Though an offshoot of the Privy Council, the High Commission represented the Queen rather than the generality of her Councillors. Indeed many of them, like Cecil himself, disliked its procedure of cross-questioning the accused under oath as redolent of the ' Romish inquisition,' and saw danger to the State in its policy of persecuting too ardent Protestants. But the Queen held on her way in spite of the advice of her Councillors and the votes of her faithful Commons, and so preserved the Anglican character of the Church at a time when popular forces bade fair either to carry it into the full stream of the European and Scottish Reformation, or haply to tear it asunder by fresh divisions.

There were Protestant as well as Catholic martyrs under Elizabeth's State-Church. Puritan controversialists like Penry, author of the ' Marprelate ' tracts, made their violent attacks on the Bishops at their peril. In the Queen's eyes, to attack Episcopacy was a political offence, because it endangered the delicate balance of her establishment in Church and State. Even the more decorous Presbyterian propaganda of Thomas Cartwright angered and alarmed her. Cartwright was imprisoned, and Penry, Barrow and Greenwood were hanged as seditionists. 1590. 1593.

There were other martyrs of conscience who had no great party at home or abroad to pity their fate or commend their fortitude, but who were more clearly innocent of all offence against the State than either Jesuit or Puritan. Several persons in East Anglia were burnt for ' diverse detestable heresies,' because they had scruples as to the orthodox doctrine of the Trinity. For such men, neither Catholic, Calvinist nor Anglican had in that age any mercy. They were the victims, not of reasons of State, but of intolerant religious prejudice and the still surviving habits of the mediæval heresy-hunt.

The Crown in Parliament, the modern State omnicompetent within its own borders, did indeed wield terrific powers after the Tudor monarchy had subdued the Church to its will. Such powers were perhaps needful to save the country from Spanish conquest, but they set a limit to the otherwise steady growth of individual liberty. Economic and intellectual freedom had enlarged their borders by the disappearance of the mediæval system. But in religion and politics the new State for awhile imposed fetters scarcely less galling than those which had been broken. The right of Catholic and Puritan to worship God each according to his own conscience was not conceded. And in politics no opposition was allowed ; no one might criticize the government. Even loyal John Stubbs, for writing a pamphlet advising the Queen not to marry the French Prince, Alençon, had his right hand cut off by the hangman. Waving the bloody 1579.

stump he cried from the scaffold ' Long live the Queen ! ' Such
was the relation of that strange, subtle woman to her simple-
hearted subjects. She had never had the remotest intention of
marrying Alençon, but no Puritan squire was to be allowed to
interfere with the mystifications of high female diplomacy.

As yet there was neither political nor religious liberty for
the individual, but a split between Crown and Parliament might
produce both. For England was not a despotism. The power of
the Crown rested not on force but on popular support. The
people still wished the Crown to exercise these coercive powers
in the public interest. But it was significant that the Parliament
men, while not denying the Queen's ecclesiastical authority which
they themselves had restored in 1559, criticized the use she made
of it against the Puritans. The English State had won control of
religion from the mediæval Church only by an alliance with the
rights of private judgment and the forces of free speculation ;
it could not permanently deny the moral origin of its new-gotten
authority. Puritan and Catholic might for awhile be a danger
and might for long be an embarrassment to statesmen. But their
claim, in the name of the higher law of conscience, to challenge
the religious decrees alike of the Crown and of Parliament must
carry weight in the end. Since the appeal to private judgment
had triumphed in England over the vast organization and immemorial prestige of the European Church of the Middle Ages,
how much more certainly would it prove stronger in matters of
religion than the secular authorities of the island State. And so,
after another century of faction, persecution and bloodshed, the
attempt to force all Englishmen inside the doors of a State Church
would be abandoned, and a larger liberty would be evolved than
any dreamt of by Penry or Parsons, Whitgift or Cecil.

But outside the politico-religious sphere, intellectual and
poetic freedom had already reached their fullest expansion by
the end of Elizabeth's reign. The Renaissance, with its spirit
of enquiry and its vision of the ancient freedom of Greek and
Roman thought, had been transplanted from Italy, where it was
fast withering away under the hands of Spaniards and Jesuits.
It bloomed afresh in England, tended by poets who grafted it on
English trees in the Forest of Arden. There the imagination was
free indeed,—freer than in our own day, when it is burdened by
too great a weight of knowledge, and hemmed in by the harsh
realism of an age of machinery. Shakespeare and his friends,
standing as they did outside the dangerous world of religious and
political controversy, enjoyed in their own spacious domains a
freedom of spirit perhaps irrecoverable.

But though Shakespeare may be in the retrospect the greatest glory of his age, he was not in his own day its greatest influence. By the end of Elizabeth's reign, the book of books for Englishmen was already the Bible, although the Authorized Version that is still in use was only drawn up by James I's Bishops in the years immediately following her death. For every Englishman who had read Sidney or Spenser, or had seen Shakespeare acted at the Globe, there were hundreds who had read or heard the Bible with close attention as the word of God. The effect of the continual domestic study of the book upon the national character, imagination and intelligence for nearly three centuries to come, was greater than that of any literary movement in our annals, or any religious movement since the coming of St. Augustine. New worlds of history and poetry were opened in its pages to a people that had little else to read. Indeed it created the habit of reading and reflection in whole classes of the community, and turned a tinker into one of the great masters of the English tongue. Through the Bible, the deeds and thoughts of men who had lived thousands of years before in the eastern Mediterranean, translated into English during the period when our language reached its brief perfection, coloured the daily thought and speech of Britons, to the same degree as they are coloured in our own day by the commonplaces of the newspaper press. The Bible in English history may be regarded as a ' Renaissance' of Hebrew literature far more widespread and more potent than even the Classical Renaissance which, thanks to the reformed Grammar Schools, provided the mental background of the better educated. The Bible and the Classics together stimulated and enlarged the culture of the British, as their ocean voyages stimulated and enlarged their practical outlook on life.

Another source of popular inspiration and refinement in the great age that lies between the Armada and the Civil War, was music and lyrical poetry. They flourished together : many of the best poems, like the songs in Shakespeare's plays, were written to be sung. Europe recognized Elizabethan England as the country of music *par excellence*. German travellers noted with admiration how they ' heard beautiful music of violas and pandoras, for in all England it is the custom that even in small villages the musicians wait on you for a small fee.' Throughout Tudor times, fine Church music was written in England, indifferently for the Roman Mass or the Anglican service, while the Renaissance inspired non-ecclesiastical music with a fresh spirit, so that it reached its zenith under Elizabeth. The genius of Byrd adorned impartially the religious and the profane sphere, and whole troops of able composers flourished in that great age of

b 1538,
d. 1623.

the madrigal. The arena of Tudor and Stuart music was not the concert-hall but the domestic hearth. In days when there were no newspapers, and when books were few and ponderous, the rising middle class, not excluding Puritan families, practised vocal and instrumental music assiduously at home. The publication of music by the printing-press helped to diffuse the habit, and Elizabeth set the example to her subjects by her skill upon the virginals.

Music and song were the creation and inheritance of the whole people. The craftsman sang over his task, the pedlar sang on the footpath way, and the milkmaid could be heard ' singing blithe ' behind the hedgerow, or in the north country crooning the tragic ballads that told of Border fight and foray. The common drama was a poetical drama, and in that age was popular because it appealed to the imaginative faculties. Poetry was not an affair solely of intellectual circles, nor was music yet associated mainly with foreign composers. It was no mere accident that Shakespeare and Milton came when they did. Among a whole people living in the constant presence of nature, with eyes and ears trained to rejoice in the best pleasures of the mind, the perfect expansion of Shakespeare's poetic gifts was as much a part of the general order of society as the development of a great novelist out of a journalist would be to-day. And in the life of John Milton, born five years after Elizabeth died, we read clearly how the three chief elements in the English culture of that day—music, the Classics and the Bible—combined to inspire the ' God-gifted organ-voice of England.'

From the age of Elizabeth down to the industrial changes in the reign of George III, the economic conformation of society was in certain respects very fortunate. The English were still country folk, not yet divorced from nature, but they were already to some degree relieved from the harsh poverty and ignorance of the mediæval peasant.

In the country towns and villages where the industry as well as the agriculture of the country was carried on,[1] a considerable proportion of the inhabitants were trained craftsmen. Apprenticeship was the key to the new national life, almost as much as villeinage had been to the old. The apprentice system was no longer left to local usage and municipal enforcement, but was controlled on a uniform national pattern for town and country by Elizabeth's Statute of Artificers, which remained in force with little modification for over two hundred years. No man could set up as master or as workman till he had served his

1563.

---

[1] See pp. 280-2, above.

seven years' apprenticeship. In that way the youth of the country obtained technical education and social discipline that went some way to compensate for the unfelt want of a universal system of school education. Youth was under control of a master, in some cases until the age of twenty-four.

Industry was conducted in the home of the employer, who worked in the same shop and usually dined at the same board with his paid journeymen and his bound apprentices. The happiness of the manufacturing household depended, not on factory laws or trade union rules, but on the temper and character of the inmates. There was often harsher dealing than would be tolerated to-day, for conscious and organized humanitarianism is of no earlier date than the Industrial Revolution. Under the old system the men slept heaven knows where, under the rafters or in the cupboards. Masters were expected to beat their apprentices and often laid angry hands on their journeymen. But there was probably more kindness than severity, for the relation was closely personal and few people like discontent in their own home. The distinction between master and man was one of rank only, not of class ; indeed, as old plays remind us, the London apprentice who happened to be cadet of a squire's family often plumed himself on being the better ' gentleman ' of the two.[1]

The work of the skilled craftsman was a joy to him, and called out the artist latent in man more than the specialized functions of modern industry, which so often consist in watching some purely mechanical process. For this reason the objects in common use—the ship, the cart, the house, the chair, and all the utensils of the field and the home—bore the impress of beauty and of individual workmanship, lacking to the machine-made article of to-day. Work was more popular then than now, partly because much of it was educative of man's best talents.

[1] Carey's ' Sally in our Alley ' portrays some of the realities of prentice life, which were just the same under Elizabeth as under Queen Anne :—

> When she is by, I leave my work,
>   I love her so sincerely ;
> My master comes like any Turk
>   And bangs me most severely.
>
> My master carries me to church
>   And often am I blaméd
> Because I leave him in the lurch
>   As soon as text is naméd.
>
> My master and my neighbours all
>   Make game of me and Sally,
> And but for her I'd better be
>   A slave and row a galley.
>
> But when my seven long years are out
>   O then I'll marry Sally,
> O then we'll wed, and then we'll bed,
>   But not in our alley !

But there was another side to the life of the pre-mechanical ages which is often forgotten by those who too indiscriminately praise the past. Besides the skilled labour, there remained a heavy weight of hard muscular toil to be done, which modern mechanism has greatly relieved. In the saw-pit, at the plough's tail, in quarrying, in moving of heavy material, man still paid very severely in his own person for the conquest of nature. The exposure and hardship which were the lot of the poorer agriculturists were terrible. The proportion of dangerous trades was great. And in cottage industries parents often employed their small children for very long hours. In the Eighteenth Century the public conscience began to be disturbed by numerous cases of cruelty to apprentices and children leading to death at the hand of their masters, and earlier generations had certainly not been more gentle.

But the Elizabethan child, when not engaged in industry, had the freedom of the fields and woods, denied by the circumstances of our modern civilization. It is small wonder if in those days he ' crept unwillingly to school,' for outside the school doors lay a world full of freedom and delight, and in school cruel flogging was still considered, by all save a few enlightened pedagogues and parents, to be an essential part of education.

Although warmth, clothing and food were more available in the Elizabethan village than in the mediæval manor, they were more often lacking than in our day. A bad harvest still meant shortage of food. Washing of clothes and person was much neglected, especially in winter. Conveniences which we consider necessities did not exist. The death-rate even in upper class families was very heavy, and the poor only expected a slender proportion of their numerous progeny to survive. Medicine was in its infancy. The aged, the sick, the debtor, and all who fell foul of the law suffered martyrdoms which were regarded as an inevitable part of human fate and fortune. If life was more full of beauty, it had less certainty and comfort than to-day, and the number of persons alive in Elizabethan England was about a seventh of the present population.

Much that would now be regarded as intolerable seemed no hardship because formerly things had been still worse. Elizabethan writers noted as innovations the use of glass instead of horn in the windows, chimneys to draw the smoke out of the poor man's cottage, and flock-beds instead of straw mattresses for some at least of the common folk.

The leading class in England was the landed gentry or squires. They were no longer a feudal or a military class, and when civil war broke out in 1642 had to be taught the art of soldiery from the beginning. So far as it is possible to define the important and recognized distinction between ' gentle ' and ' simple ' in the new England, the ' gentleman ' was a landowner who could show a coat of arms, and who had the right when he wished it to wear a rapier and to challenge to the duel any other ' gentleman ' from a Duke downwards. But yeomen and merchants were constantly finding entrance into this class by marriage and by purchase of lands, and the younger sons of the manor-house normally passed out of it into trade, manufacture, scholarship, the Church, or military service abroad, in some cases carrying with them their pretension to gentility, in other cases tacitly abandoning it.

There were infinite gradations both of wealth and rank in this peculiar upper class. At the top of the scale was the great noble, with his seat in the House of Lords, keeping semi-regal state in his castle of Plantagenet stone or his palace of Tudor brick, which served as a school of elegant accomplishments to young gentlemen pages in training for careers at Court. Broken meats were daily distributed to a crowd of poor at the great gate. In the hall, on the dais, sat his lordship with his lady and chief guests, while half a hundred hungry clients and led captains feasted at the lower tables off silver and Venice glasses, and an army of serving-men and gamekeepers caroused off pewter in the ample regions of the kitchen. At the bottom of the scale of gentry was the small squire who farmed his few paternal acres, talked in dialect with his yeomen neighbours as they rode together to market, and brought up, with the help of his hard-working wife and the village schoolmaster, a dozen sturdy, ragged lads and lasses, who tumbled about together in the orchard round his ' hall,' a modest farmstead not seldom converted by posterity into a barn.

Between these two extremes, every variety of Tudor and Stuart manor-house arose, built, according to the materials of the country-side, in stone, in new-fangled brick, or in old-fashioned half-timber. These manor-houses and their inhabitants, together with the village industries, kept the country-side in touch with the central life and thought of the new world. Shakespeare's England was rustic without being backward or barbarous, and whatever London generated the rural parts in due course absorbed.

The Tudor is the great period of domestic architecture. The Renaissance had this in common with the Middle Ages as distinguished from later times, that the investment of money with a view to its mere increase, though more possible than before, was not so customary, easy and safe as it became later on, and that wealthy persons normally put their wealth as it accumulated into art and ostentation—jewels, plate, beautiful clothes and above all beautiful buildings,—thereby adding to the pride and pageant of life. But whereas the Middle Ages had been the period of church and castle building to the relative neglect of the common dwelling house, the Tudor time brought the mansion to its perfect glory, and began to cover the English landscape with gabled farmhouses, very different from the hovels of the mediæval villein. The fine old farms which we admire in so many different parts of England were a product of modern change, improvement, cloth trade and enclosure.

The squires or smaller country gentry acquired a new importance under the Tudors. It was not merely that many of them had purchased the monastic lands at an easy rate. They were in a new social position, because the Barons and Abbots who had lorded it over them so long had been brought low. They themselves, whether as Ministers of the Crown or as local Justices of the Peace, became the mainstay of the government, the leaders of the House of Commons, the real rulers of the countryside. It was the squires, principally, who in the Stuart era led both the Cavalier and the Roundhead party.

Under the Tudors they were preparing earnestly for their new role. Some gentlemen sent their sons to travel abroad, or to study law at the Inns of Court, in order to fit them to be leaders in Parliament or magistrates in their own shires. The New Learning of the Classical Renaissance was also much to their taste. In the Middle Ages education had been sought by poor scholars destined to be clergy, while the lay upper classes had despised learning. But in Elizabeth's reign country gentlemen's sons formed an important element not only in the Grammar Schools but at the Universities, where their numbers filled the room of the departed friars and monks. There was indeed some justice in complaints that began to be heard, that the well-to-do were encroaching on educational endowments previously reserved for the humble. The movement had its scandalous side, yet it is well that the governors of a land should receive the best education that the land can give. In the Middle Ages the aristocracy had thought it enough if their secretaries came from Oxford and Cambridge, while they themselves had been schooled in the castle and the tilt-yard.

Parliament represented not unfairly the opinion of those classes which took an interest in politics or showed any desire to be heard in the counsels of the nation.

The House of Lords provided seats for the nobility, both the remnants of the old feudal baronage and royal servants of recent creation like Burghley, Leicester, and Russell, Earl of Bedford. The Bishops as nominees of the Crown added to the official vote in the Upper House. The Abbots were gone, and the independent feudal power of the great nobles was gone too, after Elizabeth's victory over the Northern Earls and the Duke of Norfolk.[1] In the latter part of her reign the House of Lords, however dignified, was less important as a force in politics than at almost any time before or after. The Tudors were not democrats, but they had prepared the way for middle-class power, because in the State refashioned by their hands there was no independent authority left between Crown and people.

1569–
1572.

The growing strength of the landed gentry, backed by that of the merchants and yeomen, found expression in the House of Commons. The elections were no longer regarded as a burden imposed by the Crown on the local bodies, but were valued as a means of gaining influence over the national policy. The local gentry competed with one another to secure the election of themselves or their friends to Parliament, for boroughs scarcely less than for shires, since there was no feeling of antagonism between town and country in England. The numerous Cornish boroughs, enfranchised by the Tudor monarchs, fell into the hands of the squirearchical Puritan opposition, and returned critics of government like Paul and Peter Wentworth under Elizabeth, and in subsequent reigns Sir John Eliot, Hampden and many others of that party.[2]

Both as supporter and as critic of government, the House of Commons was beginning to take an initiative of its own. In face of Spain and the Pope, it was more Elizabethan than the Queen herself. Members were in a perpetual fever of loyalty, urging her to more vigorous measures in self-defence—to get married, to name her heir, to execute the Queen of Scots, to persecute the Catholics more and the Puritans less—everything in short except raise higher taxes, which both Queen and members knew would be dangerous. She thought the House over-zealous, over-busy. In the earlier Tudor reigns the Crown, without packing Parliament at election time, had relied safely on the desire of the country and its representatives to follow as far as possible the lead of the King and Council even in matters of religion. Under Elizabeth the increasing Puritanism of the squires introduced a new element.

---

[1] See pp. 336–7, above.

[2] The best authorities differ as to whether or not the creation of the Cornish borough seats was intended to increase the power of the Crown in Parliament. If it was so intended, it failed.

The fear and love of God began to strive with the fear and love of the Queen in the breast of the Parliament men like Peter Wentworth. Protestantism and Parliamentary privilege were already closely connected, before ever the first Stuart came to trouble still further the seething waters.

But the House of Commons was not yet, as James I soon made it, essentially an opposition. So long as some of the ablest Privy Councillors had seats in the chamber and were responsible there for the principal legislation of each session, a close link existed between executive and legislative, which only the negligence of Elizabeth's successor permitted to lapse.

So long as the Queen was alive, the personal factor postponed the irrepressible conflict. In spite of her irritation with much that was done and said in the House, she respected its privileges, for she knew what the Stuarts never learnt, that her strength lay not in ' right divine ' but in the loyalty of these hot-headed, self-sufficient squires, and the unseen millions, far-scattered at their toil over land and sea, with whom these men were in more direct contact than herself or her courtiers. To the last she was supreme in the art of managing the other sex, even members of Parliament. Two years before she died, her gracious manner of withdrawing the unpopular trade ' monopolies ' regained their affection at a stroke. Honourable members wept for joy, and in that melting mood were summoned to Whitehall by their mother and mistress, who told them what had indeed been the secret of her long reign now drawing to its close : ' Though God hath raised me high, yet this I count the glory of my crown, that I have reigned with your loves ! '

BOOKS FOR FURTHER READING

See lists of books, pp. 287–8, above. See also :

GENERAL :—Creighton, *Queen Elizabeth* ; Pollard, *Political History*, 1547–1603 ; Conyers Read, *Mr. Secretary Walsingham*, 3 vols.

PARLIAMENT :—Articles on Peter Wentworth by J. E. Neale in the *Eng. Hist. Rev.*, 1924.

RELIGION :—*Cam. Mod. Hist.*, II., Chap. XVI., for Maitland on *The Anglican Settlement and the Scottish Reformation* ; Bayne, *Anglo-Roman Relations*, 1555–1565 (Oxford, 1913) ; W. P. M. Kennedy, *Elizabethan Episcopal Administration* (Alcuin Club, 1924) ; Gee, *Elizabethan Clergy* (Oxford, 1898). E. L. Taunton, *The Jesuits in England* ; Scott Pearson, *Thomas Cartwright and Elizabethan Puritanism* (Cambridge, 1925).

THE SEA :—Sir Julian Corbett, *Drake and the Tudor Navy*, 2 vols., and *The Successors of Drake* ; Sir Walter Raleigh, *English Voyages in the Sixteenth Century* ; Prof. Callender, *The Naval Side of British History*.

SCOTLAND :—*C. M. H.*, II., Chap. XVI., as above ; Hume Brown's and Andrew Lang's *Histories* ; R. S. Rait, *The Parliaments of Scotland* ; W. L. Mathieson, *Politics and Religion in Scotland*, 1550–1695.

WALES :—W. Ll. Williams, *The Making of Modern Wales*.

IRELAND :—Bagwell, R., *Ireland under the Tudors*, 3 vols. ; Stephen Gwynn, *History of Ireland*.

BOOK IV

THE STUART ERA

PARLIAMENTARY LIBERTY AND OVERSEAS EXPANSION

INTRODUCTION

THE Tudor period made, it is probable, more difference to the Englishman's outlook and habits of life than the Stuart period that followed. But the Renaissance, the Reformation, and the development of oceanic adventure, which changed so much for the Tudor English, had been world movements in which other countries took an equally active part. In the Stuart era the English developed for themselves, without foreign participation or example, a system of Parliamentary government, local administration and freedom of speech and person, clean contrary to the prevailing tendencies on the continent, which was moving fast towards regal absolutism, centralized bureaucracy, and the subjection of the individual to the State. While the Estates General of France and the Cortes of Aragon and of Castile were ceasing to exercise even their mediæval functions, while the political life of Germany was atrophied in the mosaic of petty Princedoms that constituted the Empire, the House of Commons, under the leadership of the squires and in alliance with the merchants and the Common Lawyers, made itself the governing organ of a modern nation. This it achieved by developing inside itself an elaborate system of committee procedure, and by striking down the royal power in a series of quarrels of which the chief motive was religious and the chief result political.

English freedom, being rooted in insular peculiarities, required, if it was ever to reach its full growth, a period of isolation from European influences and dangers. Elizabeth and Drake had rendered that isolation possible. Circumstances abroad, of which the Thirty Years' War was the chief, enabled England, behind the shield of her Navy, to work out her domestic problems undisturbed by any dread of interference by her neighbours.

It was only when the period of internal evolution had resulted in the settlement of 1688–9, that the new Parliamentary England, based on freedom in religion and politics, was matched under William III and Marlborough against the new type of continental autocracy personified in the all-worshipped Louis XIV, Grand

Monarch of France. That struggle freed Europe from French domination, and left the English fleet for the first time unrivalled mistress of all the seas of the world. The wars against Louis may be regarded as the ordeal by battle which demonstrated the greater efficiency of the free community over the despotic state.

This result greatly astonished and impressed a world that had up till that time held a diametrically opposite theory of power. Despotism, it had been thought, was the secret of efficiency ; freedom was a luxury to be enjoyed by small communities like the Cantons of Switzerland and the Seven Provinces of Holland—and Holland's power after a short period of glory was waning fast before the rising might of the French King. The victory of parliamentary England over despotic France was a new fact of the first order ; it was the prime cause of the intellectual movement abroad against despotism in Church and State which marked the Eighteenth Century, from the time of Montesquieu onwards. The British Navy and Marlborough, the battles of La Hogue and Blenheim, gave to Locke and the other English philosophers a vogue on the continent seldom enjoyed by English philosophy in its own right. English institutions for the first time became an example to the world, though they remained somewhat of a mystery and were very imperfectly understood.

Britain's successes in the reigns of William and Anne surprised men all the more, because, prior to the Revolution of 1688, the rivalry of Parliament with the regal executive had been a cause not of efficiency but of weakness to England as a member of the European polity. Under James and Charles the First, and again under Charles and James the Second, the balance between King and Parliament made England of little account abroad.

The exception that proved the rule was the period of national efficiency under the Puritan Commonwealth. Then indeed the Parliamentary, or at least the Roundhead party, was supreme. Legislature and executive were united ; and so, both before and during the period of Cromwell's personal rule, the Commonwealth Government wielded powers of taxation and of military and naval preparation which no Stuart King enjoyed. Then indeed the voice of England was heard and feared abroad. But the concentration of power in the hands of the Roundhead party was a temporary phenomenon, because it was based not on agreement but on force.

In 1660 the nation restored the balance of power between King and Parliament, between executive and legislative, in which Clarendon rejoiced as the perfection of our mixed constitution. And with this perfect balance returned financial inability to meet our engagements, national disarmament and divided counsels, making us the mock of our enemies and the despair of our friends. This balance of the constitution, more than the wickedness or carelessness of Charles II, lay at the root of the disasters of his reign. No country can remain half monarchical and half parliamentary without paying the penalty in want of power.

It was the Revolution of 1688 that gave to Great Britain freedom and efficiency together, because it tipped the balance of power permanently on to the side of Parliament, not as forty years before by the victory in arms of one party in the State over another, but by an agreement of Whigs and Tories, thrown into each other's arms by the fortunate folly of James II.

Thenceforward there was agreement in general policy between executive and legislative, between King and Parliament, as formerly under the Tudors ; but this time it was Parliament that led and the King who had to follow. Then and then only was it possible to reorganize the taxation and the credit of the country on a modern basis, to keep a small standing army on foot as well as a large fleet permanently afloat, to develop the organization necessary for a great empire, without giving rise to the jealousies which had frustrated similar attempts by Strafford and by Cromwell. Then and then only was it possible to induce the Scots to accept freely a legislative union with England, such as Cromwell had presented to them at the sword's point. At the same time, the attempt to force all Englishmen through the doors of a single State Church, the cause for so many generations past of faction and bloodshed, was at length abandoned as impracticable by the Toleration Act of 1689. The new era of latitudinarianism and religious peace greatly strengthened Britain's commercial, military and colonizing power as against that of France, then engaged in casting out the pick of her industrial population, the Huguenots, to aid the rising manufactures of England, Holland and Prussia.

It is during the Stuart period that we emerge from the arena of English history into the ampler spaces of British history in its largest sense. The modern relations of England to Scotland and to Ireland respectively had been outlined under Elizabeth. Under the Stuarts they were deeply engraved on the imagination of posterity by a series of dramatic events. After many vicissitudes, we reached, in the reigns of William III and Anne, a defined and permanent relation of England to Scotland which still gives satisfaction to-day, and a relation of Britain to Ireland that fixed the lines along which all subsequent misfortunes developed.

In the same Stuart period, England planted populous and

self-governing communities in North America. Englishmen began to live on the other side of the world, but under the English flag and under free English institutions. Before the Seventeenth Century closed they were learning so to adjust these institutions in New York and elsewhere, that Dutch and other foreigners were happy to live under the English flag. Already we see the germ of a free Empire, of a widespread Commonwealth of many races and religions, the ideal which both the United States and the British Empire of to-day realize in two different ways but in a kindred spirit. At the close of the Seventeenth Century, the colonies of other European countries were developing on very different lines. Neither religious nor political freedom existed in French Canada or Spanish America ; the Dutch colonies in Africa had no political freedom, and in America relatively little. It was England who first planted the flag of liberty beyond the ocean.

The toleration of varieties in religion, though not admitted within England herself until 1689, was part of the very liberal practice both of the Stuart Kings and of their Parliamentary enemies in colonial affairs throughout this period. Anglican, Puritan or Roman Catholic, if discontented with his lot in the old country, could go to America with the good will of government and pray there according to his own fancy, but still under the old flag. Those who were regarded as troublesome at home, would be a strength and glory to England—on the other side of the ocean. This relatively liberal principle gave England a great advantage in the race for colonial supremacy.

Another reason why the governments of the Stuart epoch favoured the planting of colonies even by their political enemies, was the increasingly commercial and industrial character of the English polity at home. Massachusetts, New York, Virginia and the West Indian Islands were valued as important markets for English manufactures, at a time when the Parliamentary regime was bringing commerce more and more to the front as a prime consideration in domestic and foreign policy.

The Revolution of 1688 established the supremacy of the House of Commons, but left it handicapped with the system of ' rotten boroughs ' which were bound to grow more unrepresentative as years rolled by. The idea of redistributing Parliamentary seats in accordance with the movement of population was buried in the grave of Cromwell. It followed that the House of Commons and the government which it controlled became increasingly identified with the landlord class who were able to control the ' rotten boroughs.' If the Roundhead party had been able to come to terms with the rest of the nation, a considerable element of democracy might have been introduced into the English State. But after 1660 the democratic spirit disappeared until the industrial changes of the following century gave it a new form of life. The Revolution of 1688, though Parliamentary and liberal, was not democratic. Partly for that reason the nascent democracies beyond the Atlantic became increasingly out of touch with the aristocratic Parliament at home, a difference accentuated by differences in the prevalent form of religious observance in old and New England.

The downfall first of King Charles, then of the Puritan Commonwealth, and finally of James II in consequence of attempts to override the squirearchy and the chartered corporations, left the State weaker than it had been under Elizabeth in its relation to the local government of the countryside. The kind of control that Cecil and Walsingham had exercised over the doings, economic and other, of the Justices of the Peace, was on the decline throughout the Stuart era, and was conspicuously absent under the early Hanoverians. The struggle of Parliament against Crown had, indeed, from the first been rooted in a struggle for local independence against the centre, a rebellion of the squires against the Court and the Privy Council. In that contest the yeomen and townsfolk had supported the squires, especially that section of squires that was most opposed to the Crown. The victory of Parliament, though it made England more united and efficient for action abroad, meant the subordination of the central authority to the will of the localities as regards their domestic affairs. And owing to the failure of the Puritan Revolution, the will of the localities from 1660 onwards meant the will of the squires.

The political victory over the House of Stuart finally rested with the Whigs—the section of the squires who were in alliance with London and the merchant community in matters of national policy. But the social power remained with the Justices of the Peace and the whole body of the squires who as a mass were less Whig than Tory.

The political and religious tyranny of the monarch had been effectively curbed. The State Church no longer pretended to be co-extensive with the nation. The individual was protected in freedom of speech and person by Parliament victorious over the Crown, and by the Common Lawyers victorious over the Prerogative Courts. Henceforth, so far as the government was concerned, ' a man might speak his mind ' as nowhere else in Europe and as never before in England. To abolish social tyranny was more difficult. But until the advent of the Industrial Revolution the need of social emancipation from the squirearchy was not seriously felt. Under the first two Georges Englishmen regarded human freedom as a science which they had perfected. That view, partly inspired by national pride in contemplation of a continent still domineered over by Kings, priests and nobles, was indeed erroneous. And yet it may fairly be doubted whether any set of men, since the victors of Marathon and Salamis, had done as much to establish human freedom on a practical basis as the Roundheads and Cavaliers, the Whigs and Tories of the Stuart Parliaments.

CHAPTER I

James I. Parliaments, Puritans and Recusants. Decline of English seapower. The Spanish match. Buckingham and the Thirty Years' War. Charles I. The King, Parliament and the Common Law. Coke and Eliot. Laud and Strafford

Kings : James I, 1603–1625 (James VI of Scotland, 1567); Charles I, 1625–1649

THE keynote of Tudor government had been King-worship, not despotism. Monarchs without an army at the centre or a paid bureaucracy in the countryside were not despots, for they could not compel their subjects by force. The beefeaters of the Palace could guard the barge in which a rebellious nobleman or a fallen Minister was rowed from Whitehall steps to Traitors' Gate in the Tower, because the London 'prentices never attempted a rescue on the way. But they could not coerce a population of five millions, many of whom had sword, bow or bill hanging from the cottage rafters.

The power of the Tudors, in short, was not material but metaphysical. They appealed sometimes to the love and always to the loyalty and ' free awe ' of their subjects. In the century that begins with Sir Thomas More and ends with Shakespeare, ' the deputy elected by the Lord ' walks girt with a sunlike majesty. In his presence rank, genius and religion vail their pride, or lay their heads resignedly upon the block if the wrath of the Prince demands a sacrifice. In the following century genius and religion were to show a less obliging temper.

English King-worship was the secret of a family and the spirit of an age. It owed much to the political talents of the two Henries and Elizabeth, and yet more to the need for national leadership in the period of transition from the mediæval to the modern world. When, after the death of the last Tudor, James I in his pedantry tried to materialize English King-worship into the political dogma of divine hereditary right, he spilt its essence in the dust.

England had found in the Tudor monarchs adequate representatives of her own spirit and policy ; but the Stuarts, while claiming yet greater powers from a higher source than English law and custom, adopted policies at home and abroad which were in some of their main lines opposed to the wishes of the strongest elements in English society. The situation thus created forced to the front claims on behalf of the House of Commons which were as new to the constitution as the claims of divine hereditary right and autocratic power on behalf of the Crown.

Whether the conflict would have come to blows without the complication and inspiration of the religious question in a religious age, may perhaps be doubted. And certainly the novel claims on behalf of the Lower House would never have been advanced, still less made good, without the preparatory work of great constitutional lawyers like Coke and Selden, and great Parliamentarians—a new profession—like Eliot, Hampden and Pym. In the reigns of James and Charles the First the manor-houses of England produced a famous breed of men to sit in Parliament. Antiquarians in learning, and devotees of law, custom and precedent, they persuaded themselves and their countrymen that they were only claiming ancient privileges, and carrying out the spirit and even the letter of Magna Carta.[1] Historical science was yet in its infancy, for in fact they were innovators, unconsciously groping after a form of government new to England and new to the world. These men were not adventurers or self-seekers, and had more to lose than to gain by quitting their broad acres and private gardens ; for Parliament was then the road not to power but to prison. The earnest personal character of their Protestant religion was combined with the cultured habit of mind and manner of gentlemen who were the ripe products of the English Renaissance. Only with the breach in the Parliamentary party in the second session of the Long Parliament did these two elements begin to divide, and to form the Roundhead party on the one hand and the Constitutional Royalists on the other. 1641–1642.

When James VI of Scotland, the comic offspring of the tragic union of Mary Queen of Scots with Darnley, succeeded to Elizabeth's throne as James I, the English rode in from far and near to catch a glimpse of their new sovereign on his slow progress from Edinburgh to London. Those whose rank gave them access through the throng in the Midland market towns, found themselves in the presence of the good-natured, conceited, garrulous King, wise in book-learning but a poor judge of men, and so ignorant of England and her laws that at Newark he ordered a 1603.

[1] See p. 172, above.

cut-purse caught in the act to be hanged without trial at a word from his royal mouth. Scotland indeed he knew and in part understood, but that knowledge would be of less than no use to him in deciphering the political map of his southern kingdom.

His new subjects, however, were in no mood to be critical. For forty years and more they had lived in the black shadow of the question ' What will befall us when the Queen dies ? ' That anxiety had been aggravated and prolonged by Elizabeth's half-politic, half-coquettish dislike of the topic, and her irritation at the demand for an acknowledged heir, who might, she feared, divide the loyalty of her servants before she herself had finished with them. But Robert Cecil, wise son of a great father, had negotiated with James and smoothed the way for his undisputed accession. The relief felt by the English people at the peaceful continuity of things after Elizabeth's death is enshrined in the hyperbolical language of the Preface to the Authorized Version of the Bible.

Since infancy, James had reigned in Scotland as his mother's supplanter. He was in no sense her avenger or the successor to her policy. He came to England on the implied condition that he should continue the Elizabethan regime, and so he did, in so far as he was capable of understanding its true nature. Robert Cecil remained chief Minister and became Earl of Salisbury. Francis Bacon acted as another adviser to James, though his sage counsels of toleration in Church and State were too often neglected. Only the Elizabethan ' men of war ' were discarded, and Raleigh was mewed up in the Tower, to gaze over the battlements of his terrace walk at the masts in the Thames below, and listen, sick with memory, to the sounds and songs of the mariners at their work.

The new sovereign brought with him one good gift that was personal to himself—the union with Scotland. Now that both crowns were set on one head, the long, romantic story of the Border came to an end. The moss-trooper's occupation was gone ; he yielded place, on the moors that had known him, to the shepherd, who could now drive the flocks in security to the very ridge of the Cheviots and to the heart of the Debateable Land. But there was no union of the Parliaments, Churches or laws of the two Kingdoms, and the Scots were disliked by their fellow-subjects as proud, beggarly rivals for the royal favour. Not till the Eighteenth Century did the Empire begin to draw its full increase of strength from the union. But the close reactions of English upon Scottish and of Scottish upon English affairs make up a great part of the tangled and sanguinary skein of politics and religion under the Stuarts.

Scotland, in losing the presence of her King, who now became
a mighty potentate at four hundred miles' distance from Edinburgh, was thereby subordinated to royal power as she had never
been before. From Whitehall the sixth James could keep the
Scots nobles in awe, and at the same time prevent the Kirk from
domineering over the State. To achieve the latter end, he successfully aroused the jealousy of the nobles against the small
lairds and ministers who were laying hands on power through the
medium of the ecclesiastical organization. He had established
some humble and ill-paid Bishops, whose functions he gradually
increased at the expense of the democratic Assemblies and Synods.
In so doing he was protecting moderate and liberal elements in
the religious life of Scotland, and preventing clerical tyranny, but
he was also thwarting the only form of self-expression that was
then open to the Scottish people. He did not, however, attempt
to destroy the Presbyterian organization in the parishes, or to
impose the English service book on the Scottish congregations.
He would never have become the dupe of the strange delusion
which betrayed Laud to his undoing, that there was ' no religion '
in Scotland ! There was a great deal more of it than James liked,
and his only desire was to keep it in its place. He knew Scotland
as he never knew England, and as his son Charles never knew
either the one land or the other.

Not only did England remain *terra incognita* to James, but he
never became aware of his ignorance. His mind was already
formed when first he came to reign in Whitehall, and the flattery
he received there confirmed his good opinion of his own penetration. Was not politics a science he had mastered ? He was
perpetually unbuttoning the stores of his royal wisdom for the
benefit of his subjects, and as there was none who could venture
to answer him to his face, he supposed them all out-argued. In
Scotland he had had no experience of anything analogous to the
English House of Commons. The Scottish ' Parliament ' was in
effect a court of record, and he could not appreciate the much
higher position of the body bearing the same name in England.
In Scotland the only opposition came from feudal Barons on their
estates and Presbyterian preachers in their pulpits. Who then
were these squires and lawyers in the House of Commons, with
their talk about ' privilege ' and ' precedents,' and ' fundamental
laws of the realm,' refusing to let him raise money from his subjects except on their conditions, and striving to dictate to him on
the weightiest affairs of ecclesiastical and foreign policy ? He
condescendingly pointed out to them their folly, and, when
they disregarded his lectures, fumed over in angry words and
deeds.

The relation of the House of Stuart to the Puritan movement in England was decided by one of the first acts of the new reign. The Church of England was then the principal arena of Puritan activity, and some leading clergy of the Establishment came to the Hampton Court Conference to beg for a legalized comprehension of men of those views within its borders.   They were in humble mood, no longer, as in the days of Cartwright and Penry, demanding the overthrow of episcopal government or the serious alteration of the Prayer Book.   They knew it was impossible to capture the Church against the will of the King, but they asked for a certain permissive variety in ritual and parish work which would regulate their position.

It was a moment when a settlement might well have been made on the basis of comprehension, by a little widening of the borders of a State Church designed to be elastic, more especially since toleration outside the Church was not then regarded as permissible.   To deny any legalized activity, either within or without the Establishment, to the movement which then had most influence on the laity and particularly on Parliament, was to sow the seeds of civil war.   That is precisely what James did at Hampton Court.   When he exclaimed ' No Bishop, no King ! ' he was well within his rights, but the existence of the episcopate was not then at issue.   When he added in a fury ' I shall make them conform themselves or I will harry them out of the land,' he evoked a feud that cost the blood and tears of three generations, and incidentally transferred the sovereign power from King to Parliament.

The refusal of James to grant toleration either inside or outside the Establishment was not the outcome of personal adherence to High Church religion such as inspired his son Charles.   He was still a Calvinist in doctrine, but he feared the political associations of the democratic and earnest type of religion of which he had seen so much more than he liked in Scotland.   ' A Scottish Presbytery,' he cried at Hampton Court, ' agreeth as well with a monarchy as God with the Devil. . . . Then Jack, Tom, Will and Dick shall meet and at their pleasure censure me and my council.'   Following on the abortive conference, three hundred English Puritan clergy were ejected from their livings.   It was the beginning of ' non-conformity ' on a large scale.   Yet for another eighty-four years non-conformist worship remained illegal and subject to penalties ; hence the earnestness and fury of all parties in the struggle for control of the State Church, since nowhere outside its bounds were men permitted to worship God.

Like so many who have been the cause of war and strife, James prided himself on being the ' peace-maker,' set on an intellectual eminence high above the angry passions of common men. He had tried his pacific hand on the position of his Roman Catholic subjects, promising them what he could not perform, a measure of toleration which was rendered impossible by the persecuting attitude he adopted towards Puritanism. A brief relaxation of the penal laws revealed the numbers of the crypto-Catholics and struck panic into the mass of his subjects. It was indeed a vicious circle. The Jesuit policy, aiming at the overthrow of the existing regime and the forcible extirpation of Protestantism in England, necessitated in the eyes of statesmen and people the degree of persecution customary under Elizabeth, and that persecution justified the Jesuit policy in the eyes of many Roman Catholics.

The re-enforcement of fines for 'recusancy,' after the royal promise of relief, so incensed a group of Catholic gentlemen of the Jesuit party that they formed the Gunpowder Plot, for the destruction of the King and the two Houses of Parliament together. In early Tudor times government could have been paralyzed or overturned by murdering the King; it was now felt to be necessary to murder Parliament too. The material preparations, made by men who had served as officers in the Spanish army in the Netherlands, were all complete when the conspiracy was revealed by a man of tender conscience. 'The attempt but **1605.** not the deed confounds us': it was the heaviest moral blow suffered by the Roman Catholics between the reigns of Mary Tudor and James II. Everything that had been said about the result of the Jesuit teaching seemed to plain Englishmen to be more than confirmed, and the Protestant feast of Guy Fawkes and the Fifth of November, decorously celebrated in the Church service, had democratic rites at the street corner in which the least mystical could heartily participate. Henceforth the anti-Roman passion in England remained a constant and often a determining factor in all the mazes of the long history of the House of Stuart.[1]

James disliked 'men of war' whether by land or sea. Until in his declining years he let the initiative pass to the volatile and ambitious Buckingham, he was the most thorough-going pacifist who ever bore rule in England. He wielded the sceptre and the pen, and held them both to be mightier than the sword. Of

---

[1] There is direct reference in *Macbeth* (1606) to the Gunpowder Plot and the Jesuit doctrine of equivocation, which was much discussed at the trial of the Jesuit Garnet. 'Here's an equivocator, that could swear in both the scales against either scale; who committed treason enough for God's sake, but could not equivocate with heaven.' There are several similar references scattered about in the lesser dialogue of the play.

naked steel he had a physical horror, perhaps because he was born three months after the terrible day when armed men had burst in upon his mother's supper party and stabbed Rizzio under her eyes.   And not only was James most unwarlike in his own particular : but being a Scot of that period he had no conception of the importance of sea-power.   He was the only Stuart King of England who utterly neglected the Navy.

Neglect of the Navy deprived his peace with Spain of some at least of its good effects.   The terms of the treaty that ended Elizabeth's war obtained for English merchants open trade with Spain and her possessions in Europe, and set some limit to the power of the Inquisition over them in Spanish ports.   But the claims of the Elizabethan seamen to trade with Spanish America and the regions monopolized by Portugal in Africa and Asia were not mentioned in the treaty, and the enforcement of these claims no longer received countenance from the English government, which let the Royal Navy decay, while it suppressed privateering to the best of its ability.

In these circumstances, private war against Spanish and Portuguese was continued without the countenance of the State. In the American Indies, the ' buccaneers ' found friends and bases in the West Indian Islands and in the New English colonies on the Northern mainland, so long as they maintained, however illegally, the interests and prestige of England against the Spaniard.   But their high-seas robbery was not always directed against Spaniards alone, and before the end of the Stuart era the buccaneers had degenerated far from the traditions of Drake and Raleigh towards the melodramatic villainies of Teach and the black-flag pirates.   Meanwhile the trade of South America remained, by law at least, closed to all save Spaniards ; but as a result of Drake's victories, North America was in practice open to English, French and Dutch settlement.

On the coasts of Africa and the East Indies the Portuguese, then subjects of the King of Spain, endeavoured to prevent the subjects of James I from trading with the natives even in time of peace.   But the English East India Company armed its ships for battle, and Captains Thomas Best and Nicholas Downton blew the Portuguese out of the water in decisive actions off Surat, and so established more regular trade with the native peoples of Asia than was as yet possible with the inhabitants of the guarded shores of the Spanish American colonies.

In their hostilities against the Portuguese in the East, the English merchants had the Dutch as allies.   But for the rest there was enmity between the trading communities of the two Protestant nations, which increased when the Portuguese power

1604.

1611.
1614–15.

See
Map XX.,
p. 338,
above.

became of no account in the Indian seas.   In the reigns of James
and Charles I the merchant of the Dutch East India Company
had greater resources behind him than his English rival.   It
was the day of the amazing wealth and power of little Holland,
safe at last from Spain and not yet threatened by France.   She
led the world in the arts and sciences, and was mistress of the sea.
The Dutch became the carriers for mankind, largely to the
detriment of English shipping.   They ousted the English from the
Russian trade, which the Elizabethans had been the first to open.
They fished where they liked, and often drove English fishermen
from their own grounds.   They expelled the Portuguese from
Ceylon and the Spice Islands of the Molucca Sea, and in 1623
massacred the English there at Amboyna ; James was helpless,
and it was left to Cromwell, a generation later, to exact compensation for the long-remembered outrage.

But the English East India Company, when driven from the
Spice Islands, pushed its trade on the Indian mainland.   In
James I's reign it founded a successful trading station at Surat,
and in Charles I's reign built its Fort St. George, Madras, and set
up other trading stations in Bengal.   Such were the humble
mercantile origins of British rule in India.   But from the first
these East India merchants were not mere ' quill-drivers ' ; they
had destroyed the Portuguese monopoly by diplomacy at the
courts of native potentates, and by the broadsides of their ships
at sea.

Meanwhile James abandoned one by one the claims of the
Royal Navy.   The salute to the flag by other nations in the English
seas was no longer demanded.   The pirates from the ' Barbary '
coast of North Africa raided in the Channel with impunity.   The
diplomatic protests of James about the treatment of his subjects
by Dutch and Spaniards were laughed to scorn.   Raleigh was **1618.**
beheaded to appease the Spanish Ambassador.   We were still
a maritime community, but for thirty years we almost ceased to
be a naval power.

One consequence was the deep and lasting resentment of the
mariners and merchants against the House of Stuart, increased
by the strong Protestant feeling of those who went down to the
sea in ships.   The new monarchy had abandoned the Elizabethan
tradition at sea and in its dealings with Spain ; the indignation
produced by this change of attitude was not removed even when
Charles I honestly appropriated the illegal Ship Money to the **1634–**
reconstruction of the Royal Navy which his father had allowed to **1640.**
decay.   In the hour of his need, the ships which Charles had
built revolted to his enemies, and the seaports of England followed
the lead of London and the House of Commons in the first Civil

War with decisive effects on its fortunes. The ghost of Raleigh pursued the House of Stuart to the scaffold.[1]

James' peaceful policy was put to a cruel test by the outbreak of the Thirty Years' War. At that crisis his neglect of the fighting fleet foredoomed his well-meant pacific diplomacy to failure, for why should Spain or Austria, France or Holland, listen to the man who had let England's national weapon rust, and could never prevent Spanish troops from sailing up the Channel to the Netherlands ?

In its origin the Thirty Years' War was a resumption of the forward march of the great Catholic reaction to which England and Holland had set a limit in the days of Philip II. Its new protagonist was Austria, with Spain assistant. Bohemia and the Rhenish Palatinate were overrun, the first by Austrian arms, the second by Spaniards from the Netherlands, and cruel persecution put down Protestantism in both the conquered lands. The Prince who had been driven from these two dominions was none other than James I's son-in-law. His wife Elizabeth, and their infant children, Prince Rupert and Prince Maurice, began thus early their long life of disinherited wandering, which never undermined the great abilities and virtues of either mother or children.[2] James vainly thought to effect their restoration by ingratiating himself yet more with their enemies, by subjecting English policy more than ever to Gondomar the Spanish Ambassador, and finally by proposing to marry his surviving son Charles to the Spanish Infanta.

The Spanish match, as the English people clearly saw, would lead to Spanish heirs and Catholic Kings who would endeavour

[1] The scene of Raleigh's execution in 1618, in Palace Yard, Westminster, was only a quarter of a mile from the space in front of Whitehall where Charles perished 30 years later. On the naval questions of James' reign and the peace with Spain, compare *Gardiner*, I. pp. 209–14, to Corbett, *Successors of Drake*, Chap. VII., and *England in the Mediterranean*, Vol. I., and Callender, *Naval Side of Br. Hist.*, Chap. VI.

[2]

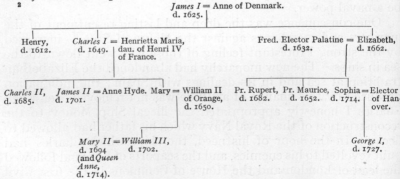

```
                        James I = Anne of Denmark.
                                d. 1625.

    Henry,      Charles I = Henrietta Maria,        Fred. Elector Palatine = Elizabeth,
    d. 1612.    d. 1649.  | dau. of Henri IV              d. 1632.           | d. 1662.
                          | of France.

Charles II,  James II = Anne Hyde.  Mary = William II   Pr. Rupert,  Pr. Maurice,  Sophia = Elector
d. 1685.     d. 1701.               of Orange,          d. 1682.     d. 1652.       d. 1714.  of Han-
                                    d. 1650.                                                 over.

             Mary II = William III,                                            George I,
             d. 1694    d. 1702.                                               d. 1727.
             (and Queen
             Anne,
             d. 1714).
```

to undo the work of Elizabeth. But James in his old age and Charles in his youth were alike infatuated with George Villiers, whom they made Duke of Buckingham ; and Buckingham's volatile imagination was for a time dazzled by the idea of giving peace to Europe through the Spanish match. When that dangerous project broke down after the escapade of the visit of young Charles and the favourite to Madrid, a marriage only one degree less fatal was carried through, Charles being mated to the zealous Romanist Henrietta Maria of France, destined to be the mother of many troubles to England and of more to the House of Stuart.[1]

1623.

James I died in 1625, but his death made little difference, for Buckingham's influence was no less strong over King Charles. The fiasco of the Spanish match was followed by a period of war-like expeditions, rashly undertaken by Buckingham, who now cast himself for the part of Protestant hero abroad. But armies and navies cannot be improvised, and the result was a series of disasters disgraceful to our arms. Some of these idle expeditions were directed to aid the Huguenots of La Rochelle against the France of Cardinal Richelieu. A wiser policy would have taken the Cardinal by the hand to resist the progress of the Catholic reaction conducted by the Hapsburg enemies of France beyond the Rhine. Other English expeditions directed against Spain were equally unsuccessful.

1625–1628.

This tale of folly and disaster lowered the prestige of monarchy in England, and brought the Crown into fierce conflict with the House of Commons. The wars, such as they were, had led to unparliamentary taxation, billeting, arbitrary imprisonment and martial law over civilians, all of which were defined as illegal in the famous Petition of Right conceded by Charles to his Parliament in return for a vote of five subsidies. Yet the Petition of Right, like Magna Carta, was the beginning, not the end, of a struggle for the principles it enunciated.

1628.

The House of Commons was not yet strong enough to dictate the foreign policy of the Crown, but it was strong enough to be a clog on the effective conduct of war. For it could not but be jealous of the taxing power and fearful of an army over which it had no control. If once the Crown established the right to tax the subject at will like the Kings of France and Spain, there might

---

[1] Henry, Prince of Wales, who died in 1612, had told his father when he proposed to him a French marriage, that he was ' resolved that two religions should not lie in his bed.' If he had lived he might possibly have become a Protestant Henry V on the continent during the Thirty Years' War, and totally changed the course of political development in England by adopting policies pleasing to Parliament and so keeping it in voluntary subordination to the Crown.

perhaps be a beginning of success abroad, but there would certainly be an end of Parliaments at home.

The squires who composed the Lower House, no longer as in Elizabeth's reign guided by tactful Privy Councillors sitting in their midst, were becoming an opposition rather than an organ of government. Their homespun wit enabled them to understand the interests of their own country better than the courtiers, but they knew nothing of the continent, and showed little wisdom in their advice as to how the Protestant cause was to be maintained abroad. With a royal executive and a tax-granting Parliament at loggerheads and both of them grossly ignorant of foreign affairs, with no army and a diminutive Royal Navy, England was a cypher in European politics at this crisis.

1628.

Buckingham, while still preparing warlike expeditions to relieve Rochelle, was murdered by a Puritan fanatic, to the shameless joy of the common folk. Charles, alienated from his people by the blood of his friend, soon abandoned warlike schemes that were clearly foredoomed to failure, and strove instead by rigid economy to govern without the Parliaments that he hated. In this design he was confirmed by a violent quarrel with the House of Commons of 1629 ; members held the Speaker down in the Chair while they passed the famous resolutions against ' Popery and Arminianism ' and illegal Tonnage and Poundage, which the circumstances of the time associated together in the minds of men. No Parliament was held again for eleven years.

1632.

Contrary to the privileges of Parliament as respected by Queen Elizabeth, Sir John Eliot and his friends Valentine and Strode were kept in prison on account of what they had done in the House of Commons. Eliot died in the Tower, refusing to obtain release by signifying his submission to these illegal proceedings, a martyr to English law and freedom ; his two friends did not regain their liberty for eleven years. The hardness of Charles in his dealings with Eliot, whom he would not even suffer to be taken for burial to his Cornish home, can most charitably be regarded as a measure of his silent grief over the murdered Buckingham, for the Commons' leader had been inveterate and even furious in his eloquent attacks upon the favourite. But such a temper in Charles towards his subjects, even if humanly excusable, was very dangerous in a king who for a dozen years to come was to rule the land at his own mere will and pleasure.

By dispensing with Parliaments and by dismissing all Judges who dared to interpret the laws impartially, Charles removed every constitutional check upon his actions. None the less, the genius of the English Common Law was still the enemy of absolute regal power, and thanks to the work of Sir Edward Coke it had become the great ally of Parliament. If Parliament ever revived and conquered royal despotism, the spirit of the Common Law would revive with it and conquer the Prerogative Courts of Star Chamber, High Commission, Requests and Councils of Wales and the North. The professional jealousy felt by the lawyers in the courts where English Common Law was administered, against these Prerogative Courts dealing out a different law by different rules of procedure, had been deeply stirred by the leadership of the fierce and arrogant Coke, and had by him been closely connected with the Parliamentary party in the House of Commons. The Petition of Right, which was largely his work and expressed his doctrine, represented the spirit of the Common Law and the vigilance of Parliament combining to protect the subject of the land against arbitrary power.

The two men who had worked together to lay the foundations of Parliamentary resistance to the Crown were strangely different specimens of humanity. Eliot was the best type of well-to-do country gentleman, seeking nothing for himself, ardent and eloquent only in the public interest. Coke was an ambitious, pushing lawyer, a bully, and in his early days a sycophant. As Attorney-General to King James in 1603 he had attacked the prisoner Raleigh in a spirit worthy of Jeffreys, crying out to the lifelong foe of Spain, ' Thou hast a Spanish heart and thyself art a viper of hell ! ' Only one thing was dearer to Coke than promotion and power, and that was the Common Law. For it he sacrificed place and royal favour, stepping down off the Bench to make on the floor of the Lower House his alliance with the Puritan squires, a union whence sprang the liberties of England. 1616–1628, d. 1634.

In essence the quarrel was this : James and Charles held, with the students of Roman Law, that the will of the Prince was the source of law, and that the Judges were ' lions under the throne,' bound to speak as he directed them. Coke, on the other hand, in the spirit of the English Common Law, conceived of law as having an independent existence of its own, set above the King as well as above his subjects, and bound to judge impartially between them. Laws were alterable only by the High Court of Parliament. The Prerogative Courts, with their reception of Roman Law and their arbitrary procedure, belonged, he thought, to an alien civilization.

The battle between these two systems of law had to be fought out, for England could no longer, as under the Tudors, be governed by both at once. The first blood was drawn by Charles, who by packing the Bench seemed to have subjected the Common Law courts themselves to prerogative ideas. But the last word was to lie with the Long Parliament.

The English Common Law was a survival from the Middle
Ages, while the Prerogative Courts and the increased deference
for Roman Law had been a Renaissance product of Tudor times.[1]
Coke and the Parliament men whom he schooled in his doctrines,
stood therefore on conservative and national ground, against
innovation of the type prevalent on the continent.   Their appeal
was made to the past,—to the past of England, not of the Roman
Empire.   Hence the antiquarian and historical character of their
arguments, not always good history in detail, but consonant
generally with a real English tradition down the ages.   ' Coke on
Littleton ' and Coke's other Institutes were less universal and less
forward-looking in their appeal than theories of the Rights of Man
by Paine or Rousseau, but they have served to underprop a vast
structure of progress and freedom in two hemispheres.

The legal issue between the King and his opponents was no
less important than the financial or the religious, and in that
litigious age it was well understood by the English people.   The
1637–8.   case arising from John Hampden's refusal to pay Ship Money,
argued fully before the Exchequer Court, was followed in its
details with intense excitement by a people better versed in legal
matters than the King or his advisers were aware.   The ruling
made by the majority of the Judges against Hampden and in
favour of the levy of Ship Money without Parliamentary sanction,
stood condemned by public opinion.   But for a short while longer
the ruling enabled the King to exact the tax and to reconstruct
the fighting Navy.   The object was worthy, but it was not by
such expedients that English maritime supremacy could be
restored and maintained by a King who had lost the loyalty of his
subjects.   It was a necessary part of the new royal policy to
abstain from all foreign entanglements, and allow the Thirty
Years' War to pass from crisis to crisis with England as a spectator, even on occasions when a mere naval demonstration would
have had important results.   The adherence of the sea-going
population and of the Royal Navy itself to the Parliamentary
side of the quarrel bore witness to the patriotic character of
Hampden's refusal to pay an illegal tax.

1629–   Laud and Wentworth, the two men with whom Charles'
1640.   period of autocratic rule is associated, were of a very different
order of character and intellect from Buckingham.

Archbishop Laud was a great churchman, who unfortunately
was called upon by the then relations of Church and State to
play also the part of statesman, for which he was unsuited alike
by temper and understanding.   His memory is cherished as the

[1] See pp. 277–8, above.

founder of the High Church party in the religious life of the Church of England. But the historian is principally concerned with the political consequences of his ecclesiastical policy, which in a Church that was then by law co-extensive with the nation could not fail to be of the utmost peril and importance. It was indeed the chief cause of the Civil War, because it provoked the furious reaction of armed Puritanism in which Laud himself perished.

If James I suffered as King of England from having been bred a Scot, Laud as Archbishop suffered from having been bred a don. He treated broad England as he had been permitted to treat Oxford, but it is easier to trim a University to pattern than a nation of grown men. The ritual side of worship in the parish churches was increased by episcopal command and visitation, while evangelical practice, preaching and lecturing were effectively prohibited within the Church. At the same time non-conformist worship outside the Church was persecuted with increasing rigour. The emigration of the Puritans to America in these years was a measure of the degree to which Laud made life intolerable to them in England.[1] Owing to his activities it became impossible for a Puritan to live in his native country and worship God freely, at a time when English Puritanism was producing men of the calibre of Cromwell and Milton, Hampden and Pym. High Anglicanism had already its men of learning and its poets, but as yet it had not won the heart of any large section of the squires, still less of the people at large. Even men like Sir Edmund Verney, Falkland and Hyde, who in time of need showed themselves ready to fight to save the Prayer Book, were hostile to Laud and his over-busy Bishops.

The zeal of the Primate roused against himself and against the King, not only the strongest religious sentiments of that generation, but the feeling, always very strong in England, that resents the interference of the religious in their neighbours' affairs. Laud, who could never be either weary or prudent in well-doing, revived the activity of the spiritual courts, and summoned influential laymen to answer for their sins before the priesthood. The Church Courts, with a truly catholic indifference, incurred the odium of the Puritan precisian, the loose-liver, and the ordinary layman who had hoped that the Reformation had delivered him from clerical control. Meanwhile Bishops were beginning to replace nobles and commoners as the favourite councillors of the Crown. And in many parishes the new school of Laudian clergy enraged the squires by setting themselves up as rival sources of authority. The censorship of the press, which was then in episcopal hands, was busily

[1] See Chap. V., p. 438, below.

employed by Laud to silence voices opposed to his own ideas.   In everything Englishmen were to toe the line drawn by a particular school of clergy.   There seemed, in short, to be an attempt on foot to restore the mediæval relation of the clergy to the laity, and such a movement gave bitter offence alike to future Cavaliers and future Roundheads.   The anti-clerical feeling which in 1661 swelled the popularity of the restored Anglican Church as the alternative to ' the rule of the Saints,' in 1640 added force to the Puritan uprising against Laud's domination.

While the Archbishop persecuted the Puritans with meticulous rigour, the growing influence of Charles' French Queen stopped the persecution of Roman Catholics.   The consequence was that they everywhere raised their heads : there were conversions, especially in the upper ranks of society, and Henrietta Maria's religion became fashionable at Court.   Meanwhile the most determined enemies of the Church of Rome were pouring out of the country to America by thousands every year.   An indefinite continuance of such a state of things must, men thought, lead to the return of England to the Papal fold.   Laud did not desire that, but he applied no remedy and suffered accordingly in men's estimation.

In these circumstances the fortunes of the High Church party, a minority attempting to coerce the principal forces in the nation, became identified with the cause of personal despotism and with the royal attempt to be rid of Parliament.   The Laudian clergy preached up the doctrine of divine right and prerogative power. To crush Laud's opponents, recourse was often had to the reserves of royal authority in the Star Chamber and the Ecclesiastical High Commission :   the Star Chamber, once popular under the Tudors, incurred the furious hatred of the Londoners for its cruel punishment of Prynne and Lilburne.   The Puritans, on the other hand, became more than ever Parliament men, looking forward to the time when circumstances would compel Charles to summon the two Houses :   all their hopes lay in the thought that— .

1637.

> That two-handed engine at the door
> Stands ready to smite once and smite no more.

The political connection of the two religious parties with King and Parliament respectively, though dictated in each case by the pressure of circumstances, was in each case a natural alliance. The authoritarian element in religion to which Laud gave renewed prominence had affinities to regal absolutism, and Parliamentary power in the State answered to the popular control of the Church, whether Presbyterian or Congregational.   Between these two parties in Church and State floated indefinite masses of moderate opinion, which were frequently to decide the balance of power in the great years now coming on.

Thomas Wentworth, afterwards Earl of Strafford, had been an active member of the House of Commons in opposition to Buckingham, whose weak and mischievous rule he abhorred. But while he felt acutely the evils of royal favouritism, he did not in his heart believe that an assembly of 500 elected persons could govern a great kingdom. Besides, he was ambitious, and thought himself more fit to rule than either Parliament or Buckingham. He who had supported the Petition of Right spent the rest of his life in trying to subvert its principles. He planned to give Britain such a royal administration as Richelieu was then giving to France and as Bismarck long afterwards gave to Germany. If this great man had been Charles' chief Minister during the years when Laud was his chief ecclesiastical adviser, he might have found means to build up an army and a bureaucracy dependent on the Crown, for lack of which the autocratic system collapsed at the first touch of determined resistance. Fortunately for the liberties of Great Britain, Wentworth only became Charles' right- Sept. hand man when it was too late, after the Scots had risen with 1639. success and Englishmen had begun to realize how unanimous was their own discontent.

During the previous decade Wentworth had been employed by the King first as President of the Council of the North and then as ruler of Ireland. In these proconsular capacities he had shown a fine administrative vigour and a ruthless contempt for opinion and intolerance of all opposition ; to this method he gave the name of ' Thorough,' while others called it tyranny. In Ireland such fearless disrespect of persons might have been useful as the instrument of an enlightened policy. But his policy was enlightened only on its economic side. Otherwise his injustice alienated Catholics and Protestants alike.

The native Irish, when he first came to rule the island, were 1632. already deeply embittered by the proscription of their religion and by the land policy of successive governments, who had handed over more and more of their soil to British landlords. The great 1608– plantation of Ulster in James' reign—the only part of the English 1610. garrison system that survives to our own day—had fixed a colony of Londoners in the good town of Derry, and some thousands of hard-working Presbyterian Scots on lands whence the Irish had been cleared. The Scots from across the narrow seas—some of whose ancestors had been in North Ireland long ago [1]—formed the most stable part of British colonization there, because they

[1] See p. 57, above.

were prepared to till the soil themselves, and not merely to exploit and rack-rent the tillers.

Wentworth harried the Protestants of Ulster for their sympathy with the Puritans of Britain, but he had not set out to propitiate the Irish Catholics. On the contrary, he planned new plantations in Connaught to deprive the natives of the lands which previous governments had left them. The fact that he ended by raising an Irish Catholic army to subdue Great Britain, certainly did not mean that he came a step nearer to solving the Irish problem than any other statesman of that century. The native Catholic rising of 1641, a terrible event in itself and yet more terrible in its consequences and its memory, was a measure of Wentworth's failure in Ireland.

Laud and Wentworth were close friends and allies, and laboured together to set up the Prerogative and its courts above Parliament and the Common Law. Laud, on his translation to Canterbury, had written to Wentworth that the Church was overmuch 'bound up in the forms of Common Law,' and his friend had replied :

'No such narrow considerations shall fall in my counsels as my own preservation, till I see my master's power and greatness set out of wardship and above the exposition of Sir Edward Coke and his Year-Books, and I am most assured the same resolution governs in your lordship. Let us then in the name of God go cheerfully and boldly. . . . And thus you have my Thorough and Thorough.'

BOOKS FOR FURTHER READING

Gardiner's *History of England*, 1603-42 (ten vols.) ; Holdsworth, *History of English Law*, Vol. V. (on Coke) ; Figgis, *Divine Right of Kings* ; Gwynn, *History of Ireland* ; Bagwell, *Ireland under the Stuarts*, 3 vols. ; *Archbishop Laud Commemoration*, 1895 (Essays on Laud by Creighton and others) ; Dowden, *Puritan and Anglican* ; John Forster, *Sir J. Eliot* ; Traill, *Strafford* ; G. M. Trevelyan, *England under the Stuarts*.

CHAPTER II

England and Scotland. The Scottish Revolt. The Long Parliament. First Session: fall of the Prerogative system and execution of Strafford. Second Session: the Church Question and the division of parties

THE divergent courses which the Reformation had followed in England and in Scotland respectively, did much to complicate the politics of the succeeding era, when the rule of a single King over both countries constantly pointed towards ecclesiastical union that was, in fact, always impossible.

At the Reformation the laity on both sides of the Border had asserted their will against the mediæval clergy, but in two very different ways. In England the Church had kept the outline of its ancient organization, remaining purely clerical in its internal structure ; it followed that the control of the laity over its liturgy and doctrine had to be exercised not from within but from without, through Crown and through Parliament. In Scotland, on the other hand, the laity took an active part in Church organization and government. Only so could there be any control of religion by the laity, because they had no real Parliament to speak for them, and in the days of Mary Stuart they could not trust the Crown as contemporary Englishmen trusted Elizabeth. The Scottish nobles had indeed helped to overthrow the old religion ; but the new religion had been fashioned, not from outside by the Crown or nobles, but from inside the Church by a democracy of ministers and laymen.

It was natural, therefore, that the English, whether Royalists or Parliamentarians, Anglicans or Puritans, should be Erastian in the sense that they wished the State to control the Church. It was equally natural that the Scottish Presbyterian party wished the Church to control the State. In these circumstances neither the Stuart Kings nor their enemies ever succeeded in imposing a uniform religious settlement on the whole island.

In those days, when the idea and practice of representation were still at an early stage of development, the English were most nearly represented by their ancient Parliament, and the Scots by their novel Church. But this difference of the position at the two ends of the island was not understood by the rulers of Britain. James I, having been brought up in Scotland, had supposed that the English Parliament, like the Scottish, existed to obey the Privy Council. His son Charles, having been brought up in England, made the corresponding error of supposing that the Scottish Church could, like the English, be moulded by royal command. Confident in the power he had recently assumed as autocratic ruler of England, and knowing that the Parliament of Edinburgh was of no account, he deceived himself into supposing that he could act as absolute monarch in Scotland, even in matters of religion. His attempt to impose Laud's English Prayer Book on the Scottish Church at the very moment when he was trying to get rid of the English Parliament, outraged both nations at once, each at the point where it was strongest and most susceptible, and broke his power in both Kingdoms. **1637– 1640.**

The revolt against Charles and Laud north of the Tweed took

the form of a religious Covenant, and of action by the Church Assembly ; the nation had to be organized on an ecclesiastical basis, because organs of political life were lacking in Scotland. This state of things naturally tempted the Church, after she had liberated the country from a foreign yoke, to claim practical control of the State and to show a most ugly temper of interference and intolerance.   This in turn enabled Charles I and Charles II after him to rally the Scottish Cavalier party, in the days of Montrose and of Claverhouse, to resist the tyranny of religion. Against it the Cavaliers of the Restoration erected the tyranny of the Privy Council.   The terrible feuds of the Scottish factions went on with many vicissitudes, till the Revolution settlement of 1689 established Presbyterianism as the national religion, but made it the subordinate partner of the State.

In Stuart England, where the Church never aspired to independence of the State, the religious quarrel lay between Crown and Parliament.   One part of the English people demanded, through Parliament, to have the Church made purely Protestant in its services, and more representative of the laity in its internal structure.   The Crown resisted this demand, backed by another part of the nation zealous for the Prayer Book, though by no means for the whole of Laud's politico-ecclesiastical system. This situation forced to the front a question that men had begun to ask themselves under Elizabeth : if Crown and Parliament disagreed, which had the right to remodel the Church of England ? That was one issue fought out in the English Civil War.   The other was the purely political question—is Crown or Parliament to nominate the executive and control the armed force ?   In practice the two issues were inseparable ; to take a side on one involved taking the corresponding side on the other.

The Scottish revolt of 1638–40 began the British Revolution. Until the Scots had successfully defied Charles, in arms upon their own Border, there had been no signs of resistance in England, though many of discontent.   For Stuart England had no centres of opposition except Parliament, which was in abeyance.   English feudalism was dead and buried.   Harry Percy's spur was cold. The squires as a class were the most peaceful and law-abiding of men,—agriculturists, sportsmen, sometimes lawyers, but very seldom soldiers.   The King, it is true, had no army to enforce his will, but the habit of obedience to the Crown was the great inheritance from the Tudor age.   It had been the custom in mediæval England for districts or persons with a grievance against government to rise in arms, but that tradition had not survived the reign of Elizabeth.   If, therefore, the modern

English were deprived of Parliament, they would be slaves to absolute power as their ancestors had never been before.

Scotland supplied what England no longer possessed, a rough and hardy population, accustomed to take up arms in their own defence. The two nations were the complement one of the other. The Scots could boast of no independent political institutions, no habit of obedience to good laws ; the English had so long enjoyed peace under Parliament and the Common Law that they were slow to defend their privileges with the sword. England was neither feudal nor democratic ; the fighting spirit of Scotland was composed of both those elements, formidably interfused.

Until very recent times every burgher and peasant in Scotland had possessed weapons which he was accustomed to employ in racial war or private broil, and along the Highland Line these habits still prevailed. Everywhere the nobles and leading gentry of Scotland, like those of England in the Wars of the Roses, still had retainers and tenants accustomed to follow them to war. In 1638 these feudal chiefs stood for the Kirk against the Crown. They had been alienated by Laud, under whose influence nobles had been superseded by Bishops on the Scottish Privy Council, and lay possessors of former Church lands had been threatened with resumption. Moreover, the nobles were true Scots, and the young Montrose himself took a leading part in armed resistance to the English-hearted King and his Prayer Book.

When Parliament was not sitting, the English were like sheep without a shepherd, but in Scotland the Church supplied a ready-made organization for political activity in every parish. It was the people themselves who had made the original Reformation by the strong hand, and it was all in the national tradition to defend it now by the same means. The Covenant with God was renewed in 1638 and embraced all ranks from highest to lowest. In every parish men signed it, weeping and lifting their right hands to heaven. When the Scots display emotion, something real is astir within them. Indeed the country had not been so moved since the days of Wallace and Bruce.

The Church Assembly at Glasgow, to which the lay members 1638. came up armed and attended, defied the King as the Long Parliament in England defied him four years later. When he dissolved the Assembly, it sat on, declared Episcopacy abolished and restored the full Presbyterian government of the Church. The action of the Glasgow Assembly was supported by the Earl of Argyle, the head of the Campbells, the most powerful fighting clan in the Highlands. That day he began the connection of his House with the Presbyterian and popular cause in the Lowlands, an alliance which for more than a century to come remained a constant and often a determining factor in Scottish history. Thenceforth till the time of Culloden the clans hostile to the Campbells gravitated for that reason towards the party of the Stuart Kings.

Not the least of the causes that wrought Charles' downfall was this : Scotland, still as poor as a thin soil and mediæval methods of agriculture could make her, and still without any considerable trade either with England or across the sea, sent forth in those days her most adventurous sons to serve abroad, not then as cashiers and foremen throughout a far-flung British Empire, but as captains and ancients in the armies of Gustavus Adolphus and other Protestant champions on the continent. These men came swarming home, eager to employ their professional skill in saving their native land from English outrage. Their leader was ' that old, little, crooked soldier,' Alexander Leslie. He and they speedily put a face of disciplined war on the enthusiasm of the Scots, and camped them advantageously on Dunse Law, ready to dispute against Charles the passage of the Tweed.

1639.

The England of the pacific James and his son had bred few ' men of war ' : Englishmen lived at home on the fat of the land, or traded oversea, or emigrated to America. There was no nucleus of a standing army, and failure attended the belated efforts of Charles and Strafford to improvise, without money and from a disaffected and unwarlike people, a force to match the army of the Covenant.

Wentworth, who was at length made Earl of Strafford, had been called over to England to be his master's right-hand man at this crisis. But he did not cease to act as ruler of Ireland, where he continued to harry the Scots of Ulster with persecution to enforce on them the ' Black Oath ' of passive obedience unknown to the law. At the same time he raised regiments of Celtic Irish to coerce the King's disobedient subjects in either island, the first of a series of Roman Catholic armies whose threatening shadow from oversea so often prejudiced the cause of the House of Stuart, without ever striking a formidable blow for it in Britain.

As yet the general temper of England had found no means of expression. Strafford guessed it wrongly. He advised Charles to summon Parliament, in the hope that it would tamely provide the money to subdue Scotland. The ' Short Parliament,' however, revealed the unanimity of English discontent, and was peremptorily dismissed, but not before Pym had spoken on the floor of the House the memorable words : ' The powers of Parliament are to the body politic as the rational faculties of the soul to man.'

Ap. 13–
May 5,
1640.

For a few months longer, Strafford, though suffering from untimely illness, strove single-handed to make the system of autocracy function again. But its wheels were clogged and would no longer revolve. The recent Parliament, though it had come and gone in a breath, had lifted a curtain, and henceforth the nation knew its collective mind and strength. Strafford's desperate efforts to gather round him some reliable regiments in his own Yorkshire, were countered by the army of the Covenant which crossed the Tweed,—Montrose the foremost horseman on the English shore—and occupied Northumberland and Dur- Aug.1640. ham. There the Scots cannily sat down, demanding as the price of evacuation not only their own terms but money ; for money, as they knew, was a commodity which Charles could obtain only if he submitted to a new English Parliament, certain to be more angry and more formidable than the last.

The Short Parliament had been summoned to vote taxes to fight the Scots ; the Long Parliament was called to buy them out of the country. But redress of grievances would certainly have Nov. to precede supply, and in the autumn of 1640 redress of grievances 1640. meant a revolution of undefined scope in Church and State.

The Long Parliament was not destined to prove, as half its members hoped, a turning-point in English religion comparable to the Tudor Reformation, though it did clear the way for the great incident in English religious history—the Puritan Revolution, the parent of the Free Churches of later times. On the other hand, the Long Parliament is the true turning-point in the political history of the English-speaking races. It not only prevented the English monarchy from hardening into an absolutism of the type then becoming general in Europe, but it made a great experiment in direct rule of the country and of the Empire by the House of Commons. In the course of that experiment the Long Parliament successfully organized the largest military operations ever till then conducted by Englishmen, in a four years' war against the King. After the victory it failed to make a permanent settlement at home, but it made England feared and honoured abroad. After all those memorable years, the House of Stuart might be restored, but it would never again be possible to govern the country without the participation of the House of Commons.

In all the actions of the Long Parliament it was the Commons who led, and the Lords who followed with ever-growing reluctance. We have then to ask, how did a debating assembly, which under the Tudors had passed the Bills drawn up by Privy Councillors of the Crown, and since Elizabeth's death had acted only as an opposition,—how did an assembly so numerous, so plebeian and so inexperienced succeed in taking hold of the helm of State and riding the most terrible storm in English history ?

One reason why the House of Commons was able to assume the government of the country has, until recently, attracted less attention than its importance deserves. The late Tudor and early Stuart Parliaments had made great progress in forms of procedure, especially by developing the Committee system. In 1640 the Lower House was no mere debating society, but an elaborately organized business body of the modern type, capable of conducting affairs as no mediæval House of Commons could possibly have done. For forty years past, Parliaments had no longer been content to have their work prepared for them by Privy Councillors, but had thrashed out subjects for themselves in committee, and so learnt to produce practical Bills and policies of their own.[1]

In the second place the Long Parliament had at its doors an enthusiastic ally, London, already the first city in the world, surpassing any other English town many times over in wealth, population and mental activity. It was in the London of these eventful years that Milton, the greatest of Londoners born, had his vision of England as ' an eagle mewing her mighty youth,' as ' a noble and puissant nation rousing herself like a strong man after sleep and shaking her invincible locks.' London was the nursery of almost every movement of that time, in whatever part of the country it had first seen light ; and ' correspondency with London ' was alleged as the reason why the Roundhead party dominated most of the boroughs of England during the Civil War. Some may think that the effervescence of London's wit and passion drew Parliament down strange and questionable courses, but none can deny that the protection which it gave to the Houses was faithful and effective.

And, lastly, there were upon the benches in 1640 members of old experience, who had sat with Eliot and Coke in committee and debate, some of whom chanced to be men of high ability, character and courage. Pym, perhaps the strongest Parliamentary leader in history, and Hampden, the best-beloved in that choice assembly of England's best, backed by members of the type and temper of Strode and Cromwell, were not afraid to seize

---

[1] The distinguished American Historian, Professor Notestein, who has made this subject his own, writes (*Journal of Sir S. D'Ewes*, 1923, Introduction) : ' It can hardly be said too often that the pre-Elizabethan House of Commons was a somewhat rudimentary body, and that the Long Parliament was in many ways a complex modern organization. A knight of the shire in 1558 who stepped into a mediæval Commons probably would not have felt much out of place, but a Commoner of 1640 would ; he would be more at home at Westminster to-day. It was in the years between that the enormous growth took place,— the rapid extension of Committees and of the work of Committees ; the hitting upon and utilization of that wonderful device, the Committee of the Whole,' etc.

and wield the power of the State. The time for mere criticism had passed, and the insufficiency of Charles' signature to Statutes had been proved. Since the struggle now was for power, these men did not shrink from evoking mob passion and armed force to protect what they did from the royal reaction which had destroyed the work of every previous Stuart Parliament.

During the first session of the Long Parliament, Pym and Hampden worked in alliance with Hyde and Falkland, a couple not unlike to themselves in ability, character and destiny. It is hard to say which pair of friends had in the end the most influence on the evolution of modern Britain. The 'constitutional Cavaliers' of 1642 were in 1640 as determined as the future Roundheads to bring about the fall of Strafford, and to abolish the Star Chamber, the High Commission and the whole Prerogative system. All were opposed to Laud, who was committed to the Tower after impeachment by the unanimous vote of the Lower House, but members were early made aware of differences among themselves on religion, and were glad to postpone the settlement of the Church till the State had first been made safe.

Nov.
1640–
Aug.1641

The work of this session, so far as it extended, was built upon the rock. It was never undone, for it was work of Puritans and moderate Episcopalians, of Roundheads and constitutional Cavaliers acting in union. It registered the great irreversible victory of 'Sir Edward Coke and his Year-Books' over Strafford and the Prerogative courts. The Star Chamber, the High Commission, the prerogative jurisdiction of the Councils of Wales and of the North were abolished by Statute, and the illegality of Ship Money and Tonnage and Poundage without Parliamentary sanction was declared beyond all cavil. Thus was the Crown put back, to use Strafford's phrase, into 'wardship' to the Common Law, and made dependent on, though not necessarily subordinate to, Parliament. The first session struck an exact balance of the constitution, the same which was restored in 1660 by Hyde, the great Common Lawyer, who believed in a precise counterpoise of Crown and Parliament. Pym, on the other hand, believed that the essential power must pass on to Parliament, or mere confusion would prevail.

The other work of the first session was the trial, attainder and execution of Strafford. In that high tragedy, unsurpassed for historical and human interest in the political annals of any time or land, Falkland and many of the future Cavaliers acted in union with Hampden and Pym. They held it necessary that the man should die who might yet, by his vigour and genius, restore the despotic powers of the Crown. Already the King was engaged in the Army Plot to rescue Strafford and dissolve Parliament. The first thing to be expected, if Strafford lived, was that as soon as Parliament was up, Charles would let him out of prison and restore him to office. So argued the Earl of Essex, typical of many members of the Upper House who feared a restoration of Strafford's insolent personal hegemony over the nobles of the land ; the Earl's conclusion was that ' stone dead hath no fellow.' It was not a policy of mean revenge, like that which four years later sent Laud to the scaffold. Strafford's enemies were in deadly earnest, because while he lived they and all they strove for were in jeopardy. They did not scruple at the last to allow mob violence to extort Charles' signature to the Act of Attainder by which his great servant perished.

With the Act of Attainder against Strafford, the King passed another Bill which forbade the dissolution of the existing Parliament without its own consent. These two measures, the first of them the bitterest humiliation of Charles' life, seemed to make the position of Parliament secure. And so it would have been, but for the religious difference which in the second session split into two hostile parties the hitherto solid phalanx of the constitutionalists. In the Commons the Puritans won, by small majorities, divisions in favour of the Root and Branch Bill abolishing episcopacy, and the Grand Remonstrance. The Grand Remonstrance demanded that the King's Councillors should be persons trusted by Parliament, and that there should be a Parliamentary reformation of the Church, on what may be described as Erastian-Presbyterian principles. It is easy now to see that the times required a compromise on religion, and that England had outgrown any orthodox strait-waistcoat which could be devised by either party. Unfortunately, it was not clear then, and no serious effort was made by Puritan or Anglican either for comprehension within, or for toleration without, the borders of the Church. Moderate episcopalians devoted to the Prayer Book, like Falkland and Hyde, saw no way of defending their religion but to go into complete opposition to Hampden and Pym.

The religious question decided the attitude of many towards the command of the armed forces of the Kingdom—the other great problem of the second session. Was King or Parliament to control the militia of the towns and shires, and the regular army which must forthwith be raised to suppress the rebellion in Ireland ? For the Catholics there had risen to recover their lands ; the Ulster plantation and the whole English interest were in the direst jeopardy, and some thousands of Protestants had perished. Law and custom assigned the command of the armed forces to the King. But if Charles had the power of the sword and Parliament had not, how much longer would he respect the concessions he had recently made ? He himself answered the question by his rash and illegal attempt to arrest Pym, Hampden, Hazlerigg, Holles and Strode on the floor of the House of Commons, which might well have been stained with blood that day by the bravoes Charles had brought with him to ' pull them out by the ears,' had not the Five Members received warning and been carried by boat from Parliament stairs to the safe shelter of the City and its trainbands.

Jan. 4, 1642.

Charles fled to the North, leaving London and Westminster to be the focus of his enemies' power and authority. Civil war was certain, and men began to choose their side, some with enthusiasm, many with dubious sighs and searchings of heart, while the majority manifested a strong desire to remain neutral if they possibly could.

Lovers of the Prayer Book for the most part remained neutral or drew sword for the King. After the disastrous fiasco of the Five Members, Charles, for the six months before the fighting began, put his case into the wise and constitutional hands of lawyer Hyde, who issued manifestos of a moderate and legal character. This and the high-handed proceedings of Pym in preparation for war won the King many friends among his late opponents ; but others reflected that Charles' word was of no value, and that the moment the sword was drawn it was in the nature of war that the control of his party should pass from Hyde and the lawyers to the swordsmen and friends of despotic power, from Falkland and the moderate Episcopalians to the High Laudian and Romanist devotees. Falkland sought death in battle for the King, because he could not bear to witness either his triumph or his defeat. Among the Roundheads also were many who lived to rue the victory of their cause. Moderates may well be loath to begin wars, for it is always extremists who end them.

Jan.- Aug. 1642.

Was it then impossible for Parliamentary power to take root in England at a less cost than this national schism and appeal to force, which, in spite of many magnificent incidents, left England humanly so much the poorer and less noble in twenty years time ? It is a question which no depth of research or speculation can resolve. Men were what they were, uninfluenced by the belated wisdom of posterity, and thus they acted. Whether or not any better way could have led to the same end, it was by the sword that Parliament actually won the right to survive as the dominant force in the English constitution.[1]

[1] In the final division of opinion on the resort to arms, the Roundhead majority in the Commons was very much larger than it had been for the Grand Remonstrance. Professor Firth calculates that in the war, 300 of the Lower House were for Parliament and 175 for the King, although only thirty Peers supported Parliament and eighty the King. Of the shire members the very great majority stood by the Parliament against the King.

CHAPTER III

The Great Civil War, 1642–1646

ALTHOUGH there were sots and swaggerers enough in the King's armies, and hypocrites and fanatics enough among those of Parliament, and plain self-seekers in both camps, nevertheless upon the whole the Cavalier, with his unselfish loyalty and careless valour, the Roundhead, with his self-discipline and steady zeal for the public cause, present a favourable contrast to the emigrant noble and the Jacobin of the French Revolution. For the English Civil War was not the collapse of an out-worn society in a chaos of class hatred and greed, but a contest for political and religious ideals that divided every rank in a land socially sound and economically prosperous.

The causes of the war were not economic, and were only indirectly social. Nevertheless the older aristocratic connection was apt to favour the King, while the world that had arisen since the Reformation was apt to favour the Parliament. The new world was centred at London, while the old was strongest in North and West at the greatest distance from the orbit of the capital.

In every shire the landlords were the leaders on both sides when the war began. The majority of the nobles fought for the King ; but a body claiming to be the House of Lords still sat at Westminster to make Pym's Parliament complete, and noblemen like the Earls of Essex and Manchester, and Lord Brooke, commanded the earlier Roundhead armies. The great strength of the royal party lay in the more rustic squires of ancient lineage, who had least connection with the mercantile community, while Parliament usually received the allegiance of squires more closely connected with the world of business—some of them recently risen into the landlord class and still twitted with their plebeian origin. The towns were predominantly Roundhead, especially those connected with the sea or the cloth trade. Most cathedral and some market towns were Cavalier. The tenant farmers followed their landlords into either camp. The agricultural labourer or cottager was for all effective purposes a neutral, except when he was pressed or bought to trail a pike or carry a musket in the ' poor foot.' The freehold yeomen supplied the best and most zealous fighting stuff in the ranks of both parties, particularly in Cromwell's regiments of East Anglian horse.

The North and West were strongest for the King, except the Puritan clothing districts and seaports. Before the time of Wesley, ' the Celtic fringe ' was untouched by Puritan ideals ; so

Charles drew his best infantry from the loyal Cornish volunteers, and filled up many of his other regiments of foot from the sturdy poverty of the Welsh hills. The South and East were firmly secured for Parliament, owing to the strength of London's arm in the Home Counties, and the activity of Oliver Cromwell in the Eastern Association of which Cambridge was the centre. But in every shire and town of the land there were two parties, and many local wars were waged more or less independent of the central campaigns. A single energetic man often determined the allegiance of a whole district, for the neutrals were many and the would-be neutrals more. Under their influence ' county treaties ' were sometimes made to exclude the war from a given area, but the rising tide soon swept down these frail barriers of peace.

All the Roman Catholics were for the King, and more particularly for the Queen, who was the real head of their party. They were strong in the Northern counties and in Lancashire, where the local civil war between feudal Catholicism and the Puritanism of the clothing districts was exceptionally bitter. Since the fines prescribed in the penal laws had been suspended during the personal rule of Charles I, the old Catholic gentry and nobles were able to pour their accumulated wealth into his empty war-chest. The Earl of Worcester, enjoying a princely rent-roll of £24,000 a year, saved the King from financial ruin in 1642 by a generosity no less princely. His castle of Raglan and the Marquis of Winchester's Basing House were strongholds of Romanism and Royalism in the war, and their fall was long delayed and widely celebrated. The Roman Catholic body was destined to suffer more serious and permanent injury in the coming strife than any other section of the community.

In the end the King lost the war for lack of money. The parts of England that owned his authority were on the average less wealthy than those which defied him. His headquarters were in Oxford, a small city more famous for learning than for wealth, a poor substitute for London left in the hands of his enemies. The rustic gentlemen who offered him their lives, their swords, their horses and their plate, could not easily realize their land until it came under the hammer within the Roundhead lines as sequestrated property. And if Charles got freewill offerings, so did Parliament. For Puritan squires and shopkeepers also had silver plate in abundance, and

> Into pikes and musqueteers
> Stampt beakers, cups and porringers.

Parliament, no less than the King, would call on gentlemen to raise private regiments, like Hampden's Green Coats. In these appeals to individual generosity the two sides were on equal terms, and that was how the war was begun. But the Roundheads had more staying power because they could do what the King could not—negotiate loans in the City, and place regular taxes on the trade of England and on its richest districts. To pay for the Civil War, the Long Parliament introduced excise duties on goods, and an improved assessment for taxes on land and property, far more profitable to the public and far less unjust as between individuals than the happy-go-lucky assessment for the old ' subsidy.' In the ordinances of the Long Parliament we find the germ of our modern fiscal system. The resources of England, which had been grudgingly doled out to Elizabeth and denied to James and Charles, were first exploited by Parliament in the war fought upon its own behalf.

The sea was held by the King's enemies. The Royal Navy revolted to ' King Pym.' The seaports made a present to Parliament of the mercantile marine. The overseas trade of England was carried on to increase the wealth of rebels, while Charles had difficulty even in importing arms from abroad. The excise levied by Parliament was largely paid for by the higher prices which upland Cavaliers had to find for articles that had been taxed in Roundhead manufacturing centres and seaports.

If Parliament could at once have translated these financial advantages into military terms, the war would not have lasted long, and would have been won by the original Parliamentary party under Pym, Hampden and Essex, without any need on their part to purchase the embarrassing help either of Covenanted Scots or of East Anglian Sectaries. In that case the history of England would have taken some totally different course. But it was not to be. The Cavaliers, though starting at a great disadvantage, rapidly improved their position, until by the end of 1643 they had conquered the South-West and solidified their position north of the Humber.

The King's generals won these early successes because they had ready to their hand human material that could be very quickly manufactured into good soldiers. In that most civilian of societies neither side had any trained force at the outset, for the militia could scarcely count as such. But the hard-riding squires and their huntsmen and grooms only wanted a soldier to teach them how to charge home as cavalry. And there was a lad of twenty-two, the King's nephew Rupert, who had actually seen a campaign in Germany and whose spirit burned like a fire. He saved his uncle from desperate straits in 1642 by making for him a body of horse that none of the Parliament side as yet could resist.

Rupert, in one of the first of his many quarrels with his brother generals, insisted that the Royalist cavalry should fight at Edge- hill in line three deep, after the Swedish fashion, and charge home with the steel, instead of lumbering slowly up in column six deep after the old Dutch fashion and halting to fire off their pistols. The more spirited modern tactics of the Swedes were soon adopted in both armies, notably by Cromwell's Ironsides.

Oct. 1642.

The infantry, however, continued to fight in masses six deep,

"Forlorne hope of musquettiers"

CAVALRY   MUSKETEERS   PIKES   MUSKETEERS   CANNON   MUSKETEERS   PIKES   MUSKETEERS   CANNON   MUSKETEERS   PIKES   MUSKETEERS   CAVALRY

INFANTRY RESERVE

WAGON-TRAIN, GUARDED BY MUSKETEERS

Note: *The general idea of this formation is based on the well known map-picture of Naseby in Sprigge's* Anglia Rediviva, *1647. The precise depth of the columns-six lines for the foot, and three for the horse-is derived from Firth's* Cromwell's Army *pp. 95-0, 131-3.*

MAP XXIII.—An Army in Battle Array : Great Civil War

occasionally reduced to three for the purpose of attacking a position. The pikes were in the centre, the musketeers on the two flanks. When 'the shot' had delivered their fire, they clubbed their muskets and closed in, 'the strongest soldiers and officers clubbing down' the enemy. But the struggle at close quarters was mainly decided 'at push of pike.' In rough or enclosed ground, indeed, well-led musketeers were more valuable than pikemen, and infantry than cavalry. But in the open, since bayonets had not yet been invented, an attack on the flank by cavalry was fatal to the musketeers, and often to the whole regiment if it was engaged on its front against other infantry and had no leisure to re-form and shelter its 'shot' under the protection of the long extended pikes. On some battlefields, like Lansdowne or Newbury, and in the later wars Preston or Worcester, hedges or woodland gave protection and scope to the activities of the foot, but much of the landscape of the North-East and Midlands of that day was open heath or unenclosed field. On Marston Moor and the gently undulating lands of Naseby, the infantry were exposed to cavalry attack as they would not have been in the woodlands that encumbered those sites in primæval times, or amid the hedges that line and traverse them to-day.

For these reasons the decisive battles of the war were won by cavalry. The man who led the best cavalry, like Rupert in 1642–3, and Cromwell in 1644–5—at least if, like Cromwell, he had also a general's eye for the course of the battle as a whole—that man would make his side master of England.[1]

In 1643 the Royalists had not only the best cavalry upon the average, but the best single body of infantry in Hopton's astonishing Cornishmen. With these advantages they overran the whole South-Western quarter of England, destroying one after another the small, ill-disciplined armies, privately or locally raised, which then represented the Roundhead cause.[2]

The Parliamentary generals wandered aimlessly about with no objective, and were cut up in detail. The Cavalier chiefs began to conceive a large strategic plan to end the war by a triple advance on London from Yorkshire, the Thames Valley, and the South-West at once. Hopton's advance on London from the South-West was to unmuzzle the suppressed Royalists of Kent upon its way. It was a hopeful plan. But it foundered on the irregular and local character of the Royal armies : the men of Cornwall and Devon were not well-paid, long-service regulars, but volunteers who were unwilling to remain indefinitely away from their work and homes, the more so as Plymouth was still held from the sea by Parliament, threatening their own county in their rear. Bristol indeed had been taken, but Gloucester and Taunton, centres of the Puritan clothing industry, still held out. It became apparent that before London could be attacked, these places must first be reduced. Close siege was laid to Gloucester, but the London 'prentice train-

---

[1] Cannon were used in the field, but decided no important battle except the peculiar battle of Langport in 1645. But once the King's armies were broken in the field, the siege train of the New Model, a fruit of Parliamentary taxation, made short work of his garrisoned towns, castles and manors, and speedily finished the war.

[2] The various bodies composing the Cavalier armies were of a no less private character than the Roundhead regiments, though at first combined under better generalship. 'The honest country gentleman,' says a Royalist playwright, ' raises the troop at his own charge, then he gets a Low-Country lieutenant to fight his troop for him, and then sends his son from school to be cornet.'

bands marched across England and relieved it, their masters being willing that work should go slow for two months while the stronghold of the ' good old cause ' in the West was being saved.

Clearly a war waged on these terms could be won by the side that should first create a long-service army with regular pay and discipline. The King had not the money to do this. Parliament had the money if it had the wit.

Meanwhile in the North the advance from Yorkshire on London was stopped, partly by the resistance of the seaport of Hull, corresponding to Plymouth in the South-West, partly by the greater solidity of Roundhead civil and military organization in the counties of the Eastern Association, where Puritanism was strongest and had found its ideal leader.

Oliver Cromwell was the Puritan type of squire, farming his land himself, closely connected with the middle and lower classes of town and country in business transactions and in local politics. As champion of the common rights of small peasants and fishermen in the matter of fen-draining, he had won the first place in the affections of his own countryside before ever the Long Parliament met. He had fought at Edgehill, and had there noted, as he told his cousin Hampden, the superiority of the high-spirited Cavalier horse over the ' old decayed serving men and tapsters ' opposed to them. Returning to East Anglia he set himself to raise, among the yeomen and small freeholding classes whom he knew and by whom he was known, well-mounted regiments of cuirassiers whom he taught to combine a strict military discipline with their religious zeal. They were ' of greater understanding than common soldiers, making not money but that which they took for public felicity to be their end.' From the first they were marked by a democratic tone on social and political questions and unorthodoxy in the forms of their Puritan faith. At this period Cromwell wrote :

I had rather have a plain russet-coated captain that knows what he fights for and loves what he knows, than what you call ' a gentleman ' and is nothing else. I honour a gentleman that is so indeed. It may be it provokes some spirits to see such plain men made captains of horse. But seeing it was necessary the work should go on, better plain men than none.

These East Anglian regiments, who began a new era in English war and politics, became best known to the world by the nickname of ' Ironsides,' which had first been applied to their leader in person. They were the real origin of the New Model and of all the later Cromwellian armies. Their first important service was to check the half-hearted advance of the northern Cavaliers

through Lincolnshire, at Gainsborough and Winceby fights, and
in doing so to get into touch with Sir Thomas Fairfax, who was
still upholding the Roundhead cause north of Humber from the
sea-base of Hull.

But it was not enough that the Cavalier advance on London
had been checked. The country was weary of the war, and a
strong party even in the Capital was clamouring for peace by
' an accommodation with His Majesty,' not very different from
surrender. In these straits Pym's last act of statesmanship was
to negotiate an alliance with the Scots. After the satisfaction of
their national demands, they had withdrawn their army to their
own side of the Tweed in August 1641. They now undertook to
send it back into England as the ally of Parliament. In return
they demanded the reformation of the English Church upon the
Scottish model.

The Parliament men could not accede to the demand in its
entirety, for although they desired to abolish Bishops and the
Prayer Book, and to introduce some lay element into the ecclesiastical organization, they were, like all Englishmen, jealous
guardians of the supremacy of the State over the Church. There
was the further difficulty that the Scots and their English partisans demanded the persecution of all unorthodox Puritan sects,
even while the war against the Prelatists was still unwon. Only
so, it was held by many, could they look for God's blessing on
their arms.

Now popular Puritanism in England, during this period of
its most rapid expansion, was markedly unorthodox, full of fresh
individual vigour and variety, and breeding a hundred different
forms of doctrine and practice. The great religious ferment of
English humble folk which laid its strong hold on young George
Fox and John Bunyan, taught men to think that—

New Presbyter is but Old Priest writ large.

Honourable members at Westminster would not indeed have
thought twice about clapping into gaol all tinkers and shoemakers
who took to prophesying, whether or not they were afterwards
going to produce *Pilgrim's Progress* and the Society of Friends ;
but it was a more serious matter that the best English soldiers of
all ranks from Cromwell downwards were the most rebellious
against orthodoxy. ' Steeple Houses ' and ' hireling ministers '
were coming in for hard words from the hardest fighters. In
half the regiments and on half the local committees that upheld
the authority of Parliament, Independents were bearding Presbyterians, and Presbyterians were demanding the dismissal of
Independents. For the Independents wanted a Church made up

of free, self-governing congregations, not under the scrutiny of any general organization bound to enforce orthodox opinion and practice.

This quarrel in face of the enemy almost ensured the triumph of the King's armies. However, in the autumn of 1643 the Scots were for the moment satisfied by Parliament itself taking the Covenant, and by vague promises of ' a thorough reformation ' of the English Church ' according to the example of the best reformed Churches,' but also, as was inserted by way of safeguard, ' according to the word of God.' On these somewhat equivocal terms Pym purchased the aid of the Scottish arms, and died in December.

Next year the policy of the dead statesman bore fruit in the victory on Marston Moor. The three united armies of Cromwell's July 2, East Anglians, Fairfax's Yorkshire Puritans, and the Scots under 1644. Alexander and David Leslie, twenty-seven thousand in all, destroyed the forces of the northern Cavaliers joined to those of Rupert, numbering together eighteen thousand. It was by far the largest battle in the war. Rupert in person and his best troops of horse, hitherto unmatched, yielded before the impact of the Ironsides. At a blow the whole of Northern England was subjected to the Roundhead power.

Marston Moor was set off by the capitulation of Essex and all Sept. 2, his infantry at Lostwithiel in Cornwall, whither he had rashly 1644. and aimlessly penetrated. Instead of trying to destroy the royal forces, he had sought prematurely to overrun the royal territories, with fatal results. This disaster cleared the way for the rise of Cromwell. The older type of general, high in social rank, moderate in politics, and orthodox in religion, which had served Parliament well to begin the war, suffered at Lostwithiel an irremediable loss of prestige. The sectaries and ' russet-coated captains ' who had reaped the bloody harvest on Marston Moor stood proportionately higher in the minds of the Parliament men. If it was a question of God's blessing, the sectaries seemed to have had the larger share of it that year.

The war was decided by the statesmanlike decisions of the House of Commons in the winter of 1644–5. The development of the Roundhead armies into the most perfect military weapon of the age was curiously involved in the quarrel of Presbyterian and Baptist over religious conformity. Parliament had to deal with the two problems together. Few members sympathized with the sectaries, and many were bitter against them as turbulent and dangerous fellows ; but, on the other hand, the House had no wish to subject the English Parliament to the Scots Kirk, and the English squires to inquisitorial boards of elders and clergy.

Of the two impending evils they chose, for the time being, the one that gave promise of immediate success in the field, although some honourable members intended to cheat the Independents of ' the liberty they fought for,' after they had safely won the war for their masters—a game that proved as dangerous as it was dishonest.

For the present, at least, the Houses supported Cromwell against his rival, the Presbyterian Earl of Manchester, because the sectary was the better soldier. By the Self-denying Ordinance they obtained the resignations of all officers who were members of either House, but the right of reappointment was reserved. When the decks had thus been cleared of every encumbrance, they chose Fairfax as their Captain-General; he added to his high military qualifications a politic indifference between Presbyterianism and the Sects. Finally they appointed Cromwell as his lieutenant, with charge of all the horse. His Ironsides constituted half the cavalry of the New Model. The position of Independents and Baptists was now safe, for just so long as the war lasted.

The ' New Model' Army which Fairfax and Cromwell were to command was a regular force, enlisted in the direct service of Parliament, and more regularly fed and rather less irregularly paid than any army on either side had yet been; it was therefore possible to enforce a proportionately stricter discipline. The good conduct which enabled the ' Saints' speedily to finish the war was due to their food and pay as well as to their religion. The Houses had now a better instrument than private regiments and local levies, badly provided for by paymaster and commissariat, and fending for themselves by plunder. For Parliament had the power of the purse and had at last learnt how to use it.[1]

On the other hand, the plundering habits of the Royalists were worse in 1645 than in 1642, in proportion as the King was more desperately bankrupt. Discipline had indeed at no time been the strong point of the gallant Cavaliers. Their commanders quarrelled with one another less often on questions of religion and politics than on points of precedence and personal rivalry. The old spirit of chivalry, the independence of each knight working counter to all regular command, was the bane of the royal armies from first to last. The common Cavalier, brave in battle, but drinking and gambling between whiles, prided himself on his

---

[1] It is true that in 1646 the pay of the New Model began to fall gravely into arrears, but the pay in 1645 must have been fairly regular; between March 1645 and March 1647 Fairfax's men actually received £1,185,551. See Firth's *Cromwell's Army*, 183–4, 202–3.

unlikeness to the precisians and psalm-singers of the rebel camp.
And as his chiefs for want of money left him more and more to
starve, he supported himself more and more by the plunder of the
countryside.   Finally even the most loyal districts of the South-
West were glad to see the back of Goring and his like, and
brought in the produce of their farms to the New Model camp
for money down.

The King's best servant saw and noted it all :

> Those under the King's commanders (wrote Clarendon) grew
> insensibly into all the licence, disorder and impiety with which they
> had reproached the rebels ;   and they again into great discipline,
> diligence and sobriety ;   which begat courage and resolution in them,
> and notable dexterity in achievements and enterprises.   Insomuch as
> one side seemed to fight for monarchy with the weapons of confusion,
> and the other to destroy the King and government with all the
> principles and regularity of monarchy.

It was indeed the task of the Long Parliament to prove that
'government' can be even more effectual when it is collective
than when it is personal.   And in the summer of 1645 that
proposition was proved up to the hilt.

Fairfax, unlike Essex before him, had for his military objective
the destruction of the King's army in the field.   At Naseby he
found it and broke it to pieces, thanks to Cromwell and his horse.
After that the moral of the remaining Cavalier armies rapidly
degenerated, while the country turned with gratitude or resignation to the side that would give it peace.   The well-provided
artillery train of the New Model Army, and the zeal and skill of
the storming tactics of its infantry, reduced with astonishing
speed the numerous garrisons of the King, scattered wide over
the West in castle, manor-house and walled town.   Twelve
months after Naseby, the capitulation of Oxford marked the
practical termination of the Great Civil War.   From Land's End
to Berwick the word of Parliament was law.

The progress of these mighty operations had not been
effectively disturbed by Montrose's romantic diversion.   Riding
from the King's camp to Scotland disguised as a groom, he was a
few weeks later sweeping victorious over the Lowlands at the
head of a few thousand Highland swordsmen.   As a general he
was Cromwell's only rival, but it was his destiny to command
brave but uncivilized tribes, who slunk back after their victories
to store their plunder in their native glens, leaving him with a
remnant to be trampled to ruin by the charge of David Leslie's
cavalry at Philiphaugh.   Of Montrose's great enterprise, which
was to have broken the secular power of the Kirk in Scotland,

June 14,
1645.

June 24,
1646.

Aug.
1644.

Sept. 13,
1645.

nothing remained except the memory, very bitter to Lowland Scots of that day, but very dear to their descendants as a point in the common national pride that has united Highlander and Lowlander ever since the days of Sir Walter Scott.

CHAPTER IV

The Failure to reach a Settlement. Regicide. The Revolutionary Govern-ments. Ireland and Scotland. Blake and the Revival of the Navy. Domestic, Ecclesiastical and Foreign Policy of the Protectorate. The Death of Oliver and the Restoration

THE victory of the Roundheads was complete, not in the material and military sphere alone. Moral disintegration had undermined their enemies' resistance. The neutrals had everywhere acclaimed the triumph of the New Model as the only road back to security and peace. Even the Cavalier gentleman who laid down his arms, disbanded his troop and rode off home in a mood between melancholy and relief, felt no such bitter resentment as he and his son were to nurse after a dozen years of military rule, accom-panied by the sequestration of half their estate, the proscription of their religion, and the execution of their King. When Sir Jacob Astley at his surrender said to the victors—' You have now done your work and may go play, unless you fall out among your-selves,' he was not using the language of irreconcilable hatred.

A great opportunity for settlement was there for the taking. In three years it had been so completely thrown away that the Empire was only saved from disruption and England from anarchy by the employment of despotic military power ; and the Restora-tion settlement of 1660–2, though in itself inferior to what might have been obtained in 1647, was actually the salvation of the country.

The execution of Charles I marks the moment at which the failure to carry on government by consent was admitted and proclaimed, and the ' forcéd power ' established, nominally in order to realize Republican ideals, but in fact to prevent utter chaos. How had that situation been reached ? Between the end of the First Civil War and the tragedy in front of Whitehall stretch a series of intrigues, proposals, coups d'état and military operations, arising out of the character and policy of the four parties actively concerned—the victorious Parliament, the captive King, the Army, and Oliver Cromwell.

Parliament is the party whose conduct in these three critical

June 1646– Jan. 1649.

years it is least easy to praise or even to excuse. It may seem strange that a civilian assembly which had learnt to take the right measures and trust the right men in war-time, should fail only when it came to make political use of its conquests. But history, from the time of the Roman Senate until the Parliaments of our own day, is full of examples of this apparent paradox. Assemblies of men of valiant blood can be made wise by the dangers of war, but the power that armed victory brings, or seems to bring, may deprive them of judgment, and subject them to the mass-emotions of a mob. So in 1647 the House of Commons thought that its hired servant, the New Model Army, had placed in its hands supreme power over the religions and estates of all the subjects of the land, and it proceeded to dispose of all things English according to its own prejudices, with no more respect for the real England than Charles had shown in the day of his supremacy.

The most important cause of the failure of the Long Parliament to make peace after the Civil War was the same error that had ruined Charles and was to vitiate the Restoration settlement, the inability of any party to admit the need for religious toleration in a divided land. But the Long Parliament had the peculiar audacity to attempt the persecution of the Anglicans and the Sectarians at the same time, on behalf of the narrow Presbyterian orthodoxy which had less hold on the future of English religion than any other movement of the day.

Simultaneously the Long Parliament yielded to the temptation of meeting its great financial difficulties by the too facile expedient of attacks upon the property of its late opponents in the field. If, with reasonable exceptions, security had been given to the lands and fortunes of both sides in the late war, it is not likely that the Cavalier squires would have conceived that intense loathing of Puritanism which governed the conduct of their class during the remainder of the century. They had hitherto felt small affection for Laud and the Laudian clergy. But when the fines on 'malignants,' as the defeated party were called, forced them to sell large parts of their estates to the victors of the hour, often to war-profiteers of lower social standing than themselves,[1] and when at the same time the Prayer Book service to which they

---

[1] These men, who bought up the land of individual Cavaliers needing money to pay fines, kept their purchases and their new social status at the Restoration. Unjustly, but not unnaturally, Charles II was therefore accused of ingratitude towards his own and his father's followers. On the other hand, the more thorough-going Cromwellians, mostly army officers, who invested their pay and gains in buying up Church or Crown land cheap, lost it when it was resumed at the Restoration; everywhere except in Ireland they sank back to the social level whence they had risen.

were accustomed was forbidden, the squires began to feel a new affection for the ejected Laudian clergy,—about 2000 in number, —fellow-sufferers at the same rude hands. The breach between clergy and laity, which Laud had made, was healed by Puritan persecution. The political alliance of squire and parson, and the hatred they so long nurtured together against the foes of Bishops and Prayer Book, date from feelings engendered at this time.

1646–
1647.

Not content with rendering the Royalist gentry irreconcilable, the Long Parliament, with almost incredible folly, proceeded to pass measures for the lifelong imprisonment of Baptists, the prohibition of laymen from preaching in public, and the dismissal of all Independent officers from the New Model. In their harsh ingratitude to the men who had saved them in the field, the Parliamentary majority was egged on by the dominant faction in the City of London. To crown this elaborate edifice of folly, it was proposed to disband the Army without cashing its considerable arrears of pay. This drew together in close alliance officers and privates, enthusiastic sectaries and men who had been attracted into the ranks by the offer of good pay secured upon the taxes. Injustice made the Army a faction in the State, united by its grievances and its anger. All ranks began to listen more eagerly to the propaganda of the radical enthusiasts in their midst, who appealed from the Long Parliament to Republican and democratic ideals based on universal suffrage. These theories proved in that age impracticable, but humanly speaking, the soldiers cannot be blamed for refusing to submit to religious persecution and neglect of their just financial claims, at the hands of the authority whom they themselves had rendered supreme in the State by their magnificent military services.

Aug.
1647.

Yet the coercion of Parliament by the Army, even if justifiable in the first instance, was necessarily fatal to constitutional rule, and led by inevitable steps to the dictatorship of Cromwell. He long strove to keep the soldiers in their duty to the Houses, and said to them with perfect sincerity as late as July 1648 : ' What we and they gain in a free way is better than thrice so much in a forced way, and will be more truly ours and our posterity's. That you have by force I look upon as nothing.' This warning, uttered by England's greatest man of action, stands as the tragic comment on all that was yet to come in his own career.

The quarrel of Parliament and Army, which Parliament had provoked, put the balance of State in the hands of the captive King. Both sides made advances to him, and he could perhaps have settled the country by casting in his lot with one or the other. But his virtues and his failings alike made that impossible. His rigid adherence to the principle of monarchical government and its corollary the episcopal regime in the Church, for which he was prepared if necessary to endure in his own person the worst that man can do, made it impossible that he should come to terms either with Army or with Parliament.   Furthermore, he was by temperament incapable of coming to an honest agreement and abiding by it.   The less admirable side of his character taught him to conceive the plan of winning back power by insincere negotiations with both parties, which should help to set them by the ears together.   To play with victorious enemies in the hope of deluding them is always dangerous.

Yet his execution was as much the catastrophe of his enemies' cause as of his own.   In the person of his son, his plan was victorious a dozen years later, for his policy had hastened and his death cemented the alliance of Presbyterians with Royalists against the Independents and the Army.   The first stage of that 1648. alliance led to the Second Civil War and the victory of Cromwell at Preston, and so to the execution of Charles.   The final result was the Restoration of his son, when the Presbyterians were the catspaw and the dupe of their Episcopalian allies.   Crown, Parliament and Episcopacy were restored together, but owing to the action of Cromwell and the Army who had defended and nursed the sects for a dozen years, it was the sects and not the Presbyterian orthodox with whom lay the future of non-conformist Puritanism.

The revulsion of feeling in favour of the King, which began during his trial and execution, and swelled to such vast proportions as years went by, was largely due to the fact that he suffered as the champion of the laws which his enemies were breaking and of the ancient institutions which they were destroying.   Apart from the personal aspect of the scene, with its overmastering appeal in favour of ' the royal actor ' who played his part with Jan. 30, sincere and simple dignity, the conservative instincts of the 1649. English nation were rudely outraged.   They felt that they were being carried beyond the historic current of English life into uncharted seas.   It was an adventure they had not bargained for.   This Republicanism, what was it ?   The rule of preaching colonels apparently.   And yet for many years to come, the men, and in particular the man, who had seized power through means of the Army but in the name of an unconscious and bewildered ' people of England,' had the courage and genius to govern, making out of an utterly impossible situation something not ignoble, and in some important respects very profitable for the future growth of Great Britain and its Empire.

The decisive factor in the triangular contest between King, Parliament and Army had been Oliver Cromwell.   As early as

1647, while he was still a back-bench Member of Parliament, and not yet in name the supreme commander of the Army, his force of character made him in effect 'our chief of men.'

King, Parliament and Army each had an *idée fixe* and consequently they could not agree.   Cromwell, who was pre-eminently an opportunist,—'none goes so far,' he once said, 'as he who knows not whither he is going,'—could easily have supplied them with a dozen possible solutions if they had been ready to listen to reason.   Far the best solution propounded by anyone was the 'Heads of the Proposals,' made by Cromwell and Ireton to Charles, based on wide toleration, the use of the Prayer Book in Church by those who wished, Bishops without coercive power, and a stop to the sequestration of Cavalier estates.   But the King was only playing at negotiation, and neither Army nor Parliament had any thought of so liberal a treatment of the conquered.   Cromwell and Ireton were speaking for themselves and common sense alone.   They found that they must either march with the Army or perish.   Cromwell underwent one of those sharp revulsions, accompanied by repentance and prayer, so timely that his enemies miscalled them hypocrisy.

The riddle of Oliver must be read not in his mutable opinions but in his constant character.   His moderation and his dislike of force were often counteracted by his instinct at every cost to find a practical solution for the problem of the moment ; if agreement failed, as it often does in revolutionary times, then, however reluctantly, he would cut the Gordian knot, for the nation's government must be carried on.   Moreover, although common-sense was the dominating quality of his intellect, it worked in an atmosphere of temperamental enthusiasm which left him no doubts or fears when once he had reached a conclusion after weeks of brooding hesitation.   For his final resolve, when at last it emerged, always seemed to him the inspiration of God.   God spoke in the victories of each successive war, pointing—whithersoever Cromwell's latest thoughts were leading him.[1]   When, therefore, he learnt at last that all his efforts to find an accommodation with the King had been wasted time, the fanatical mood of the Army about 'the man Charles Stuart' took possession of him.   When he found also that England must be ruled for awhile through the soldiers or slide into anarchy, he felt the glow of the Republican

Sept.
1647.

---

[1] Butler, the author of *Hudibras*, the famous satire on the Puritans, writes four lines not inapplicable to Cromwell :

'Whate'er men speak by this New Light,
  Still they are sure to be i' th' right.
'Tis a dark Lanthorn of the Spirit,
  Which none see by but those who bear it.'

faith in which so many of his men returned from the victory at Preston, although it was not so much his settled conviction as the apparent necessity of the moment. Ten years later he was veering round again to constitutional kingship—in his own person this time,—in order to get rid of military rule and put himself in line with the strongest current of thought of that day, ebbing back towards conservative and civil legality. For always this strong swimmer must ride on the crest of the wave. How many more successive waves would he have ridden, if death had not put an end to his titanic strife with circumstance?

Cromwell was not the only able and public-spirited man who had pushed his way to the front on the Roundhead side, under the double impulse of the emotional turmoil of the time and the number of careers opened to talent by civil war and revolution. The era of Vane, Blake, Ireton, Monk, and of Milton as pamphleteer and secretary, was an era of great public servants, worthy to be dignified by the name of 'Commonwealth.' The Regicide government, consisting partly of army officers and partly of members of the 'Rump' or minority which 'Pride's purge' had made supreme in Parliament, were neither poltroons nor blind fanatics. The position in which they found themselves on the last day of January 1649 was one which must have speedily led to their own ruin and the dissolution of the British Empire, had they not been men above the common in cool-headed courage. The state of public opinion, strongly alienated from them but divided against itself, rendered impossible the appeal to a free election, which their democratic theories demanded but their sense of responsibility and self-preservation forbade. Wherever they looked, the prospect was dark in the extreme. Their authority was denied, not only by Cavaliers and Presbyterians, but by radical democrats like John Lilburne, who at that time had a great popular following. The Navy was paralysed by mutiny; the Royalist privateers under Prince Rupert held the seas; Scotland and Ireland were in arms for the younger Charles; Virginia and Barbados repudiated the authority of the usurpers; Massachusetts, though not unfriendly, had since the beginning of the troubles in England acted as if it were an independent State. Holland, France, Spain and all the continental powers regarded the regicides as pariahs and England as a cypher. Yet in four years the Council of State had overcome these dangers with the help of Cromwell's sword and Blake's broadsides, before resort was had to the final stage of the revolutionary government, the Protectorate of Oliver.

The first step in the reconstitution of the British Empire by

Dec. 1648.

the Republican Government was the subjugation of Ireland. It was rendered easier for Cromwell and his army because the Protestants over there, whatever their political allegiance, tended to rally round him as the champion of their race and creed, while the Irish resistance became racial and Catholic instead of Royalist. After the fall of Drogheda, Wexford and Clonmel had broken the back of resistance in the East, Cromwell went home, leaving Ireton

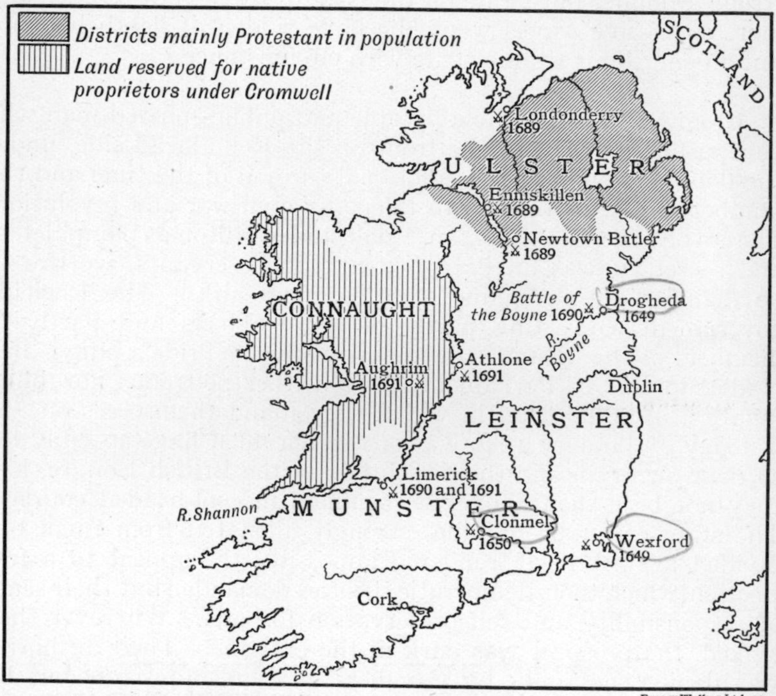

MAP XXV.—Ireland in the Seventeenth Century

to carry on the guerrilla war of Celt and Saxon in the West to its bitter end.

The land settlement in Ireland, by far the worst part of Cromwell's constructive work within the British islands, was the part that outlived him substantially in the form he gave it. It completed the transference of the soil from Irish to British proprietors, which had been begun under the Tudors and pushed forward under the Stuart Kings. The object was threefold: to pay off in Irish land the soldiers who had fought and the capitalists who had provided the money for the conquest, in the manner in which the veterans of Cæsar and of William the Conqueror had been rewarded; secondly, to render the English hold upon Ireland secure against another rebellion like that of 1641, even after the army should be disbanded ; and lastly, to extirpate Catholicism. The first two objects were attained.

Ireland west of Shannon was reserved for native proprietors. The rest of the island passed to Protestant landlords. The idea of driving the whole Celtic population beyond the Shannon was entertained but not executed. The natives remained for the most part on their farms as hewers of wood and drawers of water to the new alien landowners, who rack-rented them, according to Irish custom, without being obliged to make the improvements and repairs customary in English tenancies.

In Ulster alone had the tenant some protection, and in Ulster alone the population was largely British and Protestant, on account of the immigration of hard-working Scots from the neighbouring coast beginning from the time of James I's plantation. Elsewhere in Ireland, those of Cromwell's private soldiers who were planted out as yeomen failed to preserve their religion and nationality, because they were too widely scattered and were cut off by social barriers from the Protestant gentry. Some of the yeomen threw up their farms, while others intermarried with the natives, with the result that their descendants brought Saxon and Ironside qualities to stiffen the Celtic and Catholic resistance. The landlords were left isolated in their power and privilege, until the end began with Gladstone's Land Bills and Parnell's Land League.

In Ireland as Oliver left it and as it long remained, the persecuted priests were the only leaders of the people because the English had destroyed the class of native gentry. The Cromwellian settlement rendered the Irish for centuries the most priest-led population in Europe.

Cromwell's next task was to reduce Scotland to the obedience of the Commonwealth. North of the Tweed there was no Sectarian or Republican party and, properly speaking, no Parliamentary party. The land was divided between a rigid ecclesiastical Presbyterianism, very different from the political Presbyterianism of England, and the Cavalier interest, which in Scotland was not Laudian but represented the rebellion of the nobility and others against the rule of the State by the Church. Presbyterian and Cavalier hated each other bitterly, for the blood shed in Montrose's wars flowed between them. But they patched up a hollow alliance round the person of Charles II, whom they proposed to restore by force of arms to his throne in England. Their plans were ruined at Dunbar and Worcester, the last and, militarily, the greatest victories of Cromwell's army on British soil—

Sept. 3, 1650. Sept. 3, 1651.

When up the armed mountains of Dunbar
He marched, and through deep Severn, ending war.[1]

The only sanction of Oliver's rule beyond the Tweed was the presence of the English army and, therefore, the arrangements he made could not be permanent. But the rule of the sword, so long as it lasted, enabled Oliver to carry through without compromise his own enlightened policy for the benefit of Scotland, whose internal feuds had at length subjected her to the great neighbour she had so often defied. He united the whole island in a single Commonwealth, and Scottish members sat in the British Parliaments held under the Protectorate. For the first time Scotland enjoyed the immense advantage of free trade with England and her markets beyond sea. Order was kept and justice administered without favour, as never before in her history. Even the Highlands were garrisoned and the clans kept in awe. The government was good, but, as in England, it was costly, and the taxes were burdensome and deeply resented.

The dignity and efficiency of the Scottish Presbyterian Church were preserved, while it was no longer permitted to persecute others or to domineer over the State. ' I verily believe,' a Scottish Presbyterian wrote of the Protectorate, ' there were more souls converted to Christ in that short time, than in any season since the Reformation though of triple its duration.' The English soldiers behaved irreproachably as an army of occupation, save when they endeavoured to found Baptist Churches in an uncongenial soil, or derided the discipline of the Kirk by seating themselves on the ' stools of repentance ' during divine worship. to the displeasure of ' grave livers,' and the untimely mirth of the youthful part of the congregation.

The Scots hailed the Restoration of Charles II in 1660 as the return of their own national independence. It was indeed the end of formal union with England and therewith of free trade, but national independence was not, in fact, recovered till the Revolution of 1688. Till then the feuds of the Scots among themselves made their country an easy prey to the schemes of one English government after another ; and of these foreign governments, Oliver's was the first and very much the least bad.

Oliver as Protector realized his vision of the united British islands. Scotland and Ireland were joined to England in legislative and economic union, their members sitting in Parliament at Westminster, their traders selling and buying freely in the English

---

[1] During the raid of Scots and Cavaliers into England that ended at Worcester, it is noticeable that so far from Englishmen rising to join them, the militia turned out very readily to put them down. If the regicides were unpopular, so were their enemies, especially the Scots.

market. So long as Oliver lived, the Protestant interest in Ireland was fostered and encouraged as a part of England herself. The Restoration broke up the union of the British Isles and saw the Protestant Irish sacrificed to English trade jealousy, and to Anglican revenge on the Presbyterian religion. Not all the woes of Ireland can be laid at Oliver's door.

To the Regicide Government belongs the credit of the revival of English sea-power, and the establishment of the Navy on a basis of permanent efficiency, which every subsequent government, whatever its political complexion, honestly endeavoured to maintain. The Council of State now consisted of the men who had won two civil wars ; strong men selected from every class of the community by the test of deeds, men with soldierly and practical ways of regarding each situation as it arose, and in a position never enjoyed by the Stuart Kings of raising as much money as was needed by taxation. The revolt of a third of the **1648–** navy, and its organization in foreign ports by Prince Rupert to **1649.** avenge his uncle on the high seas, menaced the trade of London and of all England in the Channel as it had never been menaced during the Great Civil War. The men of the new government, aware that they must subdue this peril or perish, threw their energies and resources into naval organization. Their warlike training led them to infuse into the discipline and tactics of the fleet just that military element which was needed to complete the tradition of the English fighting navy. 'Their measures,' wrote Julian Corbett, 'transformed the Navy to its modern scope and established England as the great naval power of the world.' But they would not have succeeded in so doing had they not, in a fortunate hour for England, called Robert Blake to command the fleets of the Commonwealth.

Blake, in the eyes of modern naval historians, stands as a **1649–** third with Drake and Nelson. The record of his eight years of **1657.** admiralty afloat, his innumerable and successful actions with all kinds of enemies,—with Rupert, with the Barbary pirates of Tunis, with the greatest fleets and admirals the Dutch ever sent to sea, with the French and with the Spaniards who had so long despised us,—gave to the British Navy the place which it aspired to attain under Elizabeth, lost under the early Stuarts, and never after Blake's day more than momentarily relinquished. The acceptance of the Blake tradition at sea by the Cavalier and Tory party after the Restoration, while Cromwell's militarism on land was violently rejected on account of its political associations, is one of the governing facts of modern British history.

Blake himself was bred a sailor less than either Drake or

Nelson. As the son of a wealthy trader of Bridgwater, he was well acquainted with the merchant shipping of the Parret estuary and the Bristol Channel ; but he had tried to become an Oxford don, and had succeeded in becoming a fine Puritan soldier. The defence against overwhelming odds, first of Lyme Regis and afterwards of Taunton, which Blake organized when the Cavaliers swept over the South-West in the Great Civil War, stood out among the finest deeds of the Puritan spirit in arms. But he himself was more of a public servant than a zealot. When called, a few days after the execution of the King, to take command of the fleet and recover for the English marine the lost freedom of the sea, he obeyed marvelling. Doubtless he had been chosen because his knowledge of ships and seamen was at least greater than that of other soldiers. From that moment forward, his genius blazed out his path of victory upon the waters.

Rupert, fine soldier and fine sailor as he was, had the ill-fortune to meet Cromwell on land and Blake at sea. Blake blockaded him in the Irish ports, chased him to Portugal and out of it, and thence to the Mediterranean, where the bulk of the Cavalier fleet was destroyed. In these operations of civil war, English naval power was, for the first time, successfully introduced into the Mediterranean, to the astonishment and dismay of France, Spain and the Italian Princes. Taught by Blake's successes there in pursuit of Rupert, Oliver a few years later sent him again to the inland sea, not only to defend our merchants there, but to add weight to the elaborate diplomacy of the Protectorate. Thenceforward, British sea-power in the Mediterranean has remained an important factor in world history.[1]

The revival of the fighting navy under Blake, and the government of the State by a class of men closely in touch with the mercantile community and especially with London, inevitably led to renewed rivalry with the Dutch. For a generation past, the mariners of Holland had lorded it, often insolently enough, in the seas of Northern Europe and America, and in the African and Indian oceans, and had poached the fisheries and almost monopolized the carrying trade of England and her American colonies. The serious revival of English competition was marked by the Navigation Act of 1651, and the Dutch War of 1652-4. But the struggle against Dutch maritime supremacy was not decided till the early Eighteenth Century. It was not an act, but

---

[1] In 1623 James I had sent ships into the Mediterranean against the pirates of Algiers, but without success. Oliver was so much impressed with the importance of the Mediterranean to England that he contemplated taking and holding Gibraltar.

a process, of which the first conscious beginnings are visible under the Commonwealth.[1]

Navigation Acts, to set a limit to foreign shipping in English *— Nav. Acts* ports, had been passed by English Parliaments as long ago as the reign of Richard II, but owing to the scarcity of English shipping it had not been possible to enforce them. There was, therefore, nothing new in the principle of the Act of 1651, and there was equally nothing new in the failure to enforce it strictly. Nevertheless, it expressed a new spirit of revolt against Dutch supremacy, and henceforth there was at least a continuous effort of enforcement, because there were many more English ships than in former times. When the Restoration Government took New York from Holland, it removed a base of Dutch maritime activity in America and so helped to put the principle into practice in the ports of New England.

The naval war of the Commonwealth against Holland arose *1652–* out of a number of incidents in the rivalry of the two maritime *1654.* communities. It cannot be attributed to one cause alone, except indeed to mutual jealousy. It was a battle of Titans, Blake against Van Tromp, commanding the two greatest fleets in the world, already little inferior to the fleets of the Nile and Trafalgar in their ship construction and the technical skill of their crews. Holland suffered more than England, because she had fewer resources on land and now, for the first time since she had become a nation, found a hostile power blocking the Channel against the merchant fleets that brought her life and wealth from afar. The greater staying power of England was clearly indicated in this first round.

The war against Holland was more popular in the City than in the army, and Cromwell desired Protestant co-operation throughout the world. One of his first acts as Protector was to *Peace* make peace with the Dutch on good terms for England. *signed* *1654.*

But Oliver's direct rule failed to bring the immunity from foreign war which alone could have given his domestic system any chance of financial stability and ultimate popularity. His Protestantism and his desire to help English traders and colonists all the world over, led him into a quarrel with Spain. He revived the claim of Elizabethan Englishmen to trade with the Spanish colonies and to be entirely free from the power of the Inquisition.

---

[1] See p. 387 on the Dutch hegemony. The Navigation Act of 1651 'prohibited the introduction into any territory of the Commonwealth of produce of any country in Asia, Africa or America, except in vessels owned by Englishmen or by the inhabitants of English colonies, and manned by crews of which more than one half were of English nationality. Imports from any part of Europe might be brought in only in English vessels, or in vessels the owners of which belonged to that nation in which the goods were manufactured or produced.'

See
Map
XXVI.,
p. 437,
below.

The Spanish Ambassador replied that this was to ask ' his master's two eyes.' Perpetual hostilities were taking place between the Spanish forces and the English colonists, traders and buccaneers of the West Indian Archipelago, which Spain regarded as her own in spite of English settlements in so many of the islands. Oliver lent to the English of the West Indies the powerful aid of the mother country. He sent out an expedition which, though it failed at Hispaniola, captured Jamaica. This proved the most important single step in the enlargement of that West Indian island Empire which, for a century and a half to come, held so prominent a place in British trade, diplomacy and war.

1655.

As a factor in European politics Cromwellian England was feared and respected, but achieved nothing great. The protection of the Vaudois was a noble gesture, worthy of the finest sonnet ever written by a political secretary, and was very well managed as a diplomatic feat ; but it was not very important. The war with Spain, which was really a trans-Atlantic quarrel, did little good in Europe either to England or to Protestantism. There was glory, no doubt, in Blake's destruction of the Spanish fleet under the forts of Teneriffe, where Nelson afterwards lost an arm, and there was pride in the storming of the slippery sand-dunes near Dunkirk by the red-coated infantry with the army of our French allies looking on in admiration. But the perennial British interest in the Balance of Power in Europe demanded no such vigorous interference, for the balance then stood adjusted without Cromwell's heavy weight in the scale. Spain had already decayed and France had not yet grown to any dangerous height. The Thirty Years' War was finished and, for the time, no opportunities existed for a new Gustavus Adolphus. If Oliver had been on the scene with his army and his fleet in 1618 or in 1630 or again from 1670 onwards, something notable might have been achieved. In 1654 the man was there, but the hour had passed, or not yet come. History is made up of coincidences or their absence.

1655–
1658.

On the top of the expenses of the Dutch war, the Spanish war increased the burden of taxation on the country and gravely injured its prosperity and trade. Oliver's militarism and imperialism became increasingly unpopular, not only for political reasons, but because they cost too much. That one should be forced to give a large part of one's property yearly to the tax-gatherer, though accepted as a normal condition of life to-day, seemed then an intolerable outrage. Yet, in spite of the heavy taxes, the sale of Crown and episcopal lands, the fines on ' malignants,' and the confiscation of half the soil of Ireland, Oliver died in debt. From the point of view of finance alone a

change of system was necessary, which would enable the army
to be disbanded.   But the army could not be disbanded unless
some way could be found leading back to government by consent.
Oliver spent his last years in the search for that way, but he had
lost it, and was doomed to bear his load through the wilderness
to the end.

> The same arts that did gain
> A power must it maintain,

wrote Andrew Marvell, the lesser but not the less shrewd of the
Protector's two poet secretaries.

Oliver, unlike Strafford and others who have ' broken Parliaments,' believed to the last in the necessity for Parliamentary
rule.   And unlike others who have founded Republics, he began
and he ended his career as a believer in the uses of constitutional
Kingship.   Yet it was his fate to ruin the Puritan cause by dis-
sociating it from both Kingship and Parliament, and to clear the
way only by his own death for the restoration of the civil legality
which he himself desired.   It was his fate—was it also his fault ?
On that point historians who know the most are the least willing
to venture a clear opinion.

His dismissal of the Rump of the Long Parliament when it   1653.
endeavoured to perpetuate its power, was perhaps a necessity.
It pleased the nation well for a month, during which the ballad-
makers chanted :

> Brave Oliver came to the House like a sprite,
>   His fiery face struck the Speaker dumb ;
> ' Begone,' said he, ' you have sate long enough,
>   Do you think to sit here till Doomsday come ? '

But the all too dramatic march of his red-coats up the floor
of the House, and his guard-room jest about the mace, left in
longer retrospect an indelibly bad impression.   If the mace was
a bauble and the crown to boot, what counted but the sword ?

After he had become Protector, his later Parliaments, though   Dec.
elected under such restrictions as the times demanded, were not   1653.
able to agree with him.   Whether he should have risked more to
bring about an agreement so indispensable, is a question too
detailed for discussion here, although it is the heart of the problem.
The alternative was government by Major-Generals, the naked
rule of the sword, which outraged the country and his own
instincts.   His last two years were spent in the delicate operation   1657–8.
of beginning to free himself from dependence on the army by
making terms with the legalists and constitutionalists.   They

demanded of him that he should revive the Kingship in his own person. He began to fall in with their view of the matter, but some of the army chiefs on whom he most depended remained stubbornly Republican. The desire of many moderate and practical men, particularly of the lawyers, was that Oliver should wear the crown,—the same men who two years later took the lead in recalling Charles for much the same reasons. Monarchy was seen to be essential to the restoration of Parliament and the rule of law.

Sept. 3, 1658.
It was in an early stage of this new evolution that death over-took the Protector. But already he had made some headway in weeding the army of its fanatical and extremist element, and for this reason Monk, the practical man, was able to represent the strongest party among his fellow soldiers, and to possess himself of power at the end of the prolonged crisis of eighteen months that followed Oliver's death. Consequently, the desired dis-
1660.
bandment of the army, the Restoration of Monarchy, Parliament and the rule of law took place without bloodshed, in the name of the old dynasty. Whether, if Oliver had lived, it could have taken place in his name may be doubted, but it remains an open question.

Oliver would perhaps have regarded the Restoration settle-ment with more equanimity than we suppose, for he was a good patriot, a great opportunist and at heart an ardent Parliamen-tarian. His bitterest disappointment would have been the religious side of the new regime. Yet on English religion also he had left an indelible mark. His victory in the First Civil War made Parliament instead of King the ultimate authority on ecclesiastical questions, a decision upon which James II alone attempted to go back and in vain. His victory in the Second Civil War prevented the establishment of persecuting Presby-terian orthodoxy. His long rule had nursed the Sects into such vigorous life that they and not the Presbyterians gave English Puritanism its form and its character in the coming period of non-conformity. The variety of English religious thought and practice, not without its influence inside the borders of the Church itself, and tending always to freedom of opinion, springs no doubt from something fundamental in the English character, but historically it dates from the Cromwellian epoch.

The Protector's policy had combined comprehension within the Church and toleration without it. While he preserved tithe and endowments, he put down persecution. The benefices of the Church were held by Presbyterians, Independents or Baptists indifferently, while free congregations of a more fanciful kind multiplied outside. Oliver thus obtained in the field of religion a reconciliation of all the various Puritan forces which he had signally failed to obtain in politics. He even tolerated the Prayer Book surreptitiously, and would have tolerated it openly but for the political situation which more and more identified Anglicanism with the cause of the exiled Stuarts. The fatal flaw in his ecclesiastical policy was that he had not been able to give to Anglicanism that share in the life of the Church which he had offered to grant it in the Heads of the Proposals.[1] The Roman Catholics were less molested under the Protectorate than under Presbyterian or Anglican Parliaments, and though the Mass was not legally tolerated the Recusancy laws were repealed.

These conditions were much more favourable to the growth of new religious movements than any that recurred until the great age of religion had begun to wane. The Quaker movement was able to come into being, favoured by Oliver himself, though highly offensive to most persons in authority. Under the Protectorate it took such root that the fiercer persecutions of the Restoration period could not destroy it. George Fox made at least the most original contribution to the history of religion of any Englishman. His very spiritual and very unorthodox Christianity had immense success among the Puritan sectaries of the last half of the Seventeenth Century. In this first period of its power Quakerism,—based on the doctrine of the 'inner light,' that is on the direct personal inspiration of each Christian, man or woman,—was revivalist in its spirit and methods among the common people, rather than staid and 'quiet' as it became in later generations.

Both Long Parliament and Protector did their best for education, both by direct grants in aid and by donations of Church lands. The Puritan movement was in earnest about education as the Tudor despoilers of the Church had never been. Largely under Puritan influence the founding of schools went on much more rapidly in the first half of the Seventeenth Century than in the previous hundred years. The motive of educational enthusiasm was largely religious, but the connection of education with religion, and of religion with politics, had the grave disadvantage of continual proscription in the Universities and schools, first of Puritan teachers by Laud, then of Laudian teachers by the Puritans, and finally of all save Anglican teachers by the Restoration Parliaments. The effect on the two Universities, which otherwise gave signs of vigorous life, was deplorable, and ultimately reduced them to the lethargy of the Eighteenth Century. The enforcement of unquestioning orthodoxy in politics and religion is incompatible with the true life of a University.

[1] See p. 420, above.

The great fault of the Puritans as governors of the land was that they tended to exclude all who were not Puritan from power and influence in the State; by making profession of religious zeal a shibboleth, they bred notorious hypocrites. Their tyrannical and disastrous suppression of the theatre and other clumsy attempts to make people good by force were part of the same general error. When the Restoration occurred, the non-religious part of the community had come to loathe the Puritans as, twenty years before, they had loathed the Laudian clergy. In particular the squires, the strongest class in the social order of that day, had been outraged by the military rule of Major-Generals and by the overturn of the ancient institutions of the country. Whichever side they or their fathers had taken in the Great Civil War, the squires had come to associate the political and social changes which they disapproved with Puritan religion; therefore, by a strange inversion since the days of Eliot and Pym, the anti-Puritan legislation of the Clarendon Code was the work not of the King and the courtiers but of the Parliament and the squires. Yet under a Parliamentary system the Puritan sects could hope some day to obtain a measure of toleration which they would never have obtained if the Stuart despotism had been prolonged after the pattern of Laud and Strafford.

1661–
1665.

BOOKS FOR FURTHER READING FOR CHAPTERS II., III., AND IV.

Gardiner, *History*, Vols. VIII. to X.; *Civil War* (4 vols.); *Commonwealth and Protectorate* (3 vols.).

Firth, *Cromwell* (Heroes of Nations Series), much the best short book on the period; *Cromwell's Army*; *Last Years of the Protectorate* (2 vols.), completing Gardiner.

Carlyle, *Cromwell's Letters and Speeches*; Gooch, *Democratic Ideas in the Seventeenth Century*; W. A. Shaw, *History of the English Church*, 1640–60; Lady Verney, *Memoirs of the Verney Family*, vols. I.-III.; Feiling, *History of the Tory Party*, 1640–1714; R. Barclay, *Inner Life of the Religious Societies of the Commonwealth*.

SCOTLAND:—*Hume Brown* and *Andrew Lang's* histories; John Buchan, *Montrose*.

NAVY:—Callender, as before; Corbett, *England in the Mediterranean*, 1603–1713 (2 vols.)

This period is rich in particularly delightful and noble contemporary literature: Clarendon's History; George Fox's *Journal*; Milton's *Areopagitica* and *Of Reformation in England*; *Life of Col. Hutchinson* by his widow; *Clarke Papers* (Camden Soc., 1891), being the debates of the army officers and men with Cromwell etc. (See also books, p. 396, above.)

CHAPTER V

English village and town life and its expansion overseas. Character of
Colonization and Colonial policy in the Seventeenth Century. New
England, Virginia, and the absorption of the Dutch Middle Colonies.
England, France and Holland

EVERYDAY life in Stuart times, though full of hardship, ignorance
and cruelty as compared with our own, had great compensating
advantages. It was neither ugly nor unnatural. It was lived in
the country, and whatever man himself added to nature did not
detract from the beauty of things. The crafts were conducted
by men armed with tools to do their will, not as now by men
doing the will of the machines they serve ; and it is not man himself but the machine that is the enemy of grace and beauty of line.
Before the mechanical age, common craftsmen were in a sense
artists, doing nobler and more individual work than the modern
employee engaged on mass production. They were therefore
more contented with their lot in life, though many of its conditions were such as would not be tolerated in our more humane
generation.

These crafts were not carried on in immense urban areas from
which nature had been elaborately expelled. London, which
numbered half a million inhabitants by the end of the century,
was the only place in England that could answer to that description. And even there a man could take his pleasure on the
Thames, then the most glorious of city highways, or, if he could
not afford a boat, could convey himself on foot in half an hour
out of roaring Cheapside to meadows where sportsmen set
springes for snipe and partridge, close under hills haunted by
nightingales. Nature could be found and wooed even by the
Londoner without the intervention of mechanical transport.[1]

The other towns of England, all much smaller in proportion to
the capital than some are to-day, answered to the description that
Thomas Hardy has given of the Dorchester of his own boyhood :

Casterbridge [Dorchester] lived by agriculture at one remove
further from the fountain-head than the adjoining villages—no more.
The townsfolk understood every fluctuation in the rustic's condition,
for it affected their receipts as much as the labourer's ; they entered

[1] The extraordinary size of London, both absolutely and relatively to other
towns, at the end of the Seventeenth Century was due to its having become the
greatest port in the world and a vast distributing centre for both wholesale
and retail trade. Its manufactures were carried on not in factories but on the
domestic system as elsewhere ; indeed the domestic system survived longer in
London than in the North and Midlands after the coming of the Industrial
Revolution in the Eighteenth Century, when the *relative* size of London declined.

into the troubles and joys which moved the aristocratic families ten
miles round—for the same reason. . . . Casterbridge was the complement of the rural life around ; not its urban opposite. Bees and
butterflies in the cornfields at the top of the town, who desired to get
to the meads at the bottom, took no circuitous course, but flew straight
down High Street without any apparent consciousness that they were
traversing strange latitudes.

Such were the towns of England from Elizabeth to George III.
And, such as they were, they housed only a small part of the
population, for under the Tudors and Stuarts the crafts and
manufactures were increasingly carried on, not in the corporate
towns but in the country.   Many villages and hamlets manufactured for the national and international market.   The mediæval isolation of the peasant was broken down, and he came in
contact in his own village with men of various occupations dealing
much with distant shires.   Community of trade drew the whole
nation together, sharpening the wits and broadening the outlook
of the villager.   When the first Stuart ascended the throne, men
were saying to each other :

By the Lord, Horatio, these three years I have taken note of it, . . .
the toe of the peasant comes so near the heel of the courtier he galls
his kibe.

While the contemporary French and German peasants were
still depressed by the survivals of an outworn feudalism, the
English villager was ready to play an independent part in any
new development, religious or political, industrial or colonial.
The Pilgrim Fathers were most of them English villagers in origin.
The mediæval serf would never have planted the free and self-
sufficient townships of New England.   French Canada, founded
in this same Seventeenth Century, was the transplantation of the
mediæval peasant under the leadership of his feudal noble and
his priest ; while the English Colonial movement was the migration of a modern society, self-governing, half-industrial, awake
to economic and intellectual change.

The new agriculture and the enclosures had upon the whole
increased the number and importance of the well-to-do tenant-
farmers and freehold yeomen.   Thomas Fuller, writing at the
outbreak of the Civil War, thus describes the yeomen :

The yeomanry is an estate of people almost peculiar to England.
France and Italy are like a die which hath no points between sink and
ace, nobility and peasantry. . . . The yeoman wears russet clothes,
but makes golden payment, having tin in his buttons and silver in his
pockets. . . . In his own country he is a main man in juries.   He

seldom goes abroad and his credit stretches further than his travel. He goes not to London, but *se-defendendo*, to save himself a fine, being returned of a Jury, where seeing the King once, he prays for him ever afterwards.

The forty-shilling freeholder, who included many of this sturdy class, enjoyed the parliamentary franchise in the shire elections. The independent part played by the yeomen for King Charles' cause in the West, and for the Parliament in Hampden's Buckinghamshire and Cromwell's East Anglia, showed how far the better class of English peasant had progressed out of the ignorance and dependence of the serfs over whom the Norman Barons had ridden roughshod.

The small squires, freehold yeomen, leasehold farmers and craftsmen formed together a large part of the rural population. But there existed also an agricultural proletariate. Towards the close of the Stuart period the publicist Gregory King surmised that the 'cottagers and paupers' considerably outnumbered the yeoman freeholders and well-to-do tenant farmers, and slightly outnumbered the 'labouring people and out-servants.' All is extremely uncertain, local variations were infinite, and there are no figures available except such guesswork as Gregory King's. But it is probable that there was a large class of poor folk in every village, part of it landless and working for hire, part of it living from hand to mouth on a few strips in the common field, or on pasture rights or squattings on the common waste. Then, too, there was the nomad population of the roads and lanes,—the campers in the dingle, the tinker and wandering craftsman, the gipsy from far lands, the highwayman and footpad, the ballad-monger, the quack and the showman,—a world of infinite variety, entertainment and romance, which Shakespeare loved in its prime, and George Borrow portrayed on the eve of its fading away before the remorseless regimentation of modern ' improvement.'

Every class of the rural community found an additional means of livelihood and enjoyment in the snaring of hares, wild-fowl and rabbits in places where no one then cared to preserve them, besides more adventurous poaching in warrens and parks. During the Civil War, the ' poor foot,' recruited on both sides from the rural proletariate, had the gratification of breaking up innumerable deer-parks of ' rebel ' or ' malignant ' gentlemen, with the result that the stock of deer never fully recovered, and fox-hunting began after the Restoration to rival stag-hunting as the usual form of the chase. Before that, foxes had been massacred for necessity, not preserved for sport. At the same time the improvement of shot-guns presented an alternative to hawking or snaring as the sportsman's favourite method of taking game. These early gunmen usually stalked the bird for a sitting shot : pheasants were shot roosting, and partridges were shot or netted on the ground. By the end of Charles II's reign, however, many gentlemen practised the most refined form of sport, and actually ' shot flying.' [1]

England under the Stuarts was not sharply divided between an urban and a rural way of life. Since the feudal life of the manor had disappeared and municipal life had become decadent, village and town were both governed by Parliamentary Statutes rather than by local legislation, and were harmoniously related in a single economic system of national dimensions.[2]

Yet in spite of the political and economic unity of England, means of locomotion were still so primitive, and the ill-tended roads so execrable, that provincial differences in speech, custom and character still gave picturesqueness and piquancy to life. The absence of a newspaper press and of a standardized and universal system of education enabled local traditions to survive. Shire differed from shire, town from town and hamlet from hamlet. There was more individuality then than now, at least in the external expression of character.

Men and women were widely scattered through the island, thrown back upon themselves during frequent hours of solitude and isolation ; each had space to grow, like the spreading oak tree alone in the field, without troubling too much to conform to any conventional pattern. It was ' every man in his humour.' The typical economic life of the time, as conducted by yeoman, farmer and small craftsman, left the individual more unfettered and self-dependent than he had been in the corporate life of mediæval burgher and serf, or has become in our own day under great capitalist and labour combinations.

But such individualism, greater than is possible in the crowded world of to-day, was qualified by the greater subjection of women to men. It was still the exception for women of the upper and middle class to choose their own husbands, and when the husband had been assigned he was lord and master, so far at least as law and custom could make him. Yet even so, neither Shakespeare's women nor those of authentic Seventeenth Century memoirs, like

---

[1] *The Gentleman's Recreation*, 1686, says : ' It is now the Mode to *Shoot Flying*, as being by experience found the best and surest way ; for when the game is on the Wing, if but one Shot hits any part of its Wings so expanded, it will occasion its fall, although not to kill it, so that your Spaniel will soon be its Victor.' Others found the art more difficult, for in *Tom Jones* (Bk. VIII., Chap. XI.) the gentleman supposed to have been born in 1657 says of his brother's expertness with the gun ' though perhaps you may think it incredible, he could not only hit a standing mark with great certainty, but hath *actually shot a crow as it was flying in the air.*'

[2] See pp. 269, 282, above.

the Verneys and Hutchinsons, seem wanting in personality and character.

This new English world, so full of vigour, freedom and initiative, laid the foundations of the British Empire and of the United States. The migration of early Stuart times was a world-movement akin in its importance to the Anglo-Saxon and Norse settlement of England a thousand years before. The Elizabethans had prepared the sea-way for the host of emigrants who used it in the following reigns.

The great majority of the first Anglo-Americans came from the south-east of England and represented her most pronounced Nordic stock.[1] They were accustomed not to the hamlets and isolated farms of the West and North, but to the large villages of the South-East and Midlands; it was therefore natural for them, when they reached the other side of the Atlantic, to create the New England township, an institution which spread far, and did much to mould the destiny of all North America. They were indeed the very men to found solid institutions in the wilderness, because in their old homes they had combined self-help and economic individualism with residence in large village groups, where agriculture, crafts and trade had flourished together. The Pilgrim Father did not go out expecting to find a job awaiting him in some specialized employment, but was prepared to turn his hand to anything that circumstances imposed, asking only for land, of which there was abundance.

A great part of the emigration under James and Charles I ran, indeed, not to New England but to the Bermudas, the West India islands, and to Raleigh's Virginia, the first of English Colonies, refounded in 1607. In these latitudes the climate was in some respects alluring; in Virginia tobacco-culture and in the islands sugar offered a way to rapid wealth for a few. The abundant slave-labour of African negroes was only gradually introduced, but from the first there was a tendency to seek 'indentured servants,' whether convict or other, to work the 'plantations' for an aristocracy. Some of the West Indian settlers were Puritan, some Anglicans inclining towards Royalist sympathies, and some were failures of the Old World sent to make

[1] Of about 25,000 English settled in New England in 1640, it has been calculated by some statisticians and genealogists that fifty per cent. came from Suffolk, Essex and Herts; twenty per cent. from Norfolk, Lincolnshire, Nottingham, Yorkshire, Middlesex, Kent, Surrey and Sussex. The counties on the Welsh and Scottish borders supplied only scattered individuals. These original 25,000, to whom collectively may be extended the term 'Pilgrim Fathers,' were a prolific stock and their descendants were the men who did most to set the political and social tone of the United States in its great developments west of the Appalachian Mountains in later times, until about 1870.

a fresh start oversea, not always with happy results for the colony. Local self-government at once became a feature of English settlements in Virginia and the islands, distinguishing them from the colonies of other nations.

But these semi-tropical colonies, important as they became, could not have imposed the English law and language on North America as a whole. The tree whose branches were destined to cover the continent from sea to sea, had its deepest roots in the close-settled, democratic, Puritan land of the New England townships. There the winter was long and hard, the soil thin and stony, the forests came down to the sea coast, covering everything, and the Red Indians prowled around, raiding the lonely farmstead and sometimes the unwary township. Every acre had to be won from nature by axe and plough, and guarded by sword and gun. Yet all the hardships of early settlement in such a land were endured and overcome, on account of the special character of the settlers and the reasons of their coming thither from England. Laud's persecution made some of the best types of small gentry, yeomen and craftsmen, desire to emigrate. Nor were such men indifferent to the character of their new home. The English Puritan of that day sought a community large and homogeneous enough to protect him in the peculiar religious life which he wished to lead and which he wished to see his neighbours lead. The desire for free land and economic opportunity was part of the inducement, but would not by itself have filled the wilderness of New England with folk. For when in 1640 the persecution ceased, the immigration thither ceased also. But the prolific stock that had been planted there in the previous twenty years, held the key to the future of North America.

Immigrants of this type were able to endure and overcome the first winters in that harsh land of snow-bound, rocky forests. For they were picked men and women, trusting themselves and one another, with a purpose strongly held in common. Some of them were well-to-do, and the colony of Massachusetts was backed by money, supplies and good organizers in England,—wealthy Puritan Lords, squires and London merchants, who stayed at home themselves, but supported these ventures, partly from motives of religion, partly as an investment of their capital.

Charles I set no bar to these proceedings, for he was glad to see such dangerous spirits go into voluntary exile. Indeed their departure goes far to account for the non-resistance of his English subjects during his dozen years of autocratic rule. From the time of Elizabeth onwards, Anglican persecution has always been more than half political in its motive. The Roman Church persecuted to save souls, and was therefore less compromising.

Rome could not endure the thought of heresy in any part of the world ; so Louis XIV would allow no Huguenots in Canada ; and Spain would have no Protestants in South America. But Charles I, and, in later years, Clarendon, tolerated Puritan and Roman Catholic colonists on the other side of the ocean, provided Anglican conformity was observed at home, as the basis of the corresponding system in the political sphere.

New England was democratic in spirit from first to last. The Saxon township was brought across from East Anglia, but squire-archy was left behind. Abundant land, divided up into freeholds among all who were ready to clear it of trees and till it with their own hands, was the firm basis of the original North American democracy. Squirearchy continued to flourish in an island where land was limited and at a premium, and population at a discount, whereas the opposite conditions prevailed in New England. Feudalism had arisen in the Dark Ages to organize society for self-defence under warrior landlords ; but in New England the community acted as a whole, the township and the colony undertaking the organization necessary for fighting the redskins, and the mother country helping to defeat the Dutch and the French.[1]

Above all, the Church was democratic, and religion was the motive of the foundation of the colony ; the State in early Massachusetts was ruled by a democratic Church even more than in contemporary Scotland. Full political rights were confined to ' Church members,' who composed a considerable proportion of the whole population. Inside the colony there was no pretence at religious toleration. Dissidents seeking religious freedom from the particular brand of Puritanism represented in Massachusetts, moved away and founded neighbouring Rhode Island, the colony of Puritan toleration, under the leadership of Roger Williams. New England included both kinds of Puritanism, the rigid and the free.

New England was an amphibious community. The seaboard with its fine harbours and inlets, and the neighbouring fishing grounds, held the people to the coast and made them hardy mariners. Their capital was Boston, a merchant city on the sea. The forests on the water's edge of the Atlantic rendered ship-building easy for them, until the age of iron ships. Their houses were built of wood as universally as those of the early Saxons in the old English forest.

The inhabitants of New England and of all the English colonies on the American seaboard, not only found attraction on the coast

[1] See p. 88, above.

but were hindered from penetrating far inland by formidable geographic barriers.   The Appalachian and Alleghany mountains and their continuation northwards in wooded wildernesses up to the Gulf of St. Lawrence, effectually cut off the early English colonists from knowledge of the prairies of the interior and the Ohio Valley, where in fact much richer soil awaited them.   But no great rivers offered them an easy way into the interior, like the St. Lawrence, the highway of the French colonials.   This geographic restriction favoured close settlement and the growth of a number of coastwise colonies, each of great political solidity and numerical strength.   When therefore in the Eighteenth Century the English-speaking populations of the seaboard at length burst over the Appalachian barrier into the Ohio Valley and the prairies of the Middle West, they were powerful enough to sweep away their French forerunners in those regions and then to advance across the empty continent with astonishing speed, planting over immense areas the New England idea, modernized and mingled with the spirit of the ever-moving frontier.

The settlement of the shores of the St. Lawrence river by the French, though contemporaneous with the settlement of New England, was its opposite in every respect.   The one was the plantation of a seaboard, the other of a great river highway leading far into the interior of the continent.   While the early English settlers multiplied their numbers and concentrated their strength in the agricultural townships of a large but limited area, the French went up the St. Lawrence as missionaries and fur traders, discovered the Great Lakes and sailed down the Mississippi. The fur trade was their economic object, and they pursued it by keeping on good terms with the Red Indian trappers from whom they purchased the furs.   The New Englanders, on the other hand, wanted the Indian's hunting-grounds to plough, and regarded him as an enemy, only half human.   The colour-feeling of the English race is stronger than that of the French.

French Canada was as feudal and Roman Catholic as New England was democratic and Puritan.   The Breton peasant, the most religious and obedient in old France, went out under the leadership of his priest and his lord, and reconstituted on the banks of the St. Lawrence the clerical and feudal society which alone he understood.   There was no element of democracy or of self-government in the French North American settlements until those ideas were intruded late in the Eighteenth Century as a result of English conquest.   The French royal government, which had organized and subsidized the planting of the colony, kept it under close control and subjected every male inhabitant to com-

pulsory military service. No one could enter the colony without
the permission of King Louis, and that permission was not granted
to Huguenots.

The American colonies of England, the offspring of Dissent by
Self-help, were much less submissive to their home government
than the colonies of France, Spain or even Holland. The English
colonies had originated not in acts of State but in the venture of
joint-stock companies or of individual proprietors. As they were
gradually brought under the control of the Crown, the habit
of self-government within the colony had perpetually to be
adjusted, not without friction, to the authority of the Royal
Governor. It was a 'dyarchy' that caused many quarrels, but
was necessitated by the circumstances of the time.

In practice, in spite of the Governor, the colonies were self-
governing as regards their own internal affairs. Laud had contemplated an attack on the religious autonomy of New England,
and it cannot be doubted that if Charles I's despotism had become
securely established in the old country a crisis would ere long have
arisen out of an attempt to extend the system of arbitrary government across the ocean. But the civil troubles at home gave the
colonies twenty years in which to nurse their independent spirit:
Massachusetts made war and founded or annexed new colonies
without reference to the home government. It is true that the
victorious Parliament of 1649, in reasserting the unity of the
Empire on a regicide basis, had proclaimed the novel doctrine that
the English Parliament could legislate for and govern the colonies;
but Oliver as Protector had more carefully respected the sensitive
independence of New England, and the Restoration put the
colonies back in direct relation with the Crown rather than with
Parliament.

Massachusetts had, in fact, early adopted an attitude almost
amounting to a claim to independent sovereignty. This led to
a long and bitter dispute, occupying the reigns of Charles and
James II. It came to a climax in 1683, when the Charter of
Massachusetts was cancelled at the height of the Tory reaction
in England, when so many English towns were similarly deprived
of their ancient liberties. In the case of Massachusetts the provocation had been considerable, but it did not justify the attempt to
subject the colony to despotic government. The Revolution of
1689 gave the opportunity to settle this, like so many other outstanding questions. A new Charter was granted and self-govern- 1691.
ment restored on the condition that political rights should be
extended not merely to 'Church members' but to the whole
colonial community. 'Thanks to England,' writes Mr. Truslow
Adams, 'the final death-blow had legally been dealt to the

theocracy, and the foundation laid for genuine self-government and religious toleration.'

The probability that New England would some day break off from the home government was present from the first. It was made yet more probable when on the Restoration of Charles II the social and religious differences between old and New England were stereotyped. In the homeland puritanism and democracy were once more subjugated by Anglicanism and aristocracy, an arrangement which the Revolution of 1689 modified but did not overset. Cromwell had found it easy to remain on good terms with Massachusetts, though Virginia and Barbados had to be compelled by force of arms to obey the regicide Republic. If a system of religion and society consonant with the ideas of the Protectorate had become permanent in the mother country, the social and intellectual misunderstanding between old and New England would not have become so sharp as it did in the middle of the Eighteenth Century.

Cromwell was the first ruler of England who was consciously an Imperialist. Before him, the attitude of government towards colonization had been permissive only. The Protector annexed Jamaica by force of arms, thereby greatly increasing the importance of the English possessions in the West Indian archipelago.[1] He also annexed Acadia from France, but it was given back after the Restoration.

In spite of their surrender of Acadia, the governments of Charles II's reign, under the influence of Clarendon and of Shaftesbury, were imbued with the spirit of Cromwell's colonial policy. They took intelligent interest in the affairs of America, largely with a view to promoting English trade and finding markets for English goods. Prince Rupert and the Court supported the enterprise of the English fur-traders to Hudson's Bay, turning the northern flank of the French Canadian trappers. Above all, 1664. England captured and annexed from the Dutch the group of Middle Colonies between New England and Virginia, turning New Amsterdam into New York, and so forming an unbroken coastline under the British flag from Maine to the new colony of Carolina. Behind that line of coast colonies was founded the most strange settlement of all: Charles II's government, at the moment of the strongest Tory reaction in England, permitted 1681. William Penn, the Quaker courtier and organizer, to found Pennsylvania as a refuge for persecuted Friends in the wilderness,

---

[1] The Civil Wars, from the time of Cromwell till Sedgemoor and after, sent large supplies of unhappy political prisoners and prisoners of war to serve the West Indian planters as ' indentured servants,' practically as slaves, for a term of years. In this miserable way, the English stock was increased.

where they practised with success the unwonted principle of just dealing with the redskins.

The annexation and further planting of these Middle Colonies brought to the front two new principles of the utmost importance in the British Empire—the union of a number of different races with equal rights under the British flag, and religious toleration for all. Those principles had not been the contribution of New England. They were first developed on a large scale in the Middle Colonies seized from Holland, where the Dutch were quickly reconciled by the respect paid to their customs and by the enjoyment of rights of self-government such as they had not known under their own flag. In New York Colony, in Pennsylvania, in Maryland and in New Jersey, there were welded together on equal terms of freedom, English, Dutch, Swedes, Germans, French and Ulster Scots—that is to say, Anglicans and Puritans, Calvinists and Lutherans, Roman Catholics, Quakers and Presbyterians. Thither, as to a most congenial atmosphere, came the Huguenot victims of renewed Roman Catholic persecution in the Europe of Louis XIV, and the Romanist and Puritan sufferers from Anglican intolerance, which operated only in the British Islands.

The North America of the Eighteenth Century that ultimately revolted from Great Britain, was made up of the combination of three types of colony, New England, the Middle Colonies, and the Southern slave-owning aristocrats. The characteristic spirit of modern America, which eventually spread from Atlantic to Pacific, was a blend of the ideas and habits of the democratic township and self-dependent Puritanism of New England with the absence of religious and racial prejudice fostered among the races and religions that were first mingled in the Middle Colonies.

A third element, common to all the colonies from Maine to Carolina, was the frontier spirit. The frontier in American history does not mean, as in Europe, a fixed boundary paraded by sentries, but is the term used for that part of the wilderness into which the white man has most recently penetrated. The frontier was always moving, but the frontiersman was always the same. At whatever distance, small or great, from the Atlantic seaboard, whether in the Seventeenth or the two following Centuries, certain characteristics were always found among the pioneers of the advance into the West. Hardihood, resource and courage; poverty and the hope of present betterment; democratic equality and dislike of all forms of training and authority, whether political or intellectual; careless generosity and shrewd self-help; lynch-law and good comradeship; complete ignorance of distant Europe—combined to make up a well-known type of character, often in sharp contrast to the settled and conservative habits of

the comfortable folk nearer the coast, in districts which had themselves constituted the frontier a generation or two before.

If ever aristocratic Britain were to come into serious conflict
with her colonies, she would find some sympathizers at least
among the settled and well-to-do folk of the coast towns, who
grew richer and somewhat more amenable as the generations went
by ; but she would find implacable rebels not only in the Puritan
farmers of New England, but in the democratic frontiersmen at
the back of every colony, an element frequently despised or forgotten by the highly civilized part of society until it was too late.

In the last half of the Seventeenth Century England's statesmen and merchants put a high value on her American colonies.
They did not indeed foresee their enormous future expansion ;
no one dreamed for an instant that the quarter of a million
inhabitants of the coast colonies in 1700 would ever be enlarged
into a State of a hundred millions. The Appalachian Mountains
bounded the vision not only of British statesmen but of the
Anglo-Americans themselves. England prized about equally the
sugar islands and the colonies of the continental seaboard.

The overseas possessions were valued as fulfilling a twofold
purpose. First as supplying an appropriate outlet for the energetic, the dissident, the oppressed, the debtors, the criminals and
the failures of old England—a sphere where the energies of men
who were too good or too bad not to be troublesome at home,
might be turned loose to the general advantage ; as yet there was
no pressing question of a purely economic excess of population in
England. Secondly, the colonies were valued as markets where
raw materials could be bought, and manufactured articles sold,
to the advantage of England's industry and commerce. ' I state
to you,' said Chatham, ' the importance of America ; it is a
double market : a market of consumption and a market of supply.'
Cromwell and Clarendon, Shaftesbury and Somers, would all have
said the same.

The external policy of England was falling more and more
under the influence of mercantile considerations. Even the
restoration of the influence of the old social order in 1660 did not
go far enough to check this movement. The direction of the
course of external trade by government regulation from Whitehall or Westminster, a scheme of which the Navigation Laws
formed part, was worked in some respects to the advantage
of the mainland colonies ; in other respects it sacrificed their
interest to that of the home country or the sugar islands—
whereupon the New Englanders took to smuggling like ducks
to water.

At the end of the Stuart period England was the greatest manufacturing and trading country in the world, and London outstripped Amsterdam as the world's greatest emporium. There was a thriving trade with the Orient, the Mediterranean and the American colonies ; its basis was the sale of English textile goods, which could be carried to the other side of the world in the large ocean-going ships of the new era. England's commerce, in America and everywhere else, largely consisted of the sale of English manufactures. In that lay her strength as compared to her forerunners in maritime power. Venice had been the carrier, at the European terminus, of the trade between all Europe and the Asiatic markets. Spain had lived on spoil, tribute and mining for precious metals. Even Holland had lacked a sufficient hinterland of manufactures and population in her small territory.

When finally the attacks of Louis XIV drove Holland to devote her wealth and energy to self-defence on land, she gradually fell behind England in the race for commercial leadership. In spite of maritime rivalry, it was England's interest to save Dutch independence and to preserve the Spanish Netherlands from falling into French hands. For if the Delta of the Rhine had become French, the maritime power and the independence of England could not have long survived. In that respect English and Dutch interests were identical, as Charles and James II failed to see, but as the English people saw. But it was none the less to the selfish advantage of England that her two chief rivals for naval and commercial supremacy became engaged during this critical period in great military expenditure, France from deliberate choice and ambition, Holland from the necessities of self-defence.

1668–1714.

Meanwhile in the England of the Restoration and of the Revolution Settlement, the governing classes were determined to spend as much on the Navy as was necessary, and as little on the Army as they could possibly help.

Books for Further Reading

Egerton, *British Colonial Policy* ; Beer, *Origins of the British Colonial System,* 1578–1660 ; Osgood, *American Colonies in the Seventeenth Century* (3 vols.) ; Channing, *History of the United States,* Vols. I.–II. ; Truslow Adams, *The Founding of New England* (Atlantic Monthly Press, Boston) ; Parkman's works, for French Canada.

CHAPTER VI

The Restoration and the Reign of Charles II.   The Formation of the Whig
and Tory Parties

THE principles of government associated with the names of
Cæsar and Napoleon have never been popular in England.
Cromwell, like all great English soldiers, disliked the idea of ruling
his countrymen by the sword, and they disliked him for doing it.
In his last years he was seeking a path back to the rule of law,
custom and Parliament. But law, custom and Parliament were
in this island so inextricably interwoven with the Kingly office
by centuries of continuous growth and by the inherited association of ideas, that a restoration of the monarchy was needed if
the nation were to enjoy its ancient rights again.

Had Oliver himself lived, it seems likely that he would have
attempted the most difficult task of his life, to restore constitutional rule by reviving the monarchy in his own person. In the
person of his feeble son Richard it was frankly impossible. The
1659.   rule of the sword became more undisguised and more intolerable
when there was no strong hand to wield it, when regiment began
to fight with regiment, and General to rise up against General as
in the worst periods of the Roman Empire. To prevent anarchy
from becoming chronic at home, and to stay the dissolution of the
Empire overseas, there was no way but to recall the Stuart heir.
The sooner and the more willingly that was done by Parliament
and by the old Roundhead party, the greater would be the
freedom of the subject under the restored Kingship.

The lead given by General Monk to the sane and patriotic
elements in the army, enabled the Convention Parliament to
1660.   be freely elected. It consisted of moderate Roundheads of the
old Presbyterian party, with a strong admixture of Cavaliers.
It called back Charles II from his exile in Holland. At this
important crisis of the constitution, it was not the King who
summoned Parliament, but Parliament that summoned the King.
Though the principle of the Divine Right of Kings might be
preached as the favourite dogma of the restored Anglican Church,
though the lawyers might pretend after their fashion that Charles
the Exile had been Charles II from the moment his father's head
fell upon the scaffold, the fact was notorious that monarchy had
after a long interval been renewed in his person by the vote of the
two Houses, as the result of a general election.

The authority of the King and the authority of Parliament
were once more regarded as inseparable. Rivals they might

long remain, enemies they might on occasion become, but they would never again be two mutually exclusive methods of government as Strafford and the Regicides had made them. Absolutism and Republicanism both were dead; nor except by James II has any serious attempt since been made to revive either the one or the other in England.

So 'the King enjoyed his own again.' The second Charles could indeed be trusted to 'enjoy' whatever came his way, but 'his own' was no longer the full heritage of power which had descended to his ancestors. The crown had been stripped of many of its jewels in the first session of the Long Parliament, and that work was not undone at the Restoration. The great Prerogative Courts, with their rival system of jurisprudence based on the laws of ancient Rome, were not revived as an eyesore to the Common Lawyers and a weapon of the Prince against the Subject: Star Chamber and High Commission remained abolished and illegal. Taxation could no longer be imposed save by vote of Parliament. Strafford's old enemies, 'Sir Edward Coke and his Year-Books,' Hampden and his scruples on Ship-money, triumphed at the Restoration no less than Laud and his surplices. 1640-1641.

Of all that generation of the illustrious dead one survivor remained to become the architect of the Restoration settlement, —Edward Hyde, now Earl of Clarendon and Lord Chancellor, the faithful servant of the royal family in its long exile. To him the Stuarts owed it that they ever returned from foreign lands, because even there he had kept young Charles in some degree of connection with the Anglican Church and the constitutional royalists, in spite of the Queen Mother and the swordsmen. And now, in the critical first months of the reign, Clarendon's wisdom and moderation, in harmony with the King's shrewdness and loose good-nature, gave peace to the land, stayed the furies of revenge, and made it to the interest of all parties to live as loyal subjects of the restored monarchy.

Clarendon, who had been the bosom friend of Falkland and the ally of Hampden against Strafford, was still the man of 1640. To that year he undertook to bring back the body politic, as though the two most crowded decades in English History had not intervened. Nor was he wholly unsuccessful. The balance of power between King and Commons was fixed in 1660 at the point where it had been set in the first session of the Long Parliament. The restored equilibrium of the Constitution served as nothing else could have done to give a breathing space for recovery and regrowth after the storms of the revolutionary era. But mere equilibrium would not provide a permanent form of government for a vigorous and growing State, as Strafford and Pym had both foreseen. State action, especially overseas, was paralysed by the division of executive and legislative into two rival bodies, neither the acknowledged master of the other in case of dispute. Until Parliament controlled foreign policy as well as finance, until the King's Ministers were also the servants of the House of Commons, the King's government would remain suspected, impoverished and hampered ; and the struggle between Crown and Houses would proceed once more, whether the Parliament were called ' Cavalier ' or ' Whig.'

Clarendon indeed had little joy of his chosen part as mediator between King and Commons, for both fretted against the limits he set. His other sorrow was that he could nowhere find the integrity and public spirit of the men he had known in his youth. The character of English politicians, and, to a less extent, the character of the class of landed gentry as a whole had degenerated under the corroding influence of war, confiscation and revolution. Politicians and poets, with one or two grand exceptions, had learnt to change their principles and their allegiance like summer and winter clothes. And the young royalist squires who now rode roughshod over the land had been ill schooled for the parts they were to play. Some had spent what should have been their schooldays in garrets over the Arno and the Seine, amid the riff-raff of foreign cities ; while those who had stayed in England had grown up among grooms in a corner of the dismantled manor-house when the estate had gone to the hammer. Mean shifts to gain their daily bread had been their education and discipline, and hatred of the Puritan spoiler had been instilled in the place of religion.

An upper class so brought up was not likely to resist the incitement to cynicism and profligate life afforded by the spectacle of the supremacy and downfall of the Puritans. The distinction between virtue and hypocrisy was dim to the first generation that laughed over *Hudibras*. Charles II, himself a product of these conditions, made broad the primrose path for the world of fashion in his charming and heartless Court. Clarendon's antiquated virtue divided him from his master and from the new generation of Parliament men. His grave integrity might indeed, like Pitt's or Peel's, have won the confidence of the uncorrupted middle classes, where family prayers were said daily and virtue was not mocked. But political and religious affinities disabled him from becoming their leader ; he was the last man in the kingdom to court the popular suffrage, and he left to libertines like the young Buckingham and to sceptics like Shaftesbury the task of leading resurgent non-conformity and organizing the political aspirations of the mercantile world.

The greatest work of Clarendon and Charles, for which both deserve high credit, was their steady refusal to permit a general revenge upon the Roundhead party. Only so could the King fulfil the promises made in Holland that had brought him home in peace, only so could the throne be re-established as a national institution accepted by all parties. The Act of Indemnity and 1660. Oblivion was stigmatized by the Cavaliers as ' Indemnity for the King's enemies and Oblivion for the King's friends.' The royalists had looked to glut their revenge in the blood and the estates of the rival faction ; but in the main they were disappointed, and they never forgave Clarendon.

A dozen regicides, and Vane the noblest survivor of the Commonwealth statesmen, were offered up as scapegoats, and their deaths appeased the cry for blood, never prolonged in England. But the cry for land was louder and more lasting. Land was still the chief goal of ambition, the chief source of wealth, power and social consequence. On the land-question a compromise was effected by Clarendon which secured the acceptance of the new regime by the great body of former Roundheads. Church and Crown lands, and private estates of Cavalier magnates that had been confiscated and sold by the rebel governments were resumed, without compensation to those who had purchased them. But the lands which Cavaliers had themselves sold to pay the fines imposed on them as ' malignants ' were left in the hands of the purchasers. A large body of new men thereby made good their footing in the English squirearchy, at the easy price of attending the restored Anglican worship. Many of these prosperous ex-Roundheads became local leaders of the Whig party in the coming era.[1]

Under this arrangement many Cavaliers failed to recover lands which they had been forced to sell as a price of their loyalty in evil days ; they were bitterly aggrieved against the government, and continued to hate the former Roundheads of every shade with a personal as well as a political hatred. This temper dictated the policy of the Cavalier Parliament that was elected at the height of the reaction in 1661. The majority of the new members formed a party—afterwards known as ' Tory '—that was more Anglican and squirearchical than royalist : it kept the Crown on a short allowance of taxes, scouted the advice of Charles and Clarendon, remodelled the Corporations in the interest of their own Church and party rather than of the Court, and set on foot by Parliamentary statute a persecution of Puritan nonconformists more cruel than any desired by the King or even by that stout Anglican the Lord Chancellor.

[1] See p. 417, above, and note.

Indeed the so-called 'Clarendon Code' of laws against Dissenters was not the work of Clarendon, still less of Charles, but of Parliament and the squires. By insisting on a fiercer religious persecution than ever, at the beginning of a new age that needed above all else religious toleration, Parliament sowed dragon's teeth, destined to spring up in the plots, factions and violences that convulsed the latter years of the reign. The 'Clarendon Code' was the Cavaliers' revenge for their long sufferings and their lost lands. Balked by the Act of Indemnity, they found this other outlet for their feelings. They were prompted less by religious bigotry than by political passion and the memory of personal wrongs and losses, many of them still unredressed.

The root of what the Dissenters were now to suffer may be traced to the Parliamentary fines on 'malignants' and to the executions of Laud and Charles I. It was not merely vengeance : the 'Clarendon Code' was also a measure of police against the revival of the Roundhead party. The Act of Uniformity of 1662 restored the Prayer Book and turned adrift without compensation 2000 clergy who could not assert their 'unfeigned consent and assent' to everything the book contained. The Conventicle Act of two years later made prison and transportation the lot of those caught in acts of dissenting worship. These Statutes were the policy of Parliament, not of the King. Laud's religion triumphed, but not through the royal power nor through the clerical jurisdiction and authority which he had striven to restore, but through the action of the Parliament of squires whose right to pronounce upon religion he and Charles I had died rather than acknowledge.

The religious settlement of the Restoration was not conceived in the spirit of compromise which marked the political and social settlement. Yet it may at least be questioned whether it has not led to more religious, intellectual and political liberty than would have resulted from a wider extension of the boundaries of the Established Church. If the plan to 'comprehend' Baxter and the moderate Puritans had succeeded at the abortive Savoy Conference of 1661, the Quakers, Baptists, and more advanced sects, who must still have been left outside, might have been too isolated and inconsiderable ever to enforce the claim of toleration for themselves. The arrangement actually made, under which the Church of England and the various Puritan Churches followed each its own lines of development, rendered toleration inevitable ere long, and led to the variety and competition of religious bodies characteristic of modern England, utterly at variance with mediæval, Tudor or Stuart notions of Church and State.

It is true that the Puritan sects lost greatly by exclusion from the culture of the Universities and from their natural share in social influence and political power, but their very disabilities and grievances forced them to remain for two hundred years vigilant champions of liberty and critics of government. Our two-party system in politics flourished so long and so vigorously because religion also was based upon the two great parties of privileged and unprivileged.

But in the interim between the Restoration and the Revolution, the nation was torn and tortured by the active persecution of so large a body as the Protestant Dissenters. The squires indeed, Whig as well as Tory, conformed to the Anglican worship, although the two parties were diametrically opposed to each other in their attitude towards the Church. But many of the middle and lower classes, in the days of Baxter, Bunyan and George Fox, suffered ruin and imprisonment rather than give over the attendance at services which Parliament had made illegal. The merchant class suffered so severely from the penalties enforced on Dissenters, that statesmen were at length alarmed by the havoc wrought by persecution in English manufacture and commerce. They felt less concern for the grave injury done to education by the Five Mile Act, which forbade any clergyman or schoolmaster **1665.** from coming within five miles of a city or corporate town unless he swore that he would 'not at any time endeavour any alteration in Government either in Church or State.' Puritanism was strongest in the towns, and the loss thus inflicted on its culture was never completely made good.

The number of Dissenters was kept down by twenty-five years of severe though intermittent persecution. But even in their worst sufferings the faithful looked forward to the next general election to bring them relief through Parliament. For this reason there was no general exodus to America as in the days of Laud and Strafford. The Puritans continued to have faith in the House of Commons, although so long as the Cavalier Parliament sat,—and it sat for seventeen years,—it was the prime source of their troubles.

In Charles II's Court at Whitehall, where Roman Catholicism and scepticism were both more influential than among the Parliament men at Westminster, a larger measure of toleration found advocates. The King, a Romanist at heart, desired to tolerate and promote Catholics, and he knew that it was not safe to do so unless the Puritans were relieved at the same time. Moreover, his expert hedonist took less pleasure than the virtuous in punishing other people for their opinions. The persecuting **1662 and** statutes were on more than one occasion suspended by a royal **1672.** Declaration of Indulgence. This wholesale tampering with the execution of laws was declared illegal by Parliament, and the

Puritans who gained occasional respite by these Declarations, were embarrassed by the knowledge that they were acts of arbitrary power and that their benefits were shared by the Roman Catholics. Parliament was determined that both Puritans and Romanists should remain under the full weight of the penal laws. It was a curious ' triangular duel ' between Rome, Canterbury and Geneva, between King, Parliament and the distressed subject. It passed through a variety of phases until the decisive crisis of 1688–9.

In the second decade of the Restoration regime the Protestant Dissenters began to spy a hope of relief in a quarter that suited them much better than the royal prerogative. A minority in the two Houses of Parliament, that was steadily increased by the process of by-elections as the old members died off, held out the hope of statutory relief to ' tender consciences,' and opposed both the Cavaliers and the Court.

This ' Whig ' party, as it was eventually called, had religious affinities in its rank and file with Puritanism, and in its higher grades with the latitudinarianism and rationalism of the new age. Puritan and Rationalist were drawn together into common opposition to the dominant High Churchmen. The Baptist preacher, dogged by spies from conventicle to conventicle and haled from prison to prison by infuriated Justices of the Peace, when he heard that the Whig chiefs had taken up the cause of Parliamentary toleration for all Protestants, was too greatly rejoiced to enquire whether Algernon Sidney was in a state of grace, or what Shaftesbury meant by ' the religion of all wise men.'

The Royal Society and the great scientific movement that reached its full intellectual splendour in Sir Isaac Newton at Trinity College, Cambridge, was nursed in its infancy by the patronage of Charles II and the sceptical courtiers, who had at least the virtue of curiosity. The scientific and latitudinarian movement slowly created an atmosphere favourable to the doctrine of religious toleration as propounded by the Whig philosopher, John Locke, while outside the realm of politics it is noticeable that the hunt after witches, that had raged horridly in the first half of the Stuart era, began to abate, as first the Judges and then the juries began to feel the prickings of philosophic doubt.

b. 1642, d. 1727.

Within the national Church, latitudinarianism had a party, respectable for its learning and eloquence rather than for its numbers, and more powerful in London than in the countryside. This was the ' Low Church ' party, a name that then denoted not evangelicalism but what we should now call ' broad ' or ' liberal ' views. Politically the Low Churchmen, like Stillingfleet, Tillotson

and Burnet, were the advocates of Toleration and the friends of
the Protestant Dissenters. Similarly the name ' High Church,'
given to the great majority of the clergy and their more ardent
lay supporters, did not then mean ritualist ; it betokened strong
antipathy to Dissenters as well as to Romanists, belief in the doctrine of non-resistance to Kings and their divine hereditary right,
a great reverence for King Charles the Martyr and—at least among
the clergy—a high view of the authority of the Church in politics
and society.   Dr. Johnson, though he lived a hundred years later,
is an excellent example of the ' High Church' mentality any time
between the Restoration and the French Revolution.

It is, indeed, remarkable how much of Puritan, or at least of
strongly Protestant thought and practice survived the political
and ecclesiastical fall of the Puritan sects. Family prayer and
Bible reading had become national custom among the great
majority of religious laymen, whether they were Churchmen or
Dissenters. The English character had received an impression
from Puritanism which it bore for the next two centuries, though
it had rejected Puritan coercion and had driven Dissenters out of
polite society. Even the Puritan Sunday survived. The anxiety
of James I and Laud that the English people should continue as
of old to play games on Sunday afternoon, was, one would have
supposed, calculated to meet with the approval of the most
athletic and ' sporting' of all nations. Yet even at the Restoration, when the very name of Puritan was a hissing and a reproach,
when the gaols were crowded with harmless Quakers and Baptists,
the Puritan idea of Sunday, as a day strictly set aside for rest
and religious meditation, continued to hold the allegiance of the
English people. The good and evil effects of this self-imposed
discipline of a whole nation, in abstaining from organized amusement as well as from work on every seventh day, still awaits the
dispassionate study of the social historian.

A reduction in public expenditure was one of the most popular
consequences of the fall of the Cromwellian system. The King
was indeed put by the Cavalier Parliament on an absurdly short
allowance, which hampered all branches of the administration
and ere long tempted him to sell the control of his foreign policy
to Louis XIV of France. But the shortage was a natural result
of the return to ' the just balance of the constitution,' which
Clarendon believed to be the last word of political wisdom. Till
Parliament could control policy and expenditure, it would not
consent to open wide the public purse. When the Commons
insisted on searching the royal account books to trace the actual 1666.
use made of money voted for the maritime war with Holland,

Clarendon and the courtiers were scandalized at such an invasion of the province of the executive by the legislative. Yet this was a first step on the road to that Parliamentary control of expenditure, which alone could secure for the King's government the liberal and continuous supplies from the taxpayers essential to a great nation in modern times.

It was the military and not the naval establishment that bore the brunt of the reductions from Cromwell's lavish standards. By a single great financial effort, the New Model Army was paid off and disbanded at the Restoration, as might have been done thirteen years before if the Long Parliament had been well-advised. It was replaced by no other considerable force. Besides the King's splendid royalist ' Life Guards ' designed to ride by his coach and protect him from fanatics and Fifth Monarchy Men, only a few regiments were kept on foot, and those chiefly in foreign possessions like Tangier.[1] The oldest regimental traditions of the British Army derive either from the few Cromwellian units whose life was continued like the Coldstream Guards, or else from the famous regiments in Dutch service like the Buffs.

The Cavalier Parliament, reflecting the passionate feeling of the English country gentlemen, hated and feared the very name of ' standing army.' They were well aware that lawful Kings could play them tricks with such a force, as easily as usurping Protectors. The King alone, as all good Cavaliers believed, had the right to nominate to military commands and give orders to the armed forces. To claim any such powers for Parliament was to be a rebel and a Roundhead, for the Great Civil War had broken out on that issue. But it followed from these loyal premises that the Army must be kept very small, lest His Gracious Majesty should be tempted to arbitrary conduct.

How well grounded was this caution appeared too late when James II was permitted to keep on foot 30,000 men. Only as a consequence of the Revolution that he then provoked, did Parliament gain practical security that the Army would not be used against the liberties of the land. Only then, in the reigns of William III and Anne, did fear of a standing army begin to subside, first among Whig statesmen whose hearts were in the land war against Louis XIV. The mind of the Tory squire moved more slowly ; for a hundred years after Naseby the sight of a company of regulars on the march recalled to him the red-coats who had blown in the door of his grandfather's hall, ruined his

---

[1] Tangier and Bombay came as the dowry of Charles II's wife, the Portuguese Princess, Catherine of Braganza. In return England helped to maintain the recovered independence of Portugal from decadent Spain, and the commercial and political relations of England and Portugal began which have lasted over two centuries and a half.

estate, proscribed his religion and beheaded his King. The only force he trusted was the ill-trained militia of the county, officered by rustic squires like himself.

No such fears and memories affected the upkeep of the Navy. The Court and Parliament of the Restoration both accepted the traditions of the Commonwealth's fighting fleet, which the dying Blake had bequeathed to posterity. Charles II and his brother James took a personal and well-informed interest in naval matters, and the Admiralty was well served by men like Pepys and his patrons. The Cavalier Parliament and the Tory party regarded the Navy with special favour.

Navy

Another maritime war with Holland soon broke out, a resumption of the quarrel of the two mercantile communities begun under the Commonwealth. It was conducted on both sides with the same splendid qualities of fighting seamanship and on the same colossal scale as before. Again the larger country had rather the better of the war, and, at the Treaty of Breda, New York was ceded by Holland to England.[1]

1665–1667.

1667.

But while the treaty was still being negotiated, the Dutch fleet under de Ruyter, piloted by English seamen, sailed up the Thames and the Medway, and burnt and captured our finest warships as they lay at anchor off Chatham. The disgrace made no marked difference to the terms of the treaty, but following as it did close on the Plague and the Fire of London, it deeply affected the imagination and the politics of the English people. The sound of the enemy's guns in the Thames was new to Londoners. Men began to ' reflect upon Oliver,' whose corpse they had so recently gibbeted, ' what brave things he did and made all the neighbour Princes fear him.' ' The King,' the world said, ' minds nothing but his lust and hath taken ten times more care and pains in making friends between Lady Castlemaine and Mrs. Stewart, when they have fallen out, than ever he did to save his Kingdom.' Already there were rumours that we were ' governed by Papists ' at Whitehall. With less reason it was believed that the ' Papists ' had burnt down London ; a few years earlier the Fire would have been ascribed to the Puritans. In this changed atmosphere, more formidable opposition parties and policies were engendered than any that had hitherto been known in the Cavalier Parliament.

June 1667.

1665. 1666.

And yet the principal cause of the Medway disaster had been the unwillingness of the House of Commons to vote money liberally to a government it could not control and was beginning to suspect. The ships had been laid up and the crews disbanded as a forced economy. Indeed the British sailors had gone un-

[1] See pp: 427 and 442, above.

paid for so many years that large numbers had deserted to the
Dutch, who rewarded their seamen with dollars instead of
unmarketable ' Treasury tickets.'

Nov.1667.
The Plague, the Fire, the Medway, the persecution of Dissenters, and the ' flaunting of Papists at Court ' caused a temper
to rise in the nation that foreboded storm.   Yet in face of these
signs Charles decided to ' drop the pilot.'   It was indeed tempting
to make a scapegoat of Clarendon, for he was regarded by the
nation as responsible for all that had gone wrong ; he was hated
by the unpaid seamen, by the persecuted Dissenters, by the royal
mistresses to whom he would pay no court, by the Parliament
men whom he would fain keep within their appointed sphere, and
by the whole world of young ambition whose path he obstructed.
Indeed with his old-fashioned views he was no longer in a position
to render great services to England.   But the men whom Charles
chose in his place led King and country into dangers which he
would have avoided, for they betrayed the interests of the nation
to France, and some of them plotted with their master to betray
the Protestant Establishment as well.

1667–
1673.
The ' Cabal ' contained not one sound Anglican and scarcely
one true patriot.   Clifford was an ardent Romanist and Arlington
more of a Romanist than anything else ; Lauderdale and
Buckingham were unprincipled adventurers, and Anthony Ashley
Cooper, Earl of Shaftesbury, was the man destined first to found
the Whig party and then to ruin it by furious driving.   Released
by these mercurial companions from Clarendon's control, Charles,
his own master at last, entered upon strange courses.

The great fact of the new age in Europe was the advance of
French arms and influence across the continent.   The decadence
of Spain, and the failure of Germany and Italy to produce one
formidable power among the innumerable States into which their
vast territories were divided, left the way open for the ambition of
France.   Her unity and internal organization had been perfected
by Cardinals Richelieu and Mazarin, and bequeathed by them to
Louis XIV and the brilliant group of soldiers and statesmen who
served him in his youth.   In the ten years since the death of
Cromwell the danger had become apparent to all the world.   The
States of Europe, Catholic as well as Protestant, were in panic,
but their inefficiency, selfishness and mutual jealousy prevented
their union for self-defence before William of Orange arose to
marshal them.   Austria, engaged in defending the approaches
of Vienna against the Turk, could only intermittently concern
herself with the West.   Spain, stricken with the palsy of all her
once splendid energies, was fain to leave the defence of her

possessions in the Netherlands to her former enemies, the Dutch rebels.

Amid the effete monarchies and princedoms of feudal Europe, morally and materially exhausted by the Thirty Years' War, the only hope of resistance to France lay in the little Republic of merchants, Holland poised between the sand-banks and the sea. Enriched by its Eastern colonies, its world-wide commerce, and its open door for refugees of all races and beliefs, the home of Grotius, Descartes and Spinoza, of Rembrandt and Vermeer, led the world in philosophy, learning, finance, painting, gardening, scientific agriculture, and many other of the arts and crafts that liberate and adorn the life of man. Holland was a rival influence to France in Europe, and stood on this height without the parade of King, noble or prelate. Her first magistrate, the admired De Witt, kept a single servant in his house and walked unattended through the streets.

The destruction of this bourgeois, Calvinist Republic, no less than the extirpation of the Huguenots in France herself, formed an essential part of the schemes of Louis and the French Jesuit body who inspired the ideals and the policy of his reign. In that policy, strongly ' Gallican ' and nationalist in spirit, little reference was made to the wishes of the more moderate Italian Papacy, with whom both the French Jesuits and the French King eventually had bitter quarrels.

In 1668 an English diplomat in the Low Countries, Sir William Temple, negotiated with great skill the Triple Alliance of England, Holland and Sweden to check the French advance on the Rhine and in the Spanish Netherlands. The effect was instantaneous. Louis was compelled to accept the terms of the Treaty of Aix-la-Chapelle. If England had steadily adhered to this successful line of policy, she might have saved Europe an epoch of bloodshed. But our subservience to France during the twenty years that intervened between Temple's Treaty and the Revolution of 1688, raised the power of Louis to a point from which it could only be dislodged by the long wars of William and Marlborough.

The English Parliament and nation were at first well pleased with Temple's policy of the Balance of Power and the maintenance of Protestantism in Europe. But it was easy for persons secretly hostile to these interests to appeal in public to the sentiment of commercial rivalry with Holland that had already caused two popular wars. The management of foreign policy was in the King's hands as the constitution then stood. In the middle years of his reign, Charles II's Roman Catholic and despotic proclivities were stimulated by his natural irritation with the Cavalier Parliament, which had thwarted his wishes and starved his exchequer. Could he not enter instead into the pay of Louis, and introduce something of the admired French-Catholic system of government into the confused body-politic of England? Charles himself was half French in blood and breeding, and his family had little reason to love English institutions.

Moreover in 1670 the King of England had a family quarrel with Holland. The oligarchic Republic of the De Witts was keeping his nephew [1] William of Orange out of the quasi-monarchical office of the Stadtholderate, which William regarded as his birthright and which the Dutch popular party wished to restore in his person. By the Treaty of Dover that Charles made with Louis, England and France were to attack and partition the Republic and its possessions. A residue would be left, to be governed by William of Orange as the vassal of France. The idea that a young Prince would object to an arrangement so favourable to his vanity and comfort never occurred to these cynics, any more than the idea that a lad just coming of age would find the means to thwart the combined onslaught of France and England.

Such was the open Treaty of Dover, to which Shaftesbury and the Protestants of the Cabal, to their lasting infamy, consented. But there was also a secret treaty, unknown to them but signed by the Catholic members of the Cabal, by which Louis undertook to supply Charles with French soldiers and money, to enable him to declare himself a Roman Catholic and gradually raise his co-religionists to dominance in England.

The two treaties were a single plan for the subjugation of Europe and England by the French Catholic monarchy. But the finance of this hopeful project had been miscalculated. The war with Holland cost England much more than Louis could supply, and bankruptcy drove Charles to submit again to Parliamentary control. Louis no doubt expected that long before the

_1670._

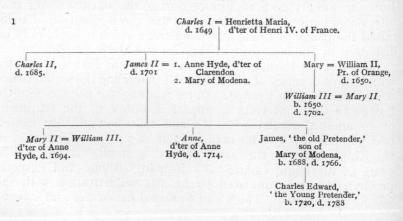

1   *Charles I* = Henrietta Maria,
d. 1649 | d'ter of Henri IV. of France.

Charles II,   *James II* = 1. Anne Hyde, d'ter of   Mary = William II,
d. 1685.   d. 1701   Clarendon   Pr. of Orange,
    2. Mary of Modena.   d. 1650.

William III = *Mary II.*
b. 1650.
d. 1702.

Mary II = *William III.*   *Anne,*   James, ' the old Pretender,'
d'ter of Anne   d'ter of Anne   son of
Hyde, d. 1694.   Hyde, d. 1714.   Mary of Modena,
    b. 1688, d. 1766.

Charles Edward,
' the Young Pretender,'
b. 1720, d. 1788

English squires discovered that they had been duped, his dragoons would be billeted at free quarters on the rich Calvinists of Hague and Rotterdam.   And so it would have happened, but for the temper of the Dutch people, the physical conformation of their land, and the qualities that William of Orange now first revealed to the world.

When the great French army entered the almost defenceless territories of Holland, the popular party rose in rage and despair, brutally murdered the De Witts, overthrew their Republic, and re-established the Stadtholderate in William's person,—but not **1672.** as a preliminary to surrender.   On the contrary they cut the dykes, letting the water of the canalized rivers flow over the low meadows, and at the sacrifice of their drowned property brought the French armies to a standstill.   Meanwhile their seamen at Solebay more than held their own against the united fleets of England and France, and William's genius for diplomacy enabled him to build in haste the first of his many European coalitions against Louis.

These unexpected events gave the squires at Westminster two years in which to take stock of the situation, and to overturn the whole policy of the Cabal and its master.   Parliament had the whip hand, for the war had made Charles bankrupt.   In 1673 he was forced as the price of supply to assent to the Test Act that excluded Roman Catholics from office under the Crown, thereby bringing to light the alarming fact that James, Duke of York, heir to the throne, was a Romanist.   Next year Parliament **1674.** withdrew England from the war.

The Cavalier Parliament had come to realize that this war, properly understood, was not a continuation of the old contest between England and Holland for maritime supremacy, but a design to put an end to Dutch independence as the chief obstacle to the French and Jesuit conquest of Europe.   Moreover, the disappearance of Holland as an independent power would be fraught with danger for England's maritime security, because the Delta of the Rhine would then fall into the hands of France.[1] France too was a maritime rival, potentially more formidable even than Holland, and if established in Amsterdam she would soon make an end of English naval supremacy.   It was the issue of 1588, of 1793, of 1914 : England could not suffer Holland and Belgium to pass under the domination of the greatest military power in Europe.

Holland was saved for the time, but the issue was not yet

---

[1] By the Treaty of Dover some of the islands of Zealand were to be attached to the British Crown, but they would not long have been tenable against French power stretching from Brest to the Zuyder Zee.

decided. It governed English and European politics for forty years to come. After 1674 Louis could no longer hope for the assistance of British arms in subjugating Europe, but thanks to the 'just balance of our constitution,' he secured our neutrality until the Revolution of 1688, by playing off King and Parliament one against the other, bribing the Parliamentary leaders and subsidizing the King. The active agents of this policy over here were his ambassador Barillon and Charles' French mistress, Louise de Querouaille, Duchess of Portsmouth, whom our ancestors spoke of as 'Madam Carwell.'

England had been saved by the narrowest of chances from laying Europe at the feet of France by the destruction of Holland. This policy, insane from the point of view of English interests, was explicable as part of the dynastic and religious designs of the House of Stuart. When this was perceived, a reaction took place against the King and his brother and their 'Popish counsels,' which gave four years of power to the Cavalier Parliament, on the basis of Anglican, national and constitutional principles. Charles, thoroughly alarmed at the storm he had raised and determined not 'to go on his travels again,' threw over his Roman Catholic schemes and sought safety in alliance with Anglican and Tory sentiment. Such was the policy which, during the remainder of his life, he played with consummate nerve and skill.

Charles' change of front involved the abandonment of the discredited Cabal Ministers and submission to the leader of the Cavalier Parliament, Thomas Osborne, Earl of Danby. A Yorkshire squire in origin, Danby sincerely held the political and religious tenets of his class. Though greedy of wealth, titles and power, and ambitious to found a great family, he was, like Clarendon, a man of principle, though with more brilliancy and versatility in his statecraft. He depended more completely on Parliament than Clarendon had done, and was indeed the first royal Minister who owed his position by the throne to the goodwill of the House of Commons. He further secured his majority in the House by systematizing the bribery of individual members which began at the Restoration and continued in the eras of Walpole and George III. The expense, corruption, and elaboration of election contests were also on the increase; in proportion as the power of Parliament rose in the State, a seat and a vote were worth more in the world's market. The patriots of an earlier age had not had their purity thus tempted.

Danby may be called the founder of the Tory party. Yet this theoretic champion of non-resistance did more than any Whig to prepare the way for the Revolution and the reign of William III.

1674-
1678.

During his four years of power he befriended Holland and opposed France. And he arranged a splendid though distant future for this system of alliance by effecting the marriage of William of Orange with Mary, daughter of James and heir after her father to the thrones of England and Scotland. James disliked the match, but Charles, convinced of the necessity of conciliating the nation, supported Danby's scheme and the marriage took place. The Tory Minister saw a thing which his party afterwards forgot for awhile, the necessity of a Protestant succession if a Parliamentary monarchy and an Anglican Church were to be maintained. 1677. See note, p. 458, above.

During the period of Danby's Ministry, the Tory party was more devoted to the House of Orange and more hostile to France than were the leaders of opposition. The Whigs feared the high monarchical principles of the young Stadtholder, and, when Danby tried to force on a war against France, they dreaded to see an army in the hands of their political enemies. These considerations were reinforced by the bribes which some of the Whig members took from the hands of Louis' ambassador. Charles and the Whigs, otherwise poles asunder, were both secretly against war, and between them they managed to prevent it.

The Cavalier Parliament had sat for over fifteen years. A general election would certainly produce a new House of Commons more favourable to Protestant Dissent, but even less favourable to the Court and the Roman Catholics. Therefore Danby and Charles had each his reason for dreading a dissolution. If Danby had already been as wise as he became in later years, he would have considered how ill the country was represented by his party and by the existing Parliament, and would have relaxed the persecuting laws. He preferred to join with Charles in evading a dissolution as long as possible, and used the precious interval to crush out the political and religious enemies of Toryism by the strong hand. The Clarendon Code was reenforced with fresh vigour, and only an accident prevented him from passing his ' non-resisting Bill,' which proposed to exclude from Parliament all who would not utter the Tory shibboleth, of non-resistance to the Crown under every provocation. A dozen years later Danby set his party the example of repudiating this doctrine by leading the rebellion of Yorkshire against King James. 1675.

The chaos and violence of British politics in the ten years before the Revolution were due to the fact that the two separate quarrels were being pressed by unscrupulous antagonists, that of Parliament against Crown involving the question of Protestant against Catholic, and that of Tory against Whig involving the question of Church against Dissent. The cross-currents and

changes of issue were consequently bewildering. Danby still calculated in the spring of 1678, that by applying the rigour of the
law he could crush the Dissenting and Whig interest before the
long overdue dissolution came, while keeping Court and Roman
Catholics subject to Parliament. It was a dangerous and unjust
policy, and it provoked Shaftesbury, now the leader of the Whig
opposition, to desperate courses.

1678.   In such a world Titus Oates' ' Popish plot ' acted like a
match applied to powder. His elaborate lies for a time
gained credit with almost everyone, and turned the Cavalier
Parliament in its last months virtually into a ' Whig ' assembly.
For the belief in Oates' falsehoods was confirmed by the publica-
tion of a truth sufficiently astounding. The correspondence of
Coleman, who acted as the Duke of York's confidential secretary,
was seized and published. It contained letters to the French
King's confessor discussing plans for the forcible reconversion of
Great Britain.

' We have a mighty work upon our hands,' Coleman had written,
' no less than the conversion of three kingdoms, and by that the sub-
duing of a pestilent heresy, which has dominated over a great part of
this northern world for a long time. There was never such hope of
success since the death of Queen Mary as now in our days when God
has given us a Prince who is become zealous of being the author and
instrument of so glorious a work. . . . That which we rely upon most,
next to Almighty God's providence and the favour of my master the
Duke, is the mighty mind of his Most Christian Majesty' (Louis XIV).

What measures should the country take to prevent the overthrow of their religion by the accession of Coleman's master to
the throne ? The Whigs proposed to exclude James from being
King even in name. The Tories proposed to limit his powers.
In the prevailing temper of party violence and religious intolerance
the attempt to carry out either ' exclusion ' or ' limitations '
would very probably have led to civil war. Nothing could have
saved the country in 1679 but a union of Whig and Tory statesmen, laying aside their mutual animosities and compromising
their rival claims, as they did ten years later after a cruel schooling
in adversity.[1]

The Whigs, with whom the game first lay, behaved disgrace-
fully. Instead of seeking to fuse the favourable heat of the hour
into a national settlement, they tried only to kindle the furnace
sevenfold and to fashion out of it their party advantage. They
pursued innocent Catholics to death, exploiting Oates' plot even

[1] Swift long afterwards wrote of the Tory scheme of ' limitations ' : ' It was
wisest, because it would be less opposed, and the King would consent to it ; otherwise an exclusion would have done better.' .

after the credibility of the evidence had begun to wear thin. The violence of the three successive Whig Parliaments against their Tory rivals no less than against the Court; the systematic intimidation of moderate men by the London mob and by Shaftesbury's 'brisk boys'; the refusal to consider for the sake of peace any compromise short of complete Exclusion; and finally the coquetting of the party with the bastard Monmouth as the candidate for the throne, in disregard of the rights of William and Mary who did not promise to be Whig puppets,—all these phenomena, and a belief that '1641 was come again,' drove a large body of moderate opinion, led by the subtle and eloquent Halifax, to rally to the Tory and Royalist side. Moreover the Tories and the Court, rivals since 1661, were consolidated into a single party by the dread of a Roundhead revival. 1679–
1681.

Whig violence was soon countered by Tory violence no less pernicious. The party that Danby had founded might perhaps have been led by him along wiser courses, but Whig malevolence kept him in prison awaiting impeachment. And although sage 'trimmers' like Halifax were the most formidable advocates of the Tory cause in Parliament, the party owed them no allegiance and hated their moderation. The rank and file of squires and High Church clergy became ultra-royalists, prostrating themselves at the feet of Charles, who had become in effect the able leader of their party, and prostrating themselves yet more abjectly before James, who enjoyed for awhile a ludicrous popularity with the Church that he was longing for the opportunity to overthrow.

After the dissolution of the Third Whig Parliament at Oxford in 1681, Tory reaction had full licence. The persecution of Protestant Dissenters, in abeyance during the Whig fury, was renewed with a redoubled zeal. Some of the Whig leaders finding themselves beaten constitutionally, plotted an insurrection, while old Roundhead soldiers planned to waylay and murder the Royal brothers at the Rye House, as they came back from the New- 1683. market races. When these villainies were discovered, the rage and power of the Tories reached their full height. The Whigs were scattered like chaff. Shaftesbury died in exile in Holland. Russell, Sidney and others perished on the scaffold. The cynicism of the age was shown in the employment against Whig prisoners of false witnesses who were known by the Court and the Tories to have sworn away the lives of Catholics.

During the last four years of the reign, Parliament did not meet. It temporarily dropped out of the constitution where for some years it had held the leading position. And whenever the House of Commons met again it would not be representative of the old constituencies, or of any free electoral body. The town 1681–
1685.

corporations, including London itself, had been ' remodelled ' to the exclusion of the Whigs. No Tudor had ever interfered in this manner with the local franchises of the English boroughs, and nothing but the assistance of the Tory party could have enabled the monarchy to strike so deadly a blow at the local liberties of England as the ' surrender of the Charters ' implied.

No more was heard of the scheme of ' limitations.' The Tories in their zeal for the Anglican Church against the Dissenters had abandoned all her defences against Rome. They were prepared to hail with enthusiasm the accession of a Roman Catholic zealot to powers greater in many respects than those of Queen Elizabeth. In their zeal against Whig disloyalty, they proclaimed the most slavish doctrines of non-resistance to the King, even if he should behave like Nero, doctrines new in the history of England and not really believed by the foolish men who proclaimed them with a violence that coming events would render absurd in the retrospect. The University of Oxford made itself conspicuous in these protestations of unconditional submission to the royal will, and James knew so little of human nature that he afterwards took the dons at their word.

The Court, completely victorious and no longer troubled by a House of Commons, was swayed in its policy by Palace intrigues alone, as in days before the Long Parliament. There were two parties at Court in Charles II's last years. Halifax and the moderates were opposed to ' French counsels ' and wished England to maintain the Balance of Power in Europe. But the heir to the throne, and the courtiers who had attached themselves to his rising star, were all for France. And Charles, being without Parliamentary supply, depended on French gold. The influence of Halifax declined. It was in these years that Louis, ever advancing into new territories on the Rhine and in the Spanish Netherlands, acquired that ascendancy on the continent which England had afterwards to wrench from him by twenty years of war.

The violence of rival factions in England had prepared slavery for Great Britain and for Europe. But these misdirected energies of the nation in the latter years of Charles II had given birth to the two great parties whose internal cohesion and mutual rivalry made Parliamentary government a success in the coming centuries, as a method of ruling the British State and Empire. From the Exclusion Bill struggle date not only the names of Whig and Tory,[1]

---

[1] In their application to English parties they were both originally hostile nicknames, ' Tory ' meaning an Irish Catholic bandit, and ' Whig ' a Scottish Covenanting zealot.

but a new perfection of party organization and propaganda, and the peculiarly English art of ' electioneering.' A country that had once excited itself so profoundly in electoral and Parliamentary strife was not likely to be long quiet under a despotism. Shaftesbury and his enemies had introduced the astonishing customs of the Eatanswill election, with all its noise, expense, anger and fun—a peculiar and valuable national heritage, because it fostered that interest in the conduct and result of elections for want of which the Parliamentary system has withered and wilted in more than one continental country in our own day.

In this same period of the Exclusion Bill struggle, the idea of ' party loyalty ' grew up among leaders and underlings ; it was indeed the only loyalty that was practised by some very important statesmen in the reigns of James, William and Anne. Party loyalty has great attendant evils, but it renders strong Parliamentary government possible. In the end Louis XIV was defeated and the Union with Scotland carried by the mutual confidence of the Whig Junta and its supporters, and the Peace of Utrecht was obtained under no less difficult circumstances by Tory cohesion.

The bond that held together the Whig and the Tory organizations respectively, so that each had a continuous life of nearly two centuries, was not altogether theory or principle,—for theories and even principles change with changing circumstances,—but permanent religious and social cleavages to which the two parties gave political expression. The Whig party founded by Shaftesbury remained, till long after the Reform Bill of 1832, the party of the unprivileged Dissenters, and of the mercantile and middle classes arrayed under a section of the higher aristocracy. The Tory party, alike in the days of Danby, Pitt and Peel, was in its heart of hearts the party of the landowners and of the Anglican clergy and their adherents, though often with strong allies in other classes. Only in the latter part of the Nineteenth Century the removal of the disabilities of Dissenters and the complete transmutation of social grades by the Industrial Revolution, led towards a gradual shifting of the party system onto new social bases, and the disappearance of religious difference as a leading motive in English politics.

Few political philosophers would have prophesied well of the party system or of Parliamentary government in the year 1685. The two parties, in their first wild boyhood, had set fire to their own house. But the severity of the immediate chastisement that fell first on the Whigs and in the new reign upon the Tories, taught them lessons of wisdom that enabled them in a few years to save Britain and to save Europe.

CHAPTER VII

James II and the English Revolution, 1685–1688. The Revolution Settlement, 1689

1681–
1685.
GOVERNMENT in the last years of Charles II had been based upon a close understanding between the Court on the one hand and the High Church and Tory Party on the other. What the Privy Council decided at Whitehall was promptly and joyfully executed by the rustic magistrate in the shire, and was praised from the pulpit in the parish church. To crush and silence their common adversaries the Whigs and Dissenters, to set the whole machinery of the law and its officers, the Justices of the Peace, the partisan Judges and packed juries to invigilate against every smallest movement of opposition or free speech, appealed alike to the Court and to the High Tories. The latter found in the Church doctrine of non-resistance to the Crown a religious sanction for these violent proceedings against all critics of the royal policy. Forgetting much and foreseeing little, they held it to be in the eternal nature of things that royal policy should be identified with their own wishes and interests. But this eternity was limited to the life of Charles. So long as he lived there was no revival of the Roman Catholic designs he had abandoned in 1674. He still, indeed, drew his pay from Louis, but it was to enable him to dispense with Parliament and to keep the peace with France, not to attempt anything active for the Roman Catholic cause at home

Feb.1685.
or abroad. Only on his deathbed was he formally reconciled to the Church to which he at heart belonged.

James II inaugurated the new reign by summoning Parliament. It was a packed assembly, in which many members owed their seats to the remodelled corporations from which every Whig had been excluded. So long as the Tories and the Court held together, they would never again have cause to dread a general election. Never again could there be a Whig Parliament. And it was only a question of years before the 'Dissenting interest' would be crushed out by the Clarendon Code, steadily applied without any more of those unsettling intervals of 'indulgence,' which the misunderstandings between King and Commons had so often caused in the past.

The Parliament of 1685 was more royalist in sentiment than the Cavalier Parliament, but there was one thing which it would never help James to do,—to subject Church and country to Roman Catholicism. The quarrel on this issue between James and the Tory House of Commons was hastened by an event which for the moment made them faster friends than ever before,—the rebellion of Monmouth in the West.

Monmouth's insurrection made no appeal to the Whig gentry or to the moderate elements that were the strength of the Revolution three years later. It was a rising of Puritans against the persecution they suffered, not in the spirit of the modern Whig but of the old Roundhead party. But whereas in Cromwell's day the Roundheads had had very effective upper-class leadership, Puritanism was now a plebeian religion, confined even in Somerset to the shopkeepers of Taunton and the yeomen and labourers of the countryside. In the campaign that ended at Sedgemoor, they gave their lives with admirable devotion, not from feudal loyalty to their chiefs such as bound so many Highland tribes to the Jacobite cause, but from the mistaken belief that the worthless Monmouth was the champion of their religion.

The revenge taken upon the rebels, first by Kirke and his barbarized soldiers from Tangier, and then by Judge Jeffreys in his insane lust for cruelty, was stimulated by orders from the King. It was the first thing in the new reign that alarmed and disgusted the Tories. In the general horror felt at the long rows of tarred and gibbeted Dissenters along the roadsides of Wessex, came the first recoil from the mutual rage of parties that had so long devastated English political and religious life, the first instinctive movement towards a new era of national unity and toleration.

But the effect of Monmouth's rising on James was to goad him on to fresh tyranny. Under French and Jesuit advice, he adopted much more rapid methods of Romanizing the country than he seems to have contemplated in the first months of his reign. He had now an excuse to keep on foot an army of 30,000 men, and to make on Hounslow Heath a great camp to overawe the capital. A mistaken reliance on the Army encouraged him to defy the Tory Parliament, the rural magistracy and the Anglican Church. Contrary to the laws of the land, which he claimed the right to suspend at will by his royal prerogative, he officered his regiments with all the Roman Catholic gentlemen whom he could induce to enter upon so dangerous a service. Their numbers were insufficient, and he was even less able to find co-religionists to fill the ranks, till he sent over to Ireland for shiploads of Celtic-speaking peasantry. English soldiers and civilians were agreed in regarding these latest recruits as foreigners and savages, whom it was the task of the Anglo-Saxon to keep docile and unarmed even in their own island. Now they were to be made masters of England herself.

By the time the Revolution broke out, James had already

ruined the discipline and loyalty of his fine army, but he had not yet converted it into a force that could be used to uproot the Protestant religion. The Revolution was, indeed, timed by its promoters to forestall the completion of that difficult military evolution. But James had done enough to confirm for another long period the antipathy of the Tory squires against standing armies, which they had twice seen employed, once by Cromwell and once by James II, to subjugate the gentry and subvert the Church.

The failure and execution of Monmouth, while it tempted James along the road to ruin, removed an obstacle from the path of William of Orange. It brought nearer by one stage the union of all English parties under his leadership. He had been on good terms with the Tories ever since Danby's Ministry, but half the Whigs had been misled by the *ignis fatuus* of Monmouth. The removal of that pretender caused all English Whigs and Dissenters to concentrate their hopes upon William and Mary. In 1687 the great majority of Englishmen were united in the hope that James would presently die, and his daughter Mary succeed him before it was too late.

The solid part of the Roman Catholic body in England consisted of country squires, excluded from the magistracy but not from society, and living on very tolerable terms with their Tory neighbours. They had no goodwill for the policy which James was adopting at the suggestion of the French and Jesuit party, and with the applause of unprincipled English sycophants like Jeffreys and Sunderland. The Catholic squires knew their countrymen well enough to be sure that supremacy could never be won for their religion, except by foreign arms and civil war ; and a second civil war might end, as likely as not, in completing the ruin of the English Catholics which the first had half accomplished. In these views they were supported by Pope Innocent XI, a man of sense and moderation, very different from the Pontiffs who had excommunicated Elizabeth. Innocent had quarrels of his own with Louis XIV and the French Jesuits ; he dreaded the French power in Italy and in Europe, and therefore watched with sympathy the sailing and the success of William's Protestant crusade, because it would release England from French vassalage.

What the Pope and the moderate English Catholics hoped to obtain in England was not political supremacy but religious toleration. This, William publicly promised to secure for them to the utmost of his power. By temper, policy and circumstance he stood for religious toleration. Holland had been successfully united on that basis under his great ancestors. He was, himself, the head of a league against Louis that sought to unite Austria,

Spain and the Roman Pontiff with Holland and Protestant Germany. James himself, with a little patience, could have obtained from his Parliament legal sanction for Catholic rites, which were in practice being openly celebrated. But neither the Tories nor William were prepared to consent to the thrusting in of Roman Catholics to officer the Army, to fill the magistrates' bench, the Privy Council and finally the benefices of the Church of England herself. Yet that was the policy pursued by James for three years, with ever-increasing violence and illegality, with no assignable object but to prepare the way for the forcible reconversion of England.

During these very years his ally, Louis XIV, was revoking the 1685. tolerant Edict of Nantes, persecuting the Huguenots of France with the utmost cruelty, forbidding them even to escape into exile, driving them by torture to the Mass, separating families as if they had been negro slaves, sending the men to the galleys and the women and children to be brought up with stripes and ill-usage in a faith they abhorred. The sum of human misery thus wantonly brought about is horrible to contemplate. In the course of years, some hundreds of thousands succeeded in escaping, mostly into England, Holland or Prussia. A large proportion were artisans and merchants of high character, who brought to the lands of their adoption trade secrets and new industrial methods. Religious sympathy prevented their welcome from being marred by trade jealousy. The transference of so many of these men from France to England was not the least of the causes why Britain so far outstripped her great neighbour in commercial and industrial enterprise. Many French industries were ruined and many English industries founded by the greater cruelty of religious persecution in France.

The effect produced on the subjects of James II by these proceedings across the Channel, and by the arrival in their midst of a host of innocent victims of Roman Catholic fanaticism, was comparable to the effect on Elizabethan England of the cruelties of Alva and the Massacre of St. Bartholomew, and to the effect on the contemporaries of Fox and Pitt of the September massacres and the cruelties of Robespierre. The Revocation of the Edict of Nantes prepared the mental and emotional background for the Revolution of 1688 and for the long wars with France that followed. They raised to a height in England the hatred of ' Popery,' though in the great division for and against Louis in which all Europe was now being arrayed, the Pope was on the side of the nation whose delight it was to burn him in effigy.

The English drew their ideas of ' Popery ' from their nearer neighbours, the French Jesuits and clergy who were eagerly preaching the extermination of the unhappy Huguenots. The terror lest their system should be extended to England as a result of James's proceedings, gave a fresh actuality to Foxe's *Book of Martyrs* and the tales of the Marian persecution. Protestants of every shade, from Archbishop Sancroft to Baxter and Bunyan, saw the necessity of forgetting old quarrels and standing together against the fanatical policy of the King, and the unlimited power he claimed to dispense with the laws of England. This union of spirit among all Protestants brought into the ascendant the Anglican Low Churchmen and the Whigs with their policy of Toleration, while the Tory doctrine of non-resistance to the Crown left the men who had rashly adopted it with the miserable choice of abandoning their political principles or watching with folded arms the destruction of their religion by the ' Nero ' of their abstract arguments suddenly incarnate.

The Tory party, indeed, was rudely thrust out not only from its moral and intellectual position but from its material and political strongholds. In 1685 the Privy Council, the rural and the municipal magistrates, the Lords Lieutenant and the Sheriffs, were almost without exception Tories and High Churchmen. Three years later, on the eve of the Revolution, Tories and High Churchmen had been excluded from positions of central and local authority as thoroughly as if Oliver himself had been at work. James attempted to replace them by Roman Catholics, all laws to the contrary notwithstanding. But there were not enough of his co-religionists ready to serve his rash designs. He therefore appealed also to the Protestant Dissenters, but found very few who were prepared to revenge themselves on the High Churchmen at the expense of the Protestant interest and the laws of the land.

Crown and Church were bidding against each other for Nonconformist support. The Crown offered religious toleration and civic equality by illegal Declarations of Indulgence suspending the obnoxious statutes. The Church promised religious toleration secured by statute, as soon as a free Parliament should meet. The Non-conformists, partly from their traditional preference of Parliamentary to Royal power, and partly from the terror of Roman Catholic despotism on the French model, accepted the less dazzling but far less dangerous offers made by the Church.

The King now openly attacked the possessions and freeholds of the Anglican clergy. The Court of High Commission was revived contrary to law, as the King's instrument for dragooning the Church. Compton, Bishop of London, was suspended for refusing to silence Protestant controversialists. A number of

Church benefices were filled with Roman Catholics. The Fellows
of Magdalen, Oxford, were illegally disseised of their property, 1687
and their great College was turned into a Roman Catholic seminary.
The effect of this act of tyranny was very great upon Oxford and
on all who looked to Oxford for their opinions. It transformed
the citadel of non-resistance and divine right into a rebel town,
that flew the Orange colours in the High Street during the most 1688–
eventful winter in English history. 1689.

Finally all the clergy were bidden to read from their parish
pulpits the King's Declaration of Indulgence, suspending the laws
against Roman Catholics and Dissenters and admitting them to
civil and military posts. Since everyone knew that the clergy
held the Declaration to be illegal, the order to read it was designed
to humiliate them ; but unless they all stood together, the High
Commission would deprive those who refused to obey. Seven
Bishops, headed by Sancroft, Archbishop of Canterbury, petitioned
the King against the order. His answer was to put them on trial
for publishing a seditious libel. The trial of the seven Bishops June 30,
and their acquittal by a jury brought the excitement in the 1688.
nation to a head, and that night an invitation signed by seven
Whig and Tory chiefs was sent over to William of Orange, whose
agents had been for some time past in close touch with various
leaders of opinion in England.

The birth of a Prince of Wales, although the identity of the June 10,
child was for many years unjustly contested by his enemies, had 1688.
served as a warning to all that James's system would not end with
his death. Neither Protestant Mary nor Anne, but their new
Catholic brother would succeed to the throne. It was this consideration that finally brought round the majority of the Tories
to reconsider their theories of non-resistance. The man who led
the party in this change of ground was its founder, Danby, ever
a man of action and reality. It was he who had signed the invitation to the Prince, together with the suspended Bishop Compton,
another Tory Peer, and four Whig Leaders.

The dangers and difficulties of William's enterprise were enormous ; half of them were European and half were English, and
only he understood what they all were and how they might all
be overcome by a rare combination of policy and luck. Unless
they could be overcome, he knew that he would not much longer
make head against Louis in Europe, so he determined to take the
risk. He needed England as much as England needed him.
Until the day of his death this mutual dependence did duty for
mutual affection.

The danger most likely to prevent William's expedition
would be a demonstration made by the French armies against

Holland. This danger was removed by James himself, who alienated Louis by publicly repudiating his protection at the only moment in his reign when he really stood in need of it. William was therefore able to use the sea and land forces of Holland to

Nov. 5, 1688.

bring over to Torbay an army drawn from all the Protestant races of Europe, large enough to protect him against a fiasco like that of Monmouth. Like Monk, he declared for a free Parliament, to which he referred all matters in dispute. The army of James, divided into factions of Protestant against Catholic, and English against Irish, was deserted at the critical moment by John Churchill, the future Marlborough, and others of its chiefs ; it fell into such confusion that James dared not risk a battle. William was for many reasons anxious to avoid fighting. Every day added to his strength. The civil population rallied to his banner and to his programme of a free Parliament. Danby himself led the Northern insurrection ; the second greatest Tory chief, Seymour, summoned the men of Wessex to William's camp, while the Whig Devonshire organized the Midlands, and the London mob rose without a leader.

Even then it was probable that James could not have been deposed, so strong was the Tory feeling for the hereditary right

Dec. 1688.

of Kings, had he not himself persisted in flying from the country and taking refuge with his wife and baby boy at the court of France.

For many generations to come the Revolution of 1688–9 was spoken of by our ancestors as 'the glorious revolution.' Its glory did not consist in any deed of arms, in any signal acts of heroism on the part of Englishmen, nor in the fact that a whole nation proved itself stronger than one very foolish King. There was indeed a certain ignominy in the fact that a foreign fleet and army, however friendly and however welcome, had been required to enable Englishmen to recover the liberties they had muddled away in their frantic faction feuds. The true 'glory' of the British Revolution lay in the fact that it was bloodless, that there was no civil war, no massacre, no proscription, and above all that a settlement by consent was reached of the religious and political differences that had so long and so fiercely divided men and parties. The settlement of 1689 stood the test of time. It led not only to a new and wider liberty than had ever before been known in Britain, but to a renewed vigour and efficiency in the body politic and in the government of the Empire. The long and enervating rivalry of Crown and Parliament gave place to co-operation between the two powers, with Parliament as the leading partner. From the external weakness that had

characterized England in the Seventeenth Century the country
rose through the successive eras of Marlborough, Walpole and
Chatham to the acknowledged leadership of the world, in arms,
colonies, and commerce, in political and religious freedom and
intellectual vigour.

The men of 1689 were not heroes. Few of them were even
honest men. But they were very clever men, and, taught by
bitter experience, they behaved at this supreme crisis as very
clever men do not always behave, with sense and moderation.
It was the gravity of the national danger in the first months of
1689, with France in arms against us, Scotland divided and
Ireland lost, that induced Whigs and Tories in the Convention
Parliament to make that famous compromise between their con-
flicting principles and factions, which we call the Revolution
Settlement. It remained the solid foundation of English institutions in Church and State, almost without change until the era
of the Reform Bill.

The Tories, who had already in the previous autumn abandoned non-resistance, found themselves in February compelled
to abandon divine hereditary right; they agreed that a slight
alteration should be made by Act of Parliament in the order of
succession to the throne. Henceforth, unless Parliament were
' divine,' the right of English Kings to reign was of human origin.
To avoid this logical defeat, many of the Tories would have
preferred a Regency in James's name; and even Danby wished
that James's daughter Mary should reign alone, with her husband
as Prince Consort only. But when these arrangements were
found to be impossible, the sense of the national danger caused
the Tories to agree to the change of succession in favour of Feb.
William and Mary jointly, the executive power being vested in 1689.
the husband.

Indeed most Tories, in spite of theory, felt so strongly in practice
the necessity of excluding a Roman Catholic from the throne,
that they took the initiative in 1701, under Harley's leadership,
in passing the Act of Settlement that vested the succession, after
William and Anne, in the Protestant House of Hanover. Only the
Right Wing of the party remained Jacobite, and a number of
High Church Bishops, including Sancroft himself, refused to take
the oath to William, becoming ' non-jurors,' and giving up their
power and preferment for conscience' sake. The reproaches of
these faithful few rendered their more adaptable brethren ill at
ease. The Tory party, though upon the whole loyal to the Revolution Settlement, remained so at the expense of its consistency
and internal harmony; a subtle transmutation towards modern
ideas was going on inside it, more painfully than in the Whig

party, leading to the Tory disruption and catastrophe on the death of Queen Anne.

But otherwise the Tory forces in Church and State lost little by the Revolution, except the power of persecuting their rivals. The Church remained Anglican, and the last attempt to extend its boundaries to 'comprehend' moderate Dissenters broke down in 1689. But the Toleration Act of that year granted the right of religious worship to Protestant non-conformists, accompanied by many limitations which read strangely to-day, but which were necessary to secure agreement in an age when Toleration was regarded by many not as a grand principle but as a necessary compromise with error.

The Roman Catholic body, being the backbone of the Jacobite party, obtained no legal relief for its adherents, and from time to time fresh laws were passed against them. But in practice the policy of William and the spirit of the times secured for them a considerable degree of free religious worship in England; the infamous penal laws were usually inoperative, and were only brought into partial vigour in times of Jacobite insurrection. Worship in private houses was hardly ever interfered with, and public chapels were erected and priests often went about openly in spite of the laws. So too the laws against the growing body of Unitarians were silently disused. In the favourable atmosphere of the new age, the spirit of the Toleration Act was practised much more widely than the letter warranted.

Substantially freedom of religious worship had, with certain exceptions, won the day. But religious Tests were fully maintained until the Nineteenth Century. Persons, whether Protestant or Catholic, who would not take the Communion according to the rites of the Church of England, were still debarred from holding office either under the Crown or in the municipalities; the doors of Parliament were still closed to Roman Catholics, and the doors of the Universities to Dissenters of every kind. The Church of England ceased to be a persecuting body, but remained throughout the coming era a body with exclusive political and educational privileges that the Whigs, in the long heyday of their power under the first two Georges, never dared to alter.

Thus the principal institutions of Church and State remained on the foundations of 1660–1, and suffered no Whiggish change. The victory of the Whigs at the Revolution consisted only in the victory of their principles—religious toleration and resistance to the power of the Crown—and in the trend towards modernity, latitudinarianism and Parliamentarism that the whole world was about to take, owing to the fact of the English Revolution and the check which it gave to the power and principles of Louis XIV.

Neither did the Whigs in 1689 gain any such monopoly of office as they gained at the accession of the House of Hanover in 1715. William was by no means their leader, though they were more bound to support him than the Tories, because they would lose more by a Jacobite Restoration. But William only looked to find men who would help him to defeat Louis ; he was purely indifferent whether they were Whig or Tory. And when in 1690 the Whigs attempted to go back on the spirit of the Revolution Compromise, and to revenge their ancient party wrongs on the Tories, he dissolved Parliament and successfully appealed to the country against them.

His successor, Anne, greatly preferred Tories to Whigs. Indeed, the only advantage that the Whigs had over their rivals prior to the coming of George I, was the fact that they were more unanimously zealous to conduct the war on land against Louis XIV than were the Tory squires with their traditional dislike of a standing army and a high land-tax.

But the Revolution had done more than arbitrate successfully between the two great parties whose feuds bade fair to destroy the State. It decided the balance between Parliamentary and regal power in favour of Parliament, and thereby gave England an executive in harmony with a sovereign legislative. It was only in the course of years that the details of that new harmony were worked out, through the development of the Cabinet system and the office of Prime Minister. But from 1689 onwards no King, not even George III in his youth, ever attempted to govern without Parliament, or contrary to the votes of the House of Commons. To bribe Parliament was one thing, to defy it quite another.

Nor did any King ever again attempt to override the local liberties of England ; indeed the central government in the Eighteenth Century became only too subservient to the Justices of Peace, and only too tolerant of abuse in any chartered corporation or vested interest. The victory of law over arbitrary power was upon the whole an immense gain for humanity ; but for the next hundred years and more the victory of law and of vested interests produced an undue admiration of things as they were, in the days of Blackstone, Burke and Eldon, all of whom appealed to the great conservative Revolution as the final standard in human affairs. Because James II had attempted to destroy the institutions of the country, it long remained impossible for anyone else to attempt their reform.

Justice and humanity, divorced from all party considerations, gained greatly from the signal overthrow of James and Jeffreys. The Judges ceased to be removable at the will of the Crown.

Trials were conducted with decency and on the whole with fairness. Cruel floggings and exorbitant fines ceased to be a usual weapon of party politics. In 1695 the Censorship of the Press was allowed to lapse, so that Milton's dream of 'liberty of unlicensed printing' was realized in England. The even balance of the powerful Whig and Tory parties protected critics of government who spoke from either camp. The cessation of persecution under the Clarendon Code put an end to a mass of continual suffering, hatred and wrong. After a thousand years, religion was at length released from the obligation to practise cruelty on principle, by the admission that it is the incorrigible nature of man to hold different opinions on speculative subjects. On that stubborn fact the modern State, like the mediæval Church, had broken its teeth in vain. The indirect consequences of this victory of the individual conscience were far-reaching and manifold, not to be revealed in the lifetime of the Whigs and Tories who worked out that curious patchwork of compromise, illogicality and political good sense, the Toleration Act of 1689.[1]

BOOKS FOR FURTHER READING (FOR CHAPS. VI. AND VII.)

Besides Ranke and Macaulay, see Feiling, *History of the Tory Party, 1640–1714*; Sir G. Sitwell, *The First Whig*; Osmund Airy, *Charles II*; H. D. Traill, *Shaftesbury*; Mahan, *Influence of Sea Power upon History* (for the Dutch wars).

CHAPTER VIII

Scotland and Ireland from the Restoration to Queen Anne.
The Two Settlements

CROMWELL'S campaigns had established English rule in both Scotland and Ireland, nor did the return of Charles II put an end to the unity of political control over the British Isles. From 1660 to 1690 Irish and Scottish affairs continued to follow the vicissitudes of revolutionary change in England.

Throughout the reign of Charles II, Scotland was governed from Edinburgh by her own Privy Council, but as that body took its cue from Whitehall, and was under no control either from the Scottish Parliament or the Church Assembly, there was no real restoration of national independence, except in the undesirable form of the loss of free trade with England and her colonies. Parliament was entirely subservient to the Privy Council, and made no attempt to voice the manifold grievances of the nation.

The Privy Council that governed Scotland in the days of

1660 1685.

[1] Further remarks on the Revolution Settlement as it worked itself out in the Eighteenth Century will be found in subsequent chapters, *e.g.* Book V, Chap. I.

Middleton, Rothes and Lauderdale, relied on the support or acquiescence of the Cavalier interest. The Scottish Cavaliers, with their traditions of Montrose, represented the fusion of aristocratic and royalist sentiment after centuries of mutual opposition ; and they represented also the determination of the less fanatical among the laity to prevent the old tyranny of the Kirk, which Cromwell had overthrown, from rising again on the ruins of his power. Many preferred the tyranny of the King's Council to that of clergy and elders. Other choice there seemed none, so long as Parliament had no power or policy of its own. The strength of the Cavalier party lay among the nobles. The alliance of the general body of the nobility with the Presbyterians had always been intermittent and half-hearted, and was already played out as a factor in history, except for the steadfast adherence of the great House of Argyle to the cause that it had chosen. Otherwise it was the smaller lairds who remained a mainstay of the Kirk.

The Privy Council had in fact a strong body of opinion behind it in maintaining the supremacy of the State over the Church. Laud's Prayer Book was not reimposed, but the Covenant was repudiated, Episcopacy was restored, and the clergy were to be appointed by patrons instead of by the democratic choice of the religious community of the parish. This programme, accepted by the greater part of Eastern Scotland, might have received the sullen acquiescence even of the South-West, had the Council proceeded with common caution and humanity. But the drunkards who ruled Scotland in the first years after the Restoration went out of their way to impose tests on the Presbyterian clergy which many of them were bound to refuse. A third of the parish 1662. ministers, mainly in the South-West, were deprived of their kirks and manses, and replaced by ' curates,' who maintained themselves, in default of popular influence, by alliance with the dragoons and the strong hand of power.

From this state of things arose the practice of ' conventicles,' where the ' outed ministers ' preached to the faithful. But whereas the ' conventicles ' of the English Non-conformists were held in barns or upper chambers, those of the Scottish Covenanters were held on solitary hillsides, in the scoop of the burn, or the heart of the birch wood, with sentinels set all round to watch for the approach of the red dragoons across the moor. And while in England the Clarendon Code was administered legally, however harshly, by civilian Justices of the Peace, in Scotland the recalcitrant districts were handed over by the Privy Council to the licence of the soldiery or the savage marauding of Highland tribes. Such ill-usage stirred to action the warrior and moss-trooper still alive in the Lowland peasant. The Pentland Rising of 1666 was followed a dozen years later by the more formidable and famous

1679

rebellion that began with the murder of Archbishop Sharp, continued with the repulse of Claverhouse by the armed conventicle at Drumclog Moss, and ended at Bothwell Brig.

The cruelty with which government provoked and suppressed these fanatical outbursts left a deep impression on the memory and imagination of the Scottish people. In happier days to come the stories of the ' killing times,' and the graves and legends of the martyrs shot down in many a solitary place or ' justified in the Grassmarket,' gave to Presbyterianism all over Scotland a hagiology and a cycle of romance, and secured its moral position as the asserter of national and religious freedom. Yet it was not freedom that the Covenanting martyrs had intended to assert, nor was it to posterity that they had meant to appeal, but to the living God whose sole servants they believed themselves to be in a world gone to perdition.

At the time when the disturbed and bloody reign of Charles II drew to a close, the Scottish people were by no means united in admiration for the zealots of the Covenant. The Privy Council and its torture chamber were indeed abhorrent to all decent folk, but the East mainly supported the government for want of any moderate leadership to follow in opposition, while the West was in a state of suppressed revolt. It was easy for Claverhouse and his dragoons to keep down a country thus divided against itself, so long as there was no revolution in England. It was James

1685–
1688.

Seventh and Second, with his Romanizing policy, who drove his subjects of both Kingdoms into the path of union and self-deliverance.

The Revolution, simultaneous in the two countries, restored Scotland to a state of practical independence of England which she had not enjoyed since Dunbar. English statesmen, Tory as well as Whig, were fain to allow her to settle her ecclesiastical and other affairs to her own liking, provided only she would follow suit by choosing William and Mary as her sovereigns. The dynastic dispute in Britain became a lever in Scotland's hand by which she won her own terms in things both spiritual and material first at the Revolution and later at the Act of Union.

1689

It was the Convention Parliament at Edinburgh that deposed James VII, chose William and Mary as sovereigns of Scotland, and dictated the terms on which they might assume the crown. And it was the Parliament that in the following year formally

1690.

restored Presbyterianism, but without renewing the Covenant. The autocratic rule of the Privy Council came to an end, as a necessary consequence of the Revolution. Henceforth the Parliament at Edinburgh was an independent force with which the government had to reckon. It was no longer a mere echo of the Church Assembly as in 1639, or a mere echo of the Privy Council as in 1661. It stood for policies of its own. The feudal method of its election rendered it very indifferently representative of the country, but it represented at least the idea of lay forces, independent alike of Kirk and King, though friendly to both. With that a better age slowly dawned for Scotland.

Yet William's was a troubled reign to the north of the Tweed, where the Jacobite party was much stronger than in England. It contained the majority of the nobles, and the respectable and influential body, specially strong in the East, who clung to the ministrations of the newly ejected Episcopalian clergy. The Episcopalian Church, thrust out of the Establishment and barely tolerated in the new Scotland, could hardly fail to be more Jacobite in sympathy than the English Tories, whose Church was left intact and highly privileged under the Revolution Settlement. Moreover, to the north of the Highland line, the great majority of the kilted tribes were Jacobites, out of jealousy of the dominant tribe of the Campbells and their chief, Argyle, the true head of the Whig and Presbyterian party in all Scotland. The Highland attack upon the South, organized by Claverhouse after the example of Montrose, was checked by his death in the hour of victory at Killiecrankie, and was terminated a few weeks later when the tribesmen were defeated by the Covenanted Cameronians at Dunkeld. But the Highland glens were never systematically conquered and occupied before 1746. The horrible Glencoe massacre did much to foster Jacobite feeling and to discredit the government. Amid all these dangers Parliament itself, though of necessity loyal to William as against James in the last resort, was factious with all the inconsequent levity and selfishness of amateur politicians, nurtured under despotism, unaccustomed to the discipline necessary for the management of affairs in a free community, and untrained in any school of public virtue or wisdom.

July 1689.

1692.

Yet William's government somehow survived in Scotland, because it was at any rate more tolerant than its predecessors, and because its settlement of Church and State was in accordance with the new spirit of the times. Though Presbyterianism was restored as the national religion, the aim of government was the gradual substitution of the secular for the theological in politics. The Church Assembly again met freely, to discuss and decide its own concerns, but no longer to dictate policies to government. The old-fashioned Cameronians, clearly perceiving that the Church had not been restored to her ancient power and glory, refused to acknowledge a King who might be a Calvinist in Holland but was a Prelatist in England, and was everywhere a Laodicean and a flat tolerationist. But the mass of the nation, sick of persecution and bloodshed, acquiesced in the new regime.[1]

An adequate solution of Scottish ecclesiastical problems had been found at last. For this reason the Scots, while continuing for two hundred years to be a profoundly religious people, were able to turn their thoughts to material problems. In 1689 their poverty was in strong contrast to their energy of mind and character. Agricultural methods were mediæval, even in the rich soil of the Lothians. For want of draining, much of the best land lay water-logged and unused, while the plough went up the barren hill-side. The primæval forests had disappeared ; and as yet no modern plantations, hedges or walls broke the monotony of the windswept landscape, where the miserable sheep and cattle shivered in the blast. Improvements were impossible because the land was let on very short leases with no security of tenure. Neither lairds nor tenants had money to put into the land, and the nobles were interested in their estates chiefly as hunting grounds. The farms were cabins of turf or unmortared stone, often without windows or chimney, the door serving for light and ventilation. Beer and oatmeal were a monotonous but a wholesome and sufficient diet, save when bad harvests brought starvation, as in the ' dear years,' dreadfully recurrent in King William's reign. Nearly half the acreage of what was nominally the Kingdom of Scotland, remained under the tribal rule of mountain chiefs, dwelling outside the law and civilization of the English-speaking lands.

Trade and industry were still on a very small scale. Glasgow had as yet no shipping of its own. Edinburgh was by far the largest and most wealthy town, but even in the towering High Street glass windows were rare. All told, there were about a million Scots in their native land and only a few thousands oversea, chiefly soldiers of fortune. This poverty-stricken population, with few political rights, and living under social arrangements still largely feudal, was more versed in Biblical knowledge and theological argument, and certainly not less independent in spirit, than the well-to-do farmers and shopkeepers of Parliamentary England. If the Scots should ever apply their well-trained minds and vigorous character to improving their lot in this life, the results might be astonishing.

The great change in the landscape and prosperity of Scotland

---

[1] An important concession was made to Presbyterian feeling by the abolition of private patronage as a means of appointing ministers ; in the following century patronage was revived with various far-reaching consequences.

which the next hundred years were to bring about,—the change
from the Scotland of Fletcher of Saltoun to the Scotland of Robert
Burns and Walter Scott,—was due to the new direction taken by
the energies of every class from landowner to cotter. Two ante-
cedent conditions of this improvement may be noticed. First the
introduction of long leases gave reasonable security of tenure,
which rendered possible plantation, hedging, walling, housing and
new methods of agriculture, grazing and breeding. And secondly
the Union of North and South Britain in 1707 opened England's
home and colonial markets to Scottish industry and agriculture,
and made the Scots participators in England's trade privileges all
the world over. In William's reign Scotland had learnt, from
the tragic failure of her national settlement at Darien, the bitter   1695-
lesson that she had not the power and resources needed to open   1702.
markets and found colonies for herself alone.

The Union involved the absorption of Scotland's Parliament   1707.
and Privy Council in those of England. Edinburgh remained the
legal and cultural capital, but was no longer the seat of political
power. It was a bitter sacrifice of Scotland's pride, but it was the
necessary price for her material and economic expansion. The
sacrifice was the more tolerable because neither Privy Council nor
Parliament were in themselves very dear to the people, except as
symbols of national independence. The Church Assembly was
more rooted in the affection and the daily life of multitudes, and
Scottish religion, like Scottish law, was left intact and separate
by the Act of Union.

The inducement that prevailed on Englishmen to invite the
Scots into partnership, was not economic but political. Scotland
was more Presbyterian but she was none the less more Jacobite
than England, and she threatened to bring the exiled Stuarts to
reign at Holyrood on Anne's death, while the House of Hanover
was being established at St. James's.[1] How far the threat was
serious, how far a mere expression of her annoyance with England
over Darien and other grievances, it is hard to say. But undoubtedly the British Empire was threatened with the possibility of disruption, in the middle of the Marlborough wars with
Louis XIV. To hold together the Empire, the Whig statesmen
of Anne's reign, supported by moderate Tories like Harley, offered
Scotland the great material advantage of union and free trade, on
condition that the Crowns and Parliaments became one. The
bargain was reluctantly accepted by Scotland, but she was greatly

---

[1] Whitehall was burnt to the ground during the reign of King William, who
himself inhabited Kensington and Hampton Court. From Anne's reign onwards
the British monarchs resided at St. James's Palace, until the move to Buckingham
Palace in the Nineteenth Century.

the gainer by an arrangement which robbed her of nominal but not of real independence, and opened out the paths of her future prosperity. England gained not only the political security which was her immediate and pressing need, but the support of Scottish brains and character in the commercial and political development of the Empire.

By this great act of modern legislation, England placed upon the world's highway of commerce, colonization and culture, a small nation hitherto poor and isolated, but the best educated and the most active-minded in Europe. The mutual advantage to England and Scotland was immense, and was not confined to the accumulation of wealth. In British literature, science, warfare, politics, administration and colonization, the Scots have played a part out of all proportion to their numbers. The mutual advantage was indeed long unrecognized by the vulgar ; it was Sir Walter Scott who first taught the English to admire Scotland, and reconciled the two nations to a joyful pride in their partnership. The statesmen of the Revolution and the reign of Anne had served Britain well. If Scottish talents and energies had for the last two hundred years been turned against England instead of being employed towards common ends, the world would be a very different place to-day. And a little more negligence or folly on either side might easily have brought it about.

On the fall of Cromwell's regime in England, the Celto-Iberian race in Ireland looked to see his work undone over there, and the chieftains of their own blood and tradition restored to the lands they had once owned, among a people who still felt for them much of the ancient tribal loyalty. But with certain exception this hope was disappointed. The Protestant landlords remained as a new race of Anglo-Irish conquerors, nor did they, like the descendants of Strongbow and the Fitzgeralds, become identified with the native peasantry around them.[1] The new barrier of religion perpetuated and emphasized the difference of civilization and idealized the politics of self-interest and racial pride. Moreover communications with England were much easier, and the arm of England was longer and more powerful than in the Middle Ages. The solid block of English and Scottish Protestants of all classes in Ulster gave a strength to the ' English interest ' in Ireland such as it had never had before. The events of 1689 were to demonstrate how much more effective the Ulster colony was as a ' garrison,' than the Cromwellian landowners thinly scattered over the island among a hostile peasantry.

James II, who tried to make his co-religionists masters of

[1] The Cromwellian yeomen, however, often did so. See p. 423, above

Britain where they were in a tiny minority, attempted the same thing with more likelihood of success in Ireland where they formed the bulk of the population.   His Catholic Deputy Tyrconnell and his Catholic Parliament at Dublin decided to undo the Cromwellian settlement and to restore the native landlords.   But before the new regime was consolidated, the Revolution in England gave the Protestants of Ireland a rallying-point and a legal position from which to defend their property and power. They were not the men to miss the chance.   William was proclaimed King at Enniskillen and Londonderry with more heartfelt loyalty than in Whitehall and Edinburgh.   The farming gentry and yeomen of the North were frontiersmen accustomed to the life of the saddle and the field, the sword and the plough, and were filled with the businesslike enthusiasm of the Puritan religion. They made Enniskillen the headquarters of a vigorous warfare in the open country.   Meanwhile the burghers of Londonderry endured the famous siege, facing starvation in the spirit that the citizens of Haarlem and Leyden had shown in like case against the Spaniard.   These men held England's bridge-head in North Ireland till reinforcements could be shipped over in sufficient strength to enable them, under the leadership of William himself, to advance southward upon Dublin.

See Map XXV., p. 422, above.

1689.

In the year 1690 Ireland was the pivot of the European crisis. The fate of Britain depended on William's campaign, and on the fate of Britain depended the success or failure of Europe's resistance to French hegemony.   William's throne was tottering in the after-throes of the earthquake of the late Revolution, which had not yet subsided.   The English Church and Army were disaffected ;   the civil, military and naval services were in grave disorder ;   the Whigs and Tories of Parliament were renewing their old feuds ;   half the public men of both parties were in secret communication with the Jacobites, not because they desired but because they expected a Restoration.   With good hope then, Louis had sent over James as his vassal, with French money, troops and generals, to complete first the conquest of Ireland, where three-fourths of the land already obeyed him.   Until Ireland was secured for William, Britain could take no part in the continental war, and might soon herself be in the throes of a counter-revolution.

The battle of the Boyne was fought upon two quarrels.   It was the struggle of the Anglo-Scots against the Celto-Iberians for the leadership of Ireland.   But it was no less the struggle of Britain and her European allies to prevent a Jacobite restoration in England, and the consequent domination of the world by the French monarchy.   The presence, on both sides of the river, of

July 1, 1690.

regiments from the continent represented the international issues at stake. The outcome of that day subjected the native Irish to persecution and tyranny for several generations to come, but it saved Protestantism in Europe and enabled the British Empire to launch forth strongly on its career of prosperity, freedom and expansion overseas.

But while Enniskillen, Londonderry and the Boyne were but a stage in the forward march of British and world history, they became the central point of time in the imagination of the ruling race in Ireland. With equal intensity of recollection the oppressed Celt continued to think of the gallant defence of Limerick, and the subsequent breach by the conquerors of the treaty they signed there with the vanquished race. Sarsfield, the hero of the Limerick campaigns, stood to the conquered as the representative man of the new Ireland, the faithful son of the *mater dolorosa*. The place occupied by Sarsfield in Irish history is significant. For he was no scion of an old tribal family, with immemorial claims on the local allegiance of a clan. The English had effectually destroyed the clan society and banished or slain the clan leaders. Sarsfield represented the new nation that was taking the place of the suppressed tribes, as Wallace had represented the new nation that in Scotland gradually took the place of old clan and feudal loyalties.

The restored English rule in Ireland reflected very little of the wise and tolerant spirit of William. In this Catholic island he was powerless to do anything to protect the Catholics, whose lot he mitigated in England. The new regime in Ireland reflected the rash ignorance and prejudice of the Whigs and Tories of the Westminster Parliament, who were the real overlords of the reconquered dependency. While the penal code placed the Catholics in Ireland under every political and social disadvantage that malice could invent, and pursued and persecuted their priests, the only leaders left to them under the Cromwellian land system,—by a masterstroke of folly the sectarian quarrels of English Protestants were transferred to Ulster ; Anglican intolerance refused political equality and for some time even religious freedom to Presbyterians who had manned the walls of Londonderry and forded the Boyne water. From the Restoration onwards, English trade jealousy had been permitted to depress the Protestant interest in Ireland by laws against the export of Irish cattle and of Irish cloth. The ruin of the Irish cloth trade, completed at the end of William's reign by the decrees of the English Parliament, effectively stopped the growth of the Anglo-Saxon colony. Many thousands of Ulster Scots who sought refuge beyond the Atlantic in the Appalachian mountains, had more real wrongs to revenge on England in the War of American Independence than had most of those who followed the standard of Washington.

Oliver had at least promoted the Protestant interest everywhere in the British Isles. He saw that if Ireland was to be an English colony it must be colonized by English. But the Protestant interest and the Anglo-Saxon colony were after his death depressed by the commercial and ecclesiastical jealousy of Cavalier, Whig and Tory Parliaments, of narrower vision in these respects than Protector or King. Yet the Catholics were still persecuted with Cromwellian vigour. All that was bad in Oliver's Irish system was preserved, all that was good in it was reversed.[1]

Such were the Scottish and the Irish settlements that resulted from the English Revolution. Very different as they were in their character and ultimate consequences, they seemed to be equally permanent and equally unchallengeable throughout the greater part of the stable and pacific Eighteenth Century. Indeed in 1715, and again in 1745, the Hanoverian government had much more trouble in Scotland than in Ireland. Yet the Scottish settlement, resting on consent, in the end outlasted the Irish settlement that reposed on force.

It is remarkable that the great events which convulsed England, Scotland and Ireland under the later Stuarts, had no repercussions of a regional character in Celtic Wales. From the Tudor settlement till the Nineteenth Century, Wales had no history except that of slow social and religious growth. The upper class were gradually becoming English in culture and connection, while the small farmers of the hills, the typical Welshmen before the modern industrial era, remained Celtic in character and largely Celtic in speech, but felt no active political hostility to England or to English institutions of which Wales was now an integral part. The level of intellectual activity was low as compared to later times, but native music and poetry persisted among the people; and all through the Seventeenth and Eighteenth Centuries the Welsh common folk were gradually moving from an indifferent acquiescence in Anglican religion towards an enthusiastic evangelicalism of their own, by means of which the national mind and spirit eventually revived.

BOOKS FOR FURTHER READING

Hume Brown, *History of Scotland*; Andrew Lang, *ditto*; Rait, *The Parliaments of Scotland*; W. L. Mathieson, *Politics and Religion in Scotland* and *Scotland and the Union*; Lecky, *History of Ireland in the 18th Century*, Vol. I; Stephen Gwynn, *History of Ireland*; Bagwell, *Ireland under the Stuarts*, Vol. III.

---

[1] See pp. 424–5, above.

S 2

CHAPTER IX

The Wars of William and Marlborough. The Downfall of Louis XIV and the Rise of Great Britain to Maritime and Commercial Supremacy. The Death of Anne and the Dynastic Crisis

Sovereigns : William and Mary, 1689–1694 ; William III (alone), 1694–1702 ; Anne, 1702–1714

IN the winter of 1688–9, foreign and domestic events combined to force England into the leadership of the alliance against France, in accordance with Danby's war plans of a dozen years before which had been thwarted by King Charles and by the Whigs.[1] After the Revolution, resistance to France became the first charge on the energies of the new King and of the reconstituted Whig party, and in a scarcely less degree of the nation as a whole. The continued attempt of Louis to reimpose upon England the rule of James and his son after him, rendered the wars of William and Marlborough unavoidable.

William's war, known as the War of the League of Augsburg, lasted from 1689 to 1697, and was ended by the indecisive Treaty of Ryswick. After an uneasy interval of four years, war broke out again on an even larger scale,—the War of the Spanish Succession,—conducted by Marlborough as Europe's general and diplomat in chief, and was ended by the Treaty of Utrecht in 1713. That Treaty, which ushered in the stable and characteristic period of Eighteenth Century civilization, marked the end of danger to Europe from the old French monarchy, and it marked a change of no less significance to the world at large,—the maritime, commercial and financial supremacy of Great Britain.

See Map XXVII., p. 493, below.

The prime condition of successful warfare against Louis, whether on sea or land, was the alliance of England and Holland. The understanding was not very cordial in 1689 between the two nations, so long accustomed to regard each other as rivals in trade and admiralty ; but a united front was demanded by the time, and was ensured by the greatest statesman in Europe who had been placed at the head of the executive in both countries. Under William's tutelage, the English and Dutch Ministers contracted habits of close co-operation for purposes of war, which survived the death of the Stadtholder-King and were continued by Marlborough and Heinsius. Co-operation was the less difficult, because England's commercial jealousy of Holland diminished as the

[1] See p. 461, above.

proportion of Dutch ships in the allied fleet dwindled year by year, and as Dutch commerce and finance fell behind the newly mobilized resources of her ally. England throve on the war,[1] while the strain of war taxation and effort slowly undermined the artificial greatness of the little Republic. In the latter part of Queen Anne's reign, the mercantile community in London had so little cause left for jealousy of Dutch commerce, that the Whigs and the 'moneyed interest' proposed concessions to be made to Holland in the terms of peace, which the Tories and the 'landed interest' justly criticized as extravagant.

Throughout this long period of war, which involved all Western and Central Europe and its American Colonies, the naval operations stood in a close causal connection with the diplomatic triumphs of William, and the diplomatic and martial triumphs of Marlborough. But it is only in quite recent times, under the influence of Admiral Mahan and his school of history, that the maritime aspect of the struggle against Louis has been rated at its true value. For although Sir George Rooke and Sir Clowdisley Shovell were fine seamen, no name like Drake, Blake or Nelson appeared as the rival of Marlborough's fame, and the single naval victory of La Hogue seemed a poor match for Blenheim and Ramillies and the long list of conquered provinces and towns. Yet all the grand schemes of war and diplomacy depended on the battleships of England, tossing far out at sea ; Louis of France, like Philip of Spain before him, and Napoleon and Kaiser William since, was hunted down by the pack he never saw. 1689–
1713.

La Hogue, the crowning victory at sea, occurred as early as the fourth year in the long contest. This is the more remarkable, because the French, as Admiral Mahan tells us, were 'superior to the English and Dutch on the seas in 1689 and 1690.' In the first months of the war Louis had the chance to perpetuate French naval supremacy and to prevent the success of the English Revolution, by the proper use of his then dominant fleet. But the irrecoverable moment went by unseized. He made no naval effort to stop William from shipping his forces to England in 1688, and to Ireland in the two following years. In 1690 the victory of the French over the inferior numbers of the combined English and Dutch fleets off Beachy Head, showed what might have been done to cut the communications between England and Ireland in the year of the Boyne. But the courtiers at inland Versailles lacked the sense of naval opportunity, which was seldom entirely 1692.

---

[1] The cost was not out of proportion to Britain's wealth, and the loss of life was trifling as compared to the losses of present-day warfare. At Blenheim the allied army in the field consisted of only 9000 British and 36,000 foreigners. And the British armies only fought one of these great battles on an average every two years.

wanting to the statesmen who watched the world's ebb and flow from the tidal shore of the Thames.

In 1692 the tables were turned by the victory in the Channel of the allied over the French fleet, followed by the destruction of fifteen French men-of-war in the harbours of Cherbourg and La Hogue. These losses were not indeed very much greater than the allied losses at Beachy Head two years before.[1] And yet La Hogue proved as decisive as Trafalgar, because Louis, having by his clumsy and arrogant diplomacy defied all Europe to a land war, could not afford to keep the French fleet up to its strength, in addition to the armies and fortresses needed for the defence of all his land frontiers at once. The French fighting navy in 1690 had owed its temporary superiority to the war-policy of the Court, and was not, to the same degree as the navies of England and Holland, founded on proportionately great resources of merchant shipping and commercial wealth. The trade and industry of France were oozing away through the self-inflicted wound of the Revocation of the Edict of Nantes. When, therefore, the war-policy of Louis induced him to neglect the navy in favour of the land forces, French naval decline was rapid and permanent, and French commerce and colonies suffered accordingly.

The battle fleets of King Louis retired from serious operations, leaving the passage to the continent open year after year to the armies of William and Marlborough with all their supplies and reinforcements, and allowing the pressure of the British fleet to be brought to bear on hesitating States at moments of diplomatic crisis. In William's reign the allied fleet saved Barcelona and prolonged the resistance of Spain against Louis. During the Marlborough wars, our alliance with Portugal and rebellious Catalonia, and our whole war-policy in the Mediterranean and in Spain, depended on our naval supremacy in those seas, of which Gibraltar and Minorca were pledges taken and kept.

1703, 1705.

1704, 1708.

The seamen of France, when their grand fleet went out of commission, turned their energies to privateering. Admiral Tourville was eclipsed by Jean Bart. English commerce suffered from him and his like, but throve in their despite, while French commerce disappeared from the seas. When the frontiers of France were closed by hostile armies, she was thrown back to feed upon her own ever diminishing resources, while England had the world for market from China to Massachusetts.

In the earlier years of the reign of the Grand Monarch, his

---

[1] Neither Torrington nor Tourville, the English and French admirals at Beachy Head and La Hogue respectively, was to blame. Both were forced to fight by orders from their governments, against their better judgments, and both made the best of a bad business.

good genius, Colbert, had nourished French industry and commerce with remarkable success, though often by State regulations more paternal than would have suited the individualist spirit of wealth-making in England. But from the Dutch war of 1672 onwards the malign influence of Louvois gradually replaced the hold of Colbert on the mind of the King. Warlike ambitions in Europe and religious persecution at home destroyed the fabric of national prosperity erected in the earlier part of the reign. Louis could indeed tax his miserable peasants at will, but even he could not take from them more than they had, and he had bled them white long before he was rid of Marlborough. Bankruptcy brought his system to the ground, and with it fell the moral prestige of despotism and religious persecution.

Meanwhile the English State, that had been so feeble and distracted in the first two years of William's reign, was gaining internal harmony, financial soundness and warlike vigour all through the long contest, so that the new English principles in Church and State were constantly rising in the world's esteem. England was paymaster to the Grand Alliance, with her subsidies to needy German Princes, and her own well-equipped armies and fleets, that increased in numbers, discipline and efficiency as the years went by.

Parliament, supreme at length in the constitution, was ready to vote supplies to William and Anne such as it had never voted to either Charles. Scarcely less important, from the point of view of the finance of the war, was the alliance between the King's Ministers and the City, leading to a new system of government borrowing on long loans. In the past, royal loans had been made in anticipation of revenue, the capital to be paid back as soon as certain taxes had been levied. Under the new system the patriotic investor, doing well both for himself and for his country, had no wish to have his capital paid back at any near day, preferring to draw a good interest on it for the rest of his life, upon the security of the State. The principal lenders to government were organized in the Bank of England, to which Ministers gave the support of public credit in its banking operations with individual traders. **1694.**

The Bank of England and the permanent National Debt were the outcome of the fertile brains of the Scot, William Paterson, and of the Whig Chancellor of the Exchequer, Charles Montagu; the whole movement was regarded with suspicion by the Tory country gentlemen, jealous of the rising influence of the 'moneyed interest' over the royal counsels. The City, prevalently Whig in political and religious sympathy, was bound still more strongly to the Whig party by this system of long loans to the governments born of the Revolution. For the Pretender would repudiate his enemy's debts if he should ever return, and to prevent that return the Whigs were pledged one degree more deeply than the Tories.

The movement towards the development of the world's resources through accumulated and applied capital, was in this era finding its principal seat of operations in mercantile England. The capitalization of industry was still in the day of small things, though the domestic cloth-workers dealt through capitalist middlemen. But the capitalization of the world's trade was already conducted on a large scale, and was moving its centre from Amsterdam to London. The London of William and Marlborough was a huge emporium, less of industry than of commerce and finance. Its work was done by a turbulent population of cockney roughs—porters, dockers, day-labourers, watermen and a fair sprinkling of professional criminals—living uncared-for and almost unpoliced in labyrinths of tottering, insanitary houses many of them in the ' liberties ' outside the City walls, especially in the over-populated area of which Fleet Street was the centre ; next, there was a large middle stratum of respectable shopkeepers and artisans, largely engaged in high-class finishing trades ; and on the top of all, a body of wealthy merchants and moneyed men to which no other district in Europe could show the equal, inhabited ' the City ' proper.

London and its leaders were once more hand-in-glove with government, as in the days of Burleigh and Gresham ; but the methods of State finance and the quantity and availability of London's wealth had made great strides since the days of Elizabeth's parsimonious warfare against Philip. If Drake had had Charles Montagu behind him, he would have done more than singe the beard of the King of Spain. The Grand Monarch of this later era was to learn by bitter experience that the English Parliament and the City of London between them commanded the deeper purse, though France had nearly twenty million inhabitants, and England and Scotland about seven.

The East India Company of London had become the rival on equal terms of the once dominant Dutch Company, that had so rudely excluded the English traders from the Spice Islands in early Stuart days. Steady trade with the Mogul Empire on the mainland was carried on from the stations at Madras, Bombay, and latterly from Fort William in the Delta of the Ganges, the nucleus of the future Calcutta. The shareholders in the joint-stock company continued to make fortunes hand over hand during the war with Louis, for although ships were lost to French privateers, the demand for tea, spices, shawls and cotton goods did not diminish, and the demand for saltpetre to make gunpowder greatly increased. The Company, though it was gradually building up a great market for English goods in China and India, was accused of exporting bullion and bringing back mere 'luxuries'; but men and women still clamoured for the 'luxuries,' and for shares in the much-abused Company. In the reigns of William and Anne, the strife in the City between the chartered traders and the interlopers, between the Old Company and the New, convulsed the House of Commons, which had stepped into the place of the Court as the State arbiter of commercial privileges. In the first half-dozen years after the Revolution, Sir Josiah Child, in defence of the monopoly of the Old Company, disbursed some £100,000 to Cabinet Ministers and members of Parliament. In these quarrels, all the furies of party passion and private greed were stimulated by the knowledge that the wealth of the East was no longer an Arabian tale, but a solid fact on which City fortunes were being built and new County families founded every year. The most remarkable and formidable of these self-made magnates was Thomas Pitt, grandfather of the great Chatham, and owner of the Pitt diamond. Having made his fortune in India first as poacher and then as gamekeeper, that is to say first as 'interloping' trader and then as Governor of Madras for the Company, he purchased a landed estate at home, together with the Parliamentary borough of Old Sarum.

The coffee drunk in the famous coffee-houses of the period was imported less by the East India Company than by the English merchants trading in the Mediterranean.[1] They had become the chief European influence at Constantinople, and were pushing the sale of English cloth in the ports of Italy, Venice and the Levant. In spite of the Barbary pirates and the privateers who dashed out from Toulon and Brest, our Turkey and Venetian merchants throve during the war. And it greatly added to their security and prestige that after the capture of Gibraltar and 1704, 1708. Minorca the Western Mediterranean was permanently occupied by the Royal Navy.

On the other side of the Atlantic, the English had the full See Map XXVI., p. 437, above. advantage of naval supremacy. There was a rehearsal of the issues brought to a final head by Wolfe and Chatham two generations later. The men of Massachusetts, much the most active of the American Colonies, twice during the wars with Louis XIV captured Acadia from the French; though given back once at the Treaty of Ryswick, it was annexed to Britain by the Treaty of Utrecht and re-christened Nova Scotia. By the same treaty

---

[1] The importation of coffee was criticized in 1680, as being ' most useless since it serves neither for nourishment nor debauchery.'

1713. Britain annexed Newfoundland, subject to certain French fishing rights which remained a constant subject of dispute until their final settlement in the reign of Edward VII.   The Hudson Bay territory was also annexed, with its snow-bound forests whence English hunters supplied the fur trade at home.   And so—
1711. although an attack on Quebec, badly concerted between the Royal and Colonial forces, had failed—the end of the war saw the British solidly planted near the mouth of the St. Lawrence, and in the arctic rear of the French settlements on the great river.

The war and the peace stimulated another British interest oversea, the endeavour to force our commerce on the great South American market, in spite of the Spanish government's decree excluding all foreign traders.   The quarrel with the Spaniards in South and Central America had been carried on by the English buccaneers ever since James I's peace with the Spanish Monarchy.[1] In the reign of Charles II, the buccaneers of the West Indian Islands were in the heyday of their romantic glory, as the unofficial maintainers of England's quarrels along the Spanish Main. In the reigns of William and Anne they were declining into the position and character of black-flag pirates of the type of Teach, their hand against the men of all nations, and every man's hand against them.   But the process was gradual ; many, like Kidd and Quelch, moved in a doubtful borderland between piracy and privateering, and the attitude of the Colonials and of the British officials differed according to the circumstances and the men.

1713. An attempt was made to regularize our relations with Spain in the Treaty of Utrecht, when the Tory government won applause even from their harshest critics by securing the famous *Asiento*, permitting England alone of foreign powers the annual privilege of sending a ship to trade with Spanish America, and of taking thither, besides, 4800 negro slaves.   But this limited monopoly was used in the Eighteenth Century as the starting-point for a larger illicit trade, and the quarrel for the open door in South America only came to an end with the termination of Spanish rule in the days of Bolivar and Canning.

With regard to the war in Europe, there is a marked distinction of character between the two parts of the struggle that brought Louis to his knees.   In the War of the League of
1689– 1697. Augsburg, of which William III was the political and military chief, France was engaged on all her land frontiers in operations against Spain, Holland and the German Princes, and even so she held her own ; neither side won any sensational victories,
1692. 1693. though Steinkirk and Landen were successes for the French ;

[1] See p. 386, above.

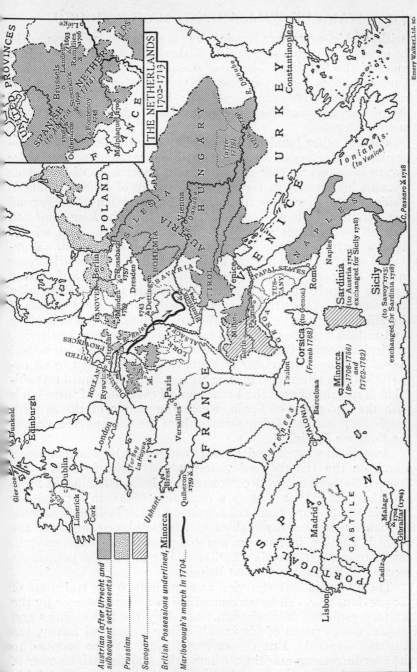

MAP XXVII.—Europe after the Treaty of Utrecht, 1713

THE NETHERLANDS 1702-1713

UNITED PROVINCES

SPANISH (to Austria) NETHERLANDS

Liège
Brussels
x Landen 1693
x1692 Ramillies
Oudenarde x 1706
Fontenoy
1745
Malplaquet 1709

Legend:
- Austrian (after Utrecht and subsequent settlements)
- Prussian
- Savoyard
- British Possessions underlined, Minorca
- Marlborough's march in 1704

Emery Walker Ltd. sc

UNITED PROVINCES

Glencoe
Edinburgh
Dunkeld
Dublin
Limerick
Cork

London
Torbay
La Hogue
Brest
Ushant
Quiberon 1759

HOLLAND
Ryswick
Utrecht
Dunkirk
HANOVER
Berlin
Minden 1759
Rossbach 1757
Dresden
Detingen 1743

POLAND

BERLIN
SILESIA
BOHEMIA
BAVARIA
AUSTRIA
HUNGARY (after 1718)
Vienna
R. Danube
TIROL
Rhine
ALSACE
LORRAINE

FRANCE
Paris
Versailles
Pyrenees

PORTUGAL
Lisbon

SPAIN
Madrid
CASTILE
Cadiz
Malaga x1704
Gibraltar 1704

CATALONIA
Barcelona

Toulon

Minorca
(Br.1708-1756)
and
(1762-1782)

Corsica
(French 1768)

GENOA
(to Genoa)
Milan
Parma
TUSCANY
Florence
PAPAL STATES
Rome
NAPLES
Naples

Sardinia
(to Austria 1713;
exchanged for Sicily 1718)

Sicily
(to Savoy 1713;
exchanged for Sardinia 1718)

VENICE
Venice
TURKEY
Constantinople
Ionian Is.
(to Venice)

R. Danube

C. Passaro x 1718

neither side anywhere made any measurable progress. The
boundary between the Spanish Netherlands and France, where
most of the fighting took place, remained practically unaltered.
Under William, who was not the man either to win or lose
campaigns on the grand scale, the British troops learnt the
art of war, and were bequeathed by him a fit instrument for a
greater captain.

1701-
1713.

On the other hand, in the ensuing War of the Spanish Succession, France began the contest with every apparent advantage
except sea-power. Her armies were in occupation of the whole
Spanish inheritance in Europe, in the name of Louis' grandson,
Philip V, the new King of Spain. The great Kingdom beyond
the Pyrenees, Italian Milan and Naples, and the long-contested
Spanish Netherlands with their famous fortresses, were all, for
fighting purposes, French territory when the war began. Moreover, Louis had as an active ally the great State of Bavaria, lying
in the heart of Germany, on the boundaries of hard-pressed
Austria, herself attacked on the other side by the Hungarian
insurrection. The situation appeared desperate for the cause of
the allies, and for the future safety of Holland and England by
land and sea : unless they could turn Louis out of these territories,
particularly out of the Netherlands, he would remain what he had
indeed become, the master of Europe. But contrary to all expectation, the allies, who in the previous war had seemed no pain-
ful inch to gain, chased the French out of every one of these lands
with the exception of Spain, where the genius of the Spanish
people for guerrilla warfare secured them the King of their choice,
the Bourbon Philip.

Austria was saved and Bavaria conquered by Marlborough's
march on the Danube and victory at Blenheim in 1704 ; the
Spanish Netherlands were conquered by him at Ramillies in 1706,
and that same year Eugene's campaign of Turin secured for
Austria Milan, Naples and the hegemony in the Italian Peninsula.
Though Spain herself remained to the Bourbon candidate, the
Spanish Empire in Europe was conquered and dismembered,
chiefly to increase Austria's territories, but also for the permanent
security of Holland and Great Britain.

These tremendous victories, as compared to the stalemate of
the previous war, can be accounted for in no small degree by the
military genius of Marlborough, backed by the fine abilities and
faithful co-operation of his friend, Prince Eugene of Savoy, the
Austrian General. But the successes must also be ascribed to
the ever-increasing maritime, commercial and financial power of
Britain and its vigorous application by Marlborough, Godolphin
and the Whig Ministers of Anne. Marlborough understood the

strategy of world war and the way to combine land and sea power
in successful operations, better than any man who has succeeded
him in control of England's destiny, with the possible exception
of Chatham. Corresponding to England's growth, was the
maritime and financial decadence of France, whose efforts at
world conquest for fifty years past exhausted and betrayed her
just when the prize was in her grasp. The national exhaustion
reflected itself in the failing ability of the new generation of Louis'
Generals, and the want of self-confidence in his troops after their
first defeats at the hand of ' Malbroucke.'

The size and armament of battleships and the tactical methods
of warfare at sea underwent no great change between the days of
Blake and the days of Nelson. But the methods of warfare on
land, when Marlborough took command at the beginning of 1702
Anne's reign, had just undergone a great change from the methods
of Gustavus Adolphus and Cromwell.[1] Ever since the Restoration
the bayonet had been gradually coming in, and, after the lesson of
Killiecrankie, William's reign saw the general adoption of the ring-
bayonet that could be left on while the gun was being discharged.
Consequently the pikemen, who had composed half the regiment
in Cromwell's day, were altogether abolished ; henceforth there
was but one type of infantry private, with his firelock ending in
the dagger-bayonet. In connection with this change of weapon,
the six-deep formation of the infantry column, suitable to pikes,
was changed to a thin line of three deep, as the method of concentrating the greatest volume of fire upon the enemy. Already we
are in the realm of the infantry tactics employed by Frederic the
Great and by Wellington, though the drill of the infantry was not
yet so perfect or their manœuvring so flexible as in those later
times. Cavalry, as at Blenheim and Ramillies, could still decide
battles, but their place in war was already smaller than in
Cromwell's day, owing to the increased efficiency of the ' poor
foot.'

The warfare of the age of Louis XIV was largely an affair of
fortresses. Readers of ' Tristram Shandy ' will remember how
the two old soldiers of William show even more professional
interest in the news of Marlborough's sieges than in his marches
and battles. King Louis' military architect, ' the celebrated
Monsieur Vauban,' carried the defensive art to a high and complicated perfection, and France and her neighbours watched each
other across a network of fortified towns, especially thick in the
Netherlands.

The result was a tendency to stagnation in military enterprise 1689-
and mobility, very marked in the War of the League of Augsburg. 1697.

[1] See p. 409, above.

1701–
1713.
But in the War of the Spanish Succession the rapid conquest of provinces recalls Gustavus and foreshadows Napoleon. The way for this change had been prepared by the unopposed advance of Louis' armies beyond the frontiers of France into the territories of the Spanish Empire and Bavaria. Marlborough, when he took over the command, found the French far in advance of their usual line of fortresses. He seized the opportunity to restore the war of movement, much to the horror of the more timid and conventional spirits on his own side. When he resolved to carry the Dutch and English armies across Europe to the Danube, to save Austria and win Blenheim, he had to deceive the vigilance of the Dutch authorities and the Tories of the English Parliament, who objected to any such dangerous use of their costly regiments.

Marlborough as a military strategist and a tactician, as a war statesman and war diplomatist, stands second to no Englishman in history. His powers resemble those of Chatham and Clive rolled into one, except that he could not, like Chatham, arouse the spirit of his countrymen at large by magnificent speech and visible ardour of soul. For the purpose of striking down a great military monarchy, he was Wellington and Castlereagh combined, and if the Whigs had left him a free hand he might have made for Europe in 1709 as good a peace as Castlereagh made in 1815,—or Bolingbroke in 1713.

Cromwell alone seems his match. But Oliver attracts or repels by the peculiarities of his character, and by his political and religious affinities; whereas Marlborough arouses no such prejudices either for or against his claims upon the gratitude of his country and of the world. 'The detested names of Whig and Tory,' as he called them, were less than nothing to him, though fate made him a Tory by birth and upbringing, and a Whig by later connection. Both sides revenged themselves upon him for not being one of themselves, the Tories assiduously blackening his character and the Whigs being lukewarm in its defence. As the contemporary of Louis' English pensioners and of the Whig and Tory correspondents of the exiled James, he was no better, indeed, than the average product of the Restoration Court and the Revolution Parliaments. But if he loved money, he gave England better value for every guinea he received from her than any other of her servants; if he looked to the main chance, his country was the gainer for his shrewdness nine times out of ten; and if he failed to arouse the personal devotion of any class except the soldiers whom he led to certain victory, his featureless calm of Olympian power is perhaps as much above as it is below Cromwell's humorous, passionate humanity, and craving, troubled spirit, never quite at rest either in this world or the other. By the light of his unclouded genius, Marlborough protected the advent of the much needed age of reason, toleration and common sense.

In the successful conduct of a world war there are two distinct operations, both very difficult,—the winning of the victory in arms, and afterwards the making of a stable peace. Unfortunately the temper and qualities required and engendered by war are not always conducive to the proper handling of peace negotiations, and for this reason it was no bad thing that our two-party system enabled the Whigs to win the war and the Tories to make the peace.

Since the Revolution, the Whigs had become the more inveterate enemies of Louis, as the representative of despotism and the patron of the Pretender. William III, who had less than no predilection in favour of the Whigs, had found in practice that only a Whig Ministry could carry on the War of the League of Augsburg with the necessary vigour and financial ingenuity ; but he himself, without help from his English Ministers, concluded peace at Ryswick. In the interval that followed before the renewal of war, the Tories rose again automatically to the surface, and on the accession of their supporter, Queen Anne, secured almost a monopoly of power. But during these four somewhat confused years of peace, it had been the moderate Tory Harley, a man of Roundhead family and connections, who exerted most influence in the House of Commons. He ' educated his party,' inducing the Tories to pass the Act of Settlement which fixed the succession on the House of Hanover, in case of Anne's death without children [1] ; and to renew the war with France, when Louis, in spite of his acknowledgment of William in the Treaty of Ryswick, insolently declared the Pretender to be James III, King of England. The control of the vast resources of the Spanish Empire had been too much for the prudence of the Grand Monarch, who already regarded himself as master of the world.

The War of the Spanish Succession was therefore begun by a combination of moderate Tories and Whigs with Marlborough and Godolphin. But events led once more to a war-Ministry predominantly Whig, because so many of the Tory party were more interested in passing laws against the Dissenters than in beating Louis. But Harley's heart was in the war, and he remained in the Whig Ministry until Louis had been driven out

margin notes: 1697–1701. June 1701. Sept. 1701. 1701–1705.

---

[1] The Tory party's support of the Act of Settlement in 1701 was probably facilitated by the discredit accruing to Jacobitism from the Assassination plot against William in 1696, curiously similar in its details to the Whig Rye House Plot against Charles II.

of the Spanish Netherlands, and the Union with Scotland had
been carried. Finally in 1708 Anne was compelled to accept
a wholly Whig Ministry without Harley. Marlborough and
Godolphin, altogether detached from the Tory party, remained
to act under the orders of the Whig ' Junto.' Mixed Ministries,
though they had often done useful work, were found increasingly
difficult under the Parliamentary system. Ever since the Revolution England had been moving unconsciously towards the modern
system of a responsible Cabinet all of one political complexion.

The Whigs, who had twice risen and thriven by war, were
slow to make peace. And unfortunately the completeness of
their political victory at home coincided exactly with the period
when peace negotiations ought to have been seriously undertaken
and pushed through. Marlborough, having won the Spanish
Netherlands for Austria at Ramillies and Oudenarde, was engaged,
during four more years of unnecessary war, in reducing the
fortresses that defended the frontier of France herself. Louis,
in terrible straits, offered in 1709 everything that the allies could
reasonably demand, including the withdrawal of all assistance
from his grandson in Spain. But the Whigs showed themselves
incapable of making peace. They demanded the one thing Louis
could not grant—that he should himself send his armies to expel
Philip from the Spanish throne on which he had placed him eight
years before. The cause of this outrageous demand was the
difficulty the allies found in expelling Philip themselves, as he was
the favourite of the Spanish people. The Whig formula of ' no
peace without Spain ' meant in practice no peace at all. Louis
appealed to his subjects, as he had never deigned to do before ;
they knew that he had made great sacrifices of his pride to buy
them a peace, but in vain, so they rallied to him with the well-
known valour of the French people in defence of the soil, and gave
Marlborough his first rebuff in his Pyrrhic victory of Malplaquet.

John Bull, also, was hungering for the victorious peace which
the Whig doctors had ordered away from his table. The cry to
stop the war swelled the Tory reaction which domestic causes
were producing. A wave of High Church feeling passed over
the Queen and her subjects, and mobs who a few years before
were chasing Jacobites and sacking Mass-houses, once more
engaged in the alternative employment of burning Dissenters'
chapels. Popular emotion was swelled by the folly of the Whig
Ministers in impeaching before the House of Lords a certain
Dr. Sacheverell, who had preached a violent sermon against the
Revolution, of a type then not uncommon in the Anglican pulpit.

The Queen's political and religious sympathies and the
influence exercised over her by Mrs. Masham, at length enabled

her to throw off the personal domination of Sarah, Duchess of Marlborough. The Whigs fell at once, ere long dragging Marl- **1710.** borough himself after them. Anne's initiative in changing her Ministers was confirmed at the General Election. Since the winter of William's coming over, no change in men and measures had been so complete and so instantaneous. Yet this was not a revolution, but a normal process of the new constitution, which was tending more and more towards party Cabinet government by Whigs and Tories in alternation. No change less complete would have secured peace for Europe at that juncture.

The new Tory Ministry took office under the double leadership of the brilliant St. John, prepared to go any lengths to crush the Whigs and extirpate Dissenters in pursuit of his political game, and the slow, moderate Harley, whose chief virtue was a desire, unfortunately rare among contemporary statesmen, to promote unity of spirit in the whole nation. But the government was at least agreed on its first necessary task—the making of peace. Except the betrayal of our Catalan allies to the vengeance of Philip of Spain, it is difficult to find serious fault with the terms of the Treaty of Utrecht. The methods by which this **1713.** excellent peace was obtained are perhaps more open to criticism. The Whigs denounced, and the nation little liked the secret negotiations with France behind the back of the allies—though William had done the same to obtain the Treaty of Ryswick,— the disgrace of Marlborough, and the withdrawal of the British armies from the field in face of the enemy. Yet it was largely the fault of Whig, Dutch and Austrian obstinacy that these methods seemed the only way to settle any terms at all with France and compel the allies to accept them.

British colonial and commercial interests were, as we have seen, amply provided for,[1] and they would have benefited still more if the Tory Ministers' Commercial Treaty with France had not been thrown out by English trade jealousy, organized by the Whig opposition. As regards territorial arrangements in Europe, See the terms of Utrecht were based on the formal assignment of the Map Spanish dominions in Europe to Austria, and the formal assignment XXVII, of Spain and her American dominions to the Bourbon Philip. It p. 493, was merely a recognition of the state of things established by the above. events of the war, which the operations of the last five years had failed to shake. England's maritime security was ensured by the transference of the Netherlands to Austria, an inland power of central Europe from whom we had nothing to fear. The French threat to the Rhine Delta had been parried until 1793.

These arrangements proved a stable basis for Eighteenth

[1] See pp. 491–2, above.

Century civilization. Europe was never again troubled by danger from the preponderance of France, until the French Revolution had given her a new form of life. If Louis had been treated with the vindictive severity contemplated by the Whigs and Austria, when Marlborough should at length have burst through the network of fortresses and reached Paris, the spirit of revenge might have made a permanent lodging in the soul of the French people, rallied them to the monarchy of the *ancien régime*, and kept Eighteenth Century Europe constantly disturbed with wars more than dynastic.

The Treaty of Utrecht remains the one great act of statesmanship of St. John, Lord Bolingbroke, wherein he showed all his natural brilliancy, together with a moderation in respect to France, that was conspicuously absent from his dealings with those of his own countrymen who were not of his political following.

The Tories, having won the peace, hoped to enjoy the fruits thereof in their domestic programme. They had passed an Act to prevent anyone from sitting in Parliament, even for a borough, unless he drew at least £300 a year from land. But the chief political passion of the fox-hunting Tory squires of the October Club was the desire for a hot run after Dissenters, and Bolingbroke, the free-thinker, was Master of the pack. The first burst had been the passing of the long-disputed Occasional Conformity Bill, which punished with ruinous fines any man who, having qualified for State or municipal office by taking the Sacrament in an Anglican church, afterwards attended a place of Non-conformist worship. But the Schism Act three years later was a much more serious affair. It took away from Dissenters the education of their own children, which was to be handed over to persons licensed by Bishops of the Established Church. The many excellent schools that the Non-conformists had established at their own cost were to be suppressed, and their teachers turned adrift. Even teachers licensed by Bishops might teach no catechism save that of the Church. Without directly repealing the Toleration Act, it was intended to circumvent it by extirpating Dissent in the next generation through this peculiarly odious and unnatural form of religious persecution. The Schism Act was the worst blot on the record of the Tory party after the Revolution, and rendered its downfall a pre-condition of religious freedom in England. For if the Schism Act had had time to come into force, it must have led to the abolition of varieties of religious belief, or else to a civil war. But the dynastic crisis precipitated by the death of Anne divided and ruined the Tory party, saved the Dissenters without resort to arms, and

1711.

1711.

1714.

Aug. 1711.

established the full Eighteenth Century era of domestic peace, latitudinarianism and toleration,

> When George in pudding times came o'er
> And moderate men looked big, Sir.[1]

The reason why the victory of the Whigs on the accession of the House of Hanover meant the victory of 'moderate men' was because the Whigs were the minority party and were in no position to persecute. On the other hand, the Tories in the last years of Queen Anne's reign showed, under Bolingbroke's leadership, a spirit of intolerance natural, perhaps, to a party conscious that it represents the strongest forces in the nation. Prior to the Industrial Revolution the landowners were the most powerful class, and prior to the growth of Wesleyanism the Established Church was by many times stronger than all other religious denominations put together. Against the landed interest and the Church interest the Whigs could put into array only half the peerage, a few of the squires, some of the yeomen, the bulk of the merchants and moneyed men, the Protestant refugees from the continent,[2] and the English Dissenters. This combination, relatively weak in numbers, was powerful in organization and intelligent unity of purpose, because its strength lay in the towns, particularly in London, and because its leaders could pursue the political advantage of their party without its counsels being distracted, as those of the Tory squires often were, by religious and class feeling. For while the ordinary Whig partisan was a middle-class dissenter, the Whig leaders were upper-class churchmen, usually of a latitudinarian or a sceptical turn of mind. Between William Penn and John Bright no Non-conformist was prominent as a leader of political life in England, though for half that period the Non-conformists were able to keep the Whig party in power.

In time of peace the Tories were normally the stronger by weight of numbers and possession of the land, and would have governed Eighteenth Century England but for the accident of the

---

[1] Both the Schism Act and the Occasional Conformity Act were repealed by the Whigs early in George I's reign, but the Sacramental Test for civil office was retained till Lord John Russell's Bill in 1828. The insistence of the High Church party on using the Sacrament as the key to political office was perhaps not very good for religion. ' I was early with the Secretary' (Bolingbroke), writes Swift, ' but he was gone to his devotions . . . to receive the Sacrament. Several rakes did the same. It was not for piety but employment, according to Act of Parliament.' But as long as they were only ' rakes ' and not Dissenters, Swift's party saw no profanation.

[2] There were over thirty French Huguenot churches in London when it had about one-tenth of the inhabitants it has to-day. Most of the worshippers in them were skilled men, many of them rising to wealth in the country of their adoption ; and almost all were Whigs, on account of the Tory hostility to their forms of religious worship.

dynastic question, which proved their division and their undoing. At the end of William's reign Harley had persuaded the party to take the initiative in passing the Act of Settlement, assigning the Crown to the House of Hanover in case of Anne's death without children.[1] This great decision represented the determination of the squires and the Anglican Church never again to trust themselves to a Roman Catholic King. The House of Stuart had only to turn Protestant and the Act of Settlement would have little binding effect on the High Tories, but neither the Old nor the Young Pretender would consent to dissemble his religious beliefs to gain a crown. The fact is greatly to their credit, and their honesty saved Britain a world of trouble and civil war.

Even as it was, the Act of Settlement represented only one-half the feelings of the Tory party on the dynastic question ; the other or Jacobite half of their sentiment had a habit of surging up in moments of emotion, and then sinking back checked and uncertain when the practical crisis came. Brought up as boys in the doctrines of Divine Right,

> In good King Charles's golden days
> When loyalty no harm meant,

the Tories of the succeeding generation were never quite at ease in opposing the House of Stuart. Old theory and old affection were moreover supported by modern considerations of party advantage and expediency : the House of Hanover was hand-in-glove with the Whigs. The future George I declined to adopt the attitude of indifference between Whig and Tory which William of Orange had shown both before and after he attained the crown. Moreover, the Tory Ministers of the dying Queen could not pay court at Hanover without quarrelling with their mistress at home. For Anne had all Queen Elizabeth's jealousy of a successor ; and, like many other Tories, she was a Jacobite in sentiment though not in practice, and detested the German Princes who were to keep her brother out of his inheritance after she herself had ceased to do so.

The Tories therefore clung to the present favour of Anne, at the sacrifice of all chance of future favour with George. The Whigs in opposition adopted precisely the opposite policy. The growing perception that the accession of George I would mean the exclusion of the Tories from power, drove Bolingbroke on his last violent courses, to prepare the way either for a Jacobite restoration on Anne's death, or at least for the complete control of the country by a Jacobitish Cabinet who could dictate terms to either one or

[1] For the Hanoverian descent from James I, see tree, p. 388, above ; for the descendants of James II, see tree, p. 458, above.

1712–
1714.

other of the claimants. This plan necessitated the extrusion of all Whigs and all moderate Tories from the magistracy, the Army, the Navy, and the government. It necessitated the dismissal of Harley, now Lord Oxford, as a preliminary to consigning the whole machinery of government, central and local, to men of Jacobite sympathy. Oxford was dismissed on July 27, and his rival's hands were free. Five months, five weeks even, might have seen the stage prepared, but the Queen died in five days, and all Bolingbroke's plans fell in ruin around him. ' Fortune turned rotten at the very moment it grew ripe,' wrote Swift, whom the disaster consigned for life to a Dublin deanery.

Aug. 1, 1714.

The outcome of Bolingbroke's intrigue was that George I came unopposed to the throne, with a rooted distrust of the whole Tory party, which was shared by large numbers of his subjects who were neither Whigs nor Dissenters but who desired undisturbed peace under a Protestant King and Parliament. For forty-seven years to come the Tory party was out of office, suspected of Jacobitism and painfully divided in its own feelings and allegiance.

1714- 1761.

Bolingbroke was prevented by the Whigs from taking an active part again in public life. After a period of service abroad as Secretary of State to the Pretender, he left that Court in disillusionment and disgust, and devoted his brilliant powers as a writer to preaching to his countrymen the moderate views of his old rival Harley, the necessity of the Revolution settlement, the evils of party spirit, and the hope of the future in a ' patriot King ' who was not to be a Stuart.[1]

The enjoyment by the Whigs of nearly fifty years of uninterrupted power at this stage in our history, though far from an unmixed blessing, secured the political and religious liberties of Englishmen, because the Whigs were the minority party and could not therefore afford to persecute, as the authors of the Schism Act had persecuted. Walpole, who held power from 1721 to 1742, had the sense to see that the Whigs would retain office for themselves and keep the House of Hanover on the throne, only if they left the privileges of the Church untouched, and allowed the government of the countryside to rest very largely in the hands of Tory Justices of the Peace. Under Whig political rule at St. James's and Westminster, the Church and the squirearchy preserved what was nearest and dearest to them in the county, the parish, and the University.

That compromise secured the *Pax Walpoliana*, and saved the

---

[1] Mr. Feiling, in his *History of the Tory Party*, says : ' The man who educated these generations (between Anne and George III) was undoubtedly Bolingbroke, who in the " Letters" and "Dissertations" of his later life Harleyized, that is to say modernized, the whole basis of Tory thought.'

House of Hanover from overthrow by the Jacobites. It was a policy very different in spirit from the violence of the original Whig party under Shaftesbury. When Walpole came to power the Whigs had learnt the lesson of 'moderation' very completely, but they had only learnt it step by step. Several times in the reigns of William and Anne they had shown a desire to persecute their political enemies, as for instance in their attempt, thwarted by William, to hold up the Act of Indemnity after the Revolution; in the trials of Fenwick and Sacheverell; finally the impeachment of Oxford in the reign of George I for his share in the Treaty of Utrecht. But a milder and more cautious spirit, which men like Somers, Cowper and Addison usually displayed, had been working in the party against the more violent elements represented by Wharton. These pacific and liberal tendencies triumphed in Walpole and his motto—'Let sleeping dogs lie.'

The contests of the two evenly balanced parties in the reigns of William and Anne, the constant appeal made by Whigs and Tories to the intelligence of the public in Parliamentary eloquence, pamphlets, electioneering and the talk of men, had instilled habits of debate and free expression of opinion which continued to mark English political life in the coming era. Though partisan bitterness was guilty of frequent acts of persecution, the shelter generally afforded by the two great parties to their respective advocates enabled freedom of speech and press to grow to its characteristic development in England.

BOOKS FOR FURTHER READING

Lecky, *History of England*, Vol. I.; Feiling, *History of the Tory Party*; C. T. Atkinson, *Marlborough*; Corbett, *England in the Mediterranean*, Vol. II.; Mahan, *Influence of Sea Power*, Chaps. IV. and V.; Coxe, *Memoirs of Marlborough*, 3 vols.

BOOK V

FROM UTRECHT TO WATERLOO. SEA POWER AND ARISTOCRACY. FIRST STAGE OF THE INDUSTRIAL REVOLUTION

INTRODUCTION

THE Eighteenth Century in England starts politically from the Revolution Settlement of 1689, on which it may be said to be a gloss or comment. The accession of the House of Hanover in 1714 was only a confirmation and extension of the principles that had placed William and Mary on the throne twenty-five years before.

The Revolution Settlement had the defects of its qualities. It was inevitably too conservative, or so at least it appears to modern eyes. It would have been better, some think in the retrospect, if the opportunity had been taken to redistribute the Parliamentary seats more nearly according to population. In the elections to Cromwell's Parliaments the rotten boroughs had been abolished as being under the influence of the local gentry, and the county representation had been proportionately increased. But the old constituencies had been restored with Charles II, and the men of 1689 left the unreformed representation to grow ever more corrupt with years, bringing thereby many evils on the country, possibly among others the quarrel with America. But the merit of the Revolution lay in being a settlement by consent, and consent could only be obtained by avoiding as far as possible the disturbance of vested interests. Now, one of those vested interests was the power of certain nobles and gentry to influence elections to the House of Commons in certain boroughs. A Reform Bill had no place in the minds of either Whigs or Tories in that era.

Indeed the ostensible object of the Revolution was not change but conservation. James II had illegally attacked a number of vested interests and chartered corporations—the Church, the Universities, the town Municipalities, the electoral rights of the parliamentary boroughs, the property of freeholders,—and he had denied the efficacy of the laws of the land. By inevitable reaction, the Revolution, in its just defence of these interests against

T

illegal assault, gave to them a sacrosanct character which helped to protect them against wise and legal reform for a hundred and forty years to come. The outrages that provoked the Revolution had engendered an ideal enthusiasm for vested interests as such, because the action of James II had for a while identified vested interests with the cause of British freedom. And this ideal enthusiasm survived the occasion that had called it forth. The existing laws, which James II in his tyranny had over-ridden, became a fetish to Judge Blackstone and the men of the Eighteenth Century.

The Revolution was a triumph of the lawyers over the executive, the close of a long struggle begun by Coke and Selden to subject the legality of the King's actions to the free judgment of the courts that administered the Common Law. The victory of law over irresponsible and arbitrary power was a splendid triumph for civilization, but it made the lawyer's point of view somewhat too predominant in the Eighteenth Century. The Revolution which had been made in order to oppose illegal changes attempted by an arbitrary monarch, was appealed to in retrospect by Blackstone and even by Burke, as a fixed standard, a criterion by which legislative reform of a popular character was to be condemned beforehand.

Partly for this reason, the period of Walpole and the Pitts was the heyday of unchallenged abuses in all forms of corporate life. Holders of ecclesiastical, academic, charitable and scholastic endowments had no fear of enquiry or reform. Schoolmasters could draw their salaries without keeping school. Universities could sell degrees without holding examinations or giving instruction. Parliamentary boroughs and municipal oligarchies could be as corrupt and ridiculous as they liked ; it was enough that they were old. ' Whatever is is right—if it can show a charter' seems the watchword of the Eighteenth Century.

It is not, therefore, surprising that the greatness of England during the epoch that followed the Revolution is to be judged by her individual men, by the unofficial achievement of her free and vigorous population, by the open competition of her merchants and industrialists in the markets of the world, rather than by her corporate institutions, such as Church, Universities, Schools Civil Service, and town Corporations, which were all of them half asleep. The glory of the Eighteenth Century in Britain lay in the genius and energy of individuals acting freely in a free community—Marlborough, Swift, Bishops Butler and Berkeley Wesley, Clive, Warren Hastings, the Pitts, Captain Cook, Dr Johnson, Reynolds, Burke, Adam Smith, Hume, James Watt Burns, William Blake, and a score of others, to whom our later ag

will find it hard to show the equals, though we have indeed
reformed and rationalized our corporate institutions.

After the prolonged political and religious crisis of the Stuart
epoch, an equally long period of stability, under laws of a generally
liberal character, was no bad thing even at the price of some
stagnation. And, indeed, the sudden vigour put forth by Britain
at Chatham's conjuring, the conquest of Canada and the founding
of the Indian Empire, showed that the political stagnation did not
mean national decadence; the British State and Constitution was
the most efficient as well as the most free of the governments of
the world in those last days of the *ancien régime*. There followed,
indeed, the loss of the American colonies, partly owing to the
defects and corruption of our home constitution, partly for more
general reasons concerned with the relations of America to
England. In imperial and foreign affairs the British aristocracy
both succeeded and failed on the grand scale, proving at least far
more successful than the contemporary despotism of Bourbon
France. On the whole, Britain flourished greatly in the
Eighteenth Century, and her civilization struck roots both deep
and wide.

But mischief lay in the fact that this period of immutable
institutions and unaltered law coincided in its later years with the
period that saw the beginning of economic and social changes of
great rapidity and of yet greater import for the future. The
Industrial Revolution began first in our island, and may for convenience be dated from the early years of George III. Throughout
his long reign, new forces of machinery and capitalized industry 1760-
worked their blind will upon a loosely organized, aristocratic 1820.
society that did not even perceive that its fate had come
upon it.

The highly civilized and well-established world of which Dr.
Johnson and Edmund Burke are the typical minds, could think
only in terms of politics and literature; men failed to observe
that a revolution, more profound than the political changes oversea that they discussed and deprecated, was taking place daily
in their own midst, and was sapping the old English order without
any proper readjustment being made by public authority.
Indeed, just when the Industrial Revolution was making reforms
in our political and municipal institutions more imperative than
ever, the reaction against Jacobin propaganda from abroad drove
the governing classes to refuse, on principle, any political change
at all, while nothing was done either to check or to guide economic
change in its fullest flood. On the top of all this came twenty
years of Napoleonic war, necessarily distracting the nation's
attention from its own grave internal affairs, and complicating the

Industrial Revolution at its most critical stage by war-time abnormality in trade, prices and employment.

After this fashion the quiet and self-contented England of the Eighteenth Century slid unawares into a seething cauldron of trouble, whence a very different world would in due time emerge. Yet even in that confused and desperate crisis, such was the energy latent in the individual Englishman, such were the advantages of the island position to the Mistress of the Seas, such was the power in war time of the new industrial machinery, that Britain, though so recently stripped of her American colonies, emerged as the chief victor of the Napoleonic wars and the mistress of a new Empire. And even while the war was raging, her creative spirit, sheltered behind her fleet, blossomed as in the age of Elizabeth. The era of Nelson and Wellington, of Fox and Pitt, of Castlereagh and Canning, was also the era of Wordsworth and Coleridge, of Scott and Byron, of Shelley and Keats, of Turner and Constable, of Cobbett and Wilberforce, of Bentham and Owen, and many more. The men of that day seemed to inhale vigour and genius with the island air. Though the social order was much amiss and the poor suffered, among the more favoured classes the individual reached a very high point of development during the early stages of the Industrial Revolution, in its first contact with the old rural life and the still surviving culture and freedom inherited from the Eighteenth Century.

CHAPTER I

Early Hanoverian England. Character of the Aristocratic Government. Prime Minister, Cabinet and Parliament. The Spirit of the Eighteenth Century. John Bull and French Influences. The Church and the Wesleyan Movement. Scotland. Universities and Schools. Village Life. Decay of the Yeomen begins. The Underworld. Humanitarianism. The Eve of the Industrial Revolution

Kings : George I, 1714–1727 ; George II, 1727–1760 ; George III, 1760

THE coming over of William of Orange had confirmed the doctrine of the Whigs and confused that of the Tories, but it gave the Whigs no mechanical advantage over their rivals. Throughout the reigns of William and Anne the two parties continued to share power evenly ; the Crown and the electorate favoured first one side and then the other, according to the circumstances of the hour ; the party contest continued to be vigorous, sometimes to fierceness, and in the main fortunate in its outcome for the country's interests. It is only in the reigns of George I and II that we find a state of things that may, with reserves and explanations, be picturesquely described as a 'Whig oligarchy.' Nor would it have come into existence even then, if half the Tory party had not been so gravely compromised with Jacobitism.

Partly for this reason, partly because George I was ignorant of English language and customs, the first two Hanoverians abandoned to the Whig leaders certain prerogatives of the Crown which William III and even Anne would never have let out of their own hands. The formation of Ministries, the dissolution of Parliament, the patronage of the Crown in Church and State, all passed, in effect, from the monarch to the Whig chiefs. In that sense a political oligarchy was indeed established after 1714. But in another aspect the change was a further development of the popular element in our constitution, by the establishment of the omnipotence of Ministries dependent on the vote of the House of Commons, and by the reduction of the power wielded by the hereditary monarch.

Later on, George III attempted in the first twenty years of his reign to take back the patronage of the Crown into the royal hands, in consonance with the undoubted intentions of those who made the Revolution Settlement. But as soon as he had recovered the patronage of the Crown, he used it to corrupt the House of Commons even more systematically than Walpole and the Whig oligarchs had done. Neither the Whig oligarchs nor George III ever tried to stand on the unparliamentary ground of the Stuarts. They never ventured to deny that the executive could only exercise power in agreement with a majority of the House of Commons. But it was possible in the Eighteenth Century to corrupt the members through the distribution of patronage, because the rotten boroughs were becoming less representative of the country with every year that passed. *1760–1780.*

Under the first two Georges the power of the House of Commons increased, while its connection with the people diminished. The long hibernation of the Tory party and the deadness of all serious political controversy damped public interest in parliamentary affairs, other than the distribution of places and bribes. The Septennial Act, passed in 1716 to secure the House of Hanover against Jacobite reaction, prolonged the normal life of a Parliament ; by rendering political tenures more secure, it further deadened political interest in the country and increased the readiness of members to enter the pay of government.

Under George III there was a great revival of public interest in politics, but no increase in democratic control over Parliament.

But when, by the Reform Bill of 1832, the middle class recovered more than their old power over the House of Commons, they found in the modern machinery of Parliament and Cabinet a far more effective instrument of government than any which had existed in Stuart times. The Parliamentary aristocracy of the Eighteenth Century had forged and sharpened the future weapons of the democracy. It is doubtful whether nobles and squires would ever have consented to concentrate such powers in the Lower House, if they had thought of it as a strictly popular body. But they thought of it as a house of gentlemen, many of them nominees or relations of the Peerage, as the 'best club in London,' as the 'Roman Senate' to which the highest interests of the country could safely be committed.

Under these conditions, the aristocratic Eighteenth Century made a great contribution of its own to the growth of British political tradition. The aristocrats devised the machinery by which the legislature could control the executive without hampering its efficiency. This machinery is the Cabinet system and the office of Prime Minister. By the Cabinet system we mean in England a group of Ministers dependent on the favour of the House of Commons and all having seats in Parliament, who must agree on a common policy and who are responsible for one another's action and for the government of the country as a whole. Neither Prime Minister nor Cabinet system was contemplated in the Revolution Settlement. They grew up gradually to meet the country's needs in peace and in war. The first approach to a united Cabinet was made by William III merely to fight the war against Louis, but he remained his own Prime Minister and his own Foreign Minister. In Anne's reign Marlborough acted as the head of the State in war time for all military and diplomatic affairs, but he left to his colleagues the management of Parliament. It was Sir Robert Walpole, the Whig peace Minister from 1721 to 1742, who did most to evolve the principle of the common responsibility of the Cabinet, and the supremacy of the Prime Minister as the leading man at once in the Cabinet and in the Commons. It was significant that, unlike his Whig and Tory predecessors in power, Sir Robert remained undazzled by the lure of peerage, and refused to leave the Lower House so long as he aspired to govern the country. When he consented to become Earl of Orford he was retiring for ever from office.

In effecting these changes in the custom of the constitution, Walpole acted not a little from love of personal power, but he did the country a great service. In driving out from his Cabinet all colleagues who did not agree with his policy or would not submit to his leadership as Premier, he set up the machinery by which

Britain has since been ruled in peace and war. The Cabinet system is the key by which the English were able to get efficient government by a responsible and united executive, in spite of the fact that the executive was subject to the will of a debating assembly of five or six hundred men. They solved this problem, which many nations have found insoluble, not, as was often contemplated in William III's reign, by excluding the Ministers from the Commons, but on the contrary by insisting that they should sit in and lead the House of Commons, like Sir Robert Walpole. The Cabinet is the link between the executive and legislative, and it is a very close link indeed. It is the essential part of the modern British polity.[1]

It was well for England that the Revolution Settlement did not supply her with a brand-new, water-tight, unalterable, written constitution. A sacrosanct written constitution was necessary to achieve the federal union of the States of North America after they had cut themselves adrift from the old Empire. For England it was not at all necessary, and it would certainly have proved inconvenient. If England had been given a rigid constitution when James II was deposed, the Crown would have had assigned to it, in perpetuity, powers which within thirty years of the coronation of William and Mary it handed over to be exercised by its Parliamentary advisers. It is probable, also, that a rigid constitution, drawn up according to the lights of 1689, would have excluded the King's Ministers from sitting in the House of Commons.

A written constitution, as distinct from the sum of ordinary law and custom, is alien to the English political genius. One of the worst signs of the straits to which Cromwell was driven by his inability to find a basis of national agreement, was the fact that he promulgated written constitutions dividing up by an absolute line never to be altered—the powers of Protector and Parliament respectively. These expedients were contrary to the real method of English progress. The London fog which decently conceals from view the exact relations of executive and legislative at Westminster, has enabled the constitution to adapt itself unobserved to the requirements of each passing age.

When we speak of the Whig oligarchy under the first two Georges, we mean (so far as we mean anything definite) about **1714-1760.**

[1] The English in those days were better politicians than political theorists. They permitted the French philosopher, Montesquieu, to report to the world in his *Esprit des Lois* (1748) that the secret of British freedom was the separation of executive and legislative, whereas the opposite was much nearer to the truth. Partly on account of Montesquieu's error, confirmed by Blackstone, partly for better local reasons, the Federal Constitution of the United States was drawn up on the idea of separating executive from legislative.

Whig
Oligarchy

seventy great families, who, in alliance or in rivalry among themselves, exercised the power and patronage of the State, on condition of retaining the constant support of the House of Commons. The heads of the great Whig families mostly sat among the Peers, and their cadets in the Commons. The Peers were able to keep the confidence of the Lower House, partly because they never seriously opposed themselves to its political ideas, and partly because they owned many of the rotten boroughs that returned so many of its members. These great noblemen had therefore no temptation to set up the claims of the more dignified but less powerful chamber in which they themselves sat. The Peers were unofficially but very effectually represented in the House of Commons, and had no objection to the constant increase of its power.

Peers

It was not until the Nineteenth Century, during and after the Reform Bill of 1832, that the Peers thought it necessary to assert the direct power of their own chamber. It was only then that they had cause to question the prescriptive right of the House of Commons to legislate at will for the nation. But in the Nineteenth Century such resistance, though by no means wholly ineffectual, came in the main too late. Englishmen had been so long accustomed to be ruled by the House of Commons when it was an aristocratic assembly, that they would not allow its power to be curtailed when it began to be more truly representative of the nation at large.

Although from 1714 to 1760 the patronage and executive power of the State rested in the hands of the Whig magnates, they were as far as possible from being absolute and arbitrary rulers like the ' Venetian oligarchs ' to whom Disraeli compared them. It was the era of the rigid reign of law in England—law that had triumphed over executive power in 1689. And in the days of Blackstone the laws of England closely limited the power of those who governed the State. The citizen had many strong bulwarks to protect him against government, and enjoyed an amount of personal freedom that was the envy of all Europe. Anything less like the arbitrary and inquisitorial government of the Venetian Republic it is difficult to imagine. If there was tyranny in the land in the mild years between 1714 and 1760 it was not the political tyranny of Parliament and Cabinet, but the social tyranny of the squires in the countryside.

All through Tudor and Stuart times the unpaid Justices of the Peace had administered and judged the English village and the English county, partly by virtue of their local importance as landlords, partly by virtue of their commissions as Justices granted them by the central government. Shakespeare has drawn such a country-bred agent of the Crown in Justice Shallow of

Gloucestershire, Falstaff's friend. Addison's Sir Roger de Coverley is another. Government relied for its working not on a paid and dependent bureaucracy, but on a political understanding with the local gentry, who acted as its unpaid agents.

Such had been the machinery of Tudor and Stuart rule. It required, like so many things English, tact and mutual understanding to ensure the co-operation of the central and the local authorities. James II broke it to pieces. He tried to bend the will of the gentry to serve the camarilla at Whitehall on the question of Roman Catholicism. But there was no organization available for such an unwonted assertion of the central power. It was impossible to use the country gentlemen against themselves, and there was no paid bureaucracy. The Revolution of 1688 in one of its aspects was a revolt of the localities against the central government; in other words, of the squires against the Privy Council. The victory of the local gentry over the King was so resounding that thenceforth they were emancipated for a century and more from all effective central control, in social and economic no less than in political and religious matters. The central power learnt to identify itself with the country gentry to such an extent that the Privy Council never again attempted to control the squires in the interest of the community in general, as had been sometimes done under Elizabeth and the early Stuarts in such matters as the Poor Law.

This part of the lesson taught by the Revolution was not forgotten. When in their turn the Whig oligarchs came to wield the power of the Crown, they were careful to leave the countryside to be administered and judged by the local squires, Tory and Whig alike. In *Tom Jones* Squire Western is a strong Tory, but he holds his commission as Justice of the Peace by the good will of the Whig Lords and the ' Hanoverian rats ' whom he is always abusing. The Justices of the Peace held their commissions from the Crown, through the selection of the Lord Chancellor, but they were not paid by the Crown, and their wealth and local influence came to them from their landed estates which the Government could not touch. Thus the political power of the Whig oligarchy at the centre was effectually limited in the localities by the oligarchy of the squires, who were mainly Tory. But there was nothing to limit the social power of the landed gentry, Whig and Tory together. It was the rural landlords who formed the true oligarchy, no longer controlled by the central power, which rather they themselves controlled. In England there was no democratic township; and elected County Councils were first set up by Lord Salisbury's Government in 1888. Until that date, the aristocratic Justices of the Peace ruled the English countryside.

Thus rural England was aristocratic, and that meant in the Eighteenth Century that most of England was aristocratic. So things remained until the Industrial Revolution made England democratic by converting her from a society mainly rural into a society mainly industrial and urban, where aristocracy had no natural power.

Two things specially distinguished the government of Britain from the governments of the *ancien régime* on the continent— Parliamentary control, and freedom of speech, press and person. Of these advantages Britons were very conscious and very proud. They looked with contempt on French, Italians and Germans as people enslaved to priests, Kings and nobles, unlike your freeborn Englishmen. Freedom had been so lately acquired in Britain and was still so rare a thing in Europe, that our ancestors prized it high among their blessings.

Nevertheless, political and social power in that easy-going century was concentrated too much in one class, the landowners. The time was coming when that defect would greatly enhance the social evils of the Industrial Revolution. But under the first two Georges, before the coming of great economic change, the wage earner, both in town and country, scarcely seems to have resented at all his want of social and political power. The British working man, then called the ' honest yeoman ' or the ' jolly 'prentice,' was quite happy drinking himself drunk to the health of the ' quality ' at election time. And even if he had no vote, he could stand cheering or hooting in front of the hustings, while the candidate, possibly a Peer's son, bowed low with his hand on his heart and a rotten egg in his hair, addressing the mob as ' gentle men,' and asking for their support as the chief object of his ambition. The sight filled foreign spectators with admiration and astonishment. The spirit of aristocracy and the spirit of popular rights seemed to have arrived at a perfect harmony, peculiar to the England of that epoch. There have been worse relations than that between rich and poor, between governors and governed. There was no class hatred, and though highest and lowest were far apart, there were infinite gradations and no rigid class barrier as on the continent. But this careless, good-natured state of society could not outlast the coming of the Industrial Revolution.

It was the special function of the Eighteenth Century to diffuse common sense and reasonableness in life and thought, to civilize manners and to humanize conduct. The century that began with the universally approved *Asiento* treaty for supplying South America with slaves, ended with the capture of national opinion by Wilberforce and the Anti-slave-trade Committee

That movement, which saved civilization in three continents, was the product of the religious and rationalist peculiarities of the epoch of Wesley and Voltaire, of Beccaria and John Howard.

When the Stuarts ceased to reign, the English upper-class could still be represented in fiction by such widely divergent types of culture and manners as Squire Western on the one side and Squire Allworthy and Sir Roger de Coverley on the other. By the end of the century, when Jane Austen began to write, there was a regularized standard of manners and speech among gentlemen.

The reign of Beau Nash at Bath taught the rules of polite society to the country squires who resorted thither with their families, and hastened the disappearance of the sword as the proper adornment of a gentleman's thigh. Largely for this reason, there was a great reduction in the number of killing affrays, and after-supper brawls of fatal issue regretted in the morning. But the regular duel with pistols did not fall into disuse until the bourgeois and Evangelical influences of the Nineteenth Century completed the work of humanity and common sense. Meanwhile, among humbler folk, the passion for pugilism made stabbing and murder 'taboo,' and the custom of making a ring to see two disputants use their fists according to rule fostered the national sentiment for 'fair play,' and tended gradually to discourage the promiscuous and barbarous melees of which we read too often in Smollett and Fielding and in memoirs of their time. *Died 1762.*

As patrons of art and letters, the English upper class reached in the Eighteenth Century a point that they had never reached before, and have since scarcely maintained. Not only great country seats like Holkham, Althorp and Stowe, with their libraries and art treasures, but many smaller houses of the gentry focussed for rural society the art, science and polite letters of the day, with which the dominant landlord class identified itself hardly less than with sport, agriculture and politics. The country houses and the world of fashion did more for culture and intellect than the dormant Universities. The upper class, under the guidance of Dr. Johnson and Garrick, imposed the worship of Shakespeare, as the greatest of mankind, on a public not very intelligent, perhaps, of Shakespeare but most obsequious to his noble patrons, and consequently very respectful to literature.

It was during the Eighteenth Century that a process, begun in the Stuart period, was brought to completion,—the establishment among the learned of the custom of writing in English instead of in Latin. This change had important consequences : British scholars became more than ever separated from their continental brethren ; thought and learning became more national, more popular, and more closely allied to literature. Bentley,

Blackstone, Gibbon and Adam Smith all made appeal to the general intelligence of their countrymen at large, rather than to a professional learned audience scattered over all the countries of Europe.

On the other hand, one of the peculiarities of the movement of English culture in the Eighteenth Century, as compared to the Elizabethan era, was the deference to foreign models. Aristocratic leadership partly accounted for this. The patrons were 'milords' accustomed to make the Grand Tour of Europe, mixing with the society of foreign courts and capitals as tourists seldom do to-day, and bringing back statues, pictures, objects of virtù, French literary and philosophic ideas, and Italian standards of music and poetry. The link with the continent was the stronger because it was reciprocal : foreign admiration of British institutions and British thinkers was a chief original cause of the 'Encyclopædist' movement of rational philosophy in France. 'Le Grand Newton,' Locke and Hume were names as highly honoured in Paris as in London and Edinburgh.[1]

It is indeed a singular fact that, during the hundred years after the Revolution of 1688, when England was in violent reaction against French religion and politics, when English and French armies and navies were in constant conflict in both hemispheres, and when the common people despised and hated everything French with a fierce ignorance and prejudice, our taste in letters, in architecture and in house decoration was to an unusual degree subjected to French and Italian ideas. In the reign of Charles II we had, like the rest of Europe, begun to submit to the cultural influences of the Court of Versailles, and we did not cease to do so after La Hogue and Blenheim. There was gain as well as loss in this temporary 'academizing' of our literary standards,—gain to English prose and loss to English poetry : gain to clearness of thought and expression, loss to imagination and native vigour. The 'romantic' and 'naturalist' movements begun in the last decade of the century by Scott, Coleridge and Wordsworth, were a revolt from foreign standards back to native traditions and native freedom. But even in the full Eighteenth Century the native English novel had been progressing freely, with little deference to foreign models, from Defoe through Smollett and Fielding to Miss Austen. Nor did our drama ever accept the French 'unities' of time and place.

---

[1] Voltaire, the dictator of continental opinion, wrote : ' La nation anglaise est la seule de la terre qui soit parvenue à régler le pouvoir des rois en leur résistant ; où les seigneurs sont grands sans insolence et sans vassaux, et où le peuple partage le gouvernement sans confusion.' ' En Angleterre communément on pense, et les lettres y sont plus en honneur qu'ici. Cet avantage est une suite nécessaire de la forme de leur gouvernement.'—*Lettres sur les Anglais*.

Neither must it be forgotten that during this period, when upper class poetry and literature were least 'romantic,' most rationalized and most academic, the imagination of the common folk was still being nurtured not only on the Bible but on ghost stories, fairy stories, ballads and tales of romantic glamour, of which their everyday rustic life seemed a part. Indeed it was precisely when 'romance' made its Nineteenth Century conquest of literature proper, that the school textbook and the newspaper began to take the place of the traditional romantic lore of the cottage fireside. It is even arguable that the Eighteenth Century, which produced William Blake and Burns and Wordsworth, was in its true nature more 'romantic' than the following century with its efforts to escape by feats of imagination from the drabness of its real surroundings.

However that may be, the artificiality of our Eighteenth Century culture was strong enough to impose an alien regime on the world of music. Handel and the Italian Opera largely took the place of our native music, which had once been reckoned the best in Europe. But the 'Beggar's Opera,' that took the char- **1728.** acteristically English form of a satire on the victorious Opera from overseas, produced a line of English popular operas, lasting into the Nineteenth Century. These operas with dialogue, of which Gilbert and Sullivan came in the end, were truly national work in a period of strong foreign influence.

Painting gained most and lost least by the close association of fashionable English society with the culture of the continent. Indeed the age of Reynolds and Gainsborough was the first notable efflorescence of a native pictorial art in the island. Its arrival to serve the 'great families' was a fortunate coincidence in time. The portraits of the native English aristocracy in their heyday of power, prestige and happiness, look down from those perfect canvasses in Olympian calm, over the heads of the so differently featured art-patrons of to-day.

The improvement characteristic of the Eighteenth Century was more marked in manners and intelligence than in morals and the stricter virtues. Gambling raged among the wealthy even more than in our own time, and drinking deep was scarce thought a blemish. The best of the upper class aimed at the full and rational enjoyment of this life, rather than at preparation for the next, of which they spoke seldom and then with a cheerful scepticism.

The accession of the House of Hanover, followed by nearly fifty years of Whig rule, left the Anglican Church with all its exclusive civil and political privileges, but imposed on its spirit the moderating influence of latitudinarian appointments to Bishoprics and other benefices in the gift of government. The Jacobitish sympathies of the High Church party, and its desire to persecute Dissenters as revealed in the last years of Anne's reign, made latitudinarian appointments necessary to keep the peace and preserve the dynasty.

The intellectual strength of the Latitudinarian party and the rational and tolerant spirit of the new century rendered this policy on the part of Government successful. Until the French Revolution and the Evangelical movement raised new issues, the clergy of the Anglican Church ceased to be zealots, whether political or religious. Goldsmith's 'Vicar of Wakefield' teaches his flock, by precept and example, those simple virtues which the pious of all denominations are too prone to under-value unless they are joined to some form of religious 'enthusiasm.' For a while the parish clergy were content to inculcate morality with little stress on dogma, and none on emotionalism, sentimentality or party spirit. The 'reasonable' character of Christianity was emphasized, and the miracles recorded in the Bible were regarded as historic proofs of a system agreeable to the philosophy and common sense of all times. The Classical learning of the period between Bentley and Porson, of which the clergy had their full share, harmonized well with this comprehensive attitude. Bishop Butler's *Analogy*, one of the world's greatest philosophic works, defended Christianity by the appeal to reason. In the England of the Eighteenth Century the Church remained on terms with the scientific and latitudinarian spirit of the age. The English spirit of compromise was suited, and the more advanced 'deism,' though it began in England early in the century, flourished only in France and was not regarded as 'respectable' over here.

1736.

The clergy, while thus inspired—or uninspired—were in certain respects in closer touch with the great body of the laity than at any time before or after. Indeed, by modern standards, the parish priests of this era became too much identified with their flocks. They rendered frequent and useful service on the magisterial bench, for the most part in a pure spirit of good citizenship. The parson as Justice of the Peace had often more law, more humanity, and a less invincible hatred of poachers than the squire at his side. The black coat in the hunting-field was little criticized prior to the Evangelical movement.

In Stuart times there had been a certain proportion of men of gentle birth among the parish clergy, but under the Hanoverians the identity of the social class of squire and parson became more close. As the value of tithe rose, the squire found it proper to put his younger son into the family living and to enlarge the parsonage into a lesser manor-house by throwing out a bay-window or two. These family arrangements were part of the great business of making life pleasant for the upper class, in which the men of the Eighteenth Century were such adepts. But the system had also its uses for the community: for, if there was any merit in the Anglican ideal of having ' an educated gentleman in every parish,' this was how it came nearest to realization. Gilbert White, a country clergyman, observing his birds, season after season, at Selborne, taught men to feel that

b. 1720,
d. 1793.

> He prayeth well, who loveth well
> Both man, and bird and beast.

Such a clergy and such a squirearchy together were able to put down popular superstitions like witch-hunting that had flourished horribly in Stuart days, particularly under the Puritans.

Thus the Established Church took an integral part in the civilizing work of the Eighteenth Century. The two leading defects of its qualities were its discouragement of all forms of zeal, and its neglect of the poor, especially in the great towns, the collieries and the industrial districts. The old parish divisions of England, no less than municipal government and Parliamentary representation, answered ill to the real distribution of population in a country that had been in constant economic change for two hundred years, and was now changing much more rapidly than ever before. Moreover, audiences as completely uneducated as were most of the English of that day, were not likely to be much impressed by arguments based on Butler's *Analogy* and by the sweet reasonableness of a learned religion.

The Dissenting bodies of the Bunyan tradition, which had been founded in the heat and zeal of the Cromwellian era and had survived the period of persecution under Charles II, still served the needs of the poor in some districts, but even they were becoming more ' respectable,' less ' enthusiastic ' and more bourgeois. The Presbyterian body had largely become Unitarian. The Quakers, ceasing to be popular revivalists, became spiritually ' quiet ' and economically prosperous.

These wide gaps in the social field left by the existing religious bodies, were filled by the full flood of John Wesley's uncompromising ardour for the salvation of souls. One of the greatest missionaries and the greatest religious organizers of all history, Wesley chanced to be contemporary with one of the greatest of popular orators, George Whitefield, who may be regarded either as his supporter or as his rival.

b. 1703,
d. 1791.

b. 1714,
d. 1770.

The zeal of these first ' methodists ' was opposed in every respect to the characteristic faults and merits of the Eighteenth

Century attitude of mind. For this reason their separation from the Established Church of the day was, perhaps, unavoidable, although Wesley to the last regarded himself as her faithful son. But the corner-stone of religion as he preached it was neither ' reason ' nor sacramentalism, but the doctrine he had borrowed from the Moravians that conversion comes as a sudden personal assurance of salvation, bringing new birth and dominion over sin. This revivalist doctrine, in the mouths of Wesley and Whitefield, had enormous power. But the indecorous field-preaching to vast audiences, the convulsions, agonies and raptures of the converted were at least as odious to the ' respectable ' classes, clerical and lay, as the early proceedings of the Salvation Army in the latter years of Queen Victoria. It was very natural that the Bishops and clergy should ostracize these Methodist proceedings, and since the Toleration Act only tolerated registered Dissenters, the Wesleyans had to choose whether they should register as Dissenters or cease to save souls. Their design to form a Church within the Church proved impossible in the circumstances of the age.

In this way it came about that the revival, after it had taken a permanent institutional form, swelled the numbers, not of the Establishment, but of the Dissenting bodies, very greatly to the future advantage of the Liberal Party in the Nineteenth Century. But early Wesleyanism, founded by a consistent Tory, was a conservative influence socially and to some extent politically. In the days of Jacobin and early Radical propaganda, Methodism proved a powerful counter-attraction among the poor. It directed into other channels the first rebellion of the uncared-for millions, for it gave them other interests and ideals besides the material, it fostered in them self-respect as citizens of another world whose franchise was not confined to the well-to-do, and it provided them with a democratic religious and educational organization of their own. But, as time went on, working-class religion became more often identified with working-class politics, and the local preacher was often a Radical agitator as well.

It was only at the very close of the Eighteenth Century that something of the spirit of Methodism began to react upon the Established Church and upon the upper classes themselves. The greater seriousness induced in those quarters by the prospect of the French Revolution, helped this change of temper. But though Evangelicalism then gained a formidable party among the Church clergy, its strength lay among the Church laity, in Wilberforce and the anti-slavery ' saints,' in Shaftesbury and the philanthropists of the new century, and in many conquerors and rulers of India and the Empire.

In the days of George II, the Wesleyan movement was carried by its founders to the American Colonies, and in the future United

States it became a force of great potency and numerical strength. In Wales, Methodism swelled to full tide a national revival springing from a native Evangelical movement. Only in Scotland it failed, because there the people already had a popularly governed Church of their own, and were well educated and deeply interested in a native system of theology.

But although Methodism, which leaped the Atlantic, was stopped on the banks of the Tweed, the religious history of Scotland in the Eighteenth Century bears a close family likeness to that of England. The middle years of the century saw the victory of a latitudinarian movement known as Moderatism, rebelling against the harsh and bigoted rigour of the older Presbyterian dogmatists. The historian Dr. William Robertson, b. 1721, Principal of Edinburgh University, is the chief figure of the d. 1793. movement. Even ' deistic ' philosophers like David Hume were b. 1711, at least tolerated in the land, and Adam Smith, as Professor at d. 1776. Glasgow University, helped to give Scotland a new intellectual b. 1723, pre-eminence. The rapidly increasing wealth of town and country d. 1790. speeded the mental liberation and growth of the society that produced Robert Burns and Sir Walter Scott.[1]

But the common people in many a rural parish never liked these modern sermons with their ' cauld clatter of morality ' instead of the old zeal and dogma. The Moderates depended dangerously on the revival of ' patronage,' by means of which individual patrons appointed ministers without regard to the wishes of the congregation—a system unchallenged in England but irregular and unpopular in the Scottish Church. In the early Nineteenth Century a great Evangelical revival in the Presbyterian body was destined to lead to renewed religious ardour and eventually to the ' Disruption ' of the Church under Chalmers on 1843. the question of patronage. But by that time Moderatism had done its work in Scotland in destroying the spirit of intolerance and enlarging the intellectual outlook of the whole community.

The slumbers of the English Universities in the Eighteenth Century were more scandalous than the lighter and more broken slumbers of the Church. There were practically no examinations held at Oxford, and few at Cambridge.[2] Our own over-examined

---

[1] There are two fascinating books on the great changes in Scotland in this period—H. S. Graham's *Social Life in Scotland in the 18th Century*, and Galt's *Annals of the Parish*.

[2] Lord Eldon, then plain John Scott, graduated at Oxford in 1770 ; he used to relate that he was asked only two questions by way of examination for his degree—' What is the Hebrew for the place of a skull ? ' and ' Who founded University College ?' By replying ' Golgotha ' and ' King Alfred ' he satisfied the examiners in Hebrew and History. At Cambridge the better men stood the test of the very serious Mathematical Tripos, still partly conducted by *viva voce* disputations. But there was no examination in Classics.

generation may think that deficiency a blessing, but the poor quality and quantity of the teaching were deplorable, taken in conjunction with the low output of valuable works of learning by communities so rich in leisure.

There were still only the two Universities to serve all England and Wales, and they had shrunk to something like half the number of students as compared to early Stuart times.   In 1750 Oxford matriculated 190 and Cambridge 127 freshmen.   Many of these were noblemen and gentlemen not intent on serious study ; others were poor scholars, either seeking to enter the Church, or at Cambridge with its North-country connection to pursue the study of mathematics after the Newtonian traditions of the place.

In the midst of a generation full of intellectual vigour and specially devoted to antiquarianism and science, the decadence of the Universities may seem very strange.   It is to be explained in part by the exclusion of Dissenters; in part by the legal reservation of University and college posts, with a few exceptions, to the clergy, in a time of great scholarly enthusiasm among laymen. Another evil was the assumption of almost all the prestige and functions of the University by the individual Colleges, at a time when each College was inspired less by academic ideals than by the spirit of a relaxed monasticism.   There was no fear of investigation or reform in that era of security for all corporate institutions. Warned by the outcome of James II's conflict with Magdalen, the Whig governments did not even attack the notorious Jacobitism of Oxford, or the not less notorious Jacobitism of certain Cambridge Colleges.   *A fortiori* there was no fear of a demand for scholastic reform.

The same spirit injured the schools and the provision of education for the poor.   No Charity Commission was to be feared in those days, no State grant was hoped for, no government inspector moved through the land.   The spirit of the Elizabethan and early Stuart Grammar Schools, inspired by the Protestant and Renaissance zeal of those earlier times, had died away.   In the villages, primary schools kept in cottages by incompetent old women purported to teach the alphabet to some of the working population.

But if the characteristic benefits of our modern systematized education were absent, so too were its defects.   Neither upper nor middle class education moulded the individual after a stereotyped pattern.   The old-fashioned Grammar School for farmers' sons at Hawkshead would not have borne modern inspection, but it allowed the shy and tender plant of Wordsworth's genius to grow naturally and in its own queer way, as would not have happened if the boy's every hour had been mapped out for organized athletics and instruction.[1] Very different from Hawkshead were the ' public schools ' of the aristocracy ; they suffered from indiscipline and bullying, but their very want of organization encouraged individual eccentricity and power. The product of genius per head of population in Eighteenth Century England seems, by comparison with our own day, to have been in inverse proportion to the amount of education supplied. But doubtless there were other causes productive of genius inherent in the general character of the life of that bygone day. And certainly the want of schooling meant the wastage of much latent talent and the denial of intellectual pleasures to thousands who might have enjoyed them.

The discipline of the home, though milder than in former ages, was still very strict for the child ; parents and schoolmasters still believed fanatically in the virtues of the rod. To some extent the want of facilities for secondary education was made good for young people by the apprentice system. Apprenticeship was not as universal as it had been in Tudor and Stuart times, but it was still very general, affording domestic discipline and thorough training in a craft to a large number of youths, during that critical after-school age for which so little provision is made in our day.

Here again there was no inspection of domestic conditions of service. The evil-minded and avaricious master could misuse his apprentice with little fear of anything beyond a bad reputation among his neighbours. Pauper children, apprenticed to the lower type of master or mistress, perished as miserably as the same class of child in the worst factories of a later generation. So far from originating cruelty to children, the factory system called attention to the evil by concentrating it where all could see, and so stimulated indignation that brought it to an end. The fate of the unfriended child under the old apprentice system may be read in Crabbe's story of Peter Grimes, and in authentic records of the doing to death of apprentices by Mrs. Brownrigg and others, which fully justify the poet's harrowing tale.[2]

On the other hand an even more common type was the ' jolly apprentice,' *alias* the ' industrious apprentice,' living with his master as one of the family, and hoping to marry his daughter

---

[1] See his *Prelude*, Books I.–II., for an Eighteenth Century Grammar School at its best.

[2]   ' Peter had heard there were in London then,—
    Still have they being !—workhouse-clearing men,
    Who, undisturbed by feelings just or kind,
    Would parish-boys to needy tradesmen bind ;
    They in their want a trifling sum would take
    And toiling slaves of piteous orphans make.'
                (*The Borough*, xxii.)

Grimes kills one apprentice after another. See also Mrs. George's *London in the Eighteenth Century*, pp. 231–3.

and succeed him. And the paid journeyman was also part of the manufacturing tradesman's ' family.' Industry was to a large extent based upon these arrangements, humanly so admirable, before the coming of the factory system segregated the classes.

These domestic industries were not all collected in towns or industrial districts, but were many of them seated in villages, amid all the amenities and traditions of old rural life. Not only did the village manufacture largely for its own needs, but the national and international markets were supplied to a considerable extent from rural England. Besides the ' spinsters ' and the weavers of cloth both coarse and fine, a great variety of the most elaborate arts and crafts, such for instance as clock-making, were carried on in small country places. Iron and wooden implements and vessels of all sorts were produced by the blacksmith, wheelwright and carpenter, and many villages were still quite able to build their own houses. The ' village shop ' dealing in every variety of article was not yet common, for that system implies the regular supply of village needs from the town. The pedlars walking their rounds normally sufficed for that.

This was the last era in our island history when the village was the normal unit of society. Under the first two Georges, most men and women, including many not engaged in any form of agriculture, were in the full sense of the word ' villagers.' They were interested, not in the political, athletic and scandalous chronicle of the world at large, of which they heard seldom and little from the news-sheets of the day, nor in the life of town, factory or trade-union, but simply in the daily human drama of their own village set amid its surrounding fields and woods, with its traditions, its ghost stories, its neighbourliness, its feuds, and its shrewd, ignorant rustic comment on the mysterious world beyond. From that frugal but digestible dish of ideas our ancestors still drew the food for their thoughts on the eve of the Industrial Revolution. What they knew of sport was what they saw and took part in for themselves at the covert side, or on the village green, or on the squire's new cricket ground.

The early Georgian village represented, on the whole, a healthy economic and social order, but with the defect that the power of the great landowners was on the increase, instead of yielding to a more diffused system of landownership and a larger measure of village autonomy. Even in the reigns of the first two Georges, the small yeomen freeholders [1] and the small squires were

---

[1] The word ' yeoman,' used in Tudor and Stuart times to include tenant farmers as well as freeholders, was used by Arthur Young for freeholders only, and came to have that narrower sense in the Nineteenth Century. But many Eighteenth Century writers, including Adam Smith, used it in the older and larger sense.

declining in numbers. The great period of the yeomen freeholders and of small, compact estates was the Tudor and Stuart epoch. In Anne's reign the acquisitive tendency of the large landowners was becoming more than ever marked. The squires were jealous of the small freeholders as being politically and socially independent of their sway. The rage for game-preserving characteristic of the epoch made them look askance at a fellow without a coat-of-arms who had the impudence to shoot partridges on his own patch of ground. Indeed, the squirearchical Parliaments of the later Stuarts had most tyrannically passed game laws which excluded all freeholders of under a hundred pounds a year from killing game even on their own land.[1]

To buy out the small freeholder was an even more satisfactory way of disposing of him. For his part, he often thought he might do better in the modern world than by staying on his farm. All through the Eighteenth Century yeoman families were drifting to the towns, often to become the founders of the great business firms of Modern England. Often, too, they became large tenant-farmers, gaining more perhaps in wealth and importance than they lost in independence.

The movements of humanism and rationalism were for a long period more observable in the educated classes than among the lower orders. The underworld of the times of Gay and Hogarth, when Wesley and Whitefield first took it in hand, was as barbarous as it was full of life and character. Long before the Industrial Revolution, governmental and social neglect were producing grave evils,—the uncared-for state of the poor in London and other rapidly growing cities ; the want of provision for popular education south of the Scottish Border ; the displacing of the Englishman's time-honoured diet of ale and beer by the cheap and deadly gin.[2]

To deal with the unsorted masses of humanity huddled together in the towns, there was no better police than the old watchman with his rattle, and police-magistrate Fielding's Bow

[1] Even the good Sir Roger de Coverley does not quite like the yeoman of a hundred pounds a year, 'just within the Game Act, and qualified to kill an hare or a pheasant ; he knocks down a dinner with his gun twice or thrice a week ; and by that means lives much cheaper than those who have not so good an estate as himself.'

[2] Gin was not seriously taxed till 1736. The yearly average of British spirits distilled rose from about half a million gallons in 1684 to nearly five and a half million in 1735. In the early Eighteenth Century, mortality and crime among the poor were increased by the new taste for gin. The retailers invited customers to come inside and get ' drunk for a penny and dead drunk for two-pence.' On the other hand tea, imported in great quantities by the East India Company, was beginning to rival alcohol as the drink of the people. As early as 1742 complaint was made that ' the meanest families, even of labouring people ' in Scotland, ' made their morning meal of tea,' to the disuse of ale.

Street runners,' fit but few. As late as 1780 the Lord George Gordon mob fairly set fire to London before the troops were called out. Mounted highwaymen beset the roads converging on the greatest capital in the world with a scandalous impunity, and were popularly regarded as the representatives of careless English valour and freedom :

> Six highwaymen shall carry me
> With good broadswords and sweet liberty ;

such was the ballad-maker's idea of a noble funeral.

Since the Revolution, trials, whether political or criminal, were more fairly conducted, and the rules of scientific evidence were gradually beginning to be understood by lawyers for the first time in history. But the prisons, still farmed out to a base type of gaoler to make his profit out of the prisoners, were, in Wesley's opinion, worse than anything ' on this side hell,' and the innocent debtor often fared the worst of all. Hanging for innumerable minor crimes against property was on the increase ; public flogging of men and women was not yet abolished. But with the last decades of the century the humanitarian movement under Howard and others had set about its task so long overdue. Humanitarianism was an Eighteenth Century product, whereas the evils it sought to remedy were, with the exception of gin, as old as civilized man.

Life under the first two Georges, though not in itself of the type we associate with the Industrial Revolution, moved under conditions that were bound to hasten that great change, if certain mechanical inventions should chance to be made. The peculiar laws and customs of Hanoverian England allowed an unusual freedom to the individual, and did little to discourage private initiative ; religious toleration left Dissenting merchants in perfect liberty to devote their energies to money-making, while they were prevented from taking part in public life ; foreign Protestant refugees, rich in trade secrets and industrial skill, were made free of the economic citizenship of the island ; commerce and manufacture were impeded by relatively few restrictions of State, municipality or guild ; a free trade area extended from John o' Groats to Land's End, in contrast to the innumerable customs barriers then dividing up Germany, Italy and the Kingdom of France ; the lords and squires who ruled the land were, unlike the French and German *noblesse*, in close personal relations with the mercantile and industrial magnates, and were often barely distinguishable from them [1] ; science in the land of Newton was honoured and exploited by the more enterprising merchants and their aristocratic patrons, on the look-out for a good thing to improve mining operations or manufacture ; capital had been accumulated as never before in the world's history, and the English moneyed men, accustomed to invest it in commerce on the grand scale, would readily apply it to industry on a scale equally profuse, if once new inventions gave capital a fresh opening there ; the markets for English goods already existing in America, Europe and the Orient could be indefinitely developed by our merchant service, to dispose of any increase in the quantity of goods manufactured at home.   In all these ways the England of that era was the predestined cradle of the Industrial Revolution.

An iron industry of immemorial antiquity was still dependent for fuel on the rapidly diminishing forests of the Sussex Weald, the Midlands and the Severn Valley ; any day the shortage of timber might suggest to ingenious minds a method of smelting iron with coal.   Since the days of the Plantagenets, coal, then easily won near the surface, had been much used for domestic purposes, especially in London where it was known as ' sea-coal ' after its voyage from Tyne to Thames mouth.   Wheeled traffic for heavy goods was still exceptional.   Where water-carriage was not available, the coal sacks were slung across the patient pack-horses, breasting the passes of the Welsh hills.   In that primitive way the textiles of Yorkshire, Lancashire and the Cotswolds had still to travel when Walpole was Prime Minister.   And when Josiah Wedgwood began his career as a master-potter in the year **1759** of the taking of Quebec, the clay and the finished crockery still entered and left the Five Towns on the back of the donkey or the horse.

Indeed, the one great remaining obstacle to the initiation of an Industrial Revolution was the badness of transport in old England.   The making of canals only began with the reign of George III.   Yet the roads in winter were often quagmires wherein loaded pack-horses sank to the girth, and waggons could

[1] It was the Duke of Bridgewater who was called ' the father of Inland Navigation,' and ' the first Manchester man.'   And are we, for instance, to count a man like Sir Walter Blackett, who died in 1777, as a squire or as a merchant and capitalist ?   He was the greatest man in Newcastle and on Tyneside, but he also developed a large agricultural estate in the heart of rural Northumberland, with all the appurtenances of a country house, grouse-shooting, tree-planting, etc. A law passed by the Tory Parliament of 1711, and not repealed by the Walpole Whigs, had closed the House of Commons to all merchants, however wealthy, who were not also landowners.   Whatever the intention of the Act, its effect was to compel merchants to become landed gentlemen also, rather than to exclude them from Parliament.   Many landed estates in the Eighteenth Century, besides Sir Walter Blackett's, were improved and embellished with money made in industry or commerce.

not be moved at all. On portions of the main roads, indeed, toll-bars were being set up by private companies, with Parliamentary powers to tax the traffic and keep the surface in repair. But during the Seven Years' War most of the mileage, even on the main roads of England, was still free to those who could force their way through the mud. The heavy coaches lumbered along in the ruts in a very different style from that in which their light-timbered successors in the era of Waterloo scoured the same roads remade by Macadam. In 1754 the Flying Coach advertised that 'however incredible it may appear, this coach will actually (barring accidents) arrive in London in four days and a half after leaving Manchester.' It took a week to travel between York and London; and in the days of Porteous riots and the rising of 'forty-five,' Edinburgh had no regular service running from the British Capital whence Scotland was supposed to be governed.

Society on the eve of the Industrial Revolution had many features most attractive to us in the retrospect : a rural population attached to the land and its labours and recreations, to the village and its traditions ; great variety and independence of type and character among men ; individual training, skill and taste in arts and crafts as a normal part of the economic life of the people. But in judging what the Industrial Revolution did to our island, it is necessary to remember that a fuel famine due to the using up of our timber was already settling down on various parts of the island in the Eighteenth Century, until relief came through the distribution of coal by canals, and afterwards by railways. The fuel famine was already putting an end to our old iron industry and was on the point of lowering the standard of comfort in domestic life. A well-to-do tradesman in Launceston was reduced to paying threepence to a neighbour for use of his fire to cook a leg of mutton ; and his poorer neighbours, like most of the South English peasantry outside coal or peat districts, lived on bread and cheese, and too seldom knew the joys of a fire. And apart from the question of fuel, it is safe to say that the population of Great Britain could not, without the great industrial and agricultural changes of George III's reign, have risen much above seven millions without a lowering of the standard of life to something nearer the level of contemporary Ireland.

CHAPTER II

George I and II. The Whig Oligarchy. The 1715 and the 1745. Social Consequences in Scotland. Walpole and the Elder Pitt. Great Britain in Peace and War. Annexation of Canada and Foundation of the Indian Empire

Kings : George I, 1714–1727 ; George II, 1727–1760

DURING the reigns of George I and II, the policy of British Ministers at home and abroad was guided by the necessity to maintain the House of Hanover on the throne. This was held to involve the continuance in office of the Whig party, on condition that political power was enjoyed only by conformists to the Anglican worship, and that the Tory squires in the countryside were given no personal ground for discontent with the rule of their political rivals. The Tories, disaffected to the House of Hanover but unwilling to take an active part in restoring a Roman Catholic Stuart to the throne, were unable to join either side in the rebellions of 1715 and 1745, or to assert themselves in a united and effective manner at elections or on the floor of Parliament.

While in England the descendants of the old Cavaliers had become, for the most part, law-abiding and home-staying Tories, who occasionally drank the health of ' the King over the water ' with a sigh and a shrug, in Scotland the Cavaliers had to a much greater extent become Jacobites, prepared to take up arms at a favourable opportunity. The habits of obedience to government and the dread of civil war were of much later growth in Scotland than in England. The Union of 1707 was still unpopular, and a Jacobite restoration might, it was hoped, mean a revival of Scottish independence. The Episcopalian Church, established and privileged south of the Tweed, could only hope to recover power in North Britain by the sword. Finally, the chiefs of the Highland tribes opposed to the hegemony of the tribe of Campbell, were longing to carry on that ancient feud after the old Highland fashion. For these reasons the rebellions of 1715 and 1745 were revolts of Scottish origin, which failed for want of English support.

In 1715 the English rising scarcely spread beyond the Roman Catholic section of the squires of Northumberland, under their leader the young Earl of Derwentwater and their Protestant stalking-horse Mr. Forster. Picking up some Scottish allies in the Borderland, they rode through Cumberland into Lancashire to rouse the Roman Catholics there. The little force surrendered to the royal troops in the streets of Preston, where Cromwell had cut off a more formidable Cavalier invasion coming south by the

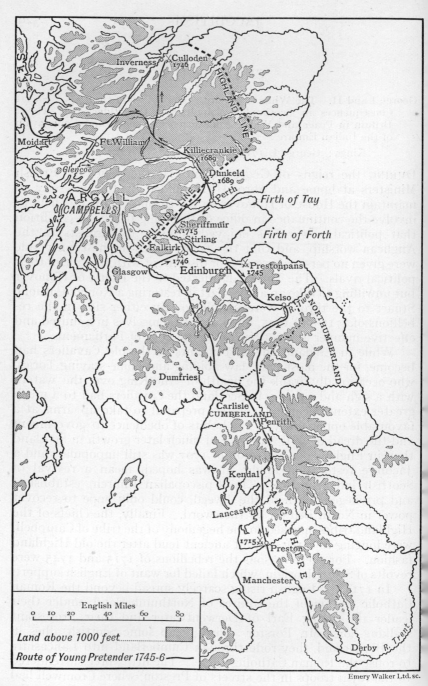

Land above 1000 feet..........

Route of Young Pretender 1745-6 ———

Emery Walker Ltd. sc.

MAP XXVIII.—Scotland and North England in the time of the Jacobites

same route. The ' fifteen ' in England was the last Pilgrimage of Grace, the dying effort of the old feudalism and Romanism of the Northern Counties, which received the *coup de grâce* from the confiscations that followed the revolt. Wesleyanism and Industrialism were soon to make a new world between Trent and Tweed.

In Scotland the ' fifteen ' was a more serious affair. The tribes opposed to the Campbells, joined with the Episcopalian congregations of the east coast, raised an army more formidable in numbers than the similar forces that followed Prince Charles Edward thirty years later. But the Whigs showed more energy and promptitude in defence of the throne upon this earlier occasion. A rising had been expected as a result of the accession of George I, and government was not taken by surprise as in 1745. John Campbell, the Duke of Argyle of the day, who commanded the royal forces in Scotland, was a better General than poor Sir John Cope who lost Prestonpans. Argyle's influence, paramount in part of the Highlands and great throughout all the Lowlands, was ably exerted at this crisis. The Presbyterians south of the Forth followed their Whig clergy ; and the burghs, with few exceptions, showed a warlike readiness in the Hanoverian cause, which was wanting in 1745, after thirty years of profound peace had relaxed the old fighting habits of the Lowlanders and disintegrated the militia of the towns. The Earl of Mar, who led the Scottish Jacobites in 1715, had no ability either as statesman or as General. The battle of Sheriffmuir, where 3500 men under Nov. Argyle held up 8000 under Mar, though indecisive at the moment, 1715. had the effect of checking the advance of the revolt and so sealed its doom. Moreover, when James, ' the Old Pretender,' son of James II, came to Scotland too late in the affair, he had none of the gifts for rousing enthusiasm which distinguished his son Charles Edward in the ' forty-five.'

It was fortunate for the stability of the new order that this first effort of the Jacobites had taken place before the House of Hanover had had time to attain its full measure of unpopularity. George I, though not quite the worst, was perhaps the least generally attractive of our monarchs. Unable to speak English, with blowsy foreign women for his mistresses, with a grim domestic tragedy in the German background, he had no redeeming touch of wit, generosity or nobleness of soul. He was, indeed, a great promoter of our constitutional liberties, because he knew and cared so little about things English that he left to his Ministers all questions of domestic policy and all patronage in Church and State. He insisted only that his Ministers must be Whigs, and fortunately had the good sense, after a little experience, to decide that Walpole was the Whig under whom the governance of England would prove least troublesome. For even under the first two Georges the King still shared with the House of Commons and with the Whig oligarchy in the selection of the chief Minister.

That Jacobitism failed to overthrow even such a King as this, was due to the admirably obstinate refusal of the exiled Stuarts to pretend to be Protestants and play Charles II's game over again. Moreover, the danger to George I's throne was reduced by the value which the French Regent Orleans, in the early years of Louis XV, placed on England's friendship. Foreign menace to the dynasty came first from the unexpected quarter of Spain, long moribund but galvanized into a brief vitality by the rule of an Italian of genius, Cardinal Alberoni. That remarkable adventurer revived the Spanish fleet and army, and entered upon schemes, somewhat too ambitiously conceived, for restoring Spain to power in Italy and the Mediterranean, and the Stuart family to the throne of Britain. His ally against Hanover was that unquestionable Protestant, the wild warrior King, Charles XII of Sweden, who

> left the name, at which the world grew pale,
> To point a moral or adorn a tale.

Charles and his lifelong rival Peter the Great of Russia were agreed in nothing save hostility to the House of Hanover, and the warlike Swede was looked to as the head of the next Jacobite invasion. But his death before a petty fortress in Norway followed close on the destruction of Alberoni's new Spanish fleet by the British off Cape Passaro in Sicily ; together, these two events confirmed the throne of George I and the British naval dominion in the Mediterranean, based on Gibraltar and Minorca.[1]

1718.

The next danger to the Hanoverian settlement came from within. A mania of speculation, known as ' the South Sea Bubble,' swept over all classes with peculiar ease in that first era of stock-jobbing. The government itself was carried into the whirlpool. State interests and obligations were most foolishly embarked in the schemes of the South Sea directors. The King's German mistresses and the Prince of Wales were deeply involved in projects which in retrospect appeared deliberate plans to exploit

1720.

[1] The British Government had been so anxious for peace that it had suggested giving Gibraltar to Alberoni as the price, which he had the folly to refuse. After Passaro, Captain Walton, who followed the flying enemy, reported progress to Admiral Sir George Byng, in a letter that ends with the often quoted words : ' We have taken and destroyed all the Spanish ships which were upon the coast, the number as per margin.' This concluding sentence was long mistakenly believed to have comprised the whole letter.

the widow and the orphan.   When the crash came, the outcry of the disillusioned and ruined filled the land.   The Jacobites never had a better chance, but their momentary good fortune proved their permanent undoing, for the South Sea affair brought Sir Robert Walpole to power, and once he had grasped the helm of the tempest-tossed State, he never let go of it for twenty years.   1721– At the height of the South Sea madness he had warned his col- 1742. leagues and the public, and had prophesied the end.   Therefore, in the hour of distress he was called upon to restore the national credit and confidence.

Hitherto the new century had been one of violent party and dynastic feuds.   It was Walpole's long rule that gave to the Eighteenth Century in England that peculiar sense of domestic peace and stability which is often regarded as its chief characteristic.   Rest after three generations of strife was Sir Robert's gift to Britain.

Apart from bitter factions arising from personal rivalry among the Whigs themselves in Parliament,—Pulteney, Carteret and Townshend against Walpole,—the real opposition to government was Jacobitism in the country.   Fear of a dynastic counter-revolution acted as a constant check upon the actions of the Cabinet.   It inspired Walpole's ' moderation ' at home, and the peace policy which he adopted abroad, lest the land-tax pressing heavily on the squires in time of war should goad them to dis-loyalty.   The same fear of Jacobitism led him to bow before the foolish storm raised against his Excise Bill, for the sake of which, 1733. as he wisely said, he was not prepared to govern by force of arms. Great Parliamentarian though he was, he never valued his ascend-ancy in Parliament at more than it was actually worth, and always calculated the effect upon public opinion of everything that he did or decided to leave undone.   With a very small army and no effective police, the British State might at this period have been defined as aristocracy tempered by rioting.

To reconcile the politically disinherited Tory squires to the House of Hanover, nothing was needed but the lapse of time with-out provocation or crises, and that Walpole procured.   Apart from politics, the Eighteenth Century world, in its laws and social customs, was perfectly constructed to suit the squires and the Anglican clergy.   The House of Hanover meant security for that world of established custom, whereas a Stuart restoration would mean putting out again on a sea of chance and trouble.   By the time George III came to the throne this had become apparent to 1760. all, and squires and clergy became once more the chief supporters of the throne.   In the interim, unity of spirit had been taught to Englishmen of all classes and denominations by Walpole through peace and prosperity, by Pitt through war and glory. Both Walpole and 'the great Commoner' ruled the Empire from the floor of the House of Commons, and through the machinery of a Cabinet dominated by a Prime Minister.[1]

1721–
1742.

To be governed by Walpole personally was no hardship to the Tory squires. A Norfolk landowner of old family and moderate wealth, who even when Prime Minister was said to open his game-keeper's letters first of the batch, who hunted with his beagles in Richmond Park when he could not get home, who drank steadily and told the broadest of stories over the bottle, was clearly a good fellow at bottom, no Presbyterian, no City upstart, no haughty and exclusive nobleman. An entirely loyal Whig, Walpole ruled by alliance with the Whig Peers, the moneyed men and the Dissenters, but in his own person he represented the squires of England.

His royal masters found him equally to their mind. He could sit by the hour with George I, drinking punch and talking dog-Latin as their only available medium of conversation. George II, a man greatly superior to his father, was almost a model con-stitutional King in his dealings with Walpole. Unfaithful as he was to his paragon of a wife, Caroline of Anspach, he valued her far above any of his mistresses, and, greatly to the advantage of his subjects, took her advice on public affairs. She was Sir Robert's wisest counsellor and staunchest friend.

Peace under Walpole

Walpole's mind and character were peculiarly adapted to the work of pacification at home and abroad. His genius lay in the arts of management, both in the good sense and the bad. No strain of idealism or romance tempted him to venturous or war-like policies. Good sense and kindliness were his dominant virtues ; cynicism his fault. The good-natured smile on his broad face was half a sneer. He would never govern by bayonets or by any form of terror, but saw no harm in allowing power to rest on the obvious and traditional basis of Parliamentary corruption, instead of making appeal to the national pride and conscience.

1757.

When the elder Pitt, in the following generation, tried to rule solely on the strength of that nobler appeal, he fell at once, and had to make terms with the arch-corruptionist Newcastle before he was permitted to win the Seven Years' War for England. Walpole, from the first, took Parliament and the world as he found them. If he laughed at the 'patriotism' of the 'boys' in opposition and thought that most Honourable Members had their

---

[1] The Prime Minister's famous residence in Downing Street dates from this period. George II presented it to Walpole, but he would only accept it as an official gift to be passed on to his successors. For Walpole's contribution to the growth of the Cabinet system and the office of Prime Minister, see pp. 510–1, above.

price, the facts of the time bore out the judgment. It was not through Walpole that moral regeneration was to come.

His love of peace abroad was genuine. It is not by idealists alone that the cause of peace has been upheld through the ages. Coarse and cynical though he was, Walpole had the humanity to keep England out of the war of the Polish Succession, in spite of the desire of his colleagues to revive the old Whig feud against the Bourbons. ' Madam,' he said to Queen Caroline in 1734, ' there are fifty thousand men slain this year in Europe, and not one Englishman.' Britain could safely stand aside from that aimless scuffle among the Powers of the continent, because the Marlborough wars had removed the danger of French hegemony. Our abstention enabled us to recruit our strength, which we would need ere long for more serious ends. Walpole took an active and successful part as ' honest broker ' in bringing about the general pacification that at length ended the war. *1733-1738.*

Sir Robert's peace policy was brought to an end by a great movement of opinion in favour of maritime war with Spain. The movement, though neither well informed nor well directed in 1739, was the same ground-swell of democratic patriotism which twenty years later bore William Pitt to power, and overwhelmed the French in India and North America. Even in 1739 the popular instinct was right in looking across the ocean for its objective. It was no question of European boundaries that excited the mob, and only the King had the interests of Hanover at heart. Popular passion was aroused by the old claim of the English, dating from Hawkins and Drake, to trade freely with South America, and by the insistence of Spain in limiting that trade to the clauses of the *Asiento* Treaty.[1] The wrongs of Jenkins and his ear, said to have been torn off by irate Spanish custom-house officials, brewed such a popular storm that Walpole yielded and unwillingly drew the sword. In his hand it seemed a clumsy weapon.

As usually occurred when England went to war after a long peace, the operations of the united services were ill-conducted, and the attacks on Porto Bello, Carthagena and Cuba left the question of South American trade very much where it had been before. But warfare on the Spanish Main had its repercussions both in England and in Europe. Walpole fell from power in 1742, as a result of an adverse vote in the House of Commons, though he still retained the favour of King and Lords ; he would have done better to resign three years earlier, instead of attempting to wage a war which he did not believe could be conducted to any decisive or profitable close.

[1] See p. 492, above.

The other consequence of the maritime war with Spain was continental war with France. The ' family compact ' between the Bourbons ruling on the two sides of the Pyrenees, dismally prophesied by the Whigs as the sure consequence of the Treaty of Utrecht, had hitherto borne no practical fruit. But as a result of the War of Jenkins' Ear against Spain, Walpole's successors inevitably drifted into hostilities against France, when the War of Austrian Succession had again set Europe ablaze. The thirty years of peace with France came to an end. The breathing space had served England well, secured her free institutions and enhanced her prosperity and power. But other men and other measures were now needed to decide new issues, drawing to a head in America and India.

The quarrel of English and French colonists in the Ohio valley for the empire of the New World, and the quarrel of the English and French companies for supremacy in the Carnatic and the Delta of the Ganges, each arose from the nature of things as an irrepressible conflict between the communities on the spot. These issues were not the outcome of the intrigues or ambitions of European statesmen, but for their solution a man very different from Walpole was required at the head of affairs in England. It was fifteen years after Walpole's resignation before he was found in William Pitt ; as Frederic the Great said, England was long in labour, till at last she brought forth a man.

Yet Walpole had been right in his warning that renewed hostilities with the French and Spanish Bourbons would mean the launching of another Jacobite attack on the dynasty, which his wisdom had so long staved off. The year of Fontenoy, a lost battle wherein our battalions of infantry distinguished themselves against the French in the Netherlands, was also the year of Prince Charles Edward's astonishing adventure in Britain. He found an island almost denuded of troops, utterly unaccustomed to war or self-defence, and so selfishly indifferent to the issue between Stuart and Hanoverian that the inhabitants let 5000 Highlanders with targe and broadsword march from Edinburgh to Derby, gaped at but equally unassisted and unopposed. The weak side of Walpole's regime of negations and management was shown by the low level of British public spirit in 1745, whether regarded from a Jacobite or Hanoverian standpoint. Such sloth compares strangely with the zeal and the sacrifices which William Pitt conjured out of these self-same Britons and their children a dozen years later.

Nothing but a fantasia of misrule could have resulted from a change of dynasty effected by Highland clans in defiance of

1745.

See Map
XXVIII.,
p. 530,
above.

Parliament and the laws, through the mere lethargy of the civilized world in defending its own institutions. Parliamentary government, deeply corrupted and not yet based on a wide franchise, could scarcely have survived the repeal of fundamental statutes by kilted swordsmen. The Stuarts, restored on these terms, must have attempted to secure their power by renewed persecution of the Dissenters, who would certainly have remained loyal to the House of Hanover ; and the conquerors must needs have proscribed every statesman, churchman, soldier and sailor who was not prepared to swallow the loyalties of a life-time— for by 1745 a whole generation had grown up in the Hanoverian allegiance. England would perforce have been governed by Irish and Scottish adventurers who knew nothing of her needs, and by a Prince whose later life became as ignoble as his youth had been gallant and brave. We might soon have been engaged in a new cycle of civil wars, fatal to civilization and industry at home, and to commerce and empire oversea.

Precise speculations are indeed idle, but the consequences of a *coup d'état* by wild Highlanders in London must in any case have been both tragic and absurd. Britain was saved from them by her small but excellent army, summoned home in haste from fields of fame abroad. In face of these gathering hosts, the veterans of Dettingen and Fontenoy, it was impossible for Charles Edward whose ranks had only been swelled by 300 Manchester men since he crossed the Border, to persuade his officers to march on from Derby to almost certain destruction. Yet the destruction towards which the Jacobites marched back into Scotland was more certain though less immediate. The advantage of surprise had been theirs, and once it was spent they had no resources in reserve.

Friday, Dec. 6, 1745.

Like Prestonpans at the beginning of the rebellion, Falkirk after the return from Derby was a victory for the Highlanders. But a few months later the last charge of the tribal swordsmen in Scottish history was broken on Culloden Moor by cannon loaded with grape-shot, and by the volleys of the long red line, three deep. After the battle, the Duke of Cumberland stained a good military reputation and great public services, by cruelties against the Highland population, then approved by the scared and angry English, but ever since held in detestation. The facts have been exaggerated, but they are bad without exaggeration. The government had throughout shown a lethargy and an incompetence which were the main cause of the rebellion. Lord President Forbes alone had shown spirit and wisdom ; if his advice had been taken earlier, there would have been no rising ; if it had been taken at the end, the poor Highlanders who had only

April 16, 1746.

followed their chiefs would have been treated with clemency and justice.

In England the consequences of the ' forty-five ' and its suppression were merely negative and merely political, involving the further decline of Jacobitism ; but in Scotland the results were positive and deeply affected the institutions of the country. The Jacobite rising had been formidable, because of the power of chiefs, lords and gentlemen over their vassals. It was, therefore, an obvious measure of policy to do away with heritable jurisdictions in Highlands and Lowlands alike. The feudalism that had so long survived in Scotland was abolished, to give the central government greater security and power. But the abolition had also the effect of further liberating the democratic and equalitarian spirit of that peasant society into which Burns was born in 1759, where ' the man's the gowd for a' that.'

It was of even greater importance that Scotland was at last enabled, with the help of the English armies, to settle her Highland question. If civilization was to go forward in the north of the island, it was essential to put down the warlike organization of the tribes and the extra-legal allegiance to the chiefs. The King's writ must run in the glens. An Afghanistan could no longer be tolerated within fifty miles of the ' modern Athens.' [1]

This most necessary change was at last accomplished, but not in the best way. Lowland law was applied to Highland tenures and customs with harsh uniformity, and with all the customary ignorance of civilized man in his dealings with a primitive society of which he despises the appearance too much to study the reality. The chiefs became landlords, on terms very disadvantageous to their late tribal followers, transformed into tenants at will. Forgetful of ancient ties, they turned the crofters off their little farms on the hillsides and transformed the glens into sheep-runs ; even before the American Revolution as many as 30,000 Highlanders are believed to have emigrated across the Atlantic.

Yet the land obtained peace, when the Highland Line ceased to have political meaning and became a geographical expression. The making of roads and the safety of travellers upon them, soon linked up all Scotland into one community. Devoted Presbyterian missionaries converted the Highlanders to the common stock of the nation's religious and educational ideas. One of the happiest and most characteristic policies of the elder Pitt was the raising of Highland regiments to fight for Scotland and the Empire in Canada and over the wide world. Modern Scotland,—the

---

[1] Besides the well-known works of Scott and Stevenson, there is an excellent picture of old Highland society and intrigue between the '15 and the '45 in Mr. Neil Munro's novel *The New Road*.

Scotland of Burns and Sir Walter Scott,—emerged as a result of
these changes, and of the great economic progress that accompanied them.   There was evolved a united people, proud of itself
and of its whole history ;   proud alike of Celt and Saxon, of
Covenanter and Jacobite ;   with a national hagiology extending
from Wallace and Bruce, through John Knox to Flora Macdonald,
representing that singular blend in the national psychology of the
dour and rational with the adventurous and romantic, of the
passion for freedom with loyal devotion to a chief.   Scotland
became more prosperous in agriculture, industry and commerce
than she had ever hoped to be in the sad days of Darien.   Yet,
for all her new material welfare, she remained full of reverence for
the things of the mind and the spirit, sending out her well-schooled
sons to develop and govern the British Empire in every clime.
When the century of progress closed, Scotland was a good neighbour and friend to England, as she had never been before and
has never ceased to be since.[1]

The period of European peace dividing the War of Austrian
Succession from the outbreak of the Seven Years' War, roughly
corresponded in England to the rule of the Pelhams,—Henry
Pelham and his brother the Duke of Newcastle, the greatest
borough-monger England ever produced.   They may be said to
have reverted to the traditions of Walpole, in an age when those
traditions were ceasing to be enough.   Within the island, these
years were the culminating moment of Eighteenth Century con-
tentment and repose, for Jacobitism was no longer a danger, and
politics had ceased to be enlivened by the epic contests between
Walpole and his personal rivals.   In the House of Commons,
Pitt's restless and haughty spirit was subject to the calming
influences of the time, and he was content to leave Ministers
unscathed for awhile by the thunderbolts of his oratory.   He was
even content to act in the office of Paymaster of the Forces.   But
in India and North America warlike operations were taking place
in time of nominal peace, that would soon cause slumbering
Britain to awake.

Both in India and America the offensive was taken by the
French.   The dissolution of the Mogul Empire and the consequent
independence of the Indian Princes of the Carnatic, had suggested
to Dupleix the idea that the French Company, hopelessly inferior
to the English in trade, should enter into military alliance with
some of the native powers, raise Sepoy regiments under French
officers, and extirpate the stations of the British East India
Company at Madras and elsewhere.   In Canada the French were

1748–
1756.

---

[1] See p. 521, above, for the Church movements in Scotland at this period.

See Map
XXVI.,
p. 437,
above.
carrying out a well-conceived plan of a line of military posts all
the way from the mouth of the St. Lawrence to the Lakes, down
the Ohio valley to the Mississippi, and thence to the mouth of the
great river in the Mexican Gulf. From this chain of river communications they intended to appropriate to France all America
north and west of the Appalachian and Alleghany mountains.

In India the English Company was older and richer than the
French, and more deeply rooted in native life. In North America
the two million colonists on the English-speaking seaboard far
outnumbered the French Canadians. The French, therefore,
must depend for success on greater unity, more vigorous leadership, and ampler naval and military support from the home
government. The Island of Mauritius, on the route from the
Cape, was their naval base for the defeat of the English in India,
and Louisburg in Cape Breton would serve the same purpose for
their conquest of North America. At first the energy of Dupleix
1751.
See Map,
XXXII.,
p. 596,
below.
carried all before him in the Carnatic, till Robert Clive left the
counter for the field, and seized and defended Arcot. Grim hand-
to-hand fighting went on along all that coast in time of peace,
gradually turning to the advantage of the English, whose resources
on the spot were much greater than those of the French owing
to their superiority as a trading community. When the Seven
Years' War broke out the French power was already on the decline
in India.

It was otherwise in North America, where the English Colonies,
except Massachusetts, were unwilling to strike in defence of their
own interests and seemed incapable of uniting in a common policy.
Physical communications between the English settlements were
difficult, and concerted action was prevented by the rivalries
between Colony and Colony, between Assembly and Governor,
and by the intense individualism of a raw new world that had
never been under feudal or royal discipline.[1]

The French settlements, on the other hand, that had never
known freedom from Church, State and seigneur, were united in
loyal obedience to their government. And they were strung
together like beads on the line of the St. Lawrence and Mississippi
waterways. Fine royal regiments and leaders from France were
there to aid and command them. Moreover, the French were in
close contact with the Red Indian tribes, whom they treated well,
but used without scruple or humanity against their European
foes. In 1753 they drove the English traders out of the Ohio
valley and erected Fort Duquesne to prevent their return. Two
years later, General Braddock's expedition, sent out by New-

[1] For the character of the English and French settlements in North America
see pp. 437-42, above.

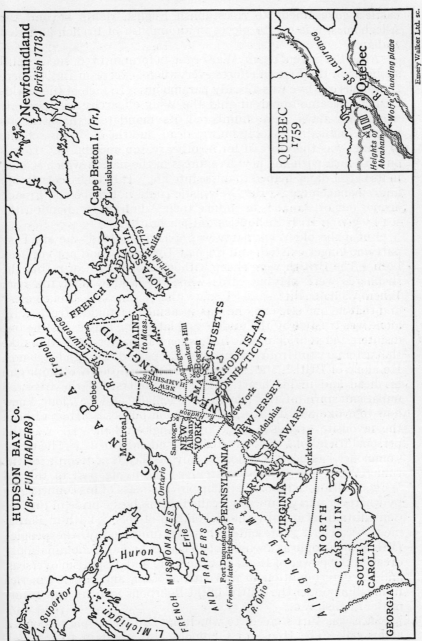

HUDSON BAY Co.
(Br. FUR TRADERS)

L. Superior

L. Michigan

L. Huron

L. Erie

L. Ontario

FRENCH MISSIONARIES
AND TRAPPERS

Fort Duquesne
(French; later Pittsburg)

R. Ohio

Alleghany Mts.

CANADA (French)

St. Lawrence R.

Quebec

Montreal

Newfoundland
(British 1718)

Cape Breton I. (Fr.)
○ Louisburg

FRENCH ACADIA

NOVA SCOTIA (1713)
Halifax (British)

MAINE
(to Mass.)

NEW HAMPSHIRE

MASSACHUSETTS

Lexington
Bunker's Hill
Boston

RHODE ISLAND

CONNECTICUT

NEW
YORK

Saratoga ×
Albany

Hudson R.

NEW JERSEY

New York

DELAWARE

PENNSYLVANIA

Philadelphia ○

MARYLAND

VIRGINIA

Yorktown

NORTH CAROLINA

SOUTH CAROLINA

GEORGIA

QUEBEC 1759

St. Lawrence

Quebec

R.

Heights of
Abraham ×

Wolfe's landing place

Emery Walker Ltd. sc.

MAP XXIX.—French and English Colonies, 1755 (see Map XXXVI for Mississippi, etc.)

castle's government to re-establish English rights beyond the Alleghanies, was cut to pieces in an ambush of French and Red Indians.

After the Seven Years' War began in form in 1756, success still shone upon the French efforts everywhere, except in India where the genius of Clive was already paramount. In face of the world-crisis, it became apparent that the Whig oligarchy was past its work. Its days were numbered, its mandate exhausted, its mission fulfilled. Jacobitism was dead, and the old Whig scheme of things was therefore, if for no other reason, moribund. It was out of touch with the new live forces in the nation which it had, in its better days, helped to nurse into life. It lived by corruption and 'management.' But Newcastle could not bribe the French armies out of Canada, or induce their Admirals to abandon the sea by giving Irish Bishoprics to their brothers.

But if the old Whig party was spiritually dead, the old Tory party no longer existed, and the new Tory party had not yet been born. The British were sheep without a shepherd, or rather the shepherds were playing cards while the wolf was in the fold. When William Pitt said ' I know that I can save this country and that no one else can,' he was speaking the modest truth. He alone was trusted by the middle and labouring classes, as the one disinterested politician, who had, when Paymaster, refused to take the customary toll from the moneys that passed through his hands. He alone of British statesmen carried the map of the Empire in his head and in his heart. He alone understood the free and impatient spirit of the American colonials, and he alone knew how to evoke and use it for the common purpose. He had been the favourite grandson of a great Anglo-Indian. He was the personal friend of London merchants and aldermen. ' The Great Commoner,' as he was called, openly displayed contempt for the ruling Whig aristocracy, but revived the living part of the old Whig tradition that could still inspire the mass of his countrymen by whatever party name they called themselves—pride in the free Constitution secured by the Revolution of 1688 ; faith in Parliament because it represented, however imperfectly, the people ; faith in the people as a whole, of all classes and all denominations ; dread of the power of Roman Catholicism and despotism overseas, and the determination to prevent the ocean and North America from falling under the control of the Bourbons ; faith in the future of the English race.

Such was Pitt's creed, to which the British people responded at his call. The House of Commons also was fain to respond, for Pitt's oratory wholly quelled and half inspired Honourable Members who had sold their souls to Newcastle for some mess of

patronage.   Pitt's manner was justly criticized as artificial, but
it represented great realities of power and passion; he was ever
an actor, but his voice and gesture dominated the auditory and
the stage.

Besides his powers, never perhaps equalled as orator and leader
of Parliament and nation, Pitt possessed in addition the qualities
of a great minister of war.   He was a master of world-strategy,
an adept in the proper combination of Britain's fleets and armies,
wherein her greatest war-strength has always lain ; he chose the
right men for command by land and sea, filled them with his
spirit, and sent them on the right errands with adequate forces.
As a war minister he surpassed Lincoln; as national leader in
time of crisis the two men may be compared and their methods
contrasted.

Chatham's world-wide conquests in 1758–1760 cannot be set
to the credit of the Whig oligarchy, though they can to some
extent be regarded as the final triumph of the old Whig foreign
policy.   But the Whig oligarchy so mismanaged the early stages
of the Seven Years' War, and brought the country into such
danger, that Pitt was called in as the People's Tribune to save
the country from defeat.   By an arrangement that suited both
parties, Parliamentary corruption and public patronage were left June
to Newcastle, and power to Pitt.   His appeal was made to the 1757.
popular elements latent in the British Constitution at home and
more fully developed in Massachusetts.   He evoked the spirit
of freedom to save the Empire.

> To glory we call you, as freemen, not slaves,
> For who are so free as the sons of the waves ?

So chants the naval war-song of the period.   Truth to tell, the
recruitenmt of the Navy by the press-gang was then the one
strikingly unfree element in the relation of government to the
citizen.   Nevertheless, the song gives the spirit in which the navy
and the Empire won the decisive war against France on the high
seas, in Canada and in the Ohio valley.   That victory decided
that free institutions instead of despotic institutions were to
dominate North America.

Pitt's ally was Frederic the Great of Prussia.   That two
million peasants scarcely yet emerging from serfdom, together
with a few score thousand Huguenot refugees, inhabiting certain
sandy regions of North Germany, should have enabled their
King to defy for seven years the onslaught of Austria, Russia and
France, may seem a miracle.   It was due not merely to Frederic's
genius in war, but to his own and his rough old father's nursing
and drilling of a docile people in time of peace.   Frederic stood

for the principle of a scientific, military autocracy, personally controlled by a self-sacrificing, laborious King, his people's stern but careful tutor. Against him were arrayed, with the blessing of the Pompadour, the self-indulgent eaters of the people's bread who presided over the decadent governments of this *ancien régime* upon the continent. Meanwhile Pitt demonstrated the power of British liberty in time of war. That Pitt and Frederic were allies against the world explains their success. The English people idealized, after their fashion, the alliance that had sprung up from the needs of the hour. They dilated warmly on the bond of common Protestantism, and saw in Frederic the Protestant champion defying the persecuting Catholicism of Austria and France.[1]

During the Seven Years' War, Frederic was engaged in defending against the three great military powers of Europe the Silesian province, which he had seized in the War of Austrian Succession in spite of his pledged word. The heroism of the defence covered the baseness of the original robbery. Yet even Frederic must have succumbed but for Pitt's subsidies and the British troops who helped to defend his Western flank against France, and in doing so won the victory of Minden. To England, the collapse of Frederic would have meant a continent united against her. Pitt's policy was ' to conquer Canada in Germany ' and he did it. Though he had formerly headed the popular outcry against Continental and Hanoverian entanglements, he now succeeded in making even the European part of the war popular. Innumerable public-house signboards were dedicated to ' The King of Prussia,' and to the gallant ' Marquis of Granby ' who charged at the head of our squadrons on the battlefields of Germany.

1759.

But all this friendship with Prussia, having served its momentary purpose, was thrown away by George III and Bute. Having got rid of Pitt, they left Frederic to his fate in 1762, an act which was never forgotten by foreign opinion down to the time of Bismarck and later. It can indeed be pleaded in mitigation that Frederic had treated his own allies yet more treacherously in the previous war. But whatever the morals of the case, it threw the Prussia of Frederic permanently outside the orbit of British influence.

The object for which Pitt fought upon the continent of Europe was nothing more than safety and the *status quo* ; his real objec-

---

[1] In spite of the growing influence of Voltaire the judicial murder of the Protestant Calas took place in France as late as 1762. An interesting comparison might be made between the position at this time of Protestants in Austria and France and of Catholics in Ireland.

tives lay oversea. The re-establishment of naval supremacy was essential to the warfare he meditated. When he took over power from Newcastle in 1757, there was serious fear of French invasion. The year before, Minorca had been lost and the unsuccessful Admiral, John Byng, had been shot, to save Ministers from the popular indignation, in spite of the manly protests of Pitt. Under Pitt's government, naval supremacy was rapidly recovered in a series of vigorous actions, culminating in Hawke's great victory off Quiberon, the Trafalgar of the war. **1756.**

1759.

Canada, which then consisted of French settlements scattered along the banks of the St. Lawrence, could be best approached and conquered by land forces conveyed and covered by the fleet. The perfect co-operation of the two services led first to the capture of Louisburg, commanding the entry to the great river, and next year to Wolfe's daring ascent of the Heights of Abraham from the river bank and capture of Quebec itself from the French royal army. Wolfe and his magnanimous rival, Montcalm, were mortally wounded almost at the same moment in that memorable day, which decided the fate of Canada. Meanwhile in the Ohio valley, Scottish Highland regiments and American Colonials, working together as everyone seemed able to do under Pitt, had crossed the Alleghanies, driven out the French and renamed Fort Duquesne as Pittsburg. Before the end of the Seven Years' War, the French power had disappeared from North America. The unexplored West was the Great Commoner's present to the English-speaking race. **1758.** **1759.** See Map XXIX., p. 541, above.

In the course of the war many French possessions in West Africa and in the West Indian archipelago were seized, and a great Empire was founded in the East. In India, indeed, another genius than Pitt's was at work in the field of war and government. The six to nine months' voyage round the Cape prevented our organizer of victory in Downing Street from planning campaigns for the Ganges as he planned them for the St. Lawrence. Indeed the battle of Plassey, leading to Clive's conquest of Bengal as the first extensive British-ruled territory in India, took place during the months when Pitt's great Ministry was painfully coming into existence. **1757.**

When George III succeeded his grandfather, the name of Britain was held, perhaps, in higher esteem by the nations of the world than ever before or since. Her free institutions, imperfect as we know them to have been, were regarded with envy by the European nations of that day. No ' anti-English ' tradition had yet arisen : the Irish were quiet and forgotten ; the American colonies were still united to the mother country and devoted to Pitt. England and ' the Great Commoner ' were as much admired **1760.**

x

as they were feared by the French themselves, a generous and
philosophic nation, at that time thoroughly out of love with their
own despotic institutions which had brought them to such a pass
The English race was at the top of golden hours. It owed it
position mainly to its own fortune and conduct over a long period
of time, but latterly to one man who had raised it in three year
from danger and disgrace. Yet in another twenty years our
fortunes were destined again to fall low in either hemisphere
And in that decline the defects of the admired constitution and o
the admired man would play no inconspicuous part.

BOOKS FOR FURTHER READING

Lecky's *England*, Vol. II ; John Morley, *Walpole*; Basil Williams, *Life c
William Pitt, Earl of Chatham* (2 vols.) ; Macaulay's *Clive* and first Essay o
Chatham ; Grant Robertson, *England under the Hanoverians* ; Hume Brown'
and Andrew Lang's *Scotland* ; P. E. Roberts, *India* (Vol. VII of Clarendo
Press *Historical Geography of British Dependencies*) ; Egerton, *History of Britis
Colonial Policy* ; Parkman, *Montcalm and Wolfe* ; Ramsay Muir, *History of th
British Commonwealth* ; Corbett, *England in the Seven Years' War* (2 vols.).

CHAPTER III

Personal Government of George III. The American Question. Th
Disruption of the First British Empire. Restoration of Governmen
by Party and Cabinet. The New Whig and New Tory Partie
Burke, Fox and the Younger Pitt

King : George III, 1760–1820

BEFORE George III came to the throne in 1760, the conflic
between executive and legislative, which had hampered govern
ment in the Stuart era, had been laid completely to rest by th
novel device of a responsible and united Cabinet, led by a Prim
Minister, but dependent on a majority vote of the House o
Commons, and with all the Cabinet Ministers seated in Parliamen
This system went several steps further than the negative settle
ment of 1689 towards rendering free government practicabl
It has since been adopted in the self-governing Dominions an
in many countries of Europe, and stands as England's chie
contribution to the science of political mechanism.

The system had served well in peace-time under Walpole, an
in war under the elder Pitt. His son, as head of the revived Tor
party, was destined to stereotype this method of government, b
which Britain has been ruled ever since his day. But betwee
the great Ministry of the elder Pitt and that of his son, intervene
twenty years when government by responsible Cabinet and Prim

1783–
1801.

1761–
1782.

Minister was in confusion, if not in abeyance. That break in the smooth development of our constitutional history was caused by the able attempt of George III to recover the powers of the Crown as they had been left by the Revolution Settlement of 1689, to make the Prime Minister a mere instrument of the royal will, and to reduce the Cabinet to a group of the ' King's servants ' in fact as well as in name. All this he temporarily achieved, after fierce and complicated struggles in the 'sixties. He succeeded because he resumed into his royal hands the patronage of the State, wherewith he bribed the House of Commons himself, instead of leaving patronage and corruption as the perquisite of the Whigs.

Obviously George III would not so far have succeeded, if Cabinet government had then rested on democracy instead of on aristocracy, on opinion instead of on ' management.' The Parliamentary and Cabinet system of the mid-Eighteenth Century, excellent as machinery, lacked moral force and popular support. It is true that, when the Seven Years' War began so ill, the Whig oligarchy had bowed to the popular demand and allowed Pitt to become Prime Minister to meet the crisis. But there was no regular method of exerting popular pressure on the House of Commons, owing to the large proportion of ' nomination boroughs ' where members were returned at the bidding of an individual. Nor had the elder Pitt any personal hold over the curious political machinery of the day. Though he had sat for Old Sarum, where sheep grazed over the mound that marked the ancient city, he was not a great borough-monger or a friend of borough-mongers. He despised, and in his haughty humour insulted the Whig oligarchs, and they feared and disliked him in return. ' Fewer words, my Lord, for your words have long lost all weight with me,' he said to Newcastle himself. It was, therefore, impossible, when the national danger had been averted by Pitt's victories, for the arrangement between him and the Whig lords to become the basis of a permanent system of government.

The other circumstance that gave George III his chance of restoring royal power through Parliamentary corruption, was the absence of a strong Tory party, capable of keeping both Crown and Whigs in check. The Parliamentary Cabinet system requires for its healthy functioning, two rival parties to criticize each other and to offer to the nation a choice between two alternative governments. Under William and Anne the Whigs and Tories, though often violent and factious, had performed that service well. But under the first two Georges there had been no real Tory opposition, owing to the ground being occupied by Jacobitism. But Jacobitism, moribund after the ' forty-five,' expired when the popular young Englishman, ' farmer George,' who 'gloried in the name of Briton,' succeeded his German grand-father. Former Jacobites and high Tories like Dr. Johnson willingly fixed their wandering and famished loyalty on so respectable a figure. The revival of a new Tory party, reconciled to the Revolution Settlement, was long overdue. But twenty years passed after the new reign had begun, before the resurrection was accomplished under the younger Pitt.

1760–
1782.

In the interval, George III governed 'without party,' making the Cabinet a mere instrument of the royal will and Parliament the pensioner of the royal bounty. The 'King's friends' in the Commons were his hired mercenaries, at best his personal devotees —not proper Tory partisans. The result was by no means in accord with Bolingbroke's prophecies of the golden age, that was to follow the advent of a 'patriot King' independent of all political factions. That ideal had caught the imagination of George himself, of Chatham, and of many others weary of govern-ment by the Whig aristocrats. But as soon as the idea was put in practice, the land was filled, not with the benisons of a grateful people on a benevolent monarch, but with the noise of unseemly

1763–
1769.

conflict between rulers and ruled. The characteristic episode of the period was the martyrdom and deification of the scandalous Wilkes, turned by government persecution into the champion of popular rights, against an encroaching executive and a House of Commons claiming to override the choice of the Middlesex electors as to the man who should represent them in Parliament. Abroad, the prestige and admiration won by England in the Seven Years' War were thrown away, first by the methods which Bute used to secure the Peace of Paris in 1763, and later by the ill-conducted quarrel with our own Colonies. When the domestic crisis of the

1775–
1782.

Empire came to a head, Britain was left face to face with a hostile Europe where she had many enemies and no single friend.

That affairs went so ill at home and abroad during the first twenty years of the new reign, must not be ascribed wholly to the faults of the King and his enemies, the Whig aristocrats. Part of the blame must be shared by Pitt himself,—or the Earl of Chatham as he became in this unhappy period. Though without a regular Parliamentary following of his own, he held the balance between King and Whigs, because he represented in some degree the spirit of the nation for which the House of Commons so very inadequately spoke. But Chatham, though popular in his political sympathies, had a personal pride that was more than aristocratic. He could be a noble and liberal-minded autocrat, but he could never be a colleague. His faults of temper and understanding made him, who should have been the umpire and abater of the strife, further confound confusion. He could work neither with George nor with the Whigs, still less effect an arrangement between them.

At one moment the government was again put into Chatham's 1766–1769. hands, and he was called upon to form a Cabinet ' above party,' and to save the State once more, this time from its internal maladies. But at that moment his physical and mental powers gave way. The gout, which he had been fighting with heroic constancy ever since his Eton days, at last overcame the resistance of a lifetime. For months together he lay in a brooding melancholy, refusing to see his bewildered colleagues, fierce and unapproachable as a sick lion in its lair. His Ministry, which had no principle of cohesion save his leadership, staggered to ruin, carrying to limbo the last hopes of the country and the Empire.

By 1770 George III had triumphed over all his enemies—over the ' Whig connection,' and over Chatham whom he detested as he did all save the second-rate statesmen who were willing to serve him without a policy of their own. ' Trumpet of sedition ' was his name for the man who had saved and enlarged the Empire that he himself failed to preserve. To criticize the royal policy was ' sedition ' in the eyes of George III, who judged the merit of all statesmen by their attitude towards himself.[1] He was not likely to be more gracious in his dealings with the colonials of New England, where ' sedition ' of a more serious nature than Chatham's was endemic in the soil, and where a problem of Imperial relations of the utmost nicety and danger was coming up for solution.

The disappearance of the French flag from the North American Continent as a result of the Seven Years' War, led to the disruption of the first British Empire. For it relieved the English colonists of the dangers which had made them look for protection to the mother country. At the same time the expenses of the late war and the heavy burden of debt and land-tax with which it had saddled Great Britain, suggested to her statesmen, in an evil hour, that the colonies might be made to contribute something towards the military expenses of the Imperial connection. An attempt to levy contributions towards the future upkeep of royal forces in America was first made through George Grenville's Stamp Duty on legal documents in the colonies. It was passed in 1765, but repealed next year by the Rockingham Whigs on account of the violent opposition which it had aroused beyond the Atlantic. In 1767 indirect taxation on tea and certain

---

[1] In 1778 he complained that Chatham's public funeral in Westminster Abbey was ' an offensive measure to me personally ' ; it never occurred to him that his subjects remembered that the dead man had won the Seven Years' War, and were momentarily indifferent whether he died on good or bad terms with the King.

other articles was imposed on America by Charles Townshend. Chatham, the strongest English opponent of the policy of taxing the colonies, was then Prime Minister in name, but in actuality he was far removed from the political scene by gout and melancholia. Of these unpopular taxes the tea duty alone was maintained in a much modified form by George III's henchman Lord North in 1773, for the sake of principle only, as the profits were utterly negligible. Unfortunately, eight years of controversy on the taxation question had so worked upon the average colonial mind, that the overthrow of that principle was regarded as worth almost any disturbance and sacrifice. ' No taxation without representation ' was the cry, and every farmer and backwoodsman regarded himself as a Hampden, and North as a Strafford.

It was natural that the Americans should object to be taxed, however moderately and justly, by a Parliament where they were not even ' virtually ' represented. They had always acknowledged an indefinite allegiance to the Crown, though Massachusetts had made very light of it at certain times in the Stuart era, and had even gone to war with France without consulting the Crown in 1643. But Americans had never admitted the supremacy of Parliament, in the sense of conceding that the two Houses sitting at Westminster could vote laws and taxes binding on the Colonies, each of which had its own Assembly. On that issue, as on most issues of constitutional law that have divided the men of our race at great historical crises, there was a good legal case pleadable on either side. But as a matter of political expediency it was most desirable that the colonists should be taxed for imperial purposes by their own representatives rather than by the British Parliament.[1]

Unfortunately they made no move to tax themselves, partly from thrift and partly from indifference to the Imperial connection. When once the French danger had disappeared, the Empire seemed a far-off abstraction to the backwoodsman of the Alleghanies, like the League of Nations to the Middle West to-day. And even on the sea coast, where the Empire was better known, it was not always better loved : it was represented by Governors, Colonels and Captains of the British upper class, often as little suited to mix with a democratic society as oil with vinegar.

---

[1] On the issue in constitutional law, see *The American Revolution, A Constitutional Interpretation*, by C. H. McIlwain (Macmillan, 1923), and a criticism of it by Professor Pollard in *History*, October 1924, p. 250. The Americans, going on precedents prior to the Revolution of 1688, distinguished sharply between the Crown, whose authority they admitted within limits, and the Westminster Parliament, which they regarded as a local assembly. To the English, this distinction was impossible, because the ' Crown in Parliament ' was for them the supreme authority.

Furthermore, the Empire was associated in the mind of the Americans with restrictions on their commerce and their industry, imposed for the benefit of jealous English merchants, or of West Indian sugar and tobacco planters who were then the favourite colonists of a mother country not yet disturbed about the ethics of slavery.

Chatham, or rather that more formidable person, William Pitt, had made the imperial connection popular in America in time of war, and might have made it tolerable even in time of peace. But Chatham had ceased to influence the politics of the Empire, except as a Cassandra prophet warning George III in vain, and being called a ' trumpet of sedition ' for his pains.

In theory,—or at least in the theory that was held in England, —the Empire was a single consolidated State. In practice it was a federation of self-governing communities, with the terms of federation undrawn and constantly in dispute. Such a situation was full of danger, the more so as the situation and the danger were alike unrecognized. The defunct Whig oligarchy can hardly be said to have had a colonial policy or any clear ideas about the future of the Empire. Pitt's great Ministry had come and gone. And now, to meet the pressing needs of Imperial finance, George III's Ministers had advanced partial and one-sided solutions that proved unacceptable, while the Americans refused to propose any solution at all. A way out could have been found by men of good will summoned to a round-table conference, at which Britain might have offered to give up the trade restrictions, and the Americans to make some contribution of their own to the military expenses incurred by the mother country on their behalf.

But such a conference was outside the range of ideas on either side the Atlantic. England was still in the grip of ' mercantile ' and protectionist theories of the old type. She still regarded her colonies primarily as markets for her goods, and the trade of the colonials as permissible only so far as it seemed consistent with the economic interest of the mother country. As the historian of our British colonial policy has remarked, ' That the measures of 1765 and 1767 precipitated the crisis is obvious enough ; but that the crisis must sooner or later have come, unless Great Britain altered her whole way of looking at the colonies, seems equally certain.' [1]

As to the hope that America might voluntarily contribute to the Imperial expenses, ' America ' did not exist. The thirteen colonies were mutually jealous, provincial in thought, divided

---

[1] Egerton, *The American Revolution*, p. 4. Adam Smith's *Wealth of Nations*, advancing Free Trade ideas, only appeared in 1776, the year of the American Declaration of Independence.

from one another by vast distances, great physical obstacles and marked social and economic distinctions. They had failed in 1754 at Albany to combine even for the purpose of fighting the French at dire need, and they were little likely to unite in time of peace for the purpose of negotiating with England on an Imperial question which they denied to be urgent.

And so things drifted on to the catastrophe. On one side was the unbending stubbornness of George III, who dictated policy to Lord North, that easy, good-natured man, so fatally unwilling to disoblige his sovereign. On the other side was the uncompromising zeal of the Radical party among the Americans led by Samuel Adams, to whom separation gradually began to appear as a good in itself.[1]

The general causes rendering it difficult for English and Americans to understand one another were then numerous and profound : many of them have been removed by the passage of time, while on the other hand the difference of race is much greater to-day. English society was then still aristocratic, while American society was already democratic. Six or seven weeks of disagreeable ocean tossing divided London from Boston, so that personal intercourse was slight, and the stream of emigration from the mother country had run very dry ever since 1640. In England politics and good society were closed to Puritans, while Puritanism dominated New England and pushed its way thence into all the other colonies ; it was Anglicanism that was unfashionable in Massachusetts. English society was old, elaborate and artificial, while American society was new, simple and raw. English society was based on great differences of wealth, while in America property was still divided with comparative equality, and every likely lad hoped some day to be as well-off as the leading man in the township. In England political opinion was mainly that of squires, while in America it was derived from farmers, water-side mobs, and frontiersmen of the forest.[2]

---

[1] The temper and programme of the party which overcame the American ' Tories ' and effected the separation from Britain is best described as ' Radical ' to English readers, whatever meaning that term may now bear in America. The Revolutionists were not ' Whigs ' in the English sense of the word, for they savoured neither of aristocracy nor of moderation. They were not ' Liberals,' for they did not wish to allow liberty of speech or opinion to their opponents, whom they eventually expelled from the country. They were not ' Socialists,' for they had no designs of redistributing property, and were individualists in economic theory. They were democrats, with less than no reverence for any authority not derived directly from the people : they sought to enforce the will of the majority on the minority and to make the poor man count as much as the rich man in politics. They can, in fact, be best described, in English political terminology, as Radicals.

[2] For some previous remarks on American society and the influence of the frontier, see pp. 443–444, above.

In two societies so widely set apart in the circumstances and atmosphere of every-day life, it required people with imaginative faculties like Burke, Chatham and Fox, to conceive what the issues looked like to ordinary men on the other side of the Atlantic. George III had strength of mind, diligence and business ability, but he had not imagination.

After the famous outrage on the tea-chests in Boston harbour, the English Government, naturally and deeply provoked, made its fatal mistake. It hurried through Parliament Penal Acts against Massachusetts, closing the port of Boston, cancelling the charter of the colony, and ordering political trials of Americans to be conducted in England. These measures rallied the other colonies to Massachusetts and ranked up behind the Radicals doubtful and conservative forces for whose support the English government might still have played with success. The Penal Acts meant in fact war with the colonies. They were defensible only as acts of war, and if adopted should have been accompanied by preparations to ensure armed victory. Yet in that very year the British Government reduced the number of seamen in the Navy, and took no serious steps to strengthen their forces in America. When the pot boiled over at last, and hostilities broke out of themselves at Lexington, Burgoyne wrote thus from Boston :

1773.

1774.

See Map XXIX., p. 541, above.

April 1775.

> After a fatal procrastination, not only of vigorous measures but of preparations for such, we took a step as decisive as the passage of the Rubicon, and now find ourselves plunged at once in a most serious war without a single requisition, gunpowder excepted, for carrying it on.

During the twelve months preceding Lexington, while the British authorities, having defied New England to the arbitrament of force, contented themselves with the inactive occupation of Boston, the Radical party in the country outside had used the respite to organize revolutionary power and terrorize, or expel, its opponents. Indeed, ever since the original passage of the Stamp Act, the ' Sons of Liberty ' had employed tarring-and-feathering and other local methods of making opinion unanimous. Even so, the Loyalists in most of the thirteen colonies remained a formidable body. Few, if any, had approved the measures by which the British Government had provoked the war, but they were not prepared to acquiesce in the dismemberment of the Empire, and for social and political reasons of their own they disliked the prospect of Radical rule. Their strength lay among the mercantile and professional men and the large landowners of the coast, and they were stronger in the Middle and Southern Colonies than in New England. Against them were arrayed the humbler folk in most sections, the small farmers and the frontiersmen of the West, organized under leaders of amazing audacity and zeal. The Loyalists were slower to move, more anxious for compromise than war, and they got little leadership either from their own ranks or from the British, who too often treated them very ill and drove them by ill-usage or neglect to join the rebel ranks.

Yet the Radicals would never have overcome the trained soldiers of George III and their own Loyalist fellow-subjects, had they not been led by a statesman of genius who was also a first-class soldier, organizer and disciplinarian. George Washington belonged by temper and antecedents rather to the Loyalist than the Radical classes. But, although he was first and foremost a gentleman of Virginia, he was also a frontiersman who had seen service against Indians and French beyond the Alleghanies, and who knew the soul of young America as it could only be known in the backwoods. Good Virginian as he was, he was no mere provincial, with feelings and experience limited to his own colony. He had a ' continental ' mind, and foresaw the nation he created. Some well-informed vision of the astounding future of his country westwards, helped to decide George Washington to draw his sword for a cause which was bound, in the stress of war, to become the cause of American Independence. The American militiamen brought to the ranks qualities learnt in their hard struggle with nature,—woodcraft and marksmanship, endurance, energy and courage. But they grievously lacked discipline, save what the Puritan temper supplied to the individual, and what Washington imposed upon the army. His long struggle, as Commander-in-Chief in the field, with the exasperating ineptitude of the Continental Congress, was a war within the war. Fortunately for him, the British army, in spite of its fine fighting qualities, made mistake after mistake not only in the military but in the political strategy of the contest.

It was a civil war, not a war between two nations, though when the battle smoke at length subsided two nations were standing there erect. Because it was a civil war, and because its issue would decide among other things whether England should in future be ruled by the King acting through Parliament or by Parliament acting through the King, opinion was divided in England no less than in America. Once fighting began, the bulk of the British people supported their government, so long as there was any hope of reconquering the colonies. But they showed so little enthusiasm for the fratricidal contest that recruiting was very difficult, and the government largely employed German mercenaries whose conduct further incensed the colonists. Moreover in England there was always a strong minority, speaking with powers as diversified as those of Chatham, Burke and young Charles Fox, that denounced the whole policy of the war and called for concession to save the unity of the Empire before it was too late.

Military operations were as ill-conducted by the British as they had been rashly provoked. The troops, as Bunker's Hill showed, were not inferior to the men of Blenheim and Minden. _{June 1775.} But the military mistakes of Generals Burgoyne and Howe were very serious, and they were rivalled by those of the government at home.   Lord George Germain in England planned the Saratoga campaign as Pitt had planned the taking of Quebec, but with very different results.   His plan gave the Americans the advantage of acting on the inner lines, for he sent Burgoyne to Canada to march down the Hudson and isolate New England, but without making sure that Howe moved up to meet him from the South.   The result was that, while Howe lingered in Philadelphia, Burgoyne _{Oct. 1777.} and his 5000 regulars were cut off in the wilderness beside the great river, and surrendered at Saratoga to the American minutemen.

After Saratoga the French despotism felt encouraged to come to the aid of liberty in the New World.   This remarkable decision dismembered the British Empire, but it did not thereby achieve its object of restoring the House of Bourbon to world power.   For it turned out that the idea of revolution, if once successful in America, could traverse the Atlantic with unexpected ease.   And no less unexpectedly, from the broken eggshell of the old British Empire emerged two powers, each destined to rapid growth—a new British Empire that should still bestride the globe, still rule the seas and still hold up its head against the Powers of the continent ; and a united American State that should spread from Atlantic to Pacific and number its citizens by scores of millions, in the place of thirteen little, mutually jealous colonies upon the Atlantic coast.

It was well that America was made.   It was tragic that the making could only be effected by a war with Britain.   The parting was perhaps inevitable at some date and in some form, but the parting in anger, and still more the memory of that moment's anger fondly cherished by America as the starting-point of her history, have had consequences that we rue to this day.

The War of American Independence ended as a war of Britain against half the world.   The Bourbon ' family compact ' of France and Spain fought her by sea and land as of old ; the French ships under Suffren seriously endangered her communications with India ; Russia, Prussia, Holland and the Scandinavian

Powers united their diplomatic and naval forces in the 'armed neutrality of the North' to defend the rights of neutrals against the Mistress of the Seas. In Ireland, for the first and last time in history, Protestants and Catholics united to overthrow the system by which their common interests were sacrificed to England.

In the hour of need, to which her fools had brought her, Britain was saved by her heroes. Among the statesmen, Carleton saved Canada, and Warren Hastings saved India ; among fighting men, Eliott defended the Gibraltar Rock against the armaments of France and Spain, and Rodney's victory recovered the mastery of the seas from de Grasse.

But the recovery of the thirteen colonies, already become the United States of America, was for ever impossible. Chatham died before he had given up hope, but three years later all King George's subjects acknowledged the fact. But nothing would bend the King's will save the positive refusal of his Ministers to proceed any longer with a task in which they had long lost faith and heart. They had even lost sure hold of their majority in a House of Commons paid to vote for them. As early as April 1780, the House had voted, by 233 against 215, in favour of Dunning's Resolution, ' that the influence of the Crown has increased, is increasing, and ought to be diminished.' It was significant that the county members who best represented any genuine body of electors, voted sixty for the Resolution and only eight against.

After the surrender of Cornwallis to Washington at Yorktown, the war in America was virtually at an end, and the news of Yorktown in England brought the system of personal government by the King to an end too.

The House of Commons accepted without a division a strongly worded motion against the continuance of the war in America. From the day of Lord North's resignation, in March 1782, Britain has never been governed save by a Prime Minister and Cabinet responsible not to the King alone but first and foremost to the independent judgment of the House of Commons. It was a matter of great importance that, owing to the catastrophe in America, the attempt to regain political power for the Crown came to an end when it did. If the personal government of George III and of his children after him had been protracted into the next century, the democratic and Reform movements of the new era, finding themselves opposed by the King as their chief source of conservative resistance, must have become anti-royalist and very probably Republican.

With the restoration of full Parliamentary government its necessary accompaniment, party government, was restored too.

George III had set out to abolish party, according to Bolingbroke's prescription, but the net result of his activities, over and above the loss of America, was to bring into being a new Whig party and a new Tory party, and to arouse a democratic interest in politics which, though it failed for fifty years to carry Parliamentary Reform, served to put the life of public opinion into the Whig party led by Lord Rockingham, Burke and Fox, and into the Tory party created by the younger Pitt, and to fill the sails of Wilberforce's Anti-Slave-Trade Crusade.

Immediately on the fall of North, the King's open enemies, **1782.** the Rockingham Whigs, came into office for a few months. They were no longer the unregenerate Whig oligarchy of Newcastle, for, though still under aristocratic leadership, they appealed first and foremost to public opinion, and seriously intended to diminish Parliamentary corruption. Their long misfortunes had taught the Whigs many things, and they had sat at the feet of Edmund Burke. His deep, sagacious insight as a political philosopher was the more powerful and the less reliable because its vehicle was a magnificent oratory, and because his Irish temper, fiery almost to madness, prevented him from seeing more than one side of a case at any stage of his career, whether as Whig, as anti-Jacobin, or as Indian reformer. When his patron Lord Rockingham took office in 1782, his political creed was still in its earlier period of liberal emphasis. The short Ministry of the Rockingham Whigs that summer, left a deep impression for good on our public life, because it passed Burke's Economic Reform Bill, which greatly reduced the patronage of government in sinecures and places, and rendered it impossible for anyone ever again to bribe Parliament wholesale, as Walpole, Newcastle and George III had done. The Augean stables were half swept out.

When, on Rockingham's death, the Whigs quarrelled among themselves over the mysterious personality of Lord Shelburne, Fox outraged the nation's sense of decency by coalescing with Lord North, against whom he had for so many years been addressing his heated Philippics. On the fall of the Fox-North Ministry, **1782–** which the King actively helped to bring about, young Pitt took **1783.** the reins of power as the head of the revived Tory party. He had strongly opposed the King's personal government and American policy, but he was ready to make an alliance on his own terms with the Crown. George, since he could no longer rule in person, greatly preferred Pitt to the Whigs.

The first decade of Pitt's Ministry, before the French Revolu- **1783–** tionary wars came to confuse the issues, was a Ministry of peace **1793.** and reconstruction, no less wise and more active than that of Walpole. Pitt reconstituted the finances of the country, restored its prestige at home and abroad, began to rebuild a new British Empire on the ruins of the old, modernized and secured the governments of Canada and India.[1] After Walpole's example, he reconstituted the power of the Prime Minister in the State as the true governor of the land, not the mere instrument of the royal will. He finally fixed the British conception of the Cabinet, as a responsible and united body, dependent on an independent House of Commons. The work of his precursors in office, the Rockingham Whigs, in re-establishing the party system, was happily rounded off by Pitt. The Tory party, as revived under his leadership, was no longer a name for the ' King's friends,' but an independent Parliamentary connection, with rotten boroughs and election funds of its own, and with roots of affection in great classes of the community. Though its heart of hearts was still the squirearchy and the Church, its young leader earned the confidence of the mercantile community, as Charles Montagu and Walpole had earned it, but as no Tory chief had ever done before. Pitt, unlike the Foxite Whigs, understood political economy and finance, subjects little studied in Brooks's. As a boy at Pembroke, Cambridge, he had sat long hours reading Adam Smith's *Wealth of Nations* when it first appeared, and a few years later, under further instruction from Shelburne, he was putting the new doctrines into practice at the Treasury. Like his father he was at home among the aldermen in the Guildhall, and the City trusted and loved the son as it had trusted and loved the father.

Owing to the personal ascendancy of Pitt, the revived Tory party became for a while an instrument of progress. By doing things which the Whigs might well have done themselves, he drove Burke and Fox round in a dance of factious opposition to liberal measures. But it was in the nature of things that the leader of the party containing the great conservative forces of the nation, should not be allowed to go indefinitely far down the path of change. When, answering to a strong movement in the country that had arisen out of the disasters of the American war, Pitt proposed a mild measure of Parliamentary Reform, his own followers would have none of it. Burke had scotched the snake of Parliamentary corruption with his Economic Reform Bill, but neither he nor his Tory adversaries wished to kill it by reducing the number of rotten boroughs. The magnificent reptile had still a long and honoured life before it. For, with the French Revolution and the wars that followed, an end was put to all political changes in England for thirty years. They were terrible years though glorious, and we might never have survived them at

---

[1] On Canada and India, see pp. 591–598, below.

all, had it not been for what Pitt had already done in the first decade of his Ministry.

As a War Minister at grips with Jacobinism and its fleets and armies, Pitt had to rely not only on the strength and confidence of workaday England, which he had himself rescued from prostration after the American war and nursed back to vigorous life, but he had also to rely on the political vested interests which he had attempted in vain to reform. And when a man, in defending his country from foreign conquest, has to rely on certain forces, he ceases to be capable of criticizing them. He becomes subdued to the material in which he works. Nor, perhaps, would the triumph of ultra-conservatism during the Napoleonic wars have done much permanent harm to the country, but for the reaction of those political habits of mind on the social and economic aspects of the Industrial Revolution proceeding all the time in our midst.

1793–
1801.

BOOKS FOR FURTHER READING

Egerton, *The American Revolution* (Oxford, 1923) ; Lecky, Ramsay Muir and Grant Robertson, as before ; Basil Williams, *Chatham*, Vol. II. ; Winstanley, *Chatham and the Whig Opposition* ; Sir G. O. Trevelyan, *The American Revolution* and *Early Life of Fox* ; Rosebery and Holland Rose for the younger *Pitt*.

AMERICAN WORKS : Channing, *History of the United States* ; Van Tyne, *Causes of the War of Independence* ; Truslow Adams, *Revolutionary New England* ; Professor Morison (Harvard and Oxford), *Sources and Documents illustrating the American Revolution, with Introduction.*

CHAPTER IV

The Tory Oligarchy and the Beginnings of the Democratic Movement. Tom Paine and the Anti-Jacobin Reaction. Burke, Fox, and the Whig Schism

AFTER the defeat of George III's attempt to revive the power of the Crown, there had been a full restoration of aristocratic, Parliamentary government. Under the wise statesmanship of the younger Pitt, a Tory oligarchy became as firmly seated as the former Whig oligarchy of the Walpole-Newcastle era. Government depended once more, not on Court favour, but on the free judgment of the Houses of Parliament ; reference to outside public opinion was secondary though not wholly neglected. Both Walpole and the younger Pitt, though supported by the Peers, were in the fullest sense House of Commons men ; their power rested on the rotten borough system more than on the House of Lords. Indeed Pitt cheapened the prestige of the Peerage by lavish creations, particularly to reward owners of rotten boroughs for their support.   The traffic in sinecures and pensions was still very brisk, although the means of corruption were more limited and less flagrant under the younger Pitt than under Newcastle or North, because of Burke's Economic Reform Bill.[1]

The old Whig and the new Tory oligarchies were much the same, in spite of the change of political label.   The monopoly of power by the landowning class remained as before.   The religious and political system with which the new Toryism was identified, was none other than the ' Hanoverian ' scheme of things which had been saved by the prudence of Walpole and the energy of Pitt's father.   But there was a change, not indeed of aim, but of emphasis, because the constitution was challenged no longer by Jacobites but by Jacobins.   The Whig oligarchs had defended the existing system against Stuart reaction supported by the French Bourbon despotism.   The Tory oligarchs defended the same system against a new democratic movement at home and against armed French Revolution abroad.   Burke's transition from Whig to Tory, in face of the changed situation, was, therefore, no more ' apostasy ' than Fox's opposite choice to move the mass of the ' Whig connection ' forward onto ground not wholly out of touch with the new democracy.

The Tory party, taught by Burke in his later anti-Jacobin mood, learnt to pride itself on being the true heir and protector of the English Revolution Settlement against the false lights of the French Revolution.   Toryism stood for Parliamentary government against the ' direct action ' of the Jacobins and against the popular autocracy of Napoleon.   In making that stand it did the world a great political service, as became fully apparent after the long wars were over, when Canning's version of Toryism became synonymous for awhile with European liberty.   But this Parliamentary constitutionalism of which the Tories were the champions was not, according to their own definition, either ' democratic ' or ' representative ' government. It was a ' mixed constitution,' mainly aristocratic, but with a popular element, and with scope left for occasional interference by the King.

At the same time the active revival of Roman Catholic claims to civil rights in England and Ireland completed the reconciliation of the Tories to the principles of 1689.   In opposing the Catholic claims, George III and the great majority of his unenfranchised subjects were in hearty agreement with the rank and file of the Tory party.   The appeal to Protestant fears ceased to be a Whig and became a Tory cry at election time.   Royalist

[1] See p. 557, above.

and popular sentiment, which it was an object of Toryism to unite, were happily reconciled on the basis of a double fear of the French Revolutionists and of the Roman Catholics. The Wesleyan movement without and the Evangelical movement within the Church, strengthened the nation's hostility to ' the infidel philosophy of Tom Paine,' and to the ' Popery ' of the Irish rebels. The fact that Jacobinism and Roman Catholicism were cutting each other's throats in Europe, did not prevent our insular conservatism from condemning and dreading them both, as fundamentally alien to the English spirit, and irreconcilable with our ' happy constitution in Church and State.' In Tory cartoons, any time between 1790 and 1830, ' Magna Charta,' the Bible, and the King's Crown on the top of those two sacred volumes, are pictured as the basis of our national ' liberties,' which the Foxite Whigs with their infidel and Popish allies were accused of desiring to destroy. This simple creed was deficient in its analysis of much that was going on in the world, it was exploited by selfish politicians and classes, and it wrought mischief in industrial England and in political Ireland ; but it served to beat Napoleon, for it appealed strongly to English nature and tradition, it was rooted deeper in men's hearts than mere politics, and it held the middle classes loyal to the government through the long years of the war.

Since the revived Tory party had become enthusiastic for the House of Hanover and the Revolution Settlement, and since the Whigs had begun to demand civil rights for Roman Catholics, it may reasonably be asked along what line are we to trace the continuity of the two parties from the days of Titus Oates and Dr. Sacheverell to these very different times. The continuity was to be found mainly in the unbroken connection of the Tories with the Church interest and of the Whig aristocrats with the Non-conformist voters. Pitt in 1787 and again in 1789 opposed the abolition of the Test and Corporation Acts which debarred Protestant as well as Catholic Dissenters from civil office. Charles Fox, on the other hand, warmly espoused the cause of religious equality, and asserted the modern principle that ' religion is not a proper test for a political institution.'

The Dissenters, therefore, saw no chance of admission to full civic rights except through the new Whig party under Fox, and through Parliamentary Reform. They believed that if once the rotten borough system were abolished, their electoral strength would compel Parliament to redress their grievances. For analogous reasons the clergy of the Established Church and their keenest supporters became determined opponents of Parliamentary Reform, which they feared might lead to disestablishment. The religious division on the great political issue of the new era continued to influence the course of politics until the Reform Bills of 1832, 1867 and 1884 laid the question to rest.

Just when English political parties were beginning thus to divide on the double issue of religious equality and Parliamentary Reform, came the great news from France. France, not yet turned Jacobin, had replaced a despotism by a constitutional monarchy, and was framing a code of laws which put men of every creed on the same platform of civic rights. The attitude of English Churchmen and Dissenters towards the early stages of the French Revolution was naturally affected by the analogy of their own position at home. And the fortunes of Parliamentary Reform, hitherto a purely and indeed peculiarly English movement, became at once deeply implicated in the affairs of a country different in every social and political aspect from our own.

1789–
1791.

1780–
1785.

The first agitation for Parliamentary Reform had arisen among the old-fashioned Yorkshire freeholders under the patronage of Whig landed gentry. It had no relation to the Industrial Revolution, or to any specifically modern conditions of society or of politics. It was not a movement to enfranchise the great towns or the new middle class. It proposed to abolish a few of the rotten boroughs and to increase the county representation. It advocated this mild measure of Parliamentary Reform, not on any theory of elevating the middle or the lower classes, or of enriching the poor, but simply to restore efficient government and to place the King and Parliament under some sort of control from public opinion. The agitation had been provoked by George III, and was intended to put an end to the personal rule which he exercised through the nominated and bribed majority of the Commons. It was as much a movement of occasion as of principle.

The wind was therefore taken out of its sails by the restoration of constitutional and efficient government under the younger Pitt. Burke's Economic Reform Bill of 1782, by reducing the power of corruption in Parliament, had acted in some measure as a substitute for electoral redistribution and reform. The rejection of Pitt's mild Reform Bill in 1785 marked the end of this first agitation, and Pitt himself soon became an anti-Reformer.

The second stage of the Reform agitation was the somewhat academic movement headed by the philosophic Dissenters, Price and Priestley. It aimed at religious equality through Parliamentary Reform, and adumbrated universal principles of democracy and the ' Rights of Man,' in general sympathy with the earlier and less extreme changes in France. As compared to the Reform agitation of the Yorkshire freeholders ten years before, the new movement was less uncompromisingly British ; it scented of America, France and the brotherhood of mankind. The Tory upper classes were alarmed by its general and philosophic character which might carry it further than even the originators meant ; Burke attacked Priestley and the French Revolution together in one of the greatest political pamphlets of all time ; and the ' Church and King ' mob of Birmingham, not **1791.** discouraged by the local authorities, sacked the philosopher's house and burnt his scientific instruments. Similar popular outrages in Manchester put an end to this movement for Reform led by the middle class philosophic Dissenters. The middle class as a whole had been indifferent and the working class had been adverse, at least in two great centres of working class life, which forty years later were prepared if necessary to fight for Grey's Reform Bill or for something yet more drastic.

The mob action at Birmingham and Manchester indicated that ' democratic ' views would for another generation be those of a minority only, even among the poor. Nevertheless Tom Paine started the democratic movement proper among a section of the working classes, precisely at this critical moment. It is here first that we see a close connection between English politics and the new social conditions created by the Industrial Revolution. The drawing together of large numbers of workmen in factories and industrial districts throughout England and Scotland, created audiences and groups where Paine's doctrines could be disseminated and discussed ; while the loss of independence and welfare suffered by many through economic changes, prompted the bewildered victims to look in sheer desperation to politics, in default of other remedy for their lot. Multitudes drifting up from the villages to the new manufacturing districts, heard there that Tom Paine declared all power to belong of right to the people, whereas in their own sharp personal experience it seemed to have been monopolized by capitalist employers, large farmers and landlord Justices of the Peace. Exploitation, resentment and mutual suspicion interrupted the harmony of classes which had so long been the mark of Eighteenth Century English life.

Perhaps it was all inevitable, but the extremism of Burke's *Thoughts on the French Revolution* and Paine's *Rights of Man* **1791–** certainly did not make for mutual understanding. These two **1792.** works had enormous influence on two separate wings of the community for forty years to come. Burke's stately periods and profound though one-sided philosophy were eminently suited to convince and alarm the educated classes of that day, while Paine's crude and homely logic was like new wine to the unaccustomed brains of classes who had never yet thought about

politics except as an occasion of riot and licence at election time.
It is a pity that great thinkers can so seldom think of more than
one side of a case.   Burke and Paine stated in their most
uncompromising form the Conservative and the Democratic
position.

The Conservatism of that day, and of many a day to come,
made no claim to be allied to Democracy.   It stood for the
' balance of the constitution ' between King, Lords and Commons
on the basis of 1689.   Pitt's Attorney-General John Scott, afterwards Lord Eldon, demanded in 1794 the condemnation of the
Radical shoemaker Thomas Hardy for High Treason, on the
ground that he had advocated ' representative government, the
direct opposite of the government which is established here.'
That the light of Burke's wisdom should have served to darken
yet further Eldon's obscurity is part of the irony of human fate.

Paine's *Rights of Man*, on the other hand, claimed that all
hereditary government, whether by King or Lords, was ' an
imposition on mankind,' that all power was derived from the
people, and that government by a properly representative chamber
should be at once established.   Then, he prophesied, the pensions
on the taxes granted to the rich would be diverted, and used,
together with a graduated income-tax, to give education to the
poor, old-age pensions and maternity benefit.   These propositions,—some of them shrewd prophecies and valuable suggestions,
—were prejudiced by his enormous folly in demanding the abolition of the Monarchy.   Paine's easily excitable nature was full
of the perfections of the new American constitution, mainly
because it had no King and no House of Lords.   His demand for
the abolition of all the antiquarian ' lumber ' of the British constitution deprived his propaganda of all chance of success, drove
him into exile, and made the circulation of his writings a criminal
offence,—though one that was very frequently committed. .

For years to come, Paine's Republicanism stuck like a burr to
everything liberal.   It was in vain for Fox and Grey to repudiate
him.   When the war with the Jacobin Republic began, the last
chance of people thinking reasonably on domestic politics disappeared.   The man in the street, as he gazed through the latticed
shop-windows at Gillray's cartoons, began to think of the aristocratic Whigs as people in red caps of liberty intent on beheading
' the good old King ' and setting up a ragged republic of *sans-
culottes*.

England was not at war with France until the beginning
of 1793.   The drama of 1792 was watched by the English as
neuters, and the spectacle had reactions of permanent import-

ance on opinion over here. The attempt of the European monarchs of the *ancien régime* to smother the French Revolution in blood, as proclaimed in the manifesto issued by their General, Brunswick ; the desperate rising of the French people in reply ; the unexpected victory of the new France in the Valmy campaign ; 1792. the simultaneous triumph in Paris of Jacobinism and Republicanism, massacre and the guillotine,—all these portentous events, which still attract the gaze of posterity, absorbed the attention of English politicians, recast our parties and determined the spirit of our government for forty years to come.

The Foxite Whigs in the fashionable purlieus of Brooks's, and the low-class Radicals of the Corresponding Society sympathized passionately with the French people against the German despotic invaders, whom Fox compared to the armies of Xerxes. In his warm-hearted, impulsive way, he wrote of the French, just before the news of the September massacres arrived, ' With all their faults and nonsense, I do interest myself for their success to the greatest degree.' Then came the first news of the massacres in the Paris prisons. ' I really consider,' he wrote, ' the horrors of that day and night as the most heart-breaking event that ever happened to those who, like me, are fundamentally and unalterably attached to the true cause. There is not, in my opinion, a shadow of excuse for this horrid massacre, not even the possibility of extenuating it in the smallest degree.'

But the sympathies of the great majority of the well-to-do classes had been all through on the side of Brunswick. And the September massacres and the regime of the guillotine aroused passions in our island akin to those aroused by the news of St. Bartholomew and the revocation of the Edict of Nantes. The democratic movement was effectively overpowered by public opinion that autumn and winter in every town and village in England. Loyalist Associations were formed all over the country, usually headed by Churchmen against their local enemies the Dissenting Reformers ; these Associations organized opinion behind the government in the demand for the suppression of Reformers at home, and stern resistance, if necessary in arms, to French pretensions to ' liberate ' Europe by the sword.

That same winter the French Republicans, intoxicated with the first draughts of victory and power, when they had expected 1792-the Prussian gallows, invaded Savoy, the Rhineland and the 1793. Austrian Netherlands, declared the Scheldt open to navigation all European Treaties notwithstanding, and prepared to invade Holland. They offered armed assistance to all countries desirous of overthrowing their old governments. The pride and ambition of Louis XIV revived in the breasts of the men who were pulling down his statues, beheading his descendants and persecuting his religion. The occupation of the Rhine Delta by the Power with the greatest military and the second greatest naval force in Europe, challenged the English sense of self-preservation, as Philip of Spain and Louis and Kaiser William challenged it by like pretensions in the same quarter of the world. Resistance to the French hegemony in Europe, and particularly in the Netherlands, was pursued by Parliamentary England with a determination more steady than that of any of the despotic Courts, that had rashly provoked the Jacobin lion with their Brunswick blusterings and then run away.

The purpose of the old English nation not to allow the newborn French nation to annex the rotten States of Europe as her vassals, was nobly personified by Pitt, and was handed on by him to his followers, who in the days of Castlereagh won success at last for an effort sustained through the vicissitudes of twenty years. Unfortunately this determination was by circumstance identified with a policy of repression of Reform and of all discussion of Reform at home and with a hardness of heart towards the victims of the Industrial Revolution and to the poor generally, as potential ' Jacobins.'

By the same process of association of ideas, often so misleading to the political mind, moderatism in politics, the mildest proclivities to Reform, and sympathy with the victims either of economic oppression or of government persecution, usually went with a want of zeal for the war, and a slowness to acknowledge the intractable character of the nationalism and imperialism of the successive governments of the new France. Fox, Lord Holland, Sydney Smith, Romilly, Whitbread, Byron, and Cobbett in his Radical period, are striking examples of this law.

The Reformers, therefore, during the coming generation, laboured under a double stigma,—as lukewarm patriots in war time, and as supposed friends of Paine's republican doctrine, in spite of their protests to the contrary. This double unpopularity made it easy, as it also perhaps made it unnecessary, for Pitt to use the strong hand of power to prohibit all discussion of Parliamentary Reform outside the privileged walls of Parliament itself. In the first two years of the war, there were constant prosecutions of editors, Non-conformist preachers, and speculative persons of a propagandist disposition, who had ventured to argue for Parliamentary Reform, often indeed with unwise and provocative phraseology borrowed from France. Muir and Palmer, tried before Braxfield, the Scottish Judge Jeffreys, were transported to Botany Bay by a most iniquitous sentence, which the ex-Reformer Pitt refused to mitigate. Sympathy with the fate of

1793.

these two 'Reform martyrs' had its part in fostering the Radicalism for which Scotland became famous in the Nineteenth
Century.

Finally, in 1794, the government was so far blinded by panic
that it sought the lives of the Reformers. A charge of High
Treason was instituted against Thomas Hardy the shoemaker,
the founder of the Corresponding Society and the principal leader
of the constitutional movement in politics among the working
classes. Other innocuous and respectable persons, like Thelwall
the lecturer and Horne Tooke the philologist, were tried on the
same capital charge. But the good genius of England came to
her rescue in her characteristic institution, the jury system. Pitt
had outraged the English sense of fair play. Thanks to Erskine's
persuasive eloquence, twelve Tory jurymen acquitted Hardy and
his fellow prisoners on the capital charge, and reminded the government that the methods of Robespierre were not wanted over here.
London, though strongly Anti-Jacobin, broke into loud rejoicings
at the acquittal.

This timely check saved England from a reign of terror and
perhaps ultimately from a retributive revolution. But the
government proceeded, with more general approval, to silence
further political discussion for many years to come. The Corresponding and other Societies were suppressed by Act of Parliament.
Habeas Corpus was suspended and numbers of men against whom
there was no evidence were kept in prison for years. Public
meetings were prohibited that were not licensed by magistrates,
and, in fact, none were any longer permitted. Except for the
Anti-slave-trade movement, which also for a time declined,
political life ceased in Britain. To make matters worse, the Foxite
Whigs, in a mood of laziness and disgust, retired to their country
houses in an aimless 'seccession' from their duties in Parliament,   1797–
where alone criticism of government was permitted.   1799.

Pitt's Combination Acts were another manifestation of the
repressive spirit of the times. These measures rendered Trade   1799–
Unionism illegal, and punished all combinations of wage-earners.   1800.
They were accompanied by no corresponding steps to enforce a
fair wage, and simply put the employee into his master's hands.
The policy represented not true *Laissez faire*, but State interference on the side of Capital against Labour. It was inspired
not merely by a desire to keep down wages in accordance with the
political economy of the day, but by Anti-Jacobin fears of all
forms of combination by the 'labouring poor.' Two Whigs,
Sheridan and Lord Holland, were the only important politicians
who opposed the Acts in either House.

The new working class that the Industrial Revolution was

bringing into existence and concentrating in the towns, had thus
early shown an instinct towards self-education and self-help,
along the parallel lines of political Associations and economic
Trade Unionism.   Pitt's government attempted to crush out
both together, though with more success in the political field
than in the economic.   When, after the war was over, the
1819.   political life of the working classes and the Trade Union movement each made fresh headway in the era of Peterloo, they had
to fight as outlaws for the right to exist.   Then indeed popular
opinion was being rapidly alienated from the Tory system, to
which it had upon the whole adhered in the time of Pitt.   But
the habit of repression, begun by Pitt against a minority in time
of war, had become custom of the country and was continued
by Pitt's successors against the majority in time of peace.   The
partisanship of government against the poor and against those
who attempted to plead their cause, however natural owing to
the French Revolution and the French war, distorted and embittered the social processes of the Industrial Revolution and
left marks which were never entirely healed in the remedial
period that followed.   It was in 1823 that the Combination Laws
against Trade Unions were repealed, the first step in a great
process of legislative evolution.

Between Anti-Jacobin Toryism and Painite Radicalism, the
Parliamentary Whigs took up a half-way position, under the now
middle-aged Charles Fox and his favourite young men, Lord
Holland and Charles Grey.   While repudiating the doctrines of
Paine they continued, in the heat of the Anti-Jacobin reaction
from 1793 to 1797, to move motions in Parliament for Reform
based on abolition of the rotten boroughs.   They were voted
down by great majorities, who regarded them with horror as
seditionists in sympathy with France; they were saved from worse
consequences by the great respect felt by all Englishmen for the
privileges of Parliament, and for the privileges of the well-
connected and fashionable to be eccentric.

In these circumstances the quarrel of the Reforming Whigs
with Burke and half the members of their own party was bitter
and complete.   But whereas the Whigs who followed Burke were
merged among the other supporters of the Tory Ministry, the
Whigs who followed Fox remained the nucleus of the party, and
the keepers of its traditions.   The continued opposition of the
Foxites to Pitt and his Tory successors, prevented the whole
machinery of Parliament from becoming a part of the Anti-
Jacobin movement, and so left a bridge, however slender and
insecure, still hanging across the gulf that divided classes in the

new era. The adherence of the Whigs to Parliamentary Reform in days when it was impracticable, enabled them, when the wheel had come full circle, to avert civil war and social catastrophe by their Reform Bill of 1832.

Until that still distant era, the position of the Whigs was one of isolation, out of touch alike with the main stream of national enthusiasm for war against the French, yet equally far removed from sympathy with the lower class Radicalism of Tom Paine and of William Cobbett after him. Thirty years of unpopularity and exclusion from power failed to make an end of the Whigs. Their strong personal ties and party traditions held them together at gatherings in their large and pleasant country houses and at Brooks's Club. They were aristocrats, scholars and sportsmen, with much to make life delightful, in default of popularity or office. Their seats were safe, for they had a modest share of the rotten boroughs. They rather despised the Tory governors of the country as people less fashionable than themselves. They were so well-connected that they could afford to toy with democracy ; they were so much in the mode that ' Jacobinism ' seemed in them only a modish eccentricity. Their attachment to the person of Fox until his death in 1806, and to his memory afterwards, was one of the accidental circumstances which moulded the course of English politics. Fox was made to be loved by his friends. Where he was, there would the Whig party be. If he had gone over to Pitt and Anti-Jacobinism, there would never have been a Whig-Liberal party, and the process of British politics in the Nineteenth Century would very probably have been by armed revolution and reaction instead of by Parliamentary Reform.

When the youthful Pitt had first been called on by George III to govern the land, the Whig satirists had made merry over ' A Kingdom trusted to a schoolboy's care.' But Parliament and country soon found in Pitt not the schoolboy but a schoolmaster, austere, reserved, dignified, didactic. It was Fox who was the eternal schoolboy. Devoted to his friends ; generous to his enemies but always up in arms against them for any reason or none ; never out of scrapes ; a lover of life and of mankind, he was born to be leader of opposition, and leader of opposition he was for almost all his long life in the House of Commons. Chatham was a greater orator, and his son perhaps a greater debater, than Fox, but for a union of oratorical and emotional with debating power, Fox has never been rivalled. His early extravagances as a gambler, his later extravagances as a politician, his coalition with North, his factious opposition to many of Pitt's best measures in the ' eighties,'—weigh heavy against him. But as advancing years and darkening public prospects sobered him, the fire of spirit of which he had wasted so much on faction, went more and more sincerely into the defence of the oppressed,—in England, Scotland and Ireland.   But the cause of the negro slave appealed to him most of all.   Pitt, ever more preoccupied by the daily care of defending the British Empire and all Europe against Bonaparte, forgot all else, and would do nothing more to assist the Anti-slave-trade cause.   But Wilberforce found in Fox an ever faithful ally.   Owing to his zeal and to the chance that put the Whig chiefs in office, in a Coalition Ministry for a few months after Pitt's death, the slave trade was abolished in 1806 instead of many years later ; that was Fox's bequest to the nation and to the world, made upon his death-bed.

The times were tragic, but the men England produced were great.   With Pitt and Castlereagh, Nelson and Wellington to lead her through the most terrible ordeal she had ever till then endured, she had Fox and Wilberforce to keep her conscience alive even in time of war.

Books for Further Reading

Rosebery and Holland Rose on *Pitt* ; Hammond, *Charles James Fox* ; Russell, *Memorials of C. J. Fox* (4 vols.) ; Moncure Conway, *Life of Paine* ; Coupland, *Wilberforce*; Veitch, *Genesis of Parliamentary Reform*; Morley, *Burke*; Graham Wallas, *Francis Place*.

CHAPTER V

The Character of the French Revolutionary and Napoleonic Wars.   Period of Pitt and Nelson, 1793–1805.   Period of Wellington and Castlereagh, 1808–1815.   The Naval, Commercial and Military Struggle.   The Final Settlement.

Modern England has four times fought with success a great war to prevent the conquest of Europe by a single Power: the Spain of Philip and the Inquisition, the France of the Grand Monarch and the Jesuits, the France of the Jacobins and Napoleon, and the German military monarchy of our own day have each in turn been foiled.   On each of these four occasions England had a double end in view,—the Balance of Power in Europe and the security of her own mercantile and colonial future beyond the ocean.   And on each occasion European and maritime considerations alike required that England should prevent the Netherlands and the Rhine Delta from falling into the hands of the greatest military and naval State of the continent.   It was no accidental coincidence, but danger to our shores and to our naval control of the Channel, that made the Netherlands the chief scene of English military interference on the continent, under Elizabeth, under William and Anne, and under George V.   And for the same reason the wars conducted in the name of George III against Revolutionary France began with the defeat of our troops in the Netherlands in 1793–4, and ended with their victory in the same sector at Waterloo.   But during the twenty years interval, the French hold on Belgium and Holland was strong enough to exclude our armies from that nerve-centre of contending interests, except for a few unsuccessful minor expeditions like those to Alkmaar and **1799, 1809.** to Walcheren.

The Napoleonic wars stand half-way between the Marlborough wars and the Great War of our own day, in time, in size and in character.   The resemblance to the Marlborough wars is the most obvious, because the weapons employed by sea and land were very similar in the two periods, and the enemy was France.   The geography and strategy, therefore, of the naval and military operations which quelled Napoleon resemble those which quelled Louis XIV.   Again, in the days of Pitt and Castlereagh, as in the days of William and Marlborough, the two props of the alliance against France were British sea-power and British subsidies, applied along all the coasts and in half the Treasuries of Europe. The huge British sailing ships whose broadsides conquered at Trafalgar were of the same general character as those which had conquered at La Hogue, while the ' thin red line ' and the British cavalry charge won Waterloo by tactics not so very different from those of Blenheim and Ramillies.   Again a British General of genius, commanding a small but excellent British army, played a decisive part among the larger military establishments of the continent.   Again British troops were landed in the Netherlands and in Spain, in Mediterranean islands and on American coasts. And again, in 1815 as in 1713, the war ended for England with the establishment in the Netherlands of a Power from which she had nothing to fear, and by great additions to her colonial Empire and her maritime prestige.

But the Napoleonic wars not only repeated the past but rehearsed the future.   The issue of the campaigns against Louis had indeed been affected by the course of trade competition between England and France, but a hundred years later the commercial struggle was more formal and more decisive as a weapon of war.   The British blockade of Napoleon's Europe, and his attempt to starve England by the Berlin and Milan Decrees, were warlike operations of the same general character as the British blockade of the Central Powers in our own day and the German submarine campaign ; they disturbed the economy of the whole world and had serious consequences for the combatants in their relations with the United States and other would-be neutrals.

Furthermore there is a political element of a distinctively modern type in the wars that originated from the French Revolution. The new regime in France, whatever its defects or crimes, filled the humblest French peasant and bourgeois with pride as a citizen and zeal as a patriot, opened military and civil careers to talent without distinction of birth, and, under the Consulate of Bonaparte, supplied the new nation with the administrative system of a wholly new type of efficiency. The other peoples of the continent were marched into the field as mercenaries or serfs, not as citizen soldiers. Britain alone could match the new spirit of France with a national patriotism of yet older date. But the Englishman's 'will to conquer' could be fully aroused only in defence of sea-power and commerce. After our expulsion from the Netherlands in 1794, it is true that we stayed in the war when others submitted to France, but we kept our armies out of Europe for a dozen years together, safe behind the shield of the Navy. We took no serious part, except naval and financial, in the wars of the two Coalitions that suffered defeat at Marengo and Austerlitz. Nor, until the Peninsular War in 1808, did we begin to fight on land as a principal, and even then with armies of not more than 30,000 British at a time.

Success only began to shine on the allies when the popular sense of nationhood was aroused in Spain, Russia and Germany, by indignation against French tyranny at length outweighing in Europe the sense of the benefits of French reform. Only in its last phase did the war become a contest between self-conscious nationalities, not altogether unlike those which fought the Great War of our own day. The horror and the slaughter increased in proportion as the peoples were aroused to fight willingly, to some extent on their own behalf and not merely as the obedient vassals of Emperors and Kings. The Moscow and Leipzig campaigns adumbrated the bloody future of nationalist Europe armed with the machinery of modern science and locomotion.

1812–
1813.

During the greater part of twenty years of war, the immense superiority of the new French national spirit and organization over the lifeless and old-fashioned machinery of the continental States of the *ancien régime*, ensured the defeat of each successive Coalition that England encouraged and financed against France. Until the Peninsular War and the popular movements in Russia and Germany made possible the grand operations of Wellington and Castlereagh, England's effective action was limited to the sea. It was much that she maintained her hold over all the waters of

1793–
1805.

1808–
1815.

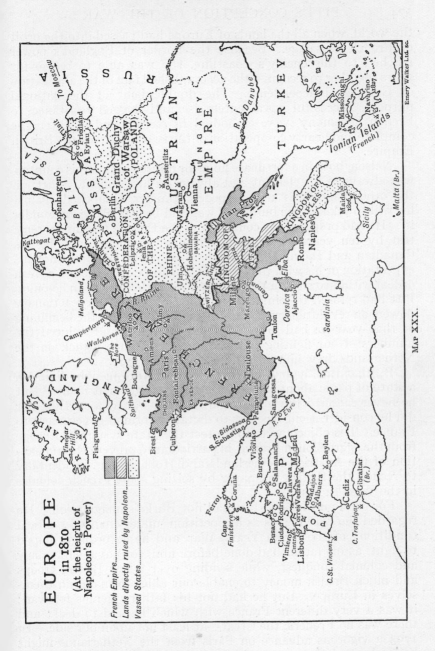

EUROPE
in 1810
(At the height of
Napoleon's Power)

French Empire..............
Lands directly ruled by Napoleon....
Vassal States...............

Map XXX.

Emery Walker Ltd. sc.

the world, when all the lands of Europe had passed into the orbit of French vassalage. Because the border of England's power reached to the enemy's coastline, she was able to refuse for years together to recognise the accomplished fact of the abrogation of Europe's independence. The double bent of the national purpose, successful naval enterprise and dogged resistance to French hegemony, were embodied in Nelson and in Pitt. The complete and hearty co-operation of the two men saved the British Empire.

Nelson, born in a fortunate hour for himself and for his country, was always in his element and always on his element. Pitt, on the other hand, was a great peace Minister, compelled against his will to take up the burden of war and bear it till he died under it. He had prepared the country and the Empire for this supreme test by ten years of sound government at home, and by his Canadian and Indian legislation.[1] But it was certainly not his expectation or his wish that Britain should be subjected to a fresh ordeal within so short a time of the loss of the American colonies. Pitt had refused to join in the original attack of the reactionary powers on revolutionary France in 1792 ; indeed, at the beginning of that year he had prophesied a long peace and reduced the numbers of our fighting forces. But the French attack on the Netherlands drew him into the war early in 1793.

By that time he had become a violent Anti-Jacobin, living in a state of panic about the activities of Reformers at home. But he never satisfied Burke by regarding the war as a crusade, nor did he consider it our business to dictate a form of government to France. His objects were to protect the State system of Europe from the aggression of France, in particular to prevent the annexation of the Austrian Netherlands and Holland, and incidentally to recoup the British tax-payer by seizing some French colonies in the West Indies.

For good and for evil Pitt had not Burke's imagination. He regarded the world crisis as a repetition, under changed political conditions, of the Seven Years' War, and he accordingly hoped to fight, as his father had done before him, for naval supremacy and colonial conquest, while sending over a few British troops and much British money to enable our allies to maintain themselves in Europe. But he had not his father's genius for war ; it was a very different France with which he had to deal ; and there was no Frederic the Great—at least not upon our side. In 1793 a vigorous advance on Paris from the Netherlands might have changed the course of history, before Carnot had time to create the new democratic army of France out of the mutinous

[1] See pp. 593–595, below.

welter of the old royal army, deserted by its aristocratic officers. But the chance was let slip, and the Revolution had time to organize its latent energies. Neither the Austrian nor the British armies then in Flanders had the training or the leadership for such an enterprise, which Wellington or even Sir John Moore might have ventured upon with the reconstituted army that we afterwards sent to Spain.

Pitt, moreover, in 1793, sent a large part of the available British forces to the West Indies. He was imitating the war plans not of Marlborough but of Chatham : the French West Indian Islands should be his Canada, which he would win for the Empire. In his generation the wealth of the sugar islands, where great fortunes were made by English planters, caused them to be much more highly regarded than Canada, and the sacrifices which Pitt made to preserve and to acquire such islands for the Empire, though severely criticized by modern historians, seemed very natural at the time. But he had no knowledge of the local conditions of warfare in the West Indies comparable to the knowledge his father had acquired of how Canada and the Ohio valley were to be won. Disease swept off the British soldiers by thousands. The slaves in the French and English islands rose, adding fresh horror and difficulty to the undertaking, and rendering it impossible to withdraw the troops and allow the whole Archipelago to sink like Haiti into black savagery. The affair, which added **1793** little to the British Empire, was only liquidated after the death **1796.** of 40,000 British soldiers in three years, a number roughly answering to that with which Wellington in six years drove Napoleon's troops out of Spain.

These fearful losses in the tropical world, and the inefficient army system of the day, crippled England's efforts in Europe. The selfish preoccupation of Prussia and Russia in sharing up the corpse of murdered Poland, prevented them from playing the part against France assigned to them in Pitt's scheme. The British and Austrian armies were driven out of the Low Countries **1793–** to the sound of the Marseillaise. Holland and the Rhine lands **1794.** were revolutionized by the French, the inhabitants half sympathizing. Finally, Bonaparte's conquest of Italy, and his establish- **1796–** ment there of vassal Republics, introduced a new era of French **1797.** conquest and of world politics. In 1797 Austria, beaten to her knees by this astonishing young genius, crept out of the war, leaving England alone against France.

' The Grand Nation,' more formidable than even the ' Grand Monarch' whom William and Marlborough had tamed, was now in the hands of the Directorate, a set of energetic ruffians, the survivors of the guillotine, the fathers of modern war and con-

quest, who were determined to re-establish the finances of France
by plundering the rest of Europe. And the ablest servant of
these men, soon to be their master, was already learning from his
Italian experience how a French European Empire might be
founded, on the basis of uniting the social benefits of the Revolution to religious toleration and political order, which the Directorate
were incapable of restoring.

England meanwhile was in a sorry plight. Her ships were
excluded from the Mediterranean waters, where the Spaniards
1797.   had joined the war on her enemies' side ; her home fleets at
Spithead and the Nore were in mutiny against the neglect and
harsh treatment which had always been the lot of the sailors who
won her battles ; on land her military reputation was at its lowest
ebb ; it seemed unlikely that she could, without an ally, hold out
against all Western Europe united for her destruction.

In this evil hour she was saved by the high quality of Pitt's
courage, and by his instinct for naval affairs.   The mutinies were
pacified and quelled, and somewhat better conditions of life on
1797.   board were established.   The late mutineers sallied out under
Duncan and destroyed the Dutch fleet at Camperdown.   Pitt
was clumsy and unsuccessful in diplomatic operations, which he
conducted through Grenville, and in military operations, which
he conducted through Dundas.   But to call him a bad war
Minister is to overlook the sea affair, which for English statesmen
comprises half the conduct of war.   He chose, in Spencer and
Jervis, the right men through whom to act ; he helped them to
pick out Nelson, one of the youngest flag-officers on the list ; and
he insisted on sending him back to recover our hold of the Mediterranean, which had been a French lake for more than a year.
The result was the battle of the Nile.

Aug. 1,   The battle of the Nile was indeed one of the cardinal events of
1798.   the whole war.   It restored British naval power at the moment
when it was wavering, and in the region whence it had been withdrawn ; whereas Trafalgar only put the crown of glory on a
campaign already decided and on a life whose work was done.

Bonaparte had been safely carried to Egypt by the French
fleet, and had seized Malta on the way from the Knights of St.
John.   The path to Constantinople and India seemed open to
the most ambitious spirit since Alexander the Great.   But when
Nelson annihilated his fleet, at anchor at the mouth of the Nile,
1799.   these Oriental visions soon faded.   Next year Bonaparte was fain
to leave his army locked up in Egypt, and slip back to France.
There he rebuilt the structure of his ambitions on a Western basis,
and only after many years attempted to cut a path back to the
East by the route of Russian conquest.   Nelson's cannonade that

summer evening off the Egyptian shore secured the full establishment of British supremacy in the Indian Peninsula, in the difficult
days of ' Tippoo Sahib ' of Mysore and of the Maratha Wars
conducted by the Wellesley brothers.

Another consequence of the Nile was the restored dominance
of Britain in Mediterranean waters. The power of our fleet was
firmly based on Malta, which we took from the French in 1800
and never relinquished, and on Sicily, where the royal family,
exiled from Naples, became Nelson's friends, and remained
England's *protégés*.

But the Nile evoked other and more formidable allies than the
South-Italian Bourbons. Austria and Russia felt encouraged to
form the Second Coalition, which after a sudden and brief day
of success in North Italy under Suvoroff, perished on the field of   1799.
Marengo at the hands of Bonaparte. As First Consul he now had   1800.
at his command all the civil and military resources of France,
which he reorganized in the four best years of his life as the
resources of no nation had ever been organized before, giving to
France the modern administrative institutions by which she has
lived ever since.

Next followed the episode of the ' armed neutrality ' formed
by Russia and the Scandinavian Powers against England, partly
on grounds of neutrals' complaints of the right of search as
exercised by the lords of the sea, partly as admirers and would-be
allies of Bonaparte, for whose friendship the Czar Paul had half-
crazy yearnings. The assassination of the Czar and Nelson's   1801
destruction of the Danish fleet under the guns of the Copenhagen
forts, put an end to the peril in that quarter. In northern as in
southern seas, the arm of Britain was omnipotent. French and
Spanish, Dutch and Danish fleets had been shattered, and Britain
helped herself at will to the colonies of the unhappy allies of
France. The Cape of Good Hope and Ceylon were taken from
the Dutch to secure the sea route to India.

But on land no one could make head against Bonaparte. The
two victorious enemies recognized their respective limits by the
Treaty of Amiens. But though hailed with joy in England, the   1802.
long-expected peace proved only a hollow truce. For it soon
appeared that Bonaparte interpreted the Treaty of Amiens to
mean the retirement of Britain behind the sea curtain, while he
remained free to annex every State of Europe to which he had a
mind. It was not so that British statesmen interpreted the peace
they had signed, which in their eyes set an agreed limit to French
expansion. So the two weary nations turned again to war.   1803.

England was once more matched alone against France. For

Y

1804.

the moment, Bonaparte had no other use for his incomparable army than to threaten 'perfidious Albion' from the camp of Boulogne. His vigorous but crude and unprofessional schemes for securing the mastery of the Channel, appointing an elaborate *rendez-vous* for the Brest and Toulon fleets in the West Indies, were baffled by the vigilance and energy of Nelson and his 'band of brothers.' Our ships hunted the French across the Atlantic and back, sometimes at fault, sometimes in full cry. The pursued ran breathless to earth in the ports of France and Spain, and no more was heard of the invasion of England. Then, when all seemed over, the anger of Napoleon against Villeneuve, his unfortunate Admiral, caused the main French and Spanish fleet to come out of harbour for the last time, to the final sacrifice off

Oct. 21, 1805.

Cape Trafalgar. It saved the British much rope and timber in blockading work during the remaining ten years of the war, and it stamped on the mind of Europe an indelible impression that England's naval power was invincible. That belief helped to make the Nineteenth Century a time of peace and security for the British, and stood them in good stead when that long period of prosperity and high civilization was at length broken by another great war on land and sea.

Nelson is the best loved name in English ears. There is more in our relation to him than can be accounted for by his genius and our obligation. For Marlborough was unpopular, and there was an element of fear in the respect and admiration felt for the Iron Duke. Indeed, Wellington's complete devotion to the public service was rooted in a noble but not very lovable aristocratic pride, which made him live reserved as a man apart, saving him indeed from mistakes and loss of dignity into which Nelson sometimes fell on shore. But Nelson entered straight into the common heart of humanity. As he lay expecting the Trafalgar fight, he chanced to discover that a coxswain, one of the best men on board the *Victory*, had been so busy preparing the mail bags that he had forgotten to drop into them his own letter to his wife, till after the despatch vessel was under full sail for England : ' Hoist a signal to bring her back,' said Nelson ; 'who knows but that he may fall in action to-morrow ? His letter shall go with the rest.' And the vessel was brought back for that alone.

Dec. 1805.

Meanwhile Napoleon, now Emperor, had turned from the useless camp at Boulogne to conquer Eastern Europe at Austerlitz. His success matched Nelson's, and men could not then see that it would be more ephemeral than the dead man's empire over the

Jan. 1806.

waves. It was an hour of gloom and glory for England. Pitt, worn out with care and disappointment and illness, died at his post. His death and Nelson's, rather than the fruitless Treaty

of Amiens, marked the close of the first half of the war of twenty
years.

The great French war,—alike in its first phase in the time of
Pitt and Nelson, and its last in the time of Castlereagh and
Wellington,—was fought by the House of Commons.   The comparison of the Roman Senate fighting Hannibal was in the mind
of every educated man.   The persons whom the House trusted
could wield the nation's power and purse, on condition of explain-
ing their plans to the benches of country gentlemen, and winning
their approval.   For this reason Parliamentary eloquence was at
its zenith ; popular oratory was not yet of importance, except
at the hustings in the few open constituencies at election time.
Public meetings there were none.   So long as the war lasted, and
longer, there was little freedom of press or speech for Reformers.
When Cobbett denounced the flogging of British militiamen by
German mercenaries, he got two years.   The restrictions on
popular liberty and propaganda were partly a measure of precau-
tion in war time, but they did not end with the war, because they
were also designed to prevent the revival of the movement for
domestic Reform, which the Anti-Jacobin mind identified with
sedition.

But though liberty was in partial abeyance, no one was
tempted to abridge the power of Parliament, or to restore the
rule of the King who had lost the American colonies.   George III
was not, indeed, entirely without power.   Even in the intervals
of the lunacy that closed gradually on his old age, he was able
to prevent Pitt from emancipating the Irish Catholics, and he   1801.
exerted a certain influence in the struggle for Cabinet office
between the groups and personages of Parliament.

The temporary revival of the group system in place of the
two-party system was indeed a feature of the period, which tended
to a certain limited extent to revive the influence of the Crown as
arbitrator.   The two-party system was no longer in full working
order, because the split in the Whig party over Reform and the
French Revolution reduced the Foxites to about a hundred
members, and left them for a generation without hope of power.
The hibernation of the Whig party between 1793 and 1830 may
be compared to the hibernation of the Tory party from 1714 to
1760, and it had the same result in the revival of a group system
on the floor of the House of Commons.   Just as the long weakness
of the Tories caused the Whigs to divide into Walpole and anti-
Walpole factions, so the Tories in the first year of the Nineteenth
Century broke up into Pittites, Addingtonians and Whig-Tory
followers of the Grenville family.   These groups, personal rather

than political in their differences, combined each in turn with the Foxite remnant to form the governments and oppositions of the remaining years of war.

In these circumstances, a certain power of selection rested with the old King, and, when his insanity was pronounced incurable, with the Regent Prince George. They both used it heavily against any combination that included the Foxite Whigs. Immediately after Pitt's death George III was, indeed, compelled to submit for a year to the coalition Ministry of ' All the Talents,' including the dying Fox, with the result that the slave trade was at last abolished. But the King managed speedily to rid himself of servants whom he so much disliked, and though the ground on which he dismissed them was indefensible, it was, perhaps, no real misfortune. For the Whig chiefs and their Grenvillite colleagues did not make good war Ministers. Ever since the camp at Boulogne the Foxites had, indeed, accepted the necessity of war with France, and their leader in his few months at the Foreign Office was converted on his death-bed to the view which he had so often denounced, that peace with Napoleon was impossible. Yet his successors in the Whig hierarchy, like Lords Holland and Grey, too easily despaired, and had neither the phlegm nor the *flair* necessary for those who conduct a long and doubtful war.[1]

The pure Tory groups combined after 1807 to govern the country and fight Napoleon through the agency of the House of Commons. The prestige of Waterloo and the final victory redounded most to the credit of the nation that had never submitted and always hoped. And, in the secure judgment of the world, the victory of the stubborn islanders was due, not to King or Regent, but to British Parliamentary institutions, to the British aristocracy, and to the steady character and rapidly increasing wealth of the British middle class.

Napoleon signalized his coronation as Emperor by conquering Eastern Europe up to the Russian border—a three years' task : each year there was

> another deadly blow !
> Another mighty Empire overthrown,

Austria at Austerlitz, Prussia at Jena, Russia at Friedland. The work was crowned in the summer of 1807 by the Treaty of Tilsit, made on a raft in the Niemen, where Napoleon embraced

---

[1] After a moment of first enthusiasm for the cause of the Spanish people risen against Napoleon, most of the Whigs took fright about the Peninsular War after Moore's retreat, and thought Wellington's campaigns there foredoomed to failure.

the Czar Alexander, an impressionable young man, destined to play many different parts in Europe's tragedy, each with the same conscientious solemnity as the last. For four years it flattered him to be Napoleon's ally and half-sharer in the rule of the continent. From the Urals to the Pyrenees the civilized world was banded against England, and closed to her shipping and her goods. But in that vast hostile camp she had many secret friends, whom it was the chief task of her statesmanship to rouse into mutiny. The prospect of British subsidies if they should take up arms, was one inducement offered ; while another and harsher was the deprivation of tea and coffee, sugar and cotton, so long as they remained French vassals.

England and France now organized the world-warfare of blockade and starvation, on a scale never before witnessed, because never in the history of war had there been sea-power like that of England after Trafalgar, or land-power like that of Napoleon after Tilsit. By Napoleon's Berlin and Milan Decrees, neutrals and French allies were forbidden to trade with Great Britain or her colonies. Britain replied by the Orders in Council, a series of measures of ever-increasing stringency, of which the general drift was that all Napoleonic Europe was subjected to blockade. *[1806, 1807.]* *[1807, 1812.]*

Of three sets of victims, which would rebel the first ? Napoleon's German vassals and Muscovite allies, deprived of their luxuries and comforts for his sake ? Or the United States, the one great neutral carrier, angry with England because her ships effectually barred the Yankee skippers from European ports, whereas Napoleon, having no submarines, could not by mere proclamation exclude them from trading with Britain ? Or, finally, as Napoleon had in 1811 some reason to hope, would the strain prove too much for the English middle and lower orders, whose business, employment and real wages were subject during these terrible years to the vagaries of war prices and war markets ?

In fact, by 1812, Russia had rebelled against Napoleon's decrees, and the United States against the British Orders in Council and the right of search as exercised by her captains. But the classes on the British ' home front ' who suffered from the war, stood firm. The mercantile community refused to submit to Napoleon, but strongly urged the Perceval Ministry to relax the Orders in Council enough to prevent war with our largest remaining customer, the United States. But the middle classes were still for the most part unenfranchised, and stood outside the close ring of the Tory governing class. Their advice was heeded too late and war broke out between England and America, causing great momentary suffering to Britain by commercial stoppage. But neither that nor the distraction of naval and military bickering on the Canadian frontier and along the American coast, proved fatal to Britain's victory in Europe, because in the same years Russia and Germany rebelled against France. The next generation of Englishmen forgot the American war as an unpleasant and unnecessary episode in the greater Napoleonic struggle ; but Americans remembered it only too well, as a patriotic landmark in their early growth as a nation. From the point of view of future Anglo-American relations, it was most unfortunate that the first foreign war of the young Republic should have been waged with the motherland, against whom also her War of Independence had been fought.

The Napoleonic struggle, though as dangerous at times to Britain as the Great War of our own day, affected the life of the community at fewer points ; above all it made a much smaller drain upon the manhood of the country. For a dozen years we

had practically no troops on the continent, except for very small and very occasional raids. The total death-roll in the whole twenty-two years was probably about 100,000, nearly half lost in the West Indies in Pitt's time and 40,000 more in the six years' fighting in the Peninsula. It was in economic suffering that England paid. The course of the Industrial Revolution, during two critical decades, was warped and diverted by the exigencies of the war.

But the economic suffering was by no means evenly divided among the whole people. The upper class throve on enhanced rents, and paid too small a proportion of the war taxes ; for revenue was raised largely by duties on articles of consumption, of which the effect was felt by the poor in the rise of prices. Pitt's useful new device of the income-tax, which was continued till the end of the war, did something, but not enough, to redress the balance. In 1815 twenty-five millions were raised by direct, and sixty-seven millions by indirect taxation. Those who enjoyed rent and tithe, composing a single governing class of the well-born, knew little of the hardships of war time.

It was, indeed, a notable period in the higher civilization of the island, where all through the war great landscape painters, poets and novelists were working for a large and eager class with the wealth and leisure to enjoy their works. Never was country-house life more thriving or jovial, with its fox-hunting, shooting, and leisure in spacious and well-stocked libraries. Never was sporting life more attractive, with its coaching on the newly Macadamized roads, and its boxing matches patronized by the nobility. In the mirror that Miss Austen held up to nature in the drawing-room, it is hard to detect any trace of concern or trouble arising from the war.

The middle classes suffered more. Many merchants, like poor old Mr. Sedley in *Vanity Fair*, were broken by the sudden opening and shutting of markets, or the rise and fall of war prices. But many also made their fortunes in new factories, and in commerce with the black and brown peoples of the world, whom England was learning to clothe, wholesale, as yet without a rival in that profitable business.

The chief sufferers by the war were the working classes, for whom little was done except the general adoption of the policy originated by the Berkshire magistrates at Speenhamland, or granting rates in aid of wages to prevent families from positively dying of starvation. But the better policy of an enforced minimum wage, though discussed, was unfortunately rejected as old-fashioned and unscientific. Meanwhile, Pitt's Act made Trade Unions illegal, so that the workmen found it difficult, in the face of hostile authority, to keep up wages in their proper relation to prices.

That sense of the brotherhood of classes in the Great War which was so marked in our own more democratic day, had no place in the Anti-Jacobin mentality. Wellington's remarks about the soldiers who won his battles, as ' the scum of the earth,' enlisted ' for drink,'[1] represent the common limitations of upper-class sympathy at that period, though Nelson and his coxswain's letter strike another note. Harshness often appeared, not only in the treatment of the much flogged soldiers and sailors, but in the attitude to Luddites and the ' labouring poor ' in general. While engaged in beating Napoleon, the authorities recognized a double duty in relation to starving men,—to keep them alive and to keep them in due subordination.

Napoleon's endeavour to enforce his ' continental system ' for excluding British goods from Europe,—his only available means of chastising the insolent islanders,—drew him into the two most fatal errors of his career, the attempt to annex Spain against the will of its people, and the invasion of the vastness of Russia. Those two acts let loose upon him the rising of the peoples, after he had dealt successfully with the Kings. The earlier and more criminal of these enterprises gave England the opportunity to commence the Peninsular War. Our operations there began very humbly in an attempt to maintain according to precedent the independence of our ancient ally, Portugal.

1808.
1812.

1808.

---

[1] We must do the Duke the justice of remembering that he added words not always quoted : ' it really is wonderful that we should have made them the fine fellows they are.'

Throughout the next six years Portugal continued to be the base, and sea-power the condition of the whole affair, as in the less lucky operations of the British armies in Spain during the Marlborough wars.

The Portuguese consented to be drilled and commanded by British officers, with the result that in this war they made very respectable troops of the line. The Spaniards, on the other hand, seldom made even tolerable regulars, but seldom failed to act with amazing efficiency in guerrilla warfare. The more primitive nature of Spanish character and society rendered the land which Napoleon had despised, more formidable to the armies of French occupation than any of the more civilized nations of modern Europe, upon which they had so long trampled. For this reason the 300,000 French in Spain were mostly engaged in guarding communications, and could never concentrate enough force to destroy the persistent British army of some 30,000 men under Moore or Wellington. Issuing from Portugal in well-planned raids across Spain, Wellington year after year carried off the

1809, 1812, 1813.

victory in an ascending scale of the decisive,—Talavera, Salamanca, Vitoria,—as Napoleon's increasing commitments in Russia and Germany gradually reduced the pressure of France upon the Peninsula. The military power and reputation of Britain, that had sunk so low at the beginning of the Revolutionary Wars, were raised to the height where they had stood under Cromwell and Marlborough. The Peninsular battles and sieges, recorded in such numbers on our flags, confirmed and perpetuated the regimental traditions which remained the true life of the British Army during the next hundred years.

The victories in Spain, though due largely to the previous work of the Duke of York and Sir John Moore in reforming the Army, and to Wellington's own strategical and tactical genius, were facilitated by the superiority of the British line over the French column. The history of that difference of formation is very curious. The dynastic wars of the Eighteenth Century, from Marlborough to Frederic the Great, had been fought in line, —three deep, reduced towards the end of the century to two. But this method of war, then universal in civilized armies, implied the perfect drill of highly professional troops. When, therefore, the first armies of the French Republic took the field with their high-spirited but ill-disciplined hosts straight from the counter and the plough, they could only be led into action in compact masses with a cloud of skirmishers flung out in front. But so great were their zeal and numbers, that in this crude formation they again and again chased off the field the well-ordered lines of the Austrian infantry. Thus defeated, the ancient monarchies of Europe imitated their conquerors by adopting their faulty tactics and formation, without the spirit that had been the true cause of the French successes. Only the British Army, guided by a combination of conservatism and good sense, continued to fight and manœuvre in line. On the rare occasions, therefore, when 1801, 1806. they had met the French in Egypt and in South Italy they had an advantage over them shared by no other nation. And now, in the more continuous campaigns of the Peninsula, again and again the narrow head of the French column was mowed down by the concentrated fire of the long red line. It is indeed remarkable that the greatest military genius of modern times never attempted to reform the retrogressive tactics of his infantry.

The Peninsular War was finally won because the French disasters in Russia and Germany continually reduced the number of their troops in Spain. Similarly, the decisive victory of our allies over Napoleon in person at Leipzig, was rendered possible 1813. by the number of French engaged by Wellington in the South. Early in 1814 France was entered by Wellington from across the Pyrences, and by the Austrians, Prussians and Russians across the Rhine. The final success had been rendered possible by the wisdom and energy of Castlereagh's diplomacy in mid-Europe in 1813–14, which held together the alliance of jealous Princes until the common object was attained.

The first fall of Napoleon was followed by his return from Elba, the rally of the veterans of the army to his standard, while the French people looked on with divided feelings. His Hundred Days' adventure ended at Waterloo. The fortunate June 18, 1815. brevity of this last war was due to the prompt and courageous action of the British Government in declaring war at once, and sending over Wellington to defend Holland and Belgium in alliance with Blucher and his Prussians, till the allied armies from the East could arrive in overwhelming numbers. The decisive character of the great battle put a sudden end to the war, because France was half-hearted in her desire that it should be renewed.

The reputation of Great Britain, as the most consistent and formidable antagonist of Napoleon, reached its height as a result of Waterloo. At the peace conference, Castlereagh and Wellington spoke with a voice of unrivalled authority among the Emperors and Kings. To the influence of these two Anglo-Irish aristocrats the merits of the Treaties of Vienna were largely due.

The most striking merit of the Settlement of 1815 lay in securing at the outset a long period of quiet for Europe by justice and even leniency to the conquered, a point on which Wellington and Castlereagh both insisted, with the aid of the Czar Alexander, against the very natural desire for vengeance on the part of

Blucher and the Germans and a large part of the British public. France,—with the Bourbons restored but the social arrangements of the Revolution left intact,—was allowed her old boundaries of 1792, was not compelled to give up Alsace or Lorraine, and received back from England most of her possessions in Africa and the two Indies seized during the war. The indemnity which she had to pay was fixed from the first at a moderate sum, and in three years her territory was completely evacuated by the allied armies. Revenge was eschewed, but security was gained by an alliance to prevent, in arms, the return of Napoleon, whom meanwhile the English kept out of harm's way on remote St. Helena.

The defect of the Settlement was that nationality and popular liberty were both disregarded on the continent, outside the boundaries of France herself. Except England, the Great Powers who had triumphed were Powers of reaction and despotism, and even Castlereagh cared nothing for Parliaments outside England. The rulers of Russia, Prussia and Austria divided up Poland, Germany and Italy as if inhabitants were so many head of population to be bartered among royal hagglers. The Temporal Power of the Pope over Central Italy was restored. The hopes of national and popular self-expression, which in Spain and Germany had partly inspired the late patriotic uprising against France, were crushed to the earth.

The merits of the Settlement of Vienna gave Europe forty years of peace. Its faults rendered war certain in the end,—war to assert national and popular aspirations which Metternich's system could not for ever keep in check. [1]

One of the points in the Treaties of 1815 in which Britain was specially interested was the restoration of the Anglophil House of Orange to Holland, and the addition of Belgium to their Kingdom of the Netherlands. The Delta of the Rhine was again in hands from which England had nothing to fear, but another sharp crisis was necessary fifteen years later, before a permanent settlement was reached by the separation of Belgium from Holland on a basis of two separate and independent States.

1830–
1831.

But the greatest interests of Britain lay beyond the ocean,

[1] Professor Webster, Castlereagh's distinguished biographer, writes : ' More worthy of reprobation is the discouragement of the idea of self-government, which had already come to a fuller consciousness than that of nationality. Alexander alone, with some of his advisers, showed any sympathy with it ; and it was he who secured the "Charte" for the French with the asistance of Talleyrand, who was also aware of the fundamental importance of this aspect of the French Revolution. To almost all the other statesmen democracy meant nothing but anarchy and revolution ; and among these must be included the Tory Ministers of Great Britain, who even secretly encouraged the attacks on the constitutions which had been set up with the direct connivance of British representatives. It was this policy that made the subsequent national movements take strange paths, instead of being an expression of the people's desires.'—*Congress of Vienna*, p. 147.

and there she was supreme arbiter.   It was for her alone to decide how many she would give back of the colonies which she had seized in the war.   On the whole she was not ungenerous in her restorations.   While keeping Ceylon and the Cape of Good Hope and Singapore, and purchasing a part of Guiana for three million pounds, Britain gave back to the Dutch their old possessions of Java and the other East Indian islands which have ever since remained the chief source of Holland's external wealth.   France and Denmark got back their most valuable islands.   But England kept Mauritius and Heligoland, and the Mediterranean vantage points of the Ionian Islands and Malta.   The network of British naval, maritime and commercial posts, soon to be used also as coaling stations, had already begun to spread over the globe. Australia, peacefully acquired by Captain Cook's voyages (1769–1775), was in process of colonization.   Upper Canada was filling with English and Scots.   A Second Empire was arising to replace that which had been lost, based like the first on sea-power, commerce and liberty.

BOOKS FOR FURTHER READING

    H. Rose, *Pitt and the Great War* and *Life of Napoleon* (2 vols.) ; Mahan, *Life of Nelson* (2 vols.) ; Corbett, *Campaign of Trafalgar* ; Sir H. Maxwell, *Wellington* ; Webster, *The Congress of Vienna* (No. 153, F.O. Handbook, H.M. Stationery Office) ; *Cam. Mod. Hist.*, Vols. VIII., IX. ; Albert Sorel, *L'Europe et la révolution française* (6 vols.).

CHAPTER VI

The Empire in the latter years of George III.   The outward expansion of the island life.   England, Scotland and Ireland.   Canada and Australia.   India.   The Anti-Slave-Trade Movement.   Wilberforce and the Evangelicals

NATURE had early decided that the inhabitants of Britain must be insular, but there are various kinds and degrees of insularity. After the Norman Conquest, the English had for several generations been to all appearance part of the feudal and Catholic world of French civilization.   Then, by a gradual process in the later Middle Ages, culminating in the Tudor revolution, they had asserted an island individuality in law and government, religion and culture, character and habits of life.   They had, in Elizabeth's words about herself, become ' mere English,' repelling the invading influences of the continent.   But as their native strength and self-confidence increased they had become every year more active beyond the seas, in that new way ceasing to be 'insular.' They appeared in every quarter of the newly discovered globe, bringing with them English ideas and standards that had come to maturity at home.

In the era of Waterloo the life of the islanders was being constantly enriched and broadened by their activities as explorers, traders, warriors and rulers in all parts of the world, both in the lands of the ever-growing British Empire, and in countries like China and South America, where the British had become the characteristic representatives of European trade and influence. The Industrial Revolution had given fresh speed and vigour to the outward expansion of English life which had been going on ever since the days of Elizabeth. The reign of George III saw, in consequence, the emergence of a number of Imperial problems of a new order, connected with Ireland, Canada, Australia, India, and the relations of the white man to the African negro. In all these the younger Pitt played a leading part.

One source of anxiety, indeed, had been removed. The relations of England and Scotland no longer formed an Imperial problem of grave difficulty, but a domestic bond of singular felicity. The Union of the two States, after a period of uneasy working, had been adjusted by time and patience. The decease of Jacobitism, the measures taken after 1745 to abolish feudalism and tribalism in Scotland, and her ever-increasing wealth since that crisis had been adjusted, led to the better appreciation in England of the Scottish qualities. 'Sir Walter's' Scottish romances, and the kilted regiments who fought so well at Waterloo, seemed to Englishmen and to the whole civilized world to represent something new added to the island tradition and power. The mutual acceptance of each other by the two peoples has remained ever since one of the chief pillars of the British State.

The era of Burns and Scott was one of expansion, new prosperity and noble pride for their countrymen, upon the whole the happiest since first they were a nation. They had, indeed, internal difficulties, but since these were of the same general character as contemporary difficulties in England, they served to unite the two ends of the island in a common *malaise*. The social and economic problems attendant on the Industrial Revolution were aggravated by antiquated political institutions in both countries, by rotten boroughs and an absence of efficient municipal and local bodies suited to the new age. In Scotland, where even County elections were a farce, the political machinery was more out of touch with modern facts than even in England, and the spirit of Anti-Jacobin repression was more severe, while the democratic spirit was more fierce. The trouble bade fair some day to be worse in Scotland than in England. But in the coming era the process of political reform and social amelioration followed the same course in both countries, tending still further to unite their fortunes in one.

While Scotland was ceasing to be regarded at Downing Street as a problem, the Irish question, after a long period of quiescence, was entering upon a new phase of virulent activity, which continued to disturb the British Empire at frequent intervals until the great events of our own day.

During the early and middle Eighteenth Century, while Jacobite Scotland had been a source of trouble and danger, the native Irish had given no sign of lifting their heads. Ever since the days of Sarsfield, the active rebels, the 'wild geese' of Irish Jacobite tradition, were serving in French armies, and had the pleasure of shooting Englishmen only on occasions like Fontenoy. The island itself, twice conquered by Cromwell and by William, lay quiet under British and Protestant ascendancy, and under the iniquitous and partially enforced Penal Laws against Catholics.

In the last thirty years of the Century the old bones in that valley of desolation began to stir under the reviving winds of a new age. In the first instance the initiative was not Catholic and Celtic, but Protestant and Liberal. It was a movement partly of Ulster Presbyterians, partly of broad-minded statesmen like Grattan, against a system of tyranny that sacrificed Ireland as a whole to English trading interests, and all other Irish denominations to Anglican ascendancy. In this generous mood many Protestants forgot their grandfathers' fears of the native Catholics, who since the Century began had done nothing more dangerous than endure wrong.

During the War of American Independence, Ireland fell into the hands of the Volunteers, who were Protestants, but the 1778– movement was supported by Catholic opinion. The Volunteers 1782. were prepared to defend the island against the French invader, but they dictated their terms to the government of England,— the abolition of Ireland's commercial disabilities, and the formal independence of her Parliament from British control. Ireland secured free markets for her goods, but her political autonomy during the next two decades was more apparent than real. For 1782– Catholics were still allowed no part or lot in the Dublin Parlia- 1801. ment, and the oligarchy in Dublin Castle manipulated the rotten boroughs so that a Reform Bill would clearly be necessary before even Protestant Ireland could practise self-government.

But there was hope in the new era. The worst of the Penal Laws were repealed. Reform was in the air, under the leadership of Grattan, who hoped to reconcile races and creeds by a gradual process of evolution. Catholic and Protestant fanaticism were both dormant. The best spirit of Eighteenth Century toleration and latitudinarianism was still widely prevalent. If British statesmen had met Grattan half way in his own spirit, much might have been done. But the spirit of Jacobinism and Anti-Jacobinism, of neo-Catholicism and Orangeism, arrived too soon upon the scene and destroyed the generous opportunity created by the time-spirit of the Eighteenth Century. The Tories in England had taken over as their own electoral speciality the old Whig cry of No-Popery, while at the same time the French Revolution made them adamant against all change. The liberal-minded but incautious Viceroy, Lord Fitzwilliam, was recalled
1795. from Dublin, after he had kindled hopes that Pitt was unable to fulfil. His recall put an end to any further attempt to gain Ireland's support for the war against France by a policy of conciliation to Catholics. When, therefore, the French military propagandists offered Republican liberty to Ireland, their aid was accepted by the leaders of the United Irishmen, Wolfe Tone and Lord Edward Fitzgerald, converts from the English garrison. These men hoped to unite the religions of Ireland in arms against England. But the actual effect of their reliance on French aid was to set Protestant and Catholic to kill each other in the old spirit of the Williamite wars. For, great as were the wrongs of the Ulster Scots and Presbyterians against the English Government, they could not join the French to set up a Celtic Republic, dominated by priests. The Rebellion of 1798 was put down by a combination of the hard-pressed British Government with the loyalists of Ireland, now reconverted to the anti-Catholic fears of their ancestors, and beginning to organize themselves in the new 'Orange' lodges. The military and political weakness of England at that critical moment made her dependent to a dangerous degree on the help of local partisans who in their panic treated the native Irish with cruel rigour. The memories of 'ninety-eight' became an heirloom of hatred, cherished in every cottage, and exploited by successive generations of patriots and agitators.

In these circumstances Pitt decided that the Union of the
Jan. 1, 1801. two islands in one Parliament at Westminster was the only method of permanently restoring order and justice. But he was able to restore only order. He had not the political authority to pass Catholic Emancipation, which he had designed to accompany the Union and render it palatable to the Celtic Irish.

FROM THE UNION TO EMANCIPATION

That hope, and an orgy of Parliamentary corruption in Dub1801–1829.had just sufficed to carry the Union. But Pitt's royal mast
many of his colleagues, his party and the majority of his countr
men feared the consequences of giving political rights to Roman
Catholics either in Ireland or in England. The two most active
forces of the day, Anti-Jacobinism and Evangelicalism, were at
one on that score. For twenty-eight years Roman Catholics
were prohibited from sitting in the United Parliament of Great
Britain and Ireland.

So the Catholic Celts were again thrust down, this time with
the whole weight of England on the top of them, and with their
fellow-Irish of the North waxing in Orange enthusiasm. The two
Irelands were once more face to face, fighting the Boyne battle
again daily with their mouths. Moreover, the land question was
beginning to take a foremost place in politics, in that over-
populated, potato-fed island of oppressed tenant-farmers.[1] In
these circumstances, a new and formidable amalgamation of
clericalism, nationalism and uneducated democracy began to be
organized by the popular oratory of the Catholic lawyer, Daniel
O'Connell.

The last years of George II's reign had witnessed the conquest
of French Canada in war. The long reign of George III saw the
reconciliation of the French Canadians to their place within the
British Empire. This was effected by complete toleration of
their religion, rights and customs, in striking contrast to the
policy of Protestant and English 'ascendancy' during the same
years in Ireland. George III's reign also saw the settlement
of English and Scottish colonists in Upper Canada on the shores
of the Great Lakes, and to a less degree in the coast colonies
of New Brunswick and Nova Scotia. The newcomers were
many of them 'United Kingdom Loyalists,' that is to say,
refugees from the intolerance and injustice of the victorious Republicans of the United States, who after the War of Independence
expelled their late political opponents from the country. The
other element in the British colonization of Canada was the
economic exodus from the homeland. This movement reached
vast proportions in the early years of the Nineteenth Century,
owing to the rapid increase of population in Great Britain, which
in spite of these emigrations rose from about seven and a half
millions when George III ascended the throne, to over fourteen
millions when he died

[1] By 1821 the Irish in Ireland had increased to the total of 6,803,000, and
added yet another million in the next ten years. Great Britain held only about
twice as many inhabitants at the corresponding dates.

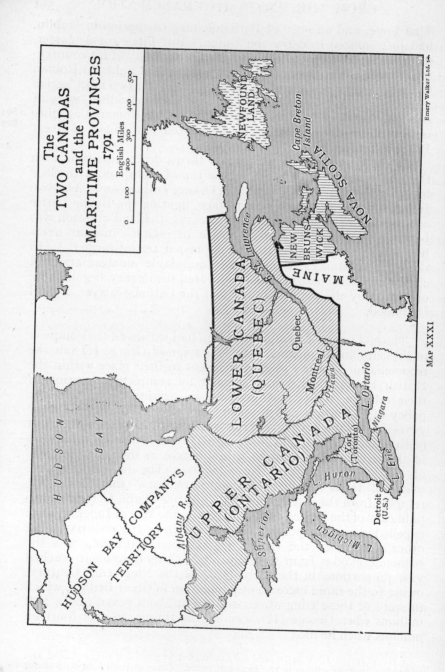

The
TWO CANADAS
and the
MARITIME PROVINCES
1791

English Miles

0   100   200   300   400   500

Emery Walker Ltd. sc.

NEWFOUND LAND

Cape Breton Island

NOVA SCOTIA

NEW BRUNS WICK

MAINE

St. Lawrence

LOWER CANADA
(QUEBEC)

Quebec

Montreal

R. Ottawa

L. Ontario

Niagara

York (Toronto)

L. Erie

L. Huron

HUDSON BAY

HUDSON BAY COMPANY'S TERRITORY

Albany R.

UPPER CANADA
(ONTARIO)

L. Superior

Detroit (U.S.)

L. Michigan

MAP XXXI

The arrival of large numbers of men and women of British stock in Canada complicated the task of governing the French there in accordance with their own very different customs and ideals. The newcomers at once demanded self-government, to which they had been accustomed in the lost English colonies, and to a less degree in England herself. But the French peasants had no use for self-government. Their seigneurs had largely returned to France after the British conquest, but they trusted to their priests, and feared that the heretic strangers would make alterations in their laws. Fortunately, a good beginning had already been made by government in winning the confidence of the French before the arrival of the United Kingdom Loyalists. Lord North's Quebec Act of 1774 and Sir Guy Carleton's wise and liberal governorship of Canada had already given them a sense of security in their rights as they understood them.

The next stage was reached when Pitt boldly and success- 1791. fully faced the complicated problem created by the juxtaposition of the two races in Canada. He determined to solve it on geographic lines, separating Upper from Lower Canada, the older district to enjoy French law and custom, the newer settlements of the Lakes to be no less completely British in their institutions. Each of the two provinces was to have its own elected assembly, not indeed with full ' responsible ' government or the right of naming Ministers, but with powers of taxation and law-making, and a fixed relation to the Governor and his executive not unlike that of an Elizabethan Parliament to the Crown. The arrangement met the needs of the time in Canada, as fully as the grant of ' responsible ' government, made fifty years later on Durham's advice, met them for the later age.   In the interval, the French were initiated into the mystery of representative assemblies, and the British population flourished and rose in the half century from 10,000 to 400,000 souls. English and 1790– Scottish immigration up the St. Lawrence largely accounted for 1840. this astonishing increase in a land where the backwoodsman had to prepare each step of the way.

The period that witnessed the plantation and early growth of British Canada, saw the same process in Australia. The occasion and method of the first settlements were different in the two cases, but the general character of the colonizing movement was much the same. Canada had been won by war, and the French were there before us to open the land to later immigrants. Australia, discovered but neglected by the Dutch in the Seventeenth Century, was still empty of men, save for a few Aborigines, when Captain Cook of the Royal Navy explored its 1769– coasts and brought it to the notice of British statesmen and 1775.

1786–
1787.

public. The first settlement was made by order of Pitt and his Home Secretary, Lord Sydney, not with a view to founding a new Empire in the Antipodes, but merely to find a new place for the deportation of convicts, since the old American colonies were now closed for that purpose by their secession. But the convict settlements and the troops that guarded them afforded a convenient base and a method of communication with distant England, very necessary for the first stages of free colonization that speedily followed. Men went to Australia for the same economic reasons which sent them to Canada. By the time of Waterloo the capitalist sheep and cattle farmers, known as ' squatters,' had already begun to create the Australia that we know.

The reign of George II had witnessed the destruction of the French power in India by Clive, and his conquest of Bengal as the first great continental area of British rule in the peninsula. Its acquisition converted the East India Company from an armed trading corporation into an Asiatic Power. The logic of the change was worked out in the reign of George III by Warren Hastings, Cornwallis and Wellesley in India, and by Pitt at home.

1757–
1805.

The design of the French to erect an Empire of their own in Hindoostan had been thwarted by Clive, but for fifty years after Plassey Frenchmen continued to be a thorn in the British side, stirring up Indian Courts and officering Indian armies, first against Hastings and then against Wellesey. In so doing, they hastened the pace at which the British power was forced to advance across the peninsula.

1772–
1785.

During the War of American Independence, Warren Hastings was left with very inadequate means to struggle against these external dangers, and at the same time to maintain his internal authority against the faction in his own Council led by his personal enemy, Philip Francis. He saved British rule in India in spite of all, but not without making the kind of mistakes which a strong man is likely to make in difficult emergencies. For these acts, much exaggerated and misconstrued by the malignity of Francis and the imagination of Burke, Fox and Sheridan, he was impeached in Westminster Hall. Those famous

1788–
1795.

proceedings, substantially unjust to Hastings even though they resulted in his acquittal, had the advantage of bringing Indian problems and responsibilities forcibly to the notice of British statesmen and the British public. Burke preached the right ideal of our obligations to the Indians, but misunderstood the relation of Hastings' governorship to the problem.

Pitt, meanwhile, after denouncing and destroying a very

similar but rather bolder Bill introduced by Fox, had by his
own India Act established the practical control of the British **1784.**
Cabinet over the administrative work of the East India Company,
while leaving its commercial monopoly intact.   At the same time
Pitt's Bill relieved the Governor General at Calcutta from the
tutelage of his Council, which became advisory only.   Such scenes
as those between Francis and Hastings were never to occur again
at the Council Board.   The Governor-General was made an autocrat in a land that only understood autocracy, but was himself
subject to the ultimate control of the Home Government through
the Board of Control under a President of Cabinet rank.   Pitt's
Indian legislation served India until the time of the Mutiny, as
satisfactorily as his Canadian legislation served Canada until the
time of Lord Durham.

Pitt had also the merit of sending out the right men to wield
as Governor-General these tremendous powers.   Lord Cornwallis
completed the internal work of Hastings, and fixed the taxation **1786–**
and government of Bengal on a system that became the model **1793.**
for all provinces subsequently administered by the British.
Indians began to find that under the British flag, and there alone,
was to be found security from warlike invasion, and from the
grosser forms of domestic oppression.   Upon that was based
both the permanence and the justification of the British raj.
The plunder and misrule that had accompanied our first conquest
of Bengal in spite of Clive's efforts to stem the passions of his
countrymen, could never be repeated under the new system and
under the influence of the new spirit.   The high traditions of the
'Anglo-Indian families' began to be formed ;   many of them
were Scottish, for Pitt's friend, Henry Dundas, cannily combined
his political jobbery beyond the Border with sending out excellent
young Scots to India.

If Cornwallis did most to justify the British power internally,
Lord Wellesley, the elder brother of Wellington, did most to **1798–**
expand it and to justify its expansion.   He broke the power of **1805.**
the fighting Mahomedan ruler, 'Tippoo Sahib' of Mysore, and
of the great Maratha Confederacy of Central India, whose horsemen had so long attacked and threatened all the neighbouring
States.   The Confederacy had recently, with the help of French
officers, armed and trained its forces after the European manner.
In effect it was the policy of Wellesley as Governor-General to
extend the protection of Britain over a number of Indian States,
such as Hyderabad, thereby stepping into the place of the deceased Mogul Empire as arbiter and keeper of the peace in the
whole peninsula.   The implications of this policy, which could
in the end have no geographic boundary save the Himalayas

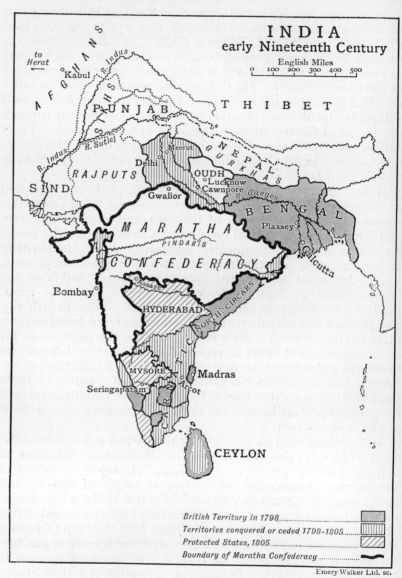

INDIA
early Nineteenth Century

English Miles

0   100   200   300   400   500

to
Herat

° Kabul

A F G H A N S

R. Indus

R. Indus

P U N J A B

T H I B E T

R. Sutlej

R. Indus

° Meerut

Delhi °

R A J P U T S

S I N D

N E P A L

G U R K H A S

O U D H
° Lucknow
° Cawnpore

R. Ganges

° Gwalior

M A R A T H A

B E N G A L

° Plassey

P I N D A R I S

C O N F E D E R A C Y

° Calcutta

Bombay °

° Assaye

H Y D E R A B A D

N O R T H E R N   C I R C A R S

M Y S O R E

C A R N A T I C

Madras °

Seringapatam °

° Arcot

C E Y L O N

British Territory in 1798 ....
Territories conquered or ceded 1798–1805 ......
Protected States, 1805 ....
Boundary of Maratha Confederacy ....

Emery Walker Ltd. sc.

MAP XXXII.

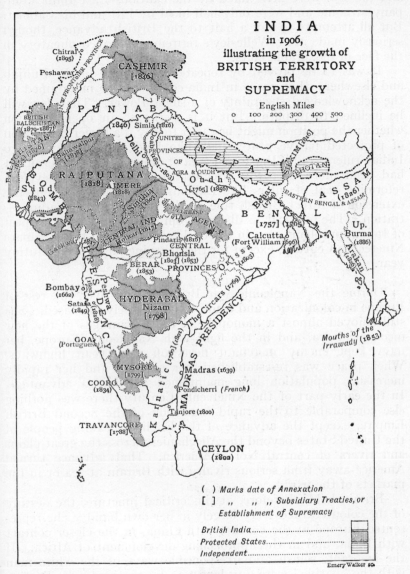

INDIA
in 1906,
illustrating the growth of
BRITISH TERRITORY
and
SUPREMACY

English Miles

0   100   200   300   400   500

Chitral○
(1895)

Peshawar○

CASHMIR
[1846]

N.W FRONTIER PROVINCE

P U N J A B
(1846) Simla (1816)

BRITISH
BALUCHISTAN
(1879-1887)

BALUCHISTAN
(1876)

Khairpur
(1832)

Bahawalpur
[1838]

Peshawar
(1849)

Delhi
(1803)

UNITED
PROVINCES
OF
AGRA & OUDH
(1801-1803)

N E P A L

SIKKIM (1816)

Oudh
[1765] [1856]

BHOTAN

A S S A M
(1826)

EASTERN BENGAL & ASSAM

RAJPUTANA
[1818]
AJMERE
(1818)

Sindhia
(1803)

Behar
(1765)

S I N D
(1843)

CENTRAL IND
Holkar (1817)

ALWAR [1803]

BERAR
(1853)

CENTRAL INDIA
AGENCY

Pindaris (1816)

B E N G A L
[1757] (1765)

Gaekwar (1817)

PRESIDENCY

CENTRAL
Bhonsla
[1803] (1853)
PROVINCES

Calcutta○
(Fort William 1696)

Assam
(1763)

Up.
Burma
(1886)

Bombay○
(1662)
Satara
(1849)

Peshwa (1802)

HYDERABAD
Nizam
[1798]

The Circars [1766] (1800)

Mouths of the
Irrawady (1853)

GOA
(Portuguese)

MADRAS PRESIDENCY

MYSORE
[1799]

Madras (1639)

COORG
(1834)

Karnatic [1763] (1801)

Pondicherri (French)

Tanjore (1800)

TRAVANCORE
[1788]

CEYLON
(1802)

( ) *Marks date of Annexation*

[ ] ,, ,, ,, *Subsidiary Treaties, or*
  Establishment of Supremacy

British India.......................................

Protected States..................................

Independent.......................................

Emery Walker sc.

MAP XXXIII.

and the sea, were little liked by the cautious East India Company at home and were only half liked by Pitt and his Cabinet. But all attempts to call a halt to the British advance, though seriously made after Wellesley's retirement, proved nugatory in the face of inexorable facts.

It was to be proved by repeated experience in the Punjab and elsewhere, that peace in India could only be maintained by the acknowledged suzerainty of a single Power. That, few will be inclined to dispute. But it is, perhaps, an open question whether the position might be easier to-day if a larger proportion of protected native States had, like Hyderabad, been left to Indian rulers, and if the actual area of direct British government had been more narrowly circumscribed. But the benevolent reforming zeal of rulers like Dalhousie made them favour the extension of direct British rule as the means of good administration. The political, as distinct from the administrative aspect of Indian problems, was in the background during the fortunate Nineteenth Century, except for the lightning flash of the Mutiny year.

1857.

During the Napoleonic war Britain's lead over the rest of Europe in colonization and trade was immensely increased. She still enjoyed almost a monopoly of the advantages of the new mechanical era, and in the fight with Napoleonic Europe, her navy kept enemy merchant fleets off the ocean highways. When peace was re-established, her energies and her rapidly increasing population long maintained the initial advantage. In the early part of the Nineteenth Century there was nothing else comparable to the rapid expansion of the Second British Empire, except the advance of the English-speaking people of the United States beyond the Alleghanies, across the great plains and rivers of central North America. That advance turned America away from serious rivalry with Britain at sea or in the markets of the world.

Britain held, therefore, at this critical juncture, the destiny of the coloured races very largely in her own hand. She represented Europe in the contact with China, in the closer contact with India, and in the approaching development of Africa. If the ignorant, selfish and irresponsible ways of the white man with the 'native' were any longer to be continued, civilization was heading fast for disaster. Could either the conscience or the good sense of England be aroused in time? In India, as we have seen, the process had begun by the growth of the fine traditions of Anglo-Indian rule, among soldiers and civil servants devoted not to personal gain but to government as a means of peace and

welfare for millions.   In Africa the first business was to stop
the slave trade and slavery, before the relation of white and
black could be anything but a mutual curse.

It was a turning-point in the history of the world when
William Wilberforce and his friends succeeded in arousing the
conscience of the British people to stop the slave trade in 1807,
and to abolish slavery in the Empire in 1833, just before the
development of the interior of Africa by the European races began.
If slavery and the slave trade had continued through the Nineteenth Century, armed with the new weapons of the Industrial
Revolution and of modern science, the tropics would have become
a vast slave farm for white exploitation, and the European races
in their own homes would have been degraded by the diseases
of slave-civilization of which the old Roman Empire had died.

Fortunately, when Wilberforce attacked the slave trade, it
was still confined to a traffic carried on by British skippers
crimping negroes along the African coast for the horrors of the
Atlantic passage.   The interior of the Dark Continent was still
closed to Europeans.   And the maritime predominance of England
was such that no power would seriously dispute her determination
that the slave trade should stop, if she once made up her own mind.
If Wilberforce could convert England, she would soon persuade
the world.

The method by which this conversion was effected, in itself
constituted a new epoch in British public life.   The anti-slave
trade movement was the first successful propagandist agitation
of the modern type, and its methods were afterwards imitated by
the myriad societies and leagues—political, religious, philanthropic and cultural—which characterized Nineteenth Century
England.   Originally promoted by the Society of Friends, who
never did a greater service to humanity, the slave trade question
was taken up by philanthropists like Sharp and Clarkson, by
Wilberforce the ‘ converted ’ man of fashion, and by Zachary
Macaulay whose eminently Scottish qualities put a stiffening
into the fibre of English Evangelicalism.   Many of the workers
in the cause were either Quakers or Evangelicals, inspired by
the practical religious zeal of so many of the Protestant laity
of that period.   This gave them an easier route to the heart of
many of their countrymen, especially the Dissenters, than if they
had appealed on grounds solely of humanity or in furtherance of
scientific plans for the future of the Empire.   But they had a
formidable ally in the non-religious humanitarianism of the new
age, in veterans like Fox and young men like Brougham, whose
zeal for the slaves waxed in opposition, while the cares of office
sprang up and choked Pitt’s first generous zeal.

The conversion of the country, begun just before the French Revolution, was carried on under difficulties during the Anti-Jacobin reaction, when the slave trade abolitionists were denounced as 'Reformers' tampering with the vested interests of Bristol and Liverpool merchants under the Leveller's plea—humanity. But after a period of depression the cause rallied, and by the Act of 1807 triumphantly put down the slave trade. The triumph was all the more remarkable for being won in the middle of the Great War, and in the middle of a period when no other agitation was permitted. In spite of much corruption in public institutions, the spirit of the British body politic was free, healthy and capable of response, as compared to any other public opinion then existing in the world. Wilberforce, the cross-bench member for Yorkshire, had found a new and nobler use for the political machinery of England.

1815.

1809–1812.

And so, at the time of the Treaties of Vienna, Castlereagh was both able and willing to induce the Powers of Europe to subscribe to the suppression of the slave trade as the rule of the sea in the new era. The Union Jack had become, by a dramatic change, specially associated with the freedom of the black man.

By this time Evangelicalism had made a strong lodgement inside the Tory party. One Prime Minister, Perceval, had been an Evangelical. Many Tories of the old school disliked the 'Clapham sect' as they were called,—for their friendship with Dissenters, their too insistent interest in their own and other people's souls, their want of appreciation of the spirit of cakes and ale, their frequent unreadiness to play the party game owing to some scruple of humanity or conscience. This duality inside the Tory fold, and a corresponding rivalry in the religious world of the hearty or fox-hunting churchman and his more serious Evangelical brother, though they caused heartburning, were signs of life. Such differences of aim helped to keep the party and the Church in some touch with outside forces in the nation, during the years after the war when the limitations of the old Toryism and of the old Establishment began to be painfully visible. Evangelicalism and humanitarianism—often though not always allied—were forces of the new age that worked upon British affairs athwart the lines of party divisions, and gave a new reality to public and Parliamentary life.

BOOKS FOR FURTHER READING

Lecky, *Leaders of Public Opinion in Ireland*, and *History of Ireland in the Eighteenth Century* (5 vols.) ; Stephen Gwynn, *History of Ireland* ; Lyall, *British Dominion in India* ; Professor Coupland, *Wilberforce*.

For the Dominions and Colonies there are two excellent series, Wyatt Tilby's *The British People Overseas*, and the more detailed *Historical Geography of the British Empire*, edited by Sir Charles Lucas.

CHAPTER VII

The reign of George III in its economic aspect. The early stages of
the Industrial Revolution. Population. Canals. Machinery. Coal.
The movement of industry from the village to the town. Enclosure.
Housing. Administrative defects. *Laissez-faire*

King : George III, 1760–1820

THE great changes in man's command over nature and consequent
manner of life, which began in England in the reign of George III
and have since spread with varying degrees of intensity over
almost the whole inhabited globe, make bewildering work for
the historian. Up to the Industrial Revolution, economic and
social change, though continuous, has the pace of a slowly-
moving stream ; but in the days of Watt and Stephenson it has
acquired the momentum of water over a mill-dam, distracting
to the eye of the spectator. Nor, for all its hurry, does it ever
reach any pool at the bottom and resume its former leisurely
advance. It is a cataract still. The French Revolution occupied
a dozen years at most, but the Industrial Revolution may yet
continue for as many hundred, creating and obliterating one form
of economic and social life after another, so that the historian can
never say—' This or this is the normal state of modern England.'
To speak, for example, in terms of traffic. Four successive
civilizations of the riding track, the canal and coach road, the
railway, and the motor have been superimposed one on the other
in the course of a hundred and sixty years.

Want of statistical and economic information lightens the
work of the historian of earlier times, while setting limits to the
scope and certainty of his deductions. The age of Blue-books
begins with the Nineteenth Century. The first census of Great
Britain was taken in 1801. Our economic information, in fact,
only becomes trustworthy in the middle of the first phase of the
Industrial Revolution. We have, therefore, very slender means
of estimating the material welfare of the majority of Englishmen
before the latter years of George III. Then, indeed, the picture
which economic historians present to us of England in the time
of Cobbett, is in some important respects very unpleasant ; but
as it is the first ' close-up ' in the cinema show of English social
history, we are unable to say whether an equally hard and precise
vision of any earlier period would be any less unpleasant to our
modern susceptibilities. Candid persons will refrain from answering the question with any approach to dogmatism.

It is possible, of course, to prefer the rural to the city life, and
to regret that the farmer and artificer have been so generally

replaced by the minder of machines ; it is possible also to hold exactly the opposite view. We must indeed all of us deplore the loss of beauty of shape and variety of surface in machine-made articles, and the landscape marred by industrialism, which have so largely deprived us of the purest æsthetic pleasures formerly common to rich and poor alike. But in no case must we imagine that Great Britain could, without modern machinery, have supported forty-two millions in 1921 at a standard of material comfort as high as that which then obtained ; or even fourteen millions in 1821 at the miserably inadequate standard, as we now hold it, of that day. What precisely was the average standard of life among the six or seven millions in 1721, is a question on which experts differ in opinion, because statistical knowledge about that early date is fragmentary or non-existent. As to the extent of true happiness and moral welfare then as compared to now, we are still more in the dark. But the interest of the enquiry loses nothing by want of certainty and finality in the answer.

The most striking accompaniment of the revolution in machinery and organization was the rise in the number of inhabitants of Great Britain in the single reign of George III, from about seven and a half to above fourteen millions. But what precise relation as cause or effect this increase had to the industrial and agricultural changes of the time, is a question not easily answered. Certain explanations, till recently accepted, now appear doubtful. It must be remembered that a similarly unprecedented rise in population was taking place in Celtic Ireland during the same years, and in Celtic Ireland there was no Industrial Revolution at all. Neither is it safe to set down the rise in population to the ' Speenhamland ' system of aiding wages out of rates, at so much per child ; for that system only began in 1795, became fully operative a good deal later, and never obtained at all in Scotland, North England or Ireland, where the rise in population was just as rapid as in the ' Speenhamland ' counties of the Midlands and South. Moreover from 1790 onwards the birth-rate slightly declined, although the population continued to multiply owing to the far more rapid fall in the death-rate.

The unexampled rise in population from 1760 onwards was due, not so much to earlier marriages and an increase in the crude birth-rate, though these had a considerable part in the affair before 1790, as to the saving of life by improvements in medical science and practice, and to an improved standard of living which may to some extent be attributed to cheap goods produced by the new mechanical inventions. The disappearance of the Plague so long endemic in the island ; the control of the ravages of scurvy and ultimately of small-pox ; the reduction of ague and fever by the draining of the land ; the advance of habits of cleanliness and the use of cheap cotton shirts ; improvements in sanitation in London and elsewhere as compared to the past, however appalling the age of Howard appears to our nice senses to-day ; and above all else, more and better hospitals and better medical care of mothers and infants which greatly reduced mortality at child-birth or by 'convulsions,' rickets and other infantile diseases,—all these were features of the Eighteenth and early Nineteenth Centuries.[1]

It is not impossible that until the very eve of the Twentieth Century the crude birth-rate has varied very little down the ages, and that the modern increase of population was due to the more successful efforts of society 'officiously to keep alive.' At the end of George III's reign the French death-rate was twenty per cent. higher than the English. With all its faults, the later Eighteenth Century in England was a period of improved science, cleanliness and humanity. The patriotic pride of the historians of the Victorian era, like Macaulay, in the perpetual progress of the nation in its social life and comfort is perhaps after all no further removed from the whole truth than the more recent view that the Industrial Revolution was accompanied by a general throw-back to harder conditions of life. Vital statistics are not everything, but so far as they go they are not unfavourable to the more optimistic doctrine of the older school.[2]

But if these causes, and others at present obscure, produced an increase in population wholly unexampled in history, it is certain that the additional millions could not have been maintained in the island, or even provided for in the colonies, had it not been for the agricultural and industrial changes of the new era. Indeed, if the old economic system had continued unchanged after 1760, it is doubtful whether the existing seven millions could have continued much longer to inhabit the island in the same degree of comfort as before. The depletion of British timber was already producing a fuel famine that left many domestic hearths cold, and was driving the iron industry across the sea to the still virgin forests of America and Scandinavia. At that moment the situation was saved by the new canal system,

---

[1] See the important work just issued (1926) by the Cambridge Press, *Population Problems of the Age of Malthus*, by S. Talbot Griffith. See also Mrs. George's *London in the Eighteenth Century*, pp. 1–61.

[2] In Ireland improvement in health conditions was less operative than in England, though not totally wanting. The increase in Irish population was due largely to the absence of potato famine in the Eighteenth Century. The potato blight of 1846–7 initiated a rapid reduction of the population from over eight millions to under five millions by stimulating emigration to America. The potato is the easiest method of supporting life at a very low standard,—until a year comes when the crop completely fails.

which brought coal to domestic hearths in inland regions of South England, and to the furnaces of the Black Country.

The way for the Industrial Revolution was prepared by the first rapid improvement in methods of transport since the Roman era.[1] From the beginning of the reign of George III, a network of canals was gradually extended over many districts, bringing to them benefits which London had always enjoyed from her maritime position and sea-borne coal. Canals were eventually made in all parts of the island, but those which paid dividends over ten per cent. were nearly all in the mining and industrial districts of the North and Midlands, or served to connect those districts with the Thames Valley. For the system of 'inland navigation,' as it was called,[2] no less than the modern merchant navy, throve by reason of the coal trade. Railways, when they came in their turn, were originally devised to serve the distribution of coal, and to link up the gaps in the canal system. But early in the days of George Stephenson it was clear to the foreseeing that the age of canals would be short in England.

b. 1781,
d. 1848.

Short, too, for the same reason was the glory of the hard 'Macadamized' road, with its Tally-ho coaches and post-chaise postilions speeding along at twelve miles an hour from the courtyards of the great London inns to Bath, or Holyhead, or York, or Gretna Green, and on over Sir Walter's Scotland. Like the contemporary canals, the hard roads were the work chiefly of capitalist companies, who recouped themselves from passengers at the toll-bars. But the movement was aided by the Post Office, one of the first Departments to conceive the modern idea of the duty of the Civil Service to the public. The gay and rapid life of the English road reached perfection only during the Napoleonic wars, and twenty years later the railways already clearly foreshadowed the end. Brief, but characteristically English while it lasted, was that age of the all-worshipped horse, with Horncastle Fair for its Mecca, with fox-hunters, stage-coachmen and jockeys as ministers to the national enthusiasm for the noblest of animals. Posterity still fondly regards that generation as the last of 'merrie England,'—except when it remembers that it was also the era of Peterloo and the very worst period of the 'evils' of the Industrial Revolution.

Indeed, when we picture the past to ourselves, it is not easy always to remember the great variety of things old and new that go on side by side in separate compartments in the life of a growing nation. We sometimes think of the factory system as the leading

[1] See pp. 45–6, above.
[2] Hence, the hosts of labourers who dug them were called 'navigators' or 'navvies.'

feature of the last years of George III. But though it was the new feature and had the future with it, it by no means as yet dominated the scene except in one or two districts. The cotton trade of Lancashire had indeed sprung into sudden being, first in small ' mills ' planted beside the water power of the Pennine streams, then with more elaborate machinery and on a larger scale in the plain below. And there had been a corresponding development of Liverpool, as the port for this new industry which bought all its raw material in America and sold most of its finished goods oversea. But when Peterloo was fought, not a 1819. twentieth part of the families of England had a member in the cotton industry. Agriculture was by far the largest occupation, and next came the building trades and domestic service ; the weaving of wool had not yet passed into the factory, though the spinning-jenny had already destroyed the cottage industry of many industrious wives and children of the peasant class ; tailoring and shoemaking, that figured among the very largest trades in the country, were still conducted on the domestic basis ; and the number of persons engaged in the service of horses must have been immense.

The Industrial Revolution was not an event but a process. It was the admixture of the old manner of life and the new that made the characteristic and vigorous Britain of the era of Wellington. Only as the Nineteenth Century wore on, an ever larger proportion of the population was harnessed to the new machinery and to big business, while the realm of the factory was extended every year at the expense of domestic and out-of-door occupations. Fortunately, as the factory had become the typical arena of work, its worst abuses were gradually remedied ; from 1833 onward it became increasingly subjected to State inspection and regulation, which employees in the older type of domestic workshop had good reason to envy.

The greatest development of the reign of George III, greater even than the Lancashire cotton trade, was the revolution involved in the application of coal to iron-smelting, which created the Black Country in the West Midland shires. In forty years the production of iron in Britain increased ten-fold. The Black Country became the chief scene of this new development, and of a great number and variety of hardware, pottery and other industries more and more dependent upon iron or coal. All over the island new businesses sprang up, each helped by some adaptation of James Watt's steam engine to the various processes of b. 1736, mining and manufacture. With iron and machinery was born d. 1819. a new class—the modern mechanic. If the great economic changes as yet brought little good to the child in the factory or to man, woman or child in the coal-mine, it created a large class of well-paid, educated engineers, whose advice was sought with respect by their employers in innumerable industries scattered all over the island. To that class of wage-earners belonged the great Stephenson family of Tyneside. There was nothing ' bourgeois ' about the origins of the man who invented the locomotive, after having taught himself to read at the age of seventeen. The motto of the coming age was ' self-help,' or individual opportunity, and its benefits were not entirely monopolized by the middle class. It was from the ' Mechanics' Institutes ' that the adult education of the new age took a start.

For the first time since Anglo-Saxon days, the North-Western half of England, the ancient Northumbria and Mercia, became of importance in rivalry to the corn-bearing lands of South and East, and to London and its satellite counties.[1] Even the old textile industries of East Anglia, of Somerset and of the Cotswolds declined before the vigorous competition of the northern dales in the age of machinery. Moorlands which had formerly been the home of the moss-trooper, the feudal retainer and the shepherd, became centres of wealth and trained intelligence of the modern order. This shifting of the geographic balance of power in the island was to be a chief cause of the demand for political change and Parliamentary redistribution in the approaching era. But so long as the Napoleonic wars lasted, and for more than a decade after they had come to an end, the new middle class was content to accumulate wealth, and did not seriously challenge the political and social monopoly that excluded it from its natural weight in the new England. And although the proletariate assembled in the new industrial districts were driven by misery to Radical agitation under Cobbett and Hunt, it was still easy to keep them down so long as they had no middle-class support, and no legal Trade Union organization of their own.

With momentum ever increasing throughout the reign of George III, men and women were flooding into the industrial districts of Clydeside, the northern coalpits, Lancashire, the Black Country, South Wales, London, and any place where ' navvy ' work was to be had on the new canals and roads. Round these centres of industry the miserably low agricultural wage was brought to a higher level than in more remote rural regions where there was no competition of alternative employment. And yet the condition of the new industrial proletariate was very miserable, and was made more miserable by the vagaries of prices, wages

[1] See p. 60, above.

and employment due to the violent fluctuations caused by the Napoleonic war.

The evils of this first period of the new economic system were great, but they were a concentration and multiplication of old evils rather than a creation of new. There had been coalmines for centuries and the miners had always been shockingly housed, paid and overworked, with little or no provision against accidents or enquiry when accidents took place.[1] Indeed, before 1815, it was not the custom to hold inquests on deaths in the mines of Northumberland and Durham. In Scotland the miners, incredible as it may appear, were bound serfs until nearly the close of the Eighteenth Century. And even in England women and children in the past had been literally harnessed to the work under unspeakable conditions in the damp darkness of the mine. The Industrial Revolution immensely increased the mining population without at first materially improving their condition, and their ill-treatment was revealed to a more humane and inquisitive generation by the epoch-making Mines Report of 1842. So, too, pauper children, who had previously been handed over individually to the domestic affections of Mrs. Brownrigg and Peter Grimes,[2] might in the new age be grouped together in a cotton mill run by a hard-bitten North country working man who had borrowed a couple of hundred pounds to start the business, and had no compunctions about making the lasses work. The 'free labour' of children who had parents to support was also passing from the home to the mill or factory, a change that must in many cases,—though not in all,—have been for the worse, before the era of Factory Inspection began in 1833. The relative misery of the poor at this period as compared to that of their forebears is hard to estimate, for want of facts about earlier times. The absolute misery of many of them is a fact incontestable.

The immigration into the new industrial districts represented the overflow of population created by the continual rise in the number of inhabitants of Great Britain from 1760 onwards. They came to be the man-power for the new industrial world, 'bowing their heads for bread,' but glad to escape from rural England, Scotland, Wales and Ireland, where only starvation awaited them. Irish immigration had been a feature of London life and of English and Scottish harvesting since Stuart times at least, but in the Hanoverian epoch it became much more pronounced. Jews from Central and Eastern Europe also began to come over in great numbers, so that by the end of the Eighteenth

---

[1] But no doubt the mines were getting deeper and the chance of accidents greater as the surface coal was exhausted.

[2] See p. 523, above.

Century there were 20,000 in London, mostly very poor. But for the attractions of America in the Nineteenth Century to these two races, the admixture of Irish and Jews in the English community would be much greater than it is. The Irish brought with them a low standard of life and wages, and helped to make the worst slums. The cellars they inhabited in London were as weather-proof as the hovels they had left in Connemara, and bread and cheese was at least better than potatoes. Partly because they tended to lower the English workman's pitiful wage, there were frequent riots against them in London and among the farm-hands. Indeed, the animosity against the Irish labourer was one of the causes of the feeling against Roman Catholics that distinguished the populace of Great Britain in the days of Lord George Gordon and for long afterwards.

1780.

A large immigration of Englishmen from the rural districts must in any case have taken place, owing to the rise in population coinciding with new facilities for employment in industrial centres. But changes at the same time occurred in the economy of the rural village itself, which, in a variety of ways, affected the pace of the exodus to the towns. The change was twofold: the removal of industries from the villages to urban areas owing to the revolution in machinery and organization; and the enclosure of commons and open fields to grow more corn. The two movements combined to revolutionize English rural life, but they had no direct causal connection one with the other.

The Industrial Revolution, by introducing machinery and so favouring concentration in factories and urban districts, gradually made an end of two kinds of village industry. It destroyed first the spinning and other by-employments of the wives and children of agricultural families; and secondly the full-time employment of villagers in such various trades as clock-making, basket-weaving, carriage and waggon building, tanning, milling and brewing, saddlery, cobbling, tailoring, and the great national industry of cloth-weaving. Some of these arts and industries supplied the village itself, others supplied the national and the world market. In the course of a hundred and seventy years, starting from the accession of George III, British industries have been almost entirely removed to the towns.

The migration of industry and craftsmanship left the village once more almost purely agricultural, as in the time of Domesday. The rural outlook was narrowed, the villager's intelligence and independence lowered, except in so far as improved school education has applied a one-sided remedy of recent years. But there was no efficient school in the English village a hundred years

ago. Apprenticeship and the craft were the old educational
forces, and they were disappearing. With the flight of the industry by which they lived, many independent families had to
obliterate themselves in the featureless streets of the modern
city, leaving, like Wordsworth's 'poor Susan,' the cottage beside
the stream,

> The one only dwelling on earth that she loves.

Those who remained behind as hands employed by the farmer
in his fields, no longer had any by-employment in their own homes
to enable them to hold out for better wages, or to eke out what
wages they got. The monotony of village life in the Nineteenth
Century was due mainly to the migration of the industries to the
urban districts, which eventually was more complete in England
than in any other country of Europe.

When George III died, the migration of industry from the
village was only half accomplished, but the enclosure of the land
was more nearly finished. The period of private Acts of Parliament for the enclosing of open fields and of common wastes
corresponds roughly to the years of George III's reign, though it
overlaps at both ends.

1760–
1820.

The survival in the best corn-growing area of the Midlands
and East Anglia of the early mediæval system of open-field cultivation,[1] was an anomaly too gross to be any longer tolerated.
The beneficial effects of enclosure in increasing production and
ultimately population, had been demonstrated in many districts
in Tudor and Stuart times.[2] And when, in the days of the elder
Pitt, the population of the island began to grow by leaps and
bounds, the enlargement of the corn supply became the first of
national necessities. It was not till after the Napoleonic wars
that Russia or any other land beyond the sea was able to supply
any appreciable quantity of grain to Britain. In those days, the
island must feed itself or starve.

It was, therefore, in the reign of George III that the Midlands
and East Anglia and much of the North English and Scottish
landscape took on their present appearance of a chess-board
pattern, made up of innumerable fields 'enclosed' by hedges or
stone walls. The extreme south-east corner of the island, and
many western counties, had displayed those familiar features for
centuries past.[3]

---

[1] Described, pp. 150–152, above.   [2] P. 286, above.

[3] See the maps at the end of Gonner's *Common Land and Enclosure* for a rapid
view of the geographic area of the enclosure in the Eighteenth and Nineteenth
Centuries. In the North-Western corner of England the enclosures were of
common of waste ; the open-field system of agriculture had never had a great
part in the life of the North, where scattered farms had been the rule.

z

The wholesale enclosures of the reign of George III, like the partial enclosures of Tudor and Stuart times, opened the way for better agriculture by farmers with a compact holding in place of scattered strips in the open village field.   These opportunities were not neglected, for the Eighteenth Century was the age of ' improving landlords,' who put their capital into the land, and who studied, practised and preached scientific agriculture and stock-breeding.   Sheep and cattle, as well as horses, were developed to the point of perfection in England during ' the century of improvement.'   Artificial grasses, root crops and proper methods of growing grain, all alike impossible in the open-field system, became the usual instead of the exceptional practice of English farmers.   The prophet of the new agriculture was Arthur Young, and its typical man was ' Coke of Norfolk,' that sturdy Whig and enemy of George III, who reigned at Holkham from the American Revolution to the premiership of Peel, increased his rent-roll from £2200 to £20,000, made the fortunes and won the affections of all classes in his neighbourhood, turning a sandy rabbit-warren into a model estate which agriculturists came from all over Britain and Europe to visit.

Scotland, when George III began to reign, was hedgeless and treeless.   It was not, like central England, a land of large villages, but, like northern England, a land of hamlets and scattered farms, set in the surrounding wilderness.   The power of the Scottish landlords was very great, and the tenants often held their farms on precarious leases of one year.   But the spirit of scientific improvement became even more prominent in Scotland than in England.   The lairds used their power to have the land enclosed and tilled on modern methods, while the new practice of giving long leases encouraged the enterprise and independence of the farmer.   The solid farm buildings, field-walls and plantations of Scotland date from the beginning of George III's reign onwards.

Rural Wales changed less than Scotland and England in this period, because in the Celtic mountain-land enclosure had been co-eval with agriculture.   But Wales was acquiring a ' Black Country ' of its own, where on its southern coast the coal measures ran down to the sea.

The enclosure movement was a necessary step to feed the increasing population.   And it increased not only the wealth of the landlords who put money into their estates, but that of the large tenant farmers who were their principal agents in the movement.   The spleen of Cobbett was moved by the number of farmers who at the end of George III's reign lived in a smart new brick house—often entitled ' Waterloo farm,'—who drove in a gig to market, had wine on their tables and a piano in the parlour for their daughters ; yet these things were a sign of increasing wealth, comfort and education. Nor had the old-fashioned small 'husbandman' by any means disappeared, although he had been long declining. The census of 1831 showed that the agriculturists who neither employed labour nor were themselves employed, were still as one to six in comparison with employing farmers and their hands. And as late as 1851 two-thirds of the farms of Great Britain were still under one hundred acres in size.

Enclosure had been a necessity, but the enclosures had not brought equal benefits to all. The share of the poor had been inadequate. The loss of their village industries has been already referred to, and accounts for half their distress or more. But the method of the enclosures had not taken enough consideration of the small man, and too little had been done to fix the lesser peasantry on the soil as part of the new scheme of things. When similar changes took place in contemporary Denmark, a land ruled by a monarch dependent on his general popularity, the interest of all classes down to the poorest was carefully considered, with excellent consequences in the agricultural Denmark of to-day. But the England of George III was completely aristocratic in the sympathies and constitution of its governing class, whether Whigs, Tories or 'King's Friends' bore rule. The Houses of Parliament which passed the Enclosure Acts were closed by law to anyone who was not a considerable owner of land. The Justices of the Peace were autocrats of the countryside and represented one class alone. The proprietorship of most of the land of England was in the hands of a comparatively small group of 'great landed families.' Under these social and political conditions it was inevitable that the enclosures should be carried through according to the ideas of the big landlord class alone. Those ideas rightly envisaged the national necessity of more food production, but not the national necessity of maintaining and increasing small properties or small holdings.

In the redivision of the open fields and common wastes among individual proprietors and farmers, there was no intention to defraud the small man, but no desire to give him more than his apparent legal claim. Often he could not prove a legal claim to the rights he exercised on the common. Oftener his legal rights to keep cows or geese there, or his personal right in one or two strips in the village field, were compensated with a sum of money which was not enough to enable him to set up as a capitalist farmer or pay for the hedging of the plot allotted to him ; the compensation might, however, pay for a month's heavy drinking in the ale-house. And so he became a landless labourer. Arthur Young himself was horrified at some of the results of the move-

ment of which he had been the chief apostle.   In 1801 he wrote
' By nineteen out of twenty Enclosure Bills the poor are injured
and most grossly.' [1]

The condition of the agricultural labourer, deprived of the
industries previously conducted by his wife and children, was,
indeed, most unhappy.   The enforcement of a living wage was
not opposed to old English theory and practice ; and it was the
labourer's due in common justice, because Pitt's Acts made Trade
Union action illegal.   But the landlord class, represented by the
Justices of the Peace, decided not to compel the farmers to pay
a living wage.   They adopted instead a policy elaborated by the
Berkshire Magistrates at Speenhamland in 1795, namely, to give
rates in aid of insufficient wages.   To keep the poor alive, it was
decided to tax the rate-payers, instead of forcing farmers and
employers of labour to shoulder their proper burden.   It was a
fatal policy, for it encouraged farmers to keep down wages.   The
system, which lasted till the New Poor Law of 1834, made the
rural labourer a pauper, and discouraged his thrift and self-respect.
It paid better to cringe to the authorities for the dole, than to
attempt any form of self-help.   The system was not adopted in
Scotland and North England, where the agricultural labourer
suffered no such moral and social degradation, though there too
times were often very hard.

Wealth was increasing so fast in town and country that the
contrasts between the life of the rich and the life of the poor were
more dramatic and more widely observable than of old.   In the
industrial world, members of the new middle class ceased to live
over the workshop, and built themselves separate villas and
mansions in imitation of the life of the gentry.   They no longer
formed one household with their apprentices and journeymen.
The landed gentry, for their part, were enlarging the manor-
house for the heir and the parsonage for the younger son, and too
often replacing a tumble of gabled roofs that had grown up piecemeal in the last three hundred years, by a gorgeous ' gentleman's
seat ' in the neo-Palladian style.   Game-preserving in the midst
of a hungry population, with man-traps and spring guns lurking
in the brambles to guard the pheasant at the expense of man's
life or limb, led to a poaching war with armed skirmishes, and
several thousand convictions a year.   It was these contrasts that
made the Radicalism of the new era, a spirit unknown in early
Hanoverian England, even though the poor may have been
materially as ill off in the one period as in the other.

---

[1] It is not true, however, that the enclosure movement sweepingly deprived
the cottagers of their gardens.   Cottage gardens and potato patches were quite
common when George III died.

Coal and iron in the Northern and Midland Shires were creating industrial cities not so immeasurably smaller than London, as Norwich and Bristol had been in the Stuart epoch. Yet London though it distanced its rivals less, was still growing with a rapidity that astounded and alarmed the world. Its prosperity continued to be based, as before the Industrial Revolution, on its unique place in commerce and distribution, and on highly skilled finishing trades still conducted on the domestic system. It still, therefore, attracted two classes of immigrants—the roughest kind of labour for porterage at the docks and in distribution, and the most skilled and intelligent workmen for the finishing trades. It had also a much larger proportion of clerks, organizers, civil servants and men of education than any other city in the world.

All round London, bricks and mortar were on the march across the green fields. When George III died, the city was linked up by an almost continuous line of houses with Hammersmith, Deptford, Highgate and Paddington. For London, like other English cities, had always grown outwards, not upwards. Paris and many foreign cities, where houses used to be forbidden outside the fortifications, being unable to expand sideways, grew towards heaven, with tenements for the poor and flats for the middle classes. But the Englishman traditionally lived in his own house, however low and small and however distant from his work. On the whole, the English system was the best, though not the cheapest.[1]

Jerrybuilding was perhaps the gravest evil of the Industrial Revolution. It was much, no doubt, that the immensely increased population was housed at all. Nor is it clear that on the average men were, in the strictly material sense, worse ' housed ' in the new urban areas than in the old country cottages whence they or their fathers had come. But cellar and one-room tenements for families were dreadfully common for the lower class of labour, whether in London, Glasgow, Manchester or the mining districts. A large proportion of the wage-earners and all the large class of commercial ' clerks ' were better housed. But even their dwellings were monotonous and sordid in appearance ; town-planning and any effort to brighten or embellish the face of the street were alien to the ideas of the age. The enterprising employer wanted dwellings where the new hands he wished to

---

[1] The tall ' wynds ' of Edinburgh, many storeys high, recalled the days when life outside the High Street region was unsafe. But in Sir Walter Scott's day, Princes Street and the new modern town down below were growing apace. Scottish housing in town and country then, as now, was behind English. One-room hovels of turf or unmortared stone could still be found in the poorer farming districts.

employ could live. The builder looked to make money on the transaction. No one else gave the matter a thought. Thus was the new England built.

Laissez-faire, or the objection to interference by government, became a theory, but it was first a fact. The whole framework of Eighteenth Century England was incompatible with efficient administration. A modern nation was being governed by Tudor machinery, or rather by what was still left of that machinery after the passage of two hundred years. In these circumstances, what little taste men had of State or Municipal control, did not encourage them to ask for more. Till the machinery of local and central government was modernized, as it only began to be after 1832, opinion based on experience said that the less government did the better. Among the few things it had actually done in recent times was the attempt to suppress Trade Unions by law, the supplementing of wages out of the rates, and the Corn Law of 1815. As to town-planning, factory-inspecting, sanitation and public education, much had to happen before either State or Municipality could dream of undertaking such tasks. Whole new generations of men and ideas had first to be born.

The political spirit of the English Eighteenth Century,— aristocratic power tempered by Parliamentary control and individual rights,—had little in common either with continental despotism or with the bureaucratic democracy of our own time. When the Reformers, inspired by Bentham, Cobbett and Brougham, took in hand the problem of the relation of this old governmental system to the new facts of the Industrial Revolution, their first belief was that the remedy lay in reduced taxation and less State interference. Such, it was expected by many, would be the result of Parliamentary Reform. The exact opposite proved to be the case. In the event, Liberalism meant not less government, but more. But the government had first to be made the instrument of the general will. The gradual creation of social services by public action and at the public expense was to be the chief contribution of the Nineteenth Century to social welfare. But this was not foreseen by anyone in 1816, when Brougham compelled the government to drop the Income Tax on the return of peace, as a sop to democratic opinion.

BOOKS FOR FURTHER READING

J. H. Clapham, *Economic History of Modern Britain*, Vol. I. *The Railway Age.* (forthcoming) ; Halévy, *History of the English People in the Nineteenth Century*, Vol. I. (*England in* 1815) ; Hammond, *Rise of Modern Industry*, and series of *Agricultural, Skilled*, and *Town Labourer* ; Mrs. George, *London Life in the Eighteenth Century* ; Lord Ernle, *English Farming* and *The Land and the People* ; Meredith, *Economic History of England*; Stirling, *Coke of Norfolk* ; Griffith, *Population Problems of the Age of Malthus.*

BOOK VI

THE LATER HANOVERIANS. SEA-POWER IN THE AGE OF MACHINERY. THE TRANSITION TO DEMOCRACY

INTRODUCTION

THE Parliamentary aristocracy under the first three Georges had developed British maritime power to the point where Nelson left it ; had lost one overseas empire and acquired another ; had completed the reconciliation of Scotland and perpetuated the alienation of Ireland ; and had guarded the arena for the early stages of the Industrial Revolution, but without any attempt to control its social effects, or any foresight of its political implications. In the course of their long hegemony the Whig and Tory aristocracies had perfected a new form of governmental machinery, hinging on the Cabinet and Prime Minister, which lent efficiency to the rule of Parliament. By the help of this system the English House of Commons had risen triumphant from a succession of wars with despotic monarchies, and under Pitt and Castlereagh had defeated Napoleon himself, given peace to Europe, and won a hundred years of security for Great Britain.

The task awaiting their successors, under the later monarchs of the House of Hanover, was to adapt this system of Parliamentary Cabinet government to the new social facts created by the Industrial Revolution. This was found to involve the admission first of the middle and then of the working class as partners in the control of the political machine. A failure to make these adjustments would have led to a breakdown of the Parliamentary system and a war of classes, such as seemed adumbrated for the future at the time of Peterloo and the Six Acts.

1832
1867.

1819.

But the good genius of English politics has often retrieved apparently hopeless situations. The last British Revolution is still that of 1688. By a gradual transition towards democracy, seldom hastening and never turning back, political rights were extended to all without a catastrophe. This great manœuvre was safely accomplished because all classes and all parties showed, upon the whole, sound political sense and good humour, because the Victorian age was a period of peace and external security for Britain, and because its middle years were years of unexampled

1870
et seq.

prosperity. Finally, the extension of the political franchise to all compelled the nation to elaborate a system of national education out of the fragmentary efforts of private and denominational enterprise.

In the main the transition was effected through the revival and strengthening of the old two-party system. The peculiarly English tradition of the two perennial parties had been to some extent replaced by a group system of politics during the unchallenged Tory predominance with which the Century opened. But at the time of the Reform Bill of 1830–1832, the Whigs furbished up their old traditions with new war-cries and programmes, and both parties thenceforth moved forward, forming as they went a kaleidoscopic succession of new social alliances in the rapidly changing world.

The underlying principle connecting the Liberals and Conservatives of Victoria's reign in an actually traceable succession with the Whigs and Tories of Charles II, was the continuous antagonism of Church and Dissent. That lasting dualism of English religious life was bound to reflect itself in a political dualism, so long as certain monopolies of the Church were maintained. For two hundred years it gave a reality to the otherwise artificial permanence of the traditions of the two parties from one changing period to another. The working-class movement at the beginning of the Nineteenth Century was in part connected with Dissent and was at that time almost altogether outside the influence of the established Church. The denominational aspect of politics therefore served to connect the Radicalism of the working classes to some extent with the Whig-Liberal party ; through that party they sought political enfranchisement, while seeking economic and social amelioration by their own methods of Trade Unionism, Co-operative Societies, and incipient Socialism. The fact that the majority of Englishmen in the middle of the Nineteenth Century were religious but not of the same religion, was a steadying influence in the strife of parties and classes, although it was in itself an additional cause of controversy.

But the gradual adaptation of Parliamentary government, and with it of local government, to the democratic character of the new age, was only a small part of the adaptations necessary if the new society was to be saved. To render life increasingly tolerable to forty millions in an island where seven millions had found it hard to live before, new organizations of the most various kinds had to be created. The Eighteenth Century had been prolific of men and great in individual energies, but its corporate and institutional life had been lethargic. The Nineteenth Century, on the other hand, not only put fresh democratic vigour into

Parliament, municipalities, Church, Universities, Schools and
Civil Service, but created a wealth of new organisms, public and
private, dealing with every department of life.   It was the age
of Trade Unions, Co-operative and Benefit Societies, Leagues,
Boards, Commissions, Committees for every conceivable purpose
of philanthropy and culture.   Not even the dumb animals were
left without organized protection.   The Nineteenth Century
rivalled the Middle Ages in its power to create fresh forms of corporate and institutional life, while yielding little to the Eighteenth
Century in the spirit of self-help and personal initiative.   The
list of great men whom the Nineteenth Century produced is often
repeated ; the list of new organizations that it created would be
yet longer and no less significant.

The new forms of government and of human activity which
were evolved are indeed too complex for brief description in this
book, but many of them are familiar to us as matters of our own
everyday life.   A characteristic of the new national machinery,
fully apparent towards the end of Queen Victoria's reign, was the
close inter-relation that had grown up on the one hand between
private philanthropic effort and State control, and on the other
between local and central government.   As Parliament and local
government began to respond to the needs of the community
as a whole, and as the State became more and more intelligently
interested in the work of private effort in education, medicine,
sanitation and a hundred other sides of life,—an elaborate system
of State aid, enforcement and control came into being, through
Treasury Grants in Aid to local bodies, State inspection of conditions of labour and of life, industrial insurance and the modern
educational system.   Voluntary and private effort aided by the
State did many things that in other countries of Europe were done
solely by the State or were not done at all.

The complicated and constantly shifting relationship between
central and local government, between private enterprise and
State undertaking, was rendered possible by the evolution of the
permanent, non-political Civil Service of Great Britain with its
accumulated stores of knowledge, experience and sound tradition.
In the third quarter of the century, the Civil Service was removed
from the field of political jobbery by the adoption of open competitive examination as the method of entrance, a device that
seemed as strange as it has proved successful.

British methods of coping with the problems of the new era
showed great practical inventiveness, and were all in the line of
a strong native tradition.   Relatively little was copied from
continental movements.   The Parliamentary system was our
own ; local government was reformed and elaborated on British

lines ; factory inspection, Trade Unionism, the Co-operative movement, were of British origin ; the Civil Service was native in its traditions, and in the peculiar method of its selection by examination.

The advance in humanity, democracy and education, and the changes in industrial method bringing large crowds of wage-earners of both sexes together in offices and factories, led to a new conception of the place of woman in society. The education of women, from being almost totally neglected, became in a couple of generations comparable to that of men. The position of women in the family was altered in law, and was yet more altered in practice and opinion. Finally the movement for their political enfranchisement ceased to seem absurd.

All these great changes would never have been carried through without disaster but for the peace, prosperity and security that marked the Nineteenth Century in Britain. Except in the episode of the Crimean War, the general policy of Britain was to abstain from taking part in the strife of continental nations, when it renewed itself forty years after Waterloo. Since the Balance of Power was for the time safely adjusted, there was no call for us to fight in order to prevent the conquest of Europe by a single nation and its vassals.[1]

So, too, relations with the United States, though of growing importance, remained peaceful from the Treaty of Ghent onwards, in spite of some ugly crises. This happy result was due in no small degree to the work of Castlereagh and Monroe in agreeing to a permanent disarmament along both sides of the Canadian frontier ; it followed that while that frontier was being prolonged further and further to the west, the grave disputes that necessarily accompanied the process were never submitted to the decision of war. Another great step forward was taken when Gladstone consented to submit the *Alabama* claims to the arbitration of a third party. So too, in the division of Asiatic and African territories, the disputes with France and Germany, though sometimes acute in the later years of the century, were settled by peaceful arbitration or agreement, largely through the action of Lord Salisbury, who held that Britain's ' greatest interest ' was peace.

Peace, then, and the amazing prosperity which the state of

Xmas
Eve,
1814.

1817.

---

[1] Speaking of our friendly relations after 1886 with the Triple Alliance of Germany, Austria and Italy, then the strongest group in Europe, Lord Grey of Falloden writes in his memoirs :—' Great Britain has not in theory been adverse to the predominance of a strong group in Europe when it seemed to make for stability and peace. To support such a combination has generally been her first choice. It is only when the dominant Power becomes aggressive and she feels her own interests to be threatened that she, by an instinct of self-defence, if not by deliberate policy, gravitates to anything that can fairly be described as a Balance of Power.'

the world in Queen Victoria's reign brought to the door of Britain's commerce and industry, formed conditions highly favourable to the solution of the grave political and social problems of the new order within the island. The chief external interests of Britain were not war or preparation for war, but her ever increasing foreign trade, more fabulous every decade, and the development of her new colonial empire bequeathed by the victors of Trafalgar and Waterloo. The over-population and unemployment in Britain after the Napoleonic wars, unrelieved in those days by any form of industrial insurance, drove English and Scots to the Colonies by hundreds of thousands. In the first half of the Nineteenth Century, many of these emigrants were agricultural or semi-agricultural labourers, glad to get hold of land and work it for themselves. Only towards the end of the period did the decay of rural life in England and the attraction of the modern town life create a danger that the English race should become a race of city-dwellers, unwilling to settle or to remain on the land.

By the beginning of the Twentieth Century, the Colonies had become Dominions, new nations in effect. After enjoying complete self-government as regards their internal affairs for fifty years or more, they began to look out upon the world, each with its own national point of view,—Canadian, Australian, South African. In these circumstances, the hopes entertained by British statesmen during the Imperialist movement at the close of the Nineteenth Century that it would be possible to unite the Empire more closely in some kind of Federal Constitution, were not destined to mature. A looser bond of common interest and affection held the Empire together when it was plunged into its next great crisis by the outbreak of the War with Germany in August 1914.

CHAPTER I

Repression and Reform, 1815–1835. Corn Law and Income Tax. Cobbett, Peterloo and the Six Acts. Tory Reform. Peel and Huskisson. Castlereagh and Canning. The Wellington Ministry. The Whigs and the Reform Bill. The Municipal Corporations Act and Slavery Abolition. Belgium

Kings: George III, died 1820 ; George IV, 1820–1830 ; William IV, 1830–1837.

THE sudden fall in prices after the peace ruined many farmers and business men, and threw multitudes out of employment, though it momentarily increased the purchasing power of wages.

Now, for the first time in English history, prices were seriously affected by the importation of foreign foodstuffs, not yet indeed from America but from Europe. The Corn Law of 1815, designed to prevent this entry of cheap grain, seemed insult and injury not only to the poor but to the manufacturing middle class, who had no wish that the poor should have to spend all their wages in buying bread alone. Industrial employers and working men for the first time found themselves combined in angry opposition to the use made by the landlord class of its monopoly of political power.

This first united movement of the middle and lower orders soon died down, though not for ever. The poor, indeed, were kept by sheer misery in a state of unrest, and went on with the agitation inspired by Cobbett and Hunt that culminated four years later in Peterloo and the Six Acts. But the middle classes retired for awhile from the political arena, contenting themselves with a victory won by their champion Henry Brougham and the Parliamentary Whig leaders, who wrested from the Government **1816.** the abolition of the Income Tax. The agitation had been carried on by Petitions to Parliament from 'the most respectable' inhabitants of town and country in all parts of the island against the continuance of Income Tax in time of peace, and especially against ' the compelling the petitioners to lay open their concerns by a train of inspectors and spies.' The Government was forced to bow to the storm. It was the first step made by popular control of policy, and unfortunately it was clean in the wrong direction. It increased the already excessive proportion of indirect taxation, which fell on the poor as heavily as on the rich, and this state of things lasted till Peel revived the Income Tax in 1842.

Because indirect taxation was employed to pay for the sinecures, pensions and places secured by aristocratic political jobbers, as well as to pay the interest on the National Debt to prosperous fund-holders, the National Debt and political jobbery were confounded together in Cobbett's sweeping censures. The poor, it was said with some justification, were being taxed to keep the rich. To the Radical of those days, the 'taxeater' seemed to belong to a separate, half-human species, with interests wholly opposed to those of the 'tax-payer.' Whigs and Radicals in opposition hoped to relieve distress mainly by retrenchment and cutting down of taxation, instead of by redistribution of its burdens. But when they came into power after the Reform Bill they soon found that 'retrenchment' was not a royal road to 'the greatest happiness of the greatest number.'

Though William Cobbett wrote a vast deal of angry nonsense

about finance and many other subjects,[1] he played a great and beneficent part in English history. He revived the political movement in the working class which Paine had begun and Pitt suppressed, and he revived it not as a Republican or Jacobin movement but as a Parliamentary movement, demanding the vote for the working classes and teaching them to look that way for relief of their distress. At the height of his influence in 1816 it stands on record that he turned many of his readers from rioting and rick-burning to political discussion and organization. They would have paid little attention to his advice if he had not been a journalist of genius in the early youth of journalism, and if he had not given expression, as no one else then did, to the insufferable position in which the poor found themselves. In town and country every person in authority in Church or State seemed to them in league with their employers against them ; they had no tribunes to speak for them ; they had no franchise in central or in local government ; they had no legal means of trade organization to make their numbers felt in the labour market. Cobbett was the first who gave effective voice to their case.

William Cobbett was the old-fashioned John Bull, a lover of the past and of the sweet-smelling countryside, of the yeoman and the plough and the thatched cottage. A despiser of foreigners, a hater of theory, he had begun his journalistic career as an Anti-Jacobin, opposed to Paine and the ' rights of man.' But when he saw, or thought that he saw, the ancient rights of Englishmen being stolen from them, he rushed noisily to the rescue, to the no small wrath and consternation of his former allies. His *Political Register* was read aloud to illiterate audiences under the hedgerow and in the workshop ; and even the ' respectable' sometimes read the rascal for his shrewd hitting, laughed and cursed his impudence, and rode off thinking on what they had read. In this way the upper world first got a glimpse of the life and sufferings of the poor. Judge, then, how the poor loved him, when everyone else seemed to them to have entered into conspiracy to rob, oppress and vilify them. A bully was needed to stand up against that host of conscious and unconscious bullies. Old England, the passing England of the yeoman and the alehouse on the heath, produced as a last effort

1802–
1835.

---

[1] Speaking of Hyde Park Corner in 1826, Cobbett wrote ' The *Great Captain of the age,* as that nasty palaverer, Brougham, called him, lives close to this spot, where also the " English ladies' " naked Achilles stands, having, on the base of it, the word *Wellington* in great staring letters, while all the others are very, very small ; so that base tax-eaters and fund-gamblers from the country, when they go to crouch before this image, think it is the image of the Great Captain himself ! '

this glorious, unchallengeable bully, with no touch of cowardice in all his vast bulk, and, when out of the ring, no malice.

Cobbett became the father of the very unphilosophic Radicalism which effected so much in Nineteenth Century Britain. It was not a doctrine but a spirit—indignation at the wrongs of the poor. It was not tied to Liberalism, though often in alliance with it ; still less was it tied to *laissez faire*. Working on and through many different politicians and parties, it passed Factory Acts, abolished Corn Laws, forced on the franchise, education, freedom of speech and press, and in the end altered the whole attitude of the upper to the lower class. Bentham and Mill were wiser men than Cobbett, but they would not without his aid have so transformed England from their study-chairs.

The history of the working-class movement, ever since the Industrial Revolution gave it self-consciousness, has moved in a perpetual alternation between political and economic action. Immediately after Waterloo its action was political. It was not yet highly organized in Trade Unions, and was not yet identified with any economic gospel or programme except an ungratified desire for better wages.[1] The Corn Law of 1815 seemed a challenge to political action; Parliamentary Reform was demanded as the first step to economic betterment of any kind.

1817–
1819

As yet the middle class stood aside as neuters, leaving the battle of Reform to be fought by unorganized labour led by Cobbett and Hunt, against the upper class and the full force of Government. The Whig, or aristocratic liberal, party also remained an impotent spectator, because it was still divided on the question of Parliamentary Reform. The Whigs, while denouncing the repressive measures of the Tories, disliked no less the tone of Radical propaganda, and could suggest no positive remedy of their own. The game therefore remained in the hands of the Tory Government of Liverpool, Wellington and Castlereagh.

Unfortunately the victors of Waterloo and of the Peace Conference were less happily inspired in dealing with the crisis that now confronted them at home. They had no economic or political remedy to propose except the severest forms of repression. Pitt's Anti-Jacobin repression had succeeded against a small minority, in time of war ; it was now applied in time of

---

[1] Robert Owen, who always decried political action, was still at this period a philanthropist employer, not yet a democratic leader. In the first years of the peace he was still engaged in trying to persuade his brother employers, the Cabinet and Parliament that improved conditions of life and education in the factories would pay the employers and the nation, as he had demonstrated in his own New Lanark Mills. If he had been listened to then, we should live in a different world to day.

peace against a majority, perhaps, of the nation. Rioters were tried for high treason, and printers and authors for sedition, but not always with success before middle-class juries. Spies and *agents provocateurs*, like the notorious Oliver, were let loose by Government among the Radicals. The Habeas Corpus Act was suspended. A tax of fourpence a copy on all periodical publications put not only Radical propaganda but knowledge of all sorts as far as possible out of the reach of the poor. Till 1836 fivepence was the minimum price for a newspaper worth a penny—so had the wisdom of Parliament decreed.

Public meetings, too, were generally prohibited. It would have been better if none had been allowed at all, for when a vast but orderly concourse of working men and women assembled on St. Peter's Fields, Manchester, to demand Parliamentary Aug. 16, Reform, the magistrates, seized by sudden panic, let loose a 1819. charge of yeomanry which killed a dozen and seriously injured hundreds of both sexes.

The Ministry approved of this tragic blunder without waiting to make enquiry. The bulk of the nation thought otherwise. Not only Radicals and working men, but Whigs in their high country-seats and merchants in their cosy parlours were horrified at the callous slaughter of their fellow-citizens. It was called ' Peterloo,' because it seemed to cancel the debt of the nation's gratitude for Waterloo. It had a great effect on the mind of the rising generation of all classes and of all parties, for it showed the end of the blind alley up which the old Anti-Jacobin Toryism of mere negation had long been leading the country. But for the moment there was no alternative to that policy. Since there was to be no conciliation, order must be rigorously maintained, as it was by the ' Six Acts,' passed in that winter.

There followed, next February, the Cato Street Conspiracy of physical-force Radicals, under Thistlewood, to murder the 1820 whole Cabinet as it sat at dinner. The reaction in favour of Government was considerable, but, considering the horrid nature of the conspiracy, curiously evanescent. The unsavoury episode of the divorce proceedings against Queen Caroline, instituted that summer by Ministers to gratify their royal master, George IV, at the time of his accession, plunged them into deeper unpopularity than ever before. The subjects of the land were in some doubt as to the Queen's character, but in none at all about the King's. The fact that he was actually married to two women at once was not then generally known, though much suspected. But the English sense of fair play was outraged by the low type of Italian witness brought over by the King's agents to swear away his wife's good name before the Peers of the land, while the

King himself was openly living with other women. The ' Bill of
Pains and Penalties ' had to be withdrawn before ever it reached
the Commons' House. The rising generation of caricaturists,
headed by George Cruikshank, were depicting George IV's no
longer elegant shape, and the yeomanry charging over the bodies
of shrieking women, with the same brutal force with which their
predecessors in the time of Gillray had attacked Fox and the
' Jacobins.'

After the fiasco of the ' Queen's Trial ' had a little cleared
the air and improved the humour of the nation by inflicting a
severe defeat on Government, the Tory Ministry began a recovery
which gave their party another decade of power. Three circumstances gave them this opportunity to make good : first,
better times in trade ; secondly, the atrophy of the Whig party,
their only rivals in Parliament ; and thirdly, the death of
1822. Castlereagh, whose genius lay in foreign not in domestic affairs,
and whose presence in the Cabinet stood effectively in the way
of the rise of Canning, the powerful representative of the new and
more liberal brand of Toryism.

During the eight years that followed, not only the rigid Anti-
1822– Jacobin structure of recent times, but the British Constitution
1829. as men had known it since 1689, began to crack and give way in
unexpected places. Although the electoral system gave little
direct representation to any large section of the public, Parliament did not altogether fail to reflect the new spirit of the age.
The old two-party system could not revive till the abolition of
the rotten boroughs gave the Whigs a fair chance, but the group
system did some service in representing varieties of national
opinion. There were two groups inside the Tory Cabinet itself :
Canning and Huskisson stood for the more liberal[1] view of things,
and Wellington and old Lord Eldon for the rigid past, with the
Prime Minister Liverpool and the judicious Peel striving to keep
the peace. Yet when, under Wellington as Premier, the Old
Guard drove out their rivals, they were compelled by the stream
1828– of events to pass measures yet more liberal than any which
1829. Canning himself had found it possible to introduce.

The outcome of the last eight years of Tory rule was a number of important reforms and the dissolution of the Anti-Jacobin
Tory party, that had borne rule for more than a generation. In
1830– its place there arose, during the crisis of the Parliamentary
1832. Reform question, a new Whig-Liberal party and a new Conserva-

---

[1] ' Liberal ' was not the name of a party till after the middle of the century.
It denoted only a man of progressive views, whether Radical, Whig or Canningite
Tory.

tive party, which governed the country in alternation in the coming epoch. Thus, after a period of peculiar confusion, Parliamentary life reverted to the two-party system in spite of greater complication of issues and the increasing number of classes and interests involved in the larger life of the reformed Parliament.

Of the liberal measures that signalized the last years of Tory rule, one of the most important, the repeal of Pitt's Combination Acts making Trade Union action illegal, can be ascribed not to any section of the Ministers, but to a change of public opinion, and to the shrewd activities of a remarkable individual outside Parliament—the Radical tailor Francis Place—acting through the Radical member of Parliament Joseph Hume. Place organized petitions and witnesses in the factory districts of the North, and brought them up to Westminster to impress and persuade members of Parliament.

1824-
1825.

To Peel's initiative as Home Secretary belongs the credit of a series of important reforms. The son of a great Lancashire manufacturer of the modern type, Robert Peel junior had been introduced into the governing Tory group through Harrow and Christ Church, and had in early youth become the favourite political agent and spokesman of the squires and clergy of England and of the ascendancy party in Ireland. His life-long connections had thus been formed in the most prosperous period of the old-fashioned Toryism, while the Peninsular War was still raging. If he had entered public life ten years later, he would probably have found out the truth that he was a Liberal-Conservative like Canning or Huskisson. Actually, the position of trust that he held among the defenders of the last ditch made that line less tenable in time of trouble than it would have been if he had fought among the recognized assailants. The Duke, it is reported, once complained of Peel that he never foresaw the end of the campaigns that he began. Though even more true of the Duke himself as a politician, the criticism of Peel is not unjust, provided we add, in Cromwell's words : ' None goes so far as he who knows not whither he is going.' It is characteristic of the England of that period of rapid transition, that her greatest statesmen could never see four years ahead.

The substitution of Peel for Lord Sidmouth at the Home Office in 1822 soon brought an end to the system of espionage and repression exercised by Government against the Radical working men, and established fairer dealing with classes and parties. Peel also put into legislative effect the principles of the crusade carried on for many years past by Bentham, Romilly and Sir

James Mackintosh for reform of the criminal law ; he abolished the death penalty for a hundred different crimes. And finally in 1829 he established for the first time in our history an efficient civilian Police, whom the populace endearingly called by either of his two names. Their social value in dealing with common crime was equalled by their political value in dealing with Radical mobs : for at last the place of the soldiers had been taken by a civic force armed only with batons, who were none the less capable of looking a crowd in the face, and who, unlike the soldiers, could be used to quell the first signs of disturbance. There would be no more Lord George Gordon riots, and no more Peterloos, in towns where ' the force ' exercised its functions. The Reform Bill riots that set Bristol on fire two years later, could have been easily stopped by a hundred of the ' new Police ' acting in good time. Set up first in London alone, they were in the course of a generation adopted all over the country, in answer to a universal demand. From the first they were dressed in civilian blue, and in their early years they wore not helmets but stout top-hats.

In the same period, the finances of the country were taken in hand by Huskisson. The tariff, whether aiming at revenue or protection, was a jungle of unscientific growths and unrelated experiments, hampering trade at every turn. Huskisson did not desire to introduce complete Free Trade, and his operations were limited by the popular objection to a revival of the Income Tax as a source of revenue. Nevertheless he greatly reduced the tariff list, and put order and purpose into what was left. One article only was sacred : ' Corn was King ' in English politics, so long as a section of the country gentry held the monopoly of power through the rotten boroughs.

Huskisson also made the first great inroad on the old system of Navigation Acts, which had for a century and a half given to British shipping monopolistic privileges in British ports.[1] The time had come when this artificial support, which had been praised in its day by Adam Smith, could be dispensed with by the full-grown strength of the British mercantile marine. The process of abolishing the Navigation Acts was completed during the later period when Free Trade was the accepted national policy, and when the remainder of the protective tariffs were abolished. The removal of the monopoly right conferred by the Navigation Acts forced British ship-owners and ship-builders to bestir themselves and improve their methods. Owing to the industrial supremacy of Victorian Britain, the coming of the age of steam and iron at sea was all to her advantage, especially

[1] See pp. 426–7 and note, above.

as she now had difficulty in obtaining timber. And the outward cargo of coal, which was saleable in most ports all over the globe, was a great stimulus to British shipping. Throughout the remainder of the century our mercantile marine continued to grow without a serious rival.

The substitution of Canning's influence for Castlereagh's as the strongest personal force in the Cabinet, gave a stimulus to the forces of change in domestic affairs. At the Foreign Office, the special sphere of these two great men in succession, Canning did not reverse Castlereagh's policy. But, in contrast to his reserved and aristocratic predecessor, he loved to appeal not only to the House of Commons but to the people at large. Foreign affairs ceased to be a mystery of Elder Statesmen, as under Grenville and Castlereagh. Canning's new methods of publicity were destined to grow under the hands of Palmerston, Gladstone and Disraeli, until general elections were lost and won on questions of foreign policy. At the end of the century, Lord Salisbury reverted somewhat to the more quiet methods of Castlereagh.

The advent of Canning meant therefore an important change of method, consonant with the more democratic and inquisitive spirit of the age. But the direction, in which British foreign policy was moving, was not altered, though the pace of the movement was accelerated, and its liberal and British standpoint were both more clearly emphasized.

Castlereagh, eminently a 'good European,' favoured periodical Congresses of the Powers to arrange international disputes. But as the Powers did not then represent the peoples, and as the States did not represent the races, there was no chance that these Congresses could develop into anything approaching the League of Nations of our own day. On the contrary, under the influence of Austria's Metternich and of the Czar Alexander, now in the final reactionary phase of his life, the Congresses were perverted into clearing-houses for the obscurantist policy of the governments of the Holy Alliance, leagued to suppress the first stirrings of liberty and of nationalism. Castlereagh, who had no wish to involve England in the internal police questions of foreign countries, was tending reluctantly to a less close participation in the congressional politics of the continent, when the strain of overwork caused him to commit suicide. But his strongly expressed dislike of the movements for Greek and Italian independence, may lead us to suppose that he would never have taken the actively liberal line pursued by his successor.[1]

Canning, in one sense the continuator of Castlereagh's work,

1822.

1815– 1822.

1822.

[1] For Castlereagh and the settlement of Europe in 1815, see pp. 585–7, above.

introduced an element of more active opposition to the reactionary parties on the continent.　He was more acutely aware
than Castlereagh that the English State stood for something
midway between Jacobinism and Despotism.　The same British
feeling that had inspired the brilliant Anti-Jacobinism of his
youth, made him, as a middle-aged Foreign Minister, the dread
of the despots and the hope of the Liberals of the continent.
He sympathized with the indignation felt by his countrymen,
that the powers which British arms and subsidies had helped to
restore to the 'legitimate' monarchs of Europe, were used everywhere, from Poland to Portugal, to trample out political, racial
1823.　and cultural liberty.　When the France of the Royalists and
Clericals was commissioned by the Holy Alliance to put down
the constitutional movement in Spain by force of arms, all
England was furious, without distinction of class or party.
But Canning, whilst protesting against the French invasion of
Spain, wisely refrained from threats which would have involved
this country either in a new Peninsular War or in an ignominious
diplomatic retreat.

But the other sphere of the Spanish question, the revolt of the
Central and South American Colonies against the old monarchy,
was more fully in Canning's control, because no crusaders of
France or the Holy Alliance could cross the Atlantic to suppress
the rebels under Bolivar, without the acquiescence of the British
fleet.　Moreover, the independence of South America was a direct
material interest of Great Britain.　The restrictions set by Spain
on English commerce with her American Colonies had been a
burning question for nearly three hundred years.　There was now
a golden opportunity for its happy solution, if the Colonies themselves should become independent States, friendly to Britain
and anxious to trade with her merchants.　The heart-burnings
that had caused the wars of Drake, of the buccaneers, and of
' Jenkins' ear ' in the time of Walpole, would at last and for
ever be laid at rest.

In these circumstances the anxiety of British merchants and
industrialists to open new markets for the congested produce of
the new English factories, was blended with a sincere enthusiasm
for the cause of liberty all the world over ; with joy in Cochrane's
gallant exploits off the coast of Chili and Peru as Admiral for
the rebel governments ; and with the satisfaction felt by all true
Englishmen at paying out the French and their perjured and
bigoted protégé Ferdinand VII of Spain for their recent military
triumphs in the Peninsula.　It was to these popular sentiments
that Canning successfully appealed when he pronounced in the
House of Commons that he had called a New World into exist-

ence to redress the balance of the Old. Eldon and Wellington, who preferred old worlds to new at any time, were disgusted beyond measure at their colleague turned demagogue, and the rift in the Tory party became deep and wide.

In proclaiming and defending the independence of South America, the statesmen and people of England were at one with those of the United States. President Monroe had seized the occasion to lay down his ' doctrine,' so famous and important in years to come, denying to European States the right to acquire new territories or political influence in the American continent beyond what they already held. This was meant as a warning to the powers of the Holy Alliance at the moment, but it was meant also as a warning to Great Britain with regard to the future. Canning did not like it. Neither he nor his pupil, Palmerston, after him, was so friendly to the United States in feeling as Castlereagh had shown himself over the Canadian boundary disarmament.[1] But in Canning's day the questions in dispute with the United States were dormant, and on the question of the hour the two branches of the English-speaking race were at one. It was not, however, President Monroe's ' doctrine,' but the British fleet, that prevented France or the Holy Alliance from suppressing the independence of the Spanish Colonies. *Dec. 1823.* *1823–1826.*

Besides the vast regions of South and Central America, a smaller spot upon the political map of the world still bears the mark of Canning's handiwork. The independence of Greece was largely due to him. In the Levant, Canning could not override the will of all the Powers of Europe, as he could on the open Atlantic. But on the question of the Greek revolt against the Turk, the governments of the Holy Alliance were at variance with one another. Austria indeed consistently supported the Turk as representing the ' anti-revolutionary ' side. Russia, for her own ends, and from traditional sympathy, was the champion of the Eastern Christians. France, partly from religious and cultural inclination, inclined the same way. Much depended therefore on England's attitude. Wellington, following the example of Castlereagh, was pro-Turk. But the British public, moved by Byron's self-sacrifice and death, and at that time profoundly ' classical ' in its culture, idealized the Greek ' Klephts ' as heroes of Thermopylae. Canning was happily inspired to put up a barrier to Russian aggression in the Levant by erecting an independent Greek nation, rather than by supporting the continued abominations of Turkish misrule. His policy of trusting to nationalism to keep Russian ambition in check, succeeded in

[1] See p. 662, below.

the case of Greece, but was abandoned by later British statesmen when Palmerston, Russell and Gladstone, at the time of
the Crimean War, and twenty years later, Disraeli, sacrificed the
interests of the Balkan Christians to British fears of Russia.

The success of Canning's policy was secured, as regards
Greece, when, a few weeks after his death, the British, French,
and Russian fleets under Admiral Codrington blew the Turkish
fleet out of the water in Navarino Bay. In that conflagration
the Holy Alliance was dissolved as a force in European politics.
Wellington, when he came to the Premiership, regretted
Navarino as an ' untoward event,' but he was unable seriously
to limit the extent of its consequences.

Canning, as Foreign Secretary in Lord Liverpool's Cabinet,
had so stirred the romantic liberalism of the new England and
the new Europe, that in the absence of effective Whig leadership
he had become the principal hero in the eyes of the forward-
looking party in Britain. When, therefore, on Liverpool's illness

and retirement, the Tory Cabinet split, and Canning formed a
government which the Old Guard under Wellington, Peel and
Eldon refused to join, the new Premier obtained the co-operation
of more than half the Whigs in Parliament and the good wishes

of liberal-minded men in the country. His own death a few
months later brought his Ministry to an end before it had accomplished anything remarkable, but the fact that it had been
formed was an important step in the break-up and reshuffling of
parties. Most of the ' Canningite ' Tories who served in it, like
Palmerston and Melbourne, soon afterward joined the revivified
and enlarged Whig Party that passed the Reform Bill.

It is remarkable, however, that Canning himself to the last
opposed Parliamentary Reform. Probably, therefore, his removal from the scene actually precipitated the speed of political
change which he had done so much to set moving. He was the
one man in England who might have preserved the rotten
boroughs for many years. But after his death everything played
into the hands of the Reformers. The hope that the unreformed
Parliament and the Tory party would lead the country forward
in the new age, which had burned brightly under Canning and

Huskisson, was effectively quenched by the High Tory Ministry
under Wellington.

But before the final reconstitution of parties on the Reform
Bill issue, important concessions to the new principle of the
civic equality of religions were wrung by events from the unwilling Cabinet of Wellington and Peel. The tide of change was
indeed coming in with an elemental rapidity, overthrowing in
turn every position taken up by embarrassed statesmen from day

to day. Whereas Canning in 1827 had thought it necessary to pledge his Cabinet to prevent the repeal of the Test Act and to leave Catholic Emancipation alone, in spite of his own views on Emancipation, fifteen months after Wellington took office on the basis of ' no-surrender,' both these relieving Bills had become law of the land under the ægis of an ultra-Tory Ministry.

The Test Act, which prevented Catholic and Protestant Nonconformists from holding State or Municipal office, had been regarded by the Church as the very ark of the Covenant ever since the reign of Charles II, and had been the condition of her accepting the Revolution settlement and the Hanoverian succession. Its repeal, on the motion of Lord John Russell, was of symbolic **1828.** importance, but was not of great immediate effect. For until the Parliamentary and Municipal elections had been democratized, Dissenters had little chance of holding office. It was only in conjunction with the Municipal Corporations Act of 1835 and the Second Reform Bill of 1867, that the Repeal of the Test Act effected the full political emancipation of Non-conformists.

In 1829 a still more remarkable surrender was made. For half a dozen years past the Irish people had been organized in the Catholic Association, under the priests as officers and under Daniel O'Connell as Commander-in-Chief. Though everyone in authority was hostile to the movement, the unanimity of the population was terrible. No great body of men moves so completely to order, as a nation consisting of a single class of ill-educated peasants, in whom the instincts of herd-morality have been fortified by centuries of oppression. O'Connell demanded Catholic Emancipation, that is to say, that Roman Catholics should not be debarred from sitting in either House of Parliament. The victor of Waterloo shrank from the contest with the Catholic Association of Ireland. The British Army had been reduced to its lowest point in pursuit of retrenchment and lower taxes, and scarcely sufficed to protect property in Britain from starving operatives and rick-burning peasants. Moreover, Wellington always abhorred the idea of civil bloodshed, though he so frequently refused until the very last moment to make concessions which were the only alternative. The surrender of Peel and Wellington to O'Connell infuriated the High Tories, **1829.** who had put their trust in them. Indeed Wellington had purged his administration of the Canningites, and of nearly every man who believed in Catholic Emancipation, only a year before he emancipated the Catholics. The fabric of the Tory party was split into three mutually enraged sections—Canningites, High Tories, and embarrassed supporters of government. The strategical and tactical errors of Wellington's political campaign had cleared the way for what he most dreaded—a real Parliamentary Reform Bill and a real Reform Ministry.

Charles, Lord Grey, the nominal chief of the Whig Party since the death of Fox, had for many years played a very inadequate part as leader of opposition—at least by our modern ideas of political leadership. The rural leisure of his home on the Northumbrian shore, with its library and his fifteen children, grew to have many more attractions for him than Westminster. But in his hot youth he had been the principal agent in leading Fox to pronounce for Parliamentary Reform in 1792, and so to break with Portland and the Whig seceders who followed Burke into the Anti-Jacobin camp. Grey had never given up his belief that a redistribution of seats, based on the abolition of a large number of the rotten boroughs, would ultimately be necessary to save Parliamentary government in Britain. He had for many years ceased to preach the doctrine, regarding it as untimely, so long as only the working-class Radicals would move in the matter. But he still maintained that it would be necessary to wait only until the time when the question should be taken up 'seriously and affectionately' by the people themselves, meaning more particularly the 'solid and respectable' middle class. That time had at length come, and greatly to the surprise of friends and the consternation of foes, the old nobleman proved as good as his word, and for three years left his rural seclusion to give Britain the reformed Parliament of which he had dreamed in his youth.

In 1830 the movement for Parliamentary Reform seemed to be generated by a natural process out of the circumstances of the hour—the return of bad times, the violence of working-class despair in town and country, the gravity of middle-class fear of a social uprising beneath their feet, and the belief that it could no longer be averted by mere repression; to all these causes were added disillusionment with the Tory party resulting from the Duke's blunders, and the example of the July revolution in Paris that put an end to Charles X's reactionary government, without, as in 1789, causing social overturn. From squire to postilion, from cotton-lord to mill-hand, everyone was talking of the need for Reform, though with great varieties of meaning and emphasis. On the extent and character of the proposed new franchise there was wide divergence, but all were united in a detestation of the rotten boroughs. Their owners, hitherto regarded with obsequious deference, were now held up to general execration as 'borough-mongers' who had stolen the nation's birthright. There was also general agreement that the new

industrial and the old rural districts ought to obtain a representation more in proportion to their wealth and the numbers
of their inhabitants.   The alliance of all classes against the
rotten boroughs found expression in the Birmingham Political
Union, ably led by Thomas Attwood.   In the Birmingham of
forty years before, the mob had sacked the Reformers' houses,
but the citizens were now agreed that the Midland capital had
a right to representation in Parliament.

Grey and his more advanced lieutenants of the younger
generation, Lord John Russell and Lord Durham, saw that the
moment had come to place the Whig Parliamentary party at the
head of this movement.   On the basis of a sweeping redistribution of seats and a level ten-pound household franchise in all
boroughs, the aristocratic Whig leaders in Parliament placed
themselves at the head of middle-class opinion in the country.
Owing to the Industrial Revolution, the middle class counted
for much more than in the Eighteenth Century ; and owing to
the growth of Wesleyanism, Dissent was reckoned at nearly half
the religious world.   Therefore the renewed leadership of the
middle classes by the Whig aristocracy, on the basis of a reformed
electoral system, was destined to remain the most stable element
in the government of Great Britain for a generation to come.
The man who represented the alliance was the plebeian Henry
Brougham, the agitator and leader of the ' intelligent middle
classes,' who with his hard but mobile features was the very
incarnation of the new age of ' machinery and the march of
mind.'   He was closely connected also with the Whig leaders
and with the *Edinburgh Review*.   No Whig Cabinet in 1830
could be formed without him.   If his wisdom and reliability
as a colleague in office had been on a level with his activity
and genius as a free lance in opposition, he would have been
the leading statesman of the new era ; but he declined, instead,
into its most magnificent oddity.

The political alliance of Whigs and middle classes was joined
by other recruits.   Canningites like Melbourne and Palmerston,[1]
and independents like young Stanley and Sir James Graham
representing the ' respectable ' classes of Northern England, had
recently come to believe that the country could only be saved
by a moderate measure of Parliamentary Reform.   In the
autumn of 1830 they still looked to Wellington to supply what
the country demanded, but he alienated all moderates by
declaring that ' the system of representation possesses the full

---

[1] The other leading Canningite, Huskisson, was killed by an engine at the
opening of the Manchester-Liverpool railway in Sept. 1830.   He was in negotiation with Grey at the time.

and entire confidence of the country,' and that to improve it was beyond the range of human wisdom. As a result of this famous pronouncement, Stanley and Graham at once entered into a temporary alliance with the Whigs to secure a Reform of Parliament, and the Canningites, Palmerston and Melbourne, became recognized as Whig leaders and remained so during the rest of their lives. Wellington's Ministry tottered, and the High Tories seized the opportunity to take their revenge on him and Peel for passing Catholic Emancipation, by voting against them in the critical division. In November 1830 the Duke fell from power, and Lord Grey was called on by the new and popular ' sailor King,' William IV, to form a Ministry based on the programme of ' peace, retrenchment and reform.'

The Cabinet formed by Lord Grey was aristocratic in *personnel*, but the aristocrats in the Whig Ministry included some of the ablest and most advanced men in Parliament. The measure of Reform which Lord Durham and Lord John Russell framed under Grey's general direction, and which Lord Althorp piloted through the House of Commons, though criticized ever since for not going far enough, in its own day astounded friends and foes by the distance that it went. It was indeed, as the Tories complained, ' a new constitution,' in the sense that it extended political power to new social classes and to new districts of the island.

March, 1831.

A Bill abolishing all the rotten boroughs at a stroke had never been expected, and its announcement aroused a shout of surprise and enthusiasm from Land's End to John o' Groat's, while throwing the Tories, who had looked for a much milder proposal, into angry opposition. The most influential working-class leaders and organizers, like Place and Cobbett, actively supported ' The Bill, the whole Bill, and nothing but the Bill,' because they knew that to pass working-class enfranchisement was impossible in the existing House and, indeed, in the existing state of public opinion. But they foresaw that it must follow some day, whatever the Whigs might say about ' finality,' if once the time-honoured system of vested interests in nomination boroughs were overset. To get that done would require the union of all classes, for the House of Lords had by the law of the constitution the power to veto the Bill, and was determined at all risks to use it.

The upper middle-class and the shopkeepers in the newly enfranchised boroughs saw in the ten-pound household franchise all that they could ask for themselves. The half of the middle class that was still excluded from the vote, looked to find indirect representation of their interests in the enfranchisement of the new industrial areas : that Manchester should have two members instead of Old Sarum, and Sheffield instead of some Cornish hamlet, would before long secure the disappearance of the Corn Laws. But the squires and tenant-farmers overlooked that danger, for they themselves were gratified by the increase of County representation under the Bill, and by the concession of a tenant-farmer franchise that rather increased than diminished landlord power in the rural constituencies.[1]

It may seem strange to-day that a proposal to divide political power between half the middle class and all the landlords should have aroused so much popular enthusiasm. But the cry of 'Down with the rotten boroughs' united almost everyone except the numerous beneficiaries, direct and indirect, of the old distribution of power, and the Church clergy, who mistakenly believed that the Reform Bill would lead to disestablishment and disendowment. It did not even lead to the abolition of compulsory Church rates, nor to the admission of Dissenters to the Universities, till yet another extension of the franchise had been granted, so imperfectly were even the middle classes admitted to power under the Bill of 1832.

After fifteen months of political agitation unparalleled in the history of Great Britain, the Reform Bill was carried in the teeth of the resistance of the Peers. The first crisis was a general election which produced a sure majority of 136 for the Bill, in place of an unreliable and evanescent majority of one. The second crisis was the throwing out of the Bill by forty-one votes in the Lords, chiefly by the Peers of recent Tory creation and by the Bench of Bishops. That winter there was great economic distress in the industrial and agricultural districts,[2] cholera was raging, and the popular anger at the Lords' action threatened society with chaos. But the Bristol riots served as a warning to all sensible men, and the movement of violence was controlled by the Political Unions that had sprung up all over the country in imitation of Birmingham. The existence of the

[margin: March 1831– May 1832. May. 1831. Oct. 1831.]

---

[1] Before 1832 there were only two members for each county in England, while there were 400 borough members, most of them sitting for more or less rotten boroughs. The Whigs in 1830 were reckoned to hold 60 out of the 200 rotten borough seats which they destroyed by the Bill. About 140 of these 200 were abolished altogether, and about 60 more had their electoral character restored by the new ten pound franchise. In a very few cases, like Preston and Westminster, the franchise was limited by the application of the uniform ten pound line, to the disadvantage of the working class in those few localities.

[2] On first taking office the year before, in November, 1830, the Whigs had been faced with 'the last peasants' rising' in some of the southern counties, to obtain the wage of half-a-crown a day. The starving agricultural labourers rioted, but shed no blood, and destroyed little property ; they were most cruelly punished by the panic-stricken Whigs, who allowed several of them to be hanged and 450 of them to be transported to Australia from all knowledge of their families.

Unions implied, however, a more serious threat of real civil war if the Bill were finally rejected.

The danger to the Bill was lest its working-class supporters should break off and begin a revolutionary movement of their own. Reaction might then ensue in the struggle to maintain order. But the middle classes had thrown off their long political apathy, and were determined to have the Bill passed before society was destroyed by a clash of the Radical with the Tory forces. The peace of the country depended, indeed, on the passage of the Bill. At length King William, a perturbed and honest sailor in such a gale as no State skipper had seen before, promised Grey to use his prerogative of creating Peers to carry the Bill. There was the useful precedent of Queen Anne's creation of Peers to carry the Peace of Utrecht for the Tory Ministry of that day. Then at the last moment William hesitated, and endeavoured to get the Tories to take office and pass the Bill in their own way. This occasioned the last crisis, the famous 'Days of May.' Lord Grey gave in his resignation, and for a week the country believed that Wellington was coming back to rule by the sword. The big towns prepared resistance. But Peel saw that the game was played out, and Grey was brought back triumphantly, on the condition of the surrender of Peers and King.

May 1832.

This final crisis, that secured the actual passage of the Reform Act, gave dramatic emphasis to the popular element in the 'new constitution.' The people, as a whole, had wrenched the modern Magna Carta from the governing class. The nation was thenceforth master in its own house. But the political extent of the 'nation' would yet need to be defined by a succession of franchise struggles, each less violent indeed than the great original. Ten-pound householders and tenant-farmers were not likely to constitute 'the nation' for ever. They had no such prescriptive right to govern the land as the borough-owners, whose vested interest had been swept away by the pacific revolt of a nation.

1867, 1884, 1918.

In Scotland the old representative system had been worse than in England, for not even the county elections had any reality north of the Tweed. Politically Scotland was one vast rotten borough. The violence of the northern democracy at the crisis had been proportionately great. In 1832 the Scots obtained for the first time popular institutions, other than the Kirk, through which to express themselves. The immediate consequence of the Reform Bill was the Burgh Act of 1833, which created the first popularly elected Municipalities that Scotland had possessed since the Fifteenth Century.

England waited till 1835 for her Municipal Corporations Act. The fall of the Parliamentary rotten boroughs involved the fall of the Municipal rotten boroughs, analogous sister bodies in the field of local government, which would never have been disturbed under the old regime. The Act of 1835 was more democratic than the Reform Bill, for it gave all ratepayers the right to vote for the new Municipalities. At last the ice-age of English institutional and corporate life had come to an end, and the life of the community began to be remodelled according to the actual needs of the new economic society. The spirit of Jeremy Bentham was abroad in the land, though the old man himself was on his death-bed. His test question—' What is the use of it ? '—was being applied to one venerable absurdity after another. The age of Royal Commissions and their Reports had begun with the Whig Reform Ministry. The Municipal Corporations Act was among its first-fruits.

The Act only applied to the larger towns. The rural districts were still left under the administrative control of the Justices of the Peace until the establishment of elected County Councils by Lord Salisbury's Ministry in 1888. This difference in types of local government corresponded to the fact that rural England was still mentally subordinate to the squires, while the new urban England was already in spirit a democracy.

Inadequate as it was in its geographical scope, the Municipal Corporations Act of 1835 established in the chief urban areas a powerful form of authority, subject to popular control, and able to levy a local rate. From this beginning there grew up a concentration of new functions ; throughout the coming century powers were perpetually being added to the Municipal Corporations. Finally they dealt with almost all aspects of local government except public-house licensing and judicial power, which were regarded as unfit functions for an elective body. In 1835 very few foresaw that the new Municipalities would end in educating the children of the people, and in supplying the public with trams, light, water, and even houses, or that they would become traders and employers of labour on a large scale.

Starting from 1835 there also grew up the connection between the governmental departments of Whitehall and the popularly elected local bodies, based on State supervision and Treasury grants of the taxpayers' money in aid of local rates. All this, though not foreseen, was rendered possible by the bold and uniform Whig legislation of 1835. In this way was begun the tardy process of catching up the uncontrolled social consequences of the Industrial Revolution. But where, in all this, was the place for ' retrenchment ' ? That panacea faded into thin air.

In 1833 Lord Althorp passed the first effective Factory Act, fixing legal limits for the working hours of children and young persons respectively. The great merit of the Bill, little recognized at the time, was the institution of government inspectors to enforce the law. It was the beginning of a whole new development in social welfare.

Another immediate consequence of the Reform Bill was the abolition of slavery in the British Empire by the Act of 1833. Wilberforce died the same year, his work marvellously completed. During the later years of his life the active leadership of the Anti-Slavery cause had been carried on by Sir Thomas Fowell Buxton, with Brougham as trumpeter. In Wilberforce's original campaign the defenders of the slave-trade had been important British shipping interests in Bristol and Liverpool.[1] But after the slave-trade had been stopped, the defenders of slavery were found less in England herself than in the colonies. If slaves could no longer be imported, they could still be bred from the existing stock. The planters of the West Indies and other tropical colonies saw ruin in the proposal to emancipate their slaves on any terms. But they did not conduct their case wisely, or treat either their negroes or the negro-phil missionaries well; their violence aroused the indignation of the British public, more particularly the religious world of Evangelicalism and Non-conformity, then very influential. The Slavery Abolition Act of 1833 gave the slave-owners twenty millions in compensation for their slaves, willingly paid by the mother country.

The other great successful action of the Whig Ministry was the settlement of the Belgian question. In 1830 the Paris revolution had been followed by the revolt of Belgium from the partnership with Holland to which the Treaties of 1815 had assigned her. The revolt was partly liberal, partly clerical, and was promoted by French influences, clerical and liberal alike. The reactionary Powers of Eastern Europe regarded a breach made in the Treaties of 1815 by a popular revolt, as a thing to be suppressed after the fashion of the Holy Alliance. That was not the view of Great Britain, especially under the liberal Ministry of which Grey was Premier and Palmerston Foreign Secretary. But Britain, for her part, objected strongly to the establishment of French influence over Belgium either by annexation or by the reign of a French Prince at Brussels. The Chauvinist party in Paris was with difficulty kept in check by Louis Philippe, ' the Citizen King,' and his Ministers, anxious on the whole for the friendship of the new liberal England in face of the hostile Powers of Russia, Austria and Prussia. It was a situation of delicacy and danger,

---

[1] See pp. 599–600, above.

but was satisfactorily solved, after a number of crises, on the basis of the adoption of Prince Leopold of Saxe-Coburg Gotha as **1831.** King of the Belgians; he was a personal friend of the British Ministers and the favourite uncle of the future Queen Victoria. In 1839 Palmerston crowned the work by a treaty which settled the vexed question of Dutch-Belgian boundaries, and guaranteed Belgian neutrality. The treaty was signed by Belgium, Great Britain, France, Russia, Austria and Prussia. In this way the perennial British interest of securing a Power in the Netherlands from which we had nothing to fear, was again made safe for a long period of years.

Books for Further Reading

Spencer Walpole, *History of England from* 1815, Vols. I.–III.; Webster, *Foreign Policy of Castlereagh*, and Temperley, ditto, *Canning*; Graham Wallas, *Francis Place*; Cole, *William Cobbett* and *Short History of the British Working Class Movement*; Dicey, *Law and Opinion in England* (on Bentham); Trevelyan, *Lord Grey of the Reform Bill*; Butler, *The Passing of the Great Reform Bill*; Porritt, *The Unreformed House of Commons* (2 vols.) for details of the old system; Sir D. Le Marchant, *Lord Althorp*; Redlich and Hirst, *Local Government in England*, Vol. I.; Sir Herbert Maxwell, *Wellington*; Atlay, *The Victorian Chancellors*, Vol. I., for Brougham; Bagehot, *Biographical Sketches*.

CHAPTER II

Whig financial failure. Peel and the new Conservative Party. The New Poor Law. Chartism. The Repeal of the Corn Laws, 1846. Disraeli and Peel. The Whig-Palmerston regime. The Civil Service. Queen Victoria. The Crimea and Italy. Prosperity and Social Assuagement. The franchise agitation and the Second Reform Bill, 1867

Queen Victoria, 1837

In the reign of William IV, the Whigs, under Benthamite inspiration and Radical pressure, had introduced into the organs of government elements of modern efficiency and popular representation, through the Reform Bill and the Municipal Corporations Act. It was only a beginning, but the first step counts. If the Whigs had produced among them a great statesman who understood the social problems of the day, or if they had even produced an able finance Minister, they might at once have led the nation far along the path of progress which they had opened out to the eager hopes of their suffering and impatient fellow-countrymen. But the party which in old times had benefited by the services of Charles Montagu, Godolphin and Walpole, was stricken with financial paralysis, and left it to Peel to discover in the Income Tax and Free Trade the key to the financial and economic enigma of that day. At the time of Queen Victoria's accession the Whig

Chancellor of the Exchequer appeared ' seated on an empty chest by the side of bottomless deficiencies, fishing for a budget,' as Peel said in one of his rare, deliberate lapses into humour.[1]

And so, within half a dozen years of the passage of the Reform Bill, it was clear to all that the Whigs had shot their bolt, and had no further programme for the relief of the still acute economic and industrial distress of the country. It was well for the fortunes of Parliamentary government under the new regime that an alternative Ministry could be formed from the opposition at Westminster. Peel had reconstituted a ' Conservative ' party out of the wreckage of the ' Tory ' party destroyed by the Reform Bill, and he was attracting back many who, like Stanley and Graham, had supported the Whigs in order to get the rotten boroughs abolished. It was characteristic of England in the Nineteenth Century, as distinct from several foreign lands, that when the various sections of the upper class lost their special privileges they did not on that account retire to private life, but accommodated themselves to the new conditions. The very limits of the Reform effected in 1832, with which modern criticism is often impatient, had the advantage of keeping unbroken the tradition of upper-class connection with political life, and avoiding the development of a class of ' professional politicians.' There may be no logic in a process of bit-by-bit enfranchisement, but there may be great practical advantages to the life of the nation in the very graduality of an uninterrupted movement towards democratic control.

Peel's ' Tamworth manifesto ' in 1834 had accepted the Reform Bill as a *fait accompli*, with all its implications, and Peel at least understood what those implications were. His ' bourgeois ' origin and natural affinity to the trading and manufacturing classes enabled him to understand the economic and financial needs of the country better than most Tories and most Whigs. Indeed, he understood the middle-class mind, on its economic side, and sympathized with the sufferings of the poor better than he understood or sympathized with the mentality of the landlord party which he led. He came to regard that party as an instrument of government given into his hands for whatever wise purpose he wished.

The majority of the new Conservative party had, however, interests and feelings of their own. They disliked Peel's

[1] O'Connell, who disliked Peel not without personal cause, said ' His smile was like a silver plate on a coffin.' His shy manners, taken for coldness and hauteur, isolated him personally from the ordinary members of his party, and go some way to account for their repudiation of him in 1846 ; his Cabinet colleagues who knew him better stood by him and became ' Peelites.' Queen Victoria also disliked him till she knew him well—not afterwards.

favourites, the manufacturers; they were deeply interested in
the defence of the Corn Laws, and equally in the defence of the
Church. They believed the Church to be in danger from the
Whig proposals to admit Dissenters to Oxford and Cambridge,
and to apply a part of the superfluous wealth of the Irish Establishment to secular purposes, although the House of Lords was
there to prevent the actual perpetration of these outrages.
Such questions, it is true, interested Peel as well as his followers,
but the leader's heart and mind were moving more and more
into the study of the financial aspects of the relief of trade, and
the ' condition of the people problem,' which Carlyle and others
were beginning to regard as the principal business of Parliaments
and Cabinets. What Peel lacked was the gifts of personality
and popular persuasiveness to draw his party after him in these
thoughts, as he succeeded in drawing many of his intimates and
colleagues, the future ' Peelites,'—Graham, Aberdeen, Cardwell
and Gladstone. He had had his political training in days before
the Reform Bill and before Canning, when the decision of the
Cabinet was law. After the Reform Bill, he understood the new
relation of the Cabinet to the people at large, better than he
understood its new relation to its own partisans.

Before the Whigs finally handed over the government of the
land to Peel as a result of the General Election of 1841, they had
taken, with the full concurrence of Peel and Wellington, an im
portant step in social reorganization, by passing the New Poor Law. 1834.
On the advice of Nassau Senior and his fellow Commissioners,
they had abolished the Speenhamland system of giving rates in
aid of wages.[1] In that way they had begun the depauperization
of the labourer in South England, and the restoration of his
qualities of self-respect and self-dependence. Unfortunately,
this necessary operation was carried through with a ruthless and
doctrinaire disregard of the human side of the problem. When
out-door relief was the means of livelihood to many thousands
in town and country, it was terrible to cut it all off at one stroke,
without at the same time enforcing a living wage, or supplying
any shelter for the unemployed and their dependents except the
workhouse. Moreover, in their just alarm at the pauperizing
effect of the system which they abolished, the Commissioners
made it a principle that the workhouse life should be more
unpleasant than the life of free labour beyond its walls. The
economic theories of the day did not permit of setting to work
at the problem from the other end, and trying by statute to raise
the condition of free labour to one of greater attractiveness than

[1] See p. 612, above.

2 A

the workhouse. Even the aged and the sick, for whom in those days there were no pensions or industrial insurance, had not the means to live at home, and yet received no better treatment in the workhouse than if they had come there through their own fault. It was in these circumstances that the youthful author of *Oliver Twist*, by describing what workhouses meant for those who inhabited them, appealed from the Benthamite abstractions in which the Commissioners dealt, to the flesh and blood realities which interested the more sensitive rising generation of the new Victorian era.

1838.

By these all too drastic measures the rot of pauperism was stopped. Too great local variation and parochial independence had been faults of the old Poor Law. The national and centralized character of the New Poor Law, though far too harshly used in the first generation, made it easier to carry out the alleviations and improvements on which later public opinion insisted. The workhouses gradually ceased to be penal settlements for the unfortunate, and in our own day of Old Age Pensions and Industrial Insurance, they have been to a very large extent emptied of their folk even in bad times.

The anger of the wage-earning classes at the New Poor Law, and the political impotence of that anger, sharply reminded them that another Reform Bill was needed before they could make their wishes directly operative at Westminster. So, too, their agitation for the Ten Hours Bill, to limit by statute the hours of work in factories, led by Lord Shaftesbury and by Fielden the great master cotton-spinner, divided both the Liberal and Conservative parties so that the Bill was not passed till 1847.[1] These continued agitations in the manufacturing districts, and the continued distress caused the rise of Chartism. Chartism demanded in effect only what was granted in 1867 and 1884, that is to say the enfranchisement of the classes left out by the Bill of 1832. The six points of the 'People's Charter' were purely political. But the motive and character of the agitation were social. It repelled middle-class aid. It was a cry of rage and class-consciousness on the part of the suffering wage-earner. It had its influence on Parliament, now a more sensitive barometer to outside opinion than of old. The ominous shadow of Chartism in the background accelerated the passage of Factory Acts, Corn Law Repeal, Acts against truck payments, Shaftesbury's Mines Act and the first belated Public Health Act of 1848 when Chadwick's Reports had at last persuaded Parliament that Sanitation was a public question.

1838.

In this way Chartism indirectly improved the lot of the

[1] See p. 647, note, below.

working classes, and so attained some of its real objective. But its political programme of Universal Suffrage had no chance of success so long as it was demanded as a class measure, to be won not by the help of middle-class organization and leadership, but as an attack on employers. The Chartist leaders themselves were of little use as practical politicians. Success crowned the movement in the 'sixties, because then the middle classes, half of whom were still excluded from the franchise, joined with the wage-earners under the leadership of Bright and Gladstone to demand the further extension of the franchise.

The better terms on which the middle and working classes stood to one another in that later decade as compared to the earlier period of Chartism proper, are to be accounted for in part by the increased prosperity that had come to all ranks of society in the interval, abating much of the bitterness engendered by want. Other causes of class reconciliation were the beneficent finance of Peel's Ministry, and the remarkable circumstances under which the Corn Laws were abolished. Cobden's Anti- **1846.** Corn-Law League skilfully combined and mobilized working and middle class opinion on a subject where there was no difference of interest between them. Their common victory, won, after half a dozen years of constant agitation, over the determined resistance of the landlord class, did much to prevent the line of political demarcation from being drawn between the wage-earners and the rest of society. It opened the way for the gradual transformation of Melbourne's and Palmerston's Whig party,—an alliance of part of the aristocracy with the middle class,—into Gladstone's Liberal party,—an alliance of part of the middle class with the wage-earners.

By these complicated movements of classes and parties, involved in an endless network of cross divisions and double allegiances—yet always with the two-party system functioning in the Parliamentary world,—the Victorian era succeeded in avoiding the sharp battle of classes which had seemed to threaten in the days of Chartism and of Robert Owen's Grand National **1838.** Trade Union.[1] Class war in some form would not have been **1833.** avoided if steady improvement had not been going on in conditions of life, at any rate outside the purely rural districts. The salvation of society was due not only to the efforts and the good sense of various sections of the community, but to the improved

---

[1] Robert Owen wanted to draw the wage-earners away from political agitation to economic action of a semi-revolutionary kind, and to socialism. He never cared about a democratic franchise, being by origin an autocratically minded employer who organized the lives of his employees for their own good. But, like Bentham, he was compelled, by facts, to realize that society would never be reformed from the top.

trade and prosperity that set in during the 'forties. In the mid-Victorian era Britain was the manufacturing centre of the world. Other nations largely depended upon her for coal and for manufactured goods in return for food and raw material.

In such a world the middle class saw its interest in a policy of complete Free Trade. In that matter it asserted itself against the landlord class, whose political leadership it otherwise accepted with gratitude. It was the old custom of England for the townsfolk to be led by the gentry, provided the followers had a say as to the direction. The ten-pound freeholders enfranchised in 1832 often chose country gentlemen to represent them. Until the Second Reform Bill of 1867, the presence on the benches of the House of Commons of persons of middle-class origin and standards like Cobden and Bright, was tolerated as a curiosity or resented as an impertinence by the Whig and Tory squires around them. For in those days the distinction between the well-to-do middle class and the gentry still existed : they had not yet been merged in one grade of society by passing through the standardising process of Public School education. There was very frequently a difference of religious observance, which counted for much in those days because it represented social facts, such as the exclusion of Dissenters from Oxford and Cambridge. The culture of the one class was based mainly on the Classics, of the other mainly on the Bible. The one was interested in sport, government and landowning ; the other stuck close to its ledgers and had fewer amusements and shorter ' week-ends ' than the business man of to-day.

Even after 1832, the middle class put up with a good deal of exclusiveness and patronage on the part of those above them, but in the matter of Free Trade in Corn they made up their minds and on that issue they had the formidable masses of the unenfranchised behind them. The Parliamentary Conservative party was opposed to Corn Law abolition and the Whig party was divided on the question. Peel, in the early days of his great Ministry, revived the Income Tax, and with its help reduced and abolished import duties on many articles with excellent results to the trade of the country. But he was in no position to abolish the duties on foreign corn. Corn remained the outstanding question. The Anti-Corn-Law League was almost as formidable in industrial England as O'Connell's Catholic League had been in rural Ireland. Peel, who had surrendered to the one in 1829, surrendered to the other in 1846, partly from a sense that government must be carried on by consent of the governed, partly because Cobden's speeches on the floor of the House had persuaded him on the economic issue, and partly because the potato-blight

1842–
1845.

in Ireland in 1845–6 left him no other choice than either to suspend
the Corn Laws or to allow the Irish to die by tens of thousands.
And the duties on foreign corn, if once suspended, could scarcely
be put on again without causing a revolutionary movement in
Great Britain.   The 'total and immediate' repeal of the Corn
Laws was an unforeseen consequence of Pitt's Act of Union.[1]

The Repeal of the Corn Laws was for a number of reasons
the most important political event between the First and Second
Reform Bills.   In the first place, it broke up the Conservative
party and so put the Whigs into power, with short intervals,
for twenty years, with the occasional addition to their counsels
and their voting strength of Peelite statesmen like Aberdeen,
Cardwell and Graham, and the much needed financial ability of
Gladstone.

The revolt of the Conservative private members against 1846.
Peel had not been generally expected.   It was the force and
quality of Disraeli's philippics against the traitor in command
that compelled the back benches to rise and mutiny, as gunpowder must needs blaze up if fire is applied.   It does not appear
that Disraeli had deep convictions on the Corn Laws as an
economic policy, and he was soon afterwards speaking uncon-
cernedly of Protection as 'dead and damned.'   But he had, like
Bolingbroke before him, attached himself in a professional
capacity to the gentlemen of the 'country party' and felt bound
to show them sport.   The 'great historic Houses' of England
appealed strongly to his imagination as a foreign observer of our
institutions, though he was obliged to except the Whig Houses
which belonged to the other side.   Peel had maltreated and
betrayed 'the gentlemen of England' in abandoning the Corn
Law, and as they found it difficult adequately to express their
own feelings on the matter, Disraeli became their champion
against the man who stood also in his own way.   His conduct
in overthrowing Peel kept the Conservative party out of power
for twenty years, but raised him from the back benches to the
direct succession of the leadership after Stanley.   It thereby
enabled him, twenty-one years later, to 'educate his party'
to the performance of a *volte-face* just as complete and just as 1867.
unpalatable as that on account of which he had put a sudden
end to the career of Peel, at the height of the great Premier's
popularity with the mass of his countrymen.

Genius has its privileges, which no one need grudge it, for

---

[1] Wellington characteristically supported Peel's *volte-face*, not because he
agreed, but because he believed in Peel as a Minister.   'Rotten potatoes have done
it,' he said resignedly ; 'they put Peel in his d—d fright.'

genius alone can make Parliamentary proceedings as attractive to contemporary observers and historical students as the more dangerous annals of war and revolution. It seemed as if Palmerston, Disraeli and Gladstone were raised up at this time to captivate, each in a totally different way, the imagination of the new democracy, and give to it that personal interest in Parliamentary government, for lack of which Parliamentary institutions in some countries have withered like waterless plants.

The victory of the Anti-Corn-Law League was the first signal victory of the middle classes over the gentry, and of the industrial over the agricultural interest. But the agricultural interest, in the wider sense of the term, had in fact been divided on the issue. If there had been a numerous peasantry owning or occupying the land in small portions, the landlords and big farmers would not have been left isolated in the struggle. The landless agricultural labourer, so far as his almost negligible opinion was asked by politicians, on the whole inclined to the policy of the cheap loaf.

But even the ' agricultural interest ' of landlords and large farmers soon found that they had not been ruined by Repeal. Free importation prevented corn prices from soaring even when the value of money fell with the gold discoveries in California and Australia, but corn prices remained fairly steady for another generation, and with better times there was a greatly increased consumption of bread. The country-houses and farmsteads of England were never more wealthy, populous and happy than during the mid-Victorian age,—the age of Trollope's novels and John Leech's pictures. Indeed, the removal of all serious cause of bitterness between town and country left the ' great houses ' in a most enviable social position for another thirty years. Then, indeed, the development of trans-continental railways and great steamships enabled America to pour forth such quantities of food that, during Disraeli's Ministry in the late 'seventies, British corn-growing was at last very seriously affected. The world-wide organization of British commerce drew food to the island from every quarter, and the agricultural situation which we know to-day began to develop itself.

The victory of the Anti-Corn-Law League in 1846 had been a victory of new methods of political education and advertisement, which were another step along the road of democracy. These methods were to some extent left in abeyance in the two following decades of prosperity and social peace, but they became the common stock-in-trade of both political parties after the enfranchisement of fresh millions in 1867 and 1884.

The sharp tussle between landlords and millowners, which

had resulted from the Corn Law controversy, had caused each party to champion the victims of its opponent. The miserable wages and housing of the rural labourer were proclaimed on League platforms; the wrongs of the factory hands were the most popular argument in reply. In this way the unenfranchised had their wrongs advertised, and in some cases remedied. The years of mutual recrimination between landlord and millowner saw the passage of Shaftesbury's Mines Act and the famous Ten 1842. Hours Bill for factories.[1] Less was done for the agricultural 1847. labourers, because they were more widely scattered than the workmen organized in Trade Unions and congregated in factories, and they were therefore less feared and less easy to help.

With the laying to rest of the Corn Law controversy there set in at the same time the great period of mid-Victorian commercial and industrial expansion, which submerged beneath a tidal wave of prosperity the social problem and the mutiny of the underworld. Politics reflected the relaxed tension. From 1846 to 1866 we have the period of quiet Whig-Peelite rule, dominated by the figure of the popular favourite, Lord Palmerston. His performances were eminently suited for a period when everything was safe, when nothing seemed to matter very much either at home or abroad, and when even to provoke a war with Russia involved only a limited liability.

Gladstone, meanwhile, at this stage of his long passage from old-world Tory to advanced Liberal, saw the duty of a statesman to the community chiefly in sound finance, and in the creation of the Treasury traditions with which he was closely associated in these years, implying strict economy and probity in the expenditure of public money. It was a great period for the growth of system and tradition in many Departments of the permanent Civil Service, preparatory to the much greater weight of administration which the next more active age would throw upon the offices of Whitehall. At the same time experiments were made in competitive examination, instead of jobbery, in making selections for the Civil Service. The idea of the value of examination as a test of men was derived from Oxford and Cambridge, where

[1] The Bill limited the hours of *young persons* and *women* in factories to ten hours a day: in effect this meant a similar limitation of the hours of male adults, on account of working arrangements in factories. This was the Bill that was opposed by Bright, who never opposed factory bills to protect *children*, as is often erroneously stated. The Ten Hours Bill divided both the Whig and Conservative parties. The effective Bill for the protection of *children under thirteen* had been the Whig government's Bill of 1833, which introduced the all-important principle of Factory Inspection to put the law in force. See on the whole subject Hutchins and Harrison, *History of Factory Legislation*, and Hammond's *Shaftesbury*.

examinations had come greatly into fashion since the beginning of the Century. Palmerston, with his Regency standards of public life, scornfully opposed the wholesale abandonment of government patronage to a board of examiners. But the tone of the new age was all against favouritism and aristocratic inefficiency, and shortly after Palmerston's death Gladstone, 1870. who was much in earnest in the matter, imposed the system of open competition on almost all the avenues leading into Whitehall.

No doubt a more far-seeing generation would have used the fat years of mid-Victorian prosperity to make provision against the return of the lean, by more social legislation, and by the establishment of a national system of primary and secondary Educa-1847– tion. Something indeed was done in the way of Public Health 1865. provision. But, on the whole, while the voice of complaint was no longer loud in the land, statesmen of all parties were glad to rest and be thankful, hoping that the ugly facts and passions which the wave of prosperity had covered from observation, would never again obtrude themselves on the notice of Parliament.

As to Education, Prince Albert, it was remembered, was a German, and popular education a fad,—fit perhaps for industrious foreigners in Central Europe who had not our other advantages of character and world-position. At any rate it would be the height of political unwisdom to touch the Education question, because nothing could be done that would not make either Church or Dissent spring up in angry protest. The new Whig policy, like Walpole's of old, was not to rouse the sleeping ecclesiastical Cerberus, chained at present at the entrance of the House of Lords. The Whigs, allied as they were to the Peelite Conservatives, could not even remedy the Non-conformist grievances of compulsory Church Rates and exclusion from the Universities. And, indeed, in a world so comfortable and prosperous, it was difficult for any set of men to feel grievances very acutely, though Bright kept up a bulldog growl of his own, that might some day swell into a chorus. |

In these circumstances at home, the main political interests of the period were those of Foreign Affairs. Here Palmerston was born to shine, and he shone with a lustre that no one can deny, though the amount of gold that went to make the glitter was then, and always will be, a subject of agreeable controversy.

Palmerston, who like Peel had begun public life as a Tory Minister in Peninsular days, had later been a follower of Canning, and in his strong old age may be defined as a cross between a Canningite Tory and a Whig aristocrat. He voiced the popular feeling of Britons against foreign despots, in the manner common to Canning and the Whigs. He was Whig aristocrat in his attitude of Gallio towards religion and the Church, and in his resistance to the influence of the Court. Opposed as he was in home politics to an increase of democracy and especially to an extension of the franchise, he was not opposed to a certain degree of popular control over Foreign Policy, for he regarded himself, when Foreign Minister, as responsible rather to public opinion than to his Sovereign or even to his colleagues. Like Canning before him, he appealed to the middle classes to defend his foreign policy against the hostility of Court and Cabinet, sometimes, it must be confessed, with less good cause than his master had been able to show.

Palmerston's popularity was great in the country, considerable in the House, small in the Cabinet, less than nothing at Court. His influence with his countrymen arose in part from a personal impression that ' Old Pam ' was a ' sportsman,' and in part from the nature of his policy. It had a double appeal. He combined the Liberals' dislike of the despotisms of Austria and Russia, Naples and Rome, with a tone in asserting purely British rights which a later generation would have called ' Jingoism.' In Palmerston's spirited language, a British subject was ' *civis Romanus*,' and even if he were only a Maltese Jew swindling at Athens, had the British fleet at his back. The same nonchalant spirit was more happily shown in the sympathy extended to the victims of Austrian and Russian tyranny in Hungary, Italy and elsewhere after the collapse of the Liberal movement of 1848 upon the Continent. The attitude then adopted by Palmerston on behalf of Britain, in defiance of the wishes of the Queen and Prince Albert, was neither ignoble nor entirely useless, for it signified that constitutional liberty had still one hearty well-wisher among the Great Powers.

The strife between Palmerston and the Court was a constant source to him of amusement and joy in adventurous living, and to the Queen of grave annoyance. The Court had under her auspices become the reverse of what it had been under George IV as Regent and King. Probably Palmerston preferred what he recollected of the Regency—though scarcely of the Regent. In those days no one had expected Monarchs, Peers or Ministers to pay their debts to tradesmen or otherwise to conduct themselves as school-models to the unprivileged. In politics the change was equally marked. George III and George IV had been identified with High Tory resistance to reform. But Queen Victoria, in her impressionable youth, had learnt from her mentor, old Lord Melbourne, what she never forgot, that the strength of the British monarchy did not lie in intriguing against Ministers or fighting against popular aspirations. At that time she had, it is true, shown too great a partiality to the Whigs, but she learnt on closer acquaintance to rate Peel at his true value. Under Prince Albert's teaching, her personal affection for foreign dynasties, particularly German, was emphasized ; but her non-partisan liberality of outlook on home affairs was perhaps increased, and was certainly rendered more intelligent, by her student Consort.

The Crown had not yet reached the full position which it held by the end of the century in the popular imagination and in the new fabric of Empire. But already it was released from the unfortunate traditions of recent reigns. All through her long life as Queen, Victoria made a habit of following the actions of her Ministers with close attention, expostulating strongly when she disagreed, often obtaining thereby modifications, but never attempting to reverse or alter policy on which her Ministers remained determined after they had fully heard her views. She also exerted an occasional influence on opposition, particularly in the House of Lords, and was singularly successful in averting conflict between the Houses on several important occasions in the last half of her reign, after the revival of a more militant Liberalism under Gladstone.

1869,
1884.

1854–
1856.

The two mid-Victorian decades of quiet politics and roaring prosperity were broken in the middle by the Crimean War. Forty years had elapsed since Waterloo, and the new generation of Britons were therefore easily stirred to a fighting mood. The modern press, especially that part of it subject to Palmerston's influence, fed the war-spirit with selected news and incitements to hatred of Russia. The choice of Russia as the adversary appears at first sight somewhat arbitrary. But the dread of Russian power had of recent years been growing both in India and in Europe. It was not, indeed, Russia's nearest neighbours, Austria and Prussia, who considered that the Balance of Power needed redressing at the Czar's expense ; it was France and England who felt called upon to champion against him, among other things, the ' independence of Germany.' The reason of this was in part political. Austria, Prussia and Russia stood together for the old principle of the Holy Alliance that had recently effected the repression of the risings of 1848. The Britain of Queen Victoria and the France of Napoleon III stood, each in a different way, for something more liberal. In England, Liberal sentiment had been outraged by the treatment of Poland, and by the aid lent by the reactionary Czar Nicholas to Austria to put down Hungary in 1849.

But the actual occasion of the quarrel of Palmerston and

Russell with Russia was their defence of Turkey. Russia, it is true, accepted our proposed terms of settlement, embodied in the Vienna Note of July 1853, and Turkey refused them. Nevertheless we fought for Turkey against Russia. Such an exhibition of diplomatic incompetence left Ministers with very little answer to some of Bright's censures in the House of Commons, but no answer was needed in the enthusiasm of war. The condition, or even the existence, of the submerged Christian nationalities in the Balkans, was little surmised in the Britain of that day. There was therefore no proposal made to check the advance of Russia by establishing a free Bulgaria and Servia, as Canning had for that purpose established the independence of Greece. The old Turkish system was regarded as the only possible barrier to Russia's ambition.

The Czar Nicholas was considered, not without reason, to be the mainstay of reaction in Europe outside the Balkans. The enthusiasm for the Crimean War was a mixture of Liberalism and Jingoism arising out of the circumstances of the period, and incarnate in Palmerston. But the war was not fought as a war of liberation, for Austria was invited to join the Anglo-French alliance. Only when Austria refused, was the proffered help of Cavour's little Piedmont accepted instead. The substitution of Piedmont for Austria in the Crimean undertaking afterwards hastened the liberation of Italy, but such was not the original intention of the makers of the war.

Among the good results of the Crimean War should be set down British friendship with France and Napoleon III, in an age when France was inclining to take the war-path once more and when British sensibilities were preparing to resist the beginnings of a new era of Napoleonic conquest. The extraordinary man who had so ably manœuvred himself onto the throne of France had not studied his uncle's career in vain. He saw that it would always be fatal to a French Empire to antagonize the Eastern despotic Powers and England at the same time. He ardently desired the friendship of Britain. Palmerston was the first to believe in his good faith, but the British in general were incredulous. The anti-Russian alliance was for awhile good security against the danger of war with France.

The course of the war exhibited the soundness of the British regimental drill and tradition, and the utter incompetence of the higher command, the lack of organization and staff work, the deficiency of commissariat and medical provision. Half a dozen miles from our fleet in Balaclava harbour, our soldiers starved and died because supplies were not brought up to them. The raw recruits, sent out to replace the splendid troops who had thus unnecessarily perished, failed in the assault on the Redan, and thereby to some extent lowered in the eyes of Europe the respect for British arms won by the victories of Alma and Inkerman the year before.

The shortcomings of our military organization formed indeed at that time a remarkable contrast to our commercial and industrial efficiency. They were the result of the obscurantist spirit of the Horse Guards and the War Office, undisturbed hitherto by any popular demand for Army Reform. Rotten Boroughs, Municipalities, Universities, Church, Civil Service

The Neighbourhood of
SEBASTOPOL
English Miles
0 1 2 3 4
Limit of ground occupied by the allies
in the early winter of 1854-5 - - - - - - -

M = Malakov Redoubt
R = Great Redan
F = Flagstaff Bastion

MAP XXXIV.—Crimea

had all in various degrees felt the breath of criticism and change. But the nation had since Waterloo been so pacific that it had never enquired into the state of its Army, so long as War Office estimates were kept well down. Then, in a sudden fit of warlike zeal, John Bull remembered that he had 'a thin red line of heroes,' and sent them out to fight the Russians, expecting results of the old Peninsular kind. But nothing was left of Wellington's army except the spirit of the regiments and the old Brown-Bess muskets with which many of them were still armed. At the time there was a great outcry against the Generals and the War Office; yet as soon as the war was over the old indifference to things military returned. Army Reform was put off for yet another dozen years, till Cardwell came to the War Office in

the first Ministry of Gladstone

The reaction of the Crimean War on the national life was not remarkable in the political sphere. There was a temporary reaction against Cobden and Bright as critics of the war policy. But many Radicals had been strong for the war. And on the whole the aristocratic system of government lost rather than gained prestige by the inefficiency with which operations had been conducted. William Russell, of the *Times*, created the new profession of war-correspondent, and subjected the Generals in the field to direct civilian criticism such as no British commanders ever had to undergo before or since. His communications to the *Times* gave away to the enemy the military secret of our army's appalling condition in front of Sebastopol; but the publicity served as nothing else would have done to rouse public opinion and Parliamentary action before it was altogether too late. It was only fitting that Palmerston should become Prime Minister at the crisis, in place of Lord Aberdeen, who had never liked the war.

But the 25,000 [1] lives that the country lost in the Crimea saved very many more in years to come. For the real hero of the war was Florence Nightingale, and its most indubitable outcome was modern nursing, both military and civil, and a new conception of the potentiality and place in society of the trained and educated woman. And this in turn led, in the 'sixties and 'seventies, to John Stuart Mill's movement for woman's suffrage, which Miss Nightingale supported, and to the founding of women's colleges and the improvement of girls' schools, when at length some provision was made for the neglected higher education of one-half of the Queen's subjects. From the frozen and blood-stained trenches before Sebastopol, and from the horrors of the first Scutari hospitals, have sprung not only a juster national conception of the character and claims of the private soldier, but many things in our modern life that at first sight seem far removed from scenes of war and the sufferings of our bearded heroes on the winter-bound plateau.

In the Victorian era, the field of action where British foreign policy was most obviously successful was the Italian. Without war or serious danger of war, by legitimate diplomatic action in unison with strongly expressed popular sympathy, Britain helped the creation of a new independent Power in the Mediterranean and in the counsels of Europe, contrary to the wishes of the other Great Powers. This event removed a running sore in the body politic of Europe, and started a tradition of

[1] According to Miss Nightingale 16,000 of these lives were lost by bad administration. She brought down the death rate in the Scutari hospitals from 42 per cent. to 22 per thousand.

Italian friendship for England which continued to be an important element in affairs down to Italy's participation in the Great War of our own day.

In 1848 Palmerston was at the Foreign Office. British opinion was then divided about Italy, more or less on party lines. Palmerston was favourable to Italian autonomy, and hoped to negotiate Austria out of the Lombard plain by appealing to her enlightened self-interest. But in that year of revolutions, Palmerston did not hold the key to the Italian question. For as British Minister he felt it his first duty to prevent a general European War, particularly one in which France might attack Austria, and so launch out on a new era of conquest and militarism. Yet without a war between France and Austria it proved impossible for Italy to make any advance towards freedom.

1859–1865.

When next the Italian question became acute in the summer of 1859, Palmerston formed his second Ministry, which lasted till his death half a dozen years later. Russell was his Foreign Minister, and Gladstone as Chancellor of the Exchequer was the third of the controlling members of the Cabinet. Much as these three differed on other subjects, they agreed about Italy ; and by a remarkable chance each of the ' Triumvirate ' had an intimate knowledge of things Italian, in contrast to the ignorance from which all three then suffered as regards America, Germany and the Near East. The result was that they acted with wisdom and vigour in the decisive Italian crisis of 1859–60 with very happy results.

1859.

England held the key to the Italian situation, as she had not done in 1848. In spite of the efforts of Lord Derby's late government, Napoleon III in alliance with Cavour's Piedmont had gone to war with the Austrians. His object was to expel Austrian influence from the Italian Peninsula and substitute French influence, in forms less galling and injurious to the Italians, for whom he had a real sympathy. But he wished to erect, not an independent Italian State, but a number of Italian States dependent on himself. Cavour, on the other hand, used Napoleon to expel Austria, but hoped then to effect a liberation of all Italy on such terms as would render her truly independent. Cavour was the cleverer man of the two, and won the game : but he could scarcely have done so without British help.

Russia and Prussia supported Austria in opposition to Italian liberation of any sort or kind, though since the Crimean War Russia was neither so powerful nor so friendly to Austria as before. In this complicated situation England, by taking up the cause of Italian independence and unity more thoroughly and more sympathetically than France, helped Cavour to force the pace. After Garibaldi's liberation of Sicily, the fall of the reactionary 1860. Neapolitan kingdom and of the Papal government in most of Central Italy followed, with Napoleon's enforced consent; for, since he could not permit Austrian reconquest, he was in no position to oppose the full flood-tide of Italian national movement sweeping on to unity under the Crown of Piedmont, when that movement received the diplomatic countenance of British Ministers and the enthusiastic encouragement of the British people.

A less fortunate episode in European affairs closed the epoch of Russell and Palmerston. A dispute lay between Denmark and her German neighbours, over the Schleswig-Holstein provinces, whence fourteen hundred years before a large part of the English people had migrated to Britain.[1] The merits of the case were divided, and there was room for the good offices of a judicious third party, friendly to all concerned. But Palmerston and Russell took up a position of bravado in encouraging ' little Denmark,' which they could not make good when Bismarck called their bluff. Palmerston had declared that ' it would not be Denmark alone ' with whom her assailants would have to contend. Yet when war came, she found no ally, for our still unreformed army was in no condition to take the field against the united forces of Prussia, Austria, and indeed of all Germany. And the famous Volunteer movement of the mid-Victorian epoch was as yet for home defence alone. Nor could we expect the help of France and Russia, whom our diplomacy on other questions had recently offended.

The Palmerstonian era ended therefore with a humiliating rebuff. The importance of the case was even greater than men knew at the time, for the full meaning of the modern military monarchy of Prussia had yet to be revealed by the victories over Austria in 1866 and France in 1870. Palmerston's popular and jaunty diplomatic performances had had their day. If longer continued, they would have become a serious danger in the terrible new world that was coming into existence, as nationality learnt to prepare for war with all the prodigious powers of modern science and modern locomotion.

The fact that of ' the two old ringleaders ' Palmerston died the first, had important consequences in political history. 1865. Russell, now become an Earl, was left as chief of the Whig-Liberal party, and, in spite of the fact that he had once been called ' finality John,' he had long favoured a further extension

[1] See pp. 31, 42, above.

of the franchise, and a development of the party out of aristocratic Whiggism into democratic Liberalism. If Palmerston had survived Russell, he would have opposed any such growth and would probably have broken with Gladstone, who was his opposite both in temperament and in policy. Russell, too old to take a leading part in the new age of transition, became Prime Minister, but permitted Gladstone, now at the zenith of his powers, to take over the virtual headship of the party.

1866. Gladstone, thus become the leading man in the State, formed an alliance with John Bright, who stood at the head of the movement for the enfranchisement of the town artisans and of the lower middle-class. The strength of the working-class movement on its political side lay, during this decade, in its alliance with the middle-class Radicals, on the ground of their common exclusion from the franchise. The class-consciousness that had inspired the older Chartist movement had died away, largely owing to better times.[1] Bright was the leader in the country and the spokesman in the House of this combined movement. Both he and the cause he advocated had recently gained prestige by the correctness of his judgment on the American Civil War, in which he had been a strong and well-informed advocate of the Northern cause. Most Whig and Conservative statesmen had in various

1861– degrees inclined to favour the cause of the South. While the
1865. war was raging, opinion in Britain had been largely divided on the issue according as men wished for democracy or aristocracy, a wide or a narrow franchise, in their own country. The ordeal by battle had gone in favour of Abraham Lincoln and the Northern Democracy, and the effect upon internal English affairs, though not clearly measurable, was certainly very great. Gladstone, an exception to many rules, had indeed been a hot 'Southerner,' although he was moving fast to democracy in home affairs. His alliance with Bright after the end of the American War and the death of Palmerston, brought the franchise question straight to the forefront of British politics.[2]

The manner in which the Second Reform Bill was carried was very different from the passage of the First. And the difference indicated how much in the last thirty-five years the governing and conservative classes had grown accustomed to change as a normal condition of political life, instead of regarding it as the end of all things. One might almost say that Darwin's then much contested doctrine of 'evolution' had already won its place in political consciousness.

There was, however, a sharp struggle. A very moderate

[1] See pp. 642–3, above.
[2] See pp. 664–5, below, on Britain and the American Civil War.

measure of working-class enfranchisement was introduced by **1866**
Gladstone. But the Whig-Liberal majority had been elected
the year before to support Palmerston, not to enfranchise the
working classes. Under Robert Lowe's eloquent but imprudent
leadership, a group of discontented Whig members, nicknamed
by Bright ' the cave of Adullam,' joined with Disraeli and the
Conservatives to defeat this very moderate instalment of Reform.
It was bad tactics from their own point of view, more particularly
since Lowe openly based his objections to Reform on the moral
and intellectual inferiority of wage-earners as compared to the
bourgeoisie. His incautious eloquence on this interesting theme
roused the working classes to fury, and the agitation for enfranchisement became formidable and threatening. The Trade
Unions in the great industrial centres joined with the middle
classes to organize monster out-door demonstrations, addressed
by Bright, in an age when political meetings were still a rarity.

After the defeat of Gladstone's Reform Bill, the Liberal
Government had resigned ; there was no dissolution, but the Conservatives took office. Disraeli, as Chancellor of the Exchequer
in Lord Derby's new Ministry, led the Commons and dominated
the Cabinet, just as his rival Gladstone had done in Earl Russell's
government a few weeks before. Now Disraeli, when he was not
consciously allowing his oriental fantasy to roam upon some
useful errand, had a shrewd eye for facts He understood the
situation of the country and saw that it required settlement by
concession. Moreover, he had more real sympathy than Lowe
with the working class, and in theory he had sometimes spoken
well of the working man with no vote, as against his employer
who wasted his franchise upon Whig candidates. It is true that
Disraeli had recently denounced Gladstone's argument for an
extended franchise as ' the doctrine of Tom Paine,' but, Tom
Paine's or another's, he now saw that the time had come to put
it into force.

Moreover, Disraeli could not keep control of the Parliamentary
situation on any other terms, for the Conservative Government
had no majority of its own, and the bulk of the Liberal party was
no longer willing to be put off with a mere instalment of Reform.
Outside, the country was in a ferment, The advice of Queen
Victoria was all in favour of a ' settlement ' of the question.
Lord Derby, who as young Stanley, 'the Rupert of Debate,' had
taken a leading part in passing the First Reform Bill, was now
quite prepared to ' dish the Whigs ' and to ' take a leap in the
dark.' So Disraeli very ably settled the question and pacified
the country by carrying a measure which, as finally amended,
was much stronger than the Bill which the Adullamites and

Conservatives had thrown out the year before as being too strong.
The agricultural labourer and the miner in county constituencies
were indeed still left unenfranchised, but household suffrage in
the boroughs was in effect the principle of the Second Reform
Act. Being the measure of a Conservative government it easily
passed the Lords.

1867.

Lord Cranborne, afterwards the famous Lord Salisbury, was
not alone in considering the transaction as a dishonest betrayal
of principle. Perhaps it was rather the growth of political good
sense. But in any case there was no one capable of treating
Disraeli as Disraeli had treated Peel on a like occasion. By
accepting the great change without undergoing internal schism,
the Conservative party prepared a future for itself in the new
democratic world. But the immediate advantage accrued, at
the General Election of 1868, to Gladstone and the Liberal party,
which had a programme of overdue reforms to carry through
before a real age of Conservatism could set in.

BOOKS FOR FURTHER READING

Queen Victoria's Letters (5 vols.) ; Spencer Walpole, *History of England*,
Vols. IV.–VI. ; Thursfield, *Peel*; Disraeli, *Lord George Bentinck*; Strachey, *Queen
Victoria* ; Buckle, *Disraeli* (6 vols.) ; Morley, *Gladstone* (2 vols.) and *Cobden*
(2 vols.) ; Cook, *Florence Nightingale* (2 vols.) ; Trevelyan, *Bright* ; Hammond,
Shaftesbury ; Cole, *Robert Owen* and *Working Class Movement* ; Halévy, *Histoire
du Peuple Anglais*, Vol. III. (1830–1841).

CHAPTER III

External Development in the Latest Era. Character of the Second
British Empire. Growth of Canada. Relations with the United
States. Australasia. South Africa. India

THE Second British Empire, as we have already seen, was a
flourishing child when the Napoleonic Wars came to an end.[1]
In the following century its growth was enormous in area, wealth
and population, owing to the developments of commerce, communication and transport due to steam and iron, electricity and
petrol, and applied medical science in the Tropics. Conditions
at home favoured emigration. Little check was placed on the
increase of population in Great Britain until the last decades
of the Nineteenth Century, and for long there was no other
provision for unemployment save the workhouse. A constant
stream of emigrants, therefore, poured out of the island ; part
flowed into the United States then engaged in peopling the vast

[1] See pp. 587–8, above.

plains beyond the Alleghany mountains, but a large part went
to Canada, Australasia and South Africa. The Colonial Office
in the 'thirties was lethargic and stupid as regards emigration,
but Lord Durham and Gibbon Wakefield, helped by the Churches
and by private organizations, set going a movement for scientific
care and encouragement of British settlement in British Colonies,
which eventually made a convert and ally of Downing Street.

Until the end of the Victorian era there were still large
numbers of persons in Great Britain born and bred as agriculturists, and desiring no better than to obtain land of their
own beyond the ocean. It is only of recent years that a fear has
arisen lest the English race, at home and in the Dominions, may
by choice and custom eschew the rural life and crowd too
exclusively into the cities.

The other aspect of the Second British Empire has been the
development of vast portions of Asia and Africa by commercial
intercourse and by political rule. The political rule has been
conducted in Africa and in the East and West Indies, according
to the benevolent ideals that have been generally prevalent in
Downing Street since the days of Wilberforce and since the reorganization of Indian Government by Pitt and his Governors
General. Great benefits have been conferred on a very large proportion of mankind: in Africa, inter-tribal war and slave-raiding have
been stopped; in India, Egypt and elsewhere the material benefits
of modern science and organization have been applied for the
advantage of all, not least of the humblest cultivators of the
soil.

But two difficulties have beset the path of executive rule over
the non-European races. First, the counter-claims of white
farmers and traders, especially where, as formerly in the West
Indies and permanently in South Africa, they are numerous
enough to practise self-government. And, secondly, the class
of difficulties which inevitably arise, particularly in India, when
a long period of peace, good government and contact with
Western civilization has caused the ruled to desire to become
self-rulers. The questions how best, how fast and how far this
demand can be met without disaster, form perhaps the most
difficult problem that good government has ever created for
itself.

The new conditions of the Industrial Revolution for some
time only increased the advantages of Britain as the clearing-
house for the world's trade and finance, and as the manufacturing
centre for less developed countries. These circumstances led
to the adoption of Free Trade and the abolition of tariffs and
Navigation Acts. The change of policy put an end to the old

'mercantile' theory, which had regarded the commercial interests of the Colonies as involved in but subordinate to those of Britain. It was no longer desired to control British Colonial trade as a British monopoly. The end of the mercantile system led, by the inevitable logic of liberty and equality, to the grant to the self-governing Colonies of permission to decide each for itself whether it wished to protect its own manufactures by tariffs, even by tariffs against the mother country. In our own day this principle is being applied even in the case of India.

But taken in its largest aspect, the Free Trade policy of Britain, and the refusal any longer to keep trade with our colonies and possessions as a reserve of our own, removed many sources of friction with other nations, which could not have willingly seen themselves shut out from trade with so large a portion of the world as came to be included in the Second British Empire.

The principle of self-rule for the communities oversea was only an extension of the methods of government which had formerly prevailed in the lost Thirteen Colonies, and which had been initiated by Pitt in the two Canadas.[1] But the logical and complete application of the principle of responsible Parliamentary government for the Dominions, owes its timely triumph to the wisdom and energy of Lord Durham. He had the peculiar merit of regarding freedom as the means of preserving the Imperial connection, and not as a step towards separation, which most Whig and Conservative statesmen in that era believed to be inevitable.

1838–1839.

Towards the close of the century a full consciousness of the meaning of the Empire swept over Great Britain and the Dominions in the days of Joseph Chamberlain. But the hope of the later Victorian age that this consciousness could be expressed in some form of Imperial Federation and a more unified constitution has not been fulfilled. Rather the Colonies, which had already developed into Dominions, are now developing into separate Nations. The Second British Empire is becoming an English-speaking League of Nations, officially united by the Crown. How strong the indefinable bonds of that Imperial unity may prove, was shown by the events of the Great War, an ordeal that no merely paper constitution could have survived.

The North American policy of British statesmen in the Nineteenth Century had two fields,—Canadian problems and British relations to the United States : they reacted closely on each other. The Canadian problem, thanks to Lord Durham and Lord Elgin after him, received wise attention and treatment

[1] See pp. 441 and 593, above.

at an early date. But the full significance of our relations to the
United States was not recognised by Whig and Conservative
statesmen or by British public opinion in general, until after the
American Civil War.

1861–
1865.

In 1837 two easily suppressed rebellions flared up in Canada,—
one in the Lower Province among the French *habitans*, the other
in the Upper Province among the English-speaking settlers.
Fortunately for the British connection, the two sections were
mutually antagonistic and neither had any desire to join the
United States. But both had grievances against an unsym-
pathetic administration. The two Provincial Assemblies which
Pitt had set up possessed the power to embarrass but not to
nominate or control the executive.[1] The time had now come
for the grant of full responsible government. But it by no
means followed that British statesmen at home would believe
that such was the cure, or have confidence that it could be safely
applied immediately after an armed rebellion. Ignorance of
Colonial conditions was great, and consistent belief in democracy
was rare among the statesmen who had opposed and passed the
First Reform Bill. Fortunately Lord Melbourne's Whig government had the happy inspiration to transport to Canada their able
but sharp-tempered colleague, Lord Durham. He was both an
Imperialist and a democrat at a time when hardly any other
person of Cabinet rank was either the one or the other. He and
his secretary, Charles Buller, were capable of seeing that full
self-government was required, and of saying so very effectively
in the famous ' Durham Report.'

See Map
XXXI.,
p. 592,
above.

1839.

The problem, however, was far more complicated than anyone
in England realised or than Durham himself knew before he
arrived on the spot. He found two nations, French and English-
speaking, bitterly opposed to each other as well as to the government. British immigration and farming in the West had now
put the French in a very decided minority in Canada as a whole ;
but in their own Lower Province the French peasants still outnumbered the English-speaking traders and business men.
Religious and cultural differences made the schism profound.
To establish responsible self-government in Lower Canada would,
in that generation, have led only to the breakdown of government, and probably to armed conflict between the two sections
of the community. Durham's bold advice was to unite the two
provinces in one, and to set up a single elective Assembly with
full power over the executive, which would thus be in the
hands of the English-speaking majority. This plan was carried
out in the Canada Act of 1840. The French protested, but

---

[1] See p. 593, above.

submitted. The new Canadian constitution functioned, with the help of Lord Elgin's shrewd and liberal guidance, until the next great crisis of Canadian history in 1867.[1]

But, in order to understand the circumstances that led to Canadian Federation in 1867, it is necessary to take up the thread of British relations to the United States. Castlereagh, as Foreign Minister, has many claims on the gratitude of posterity, but none greater than his part in the mutual agreement to disarm along both sides of the Canadian border, and in particular to suppress the war navies on those Great Lakes that still divide British territory from the United States. Next year, in the same spirit, he began the determination of the boundary westward. This dangerous process, which occupied the joint attention of statesmen at Downing Street and Washington for a generation to come, could never have been brought to a peaceful conclusion if large armed forces and military traditions had existed on either side of the disputed line.

In Castlereagh's day, the line was carried forward by agreement from the Lake of the Woods to the summit of the Rockies, along the line of latitude 49°. It was wisely agreed to leave the eventual settlement of the lands between the Rockies and the Pacific still undetermined. That vast region, then all of it collectively known as 'Oregon,' was inhabited as yet only by hunters and trappers of both nations, dependent on the Pacific Coast for their communication with the outside world. The 'joint occupation of Oregon' by the United States and Great Britain kept the peace in these thinly peopled lands, until in 'the roaring forties' the head of the column of American democracy, hot on 'the Oregon trail,' burst over the barrier of the Rockies.

Americans were in an expansive mood. They were conquering nature and peopling a continent with a speed never before known in the world's history. It was a period of the Mexican War and of much tall talk, that represented somewhat crudely a genuine exhilaration in the sense of boundless expansion and a great new destiny discovered. In 1844 a United States Presidential Election was won on the cry of 'fifty-four forty or fight,' implying a territorial claim as far north as latitude 54° 40', that would have altogether excluded the British Empire from the

---

[1] Though Durham's Report was acted upon in 1840, thanks to Lord John Russell, Durham himself had been most unhandsomely recalled in 1839 by Lord Melbourne, owing to Brougham's intrigues, which were naturally made the most of by the Conservative Peers. Brougham's version of Durham's performance, and his false statement that Durham wrote none of the Report that goes by his name, still find a most inappropriate place in the *Dictionary of National Biography*, —I hope not for ever.

1847–1854.

1817.

1818.

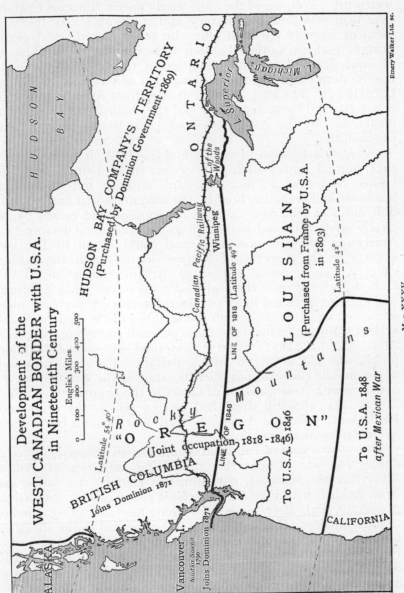

Map XXXV.

Pacific Coast.   But Canada, too, had her rights of future expansion westward.   Peel, one of the most wisely pacific Ministers England ever had, was firm, conciliatory and reasonable.   At the very **1846.**   moment when he fell from office, he accomplished a feat as important, perhaps, as the Abolition of the Corn Laws ; he obtained an equitable and peaceful definition of the boundary down to the Western Ocean, by the prolongation of Castlereagh's line of latitude 49°.   The long, invisible border from Atlantic to Pacific is not guarded by sentry boxes and the challenge of rival armaments, but by the good sense and good feeling of two great communities.

After this triumph of reason and goodwill, it seemed likely that mutual understanding between Great Britain and the United States would move forward steadily out of mutual ignorance and prejudice, bred by the wars and social and religious differences of long ago.   British institutions had ceased to be rigidly aristocratic and were in process of becoming democratic ; Americans were less provincial and could afford to live less entirely on the memories of bygone disputes with the mother country.   The renewed stream of British emigration to the United States, greater than any since the Seventeenth Century, was creating personal links between families on the two sides, often well maintained through the facilities of the modern postal system.   But, unfortunately, these personal connections between America and England existed at that time only among the plain people, who had, as yet, no votes in Britain.   The aristocratic and upper middle class had not then contracted the habit of intermarriage with Americans, or of travel in the United States ; and it was they who still controlled foreign policy, the Press and **1861–**   Parliament, when the American Civil War made a fresh crisis **1865.**   in our international relations.

The government of Palmerston and Russell behaved correctly **1861–2.**   during the war.   Under the restraining influence of Prince Albert on his deathbed, our Ministers enabled the dangerous *Trent* incident with President Lincoln's government to be settled pacifically, and, after some unfortunate hesitation, they refused to join Napoleon III in interfering to put an end to the struggle, for the benefit of the Southern slave-holding Secessionists. But the sympathies of the British upper class were mainly pro-Southern, and were expressed most crudely in the *Times, Punch* and other newspapers to which opinion in New England was peculiarly sensitive.   There was, indeed, no sympathy over here with the cause of slavery, but when President Lincoln began the war by declaring that the Union and not Slavery was the issue, many English people did not know enough about

America to understand the relation which that statement bore to the whole truth. It was not inexcusable that Englishmen should doubt whether the South could be permanently coerced into membership of the Union. But when Lincoln declared the emancipation of all slaves in the rebellious Southern Confederacy, Oct. opinion in England began to swing round to the North. And 1862. from first to last the working classes and the lower middle classes, kept well informed by John Bright, W. E. Forster and others, had been on the side of the Northern democracy against the creation of a Republic based on slavery. After the victory of the North and the assassination of Lincoln, everyone else hastened to take the same side. But so long as the war lasted there was a tendency for British sympathy to divide according as men desired or deprecated the extension of the franchise in our own island.

The North had been deeply incensed by what they took to be British opinion during the struggle ; and the South, which had expected more active help, was little better pleased. American feeling took a strong turn back against England, at the very moment when the general trend of development on both sides of the Atlantic was preparing the way for a better understanding between the two peoples. This alienation, due to the accidental circumstances of the Civil War, has not indeed been permanent, but it occurred at a time very detrimental to the progress of Anglo-American understanding. The great influx of Irish hostile to Great Britain, and of Europeans who were of a different tradition and culture, was beginning to take place on such a scale that the prevalently Anglo-Saxon character of the American Republic was, by the end of the century, considerably modified.

The outstanding diplomatic inheritance from the Civil War was that of the *Alabama* claims. Russell, as Foreign Minister, had carelessly permitted that ill-omened steamship to escape from Laird's yards at Birkenhead ; she had proceeded to prey upon Northern commerce under the flag of the Southern Confederacy. The irritation of the North against England, after the war was over, expressed itself in the form of excessive claims for damages on this score. The crisis continued grave for several years, but was honourably settled at Geneva in 1872. Gladstone, now Prime Minister, atoned for his unwise expressions of Southern sympathy during the war by consenting to leave the award of damages to the decision of a third party—a great step forward in the history of world-arbitration and peace. In the last decade of the Century, the sharp crisis of the dispute over the Venezuela boundary between President Cleveland and Lord Salisbury was also settled by 1895. arbitration ; and during the subsequent war between Spain and

1898. America over the Cuban question, public opinion in England was markedly more favourable to America than was opinion in continental Europe. Both these incidents testified to the friendly attitude which British policy and feeling had permanently assumed towards the United States.

The irritation of the Northern States against Britain during and immediately after the Civil War, and the activities of the Irish Fenians on the Canadian border, had warned Canada that her independence was in danger. Fortunately, a generation of full self-government had by that time done its work. The autonomous Colonies of British North America, with the exception of New-1867. foundland, voluntarily formed themselves into a close Federation, of which the immediate motive was moral resistance to annexationist tendencies in relation to the great neighbour Republic. The Canadian statesman to whom Federation was chiefly due, was Sir John Macdonald. Incidentally, the Federation Policy restored to the French Lower Province its separate autonomy, subject now to the bond of general Canadian unity. By this time the British and French communities had learnt to live side by side with diminished friction, and the French had adapted themselves to Parliamentary government.

As a result of successful Federation, the Dominion of Canada has been able to deal with the United States more and more on her own account, and no longer merely through the agency of Great Britain. The new sense of Canadian unity also produced See Map XXXV., p. 663, above. in the decades following Federation, the Canadian-Pacific Railway, which opened the vast regions of the remote West to English-speaking settlement under the British flag. That railway is the spinal cord of the new Canadian nation.

Australia in the Nineteenth Century moved in a world remote from outer contact. She inherited no problem like that of the French Canadians. She had no neighbour like the United States. But her history, like Canada's, is that of the formation of a number of separate colonies, divided by great distances of desert, which become completely self-governing in the middle of the century, and by the end of the century have been linked up into an economic unity by long lines of railway. And, as in Canada in 1867, so in Australia in 1901 the time had come for a Federal Union. But the Federal Union of the Australian Colonies is not as close as that of the Canadian. The peculiarity of Australian politics has been the early strength of the Labour party, and the struggle of the democracy with the 'squatters' for the equal division of land and the break-up of great estates. The policy of excluding all coloured races from the continent, and its possible consequences in relation to modern Japan, has in recent years brought the strong nationalism of Australia into a closer sense of outside diplomatic relations with other countries, and of the importance of the British connection. Australia's ideal, which she is determined to maintain even at the expense of rapid development, is an equalitarian society of white men, of high physique and a high average standard of life.

It was Gibbon Wakefield who had brought the public to believe that New Zealand might accommodate other races as well as the Maori tribes. His New Zealand Association, founded in 1837, made the first British Settlements there, only just in time to prevent the annexation of the islands by France. New Zealand, with its one and a half million inhabitants, remains one of the smallest but not the least happy and well-beloved of the British self-governing Dominions.[1]

The history of South Africa presents points of likeness and of contrast to those of the other Dominions. As in Australia and Canada, the formation of a number of large but isolated communities, widely separated by great spaces of desert, preceded the age of railway connection and of political Federation. As in Canada, the problems of colonization and self-government were complicated by the presence of another European race settled there before the coming of the English. As in the days of Wolfe and Montcalm, so in the days of Kitchener and Botha, there was bloodshed before peaceful settlement was reached. Yet the white population is in a minority of about one to four in the South African Union of to-day, excluding the native Protectorates. Canada is a white man's country, alike by nature and by settlement ; parts of Australia could support coloured folk, but policy has reserved the whole continent for whites alone ; but South Africa is a land where the European and African races flourish side by side, on the healthy upland plateau of the interior. The white South Africans have been numerous enough to claim self-government and to conduct it successfully; this fact has had constant reactions upon the native problem.

[1] The population of the self-governing Dominions in 1921 (since increased) was :

Canada .	8,788,483
Newfoundland .	263,000
Australia .	5,435,734
New Zealand .	1,320,275
South Africa .	1,538,920 (whites)

while Great Britain (England, Wales and Scotland) contained 42,767,530. Since the War, the Irish Free State has acquired Dominion Status, and Ulster responsible self-government. No census could be taken in Ireland in 1921, but its population is over four and a half millions.

The first stage of British South African history, after the annexation of the maritime station of the Cape of Good Hope during the Napoleonic Wars, was the government of the small community of Boers by British officials near Table Mountain. There was at first the less difficulty because the Boers had not been accustomed to self-government under the Dutch flag, and because there was as yet no large body of British Colonists. But in the third and fourth decades of the Century British immigrants began to arrive in such numbers as to raise difficult questions of language, law and custom. At the same time all slaves in the British Empire were emancipated. The Boers did not raise difficulty about emancipation, but considered, not without some reason, that the promised compensation was not paid them in full. In the same years they received inadequate protection in their outlying farms from the raids of the warlike native tribes of the interior. Lord Melbourne's incompetent Colonial Secretary, Lord Glenelg, represented a type of British official of that day who listened too exclusively to a certain kind of missionary on all native questions. These grievances of the border farmers, and perhaps some restless impelling spirit of adventure, were the causes of the Great Trek. The Boers started out, taking their wives and children with them in their ox-waggons, across the veld into the far interior. There they lived, after their own free patriarchal fashion, reading their great Bibles, multiplying their herds of cattle, shooting the big game that swarmed around, and watching the native warrior tribes from behind the protection of unerring musket and rifle.

But such isolation could not last long in the Africa of the Nineteenth Century. First in Natal, then on both sides of the Vaal river they were followed up by British and European immigrants of the most various kinds,—missionaries, hunters, farmers, gold and diamond diggers, and capitalist speculators. The clash of the old and new type of white society was repeated again and again in South Africa, in various forms, throughout the century.

For a long time the presence of the warrior native tribes restrained the Boers and British from coming to blows with one another. But after the suppression and pacification of the Zulu warriors by British armies and officials, the Boers felt a little more secure. At this critical moment the vacillation of the British governments, particularly Gladstone's, in deciding on a settlement of some kind with the Transvaal Boers, led to the conflict at Majuba. Gladstone accepted that British defeat for fear lest the Dutch of Cape Colony should throw in their lot with their blood-brothers beyond the Vaal; and so the Transvaal

1833.

1836.

1879.

1881.

recovered its independence as the South African Republic. The
' Majuba Policy ' was deprived of any chance it had of success, by
the development of gold and diamond diggings in the Transvaal.
The scramble for wealth produced a sharper contrast than ever
before between the cosmopolitan man of business and the shrewd
old Dutch farmer, who wished to exploit the mines without
yielding political power in his country to the miners.

At the same time Cecil Rhodes and his Chartered Company [1]
were developing new British territories to the west and north of

MAP XXXVI.

the Transvaal. Rhodesia came into existence. This ambitious
thrust into the interior was in part prompted by the fears which
Rhodes entertained lest the Germans should spread their territories across the continent from German South West Africa to
join Portuguese territory ; such a development, if made in time,
would cut off for ever the northward advance of the British race.
Rhodes, therefore, aimed at establishing in good time a link
with the regions beyond the Zambesi, where Livingstone and
other British missionaries had in the previous generation showed
the way into the heart of Central Africa, and had shown also how
the natives could be led and guided aright. Still further to the
north, Britain was in occupation of Egypt. To Rhodes' sanguine

[1] See p. 346, note, above.

spirit, therefore, the Cape to Cairo railway through British territory seemed by no means impossible.

This practical dreamer left a great mark on African geography and history. But not all that he did was what he originally wished to do. He wished to reconcile the British and Dutch races, but he alienated them for a number of tragic years. While he was Premier of Cape Colony, he gave way to his impatience with Paul Kruger, President of the South African Republic, the old-world type of conservative Boer, and in an evil hour planned Xmas, 1895. an armed attack on the Transvaal. ' Jameson's raid ' united the whole Dutch race in Africa in just resentment and suspicion, enabled Kruger to arm to the teeth, and led up to the second Boer War. For Chamberlain in the Colonial Office at home, and Sir Alfred Milner in South Africa, could see no alternative but to bring the questions at issue at once to a head.

1899– 1902. The Second Boer War, with its unexpected reverses and its long protraction by the spirited guerrilla resistance of the Boer farmers, had a number of important reactions on the British Empire. It put an end to the somewhat boastful type of Imperialism which dominated the last years of the Nineteenth Century, a spirit which, though it served its purpose in its day to popularize the idea of the British Empire, would have made trouble in the dangerous epoch now approaching. The serious character of the Boer War made men of all parties take a more sober and broad-minded view of Imperial duties and destiny. It gave a fresh impetus to military efficiency and Army Reform, destined to be of great consequence a dozen years later : if we had won the Boer War too easily we might never have won the German War at all. Finally, it called out the active and enthusiastic help of Canadians and Australasians, who came to South Africa to fight for the cause of the Empire in distress.

The victory in the field, won by Lord Roberts and Lord Kitchener, led to the annexation of the Transvaal and the Orange May, 1902. Free State. Peace was secured at the Treaty of Vereeniging, where honourable terms were granted to the Commandos who still held out on the desolated veld. The material restoration of the farms was to be undertaken at once by Great Britain, the Dutch and English languages were to be put on an equal footing, and in course of time complete responsible self-government was to be granted under the British flag. All these promises were kept. Responsible self-government was set up as early as 1906 by Sir Henry Campbell-Bannerman, with the result of the pacification of South Africa. Four years later the whole sub-continent was 1910. federated in the South African Union, except only Rhodesia and certain native Protectorates. In 1914–18 Generals Botha and

Smuts, who had held out to the last against the British armies
in 1902, headed the Union of South Africa in the war against
Germany, and thereby added greatly to the material and yet
more to the moral strength of the Empire, at its moment of
greatest danger.

The collapse of the Mogul Empire in the Eighteenth Century,
and the reduction of India to an anarchy of warring rulers, chiefs
and warrior bands, had compelled the British East India Company to undertake military operations and political responsibilities on the great scale. The process had been hastened by the
French effort to drive their European rivals out of India. Lord
Wellesley had been the first Governor-General to envisage the 1798–
necessity of going forward till the *Pax Britannica* was everywhere 1805
accepted within the circle of Indian States. But although his
Maratha wars checked the assaults of anarchy upon the Eastern
and Southern portions of the Peninsula, the great sources of See
unrest in Central India were still left uncontrolled. After Map
Wellesley's retirement, an attempt was made to limit British XXXII.,
liability and to stop any further advance across India.[1] p. 596, above.

But events soon showed the impossibility of leaving confusion to welter on the other side of a long, unguarded line in
the vain hope that it would confine itself to agreed limits. The
disturbed state of Northern and Central India rendered peace
in other parts impossible. Lord Wellesley's forward policy was
resumed by Lord Hastings. In his day the Gurkha hillmen of
Nepal were reduced by war, and their land has ever since remained 1814–
our friendly ally, and a great recruiting ground for our Indian 1816.
armies. Also in the time of Lord Hastings, the Maratha Chiefs
and the robber hordes of Central India were finally conquered in 1816–
the Third Maratha War and the Pindari Wars. Half a dozen 1818.
years later, an attack on North-East India by the irruption of
Burmese armies into Assam, led to the First Burmese War, 1824–6.
and the beginning of the annexation of Burmah, which was
completed in 1853 and 1886. The Burmese, a Buddhist people of
Thibeto-Chinese origin, are in no sense a part of the religious and
racial mosaic of India proper ; but the systems of government
applied by the British to India were with modifications applied
to this eastward extension of their territory.

After the forward movements and wars of the governorship
of Lord Hastings and his immediate successor, there was a pause
of some years before the problems of the North-West frontier,
and the contact opened out with the Pathans of Afghanistan and
the Sikhs of the Punjab led to a fresh cycle of wars and annexa-

[1] See pp. 595–8, above.

tions. During this pacific interval, the benevolent side of British rule, and the sense of trusteeship for the Indians was strongly emphasized by Lord William Bentinck and by other able and earnest public servants. Nor, indeed, had the sense of trusteeship been lacking among the British rulers who had ·dealt in war and annexation, from Clive and Warren Hastings down through Wellesley and Lord Hastings to Metcalfe and the Lawrence brothers. But Lord William Bentinck was not called on to conquer anyone more formidable than the Thugs, the caste of hereditary murderers on the Indian roads, or to beat down any resistance other than that of the half-hearted defenders of Suttee,— the burning of Hindoo widows. His victories were those of peace.

1828– 1835.

In 1813 the monopoly of the East India Company for British trade with India had been abolished, and twenty years later its monopoly of British trade with China also came to an end. ' John Company ' ceased to be a trading concern, but retained until 1858 the shadow of political power, of which the substance had long since passed to the Ministers of the Crown. The new Charter of 1833 embodied one tendency of Bentinck's policy in the words, ' No native of India, or any natural-born subject of His Majesty, shall be disabled from holding any place, office or employment by reason of his religion, place of birth, descent or colour.' But the business of training Indian administrators to render them capable of joining in the work of the British, had yet to be begun. Bentinck and his contemporaries addressed themselves to the task and its problems with an eager and generous zeal.

1833.

At this period there was singularly little ill-feeling between Europeans and Indians. The recollection of what had preceded British rule was so fresh that gratitude was still felt. The English and Scots in India were still very few and for the most part select. They were not yet numerous enough to form a purely English society of their own. They were cut off from home by a six months' voyage, often for life. India was their second home. Inter-marriage, though rare, was not *taboo*. Colour feeling was not yet as strong on either side as it became at the end of the century. The Indians knew nothing of England or of Europe ; their rulers seemed to them strange, invincible men dropped from the skies, more benevolent than most gods or kings whom they knew. Nothing could have made this happy state of things permanent. It is only a question whether inevitable change could have been made better or worse by any system of education for India other than that actually adopted.

It was under Bentinck's rule that the decision was made in favour of English as the medium of education and administration.

The controversy was decided by the strong but over-confident arguments of Macaulay, then at Calcutta as a Member of Council. It is difficult to believe that any other language than English could have been permanently accepted. Since India was to be ruled as one, there must be a common official language. And who was going to compel British and Indians, in their dealings with education and government, to employ one of the innumerable languages of the East, arbitrarily selected for precedence over the others ?

The teaching of English involved, however, certain dangers which subsequent generations did not take the right means to avoid. An energetic white race, trained in all the uses of self-government for centuries past, and assuming self-discipline and public order as things granted and certain, naturally lays stress in its poetry and its political philosophy on freedom as the crown of life. But these home-bred ideals may have strange consequences when overheard by an audience at the other end of the world and of human experience ; there is some truth in the saying that we have attempted in India to ' rear a race of administrators on the literature of revolt.' Mistakes were certainly made in the curriculum of education. But those who argue that all our difficulties of recent years could have been avoided by the simple expedient of keeping Western literature and language out of Indian schools, do not stay to consider how strongly the Indians were even in 1835 demanding to learn English, how much the revival of their own literature and thought since then has owed to contact with Western knowledge, how utterly ungenerous and ultimately impossible it would have been to exclude our fellow subjects permanently from the science and learning of the West, and how dangerous might have been the unsuccessful attempt on the part of government to keep them in ignorance against their own loudly expressed wish.

After the interval of pacific consolidation under Bentinck, the forward movement began again. The wars and settlements of the 'forties decided in broad outline the policy and geography of the North-West frontier. An attempt to bring the mountain tribes of Afghanistan within the radius of British India, led to the famous disaster when a whole army perished in the retreat from Kabul. It was perhaps a blessing in disguise, for the 1839– 1841. ultimate peace and safety of the Indian Peninsula have since been found to rest securely on the policy of friendship with Afghanistan as a buffer State, that jealously guards its mountain freedom between the Asiatic possessions of Russia and Britain. Owing to the existence of an independent Afghanistan we have never been in armed conflict with Asiatic Russia.

In the years immediately following this check in the mountain region, the annexations of Sind and the Punjab gave into British hands the great river system of the North-Western plains. The Sikhs of the Punjab were a democratic religious brotherhood, of what we may call ' Protestant ' Hindoos, who had long guarded the plains of India against the debouchment of Mahommedan hill tribes, or of invaders from Central Asia. Their great chief, Ranjit Singh, had trained the Sikh warriors in European methods, and had kept friends with the English. But after his death this splendid soldiery poured across the Sutlej to attack British India. The ensuing struggle, with battles like Moodkee, Sobraon and Chillianwallah, was as severe as any that the British have ever fought on Indian soil. The victory in war was followed up by the work of the Lawrence brothers in winning the confidence and attachment of the Sikhs by the good government of the Punjab. When therefore the storm of the Mutiny broke, John Lawrence was able to use the newly acquired Punjab, as a place of arms for the reconquest of revolted Oudh. Afghanistan also was friendly to the English during the crisis, so that the North-West frontier could be safely denuded of troops till the Mutiny was suppressed.

See Maps XXXII. and XXXIII., pp. 596-7, above.

1857.

The Mutiny, as its name implies, was a rising of some of the Sepoy regiments in British pay, including a large part of the artillery. The civilian population was rather a spectator than a participant in the event. The grievances that caused the outbreak were the grievances of soldiers, caused by mismanagement such as that which had undesignedly served out cartridges greased with the fat of the sacred cow and the abhorred pig.

The Mutiny of the Bengal army began at Meerut. Its immediate occasion was unwise severity by incompetent officers, who proved helpless before the storm they had raised. Some of the mutineers made straight for Delhi where there was no British regiment. Delhi fell at once into the hands of the movement ; and Cawnpore, after three weeks' gallant defence ; and Lucknow, all except the Residency defended by the heroic band under Sir Henry Lawrence. It was in this Upper Ganges region that the issue was fought out and won during the summer of 1857, by the British then actually in India and the faithful Indian troops. Their boast that ' alone we did it ' is substantially true, though there were many months of severe fighting after the arrival of reinforcements from England. The deeds of Nicholson and the Lawrences, of Havelock and Outram, of Colin Campbell and Hugh Rose, and the little armies which they formed and led, the stories of the Delhi Ridge, the Kashmir gate, and the relief and final capture of Lucknow, re-established the prestige of Britain not

May 1857.

only in India, but in Europe also, where the Crimea had exhibited our want of army organization no less strikingly than the fighting qualities of our seasoned troops.

The flame had been stamped out in Central India before it could spread. Most of Bengal, all Madras and Bombay and the North-West had remained loyal. So too had the great Native States like Mysore and Hyderabad. One result of the Mutiny was to put a stop to the course pursued by the over-eager spirit of the Governor-General Lord Dalhousie, of absorbing the territories of protected Indian rulers into actual British territory, in order to enlarge the area of benevolent administration. Indeed Dalhousie's annexation of Oudh, the seat of the Mutiny, had indirectly helped to provoke it. The Native States have, ever since 1857, been regarded as essential pillars of the British raj, not least during the political troubles of more recent years which are bred in the provinces directly ruled by Britain.

Although it was a Mutiny of the troops and not a revolt of the population, the outbreak was related to a dim general uneasiness and fear in the great mass of Indian opinion, at the pace with which Westernization was proceeding. Dalhousie's zeal for reform and progress was seen in many strange novelties—the railways, the telegraphs, and the European standards of efficiency and sanitation.

After the Mutiny these things indeed continued, and India grew accustomed to them. A long period of peace and sound administration followed, the British Government after 1858 replacing the East India Company in name, as it had long done in fact. In 1877 Queen Victoria, on Disraeli's advice, assumed the title of Empress of India.

The memory of bloodshed and racial feud now lurked like a phantom in the secret consciousness of rulers and ruled. Nevertheless, for many years after the Mutiny, the work of good government proceeded without an interruption. Famine and plague were fought by scientific methods. Wealth and population increased as never before.

It was a noble work for the benefit of helpless millions. Yet the bureaucracy, as the useful years went by without incident, contracted the inevitable limitations of any government that is purely autocratic. It considered too exclusively the good work done, and gave too little attention to changes in the political atmosphere. It is possible that the path of the future would have been eased, if hands had been held out from above to the nationalist movement in its earlier and loyal stages, as for instance, to the Indian National Congress in the 'eighties and 'nineties. But when criticism of a mild kind was first uttered, it was too often regarded by the English as sedition, until indeed it became no less.

In the last decades of the century, colour consciousness hardened on both sides. English society in India had become larger, more self-sufficient, more closely connected by short voyages with home. On the other side the educated Indians began to know more of the world across the mountains and the seas, whence the English and others came, and to understand that the phenomenon of white rule was a fact of history and science, not a sending of heaven. The political ideas of national-ist and liberal Europe were terribly familiar to them, mingling in their minds with a racial and conservative revolt against the modern ways of their alien overlords. The Japanese victory over Russia affected the attitude of all Asiatics toward white domination. In the new century many of the educated Indians developed an attitude of hostility, and often of sedition and poli-tical crime. The anti-English propaganda of the educated was not altogether without effect on the vast uneducated masses of conservative-minded peasantry.

1904.

The era of concession from above set in, to meet and control such serious unrest. In the question of the Partition of Bengal, an administrative decision made by a great Viceroy was reversed some years later, in deference to the strength of popular opinion. And the India Councils Act of 1909, the joint work of Lord Minto at Calcutta and of John Morley at Whitehall, enlarged the Legislative Councils by introducing into them a considerable elective element, with powers of consultation and criticism of the actions of the Government. In 1911 George V, as King Emperor, held a great Durbar at Delhi, to which the capital was moved. He was the first reigning sovereign to visit India.

1914–
1918.
1919–
1926.

When the Great War came, India remained loyal and helped the Empire both in Asia and in Europe. Afterwards, again there were troubles, concessions, movements and counter-movements, amid which we live, not without anxiety and hope.

BOOKS FOR FURTHER READING

Egerton, *Short History of British Colonial Policy* ; W. A. Dunning, *The British Empire and the United States* ; E. P. Adams, *Great Britain and the American Civil War* (2 vols.) ; Stuart Reid, *Life of Lord Durham* (2 vols.) ; Lyall, *British Dominion in India* ; Chirol, *India* (The Modern World Series, ed. Fisher, 1926) ; Basil Williams, *Cecil Rhodes* ; Ramsay Muir, *Short History of the British Common-wealth*, Vol. II. ; Theal, *South Africa.* (5 vols.) ; Pember Reeves, *The Long White Cloud* (New Zealand). See also foot of p. 600, above, for Lucas and Wyatt Tilby.

CHAPTER IV

The new Reform era. Gladstone's First Ministry, 1868–74. Disraeli and
modern Conservatism. Gladstone, Egypt, Home Rule. Lord
Salisbury's Ministries. The era of the Jubilees. Social Reform and
Imperialism

THE victory of the North in the American Civil War and the
death of Palmerston together gave the signal for another period
of rapid change in the world of English politics. The leader in
the new age of transition was Gladstone, who embodied the
political spirit of the time with its earnestness, its optimism, its
trust in human nature, and its diligent mastery of legislative and
executive detail that saved its idealism from running to waste
in words. Gladstone completed the transmutation of the old
Whig into the new Liberal party, and by the legislation of his
first and greatest Ministry of 1868–74 made up the arrears of
institutional change overdue. Palmerston's leadership had long
imposed delay on the activity of the party whose special function
it was to make the pace of progress. Reform now came with a
rush, but with no violence, because the resistance made to it was
slight.

For at the same time the Conservative party, and therewith
the control of the House of Lords' veto on legislation, fell into
wise hands. Not without a double personal application, Disraeli
in 1868 wrote to the Queen that ' a fund of enthusiasm ' ' ought
never to be possessed ' by a Prime Minister of England—nor, he
might with equal relevance have added, by a leader of Her
Majesty's Opposition. Certainly the Conservative chief's own
sceptical and clear-sighted temper was admirably adapted to the
task of ' educating his party ' to accept the democratization of
our institutions as inevitable, and even to preside over important
parts of the process. But Gladstone's more ardent nature was
required for the great legislative achievements of 1868–74.

Behind the statesmen of the transition stood the political
philosopher John Stuart Mill, whose writings exerted in the
'sixties and 'seventies a wide influence over educated opinion.
He brought Bentham's Utilitarianism up to date, and emancipated it from the stricter bonds of the *laissez faire* theory. Mill
preached the doctrine of complete democracy in the sense that
every man and woman ought to take part not only in national
but in local elections. But he knew the limits of the work suited
to the democratic machine. He desired to see specialist Departments of State guiding the democracy and keeping politicians
properly informed. ' Power,' he said, ' may be localized, but

knowledge, to be useful, must be centralized.' The dovetailing of the functions of the Whitehall Civil Service with those of the Downing Street politicians and of the electorate in the country was an essential part of Mill's doctrine of good government. There had been nothing of that in the older Radicalism of Cobbett or the pure *laissez faire* school.

His advocacy of women's rights, in *The Subjection of Women* (1869), though in his own day it was not allowed to affect the political franchise, helped to increase the respect for women's personal liberty, and the belief in the importance of their proper education which characterized the later Victorian age. Mill and Florence Nightingale [1] were the two principal pioneers of the position that women hold in our society to-day.

Mill's treatise *On Liberty* was a plea for freedom of thought and discussion, then much limited by social convention though not by law. The rising generation grew up with this creed of freedom, by no means confined to politics. It was the age of the first heart-searching controversies on Darwin's startling hypothesis of evolution, with its reaction on the literal acceptance of parts of the Bible. *The Origin of Species* and Mill's *Liberty* appeared in the same year—1859. The Natural Science Tripos was being started at Cambridge. The 'movement' begun at Oxford by Pusey, Keble and Newman, before Newman went over to Rome, had since gone out from its academic home to meet, and in some cases to blend, with other fresh sources of energy in the Church and country at large. The so-called 'Christian Socialism' of Frederick Denison Maurice and Charles Kingsley began a fresh orientation of the Church in relation to democracy and the social problems of the Industrial Revolution. Modernist theology, under Jowett, Stanley, and Colenso, gained toleration and importance through the Darwinian controversy and the growth of historical method and knowledge. The Church was beginning to contain within her own body something answering to each of the currents of the heady fight going on in the world outside. Much had been gained in knowledge in several different directions—in earnestness yet more. Missionary energy at home and overseas took on fresh life. Selwyn, Bishop of New Zealand in its earliest days of colonization, had an apostolic and democratic spirit which reacted on the Church at home. The merits and demerits of the Church clergy in their relation to the laity were very different from what they had been in the easy-going Eighteenth Century.[2]

1833–
1845.

[1] See p. 653, above.

[2] See pp. 518–9, above. For Church history in the 'thirties and 'forties see Dean Church, *The Oxford Movement*, and W. L. Mathieson, *English Church Reform 1815–40*.

The grave abuses in the uneven distribution of Church revenues had been reformed by Peel and the Whigs, and by the Ecclesiastical Commissioners whom they set up after the First Reform Bill. In many different ways, therefore, the Church was newly prepared to stand any assault which might be made on her as a result of the further extension of the franchise of 1867. No doubt many of her exclusive privileges would have to be surrendered, particularly in the Universities. But the resisting power of the Establishment was at once more solid and more elastic than it had been in 1832, when zealous Churchmen had opposed even the First Reform Bill on the ground that it must lead to disestablishment and disendowment.

It would be tedious to enumerate the many other movements of intellectual activity and social change that were stirring in the 'sixties. Among the most important was the organization of the great Trade Unions in the skilled trades, especially engineering, and the growth of the Co-operative movement, which trained so many of the working classes in business habits, thrift and mutual reliance, released them from exploitation by the shop-keeper, and gave them ' a stake in the country.'

The classes newly enfranchised by the Second Reform Bill,[1] in their first use of the vote in 1868, greatly strengthened the Radical element in the party commanded by Gladstone and placed the weapon of a large majority in his active hands. His first Ministry was the first in English history that can be called distinctively Liberal instead of Whig. In 1868 Conservatism and Socialism were both temporarily in abeyance. It was a mood not likely to last long, but the use made of it by Gladstone in the greatest half-dozen years of his life, went far to equip the country with modern services and institutions, without which she would have been ill-prepared to face the social and imperial problems of days to come. In those years the Universities were opened to men of all creeds, a national system of Primary Education was established, Army Reform was initiated, the throwing open of the Civil Service was completed, the Ballot Act was passed, and the first steps were taken towards the conciliation of Ireland.

1868–
1874.

The Irish famine of 1845–6, due to the failure of the potato crop, had set going the wholesale emigration to the United States and the Colonies, which by the end of the century had reduced the population of the overcrowded island, in spite of a high birth-rate, from eight to four and a half millions. But for more than twenty years after the famine nothing was done to remedy

[1] See pp. 656–8, above.

the wrongs of the Irish peasant in relation to his English landlord. In accordance with the ancient custom of Ireland, the landlord could rackrent and evict his tenants, but he himself put no capital into the land, made no improvements, and left the small peasant farmer to build and maintain his cabin and everything else on the farm. This system, very different from that of England, was exploited by landlords who were divided from their tenants by race and religion, and who often resided in the neighbouring island, spending there the revenues which their agents wrung from the tillers of the Irish soil.

For twenty years after the famine, Celtic Ireland was prostrate and incapable of agitation. But the relative wealth and importance acquired by the Irish emigrants in the United States and the Colonies, and their organized hatred of England, ere long reacted on the home lands. After the end of the American Civil War, the Fenian Movement, separatist in its objects and criminal in its methods, reminded the English very unpleasantly that the quiescent Irish problem had only been neglected, not solved.

Gladstone was the first statesman to take the conciliation of Ireland seriously in hand. His Irish Land Act of 1870 went a very little way, but it marked the first English recognition of the problem, and he followed it up a dozen years later by more

1881.

effective legislation for fair rent and security of tenure. The land question, kept alive by boycotting and agrarian crime in the days of the Land League, was destined to end in the buying out of the

1903.
1868-
1874.

English landlords from Ireland by a Conservative Government. But during Gladstone's first Ministry few people in England, except Gladstone himself, understood the real meaning of the Irish land question and its essential difference from the English. Many Liberals were as much averse as Conservatives to interfere with ' free contract,' which they imagined to exist in Ireland between landlord and tenant.

On the other hand, religious equality was an ideal taken to heart by the intellectual classes trained in the philosophy of Mill, and by the Nonconformists whose effective emancipation had been accomplished by the Second Reform Bill. Their common leader, Gladstone, a High Churchman of the new school, had accomplished in his own mind the wedding of the Oxford religious doctrines with political Liberalism ; his views of Church and State were no longer those he had advocated thirty years before in the book reviewed by Macaulay. In so far, therefore, as Ireland could be conciliated by religious equality, that part of the task was possible in 1869, and it was done. The disestablishment and partial disendowment of the Irish Protestant Church was carried out in a masterly and sympathetic manner by Gladstone, whose known position as an enthusiastic Churchman stood him in good stead during the negotiations. The House of Lords and the Bishops, in a very different mood from that which their predecessors had displayed on Church questions in the 'thirties, made the best terms they could and allowed the Bill to pass.

Gladstone's Liberal Churchmanship, and his political leadership of the Nonconformists and of the academic advocates of religious equality, were of no less importance in the purely English questions of the Universities and Education. The long overdue reform of Oxford and Cambridge by Act of Parliament had first been taken in hand in the 'fifties, when under Gladstone's able management the First University Commission had begun the work. But at that time the Church monopoly could not be abolished. Only as a result of the Second Reform Bill and the election of 1868 was it possible to throw open College Fellowships **1871** and University posts to persons of every, or of no, religious denomination. London and Durham Universities had already been founded, and in the closing years of the Nineteenth Century and the early years of the Twentieth, a number of other Colleges and Universities grew up all over England and Wales. Scotland was already well supplied.

As University teaching ceased to be the monopoly of a very few, secondary teaching improved and spread. By the end of the century much had been done to amend the backward condition of English middle-class education, which Matthew Arnold had once declared, with oratorical exaggeration, to be the worst in Europe. As education and culture spread among the middle classes, athleticism and the pursuit of pleasures other than the intellectual spread quite as fast. The demand for leisure and amusement grew in all classes with each new decade, as the hardworking mercantile Puritanism of the early Nineteenth Century yielded more and more to new and more varied standards of life, not all of them, perhaps, improvements upon the old.

Primary Education was also established on a national basis by the Education Act of William Edward Forster. Where there **1870.** was no school, a school was set up subject to an elected School Board, the only religious teaching permitted being undenominational. On the other hand, in areas where schools already existed, these 'voluntarily supported' schools were preserved by a largely increased grant from the Treasury, and the Church character that most of them possessed remained intact. The increased grant was a bitter disappointment to the Nonconformists, whose children in rural areas still had to attend these

Church schools. But the compromise carried the Bill through the Lords, and if it did harm to the Liberal party by causing discontent in its ranks, it did a great work for the country ; it supplied England at last with a population that could read and write, gave training and discipline to the herds of uncared-for children of the slums, and initiated the great educational progress of the next half century.

Gladstone's first Ministry also began the long overdue reform of the Army, and created the modern military system, as distinct from Peninsular and Crimean organization. These reforms are associated with the name of Cardwell, the Secretary for War. Against him were arrayed the vested interests and prejudices of the old Army chiefs, formidably headed by the Queen's cousin, the Duke of Cambridge. But the Government succeeded in carrying a number of very important reforms. They abolished the system of dual control over the Army, definitely subordinating the Horse Guards to the War Office, that is to say the Commander-in-Chief to the Secretary for War. They abolished the system of Purchase of Commissions, which prevented the promotion of men of moderate means. They established the short-service system of enlistment, thereby supplying for the first time a proper Army Reserve. These changes rendered possible a greater efficiency in war in the later years of the century, connected with Sir Garnet Wolseley and put to the test in a number of campaigns against coloured folk in Asia and Africa. The sharper lessons of the Second Boer War gave a stimulus to further changes, which left us in 1914 with an effective Expeditionary Force and a Territorial Army.

The same set of ideas that had led to the abolition of Purchase in the Army, led to the opening of the Civil Service to competition by public examination, completed by Gladstone's action in 1870.[1]

After half a dozen years of activity, Gladstone's first Cabinet had done its work : Ministers could be fitly compared by Disraeli to ' a range of exhausted volcanoes.' For he himself had very shrewdly allowed their lava to exude. The House of Lords had not prevented their policy from taking effect. The work that the country had expected of them was substantially done, and a natural Conservative reaction therefore took place at the election of 1874.

Thus Disraeli, in his seventieth year, first attained to real power as Prime Minister. The work of his Ministry bore the impress of his own ideas both in domestic and in foreign policy.

1874–
1880.

[1] Sir Charles Trevelyan, an Indian and English Civil servant, had a large part in initiating both these movements.

At home he was anxious to demonstrate the connection of the
new Conservatism with social reform and with conciliation of the
working classes. Aided by his able Home Secretary, Richard
Cross, he waged war on slums and insanitary conditions with
the Public Health Act of 1875 and the Artisans' Dwelling Act.
Such measures, and the continuous work of the Local Government
Board set up by Gladstone in 1871 to co-operate with the ever-
increasing activities of the local authorities, were important
palliatives. But bad building and bad town-planning had got
such a start in the previous hundred years, that they have never
been properly overtaken.

Much less could anything be done to set a limit to the ever-
advancing bounds of the realm of ugliness and uniformity, in its
constant destruction of the beauty and variety of the old pre-
industrial world. Indeed the more prosperous and progressive
the country was, the more rapidly did that unceasing work go
forward. Man when armed with the machine could not help
destroying beauty, whatever the work to which he set his hand.[1]

Disraeli also settled an acute stage of the ever-recurring
problems of Trade Unionism in relation to the community. In
1867, partly as a result of criminal outrages at Sheffield and
elsewhere by some of the more badly managed Unions, a judicial
decision in the courts seemed to deprive the Unions as a whole
of the freedom which they had enjoyed ever since the legislation
of 1824-5.[2] A prolonged crisis followed, the Unions being well
advised and advocated by Tom Hughes and Frederic Harrison.
The working men had voted for Gladstone in 1868, but did not
get satisfaction in this matter from his Ministry. This had
caused much discontent in their ranks, but Disraeli in 1875
settled the question satisfactorily for a number of years to come
by his Combination Act.

In foreign policy Disraeli renewed the connection between
the party he led and the dramatic assertion of British national
interests. That connection had not been specially marked since
Waterloo. After the Treaties of Vienna, the Tory or Conservative party, that had done so much to make that settlement of
Europe, was sometimes more pacific than Palmerston and his
followers, because Whigs and Radicals had less veneration for
the settlement of 1815 and more sympathy with the nations and
parties on the Continent who wished to disturb it. Nor had

---

[1] It has been well written : ' The Nineteenth Century did not attack beauty.
It simply trampled it under foot, with the result that our modern democracy is
born atrophied, and has painfully to recover that love of significant form which
has been one of the marks of civilized man from the Bronze Age until the Industrial Revolution temporarily destroyed it.'—*Times Lit. Suppl.*, April 25, 1924.
[2] See p. 625, above.

the Colonies interested the Conservatives any more than their rivals, who could boast of Lord Durham. In 1852 Disraeli himself had spoken of 'these wretched Colonies' as 'a millstone round our necks.' But his keen sense of the new situation led him in his old age to appeal to the newly enfranchised British democracy to take a pride in the Empire and an interest in 'spirited foreign policy.' It is true that interest in the Colonies was still only nascent, and was developed much more fully in the following generation, under the leadership of Joseph Chamberlain. Disraeli's principal field of operations was the Near East. His purchase of shares in the Suez Canal for England began the connection with Egypt which shortly after his death led to great developments. And in 1876-8 he and Gladstone, in their angry and magnificent disputation, aroused the passions of their fellow-countrymen over the details of Balkan wars and massacres, which but for these two men of genius would have seemed a far-off battle of kites and crows, and certainly none of England's business.

Disraeli, now Lord Beaconsfield, made the British Government the principal supporter of the Turk in Europe as the barrier against Russian influence ; while Gladstone in opposition, by his campaign on the 'Bulgarian atrocities' of Turkey, made one half of British opinion the principal hope of the oppressed Christian races of the East. It was a strange situation, full of danger to our divided land. Fortunately it ended at the Treaty of Berlin without war between Russia and Britain. This was Disraeli's 'peace with honour.' He had certainly made England again important in the councils of Europe, and had forced attention to her wishes. But whether the restoration of the liberated Macedonians to the Turkish rule for another generation was precisely what England should have wished, will remain an open question. Many who know the Balkans regret that, since Disraeli was determined, perhaps rightly, that Macedonia should not be added to the newly formed Bulgarian State, he did not in the Treaty of Berlin insist on its being placed under a Christian governor with proper securities for its good government. It is at least conceivable that such an arrangement might have mitigated the ferocity of racial passions in the Balkan cockpit in the Twentieth Century.

The General Election of 1880 put an end to Disraeli's Ministry, and a year later he died in retirement. He had given the Conservative party its orientation in the new world of democracy, by a frank acceptance of changed conditions at home ; he had taught the upper classes not to retire to their tents in anger at lost privileges, but to go down into the street and appeal to the

1878.

masses on grounds of patriotic sentiment and Imperial interest. Gladstone's mistakes in South Africa and Egypt in the following decade, and his Home Rule proposals, supplied material for such propaganda. The principle of appeal from the upper to the lower classes, made on the ground of identity of interest in the nation as a whole, found expression, after Disraeli's death, in the Primrose League, founded in his memory, and in a network of Conservative Clubs and Associations all over the country. In the early 'eighties the idea of ' Tory democracy ' received a great stimulus from the brief meteoric career of Lord Randolph Churchill.

At the same time the National Liberal Federation of local Associations, nicknamed the ' Caucus,' was being organized by the other party through the energy of the Radical leader, Joseph Chamberlain, whose political power was rooted in his personal control over the local politics of Birmingham. Democratic appeal and elaborate mechanical organization were entering into the electoral methods and political programmes of both parties. New forms of influence and of veiled corruption were arising in place of the old, new forms also of idealism and devotion to the public service. The thoroughness of modern organization and party propaganda at least secured that Parliamentary government should not fail in Great Britain for want of popular interest in elections and in politics. And the presence of real dividing principles, the rival interests of classes, and great questions like Home Rule, prevented the highly organized two-party system from becoming in England a mere lifeless machinery, representing nothing but a struggle for office.[1]

Gladstone's Second Ministry was not so triumphant an affair as his First. In 1880 the Liberal party had not, as in 1868, a definite political philosophy of its own, nor an agreed political programme. It was borne into power by reaction against Disraeli's ' Jingoism,' and by vague democratic aspirations not yet formulated into any clear programme of social reform. And it was at once faced with unavoidable problems in Ireland, Egypt and South Africa, about which, in the year 1880, Liberals, like other Englishmen, knew little and cared less. Gladstone indeed knew and cared about Ireland, and his Land Act of 1881, giving fair rents and security of tenure, was a real measure of amelioration. But it did not solve the land question, still less break up the formidable union of land agitation with the political demand for Home Rule, which Parnell's new policy of ' obstruction ' was forcing on the notice of the British House of Commons.

1880–1885.

[1] The changes of this period in British politics are coldly and severely analyzed in Ostrogorski's *Democracy and the Organization of Political Parties*, Vol. I.

The principal achievement of the Ministry was the Third Reform Bill, which extended Household Suffrage to the county constituencies. The agricultural labourer and the miner were at last enfranchised. Till then their conditions of life had received all too little attention. The attempt of Joseph Arch to start Agricultural Labourers' Trade Unions had failed in the previous decade for want of political power behind it. The agricultural labourer had been ill-used even in times of prosperity, and he fared still worse in the years of agricultural depression, due to the great increase of American importation in the late 'seventies.[1] His enfranchisement in 1884 combined with other economic and social circumstances to initiate a slow, continuous improvement in his lot, but not before the villages had been desperately depleted by the ' rural exodus ' to the towns. The social history of rural England in the Nineteenth Century is in many respects a chronicle of disaster.

The Parliamentary enfranchisement of the rural labourer soon led to the establishment of elective local self-government for the country districts. Hitherto they had been not only judged but administered by the patriarchal rule of the nominated Justices of the Peace. The Conservative Government in 1888 set up elected County Councils ; and in 1894 the establishment of Urban and Rural District Councils and Parish Councils by the Liberal Government completed the machinery of rural democracy. Judicial powers and public-house licensing were still left to the Justices of the Peace, but their great administrative powers passed to the new elected bodies.

The neglect of the South African problem in the first months of Gladstone's Ministry led to the Majuba tragedy.[2] The Egyptian affair began more brilliantly. The breakdown of Turkish and native government in Egypt, where European countries had many financial and personal interests, led to the occupation of Egypt by the British troops under Wolseley,

victorious over Arabi at Tel-el-Kebir. France had refused at the critical moment to participate, though Egypt had hitherto been more under French than English influence. British control in Egypt began, greatly to the material benefit of the Egyptian peasant. The Nile valley prospered, ruled by the all-potent ' advice ' daily given by Sir Evelyn Baring, Lord Cromer, to the Khedive's government. The French regarded our presence there with jealousy, and many unpleasant incidents resulted, until the important agreement with France on Egypt and other subjects was made by Lord Lansdowne in 1904.

---

[1] See p. 646, above.   Between 1881 and 1921 the proportion of the population engaged in agriculture fell from about 12 to about 7 per cent.
[2] See p. 668, above.

But closely attached to the Egyptian question was the Sudanese, and it was here that Gladstone came to grief. While the lower reaches of the Nile held the ancient civilization of Egypt, its upper reaches contained the barbarism of the Sudanese tribes, at that period organized under the Mahdi and his successors as the centre of slave-raiding in the interior of Africa, and a constant threat to Egypt. Any conscientious ruler of Egypt, or indeed any Power sincerely interested in the fate of Africa as a whole, must needs aspire to deal with the plague-spot of the Sudan. But the time was not yet. Egypt had first to be set in order, and her financial and military resources built up.

But in the course of the necessary withdrawal of Egyptian garrisons from the Sudan, Gladstone's Government made errors. Spurred on by William Stead, the father of modern sensational journalism, the Ministry selected for the work Charles Gordon, a strange and single-minded hero fit for any service except that of initiating retreat. Instead of successfully evacuating the Sudan he was soon shut up in Khartoum, besieged by the Mahdhist hordes. The British Government failed to send the relief expedition until too late. Gordon perished, and with him Jan. perished much of Gladstone's influence over his own countrymen 1885. at home. In Africa the defeat made less difference. The Sudan would in any case have been evacuated at that time. Only after Cromer had done his work in Egypt, was Lord Salisbury's Government able to conquer the Sudan with the British and Egyptian armies under Kitchener in 1898.

The General Election of 1885 resulted in a great defeat of the Liberal party in the boroughs, largely owing to Gordon and Khartoum. But the newly enfranchised agricultural labourer cast his vote for the party to whom he owed it, in the hope of obtaining some real improvement in his miserable lot. Lord Salisbury therefore did not obtain a clear Conservative majority with which to govern the country. The notable consequence was that the balance of power at Westminster lay in the hands of a strange man who, though himself of Anglo-Saxon origin, regarded British Liberals and Tories with a cold, indifferent hatred. Charles Stewart Parnell had established the iron discipline of his personal ascendancy over the Home Rule party from Ireland, numbering eighty-five members of the new British Parliament. Henceforth, so long as the Union of 1801 was maintained, Irish affairs must clearly be a controlling factor in British politics, as they had not been in the early and middle parts of the century when the Irish Representatives were many of them attached to one or other of the two British parties. Politics could not go on as before. Either the two British parties must unite against Parnell, or one of them must come to terms with him. Gladstone came to terms with him, and introduced a Home Rule Bill.

In the light of subsequent events, many in our generation will be disposed to consider such a decision natural and even obvious, and to wish that the question of Irish self-government could have been settled then in peace, instead of in 1921 after a series of horrible events. But it is difficult to say whether the cause of Irish conciliation was retarded or advanced by Gladstone's proceedings. The speed of his *volte-face* on a subject of such immense importance bewildered and exasperated the British electorate. The Home Rule question broke up the Liberal party and greatly weakened it for twenty years to come, while Conservatism became closely identified with Unionist doctrine for Ireland. Above all, Gladstone's acceptance of Parnell's claim to have Protestant Ulster as a part of the new Ireland, was more than an error in tactics. It flew in the face of racial and political possibilities.

The Conservative party had been courting the Irish vote not without success during the election of 1885. But it seized the opportunity given it by Gladstone's compact with Parnell to appeal to British national feeling. Home Rule was read in the light of Khartoum. The growing Imperialist sentiment of the *fin-de-siècle* did not recognize Home Rule for Ireland as an essential part of the new creed of Empire, in spite of much support for Irish Home Rule in the self-governing Dominions oversea. The passions aroused by the Home Rule controversy in England, marked by such episodes as the publication in 1887 of forged ' Parnell ' letters in the *Times*, rendered rational states-manship by an agreement of parties impossible. Yet nothing else would have served the case.

The reaction against Gladstone and Home Rule was strong enough at the election of 1886 to secure an independent Conservative majority over Gladstonian Liberals and Irish combined. There followed an era of strong Conservative government under Lord Salisbury in alliance with the Liberal Unionists, especially with Joseph Chamberlain, who became the champion of the new Imperialism. In that way the country was ruled until after the Boer War at the end of the century, with the exception of the three years of Liberal rule (1892–5). The Liberals and Irish under Gladstone then forced a Home Rule Bill through the Commons by a majority of thirty-four. It was thrown out by the Lords, and in the election of 1895 the country ratified their action. This event gave to the Conservative chiefs a new idea of the function of the Upper Chamber in modern politics, more ambitious than that adhered to in practice by the cautious Peel and Disraeli. The consequence in the following century was that as soon as the next big change in democratic opinion took place, a contest between the two Houses led to a very grave constitutional crisis, such as had been conspicuously absent from our politics since 1832.

The defeat of Home Rule at the polls in 1895 was definitive for a number of years to come, and there was a temporary lull in Irish affairs. The Conservative Ministry who had previously relied on coercion to govern Ireland, developed a policy of ' killing Home Rule by kindness.' They enlarged local self-government, and, by buying out the English landlords, ended the Irish land question, at least in its old Cromwellian form. But the political demand for Home Rule, or something more, remained unabated. In the Twentieth Century the national demand for self-government was so deeply implanted in the mind of the Irish Celts, that it survived not only the fall and death of Parnell (1890–1), but the subsequent removal of the land grievance—the man and the question which had first given it power seriously to disturb the politics of the British Empire.

Gladstone died in retirement at the age of eighty-nine. **1898.** The impassioned efforts of ' The Grand Old Man ' for Irish Home Rule had been the most dramatic and extraordinary part of his life, but the least successful. It is possible that the Liberal party, and the politics of the Empire as a whole, would have developed more naturally towards the end of his life, if they had been left by him to the men of that generation. Gladstone's immense activity overshadowed friends and foes, and pushed them into positions not of their choosing. But, viewing his life down its whole length, many will conclude that he did more than any other man to adapt the machinery of the British State and the habits of British politicians to modern democratic conditions, without a total loss of the best standards of the older world. The legislation of his First Ministry had done most to modernize our institutions. The Second and Third Reform Bills largely resulted from the lead he had himself given the country after the death of Palmerston. He had interested the new democracy in Parliamentary government by constant popular appeals, not to sensationalism or self-interest, but to men's reasoning faculties and their sense of right. His reasoning may often have been defective and his appeals to moral indignation may have been too often and too easily made, but on the whole his habit of carrying public questions in their serious aspect before the tribunal of great popular audiences was a fine and fruitful example, made at an important period of transition in our public life.

The government of Great Britain by Lord Salisbury's Conservative Ministries, in alliance with the Liberal Unionists, covered a period of trade prosperity and, until the Second Boer War,[1] of peace with civilized peoples. Good relations with the Continental Powers were maintained on the basis of the ' splendid isolation ' of Great Britain. The other Great Powers, preparatory to the great act of world-destruction in our own day, were already dividing themselves into two camps, arming in nervous rivalry—the Triple Alliance of Germany, Austria and, at that time, of Italy, against the Dual Alliance of France and Russia. Great Britain remained outside both these groups, but owing to the hostile attitude of France as our colonial rival in Asia and Africa, and to the continual dread of Russia's intentions towards Afghanistan and India, Lord Salisbury was upon the whole in a relation of greater friendliness to the Germanic Powers. But always a certain uneasiness attended the relations of a government based on Parliamentarism and popular rights with the great militarist bureaucracy created by Bismarck ; the new leaders of the German destiny inherited an instinctive distrust of the influence of British political institutions. But the general orientation of British policy was not affected by this *malaise* until Kaiser William's admiration of the British Navy led him to build a rival fleet—a development that only became dangerously noticeable in the following century. Under Lord Salisbury's management, the African continent was divided among the Great Powers by peaceful agreement. The interior of the Dark Continent was now in rapid process of exploitation by Europeans armed with modern means of locomotion, and protected by modern knowledge of tropical medicine.

At home the last two decades of the century, and of Queen Victoria's reign, whether under Liberal or Conservative Ministries, were years of social and administrative progress, particularly in the direction of what was known as ' municipal socialism.' [2] Baths and wash-houses, museums, public libraries, parks, gardens, open spaces, allotments, lodging houses for the working classes were acquired, erected or maintained out of the rates. Tramways, gas, electricity and water were in many places municipalized. It was also a great period of voluntary effort, of ' Settlements ' like Toynbee Hall, and of a very general awakening of all classes to the terrible consequences of ' environment ' in the slums, in ' the richest country in the world '—as England

---

[1] See p. 670, above.

[2] In 1888 the Conservative Minister, Mr. Ritchie, passed his County Council Act, which not only set up popularly elected bodies to rule the counties, but enlarged the existing machinery of urban democracy by turning all towns of over 50,000 inhabitants into County Boroughs, and by erecting the elected London County Council to govern all London except the old ' City ' area.

was then still accounted. The scientifically guided Christian inspiration of Canon Barnett ; the statistical investigations of Charles Booth and his helpers into the real facts of London life and his reasoned advocacy of Old Age Pensions ; the social side of ' General ' William Booth's work of redemption through the Salvation Army, and Church work on similar lines ; the civic patriotism of the new London, and its activities initiated by John Burns of Battersea and the Progressive party of the London County Council in its early years ; the investigations and ' Fabian ' tactics of the Sidney Webbs, to manœuvre instalments of socialism out of Liberal and Conservative governments and parties ; the more militant life breathed into Socialism by Henry George's *Progress and Poverty* and by Hyndman's Social Democratic Federation ; the extension of Trade Union activity from the highly skilled to the ill-paid and unskilled trades signalized by the Dockers' strike of 1889,—all these and many other movements and forces indicated that the social problem was not at its end but at its beginning, and might well in the coming century devour the other aspects of political life.

Meanwhile, apart from the conscious action of politicians or of social reformers, the continual and ever-increasing rapidity of the Industrial Revolution was year by year silently transmuting social habits, obliterating old distinctions of rank and creed, and turning a Bible-reading people with ideals based on reminiscences of rural or burgher life and a hierarchy of classes, into the city population that we know. A significant portent was observed in the growth of Harmsworth's *Daily Mail*, catering for the new half-educated democracy of all classes, in a fashion quite different from that of the more solemn political organs which had satisfied the Victorian *bourgeoisie*.

At length, in January 1901, the figure passed away that had presided over the changing scene during a period of transition longer and no less momentous than the reign of George III himself. ' The Queen ' had reigned so long that in the minds of her subjects the Monarchy had become female in its attributes. All through her long reign—alike before, during, and after her married life, alike in her period of Whig and her period of Conservative preferences, in dealing with Ministers to whom she was attached and with Ministers whose policy she abhorred and whose personality she disliked—Victoria had with fixed steadiness of principle adhered to a settled constitutional practice of her own. She always insisted on knowing what was being done ; she compared it in the vast store-house of her memory and experience to what had been done in the past ; if she disagreed, she protested ; if the Minister still adhered to his decision, she gave way. But not all Ministers adhered in every case to their first decisions, particularly in questions of appointments or in the phraseology of documents. The Queen's practice of this method for more than two generations of men, definitely fixed the position of the Crown in the Constitution, so that the storms of the Twentieth Century, which have raged round so many other institutions, have left the Monarchy unchallenged. Victoria's successors, by evincing a more complete absence of party predilection than she showed herself, have further smoothed the path of constitutional kingship in the new age.

At the same time, since the idea of a Federation of the Parliaments of the Empire has failed to materialize, the Crown has been left as the sole official bond of the whole Imperial fabric. Here, too, the Queen was in her element. In her latter years she admirably filled and greatly enjoyed her new position as Empress of India and as head of a great association of free peoples, which was proclaimed and dramatized by the Imperial pageantry of her two Jubilees.

1887,
1897.

Victoria was possessed in a high degree of queenly instincts and dignity, but they were softened and popularized by a mind and an emotional nature of great simplicity. In herself she was not very different from her female subjects in humble stations of life—except that she was also a great Queen. She was not at all an aristocrat ; the amusements and life of the aristocracy and their dependents and imitators meant little to her. She was above the aristocracy, not of it. With the other side of her nature she was a simple wife and widow-woman, who would have been at home in any cottage parlour. So, too, the intellectual and artistic currents of the age flowed by her unnoticed—except when Prince Albert was there to instruct her. The common people understood her in her joys and sorrows better than they understood those who stood between themselves and her, raised on the platforms of aristocracy or of intellect.

For these reasons, political and personal, the coming of democracy had, contrary to general expectation, coincided with a revival of popular affection for the royal office, disjoined as it now was from pretensions to direct political power.

BOOKS FOR FURTHER READING

Queen Victoria's Letters ; Morley's *Gladstone* (2 vols.) ; Buckle's *Disraeli* (6 vols.) ; Winston Churchill's *Lord Randolph Churchill* (2 vols.) ; John Bailey, *Some Political Ideas and Persons* (on Queen Victoria and Disraeli) ; John Stuart Mill, *Autobiography* ; Francis Darwin, *Charles Darwin* ; Lytton Strachey, *Queen Victoria* ; Redlich and Hirst, *Local Government in England* (2 vols.) ; Lady Gwendolen Cecil, *Lord Salisbury* (2 vols. ; more to follow) ; Barry O'Brien, *Parnell* ; Stephen Gwynn, *History of Ireland* ; Webb, *History of Trade Unionism* ; Beatrice Webb, *My Apprenticeship* ; Warre Cornish, *The English Church in the Nineteenth Century* (2 vols.) ; Herbert Paul, *History of Modern England* (5 vols.); Halévy, *Histoire du Peuple Anglais* (later vols. forthcoming).

THE close of the Nineteenth Century, the Second Boer War, and the deaths of the Queen and of Lord Salisbury, coincided so nearly in time as to mark the end of a definite epoch. The Victorian age had been a long period of ever-increasing prosperity at home, of gradual, uninterrupted, pacific transition from the old to the new society, and of peace and security for Britain in her most important foreign relationships.

But the first two decades of the new century involved the world in the greatest catastrophe of modern times, and even before that catastrophe had taken place, the relations of nations, races and classes had taken on a hard and hostile aspect. Man's power over nature far outstripped his moral and mental development. In a single generation came the motor-car, wireless telegraphy, and the conquests of the air and of the world under the sea. Such inventions, and the application on a colossal scale of older processes of steam and electricity, were perpetually transmuting the economic, social and international fabric before it had time to solidify ; linking up distant races too closely and too suddenly ; and putting into the hands of personal and national ambition new weapons of conquest and self-aggrandisement which have proved the means of mutual destruction.

The Second Boer War,[1] about which the Liberal party had been divided in opposition, left the Conservatives with a large majority to begin the business of the new century. The two leading Ministers were Arthur Balfour, Salisbury's successor in the Premiership, and Joseph Chamberlain, who as Colonial Secretary had done much to arouse the British Empire to a state of self-consciousness.

Balfour's Bill of 1902 added another storey to the edifice of National Education begun in 1870, by handing over the management both of Primary and of Secondary Schools to the County Councils, rural and urban. In this way Secondary Education for the first time received proper financial support, and was co-ordinated with the rest of the national system. The new local authority—the Education Committee of each County Council—was able to devise broader schemes of policy than the old School Board, which had usually administered too small an area. The Church ' Voluntary ' Schools were also placed to a considerable

1 See p. 670, above.

degree under the new local authority, in return for support given them out of the rates. But the Nonconformists and others resented the perpetuation of the Church Schools, particularly in single-school areas, by means of rates levied on all. An embittered controversy followed, during which began the revival of Liberalism and indirectly of the general democratic and Labour movement in the country.

At this stage, the fortunes of Unionist Conservatism, which were already beginning to decline, were put to a hazard certain either to check or to precipitate that process. Chamberlain preached the adoption of Protection, renamed Tariff Reform. The double object was to protect British industries against foreign competition, far stronger now than in the age of Peel and Cobden, and at the same time to weld the Empire together by Imperial Preference. Imperial Preference in Great Britain would involve placing a tax on foreign foodstuffs, to be remitted in case of imports from the Colonies. Popular tradition about the old Corn Laws told against it. Chamberlain's proposals, driven forward with all his unrivalled energy and influence, divided the Conservatives and united the Liberal and Labour forces. The General Election of 1906 sent back about 380 Liberals, 80 Irish Nationalists and 50 Labour Members, against a Conservative Opposition scarcely numbering 160.

During the ensuing decade, up to and after the outbreak of the war, Liberal Ministers remained in power, surviving two general elections in 1910, by dint of maintaining the Irish alliance unimpaired, and the alliance with Labour in a more precarious, but in the main an effective, condition.

The life of the Liberal Ministry was probably protracted by the hostile action of the House of Lords. Encouraged by the popularity which they had achieved by throwing out the Home Rule Bill of 1893,[1] the members of the House of Lords and the Conservative Leaders put the Upper Chamber in the forefront of the political battle, where it had never stood since 1832.

The Lords allowed passage, indeed, to many measures of social reform, and to measures in which the working classes were peculiarly interested, including even the much disputed Act of 1906, which gave the Trade Unions a privileged position in the law courts, releasing them from legal responsibility for their own actions.[2] Other measures which did not encounter the Lords' Veto were the Old Age Pensions Bill, that did much to empty

[1] See p. 688, above.
[2] In 1912 another Act legalized a political levy raised by the majority of members of a Trade Union, but allowed any member to claim exemption from the levy if he had the courage to do so.

the workhouses, Workmen's Compensation, Miners' Eight Hours, Medical Inspection of Children and the Children's Bill, the Town-planning Act, the Sweated Industries Act, measures of Unemployment and Health Insurance, and the Small Holdings Act for rural districts. Many such measures, supported by voluntary or municipal effort through Care Committees, Play Centres, Boy Scouts, Adult Education and other such activities outside the harsh discords of politics, together with constantly advancing medical science and practice, have in the present century, in spite of the war, raised the standard of children's health and happiness, reduced the death-rate and prolonged the average of human life by several years.

But the Upper Chamber refused to pass a number of the Government's measures, including a Licensing Bill and the Education Bill of 1906, by which the Liberals in the first flush of their great electoral victory attempted to settle by compromise the difficult points of religious dispute outstanding from Balfour's Education Act. And finally the Lords raised a constitutional issue of the first order by throwing out Lloyd George's Budget of 1909.

The Budget was unpopular with many influential people on account of its Land Tax clauses, and its heavy increase of direct taxation on the well-to-do classes to pay for social reforms which more immediately benefited other sections of the community. But the rejection of the year's Budget by the Lords, though not illegal, was without precedent, and meant that the Lords could force a dissolution any year they wished. It gave the Liberal Cabinet strong constitutional ground whence to appeal to the body of moderate opinion in the country that was drifting back to the Conservative side. And at the same time, Ministers were able to rally the Labour and Irish forces to a joint effort against the Peers. The vehemence of Lloyd George's democratic harangues sharpened the edge of controversy. The fate of Home Rule was directly involved in the struggle, since it could never pass into law until the Lords' Veto were abolished. Another issue between parties was Tariff Reform : it was urged by Conservatives as a method of raising money alternative to the very heavy items of direct taxation that were necessary under a Free Trade government, which had to foot the bill for ever-increasing armaments and ever-multiplying social reforms.

All these issues were brought to a head together by the fight over the rejected Budget and over the Parliament Bill ; that measure proposed to limit the absolute veto of the Peers to a suspensory veto, and to take away all their power over financial measures. The country was twice consulted in 1910—once under King Edward, and once under the new King, George V—with the result that in both elections a majority of about 120 was secured by the Liberal-Labour-Irish combination. The Liberal party was therefore master of the Lords, but at the mercy of its own allies. George V, after the second election had confirmed the result of the first, compelled the Peers to pass the Parliament Bill, using, at Asquith's behest, the same method **1911.** of threatened creations of Peers *en masse* which William IV had, at Grey's dictation, employed to pass the First Reform Bill.

But 1911 was not, like 1832, the end of the worst trouble. For opinion in the country was much more evenly divided than in that famous year of old, when the Lords had little save their own constitutional powers with which to maintain the fight. The Home Rule question now came up in earnest, for under the Parliament Act the Peers could no longer defeat it, but only delay its passage. The disestablishment of the Church in Wales, the long-standing demand of Welsh Nonconformity and of the majority of the Welsh members, was also now a practicable proposition, heaping yet more fuel on the fire of men's wrath.

Unhappily the worst exacerbation of parties in Great Britain —a mixture of old constitutional and denominational with new social and financial antagonisms—corresponded in time with the climax of the older and more intense antagonisms of race and religion in Ireland. The prevailing spirit of the day was violence and anger : many even of the female advocates of Votes for Women—the most important of the many political cross-currents of that distracted era—resorted to organized outrage on persons and property, to advertise their cause ; they were distinguished from the law-abiding Women Suffragists by the title of ' Suffragettes.' Labour troubles, too, were acute and strikes constant ; industrial strife between the vast national organizations of capital and labour in mines and railways were a new feature of life in the last years before the War. As in the Middle Ages, great corporations were threatening to become stronger than the unorganized community.

Ireland, whose case had long demanded impartial considera-tion as an Imperial problem, had for a whole generation been used as a stalking-horse by British parties. Nemesis now descended **1914.** upon al concerned. It is true that at late last the issue as between parties in England had been narrowed down to the degree and method of ' contracting out ' of Home Rule to be permitted to the several Counties of Ulster. But political tempers in England after the Budget crisis and the Parliament Act were so bad, and the passions aroused in Ireland were by this time so strong—Sinn Fein gaining ground on constitutional

Nationalism and Orange feeling worked to its height—that civil war in one at least of the two islands seemed unavoidable.   Then suddenly, in August 1914, a greater quarrel and a more terrible danger reunited in a week Liberal with Conservative, capital with labour, man with still unenfranchised woman, and even, for a few months of tense and novel emotion, Ireland with England and Orange with Green.

From Canning to Salisbury the 'splendid isolation' of Great Britain served her interests well.   She avoided a whole series of continental wars—except the adventure of the Crimea which was of her own seeking and the consequences of which were easily liquidated.   In the then state of scientific invention and warlike armament, the Navy was still her sure and sufficient shield, and for a hundred years after Trafalgar no Power attempted to build a rival fleet.   The Balance of Power in Europe was adequately adjusted without Britain's make-weight, and the independence of the small countries of the Rhine Delta was not seriously threatened.   During the Franco-Prussian War of 1870, Gladstone had, in pursuance of the terms and the policy of the Treaty of 1839,[1] announced Britain's intention to take arms against either French or German violation of Belgium's neutrality, and on that occasion the warning was enough.   In spite of Colonial difficulties with France, and Asiatic difficulties with Russia, Salisbury in the 'eighties and 'nineties saw no necessity to attach our fortunes to those of the Triple Alliance of Germany, Austria and Italy.

But with the new century, the period of 'splendid isolation' came to an end.   The first steps on the new road were taken by Lord Lansdowne as Foreign Minister.   To his thinking, the number, size and ubiquity of armed forces by land and sea all over the world, rendered it necessary that we should have at least some understandings and defined friendships.   An understanding with America would have been preferred, but her traditional policy of isolation rendered it out of the question.   So the Japanese Alliance was made, originally to counterbalance the **1902.** advance of Russia onto the Pacific, and to prevent the partition of China by Russia, Germany and France, which America disliked as much as we, but would do nothing active to prevent.   The Japanese Alliance also enabled us to dispense with the creation of an immense naval establishment in the Pacific.   Britain's friendship served to keep the ring for the rise of the first 'coloured' Great Power, to which the other European Powers were hostile.   Its triumph over Russia in war had many reactions **1904.**

[1] See p. 639, above.

upon India and on the world at large. Ten years later, the Japanese, ever faithful to their alliance with us, safeguarded the waters and coasts of the Far East against German designs during the Great War, besides giving effective help in the Mediterranean.

More important even than the Japanese Treaty was the simultaneous evolution in our relations to France and the German Empire respectively. The state of the Balance of Power in Europe was again giving cause for anxiety. Germany was more and more overshadowing Europe by her unparalleled military preparations, based on ever increasing population, wealth and trained intelligence ; and moreover she was adding to her predominant army a fleet built in rivalry to our own. To Britain the sea was the primary consideration of her very existence, as it was not to Germany. It was this naval rivalry which altered Britain's attitude to the European Powers. In 1904 Lord Lansdowne settled the outstanding differences between Great Britain and France in Egypt and Morocco, and so permitted the growth of the *entente cordiale*, not yet an alliance, and not on our part hostile to Germany—unless indeed Germany would have it so.

During the next ten years the nations armed themselves in rivalry by land and by sea. It was a race of which the only possible goal was war. *Si bellum vis, para bellum* was the fatal truth, about to be demonstrated by the most frightful of all object-lessons. Britain indeed endeavoured to reach an arrangement with Germany for the limitation of their two navies, but these approaches were repulsed. For the military party that ruled the policies of Kaiser William's Empire had become a naval party as well. So Europe drifted on to the catastrophe, this time with England in tow.

The quarrel, though it broke out on Balkan and Russian questions which did not concern Britain, threatened at the very outset to put an end to the independence of France and Belgium, in circumstances which would have prevented those countries from ever raising their heads again, otherwise than as vassals of Germany. The victory of the Central Powers would have meant the subjection of Europe to an Empire better calculated to survive and rule in perpetuity than ever Napoleon's had been. The very virtues of the German people, as the servants of their rulers' ambitions, made the danger of permanent slavery for Europe extreme.

July–
Aug.
1914.

In the days of crisis precipitated by the murder of the Austrian Archduke, Sir Edward Grey, as British Foreign Secretary, made every effort to avert the war, and thereby helped to win for Britain and her Allies the moral sympathy of a large part of mankind, particularly in America. But when those efforts failed, self-preservation dictated that we should not permit the Channel Ports, the Netherlands, and indeed all Europe, to fall into vassalage to the most powerful Empire in history, that was already openly our rival at sea. The violation of Belgian neutrality and the invaders' treatment of Belgian resistance was a drama that brought home, on a wave of generous emotion, the dreadful facts and necessities of the hour to the unwilling mind of the British public, which craved for nothing but peace.

The events of the Great War are so well known to all that an attempt to summarize them in the few remaining pages of this book would be intolerable. But some points of comparison with the conditions and methods of the Napoleonic Wars may be a not unfitting way to end this long History of our land.

First, there was the difference of geographical situation. Jacobin and Napoleonic France attempted to conquer Europe from the base of its North-West angle; the Germanic Powers made the same attempt from the more formidable strategic centre which gave to them ' the inner line ' of battle against all-comers—Russian, Balkan, Italian, French and English-speaking. Britain's communications with her allies in the East, particularly with Russia, were therefore more liable to interruption by the enemy. Also, in case the enemy won the war, it would be far more easy for the ' Central Powers ' to hold Europe and Western Asia in permanent subjection than it would have been for the successors of Napoleon, who could not have kept the Germans down for ever, even if the battle of Leipzig had gone the other way.

As regards the strategy and tactics of the two struggles, Britain's part in both was to supply the money and maritime power of the Alliance, and to blockade the enemy by sea. But in the later war we also undertook another duty : we ' paid in person,' sending over armies numbered in their millions, and counting our dead at almost a million and our wounded at over two million in the four years. In the French wars from 1793 to 1815 our military effort, though important, had been small, and our average annual loss of life not above five thousand. Against Germany our average annual loss of life was nearly two hundred and fifty thousand. We found it necessary to make the greater military effort on the later occasion, partly because of the more formidable geographic position of the ' Central Powers ' ; if once we allowed the Germans to overrun all Europe as Napoleon had done, we should never get them out again.

But our fuller participation in the war by land was dictated also by the changes in military and naval weapons and tactics, which had already shaken the old security of our island position. The possessor of the Channel ports could, by long-distance guns, aeroplanes and submarines, threaten our existence much more formidably than Napoleon and his flat-bottomed boats at Boulogne. So the British people themselves, as soldiers, took a leading part in the decisive operations of the war. The modern Leipzig and Waterloo consisted of a continuous battle, fought day and night for four years along a line hundreds of miles long. Modern financial credit, and means of transporting men, food and warlike stores, enabled the opposing nations to maintain millions of fighters continuously in the trenches, year after year, on each of the principal fronts.

The most marked difference between the two wars lay in armaments and tactics : the long Napoleonic wars began and ended with the Brown-Bess musket and close-order fighting of British line and French column. Invention continued all the time to be applied by England to industry, but was not applied by any country to war. Napoleon recognized the relation to war of modern administration and organization, but he was fortunately blind to the military possibilities of modern science. But on the later occasion the methods of warfare, which in 1914 began with all the latest mechanical appliances and in Germany at least with the fullest national organization, were revolutionized several times over in the course of four short years. Not only did trench-warfare take the place of the war of movement, but the development of aerial and submarine warfare on a great scale, and the invention of gas-warfare by the Germans and of tank-warfare by the British, are changes without any parallel among the slow-witted and unscientific wars of Napoleon. Science was harnessed, and the whole civil population was mobilized. Instead of producing Scott's lays and novels, Wordsworth's poems, Constable's and Turner's pictures, safe behind Nelson's shield, the civil population of Great Britain devoted its whole energy and its best brains for four years to the business of slaying and being slain.

In the days of Pitt and Castlereagh we increased our Colonial Empire at the expense of France and her allies, and we did so again at the expense of Germany a hundred years later. But the Colonies had taken no part in the earlier struggle, for in Pitt's day the First British Empire had already been lost and the Second was still in its infancy. A hundred years later it was fully grown. There was indeed no machinery of Imperial Federation to bid the Empire march into line, but by free individual choice, Canada, Australia, New Zealand, and Anglo-Dutch South Africa took each its full share in the whole long contest. Between them they raised colonial armies of a million and a half men.

India in the time of Pitt and Bonaparte had been the scene of the final struggle against French influence among the native Courts and armies. But India in 1914–15 sent over great bodies of troops, enthusiastic to take part in the European contest. Unfortunately in India, Egypt and Ireland the protracted and deadly character of the war gave rise to unrest and political exacerbation of which the early months had shown no sign. But the attitude of Britain to Ireland during the war, though not always wise in detail, was at heart friendly and very different from the spirit of 1795–1800. The ultimate solution of the Irish question was not therefore rendered impossible by the Rising in Dublin at Easter 1916, and the other unfortunate developments of war time.

Relations to the United States were subject to somewhat the same general conditions as in Napoleon's time, but owing to wiser management and a better spirit, took an opposite turn. On both occasions, the interests of England as the great blockading Power necessarily clashed with those of the neutral merchant Power, desirous of sending her goods as usual to the European market. But whereas the Perceval Ministry had acted as though war with the United States were a matter of indifference, and had idly drifted into that catastrophe, no such mistake was made by Sir Edward Grey, who sacrificed points of real military value in permitting the passage of cotton and other articles of value to the enemy, in order to prevent an early explosion of American opinion against us. The Germans did the rest. Owing to the careful methods of British blockade-diplomacy, the pro-Ally feeling in the States and the German submarine attack on American persons and shipping were given time to operate and draw the great neutral into the contest on our side.

Blockade conditions differed in several vital respects from those of Napoleonic times. It is true that our blockade of the enemy's principal Fleet, though conducted at long distance from Scapa Flow, was at least as effective as Nelson's close watch off Brest and Toulon in stopping all chance of invasion and in paralysing the enemy's great ships. But the Napoleonic privateers and frigates that skirmished against British commerce in spite of Nelson, were as nothing to the German submarine, which in the latter part of the war threatened to starve England out. New methods of fighting the new danger were devised and carried out with a scientific efficiency wholly modern, and an old-fashioned skill and courage at sea of which the Royal Navy and the Merchant Service had not lost the secret.

England no longer fed herself, as in Napoleonic times, and the command of the sea was therefore more than ever essential to her very life. But neither, it appeared in the event, could the Central Empires feed themselves for an indefinite period. As the British blockade tightened, especially after the American entry into the war enabled the stranglehold to be increased diplomatically and navally, Germany and Austria began to starve outright. Since the Industrial Revolution, European countries have ceased to be self-supporting in proportion as they are highly civilized and modern. The economic fabric by which the modern millions live is too international and too delicate to survive for long the injuries done by acts of scientific war. It survived them after a fashion for four years, during which the accumulated wealth and civilization of a hundred were used up. But already, since the Armistice of 1918, the destructive powers of applied science have been indefinitely multiplied. If there is another European war it will differ from the Great War at least as terribly as the Great War differed from the lesser operations of Napoleon. It may soon be as easy to destroy half a nation as it was in his day to destroy half a battalion.

A remarkable contrast appears between the two historic wars, as regards the position of the working classes and the relations of Britons to one another. Pitt and Castlereagh fought the French as constitutional statesmen, by and through the House of Commons ; but it never occurred to them or to any of their colleagues that the common people required, in time of national peril, any management or consideration beyond anti-Jacobin repression and the silencing of Parliamentary Reformers. Nor, as regards the mere winning of the war, did this reckoning prove wrong. But the dangers of the Home Front in 1914–18 had to be met by very different methods. Early in 1918, while the war was still raging, the Fourth Reform Bill was passed by universal consent, giving what was practically Manhood Suffrage and a large instalment of the new principle of Woman's Suffrage. The element of Dictatorship was perhaps stronger than in Pitt's time, as regards the relation of the Government to the House of Commons. But the English Cabinet Ministers of 1914–18 had always to appeal deferentially to the people. For they knew that if munition workers slacked or stopped work, it was no longer in the skill of ' magistrates and yeomanry ' to make them go on. Since ' the lower orders ' had developed into an enfranchised and partially educated democracy, only persuasion could effect what repression had accomplished in the days of the Luddites. In the struggle with Jacobin France, the war-time specific was Combination Acts to suppress Trade Unions; in the struggle with Germany it was the raising of wages to an unprecedented height, and inducing leaders of the Labour Party to enter the Coalition Cabinet. The hardships of wartime did not, as a hundred years before, fall with their greatest force on the fortunes of the wage-earner. So long as the common danger of the war lasted the spirit of brotherhood in the British people of all classes, both at home and in the field, was at any rate much deeper and more widely spread than during the wars against Napoleon.

In seven hundred pages I have tried to set down some aspects of the evolution of life upon this island, since the ages when it lay as nature made it, a green and shaggy forest, half water-logged, while here and there, on the more habitable uplands, the most progressive of the animals gathered his kind into camps and societies, to save himself and his offspring and his flocks from wolves and bears and from his fellow-men—down to that November day, still so recent, when forty millions, gathered for the most part in streets whence everything of nature had been excluded save a strip of sky overhead, broke into ecstasies of joy at the news that the imminent danger of destruction afflicting them for four years had at length passed away. In the earlier scene, man's impotence to contend with nature made his life brutish and brief. To-day his very command over nature, so admirably and marvellously won, has become his greatest peril. Of the future the historian can see no more than others. He can only point like a showman to the things of the past, with their manifold and mysterious message.

LIST OF MINISTRIES

1770–1782. North Ministry (Tory, King's Friends).
1782. Rockingham Ministry (Whig).
1782–1783. Shelburne Ministry (King's Friends and Chathamites).
1783. Coalition Ministry of North and Fox (Whigs and Tories).
1783–1801. First Pitt Ministry (Chathamites and King's Friends, gradually becoming Tory ; Conservative Whigs join in 1794).
1801–1804. Addington Ministry (Tory).
1804–1806. Pitt's Second Ministry (Tory).
1806–1807. Ministry of All-the-Talents (Whigs and Tories).
1807–1809. Portland Ministry (Tory).
1809–1812. Perceval Ministry (Tory).
1812–1827. Liverpool Ministry (Tory), becoming more liberal in policy after 1822.
1827. Canning Ministry (Liberal Tory).
1827. Goderich Ministry (Liberal Tory).
1828–1830. Wellington-Peel Ministry (Tory).
1830–1834. Grey Ministry (Whig).
1834. First Melbourne Ministry (Whig).
1834–1835. First Peel Ministry (Conservative).
1835–1841. Melbourne Ministry (Whig).
1841–1846. Second Peel Ministry (Conservative).
1846–1852. Lord J. Russell's Ministry (Whig).
1852. First Derby-Disraeli Ministry (Conservative).
1852–1855. Aberdeen Coalition Ministry (Peelites and Whigs).
1855–1858. First Palmerston Ministry (Whig).
1858–1859. Second Derby-Disraeli Ministry (Conservative).
1859–1865. Second Palmerston Ministry (Whigs and Peelites, Liberals)
1865–1866. Earl Russell's Ministry (Whig and Liberal).
1866–1868. Third Derby-Disraeli Ministry (Conservative).
1868–1874. First Gladstone Ministry (Liberal).
1874–1880. Disraeli Ministry (Conservative).
1880–1885. Second Gladstone Ministry (Liberal).
1885–1886. Salisbury Ministry (Conservative).
1886. Third Gladstone Ministry (Liberal).
1886–1892. Salisbury Unionist Ministry (Conservative, supported by Liberal Unionists).
1892–1894. Fourth Gladstone Ministry (Liberal).
1894–1895. Rosebery Ministry (Liberal).
1895–1902. Salisbury Ministry (Unionist).
1902–1905. Balfour Ministry (Unionist).
1905–1908. Campbell-Bannerman Ministry (Liberal).
1908–1915. Asquith Ministry (Liberal).
1915–1916. Asquith Ministry (Coalition).
1916–1918. Lloyd George Ministry (Coalition).

INDEX

474-5, 497-504, 508-9, 512, 542-3,
547-9, 557-70, 579-80, 600, 616, 622,
632-4, 639-40, 643 ; Liberal, 643,
656-8, 677-9, 685, 688-9, 693-7 ;
Conservative, 640-1, 645, 657-8, 677,
683-5, 688, 690, 693-9 ; Labour, 694,
696-7, 702-3 ; 'Group' system,
occasional recurrence of, 579-80,
616, 624-5. *See also* Radicals
Passaro, Cape, battle of, 532 *and note*
Paston Letters, 259, 261
Paterson, William, 489
Patrick, St., 53
Paul, Czar, 577
Paulinus, 51, 57, 60
Pavia, battle of, 293
Pearsall Smith, L., 184 *note*
Pecock, Reginald, Bishop, 288
Peel, Sir Robert (junior), early career
and character, 448, 624-6, 630-1,
636, 640-1 ; his Ministry, 643-6,
650, 664, 704
Pelham, Henry, 539
Pembroke, 208
Pembroke, Richard, Earl of (Strong-
bow), 6, 202
Penal Acts *v.* Massachusetts, 553
Penal Laws (Ireland), 484, 589-90
Penda, King of Mercia, 59, 60, 70
Peninsular War, 572, 580 *note*, 582-5
Penn, William, 442, 501
Pennsylvania, 442-3
Penry, John, 365
Pepys, Samuel, 455
Perceval, Spencer, 581, 600, 701, 704
Percy, house of, 121, 248, 254, 334, 336
Peru, 295, 338, 628
Peter the Great, 532
'Peter Grimes,' 523, 607
Peterborough, 94, 139
'Peterloo,' 568, 605-6, 615, 620, 623, 626
Petition of Right, 389, 391, 395
Pevensey, 108, 115, 116
Philip II, King, 318, 325, 337, 349, 353, 487
Philip V of Spain (Louis XIV's grand-
son), 494, 498-9
Philip Augustus, King, 168
Philipshaugh, battle of, 415
Picts, 34, 46, 57, 79
Piers Plowman, 143, 240
Pilgrimage of Grace, 271, 308, 315, 531
Pilgrim Fathers, the, 434, 437-9
Pilgrims' Way, 9
Piltdown man, 2
Pindari Wars, the, 671
Pinkie, battle of, 331
Pitt, Thomas, 491
Pitt, William, Earl of Chatham, 444,
569 ; leads country in Seven Years'
War, 491, 495-6, 536, 539, 542-6 ;
later career, 546-9, 551, 555-6

Pitt, William, the younger, 448, 508,
548, 704 ; his ministry, in peace,
557-61, 569 ; in war, 559, 566-70,
574-6, 578-9, 702 ; Ireland, 590-1 ;
Canada, 593, 661 ; Australia, 594 ;
India, 594-8, 659
Pittsburg, 545
Place, Francis, 625, 634
Plassey, 545
Plymouth, 352, 411
Poitiers, battle of, 226, 229
Poland, 575, 586, 628, 650
Pole, Reginald, Cardinal, 321
Pole, William de la, 188
Police force, 525-6, 626
Polish Succession, war of, 535
Political Unions, the, 633, 635-6
Polo, Marco, 164
Pompadour, the, Louis XV's mistress, 544
Poor Law, 269, 283-5, 358 *and note*,
513, 523 *and note*, 583, 602, 612, 641-2
'Popish Plot,' the, 462
Population, increase of, 148, 237, 243,
271, 444, 480, 490, 591 *note*, 602-3, 667 *note*
Porson, Richard, 518
Portland, Duke of, 632, 704
Porto Bello, 535
Portugal, 294-5, 339, 341-2 *note*, 345-7,
349, 356, 386-7, 454 *note*, 488, 583-4, 628
Powys, 208, 211
Præmunire, 247, 297, 303
Prayer Book, the : Tudor times, 235,
310, 312-16, 328, 336, 353, 360, 362-3
364 *note* ; Stuart, 384, 393, 397-9,
405, 412, 417-18, 420, 431, 450
Prerogative Courts, 277-8, 379, 391-2,
403, 447. *See also* High Commission
and Star Chamber
Presbyterians (English), 364-5, 404,
412-14, 417-19, 421, 430-1, 519.
See also Scotland *passim*
Press, censorship and freedom, 297
note, 393-4, 476, 504, 566-7, 579, 623
Preston, battle of, 410, 419, 421 ; surrender at (1715), 529-30
Prestonpans, 530-1, 537
Prime Minister, office of, 475, 510-11,
534, 547, 556, 558
Primogeniture, 145-6, 286-7, 371
Protection and Free Trade, 444, 499,
551, 558, 626, 639, 644-6, 659-60,
694-5 ; as regards Ireland, 424-5,
484, 589 ; as regards Scotland, 424,
476, 481, 526. *See also* Navigation
Laws, *and* Corn Laws
Provisions and Statute of Provisors,
174, 247

Printed in England at THE BALLANTYNE PRESS
SPOTTISWOODE, BALLANTYNE & CO. LTD,
Colchester, London & Eton.